Mastering Enterprise JavaBeans™ 3.0

Mastering Enterprise JavaBeans™ 3.0

Rima Patel Sriganesh
Gerald Brose
Micah Silverman

Wiley Publishing, Inc.

Mastering Enterprise JavaBeans™ 3.0
Published by
Wiley Publishing, Inc.
10475 Crosspoint Boulevard
Indianapolis, IN 46256
www.wiley.com

Published simultaneously in Canada
ISBN-13: 978-0-471-78541-5

10 9 8 7 6 5 4 3 2
1B/SS/QW/QW/IN

For general information on our other products and services or to obtain technical support, please contact our Customer Care Department within the U.S. at (800) 762-2974, outside the U.S. at (317) 572-3993 or fax (317) 572-4002.

Library of Congress Cataloging-in-Publication Data
Sriganesh, Rima Patel.
Mastering enterprise JavaBeans 3.0 / Rima Patel Sriganesh, Gerald Brose, Micah Silverman.
p. cm.
Includes index.
ISBN-13: 978-0-471-78541-5 (paper/website)

1. JavaBeans. 2. Java (Computer program language) I. Brose, Gerald. II. Silverman, Micah. III. Title.
QA76.73.J38S756 2006
005.13'3--dc22

2006011333

Wiley also publishes its books in a variety of electronic formats. Some content that appears in print may not be available in electronic books.

Rima wishes to dedicate this book to her dearest and most loving Mummy and Papa, on their completing 60 years of a wholesome and exemplary life this year, and to her beloved husband, Sriganesh.

To my wonderful wife, Christine, and my sons Johannes and Julius.

For Dr. Charles Marshall, who taught me Excellence.

About the Authors

Rima Patel Sriganesh is a staff engineer presently working in the Technology Outreach group at Sun Microsystems, Inc. She specializes in Java, XML, and integration platforms. Rima represents Sun at various financial services standards. She is a coauthor of three books and usually publishes her take on technology in the form of papers and blogs. She also speaks frequently at various industry conferences.

Rima graduated in Mathematics from M.S. University, Gujarat, India. She currently lives with her husband in the Greater Boston area.

Gerald Brose works as head of software development for Projektron, a software vendor that produces project management software. In previous jobs he has worked as a product manager, software architect, and researcher. He holds a Ph.D. in computer science.

Gerald is an expert in distributed object computing and middleware security, including CORBA, J2EE, and Web services. Gerald also coauthored *Java Programming with CORBA,* also published by Wiley.

Gerald is the maintainer of the JacORB project, the most widely used open source ORB for Java, which is part of the JBoss and JOnAS J2EE application servers. He lives with his wife and two sons in Berlin, Germany.

Micah Silverman has been a professional software architect and consultant for over 15 years. He has been developing with Java since its release in 1995. In that same year, he founded M*Power Internet Services, Inc., a consulting company providing software architecting, development, and security services. He has written numerous articles on software development, information security, and operating systems.

Credits

Executive Editor
Robert Elliott

Development Editor
Tom Dinse

Technical Editor
Daniel Rubio

Production Editor
Felicia Robinson

Copy Editor
Foxxe Editorial Services

Editorial Manager
Mary Beth Wakefield

Production Manager
Tim Tate

Vice President and Executive Group Publisher
Richard Swadley

Vice President and Executive Publisher
Joseph B. Wikert

Project Coordinator
Michael Kruzil

Graphics and Production Specialists
Jennifer Click
Lauren Goddard
Joyce Haughey
Stephanie D. Jumper
Barry Offringa
Lynsey Osborn
Heather Ryan
Brent Savage
Alicia B. South

Quality Control Technicians
Amanda Briggs
Jessica Kramer

Proofreading and Indexing
Techbooks

Contents

Acknowledgments

This book has been a project spanning several years. Many have commented that the first edition was one of the best technical books they've ever read. What's made this book a reality are the many people who aided in its development.

As a special thanks, we'd like to acknowledge the great folks at John Wiley & Sons. They have been absolutely outstanding throughout this book's evolution. In particular, we thank Bob Elliott, Tom Dinse, and Mary Beth Wakefield for their incredible efforts. We also thank Daniel Rubio for his insightful technical reviews, and Linda DeMichiel for lending her help to the authors in understanding the evolution of EJB 3.0 standard.

I would like to thank my wife, Tes and my daughter, Shaina for being so patient while I worked on this book.

—Micah

Introduction

This book is a tutorial on Enterprise JavaBeans (EJB). It's about EJB concepts, methodology, and development. This book also contains a number of advanced EJB topics, giving you a practical and real-world understanding of the subject. By reading this book, you will acquire a *deep* understanding of EJB.

Make no mistake about it—what you are about to read is *not* easy. EJB incorporates concepts from a wealth of areas, including distributed computing, databases, security, component-based architecture, message-oriented systems, and more. Combining them is a magnificent stride forward for the Java community, but with that comes a myriad of concepts to learn and understand. This book will teach you the concepts and techniques for authoring distributed, enterprise components in Java, and it will do so from the ground up. You need only to understand Java to understand this book.

While you're reading this book, you may want to download the EJB specification, available at `http://java.sun.com/products/ejb/docs.html`.

Goals for This Edition

This book has had a long run and hence, a long history. The first edition of this book came out in 1999, followed by second and third editions in 2002 and early 2005, respectively. Writing the latest edition of this popular title was not an easy thing. There was an endless exchange of emails back and forth between the authors before arriving at decisions about the topics to cover, the approach and the tone that should be used to cover them, and so on. We had to make some tough calls when writing the second and third editions, and that did not change in this edition. However, we are confident you'll like them. Here are our goals for this edition:

- **To update the book for EJB 3.0.** EJB 3.0 is a sea change from the previous versions of EJB technology in that the programming and deployment model is very different from its precursors. We take a top-down approach in explaining these changes. We do not just talk about the changes themselves but also discuss the rationale for making these changes to the existing EJB technology. In addition, this book goes an extra mile in providing in-depth coverage on the Java Persistence API and the entities defined therein. The ability to use POJO (plain old Java object) style entities with enterprise beans is a much sought after feature, and this book doesn't save pages when it comes to providing real implementation tips and best practices on how to use POJO entities with Enterprise JavaBeans.
- **To be broad and also deep.** We do not regurgitate the complete EJB specification in this book, nor do we cover every last detail of EJB. Rather, we cover the most important parts of EJB, leaving room to discuss advanced issues. For a complete reference while you are coding, search through the EJB specification using Adobe Acrobat. Readers who are looking for a well-written book that is interactive and fun to read, and that covers the basics through advanced subjects in adequate details have come to the right place.
- **To be concise.** Your time as a reader is extremely valuable, and you're likely waiting to read a stack of books besides this one. Given that most people don't have time to read 1,000-plus-page books, we actually wanted to reduce the size of this book as much as possible. So we've tightened things up and eliminated redundant examples. This way, you can get to actually program with EJB immediately, rather than read a book for months on end. The irony of this story is that it was harder for us to write a shorter book than a long book!
- **To be a book for developers.** This book is not intended for high-level businesspeople. This is a technical book for a technical audience.
- **To write a book the right way.** The authors of this book have taken their skills in architecture, development, consulting, and knowledge transfer, and applied them to this book. Thus, we've infused this book with the following attributes:
  - **A conversational style.** When you read this book, sometimes you'll feel like you're almost having a discussion with us. We think this is far superior to spending eons trying to reread a formal writing style over and over again.

- **Use of diagrams and bulleted lists.** The adage "a picture is worth a thousand words" applies here. These tactics are great for breaking up blocks of text. They keep things varied and make the book a much faster read.
- **A consistent voice.** Even though several coauthors wrote this book, you'll hear one voice. This was done to combine best-of-breed knowledge from several expert coauthors, while maintaining a uniform look and feel throughout the book.

- **To be an introductory book, but also to get quickly into advanced topics.** We figured that the average developer has had enough of books that merely skim the surface. We wanted to write a book that pushed beyond the basics. Our approach when writing this book was always to err on the side of being advanced. To achieve this, we did an immense amount of research. We have participated in the forums, worked on many real-world projects, attended conferences and seminars, talked to the people who have worked on the actual EJB specifications, and networked with the top experts throughout the world.
- **To be vendor-neutral.** The code listings for the examples in this book will work on any EJB application server, thereby making the book useful immaterial of the vendor you use. To stay away from the vendor wars, we have a policy to deploy all of our examples on the Java EE reference implementation rather than on a specific vendor's platform.
- **To take all the source code and make it available online.** Because we've made the code available on the Web, you know it's tested on the latest version of the EJB application server. This will ensure that the code you receive works right the first time.

Organization of the Book

The text is organized into the following five parts:

- **Part I** is a whirlwind introduction to EJB programming. Part I serves as a great overview for people in a hurry. While Part I is essential information for EJB newcomers, veterans will also find nuggets of useful knowledge. The following chapters are included:
  - **Chapter 1** is a tour of enterprise computing. We'll talk about component-based software, distributed computing frameworks, application server–class software, service-oriented architectures, and containers. In this regard, we'll introduce EJB and Java Enterprise Edition (Java EE).

- **Chapter 2** sets the scene for introducing the changes of EJB 3.0 in Chapter 3. This chapter is a must read for long timers in EJB in that it explains why a drastic change was needed in the programming and deployment model of EJB.
- **Chapter 3** shows you how to put together a simple EJB 3.0 bean of the *HelloWorld* fame. It introduces the EJB technology at a more fundamental level by bringing the discussions on IIOP, location transparency, JNDI naming services, annotations, deployment descriptors, and so on, to the fore.

- **Part II** devotes exclusive attention to programming with EJB. We'll see how to use the trio of session beans, session bean Web services, and message-driven beans. More interestingly, we will learn programming of the new and cool Java Persistence API based POJO entities. Needless to say, our discussions are accompanied with working examples.
  - **Chapter 4** introduces session beans. We'll look at the difference between stateful and stateless session beans, how to code a session bean, and what's going on behind the scenes with session beans.
  - **Chapter 5** shows how Web services can be implemented using the EJB model. In particular, we show how a stateless session bean can be made available as a Web service.
  - **Chapter 6** introduces the Java Persistence API, which is a specification created within the EJB Expert Group hosted at `http://www.jcp.org`. The mechanisms for development and deployment of POJO style entities defined in this specification are crucial in eliminating the complexity from EJB applications. This chapter explains the basics of object-relational mapping and the notion of an *entity* with respect to Java Persistence API.
  - **Chapter 7** covers message driven beans. We'll begin with a review of message-oriented middleware (MOM) and the Java Message Service (JMS), which forms the backbone of all Java based MOM software. Underneath, message driven beans use the JMS framework This is followed by an extensive discussion on various aspects of writing message-oriented EJB applications and their respective examples.
  - **Chapter 8** discusses the useful bits and pieces of EJB technology such as how to access resources made available using JNDI naming services, how to use annotations in conjunction with EJB, and so on. It further explains the resource and dependency injection mechanisms as well as interceptors introduced in EJB 3.0 with examples.

- **Part III**, the most exciting part of the book, covers advanced EJB concepts. The following chapters are included:
  - **Chapter 9** provides a comprehensive discussion on the advanced concepts of persistent entities such as inheritance, polymorphism, entity relationships, and EJB Query Language (EJB-QL) enhancements. This chapter has a wealth of information for anyone who wants to get deeper into the world of persistent entities.
  - **Chapter 10** tackles transactions. Transactions are a crucial topic for anyone building an EJB application where ACIDity (Atomicity, Consistency, Isolation, and Durability) is a prerequisite. We'll discuss transactions at a conceptual level followed by a discussion on how to apply them to EJB. We'll learn a lot about the Java Transaction API (JTA) in the process.
  - **Chapter 11** provides in-depth coverage of EJB security and covers *Java Authentication and Authorization Service* (JAAS), secure interoperability, and Web Services security, within the purview of enterprise beans.
  - **Chapter 12** introduces the EJB Timer Service, which lets you schedule tasks for automatic execution at given point(s) in time.
  - **Chapter 13** explains guidelines for using various Web application frameworks, model-driven development tools, and so on, in EJB applications. It also presents proven best practices for EJB design, development, and testing.
  - **Chapter 14** covers EJB tips and techniques for designing and deploying EJB for better performance. You'll learn about design strategies that will help you make decisions such as when to choose between stateful versus stateless session beans, when to choose between local and remote interfaces, and so on. The chapter also focuses a great deal on providing performance tuning tips for different types of beans as well as for Java Persistence API–based entities.
  - **Chapter 15** covers integration to and from EJB platform in depth. It provides an introduction to the various styles of integration, followed by a discussion of various techniques for integrating EJB with the outside world. It explains the Java EE Connector Architecture, a predominant framework for integrating EJB with back-end enterprise applications, and discusses a connector example.
  - **Chapter 16** discusses clustering in large-scale EJB systems. You'll learn about how clustering works behind the scenes and learn a few strategies for how containers might support clustering. This is a critical topic for anyone building a system that involves several machines working together.

  - **Chapter 17** shows how to build a real-world Java EE application containing EJB components. We'll see how the EJB components should be used *together* with other technologies of the Java EE stack such as the persistent entities, as in an enterprise, as well as how to connect them with clients using Java servlets and JavaServer Pages (JSP) technologies. We'll also demonstrate how to design an EJB object model using UML.

- **The Appendices** are a collection of ancillary EJB topics. Some developers may want to read the appendices, while some may not feel the need to do so. Appendices A and B are provided in the book, whereas Appendices C, D, and E have been made available on the companion web site.
  - **Appendix A** teaches you Java Remote Method Invocation over the Internet Inter-ORB Protocol (RMI-IIOP) and the Java Naming and Directory Interface (JNDI). These technologies are prerequisites for using EJB. If you're just starting down the EJB road, you shall find it very helpful to read this appendix first.
  - **Appendix B** discusses the newly introduced annotations feature for the Java platform. It provides a quick reference of various annotations supported by the EJB 3.0 specification. This can come in handy while writing EJB code.
  - **Appendix C** is a deployment descriptor reference guide. This will be useful to you especially when you're examining deployment descriptors and if you ever find yourself in a situation of modifying the deployment descriptors manually.
  - **Appendix D** covers the EJB query language (EJB-QL) in detail.
  - **Appendix E** is an API and diagram reference guide. This is useful when you need to look up the purpose of a method or a class in the EJB programming API.

NOTE **Throughout the book, this icon will signal a tip, note, or other helpful advice on EJB programming.**

Illustrations in the Text

Almost all of the illustrations in this book are written in the Unified Modeling Language (UML). UML is the de facto standard methodology for illustrating software engineering concepts in an unambiguous way. If you don't know

UML, pick up a copy of The Unified Modeling Language User Guide (Addison-Wesley, ISBN 0201571684), which illustrates how to effectively use UML in your everyday software. UML is a highly important achievement in object-oriented methodology. It's a common mechanism for engineers to communicate and design with, and it forces you to abstract your object model prior to implementation. We cannot stress its use enough.

The Accompanying Web Site

This book would not be complete without a way to keep you in touch after it was published. A Web site is available for resources related to this book. There you'll find:

- All of the source code you see in this book. The code comes complete with Ant scripts, ready to build and run. It can be deployed on any application server that is Java EE 5–compliant.
- Updates to the source code examples.
- Error corrections from the text.
- A PDF copy of this book.

The Web site is at `www.wiley.com/go/sriganesh`.

Feedback

When you begin your EJB programming, we're sure you'll have many experiences to share with other readers. Feel free to e-mail examples, case studies, horror stories, or tips that you've found helpful in your experience, and we'll post them on the Web site.

From Here

Now that we've gotten the logistics out of the way, let's begin our exploration of Enterprise JavaBeans 3.0.

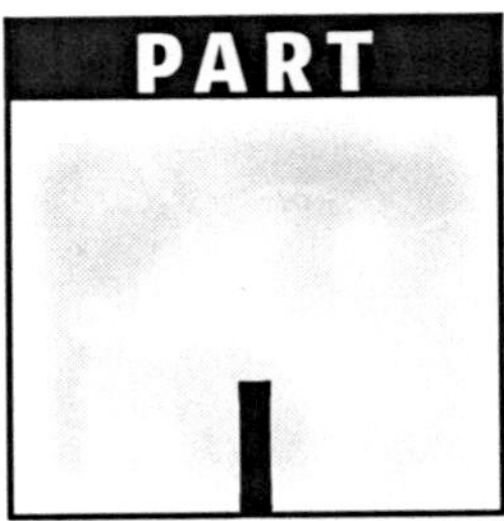

Overview

In Part I, we introduce the server-side development platform, the *Java Enterprise Edition* (Java EE), of which the *Enterprise JavaBeans* (EJB) component architecture is a vital piece. Java EE is a conglomeration of concepts, programming standards, and innovations—all written in the Java programming language. With Java EE, you can rapidly construct distributed, scalable, reliable, and portable as well as secure server-side deployments.

- **Chapter 1** begins by exploring the need for a server-side component architecture such as EJB. You'll see the rich needs of server-side computing, such as scalability, high availability, resource management, and security. We'll discuss how EJB architecture relates to the Service-oriented Architecture (SOA) paradigm. We'll also take a look at the Java EE server-side development platform.
- **Chapter 2** focuses on explaining why the existing EJB technology, especially the programming and deployment model, has to change to something much simpler. Chapter 2 makes this point by walking us through an example of developing and deploying an EJB 2.1 bean.
- **Chapter 3** gets down and dirty with EJB programming. Here, we'll write our first truly simple EJB 3.0 bean. In this chapter, we will also introduce other technologies and concepts that go hand in hand with EJB such as IIOP, JNDI naming services, annotations, deployment descriptors, and so on.

CHAPTER

1

Overview

Enterprise JavaBeans (EJB) is a server-side component framework that simplifies the process of building enterprise-class distributed component applications in Java. By using EJB, you can write scalable, reliable, and secure applications without writing your own complex distributed component framework. EJB is about rapid application development for the server side; you can quickly and easily construct server-side components in Java by leveraging a prewritten distributed infrastructure provided by the industry. EJB is designed to support application portability and reusability across any vendor's enterprise middleware services. For the benefit of those new to enterprise computing, these concepts will be clarified shortly. EJB is a complicated subject and deserves a thorough explanation.

This chapter introduces EJB by answering the following questions:

- What plumbing do you need to build a robust distributed object deployment?
- What is EJB, and what value does it add?
- How does EJB relate to SOA?
- Who are the players in an EJB ecosystem?

Let's kick things off with a brainstorming chapter.

A Prelude to Enterprise JavaBeans

Simply put, an EJB is a component. What are components? Unfortunately, over the years, this question has become a bit rhetorical, especially in the context of software engineering, because there is no exact or widely accepted answer to it. Henceforth, we will present *our* understanding of components.

Software Components

The online WordNet service hosted by Princeton University (`http://wordnet.princeton.edu/perl/webwn`) defines *component* quite simply and succinctly as "an abstract part of something." A software component goes one step beyond. It is a *concrete* part of something. A software component is a piece of code written to manifest the behavior of a corresponding abstract concept. Mostly, these abstract concepts find their underlying basis in the real world. For example, a `MortgageDebt` component might emulate the nuances associated with actual mortgage debts of real-world entities such as people, corporations, and so on. This explanation of components probably sounds a lot like how objects were explained in the late 1980s. Even so, components differ from objects in a substantial manner—they live an independent existence. Therein lies all the difference between objects and components.

A component is a self-contained entity such that it can be *reused* in a similar or a completely different application, as long as the semantics of the component are well understood. A component must be packaged with all the requisite artifacts so that it can live an independent, reusable existence outside of the original application. A business or system application can thus be designed to consist of multiple such *reusable* software components, each tasked with a certain functional responsibility.

So what do we stand to gain by designing software applications in terms of components? How did we reach the conclusion that componentization was the right approach to take? Well, continue reading.

The Need for Componentization

One of the fortuitous by-products of a more than decade-long *U.S. Justice Department vs. IBM* antitrust lawsuit (more details of this landmark trial can be found at `http://www.hagley.lib.de.us/1980.htm`) was the emergence of a burgeoning software industry. The U.S. Justice Department based the antitrust lawsuit on the premise that IBM's bundling of software, hardware (including peripherals), and services under a single pricing model marred the independent players in the software as well as the peripherals markets. Up until then, IBM and other hardware vendors did not sell software but rather bundled it with hardware almost for free, thereby making the survival of independent software vendors impossible. Even though the Justice Department eventually withdrew their charges against IBM in 1982, the impact that this case had on IBM and other players was profound. Suffice it to say that the 1970s marked the dawn of the software industry.

The emergence of the software market led to the advent of new software architectures and development paradigms. In the ensuing 25-odd years, the software industry became increasingly sophisticated in terms of architecture and development methodologies. The industry had begun deploying two-tier architectures where monolithic applications communicated with large databases running on a different system. Object-oriented development in older as well as newer languages such as C++ and Java, respectively, was in full swing. People were trying to fathom the potential of the public Internet. Corporations were beginning to realize that having a corporate Web site was as important as having phones and fax machines for communication with customers and partners.

It was at this juncture that software architects started recognizing the lack of flexibility and interoperability in existing application deployments. The inflexibility was attributed to the inherent nature of monolithic applications that inhibited the ability to repurpose and reuse existing functionality. Even though these monolithic applications were developed using object-oriented languages, object technology by itself was not fully equipped to garner optimum levels of reuse. Dividing functionality into independent and self-contained components that can interoperate with each other to assemble an application was deemed the better solution for building applications.

The preference for component-based architectural principles gradually gave way to *component frameworks* such as Common Object Request Broker Architecture (CORBA), ActiveX/COM, EJB, and so on. In keeping pace with other disruptive forces at work in software design (mainly distributed multi-tier computing), these frameworks ended up providing much more than merely the mechanisms for component development. Component frameworks evolved sufficiently to support development and deployment of enterprise applications comprising components distributed over various tiers.

To dive further, let us identify the infrastructure needs of multi-tier enterprise applications that could be provided by component frameworks.

Infrastructure Needs of Distributed Applications

Figure 1.1 shows a typical business application. This application could exist in any industry and could solve any business problem. It could be an equity trading system, a corporate banking application, a call center application, a sales automation application, and so on.

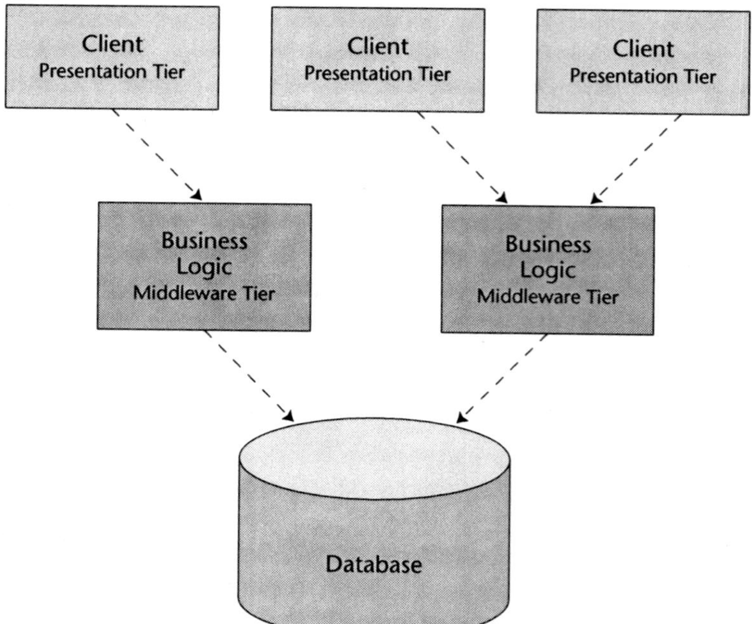

Figure 1.1 A typical multi-tier deployment.

Notice that this enterprise application is a *distributed system*. We broke up what would otherwise be a large, monolithic application and divorced each layer of the application from the other, so that each of these layers is independent and serves a distinct purpose. For instance, the presentation layer carries the logic to provide a user interface to the client, the middleware tier consists of the logic to provide the actual business functionality and other services, whereas the database tier provides data services.

Now look at this picture and ask yourself which issues would need to be taken care of for such a deployment? Take a moment to reflect on this question before proceeding to the following list of aspects worth considering in such a distributed deployment.

- **Remote Method Invocation.** We need logic that connects one tier to another via a network connection—viz. logic to connect presentation tier to middleware tier and middleware tier to database tier. This includes dispatching method requests, brokering parameters, dispatching SQL statements, and more.
- **Load balancing.** Presentation clients must be directed to the middleware (as well as database) servers with the lightest load. If a server is overloaded, a different server should be chosen.

- **Transparent failover.** If a server crashes, or if the network crashes, can clients be rerouted to other servers without interruption of service? If so, how fast does failover happen? Seconds? Minutes? What is acceptable for your business problem?
- **Back-end integration.** Code needs to be written to persist business data into databases as well as integrate with legacy systems that may already exist.
- **Transactions.** What if two clients access the same row of the database simultaneously? Or what if the database crashes? Transactions protect you from these issues.
- **Clustering.** What if the server contains state when it crashes? Is that state replicated across all servers, so that clients can use a different server?
- **Dynamic redeployment.** How do you perform software upgrades while the site is running? Do you need to take a system down, or can you keep it running?
- **Clean shutdown.** If you need to shut down a server, can you do it in a smooth, clean manner so that you don't interrupt service to clients who are currently using the server?
- **Logging and auditing.** If something goes wrong, is there a log that you can consult to determine the cause of the problem? A log would help you debug the problem so it does not happen again.
- **Systems management.** In the event of a catastrophic failure, who is monitoring your system? You want monitoring software that pages a system administrator if a catastrophe occurred.
- **Threading.** Now that you have many clients connecting to a server, that server is going to need the capability of processing multiple client requests simultaneously. This means the server must be coded to be multithreaded.
- **Message-oriented middleware.** Certain types of requests should be *message-based*, where the clients and servers are very loosely coupled. You need infrastructure to accommodate messaging.
- **Component life cycle.** The components that live within the server need to be created or destroyed when client traffic increases or decreases, respectively.
- **Resource pooling.** If a client is not currently using a server, that server's precious resources can be returned to a *pool* to be reused when other clients connect. This includes sockets (such as database connections) as well as components that live within the server.

- **Security.** The servers and databases need to be shielded from saboteurs. Known users must be allowed to execute operations for which they have adequate rights of execution.
- **Caching.** Let's assume that there is some database data that all clients share and make use of, such as a common product catalog. Why should your servers retrieve that same catalog data from the database over and over again? You could keep that data around in the servers' memory and avoid costly network roundtrips and database hits.
- And much, *much* more.

Each of these aspects should be addressed to enable deployment of robust large-scale distributed applications. Consequently, each of these aspects can be thought of as a service—a service to do resource pooling, a service to provide message-based communications, a service to provide authentication and other security facilities. These services are termed *middleware services* due to the fact that they are commonly required in the middleware layer of a multitier application.

Application Server–Class Software

Clearly middleware services are a must for an enterprise application to function successfully. So how should one go about availing such infrastructure services? What greater role can component frameworks play in this regard? IT and technology organizations around the world can do one of the two things—build these services or buy them.

Building Middleware Services from Scratch

This approach could be considered perilous because building and maintaining middleware services is a complicated affair. It requires expertise in system-level programming semantics such as multithreading, pooling, transaction management, clustering, and so on. Most business application developers employed by IT departments are not skilled enough in system programming. Undertaking such a development would therefore require additional investment in hiring system programmers proficient in this arena.

Moreover, such infrastructure services are orthogonal to the core business of most corporations using IT. Therefore, building such infrastructure services in-house would divert IT departments from the business information services that they are supposed to be delivering to the rest of the organization. Nonetheless, quite a few companies have taken this route, mainly due to the absence of frameworks to provide such distributed computing services, out of the box, at the time.

Buying Middleware Services via Application Server Software

The increasing popularity of component-based development and distributed computing gave rise to component frameworks that provided not only the basic component development facilities but also commonplace infrastructure services—a.k.a. quality of services (QoS)—for multi-tier enterprise applications. These QoS are rendered to the components hosted within an environment, namely *application server*, which implements a distributed component framework such as EJB.

Application server–class software came into existence to let you buy these middleware services rather than build them yourself. Application servers enable you to focus on your business application and not worry about the middleware plumbing you need for a robust server-side deployment. You write the code specific to your business and industry, and deploy that code into the runtime environment of an application server. You've just solved your business problem by *dividing and conquering*.

Standardization of Component Frameworks

It has been a number of years since the idea of multi-tier server-side deployments surfaced. Since then, more than 50 application servers have appeared on the market. At first, each application server provided component services in a nonstandard, proprietary way. This occurred because there was no agreed-upon definition of what a component should be or how it should be provided with services or how should it interact with the application server. The result? Once you bet on an application server, your code was locked into that vendor's solution. This greatly reduced portability and was an especially tough pill to swallow in the Java world, which has always promoted openness and portability.

What we need is an *agreement*, or a set of standard interfaces, between application servers and components. This agreement will enable any component to run within any application server. It will allow components to be switched in and out of various application servers without having to change code or potentially even recompile the components themselves. Application server vendors that implement such a standardized component framework secure their business by providing a higher quality of implementation of the standard, rather than locking in their customers.

Figure 1.2 depicts an application server that implements a standard component framework such as EJB.

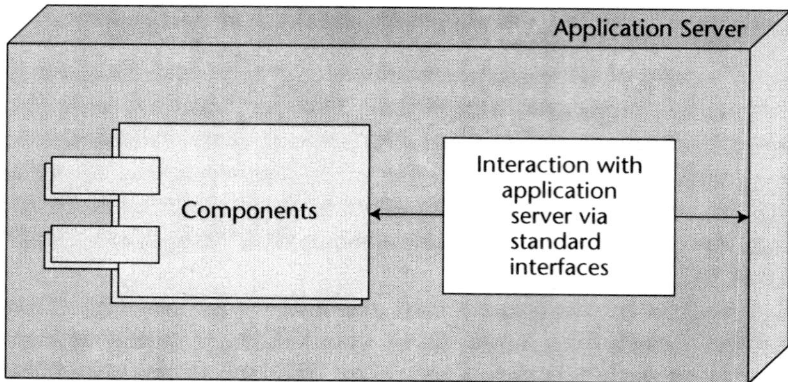

Figure 1.2 A standard component framework.

NOTE Even though software is regarded as one of the most cutting-edge industries, it has lagged behind in the trend to standardize component interfaces. Other industries, such as consumer device manufacturers, began following this path long before the software industry. For instance, television vendors started supporting NTSC (National TV Standards Committee), a standard for broadcasting, in TV sets almost five decades before we started seeing similar design principles in software.

Enterprise JavaBeans Technology

Let us finally define EJB properly. EJB is a standard for developing and deploying server-side distributed components in Java. It defines an agreement (contract) between components and application servers that enables any component to run in any compliant application server.

The three main value propositions of EJB are:

- **It is a ubiquitous industry standard.** EJB has benefited from its widespread use—it is easy now to hire staff with a good knowledge of EJB to develop and maintain your systems. Also, due to the maturity of the technology, numerous best practices for implementing EJB are available to those who use it.
- **Portability is possible.** The EJB specification is published and available freely to all. Since EJB is a standard, you do not need to gamble on the long-term viability and proprietary architecture of a single vendor. And although porting applications from one platform to another will never be without its costs, it is easier to get it done working with a standard than without it.

- **Rapid application development.** Your application can be built faster because you get middleware infrastructure services such as transactions, pooling, security, and so on from the application server. Also, innumerable tools have been made available by vendors as well as the open source community over the years to do rapid application development using EJB.

Note that while EJB does have these virtues, there are also scenarios in which EJB is overkill. Hopefully, with the simpler programming model introduced in EJB 3.0, its usage in smaller applications will increase. See Chapter 13 for best practices and discussions surrounding the issue of when to (and when not to) use EJB.

NOTE **Physically, EJB is actually two things in one:**

- ***Specification.*** **With EJB 3.0, the specification has been divided into three documents, which are all freely downloadable from `http://www.jcp.org/en/jsr/detail?id=220`. The specification lays out the rules of engagement between components and application servers. It constricts how you code enterprise beans to enable "write once, run anywhere" behavior for your EJB application.**
- ***A set of Java interfaces.*** **Components and application servers must conform to these interfaces. Since all components are written to the same interfaces, they all look the same to the application server. The application server therefore can manage any EJB-compliant components.**

Why Java?

The EJB framework has supported only the Java language thus far, unlike the .NET framework that supports multiple languages. Though this sounds a bit restrictive, the good news is that Java is one of the best-suited languages for building distributed components for the following reasons:

- **Interface/implementation separation.** We need a language that supports clean separation between the interface and implementation mainly to keep the component upgrades and maintenance to a minimum. Java supports this separation at a syntactic level through the *interface* and *class* keywords.
- **Safe and secure.** The Java architecture is much safer than traditional programming languages. In Java, if a thread dies, the application stays up. Pointers are not an issue since the language never exposes them to the programmer. Memory leaks occur much less often. Java also has a rich library set, so that Java is not just the syntax of a language but a whole set of prewritten, debugged libraries that enable developers to

avoid reinventing the wheel in a buggy way. This safety is extremely important for mission-critical applications.

- **Cross-platform.** Java runs on any platform. There is a Java Virtual Machine (JVM) for all platforms. Vendors provide support for their application servers across all the platforms most of the time. This means that EJB applications could be deployed on all these platforms. This is valuable for customers who have invested in a variety of hardware platforms, such as Intel, AMD X32-X64, SPARC, and mainframes, as well as operating platforms, including various flavors of UNIX, Windows, and so on, in their data centers.

NOTE **If you don't want to go the EJB route, you have two other choices:**

- **Lightweight open source Java frameworks such as Spring. In Chapter 13 we discuss when to use EJB versus such nonstandard frameworks.**
- **Microsoft .NET–managed components, part of the Microsoft .NET platform.**

EJB as a Business Tier Component

The real difference between presentation tier components, such as standalone applications and applets, dynamically generated Web pages, or Web service clients, and enterprise beans is the domain in which they operate. Presentation components are well suited to handle *client-side* operations, such as rendering GUIs, executing client-side validations, constructing appropriate Simple Object Access Protocol (SOAP) messages to send them back and forth to a Web service, and so on. They deal directly with the end user or end application.

Enterprise beans, on the other hand, are not intended for the client side; they are *server-side* components. They are meant to perform server-side operations, such as executing complex algorithms or performing highly transactional business operations. The server side has different kinds of needs than GUI clients do. Server-side components need to run in a highly available (24x7), fault-tolerant, transactional, multi-user, secure environment. The application server provides such a server-side environment for the enterprise beans, and it provides the runtime services necessary for the functioning of enterprise beans.

Specifically, EJB is used to help write logic that solves *business problems*. Typically, EJB components (enterprise beans) can perform any of the following tasks:

- **Perform business logic.** Examples include computing taxes on a shopping cart, ensuring that the manager has authority to approve the purchase order, or sending an order confirmation e-mail using the *JavaMail API*.

- **Access a database.** Examples include submitting an order for books, transferring money between two bank accounts, or calling a stored procedure to retrieve a helpdesk ticket in a customer service application. Enterprise beans can achieve database access using many techniques, one of which is the *Java Database Connectivity* (JDBC) *API*.
- **Integrate with other systems**. Examples include calling a highly transactional *CICS* legacy system written in C that computes the risk exposure for a new insurance customer, using a legacy VSAM (Virtual Storage Access Method) data store, or accessing *SAP R/3*. Enterprise beans can be integrated with other applications in multiple ways, one of which is through the *Java EE Connector Architecture*, which we will cover in detail in Chapter 15.

Thus, EJB components sit behind the presentation tier applications or components and do all the hard work. Examples of EJB clients include the following:

- **Application clients.** Application clients execute on a user's desktop, either within an Internet browser environment as an applet or alone. They connect through the network to EJB components that live on a server. These EJB components may perform any of the tasks listed previously (business logic, database logic, or accessing other systems).
- **Dynamically generated Web pages.** Web sites that are transactional and personalized in nature need their Web pages generated specifically for each request. For example, the home page for Amazon.com is completely different for each user, depending on the user's personal preferences. Core technologies such as Java Servlets and Java Server Pages (JSP) are used to dynamically generate such Web pages. Both servlets and JSPs live within a Web server and can connect to EJB components for business logic, thereby generating dynamic Web pages based upon the results returned from the EJB layer.
- **Web service clients**. Some business applications require no user interface at all. They exist to interconnect with other business partners' applications, which in turn may provide their own user interface. For example, consider a scenario where Dell Computer Corporation needs to procure Intel chips to assemble and distribute desktop computers. Here, Intel could expose an *Order Parts* Web service that enables the Dell *Procurement* Web service client to order chips. In this case, the Intel system does not provide a graphical user interface per se, but rather provides a programmatic Web service interface that can be used by a system instead of a human user. This scenario is shown in Figure 1.3.

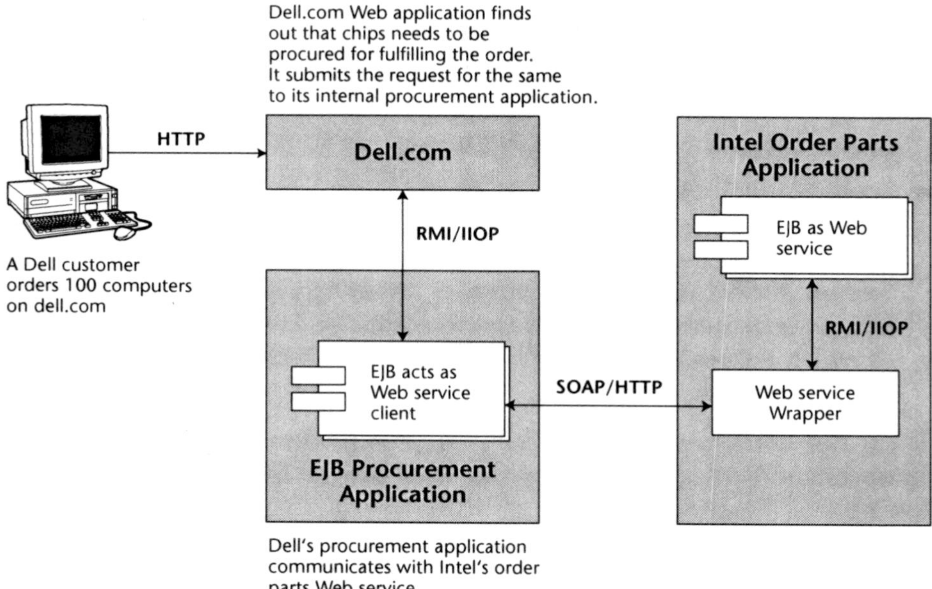
Dell.com Web application finds out that chips needs to be procured for fulfilling the order. It submits the request for the same to its internal procurement application.
HTTP
Dell.com
Intel Order Parts Application
EJB as Web service
RMI/IIOP
A Dell customer orders 100 computers on dell.com
RMI/IIOP
EJB acts as Web service client
SOAP/HTTP
Web service Wrapper
EJB Procurement Application
Dell's procurement application communicates with Intel's order parts Web service.

Figure 1.3 EJBs as Web service clients.

Distributed Computing: The Foundation of EJB

EJB enables development and deployment of distributed components. A *distributed component*, also commonly referred to as *distributed object* or *remote object*, is callable from a remote system. That is, not only can it be called from an in-process client but also from an out-of-process client that might be located on a different system on the network.

A remote invocation of a method on a distributed object follows a common process that is similar across almost all distributed computing technologies. The main steps of this remote method invocation process are:

1. The client calls a *stub*, which is a *client-side proxy object*. This stub is responsible for masking network communications from the client. The stub knows how to call over the network using sockets and also how to massage parameters from their Java representations to the corresponding network representations.

2. The stub calls over the network to a skeleton, which is a server-side proxy object. The skeleton masks network communication from the distributed object. The skeleton understands how to receive calls on a socket as well as how to massage parameters from their network representations to their Java representations.

3. The skeleton delegates the call to the appropriate implementation object. This object serves the call and does its work, and returns control to the skeleton, which returns it to the stub, which finally returns control to the client.

Figure 1.4 depicts the method invocation on a remote object.

A key point here is that both the stub and the server-side implementation object implement the same interface (called the *remote interface*). This means the stub clones the distributed object's method signatures. A client who calls a method on the stub *thinks* he is calling the distributed object directly; in reality, the client is calling an empty stub that knows how to go over the network. This is called *distribution transparency*. In fact, the distributed object is an abstraction that is created by the cooperation between the stub, skeleton, and implementation objects. No single entity in this scenario *is* the distributed object.

You can develop and deploy distributed objects using many other technologies, including CORBA (OMG), Distributed Component Object Model or DCOM (; Microsoft), and Java RMI-IIOP (Sun).

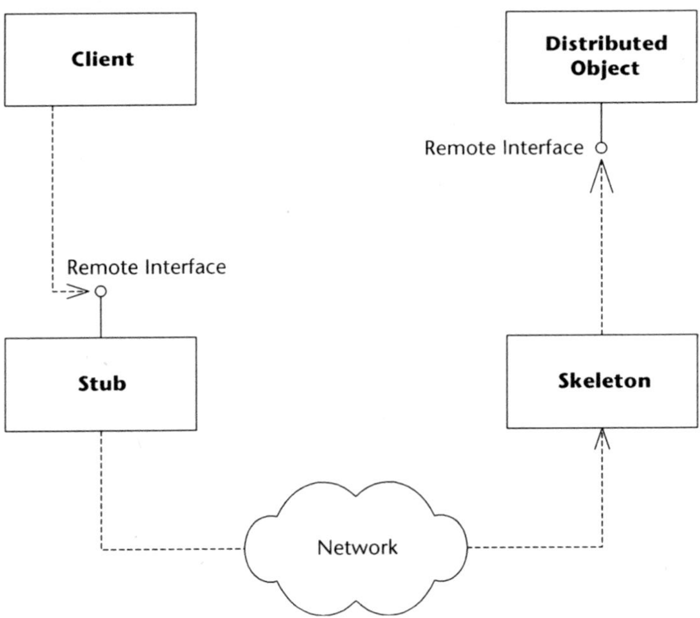

Figure 1.4 Remote method invocation.

DISTRIBUTION TRANSPARENCY

Distribution transparency is the Holy Grail in distributed systems technology and is very hard to achieve. Perfect distribution transparency would mean that a client never sees any differences between local and remote interactions. In the presence of the more complex failure modes of remote operations and network latency, this is not possible. Most of the time, the term distribution transparency is used rather loosely to mean that the syntax of the client code making invocations is the same for both remote and local invocations. Even this is not always the case when you consider the different exceptions found in remote interfaces that in turn require different exception handling, and the subtle differences between the pass-by-reference and pass-by-value semantics that local and remote invocations sometimes exhibit.

For these reasons, most middleware systems settle for a less ambitious form of transparency, viz. location transparency. We will explore location transparency further in Chapter 3.

EJB Middleware Services

Although we expound upon the EJB middleware services such as transaction management, persistence, messaging, security, clustering, and so on throughout this book, we think it is about time to introduce you to the approach taken by EJB in provisioning them.

There are two ways in which a framework such as EJB can provide middleware services—explicitly and implicitly. To use explicit middleware services you must *explicitly* call the middleware services' APIs. Implicit middleware services can be used without having to write against the middleware APIs viz. *implicitly*.

Explicit Middleware Approach

Traditionally, transactional systems such as CORBA, Tuxedo, and COM/DCOM have made available middleware APIs; your code uses them to request the framework to provide the requisite services. This explicit approach can be illustrated using pseudo-code. The following example shows a `transfer` method on the `Bank` distributed component that performs transfer of funds between two accounts.

```
transfer(Account account1, Account account2, long amount) {
// 1: Call middleware API to perform a security check
// 2: Call middleware API to start a transaction
// 3: Call middleware API to load rows from the database
// 4: Subtract the balance from one account, add to the other
```

```
// 5: Call middleware API to store rows in the database
// 6: Call middleware API to end the transaction
}
```

Clearly, although we are serviced with the requisite middleware by the framework, our business logic is intertwined with the logic to call these middleware APIs. This approach has some major downsides:

- **Lowers developer productivity.** Even though the framework provides middleware services, the developer is still supposed to write the code to use them. Writing and testing this code obviously takes time, thereby leading to lower developer productivity.
- **Difficult to write.** The code is bloated. We simply want to perform a transfer, but it requires a large amount of code due to the mingling of middleware service interaction code with the business logic code.
- **Difficult to maintain.** If you want to change the way you consume middleware services, you need to rewrite your code.

Implicit Middleware Approach

Using this approach, the framework would not only provide middleware services but also an easier way to use them. An implicit middleware framework will let you declare the middleware services that you need for your application in a separate descriptor file or even through simple annotations within the code. Hence, your code contains no cumbersome API calls to use the middleware services. The code is clean and focused on business logic. To use the earlier illustration, below is how the pseudo-code for the `transfer` method on the `Bank` component will look:

```
transfer(Account account1, Account account2, long amount) {
     // 1: Subtract the balance from one account, add to the other
}
```

At the time the preceding code is compiled, the framework will peruse the descriptor and/or annotations within the code (depending on the approach used) and will provide the requested middleware services. A framework may or may not prescribe a methodology as to how to implicitly render these services. For instance, the EJB framework does not define a specific way of doing this, and different EJB vendors use different mechanisms to provide these services implicitly. For instance, some vendors choose to consolidate all calls to middleware services in the skeleton of the given EJB component, whereas some vendors put these calls in a different object, which is then called by the

EJB skeleton. Thus, the mechanism used to provide the middleware services implicitly is an implementation detail of the EJB server and is left to the product vendors to decide individually.

Most contemporary computing frameworks, standard or not, follow this approach. The examples include EJB, Microsoft .NET, Hibernate, and so on. The upsides to this approach are:

- **Increases developer productivity.** Developers do not have to write the code for invoking middleware services. All they have to do is declare the services they require in a descriptor file or as annotations in the code itself. This increases their productivity.
- **Easy to write.** Since no code needs to be written to call middleware services, your component code is focused on business logic.
- **Easy to maintain.** The separation of business logic and middleware logic is clean and maintainable. Changing middleware service consumption does not require changing application code.

NOTE Annotations or metadata facilities have been introduced in the Java platform from J2SE 5.0. Annotations are a powerful concept and play an important role in EJB 3.0 and Java EE 5.0 at large. We will introduce annotations in Chapter 3, while discussing the EJB 3.0 programming model.

Implicit vs. Explicit Middleware Services in EJB

EJB uses the implicit middleware approach—however, it also provides a simple API to explicitly interact with middleware services. Although the API approach is a complex one, it puts greater control in the hands of a developer.

For instance, imagine a scenario where a developer does not want to mark an entire method on an EJB as transactional. In this case, he can use the Java Transaction API to interact with the transaction management services of EJB. Using this middleware service API, the developer can mark the beginning and end of the transaction at specific points within the method code, thereby wielding better control.

Although developers usually use middleware services implicitly, it is helpful to know that the EJB framework provides a choice. Also, it is good to know that you can use some middleware services implicitly and some explicitly, which leads to a hybrid approach to using middleware.

Roles in the EJB Application Life Cycle

An EJB application's life cycle involve three main phases—development, deployment, and administration. Depending on the size and scale of the application, the activities related to each of these phases can range from simple to complex. In the latter case, the time required to take an EJB application live can be significantly reduced if responsibilities across the life cycle are divided among various parties. Each of these parties will play a role, so to speak, in the EJB application's life cycle. These parties can be made up of a single person or groups of 10s or even 100s of developers. As long as the individuals playing these roles are well trained in the given area of application life cycle, this division of labor can yield the maximum possible efficiency. We have seen such role-based development practice used widely, especially in medium and large-scale projects.

The following sections discuss the responsibilities handled by these roles and clarify the issues that could surface.

The Bean Provider

The *bean provider* supplies business components, or enterprise beans. It is tasked with writing the code of enterprise beans and also unit testing their beans. The bean provider can be an internal department providing components to other departments, or it can be a group of developers in a team responsible for writing EJB components, which can subsequently be used by other developers in the same team.

The Application Assembler

The application assembler is the overall application architect. This party is responsible for understanding how various components fit together and writes the glue code, if required, to make the components work together in a meaningful manner. An application assembler may even author a few components along the way for this purpose. The application assembler is mostly the *consumer* of the beans supplied by the bean provider.

The application assembler could perform any or all of the following tasks:

- Using an understanding of the business application to decide which combination of existing components and new enterprise beans are needed to provide an effective solution; in essence, plan the application assembly.
- Supply a user interface (perhaps a Swing-based application or applet, or servlet, or JSP) or a Web service.
- Write the client code to access components supplied by bean providers.
- Write integration code that maps data between components supplied by different bean providers. After all, components won't magically work together to solve a business problem, especially if different parties write the components.

The role of application assembler can be played either by a systems integrator, a consulting firm, or an in-house developer.

The EJB Deployer

After the application assembler builds the application, the application must be *deployed* (and go into production) in a running operational environment. Many times, the bean provider or an application assembler is unaware of the issues involved in a production environment. Invariably, the environment in which EJB applications are developed is not the same as the one in which they are deployed. Hence, definite skills are required to take care of such differences in system and software infrastructure products used in development versus production to ensure a smooth transition to the live environment. This need is fulfilled by the role of an EJB deployer. The EJB deployer should be well acquainted with the portfolio of systems, storage, software, and so on in use in production, at least for that specific application. For instance, an EJB deployer should be able to work with the various application server(s) used in the production environment.

Some of the responsibilities of an EJB deployer include:

- Securing the deployment with a hardware or software firewall and other such security measures. Usually, enterprise applications are hosted within managed data centers. In which case, the EJB deployer will interact actively with the data center staff and co-manage the deployment of EJB applications.
- Choosing hardware that provides the required level of robustness and quality of service. Again, if your enterprise application lives within the walls of a data center, the EJB deployer will work with data center staff to identify the systems that meet the needs in terms of resources such as storage, network bandwidth, memory, and so on.
- Providing redundant hardware and other resources for reliability and fault tolerance. This involves configuring the EJB deployment for fault tolerance at the system level and/or application level.
- Tuning application performance. EJB deployment is not considered complete without ensuring that its performance meets the defined requirements. If the application does not meet the desired performance, then it will need tuning. Deployers can conduct this exercise in coordination with other performance experts in their organization.

The System Administrator

Once the deployment goes live, the system administrator steps in to oversee the stability of the operational solution. The system administrator is responsible for the upkeep and monitoring of the deployed system and may make use of various performance monitoring and application management tools in the process.

For example, in the event of failures or disruptions, a sophisticated EJB application-monitoring tool can send an alarm to the designated administrator, calling for their immediate attention. Some EJB server vendors have supplemented their server offerings by integrating with widely used management tool product lines such as OpenView, Tivoli, Unicenter, and so on. Others such as JBoss have written their own support for EJB application monitoring and management using technologies such as JMX.

Figure 1.5 highlights the coordination between the various parties throughout the EJB application's life cycle.

Note that some of these roles could be combined as well. For example, at a small startup company, the bean provider, application assembler, and deployer could all be the same person who is trying to build a business solution using EJBs.

DATA CENTERS

A data center is a consolidated facility that houses computer systems, storage, and communication related equipment needed to run information technology operations. In a typical data center, a dedicated staff manages not just hardware systems but also the hosted software applications. Depending on how critical the 24x7 functioning of a hosted application is, a data center would provide various levels of service agreements to their clients.

In years gone by, almost all companies operated an in-house data center. Many business models bloomed during the Internet revolution of the late 1990s, and outsourcing data centers was one. Most of the dotcoms at the time outsourced the hosting and operations of their Web sites to professional data center businesses. Even today, small as well as most medium-sized businesses continue to outsource data center operations. However, larger companies, such as the large commercial banks, continue to manage their own in-house data centers.

Data centers are one area where these companies are incurring large capital as well as operational expenditure today—even more than for new IT development. Therefore, it is one of the prime targets that CFOs are focusing on to reduce costs and increase efficiency. If you work in the role of an EJB application architect, a deployer, or even a system administrator who manages systems hosting EJB applications, it would be beneficial for you to find out about your company's data center optimization strategy. Knowing about it will help you make the right decisions in terms of product and architecture selection, thereby reducing the cost and complexity of your data centers.

QUALITY OF SERVICE(S) AND THE EJB SPECIFICATION

Quality of Service (QoS) in our industry refers to the types of services offered by infrastructure software such as operating systems, application servers, databases, and so on to the applications that run on them. Different QoS levels will impact the health of applications differently. For example, an application running on an application server that has support for transparent failover mechanisms will be much more robust (assuming it uses the facility) than the one deployed on a product that does not provide such QoS.

The EJB specification has mandated that application server vendors provide certain crucial QoS such as transaction management, resource pooling, component life cycle management, and so on to enable faster development of relatively sound enterprise applications. However, other enterprise-level QoS are still considered as optional by the EJB specification expert group. QoS such as clustering or caching of data or load balancing, and monitoring and management capabilities, fall into this category. The specification does not force vendors to provide these optional QoS. Vendors provide them if their customers demand them. However, they do not need to support such optional QoS to be compliant with the EJB specification.

Because the specification does not mandate the support for such QoS or even specify how vendors should implement them, the question is—does using such nonstandard QoS hamper application portability? The answer is—it depends. If you are making changes in your EJB code to be able to use these QoS, then you are most likely making your code nonportable. Why? Because you could be using nonstandard programming APIs supplied by the vendor to access these vendor provided services. When you hop application servers, the new application server may or may not provide that QoS. If in fact the new application server does provide that QoS, it definitely will be using different APIs to provide for that. However, if you are availing these QoS transparently or through out-of-the-code configurations, then you are protecting your code from becoming nonportable.

Bottom line—be aware of the portability issues that could arise when using proprietary vendor features.

EJB Ecosystem

The EJB *ecosystem* comprises literally, thousands of tools, servers, utilities, IDEs, and so on that are available to the developers for all stages of EJB application development and deployment. Out of them all, developers most certainly interact with two categories of products in their EJB projects—EJB containers and development tools. Let us give you a taste of these two classes of products in terms of what is available today.

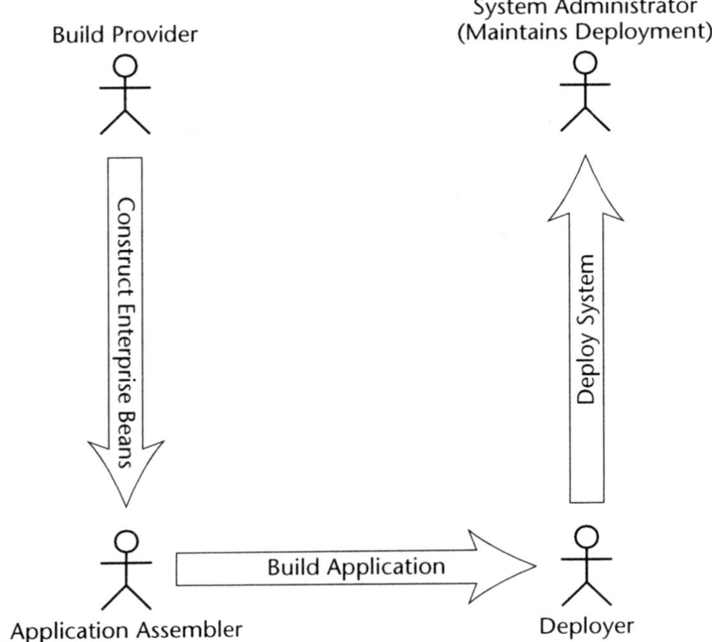

Figure 1.5 EJB role-based development.

REBRANDING OF JAVA ENTERPRISE EDITION AND STANDARD EDITION

Sun Microsystems recently rebranded the J2SE and J2EE stacks to Java SE (Java Platform, Standard Edition) and Java EE (Java Platform, Enterprise Edition), respectively. This change is in effect from the 6.0 version of Standard Edition and 5.0 version of Enterprise Edition. This means that what could have been J2SE 6.0 will now be Java SE 6.0 and what could have been J2EE 5.0 will now be Java EE 5.0. It is important to get used to calling these platforms by their newer names, since the entire industry has started using them. Everywhere in this book, we have used the newer branding for both these technologies wherever applicable.

Since these naming conventions only apply to the upcoming versions of standard and enterprise stacks, we should continue using J2SE and J2EE convention for the older versions. For example, we can refer to version 5.0 of standard edition as J2SE 5.0 instead of Java SE 5.0. Similarly, we can refer to version 1.4 of enterprise edition as J2EE 1.4 instead of Java EE 1.4.

EJB Container

The *EJB container* is the piece of software that implements the EJB specification. The reason it is called a container is that it provides an environment within which EJB components live and breath. In other words, it provides containment to the EJB components. An application server provider usually also provides an EJB container. The container supplies middleware services to the beans and manages them. More than 30 application servers have been certified by Sun Microsystems to date for previous versions of Java EE (J2EE 1.2, 1.3, and 1.4). A complete list can be obtained from `http://java.sun.com/j2ee/licensees.html`, but some of the popular commercial application servers include BEA WebLogic, Sun Java System Application Server (formerly, Sun ONE Application Server), IBM WebSphere, and Oracle Application Server. In the open source arena, JBoss, Glassfish, and Apache Geronimo are the notable application servers.

NOTE We will use the terms *EJB container* and *EJB server* interchangeably in this book.

EJB Tools

To facilitate EJB development and deployment, there are numerous tools you can use. The EJB tools ecosystem consists of several *integrated development environments* (IDEs) that assist you in rapidly building, debugging, and deploying components. IDEs encompass most of the major phases of the EJB application life cycle, except monitoring and management. Most IDEs provide a mechanism to design, develop, test, document, and deploy EJBs. Some of the popular commercial and open source EJB IDEs are Borland JBuilder, Oracle JDeveloper, BEA WebLogic Workshop, IBM WebSphere Studio Application Developer, Sun Microsystems Java Studio Enterprise, NetBeans, and Eclipse. This list is by no means exhaustive.

Most of these tools enable you to model components using unified modeling language (UML), which is the diagram style used in this book. You can also generate EJB code from these UML models. Some of the examples of specialized commercial products in this space include Borland Together and IBM Rational line of products. Also, there are a bunch of open source code utilities and tools, covered in Chapter 13, that can be used for UML modeling and code generation.

There are other tools as well, which you can use to develop your EJB applications rapidly and successfully. For example, you can use Junit for testing, Ant/Xdoclet for building your EJB projects, and performance analyzers (Borland OptimizeIt or Quest Software JProbe).

JAVABEANS VERSUS ENTERPRISE JAVABEANS

You may have heard of another standard called *JavaBeans*. JavaBeans is a different technology from Enterprise JavaBeans.

In a nutshell, JavaBeans are Java classes that have `get`/`set` methods on them. They are reusable Java components with properties, events, and methods that can be easily wired together to create Java applications.

The JavaBeans framework is lightweight compared to Enterprise JavaBeans. You can use JavaBeans to assemble larger components or to build entire applications. JavaBeans, however, are development components and are not deployable components. You typically do not deploy a JavaBean; rather, JavaBeans help you construct larger software that is deployable. And because they cannot be deployed, JavaBeans do not need to live in a runtime environment and hence, in a container. Since JavaBeans are just Java classes, they do not need an application server to instantiate them, to destroy them, and to provide other services to them. An EJB application can use JavaBeans, especially when marshaling data from one EJB layer to another, say to components belonging to a presentation tier or to a non–Java EE application written in Java.

NOTE Given that this book is technology focused, we will obviously not be spending much time on in-depth coverage of any specific product. However, every now and then we will use some interesting products (open source and closed source), to make our point.

Service-Oriented Architectures and Enterprise JavaBeans

Service-oriented architecture (SOA) has gained stupendous momentum in the recent years. As with all new ideas, there is a lot of confusion while everyone is trying to understand the core principles underlying SOA—while they are still attempting to discern what characterizes an architecture as SOA-based or otherwise. The fact that different vendors define SOA in various ways, mostly to suit their purposes, does not help reduce the SOA tumult either.

In this section, we strive to provide a workable understanding of SOA. It is essential for EJB developers and architects to understand that SOA and EJB are not mutually exclusive but rather are symbiotic. You can write robust SOA architectures using EJB. You might be called upon to implement SOA projects using EJB. Hence, it is imperative that you understand the basic principles of SOA and correctly juxtapose SOA and EJB.

Defining Service-Oriented Architectures

At the core of a service-oriented architecture lies the concept of *service*. A simplistic definition of service is a group of related components that carry out a given business process function, for example transferring funds between banks or booking an itinerary. An SOA, thus, is a paradigm focusing on development of services rather than piecemeal components such that these services provide a higher level of abstraction from a functional standpoint. Of course, there are more properties to SOA than mere coarse granularity. One such characteristic property of SOA is that they are autonomous in nature. These independent entities can interact with others in spite of differences in the way they have been implemented or the platform they have been deployed on. The notion of putting together (integrating) such autonomous and loosely coupled services to address the changing business needs has a huge value proposition, and it is well on its way to realization with the emergence of various choreography, orchestration, and collaboration technologies such as WS-BPEL (Web Services Business Process Execution Language), EbXML BPSS (Electronic Business XML Business Process Specification Schema), and WS-CDL (Web Services Choreography Description Language)

SOA and Web Services

The terms Web services and SOA are often used interchangeably and wrongly so. SOA is a paradigm. There are many possible ways of building software so that it implements salient features of SOA (mainly coarse granularity and loose coupling). One such way is Web services. Web services are a group of XML technologies that can be used for implementing SOA. Core Web service technologies—mainly SOAP and WSDL—form the basis of most of these Web service implementations today.

Simple Object Access Protocol (SOAP) is an XML-based application-level protocol intended for exchanging information in a distributed network. SOAP supports both the models of distributed computing: RPC as well as document-style messaging. RPC style SOAP allows remote invocation of operations. The RPC in-out parameters and return values of these operations are serialized into XML, whereas in document-style SOAP, because an operation's input and output are XML fragments, serialization of parameters and return values to XML is not needed. Although most of the Web service applications use SOAP over HTTP today, the standard does not preclude using SOAP over other Internet protocols, such as Simple Mail Transfer Protocol (SMTP). The latest version of SOAP, SOAP 1.2, is a World Wide Web Consortium (W3C) Recommendation.

Web Service Description Language (WSDL) is an XML-based metadata standard that is used to describe the service interface as well as service binding information. For RPC style services, a WSDL service interface consists of the supported operations, the input-output parameters that these operations accept, and their return values. For document-style services, the service interface description contains the XML schema fragments for the input-output messages of the service operations, whereas the service binding description specifies communication protocols, ports, the service URL, and other such binding information. At the time of this writing, the latest version of WSDL, WSDL 2.0, is well on its way to becoming a W3C standard.

It is noteworthy that these key Web service technologies are neutral to specific programming languages or development platforms. Support for these technologies is ubiquitously found on disparate systems ranging from mainframes to mobile devices such as cell phones. Web services can thus be employed effectively to implement service architectures encompassing such otherwise incompatible language and systems platforms. No doubt Web services present a powerful technological solution for implementing SOA.

We will spend some more time explaining technical aspects of implementing Web services on an EJB platform in Chapter 5; however, explaining Web services, and SOA for that matter, in their entirety is outside the scope of this book. If you are new to Web services, there are many books and online papers that you can refer to get started. Given the widespread adoption of this stack in the industry, we suggest that you familiarize yourself properly with Web services.

SOA and Component Architectures

SOA is *not* a replacement for component architecture; rather it neatly complements the component architecture. While component architectures enhance reusability at a finer-grained level, SOA can enhance reusability at a coarser-grained level. Hence, from an implementation standpoint, a *service* might very well be developed using well-defined component frameworks such as EJB. The EJB standard, therefore, has in-built support for Web services, the most popular stack for building SOA. So EJB is still very much in demand!

Divide and Conquer to the Extreme with Reusable Services

We have been seeing a slow but steady shift in the "build-from-scratch" trend for years now. More and more businesses want CIOs to stretch their IT dollars to the maximum. Naturally, this has led the IT departments to think of reuse; reuse in terms of systems as well as software. What better candidate than highly functional and autonomous services to fulfill this promise of reuse? SOA offers maximum reuse, especially when implemented using ubiquitous protocols such as those supported by Web services. Architects want to design their software as a composition of services such that these services can be used from any platform through well-defined service interfaces.

Why just stop at corporate ITs? Even independent software vendors (ISVs) are thinking of providing their software as services. Prime examples of "software as a service" include Salesforce.com and Siebel (now Oracle). Both these companies have made their enterprise software available to customers as hosted services. Many other businesses such as Amazon.com and Google provide their core business services—e-commerce and Web searching respectively—as reusable services to customers and end users.

Reusable services are a very powerful concept, because:

- **Businesses can focus on strategic software development.** In cases where business functionality is horizontal and cuts across multiple business domains, the related software applications can be treated as a shared commodity and can be procured from a specialized ISV in the form of services. For example, each business requires a corporate treasury management and cash management system. For such a commodity business need, it is best to acquire software from an outside vendor than to build it. This will relieve the IT staff from having to deal with complex treasury functions involving millions of regulations, which anyway does not have direct relevance to the business's core function.
- **The business processes can be assembled faster.** The autonomous and loosely coupled nature of services makes it easier to assemble them into business processes. This strength makes services the chosen paradigm for encapsulating business logic.
- **There is a lower total cost of ownership.** Businesses that build their software as services end up with a lower total cost of ownership in the long term because they are building software such that it can be easily reused and assembled into business processes. This is a definite plus when businesses are frequently expected to adapt business processes to swiftly address the changing market needs or when they are required to integrate with the IT systems of new customers and partners. Businesses that sell software as services, on the other hand, can benefit their customers by offering flexible software RTU (right to use) options, such as per-month or per-year software subscriptions, thereby setting up their customers with a lower total cost of ownership for the software solution.

Remember that these services can and should be built using components. Therefore, the component architectures are very much here to stay. Figure 1.6 depicts a treasury management service built using EJB components.

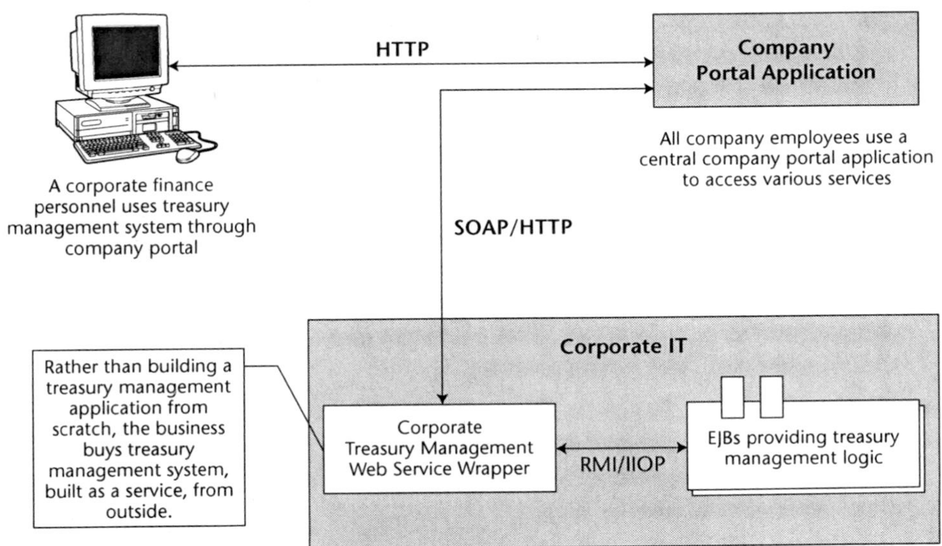

Figure 1.6 Reusable services built using EJB.

The Java Platform, Enterprise Edition 5.0 (Java EE)

EJB is only a portion of a larger offering called Java Platform, Enterprise Edition, or Java EE, also known previously as Java 2 Platform, Enterprise Edition, or J2EE. Java Community Process (JCP) members define Java EE just like all other standard Java technologies. The mission of Java EE is to provide a platform-independent, portable, multi-user, secure, and standard enterprise-class platform for server-side deployments written in the Java language.

Java EE is a specification, not a product. It specifies the rules of engagement that people must agree on when writing enterprise software. Vendors then implement the Java EE specifications in their Java EE–compliant products.

Because Java EE is a specification (meant to address the needs of many companies), it is inherently not tied to one vendor. It supports cross-platform development and deployment, since it is based on Java. This encourages vendors to compete, yielding best-of-breed products. It also has its downside, which is that incompatibilities between vendor products will arise—some problems due to ambiguities with specifications, other problems due to the human nature of competition.

Java EE is one of the *three different* Java platforms. Each platform is a conceptual superset of the next smaller platform.

- *The Java 2 Platform, Micro Edition (J2ME)* is a development platform for applications running on mobile Java-enabled devices, such as phones, Palm Pilots, pagers, set-top TV boxes, and so on. This is a restricted form of the Java language due to the inherent performance and capacity limitations of small-form-factor wireless devices.
- *The Java 2 Platform, Standard Edition (J2SE)* defines a standard for core libraries that can be used by applets, applications, Java EE applications, mobile applications, and the like. These core libraries span a much wider spectrum, including input/output, graphical user interface facilities, networking, and so on. This platform contains what most people use in standard Java programming.
- *The Java Platform, Enterprise Edition (Java EE)* is an umbrella standard for Java's enterprise computing facilities. It basically bundles together technologies for a complete enterprise-class server-side development and deployment platform in Java.

Java EE is significant because it creates a unified platform for server-side Java development. The Java EE stack consists of the following:

- **Specifications.** Each enterprise API within Java EE has its own specification, which is a PDF file downloadable from `www.jcp.org`. Each time there is a new version of Java EE, the Java EE Expert Group at JCP locks down the versions of each enterprise API specification and bundles them together as the de facto versions to use when developing with Java EE. This increases code portability across vendors' products, because each vendor supports exactly the same API revision. This is analogous to a company such as Microsoft releasing a new version of Windows every few years: Every time a new version of Windows comes out, Microsoft locks down the versions of the technologies bundled with Windows and releases them together.
- **Test suite.** Sun provides a test suite (a.k.a. Test Compatibility Kit, or TCK) for Java EE server vendors to test their implementations against. If a server passes the tests, Sun issues a Java EE compliance brand, alerting customers that the vendor's product is indeed Java EE–compliant. There are numerous Java EE–certified vendors, and you can read reviews of their products for free on TheServerSide.com.
- **Reference implementation.** To enable developers to write code against Java EE, Sun provides its own free reference implementation for each version of the stack. Sun is positioning it as a low-end reference platform, because it is not intended for commercial use. You can download the reference implementation for Java EE 5.0, the latest version of Java, EE platform that includes EJB 3.0, the technology of focus in this book, from `http://java.sun.com/j2ee/download.html`.

The Java EE Technologies

Java EE is a robust suite of middleware services that make life very easy for server-side application developers. It builds upon the existing technologies in the J2SE. J2SE includes support for core Java language semantics as well as various libraries (.awt, .net, .io, and so on). Because Java EE builds on J2SE, a Java EE–compliant product must not only implement all of Java EE stack but also implement all of J2SE. This means that building a Java EE product is an absolutely *huge* undertaking. This barrier to entry has resulted in significant industry consolidation in the enterprise Java space, with a few players emerging from the pack as leaders.

In this book, we discuss EJB 3.0, an integral part of Java EE 5.0. Some of the major Java EE technologies are shown working together in Figure 1.7.

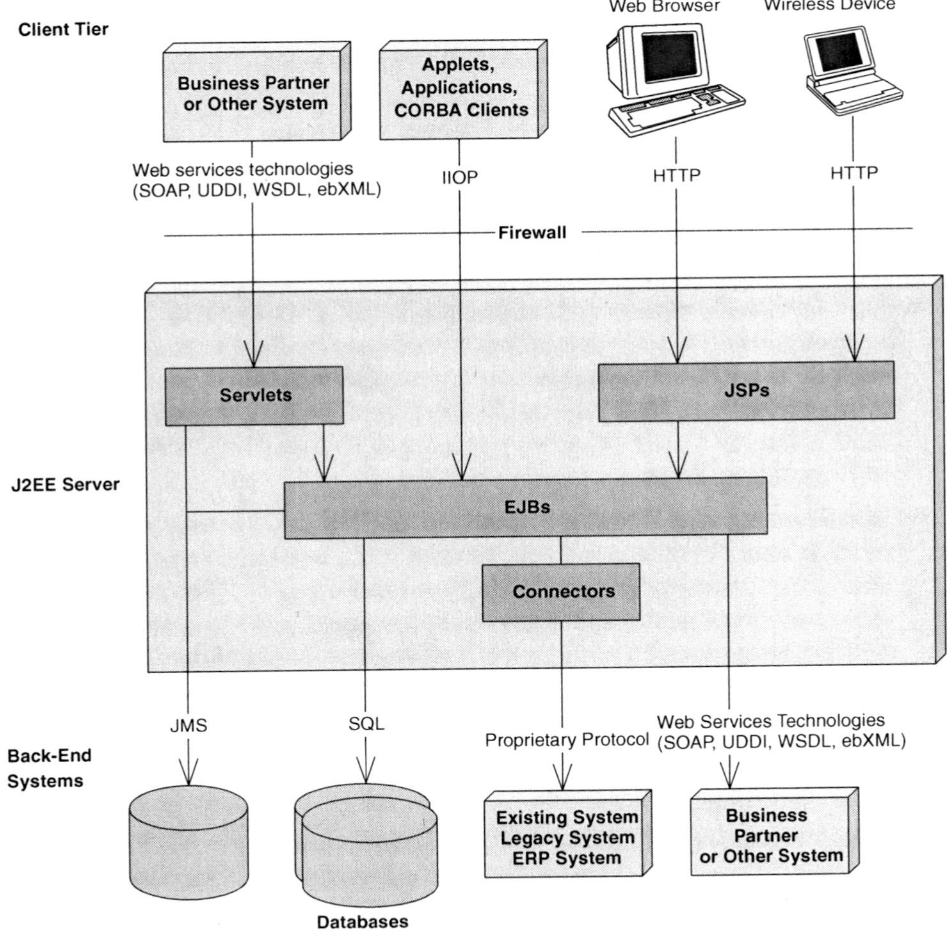

Figure 1.7 A Java EE deployment.

To understand more about the real value of Java EE, here are some of the important technologies and APIs that a Java EE 5.0–compliant implementation will support for you. Note that this is not a complete list of Java EE technologies.

- **Enterprise JavaBeans (EJB).** EJB defines how server-side components are written and provides a standard contract between components and the application servers that manage them. EJB is the cornerstone of Java EE.
- **Java API for Web Services (JAX-WS)** Previously known as JAX-RPC, JAX-WS is the main technology that provides support for Web services on the Java EE platform. It defines two Web service endpoint models—one based on servlet technology and another based on EJB. It also specifies a lot of runtime requirements regarding the way Web services should be supported in a Java EE runtime. Another specification called Web Services for Java EE defines deployment requirements for Web services and uses the JAX-WS programming model. Chapter 5 discusses support of Web services provided by both these specifications for EJB applications.
- **The Web Services Metadata for the Java Platform.** It specifies the various annotations for Web services development and deployment. It is newly introduced in the Java EE 5.0. Its goal is to provide ease of development and an easy model for deployment for Web services on the Java EE platform.
- **Java Remote Method Invocation (RMI) and RMI-IIOP.** RMI is the Java language's native way to communicate between distributed objects, such as two different objects running on different machines. RMI-IIOP is an extension of RMI that can be used for CORBA integration. RMI-IIOP is the official API that we use in Java EE (not RMI). We cover RMI-IIOP in Appendix A.
- **Java Naming and Directory Interface (JNDI).** JNDI is used to access naming and directory systems. You use JNDI from your application code for a variety of purposes, such as connecting to EJB components or other resources across the network, or accessing user data stored in a naming service such as Microsoft Exchange or Lotus Notes. JNDI is covered in Appendix A.
- **Java Database Connectivity (JDBC).** JDBC is an API for accessing relational databases. The value of JDBC is that you can access any relational database using the same API.
- **Java Transaction API (JTA) and Java Transaction Service (JTS).** The JTA and JTS specifications allow for components to be bolstered with reliable transaction support. JTA and JTS are explained in Chapter 10.

- **Java Messaging Service (JMS).** JMS allows your Java EE deployment to use message-based communication. You can use messages to communicate within your Java EE system as well as outside your Java EE system. For example, you can connect to existing message-oriented middleware (MOM) systems such as IBM MQSeries or Microsoft Message Queue (MSMQ). Messaging is an alternative paradigm to RMI-IIOP, and has its advantages and disadvantages. We explain JMS and message-driven beans (MDB) in Chapter 7.
- **Java servlets.** Servlets are networked components that you can use to extend the functionality of a Web server. Servlets are request/response oriented in that they take requests from some client host (such as a Web browser) and issue a response back to that host. This makes servlets ideal for performing Web tasks such as rendering a HyperText Markup Language (HTML) interface. Servlets differ from EJB components in that the breadth of server-side component features that EJB offers, such as declarative transactions, are not readily available to servlets. Servlets are much better suited to handling simple request/response needs, and they do not require sophisticated management by an application server. We illustrate using servlets with EJB in Chapter 17.
- **Java Server Pages (JSP).** JSP technology is very similar to servlets. In fact, JSP scripts are compiled into servlets. The largest difference between JSP scripts and servlets is that JSP scripts are not pure Java code; they are much more centered on look-and-feel issues. You would use JSP when you want the look and feel of your deployment to be physically separate and easily maintainable from the rest of your deployment. JSP technology is perfect for this, and it can be easily written and maintained by non-Java-savvy staff members (JSP technology does not require a Java compiler). We illustrate using JSP with EJB in Chapter 17.
- **JavaServer Faces (JSF).** JSF was made a part of the platform from Java EE 5 onwards. JSF was designed to support rapid application development of Java based Web applications by providing a framework that allows reuse of server-side user interface components. The JSF user interface (UI) components can be used in JSF pages, which are basically JSP pages that use JSF tag libraries, as drag-and-drop components. JSF also has provisions of a typical Web application framework such as Struts in that it provides control flow and data flow between various components of a Web application.
- **Java EE Connector Architecture (JCA).** Connectors enable you to access existing enterprise information systems from a Java EE application. This could include *any* existing system, such as a mainframe

system running high-end transactions (such as those deployed with IBM CICS, or BEA TUXEDO), Enterprise Resource Planning (ERP) systems, or your own proprietary systems. Connectors are useful because they automatically manage the details of middleware integration to existing systems, such as handling transactions and security concerns, life-cycle management, thread management, and so on. Another value of this architecture is that you can write a connector to access an existing system once, and then deploy it into any Java EE–compliant server. This is important because you only need to learn how to access an existing system once. Furthermore, the connector needs to be developed only once and can be reused in any Java EE server. This is extremely useful for ISVs such as SAP, Siebel, Peoplesoft and others who want their software to be accessible from within Java EE application servers. Rather than write a custom connector for each application server, these ISVs can write a standard Java EE connector. We discuss legacy integration in more details in Chapter 15.

- **The Java API for XML Parsing (JAXP).** There are many applications of XML in a Java EE deployment. For example, you might need to parse XML if you are performing B2B interactions (such as through Web services), if you are accessing legacy systems and mapping data to and from XML, or if you are persisting XML documents to a database. JAXP is the de facto API for parsing XML documents in a Java EE application and is an implementation-neutral interface to XML parsing technologies such as DOM and SAX. You typically use the JAXP API from within servlets, JSP, or EJB components.
- **The Java Architecture for XML Binding (JAXB).** JAXB specifies a binding of XML documents to JavaBean objects based on XML document's XML schema. Also, in the latest version of JAXB 2.0, Java can be mapped to an XML schema. JAXB is leveraged by JAX-WS as a data-binding technology.
- **The Java Authentication and Authorization Service (JAAS).** JAAS is a standard API for performing security-related operations in Java EE. Conceptually, JAAS also enables you to plug authentication and authorization mechanisms into a Java EE application server. See Chapter 11 for more details on security pertaining to EJB applications.

Summary

We've achieved a great deal in this chapter. First, we brainstormed a list of issues involved in a large, multi-tier deployment. We then understood that server-side component framework enables us to write complex business applications without understanding tricky middleware services. We then introduced the EJB standard and fleshed out its value proposition. That was followed by a discussion of the basics of distributed computing and the various approaches used by frameworks to provide middleware services. Then, we established relationship between SOA and EJB. And last but not least, we investigated the different players involved in an EJB deployment and wrapped up the chapter by exploring the various technologies bundled in the Java EE platform.

That was quite a good beginning (and we're just getting started)—many more interesting and advanced topics lie ahead. The next chapter attempts at providing the rationale for much of the work that has gone into EJB 3.0. It explains what was wrong with the previous versions of EJB and how and where the changes to the existing technology should be made in order to improve it. Thus, the next chapter builds a foundation for you to understand why EJB 3.0 needed to change the way it did. Let's go!

CHAPTER

2

Pre-EJB 3.0: The World That Was

Chapter 1 introduced you to the motivation behind EJB technology. In this chapter, we will briefly introduce you to the programming and deployment model used in the previous versions of EJB technology, viz. version 2.1 and earlier. EJB 3.0 has undergone major changes; changes of this magnitude have never been made to EJB, not even when container-managed persistence entity beans were redesigned in EJB 2.0. It is essential that we take you through the pre-EJB 3.0 world for you to realize the breadth and depth of enhancements made in EJB 3.0. After reading this chapter, you will understand what a pre-EJB 3.0 enterprise bean component was composed of as well as its programming model. We will provide an example of an EJB 2.1 bean to help you understand further. Most importantly, in this chapter you will recognize the drawbacks of the present EJB programming model. Comprehending these limitations will prepare you for the exultation you shall experience peeking at EJB 3.0 in Chapter 3!

If you are new to EJB technology and so haven't worked with EJB before, you might want to proceed straight to Chapter 3. Chapter 3 focuses on fundamentals—from an EJB 3.0 vantage point.

What Constituted a Pre-EJB 3.0 Enterprise Bean?

An *enterprise bean* is a server-side software component that can be deployed in a distributed multi-tiered environment, and it will remain that way going forward. Anyone who has worked with Enterprise JavaBeans technology before knows that there are three types of beans—session beans, entity beans, and message-driven beans (MDBs). Historically an EJB component implementation has never been contained in a single source file; a number of files work together to make up an implementation of an enterprise bean. Let us briefly go through these EJB implementation artifacts:

- **Enterprise bean class.** The primary part of the bean used to be the implementation itself—which contained the guts of your logic—called the enterprise bean class. This was simply a Java class that conformed to a well-defined interface and obeyed certain rules. For instance, the EJB specification defined a few standard interfaces that your bean class had to implement. Implementing these interfaces forced your bean class to expose certain methods that all beans must provide, as defined by the EJB component model. The EJB container called these required methods to manage your bean and alert your bean to significant events. The most basic interface that all of the session, entity, and message-driven bean classes implemented is the `javax.ejb.EnterpriseBean` interface. This interface served as a marker interface, meaning that implementing this interface indicated that your class was indeed an enterprise bean class. Session beans, entity beans, and message-driven beans each had more specific interfaces that extended the component interface `javax.ejb.EnterpriseBean`, viz. `javax.ejb.SessionBean`, `javax.ejb.EntityBean`, and `javax.ejb.MessageDrivenBean`.
- **EJB object.** When a client wants to use an instance of an enterprise bean class, the client never invokes the method directly on an actual bean instance. Rather, the invocation is intercepted by the EJB container and then delegated to the bean instance. By intercepting requests, the EJB container can provide middleware services implicitly. Thus, the EJB container acted as a layer of indirection between the client code and the bean. This layer of indirection manifested itself as a single network-aware object called the EJB object. The container would generate the implementation of `javax.ejb.EJBObject` or `javax.ejb.EJBLocalObject`, depending on whether the bean was local or remote, that is whether it supported local or remote clients, at deployment time.
- **Remote interface.** A remote interface, written by the bean provider, consisted of all the methods that were made available to the remote

clients of the bean. These methods usually would be business methods that the bean provider wants the remote clients of the bean to use. Remote interfaces had to comply with special rules that EJB specification defined. For example, all remote interfaces must be derived from the `javax.ejb.EJBObject` interface. The EJB object interface consisted of a number of methods, and the container would implement them for you.

- **Local interface.** The local interface, written by the bean provider, consisted of all the methods that were made available to the local clients of the bean. Akin to the remote interface, the local interface provided business methods that the local bean clients could call. The local interface provided an efficient mechanism to enable use of EJB objects within the Java Virtual Machine (JVM), without incurring the overhead of RMI-IIOP. An enterprise bean that expected to be used by remote as well as local clients had to support both local and remote interfaces.
- **Home interface.** Home interfaces defined methods for creating, destroying, and finding local or remote EJB objects. They acted as life cycle interfaces for the EJB objects. Each bean was supposed to have a corresponding home interface. All home interfaces had to extend standard interface `javax.ejb.EJBHome` or `javax.ejb.EJBLocalHome`, depending on whether the enterprise bean was local or remote. The container generated home objects implementing the methods of this interface at the time of deployment. Clients acquired references to the EJB objects via these home objects. Even though the container implemented home interfaces as home objects, an EJB developer was still required to follow certain rules pertaining to the life-cycle methods of a home interface. For instance, for each `createXXX()` method in the home interface, the enterprise bean class was required to have a corresponding `ejbCreateXXX()` method.
- **Deployment descriptor.** To inform the container about your middleware needs, you as a bean provider were required to declare your components' middleware needs—such as life-cycle management, transaction control, security services, and so on—in an XML-based deployment descriptor file. The container inspected the deployment descriptor and fulfilled the requirements laid out by you. The deployment descriptor thus played the key role in enabling implicit middleware services in the EJB framework.
- **Vendor-specific files.** Since all EJB server vendors are different, they each have some proprietary value-added features. The EJB specification did not touch these features, such as how to configure load balancing, clustering, monitoring, and so on. Therefore, each EJB server vendor

required you to include additional files specific to that vendor, such as a vendor specific XML or text-based deployment descriptor that the container would inspect to provide vendor-specific middleware services.

- **The Ejb-jar file.** The Ejb-jar file, the packaging artifact, consisted of all the other implementation artifacts of your bean. Once you generated your bean classes, your home interfaces, your remote interfaces, and your deployment descriptor, you'd package them into an Ejb-jar file. It is this Ejb-jar file that you, as a bean provider, would pass around for deployment purposes to application assemblers.

Figure 2.1 schematizes an Ejb-jar file, the EJB artifact that is ultimately deployed.

With this primer on the pre-EJB 3.0 constituents, let us go through with the development and deployment of a simple stateless session bean. This will set the stage for us to explore further the shortcomings of the programming model of the previous versions of the technology.

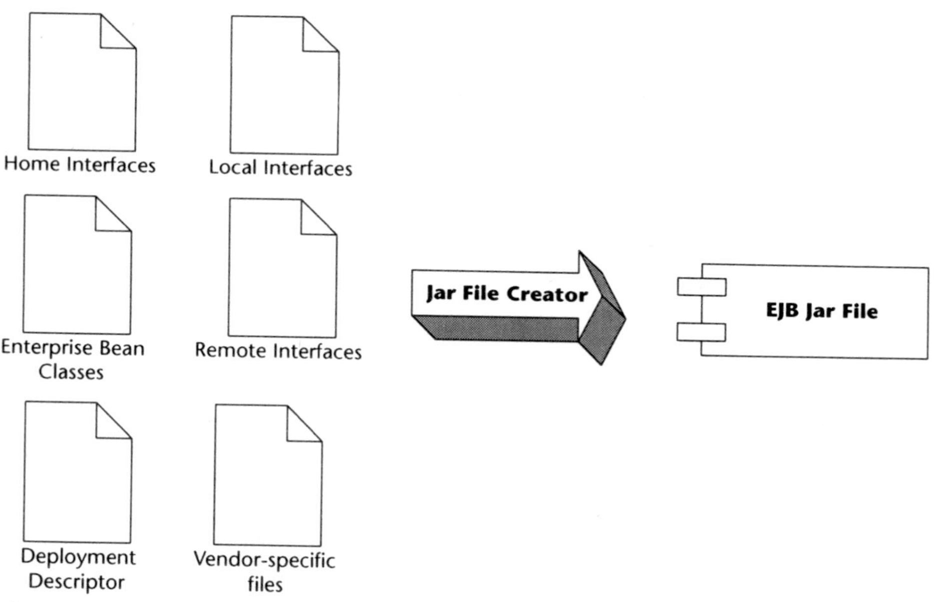

Figure 2.1 Pre-EJB 3.0 constituents.

Developing and Deploying a Pre-EJB 3.0 Enterprise Java Bean

In this section, we will conduct a simple exercise: developing and deploying the universal `HelloWorldEJB` stateless session bean using EJB 2.1. The following are the typical steps involved:

1. Write the Java code for the files composing your bean—the remote and/or local interface, the bean class, and the home interface.
2. Write the deployment descriptor or have it generated by using an IDE or tools such as XDoclet.
3. Compile the Java source codes from step 1.
4. Using the *jar* utility, create an Ejb-jar file containing the deployment descriptor and the `.class` files from step 3.
5. Deploy the Ejb-jar file into your container in a vendor-specific manner, perhaps by using a vendor-specific tool or perhaps by copying your Ejb-jar file into a folder where your container looks to load Ejb-jar files.
6. Configure your EJB server so that it properly hosts your Ejb-jar file. You might tune things such as database connections, thread pools, and so on. This step requires vendor-specific configuration and might be done through a Web-based console or by editing a configuration file.
7. Check your EJB container and confirm that it has loaded your Ejb-jar file.
8. Optionally, write a standalone test client `.java` file and let vendor tools generate stub classes for remote access, if required. Compile that test client into a `.class` file. Run the test client from the command line, and have it exercise your bean's APIs.

Figure 2.2 shows the class diagram for our `HelloWorldEJB` stateless session bean.

Now, let us go through the programming artifacts, one by one.

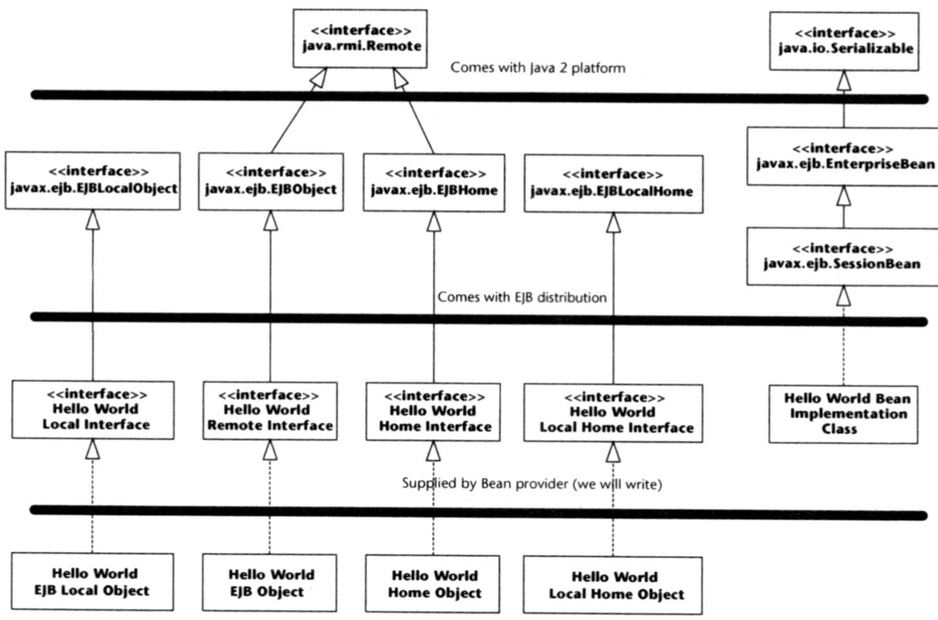

Figure 2.2 HelloWorldEJB class diagram.

The Remote Interface

The remote interface for `HelloWorldEJB` extends `javax.ejb.EJBObject`, which in turn extends `java.rmi.Remote`. Note that the container implements the bean's remote interface, not us. Also `HelloWorldEJB` remote interface consist of one business method, `hello()`, which needs to be implemented in the bean class. Because the remote interface is an RMI-IIOP interface, that is it indirectly extends `java.rmi.Remote`, all its methods must throw a `java.rmi.RemoteException`. However, the implementation of `hello()` in the bean class does not have to throw a remote exception. Why? It is not directly accessed by the client over the network and hence does not need to foresee a networking-related issue.

The source for `Hello.java`, the remote interface of `HelloWorldEJB`, is given below in Source 2.1.

```
/**
 * This is the HelloBean remote interface.
 *
 * This interface is what clients operate on when
 * they interact with EJB objects.  The container
```

Source 2.1 Hello.java. *(continued)*

```
 * vendor will implement this interface; the
 * implemented object is the EJB object, which
 * delegates invocations to the actual bean.
 */
public interface Hello extends javax.ejb.EJBObject
{

  /**
   * The one method - hello - returns a greeting to the client.
   */
  public String hello() throws java.rmi.RemoteException;
}
```

Source 2.1 *(continued)*

The Local Interface

If HelloWorldEJB were to support access by local clients within the same JVM, it would need a local interface.

Source 2.2 shows the local interface for HelloWorldEJB.

```
/**
 * This is the HelloBean local interface.
 *
 * This interface is what local clients operate
 * on when they interact with EJB local objects.
 * The container vendor will implement this
 * interface; the implemented object is the
 * EJB local object, which delegates invocations
 * to the actual bean.
 */
public interface HelloLocal extends javax.ejb.EJBLocalObject
{

  /**
   * The one method - hello - returns a greeting to the client.
   */
  public String hello();
}
```

Source 2.2 HelloLocal.java.

Notice that there are differences between the local and the remote interface for the same bean:

- The local interface extends `javax.ejb.EJBLocalObject` instead of `javax.ejb.EJBObject`.
- Our business method, `hello()`, does not throw a `java.rmi.RemoteException`, since there is no need to take care of network contingencies in local JVM communication.

The Home Interface

The home interface has methods to create and destroy EJB objects of the bean. The EJB container generates the home interface implementation.

The code for home interface is given in Source 2.3.

```
/**
 * This is the home interface for HelloBean.  This interface
 * is implemented by the EJB Server's tools - the
 * implemented object is called the Home Object, and serves
 * as a factory for EJB Objects.
 *
 * One create() method is in this Home Interface, which
 * corresponds to the ejbCreate() method in HelloBean.
 */
public interface HelloHome extends javax.ejb.EJBHome
{

    /*
     * This method creates the EJB Object.
     *
     * @return The newly created EJB Object.
     */
    Hello create() throws java.rmi.RemoteException,
        javax.ejb.CreateException;
}
```

Source 2.3 HelloHome.java.

Notice the following in the home interface:

- It extends `javax.ejb.EJBHome` as required for all home interfaces.
- We provided a `create()` method that will act as a factory method for getting a reference to an EJB object; the EJB container initializes the bean when this method is called.

- The create() method throws remote exception given that the home object is a networked object. Also, javax.ejb.CreateException is thrown, to cover for situations where creation of a bean failed due to some application-level error.

The Local Home Interface

The local clients use a local home interface in order to access the local EJB object of the bean.

The local home interface code is shown in Source 2.4.

```
/**
 * This is the local home interface for HelloBean.
 * This interface is implemented by the EJB Server's
 * tools - the implemented object is called the
 * local home object, and serves as a factory for
 * EJB local objects.
 */
public interface HelloLocalHome extends javax.ejb.EJBLocalHome
{

    /*
     * This method creates the EJB Object.
     *
     * @return The newly created EJB Object.
     */
    HelloLocal create() throws javax.ejb.CreateException;
}
```

Source 2.4 HelloLocalHome.java.

Notice the differences between local and remote home interfaces for the bean:

- Whereas the remote home interface extends javax.ejb.EJBHome interface, the local home interface extends javax.ejb.EJBLocalHome. This means that the generated local home object is not a remote object.
- Unlike the methods on the remote home interface, the local home interface methods, such as create(), do not throw remote exceptions.

The Bean Class

Now let us take a look at our bean class code, shown in Source 2.5.

```
/**
 * Demonstration stateless session bean.
 */
public class HelloBean implements javax.ejb.SessionBean {

    private javax.ejb.SessionContext ctx;

    //
    // EJB-required methods
    //
    public void ejbCreate() {
        System.out.println("ejbCreate()");
    }

    public void ejbRemove() {
        System.out.println("ejbRemove()");
    }

    public void ejbActivate() {
        System.out.println("ejbActivate()");
    }

    public void ejbPassivate() {
        System.out.println("ejbPassivate()");
    }

    public void setSessionContext(javax.ejb.SessionContext ctx) {
        this.ctx = ctx;
    }

    //
    // Business methods
    //
    public String hello() {
        System.out.println("hello()");
        return "Hello, World!";
    }
}
```

Source 2.5 HelloBean.java.

This is, of course, a simplistic bean, and hence our bean class, which holds the logic for the bean, is quite simple. Notice the following:

- It implements a `javax.ejb.SessionBean` interface, since it is a session bean. The bean class therefore must implement `SessionBean` interface methods, most of which are the hooks for the container to manage the bean. Via such methods, the container lets the bean know of its life cycle—when it is being created, destroyed, passivated, activated, and so on.

- The bean has an `ejbCreate()` method that matches the home object's `create()` method and takes no parameters.
- The `setSessionContext()` method provides a way for the container to set the EJB context-specific to your bean, which in the case of our session bean, is a session context. The bean can then use this context object to get information about its status changes from the container.

Deployment Descriptor

The deployment descriptor carries the configuration information about the bean, things such as its middleware requirements, which the container could use to set up an appropriate environment for the bean. It is an XML document, usually generated by the tools. The deployment descriptor for our bean is shown in Source 2.6.

```
<?xml version="1.0" encoding="UTF-8"?>

<ejb-jar
  xmlns="http://java.sun.com/xml/ns/j2ee"
  xmlns:xsi="http://www.w3.org/2001/XMLSchema-instance"
  xsi:schemaLocation="http://java.sun.com/xml/ns/j2ee
  http://java.sun.com/xml/ns/j2ee/ejb-jar_2_1.xsd"
  version="2.1">
 <enterprise-beans>
  <session>
   <ejb-name>HelloWorldEJB</ejb-name>
   <home>examples.ejb21.HelloHome</home>
   <remote>examples.ejb21.Hello</remote>
   <local-home>examples.ejb21.HelloLocalHome</local-home>
   <local>examples.ejb21.HelloLocal</local>
   <ejb-class>examples.ejb21.HelloBean</ejb-class>
   <session-type>Stateless</session-type>
   <transaction-type>Container</transaction-type>
  </session>
 </enterprise-beans>
</ejb-jar>
```

Source 2.6 ejb-jar.xml.

Deploying The Bean

Once we have all the required artifacts for the `HelloWorldEJB`, we will package them into an Ejb-jar file. Typically, your EJB development environment would do this packaging, so that you don't have to use another jar tool exclusively to do it. We then deploy this Ejb-jar file on the container of our choice. The steps of deployment, though tentatively are the same, vary in specifics from container to container.

Once the bean is deployed and working, develop, compile, and test the bean with a client.

HelloWorldEJB Client

Examine the code for the bean client. It is a standalone Java application, as shown in Source 2.7.

```
import javax.naming.Context;
import javax.naming.InitialContext;
import java.util.Properties;

/**
 * This class is an example of client code that invokes
 * methods on a simple stateless session bean.
 */
public class HelloClient {

     public static void main(String[] args) throws Exception {
          /*
           * Setup properties for JNDI initialization.
           *
           * These properties will be read in from
           * the command line.
           */
          Properties props = System.getProperties();

          /*
           * Obtain the JNDI initial context.
           *
           * The initial context is a starting point for
           * connecting to a JNDI tree. We choose our JNDI
           * driver, the network location of the server, etc.
           * by passing in the environment properties.
           */
          Context ctx = new InitialContext(props);

          /*
           * Get a reference to the home object - the
           * factory for Hello EJB Objects
           */
          Object obj = ctx.lookup("HelloHome");


          /*
```

Source 2.7 HelloClient.java. *(continued)*

```
             * Home objects are RMI-IIOP objects, and so
             * they must be cast into RMI-IIOP objects
             * using a special RMI-IIOP cast.
             *
             * See Appendix A for more details on this.
             */
            HelloHome home = (HelloHome)
                javax.rmi.PortableRemoteObject.narrow(
                    obj, HelloHome.class);

            /*
             * Use the factory to create the Hello EJB Object
             */
            Hello hello = home.create();

            /*
             * Call the hello() method on the EJB object.  The
             * EJB object will delegate the call to the bean,
             * receive the result, and return it to us.
             *
             * We then print the result to the screen.
             */
            System.out.println(hello.hello());

            /*
             * Done with EJB Object, so remove it.
             * The container will destroy the EJB object.
             */
            hello.remove();
        }
}
```

Source 2.7 *(continued)*

`HelloClient.java` does some interesting things:

- It creates a JNDI initial context object by supplying the container with the appropriate information such as the network location of the JNDI service, JNDI driver, and so on.
- It looks up the home object for the bean, `HelloHome`, implemented and registered by the container under the name specified in `<ejb-name>` of the deployment descriptor in a JNDI directory, so that it can create EJB object for `HelloWorldEJB`.
- Once it gets the home object for `HelloWorldEJB`, it gets a reference to the EJB object by calling `create()` method on the home object.

- After calling the business method, `hello()`, on the `Hello` EJB object, it informs the container that it is done using the EJB object and that the container can destroy it or return to the object pool, if it so desires.

The client is then compiled and run. This brings our example to completion.

Dissecting EJB 2.x

The preceding example is a good preamble to start our discussion of the shortcomings of the EJB 2.x model. Mind you, our example is a session bean—a stateless session bean to be more specific. However, the way we develop and deploy a stateful session bean is quite similar to that of the stateless session bean, so our examination is relevant to both stateless and stateful session beans, as well as to the greater EJB architecture.

The message-driven beans slightly differ in that they do not have a home or a remote interface. However, some of the issues are applicable to MDBs as well. So let's begin!

Complexity: The Overarching Issue of EJB 2.x

As a consultant, a compatriot once gave me the key to his booming consulting practice. His mantra: complexity is a virtue you could never have enough of. Of course, this mantra was convenient for his consulting business. However, imagine yourself in the position of an IT manager hiring one of his consultants. Well, you get the picture. You do not want code that is so complicated to develop, deploy, test, and maintain, that you'd rather sell it at a dime a pound, assuming there were such a junk code marketplace, and be rid of it. And the last thing you'd want is architecture such as EJB to aid to make this nightmare a reality.

WHAT ABOUT ENTITY BEANS?

Entity beans in EJB 2.x do have issues, as all of us who have worked with that technology are aware. After much contemplation, the EJB 3.0 specification expert group decided to leave entity beans alone in this version. That is, entity beans will remain as they were in EJB 2.x without undergoing any enhancements. Instead, the expert group worked on making available another API called Java Persistence API to EJB developers. This API aims at providing a very simple yet effective persistence technology for EJB applications. Therefore, our scrutiny of EJB 2.x drawbacks will not address entity beans, even though it might be applicable to entity beans as such.

EJB was designed to meet almost all of an enterprise application's middleware needs. In doing so, it also ended up adopting leviathan ways for enterprise programming. In all fairness, EJB visionaries have continually improved the technology from what it was at the time of its debut in early 1998. However, to deal with the all-encompassing convolutions of EJB, serious measures are called for. These measures are the sole focus of EJB 3.0 and Java EE 5.0 enhancements, and most rightly so.

Development Complexities

Developing a typical enterprise bean consisted of three—and many times more than three—Java sources. For our simplistic `HelloWorldEJB`, we were required to write five Java sources, including the sources for home and EJB object interfaces to support local clients, remote clients, and a bean class. The concern is that often these sources contain boilerplate stuff and yet they are cumbersome to write without the help of IDE wizards. Below are some of the examples of vanilla coding requirements that exist throughout the EJB programming model. To reduce development complexity, such coding requirements should be made the first targets of any simplification exercise.

- For session beans, home interfaces exist so that the clients can look them up and create references to the bean, which they can then use. Now EJB programming restrictions mandate that every stateless session bean have exactly one `create()` method. This `create()` method needs to be without arguments, since stateless session beans are without state and hence don't need to be equipped with a state-passing mechanism such as arguments. Therefore, given a way to somehow create and pass the stateless session bean reference to the client, stateless session bean development can be simplified by getting rid of this otherwise unnecessary home interface.

  Similarly, for a stateful session bean, its home interface serves the purpose of creating bean references and initializing their states via the create methods. If there were a way of putting these create methods elsewhere, we could get the home interface completely out of the session bean programming model. This would save developers the time and effort of developing home interfaces.

- The remote interface for `HelloWorldEJB` carries methods that are made available to the remote clients. Similarly, the methods that should be made available to the local clients are provided as part of local interface. And the ones invoked by Web service clients are made available via a Web service endpoint interface. Almost always the business methods that go into remote and local interfaces are the same, except that the former has remote invocation semantics with regard to serialization, exception handling, and so on taken into consideration, while the latter doesn't. If somehow the client view of the session bean can be provided irrespective of the client invoking its business methods, this can further help simplify the EJB programming model. In short, EJB need not worry about the location of the client invoking it. It should just be able to provide the business methods in a business interface and leave it up to the container to handle the support for local or remote client invocation of the beans using this business interface.

- The `HelloWorldEJB` bean class requires implementation of component interface, `javax.ejb.SessionBean`. As a result, our bean class has to provide implementation for four methods, namely `ejbActivate()`, `ejbPassivate()`, `ejbRemove()`, and `setSessionContext()`. The `ejbPassivate()` and `ejbActivate()` callback methods are called before the container passivates your bean and after it activates it, respectively. Naturally, these methods are not applicable to stateless session beans, which are never passivated or activated. The `ejbRemove()` callback method is invoked by the container before it removes your bean instance. The `setSessionContext()` callback is called right after the bean class instance is created. The bean can then do whatever it chooses to do with this `SessionContext` object—get access to the transaction object and manage transactions for the bean manually, get access to the local and remote home objects associated with the bean instance, get access to local and remote EJB objects associated with the bean instance, and so on. The `SessionBean` interface, thus, can have an important role to play in your bean's existence in that it provides your bean with useful information about its environment as well as letting the bean find out about its life cycleevents and take action appropriately.

  In spite of all this, however, there are times when implementing this interface can be overkill. Not all the beans need these callbacks. In our `HelloWorldEJB` example for instance, we simply did not have a reason to use the callbacks and so we ended up putting pointless `System.out.println()` calls in their implementation. Nonetheless the restrictions of EJB programming made us take on the extra burden of implementing the `SessionBean` interface. Therefore, if there were a way to implement such callbacks if need be and not have to implement them when there is no need, this would clean up a lot of bean classes with unnecessary implementations of `SessionBean` component interface methods.

- Let us talk about the `HelloWorldEJB` client now for a moment. In order to use the bean, the client has to work with the JNDI APIs. The JNDI registry holds the EJB home object references and all the other resources such as JMS topics, JMS queues, JDBC connection factories, JMS connection factories, and so on in a Java EE server. Making available the factories and other distributed resources in a registry such as JNDI registry is a good thing. However, the EJB client programmer shouldn't have to learn JNDI intricacies. The client programmer shouldn't have to know how to work with JNDI APIs. This is definitely one area where EJB programming can be simplified; provide an easier way to get resources such that using JNDI APIs isn't a requirement for clients.

The preceeding list of major EJB development complexity issues hints at the areas of focus for EJB 3.0 enhancements.

Deployment Complexities

The original EJB designers thought of a wonderful architectural concept that separates middleware issues and concerns and how these concerns are addressed from the actual business logic. In doing so, they realized that there has to be a way for a bean to let the container know about the middleware services that it will need for successful execution. The designers thought of a configuration file that is essentially used by the bean to put its needs in terms of middleware. This configuration came to be known as a deployment descriptor. It is uncanny how an artifact born of such an incandescent idea can come to be so disliked by almost all EJB programmers on the planet!

The separation of deployment information from the actual business logic in itself was a brilliant idea; however, its implementation isn't exactly to the liking of a good many EJB architects and developers. The reasons are many; some of these are:

- A deployment descriptor is a piece of XML and as such is not very straightforward to edit; a single misplaced or mistyped character can render XML invalid and lead to errors in the deployment process. Although tools usually generate these deployment descriptors, the fact that descriptors are the only way of letting the container know about bean's deployment needs means that developers are required to have a good understanding of them. If there were yet another way—a more programmer-friendly alternative—of specifying the bean's deployment needs, it would surely provide a choice for those of us who are XML-phobic.
- One of the main purposes of making the deployment descriptor a part of the EJB specification was to devise a standard way of communicating configuration information from the bean to the container such that even if the bean were to be ported to a different container, the deployer would not need to change this configuration and the deployer could deploy the bean as is. Although this has been achieved, the question is, to what extent? For example, even though our bean can specify its needs to the container with regard to transaction in a vendor agnostic way, it is not yet possible to let the container know about the clustering

or caching needs of a bean without resorting to vendor-specific deployment descriptors. Over the years, EJB application implementers have felt a surging need to insert more and more of such configuration information into the standard to make the *write once, deploy anywhere* promise of enterprise Java a reality.

Not all of the deployment descriptor flaws mentioned above have been rectified in EJB 3.0. However, the fact remains that enhancing a technology as comprehensively defined and widely deployed as EJB is not going to be an overnight process. We will get there, nonetheless, slowly and steadily.

Debugging and Testing Complexities

Debugging and testing EJB introduces us to a different set of issues. No wonder there are dozens of EJB testing and debugging utilities available, both in open source as well as in commercial/closed source domains. The reason we have to fall back on using these utilities and tools for something as intrinsic to the software development life cycle as testing and debugging is because the EJB architecture doesn't facilitate these to developers out of the box, not without ramifications.

There are two ways in which a bean could be tested—within the container or outside the container. For the former, we have to deploy the tests within the container, that is, essentially our tests have to become Java EE components such as servlets/JSPs or an EJB that implements the test case. For the latter, we need to deploy the EJB in the container such that it supports remote invocations. What if you have an EJB that supports only local interface? Would you put remote interfaces on your bean just to support the remote test clients? As you can see, testing is not as simple as it ought to be. Test frameworks, utilities, and IDEs have tried over the years to make testing enterprise beans simpler and provide an out-of-the-box experience. We are reaching that destination, but we are not there yet.

By the same token, there are two ways in which debugging an enterprise application deployed on an EJB container is accomplished—by reading the application server log files or by attaching a debugger process with the application server's JVM. Most times, especially if an application server is configured to be verbose (which, by the way, needs to be done if we want to know what is going on inside the application server), log files tend to get bulky. Scouring such log files to find exactly where your application could have gone wrong is an inefficient technique for debugging. The latter approach of attaching a debugger with an application server sure sounds more promising, and it is. Most of the IDEs today come with debuggers that attach to EJB containers so as to be able to write and debug code from within the IDE. The only issue here is that not all EJB compliant application servers are supported by the

IDEs. The IDE-to-EJB-server integration is posing issues to developers who want ubiquitous debugging support across all EJB server platforms from their favorite IDE.

What Needs to Be Done to Improve EJB 2.x?

Our example and the examination of EJB technology that followed it, specifically session beans, make one thing very clear—EJB needs to be simplified to address the issues surrounding development, deployment, testing, and debugging. Please don't mistake us; we are not in the least suggesting that EJB be made into a child's play. On the contrary, we believe that EJB programming model should be changed so as to make mundane things simpler, thereby increasing developer productivity. Developer productivity sits right at the heart of every IT organization that is a consumer of technology. Indeed, the time has come for us to make life easier for developers, so that their resulting increase in productivity can make life easier for businesses, which in turn is good for all of us.

We do believe that enterprise software development is no fool's business, although we don't think that it should be made into a rocket science either. We do acknowledge that enterprise software development demands sound knowledge of architectural principles; however, our task would be made much easier if we could get cooperation from frameworks to implement these principles.

Summary

In this chapter, we examined the past; we looked at a very simplistic example of a 2.x stateless session bean, which helped us understand the development and deployment shortcomings of the EJB 2.x model. It helped in setting us to the right speed for diving into the depths of EJB 3.0.

We are now fully prepared to get into the ocean of EJB 3.0!

CHAPTER

3

The New Enterprise JavaBean

Okay, so now we have witnessed the excessively difficult development of a very simple EJB in Chapter 2. What did that make you want? EJB 3.0 should be the answer there. Without further ado, here is brand new introduction to the EJB technology within the context of EJB 3.0.

NOTE **It is of the utmost necessity that you understand that while a lot of changes have been made to the programming model in EJB 3.0, fundamentally EJB technology continues to address the same need, that is, it serves as the server-side software component framework. The development and deployment model of EJB has been revamped, not its core framework and architectural principles. Obviously, some current best practices and design patterns might lose their applicability to EJB 3.0 solutions; however, many of them still hold water in EJB 3.0.**

Introducing EJB 3.0

An enterprise bean is a server-side software component that can be deployed in a distributed multi-tier environment. A bean is written using the EJB APIs (The `javax.ejb.*` package) and is deployed into an EJB container. The EJB container then provides the bean with various services such as life cycle management, security, transaction management, and much more. The client of an EJB bean could be anything—a servlet, a JSP, a standalone Java application, an applet, a SOAP-based Web service client, or even another EJB. One can divide a complex task into multiple beans such that a client invokes an entry point method on one of these beans, which in turn invokes the others in the group. Thus, one can use a divide-and-conquer strategy in the EJB application design.

As a real-world example, imagine for a moment what happens when you go to an ATM to withdraw some money from your checking account. Imagine what takes place underneath the ATM screen from the architecture standpoint. The ATM front-end user application can very well be a standalone Java application running on the client-side JVM. This Java application takes details such as your debit card info, pin, withdrawal amount, and so on and sends that data across the wire (often in a compressed format) to a Web service hosted by the ATM host processor, also known as the *acquirer*. It is the acquirer that then communicates with the ATM user's financial institution (bank, credit card company, and so on) to accomplish the payment transaction. The acquirer Web service can be implemented as an enterprise bean and as part of the invocation of a method—named as, say, `processWithdrawal()`—on this bean, a bunch of other invocations potentially on a number of different beans ensues.

1. Call `logTransaction()` on `ATMLog` bean, to log the date, time, and coordinates of the withdrawal transaction.
2. Invoke `doEFT()` on `ElectronicFundsTransfer` bean to transfer the withdrawal amount from ATM user's checking account to the acquirer's account.
3. Invoke `dispenseCash()` on `CashRegister` bean once the EFT transaction goes through successfully and the acquirer receives an approval code from the ATM user's financial institution authorizing it to dispense cash.

This flow is depicted in Figure 3.1. As is evident, this is a powerful way to design complex applications using EJBs.

For those who are EJB veterans, it is important to note that the core participants have remained the same for EJB 3.0, that is, a bean, a container, and a client. The difference between the old and the new is apparent when we examine the development and deployment semantics of these participants across the versions of EJB.

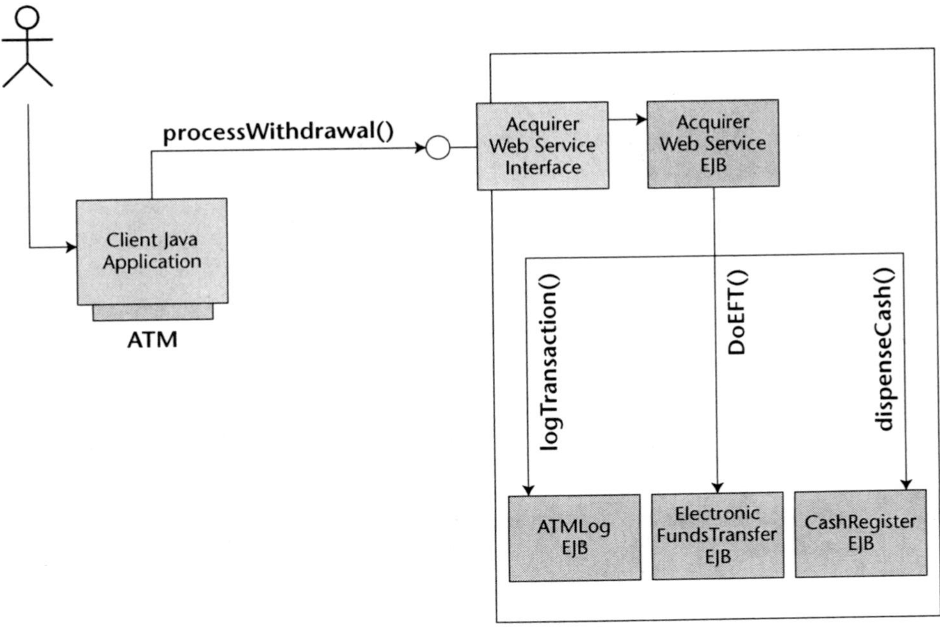

Figure 3.1 ATM cash withdrawal scenario accomplished using EJBs.

EJB Container

As you know by now, an EJB container is responsible for managing your enterprise bean. The most important responsibility of the container is to provide a secure, transactional, distributed environment in which enterprise beans can execute. However, neither the beans nor the clients that call these beans are required to explicitly code against the EJB container APIs to avail themselves of these container services. They can instead let the container know about their needs implicitly by specifying the necessary configuration information within an XML-based *deployment descriptor* or within the bean's code using *deployment annotations* (discussed later in this chapter). In essence, EJB containers act as invisible middlemen between the client and the bean. They provide the beans with suitable services *implicitly*. Described in the following list are just a few of the many services that are made available by the bean container.

Transaction management. Transactions enable you to perform robust, deterministic operations by setting attributes on your enterprise beans. The EJB container provides a *transaction service*, a low-level implementation of transaction management and coordination. The transaction service is exposed through the Java Transaction API (JTA). JTA is a high-level interface that you can use to control transactions. We will get into the details of EJB transactions, JTA, and much more in Chapter 10.

ORGANIZATION OF EJB 3.0 SPECIFICATION DOCUMENTS

The EJB 3.0 specification developed under Java Specification Request (JSR) 220 has been divided into three specification documents, as under:

- **The EJB Core Contracts and Requirements document defines the service provider interfaces (SPIs) between the bean instance and the container; application programming interfaces (APIs) between the bean provider and the container, protocols, component and container contracts, system level issues, various infrastructure services to be provided by the container to the bean; and other such details regarding the development, packaging, and deployment for all the types of beans.**
- **The EJB 3.0 Simplified API document provides guidelines on the areas where simplification to the preexisting EJB APIs and SPIs have been done to achieve simplified development and deployment model in EJB 3.0. For developers who are familiar with the previous versions of EJB technology, we recommend quickly skimming through this document to get a very good idea of how and where the EJB 3.0 technology has been simplified.**
- **The Java Persistence API document specifies the POJO-style persistent entity development guidelines. Even though the Persistence API specification was developed within the EJB 3.0 Expert Group, we believe that any enhancements or changes to this work would be carried out in a separate working group in the future. It makes a lot of sense to evolve this work independent of EJB technology in the future, given that Persistence API–based entities can be used not just in EJB applications but in any other kind of Java application.**

Security. Security is a major consideration for multi-tier deployments. The Java SE platform already enables a secure environment that authenticates and authorizes access to the Java code. EJB adds to this the notion of transparent security such that the access to the bean methods is secured by setting the security attributes instead of coding against a security API.

Resource and life cycle management. The EJB container manages resources, such as threads, sockets, and database connections, on behalf of the enterprise beans. In fact, the container manages the life cycle of enterprise beans as well. The container creates the bean instances, destroys them, passivates them by serializing them to a secondary storage (when needed), activates them by reading their serialized state from the secondary storage, and so on. Thus, the container has the ability to reuse the bean instances as and how it wants.

Remote accessibility. Clients located in a remote JVM can invoke methods on an enterprise bean. As with everything else, the container makes this happen without requiring the bean provider to code for such remote accessibility of the bean. The container converts our networkless beans into distributed, network-aware objects in order to service the remote clients.

Support for concurrent requests. The container also takes care of servicing concurrent requests from clients without making the bean provider write multithreading code to handle them. EJB containers provide built-in thread management support. For instance, it can instantiate multiple instances of the bean—maintain a pool of bean instances, so to speak—to efficiently service the concurrent client requests. If multiple clients call the methods on a bean's instance, the container can also serialize the requests, thereby allowing only one client to call the bean instance at a time. When this happens, other clients are either routed to a different bean instance or are forced to wait till the original bean instance becomes available. This thread management performed by container has a lot of value to the EJB developer, because after all, who enjoys writing synchronized multithreaded code?

Clustering and load-balancing. Although, an EJB container is not required by the specification to provide these, most of the containers come equipped with clustering and load-balancing support. Obviously, this is a tremendous value addition to any deployment that wants to handle a large number of requests in a fail-safe and scalable manner. At the same time, because these are essentially nonstandard services, their configuration varies from container to container. Also, if your code relies on these services for smooth functioning, porting it to another container can become a little tricky. But all things considered, these services still make a highly scalable and fail-safe deployment possible.

Types of Beans

Enterprise JavaBeans are categorized into various types. Depending on the design requirements you can use the suitable bean type.

Session beans. Session beans model business processes. They are like *verbs* because they perform actions. The action could be anything, such as adding numbers, accessing a database, calling a legacy system, or calling other enterprise beans. Examples include a pricing engine, a workflow engine, a catalog service, a credit card authorization service, or a stock-trading service. Session beans are further divided into two categories—*stateful* session beans and *stateless* session beans. As their names suggest, stateful session beans maintain state, encapsulated within the bean instance, across multiple client requests, whereas stateless session beans are not tasked with retaining the state across multiple client requests. Chapter 4 explores both stateless and stateful session beans in detail.

Message-driven beans (MDBs). Message-driven beans are similar to session beans in that they perform actions. The difference is that you can call message-driven beans only implicitly by sending *messages* to those beans. That is to say that there is no direct way of invoking a method on the message-driven bean. Examples of MDBs include beans that receive stock trade messages such as trade acknowledgment messages, credit card authorization messages, or messages within a given workflow or a business process where interactions are loosely coupled. These MDBs can in turn call the invoke methods directly on other EJBs or indirectly by sending a message to be received by another MDB. Chapter 7 provides a comprehensive discussion of message-driven beans.

Entity beans. Entity beans model business data. They are like *nouns* because they are data objects, that is, Java objects that cache database information. Examples include a product, an order, an employee, a credit card, or a stock. Session beans can harness entity beans to accomplish business transactions. Note that entity beans haven't been enhanced in EJB 3.0. Since there have been no changes made to entity beans in EJB 3.0, we have decided that this edition of our book shall not address entity beans at all. For readers who wish to educate themselves on entity beans, we suggest reading the third edition of this book. The third edition provides up-to-date guidance on developing and deploying entity beans, as well as related best practices and performance-tuning guidelines. Please read the sidebar "The Future of Entity Beans" to get an idea of where we think entity beans are headed and what made us drop entity beans coverage from this edition.

When we compare EJB architecture to other component based computing architectures such as DCOM, .NET, and CORBA, one of the obvious questions that arises is: Why does EJB have different types of components when other architectures don't? In other words, why does EJB have session beans, message-driven beans, and entity beans instead of just having, say, a *generic bean*? EJB is the only component framework that differentiates between components that represent domain business logic versus components that represent domain model versus components that *react* to messages passed as part of some business process. We think that this differentiation, even though not called out explicitly in other frameworks, is one of the salient features of EJBs. We can utilize various component types to suit specific purposes in accordance with the designated functions of our components right at the design time. This, in turn, further clarifies our component model and that directly translates into a better design. Admittedly this does increase the learning curve for EJB, however, it pays off in the long run with increased functionality.

Figure 3.2 is an illustration of various types of clients tapping into an EJB application comprising different types of EJBs. Also notice the protocol that is used by these clients to communicate with enterprise beans in a distributed environment. This brings us to our next topic, RMI-IIOP, the protocol of the enterprise bean.

NOTE **EJB 3.0 style POJO EJB programming is only applicable to session beans and message-driven beans. Entity beans, as noted previously, have not been enhanced to benefit from the simplicity of the POJO model in EJB 3.0. Hence, even though entity beans are very much a part of the EJB 3.0 specification, they are not "POJO-fied" as is the case with session beans and message-driven beans. Instead, Persistence API–based entities are recommended for applications that want to utilize POJO entities. This basically means that there is no real notion of "EJB 3.0 entity beans"; there is only "EJB 2.1 entity beans" given that entity beans as specified in the EJB 3.0 specification are exactly the way they were in EJB 2.1 specification. Hence, anywhere in this book, the term *EJB 3.0 bean* essentially implies session beans or message-driven beans but not entity beans.**

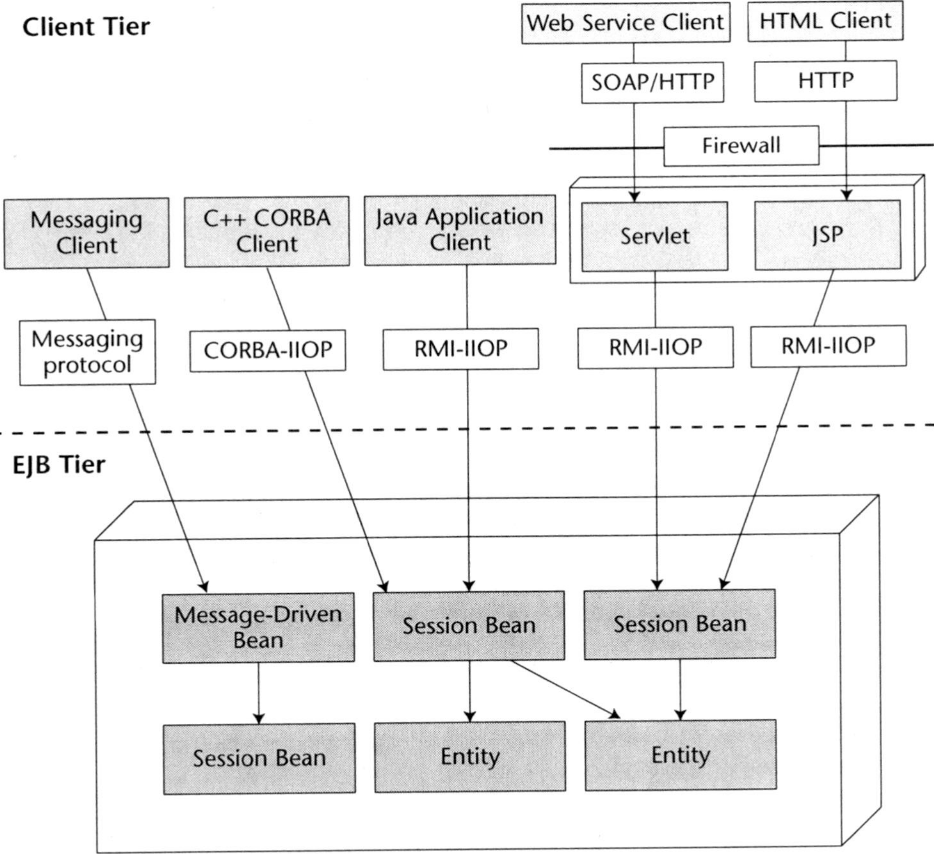

Figure 3.2 EJB sub-system: The various clients and beans.

THE FUTURE OF ENTITY BEANS

Entity beans have been a part of EJB technology ever since it was introduced. Throughout their history, entity beans have managed to cause ambivalent feelings among the industry experts and EJB application architects/developers alike. Mostly, entity beans have been projected as a heavyweight approach to handling persistence in enterprise applications. Many times entity beans have been accused, rightly or wrongly, of poor performance and heavy resource consumption of the enterprise servers. Entity beans, in short, are controversial and not surprisingly, many architects and developers tried to steer clear of using them in their applications.

Meanwhile, the rapid adoption of alternative persistence technologies and products fashioned around POJO-style entities roused the EJB community to demand that POJO-style entities be blessed by the EJB Expert Group, that the EJB Expert Group undertake providing a standard mechanism to develop and deploy such lightweight yet fully functional POJO entities. As a result, when the EJB 3.0 Expert Group was formed, one of their loftiest goals was to provide a standard lightweight persistent entity alternative to entity beans. Thus was born the Persistence API specification under the EJB 3.0 umbrella. Hence, EJB 3.0 gives you multiple alternatives for persistence:

- Use entity beans for persistence. If your application presently uses entity beans and you are happy with the way it performs, you can migrate that application as it is to EJB 3.0. All EJB 3.0 containers have to support entity beans in their entirety. Now, if you are designing a new application and if you and your developers truly feel comfortable and confident using entity beans, there is no reason not to use them in the new applications. Also note that right now there are no plans to deprecate entity beans from the EJB specification. In fact, even though there are no enhancements made to entity beans in EJB 3.0 specification, there could very well be enhancements made to them in the future versions of EJB specification. It is all based on what the industry desires and needs at the time. For now, the Expert Group has decreed that we have everything we need to get going with entity beans.
- Use Persistence API entities, also known simply as entities. Persistence API has been defined in response to the heavy demand for a standard lightweight mechanism of persistence in EJB applications. If this style of persistence suits your needs, go for Persistence API. We believe that entities are a way to go because of the sheer simplicity and ease of development and productivity that they provide, so we provide a lot of in-depth information about entities in this edition. Not only do we discuss API-level details of developing entities, but we also provide a lot of guidelines and best practices to help you optimally design and deploy the entity-based EJB applications.
- Use other persistence technologies such as Java Data Objects (JDO) or JDBC in your applications for persistence.

Again, we want to emphasize that we have made a conscious decision of not addressing entity beans in this edition. Our reasoning is that entity beans haven't changed a bit in EJB 3.0. There was no need to duplicate the same entity bean information across the two editions. Besides, we believed that using the space freed up by entity beans to cover Persistence API entities better served our readers. Hence our decision to discard entity beans related information from this edition. But this in no way reflects our take on entity beans as a less or a more viable technology for handling persistence. That decision needs to be made after considering your architecture and design requirements.

RMI-IIOP: The Protocol of the Bean

Internet Inter-ORB Protocol, also known in short as IIOP, was originally introduced within the Object Management Group (OMG), the standard-setting organization for the CORBA world, as a mechanism to enable ORB-to-ORB internetworking. The IIOP protocol connects CORBA products from different vendors, thereby ensuring interoperability among them. Later on, the preceptors of EJB understood that a similar need for interoperability among the containers from different vendors existed in the EJB world as well. They looked around to see if a solution in the form of an inter-ORB protocol already existed and that exercise brought IIOP to the EJB world.

Today every EJB container has to support IIOP. To be precise, it is RMI-IIOP that they are required to support. So what is RMI-IIOP? It is essentially marriage of CORBA's IIOP with the RMI programming model. CORBA and RMI were developed independently as distributed object programming models. RMI served as a foundation for EJB. In fact, the early days, EJB containers were based on RMI's native JRMP (Java Remote Method Protocol) protocol for remote method invocation. Although JRMP is good enough for interoperability as long as both ends of the wire are Java based, it is inadequate in scenarios where either of the client or server belong to a different programming platform. Moreover, JRMP did not address the critical question of intercontainer interoperability. However, in spite of its shortcomings, RMI did provide a very simple-to-use API for developing distributed applications on a Java platform. Hence, instead of discarding RMI completely, the Java community moved on to defining RMI-IIOP, a combination of RMI distributed computing APIs with IIOP as a protocol underneath. This way, the Java world got the best of both these technologies.

An EJB vendor can provide support for another protocol in addition to RMI-IIOP. An EJB deployer can use this vendor-specific protocol for his application as long as the communication is between the components deployed in the same vendor's container and both ends of the wire can understand RMI. However, if an EJB gets requests from other EJBs deployed in a different vendor's container or if it services requests from CORBA clients written in a different language, RMI-IIOP protocol is needed to enable interoperable communications to take place. Appendix A discusses RMI-IIOP in further detail.

EJB and Location Transparency

Distributed computing systems that offer location transparency essentially offer an ability for the clients to communicate with the remote object without them having to be aware of the remote object's machine location. The servicing object can be located on the same machine or on a different machine; the client doesn't have to care. The location transparency is usually attained via an intermediary, such as a registry, wherein the distributed objects are registered along with information such as their exact machine location. All the client has to do is search this registry for the requisite remote object, and it is the registry that hands over the remote object to the client.

In the EJB world, location transparency translates to the ability of the client to communicate with the EJB that is deployed in a JVM other than the client's JVM. The clients of the EJB that support remoting are not required to be located within the same JVM; they can be in the same JVM, but they don't have to be. JNDI is an enabler of location transparency in the EJB framework. A remote client of a bean can be located on any system—as long as it can communicate with the JNDI service of the EJB container, it can get to the bean.

EJBs also support local client view. This functionality was added in the 2.0 version of EJB technology so that the clients co-located in the same JVM as the bean can bypass the performance inefficiencies of pass-by-value semantics inherent to the distributed programming models. For such invocations on the bean's local client view, the container passes method parameters by reference. Similarly, the container passes method return values by reference from bean to the client. Pass-by-reference basically leads to sharing of the state between caller and the called. Hence, if the bean does not want the client to modify the returned value, it needs to explicitly copy the return data into another variable and pass that to the client. Local clients of EJB do not benefit from location transparency as such, since they have to be, by definition, co-located in the same JVM as the bean.

EJB 3.0 does support both local and remote client views, as it did in the previous versions, except that the bean developer is no longer required to provide definitions of `EJBObject` interfaces for local and remote client views. Instead, the bean developer is just required to define POJI (plain old Java interface) business interfaces for local and remote clients of the bean. Alternatively, the same business interface can be used to serve both local and remote clients.

JAVA NAMING AND DIRECTORY INTERFACES (JNDI)

JNDI provides a standard API to access different kinds of naming and directory services within a Java program. It is not specific to a specific naming or directory service and instead can be used to access any given naming or directory service, such as a Lightwieght Directory Access Protocol (LDAP) directory, COS (CORBA Object Services) naming, and so on, from within Java code as long as a corresponding JNDI provider for that specific naming or directory service is used. JNDI provides two APIs—one for accessing naming services, called Naming API, and another for accessing directory services, called Directory API. The power of JNDI is in the fact that a Java developer only needs to learn one set of APIs to access almost any naming or directory service, that is to say that the knowledge once acquired can be reused again and again. The question to ask henceforth is what are naming and directory services?

A naming service maintains a set of name-object *bindings*. Basically, these bindings associate names with objects such that a naming service client can provide this name to the service and the service retrieves the corresponding object bound to this name and sends it to the client. Some of the examples of naming services include COS Naming (naming services for CORBA objects), DNS (naming service for IP addresses), NIS/NIS+ (naming services developed by Sun as part of enabling network access of files and applications), and so on.

A directory service, on the other hand, provides an information model to organize and store the objects and a protocol to query and manipulate this information model. A very well-known example of directory service is LDAP. LDAP is a subset of X.500 directory services designed to address the directory services needs of smaller clients. Another example is Active Directory from Microsoft.

JNDI provides a single abstraction in the form of an API to these various naming and directory services. JNDI plays an important role in EJB programming, as we shall see in this chapter and throughout this book. Appendix A discusses the further details of JNDI technology.

Enterprise Bean Environment

The enterprise bean's environment provides a way for a bean to refer to any externally defined name-value property, resource, or even another bean such that the bean's code can remain independent of the actual referred object. In other words, an environment enables the bean to access properties; resources such as connection pools, connection factories, topics/queues, and so on; and enterprise beans, from within the bean's code without actually resolving them. The resolution can happen at the time of deployment, when the actual values of the environmental properties or references are set. The bean's environment thus provides a level of indirection to enable the bean to stay independent of referred objects so that any change to the referred object's configuration does not have to trickle down to the bean's code. The container implements the enterprise bean's environment and makes it available to the bean through the JNDI context, `java:comp/env/`

Why do we need such an indirection? As we know, enterprise beans are designed to be reusable components from the get-go. And potentially, the beans can be reused in different operational environments too. Also, most of the beans have a need to access external world. The key issue then is how to enable an enterprise bean to locate this external information/resources without it requiring knowledge of how this information/resources are named and organized in various operational environments.

For example, take an independent software vendor (ISV) that ships an EJB application to multiple customers. Obviously, the ISV expects the application to be deployed in different operational environments. In this case, any access to externally defined properties and resources from within the bean's code should be shielded of the differences in the actual environments. So if say one of the beans is trying to access a JMS topic, the code can refer to this topic as `MyTopic`, which then can be mapped to the actual JMS topic, named say `MyJMSTopic`, at the time of deployment. This ensures that the code does not have to change the reference to the topic from `MyTopic` to `MyJMSTopic` or from `MyTopic` to `MyWonderfulJMSTopic` and so on, each time it is deployed in a different environment.

Thus, a bean's environment is a powerful enabler of its reusability promise.

Anatomy of the "New" Bean

So what does an EJB 3.0 bean look like? What artifacts are required to develop this *new* bean? As we have hinted many times before this point, EJB 3.0 beans are POJO styled as opposed to their precursors that used to constitute multiple Java classes per EJB. The EJB 3.0 bean has all its code contained in a single Java class.

An enterprise bean can be a distributed component—its clients can live in the same virtual machine as the bean (say, another codeployed bean) or it can reside in another JVM potentially on a different machine. EJBs that want to service remote clients have to be equipped to handle the nitty-gritty of distributed communication ranging from error handling to marshaling and unmarshaling method parameters and return types. And as we already know, the enterprise bean is a *managed* component due to the fact that the container in which the bean is deployed manages the services that the bean needs as well as the environment in which the bean lives. The container takes care of such things as when to create the bean's instance, how to make available a reference to this instance to the remote and/or local clients of the bean, how to make available the various resources—such as connection factories, messaging queues/topics, connection pools, transaction contexts, security contexts, and so on—that the bean is dependent on within its environment and so on. The bean should thus be prepared to take notifications from the container about changes to its environment and should in general be provisioned to communicate with the container during its lifetime. Another remarkable feature of EJB architecture is location transparency, explained later in this chapter.

Up until now the enterprise beans exposed developers to a lot of these intricacies. The developer had to take care of handling system exceptions that a bean is susceptible to, given its distributed nature, within the bean code. So also, the developer had to write code for implementing the various component interfaces such as `javax.ejb.SessionBean` or `javax.ejb.MessageDrivenBean` to enable the container management of the bean. In addition to these, the bean developer had to deal with the complexity involved around coming up with the rightly configured deployment descriptor, a bunch of XML-based metadata, to further specify how the container should manage the bean. An EJB client wasn't excused from this web either; a client was required to possess knowledge of working with JNDI registry services and deal with JNDI APIs to obtain a reference to the EJB factory (EJB home interface) in order to construct a reference to the actual bean (EJB object interface).

Yielding to the popular demand of the developer community, the Expert Group had to come up with a way to take all these complications out of the EJB developer's hands and yet retain the power and flexibility that the distributed component model of EJB APIs as well as implicit middleware services of the EJB container provided. The new bean therefore is anatomized into a single Java source that almost exclusively consists of only the business logic code. In other words, this POJO class is devoid of the code that handles the horizontal concerns pertaining to distributed computing such as throwing RMI remote exceptions from all methods that could be invoked remotely or the code to implement component interfaces so that the container can provide its implicit middleware services such as life cycle management, transaction, security, and so on to the bean. Similarly, the EJB 3.0 bean developer can also forgo a deployment descriptor file and get away from that morass.

Let us take another moment and examine Figure 3.3, which illustrates the old EJB programming model, and then compare it with the new EJB 3.0 programming model given in Figure 3.4.

Figure 3.3 highlights the flow of the business method invocation in EJB 2.x as under:

- Steps 1a and 1b show a local or remote client application of the EJB—might be a servlet/JSP, a standalone application client, an application container client, or another enterprise bean—creating a corresponding local or remote EJB object reference using the EJB home reference. The client gets hold of the EJB home reference from JNDI registry and naming services. Depending on whether the client is local or remote, the client retrieves local or remote EJB home reference from JNDI. In steps 2 and 3, an EJB object is created and returned back to the client. During EJB deployment, it is the container that generates implementations for EJB home and EJB object interfaces provided by the EJB developer.

- The client makes a business method invocation on the local/remote EJB object interface in step 4.
- In old-style EJB, the container generates implementations for EJB home and EJB object interfaces, written by the bean provider, at the time of deployment. The business method invocation on EJB object reference thus is handled by the container-generated EJB object implementation. This implementation calls container-specific APIs to provide implicit middleware services prior to calling the actual business method on the EJB developer provided bean class. Similarly, the container-generated EJB object implementation will call upon container middleware services APIs after the business method invocation on the bean class. This sequence is shown in steps 5, 6, 7, and 8.
- Step 9 concludes the method invocation with a return value (if any).

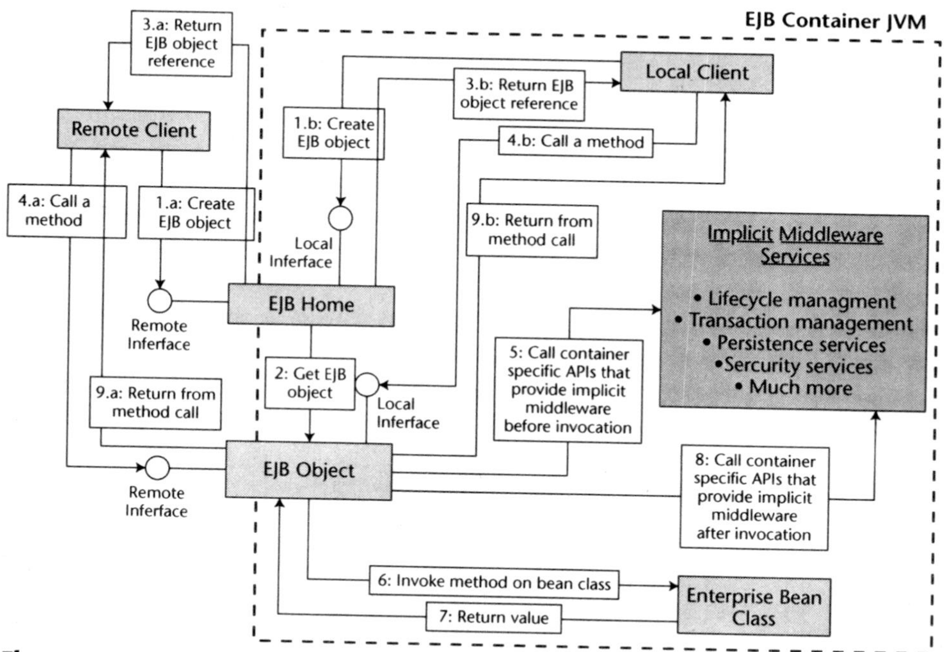

Figure 3.3 Pre–EJB 3.0 programming model.

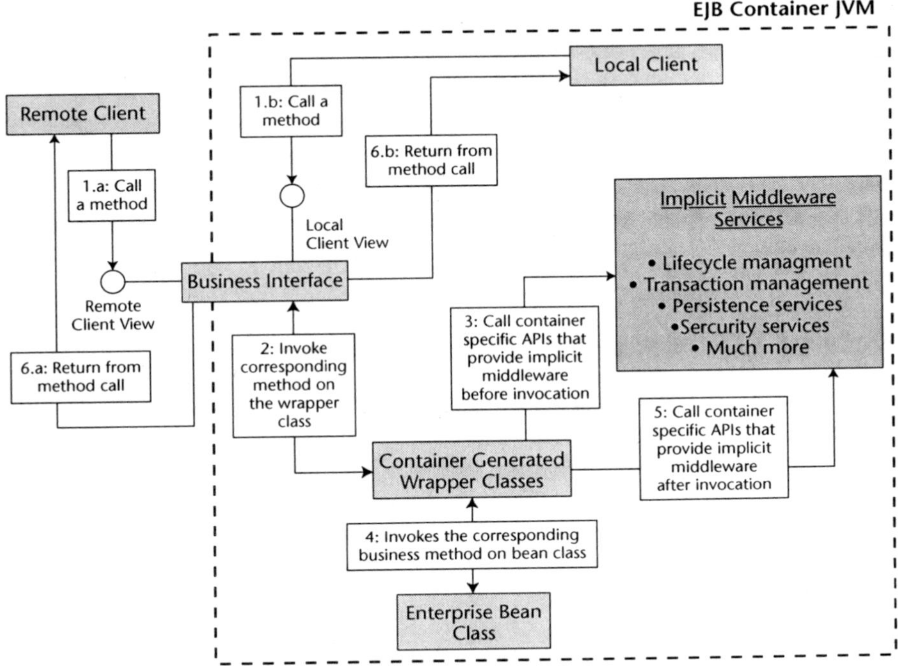

Figure 3.4 EJB 3.0 programming model.

Figure 3.4 highlights the invocation from an EJB 3.0 client's perspective.

- Steps 1a and 1b show a local or remote client application of the EJB calling a business method on the local or remote business interface. Clients retrieve this business interface reference from the JNDI naming and registry services (using JNDI APIs or dependency injection mechanisms discussed later in this chapter).
- Obviously, EJB container services have to be applied to the business method invocation. Hence, figuratively speaking, some kind of a container-generated wrapper class for remote and/or local business interface is needed so that it will call the various container middleware APIs both before and after invoking the actual business method on the bean class. This flow is shown in steps 2, 3, 4, and 5.
- The call finally concludes upon the method return.

NOTE **Java EE application clients are standard Java applications that execute within their own JVM. They are invoked via the static main() methods like their standalone Java application brethren. The only difference between the two is that the Java EE application clients run within a container, albeit a lightweight container, which is devoid of many middleware services such as transactions, as compared to a full-fledged Java EE container that provides such services. Java EE application clients are packaged with their own deployment descriptor within a .jar file.**

The Role of EJB Home and Object Interfaces

The major difference between the old and the new bean is that while the old bean was exposed to a lot of contractual requirements, such as providing a home interface, an EJB object interface, and a bean class, the new bean is limited in its contractual obligations. As you can see in Figure 3.4, it only has to provide a business interface (for local and remote clients) and a bean class that provides definitions of the methods on this business interface. The big question is why doesn't an EJB 3.0 bean require a home interface and an object interface? How can it get away with these requirements? The answers lie in understanding the purpose of home and remote interfaces and how that purpose is served in EJB 3.0 without them.

In previous versions of EJB, the home interface served as a factory for creating references to the EJB object. Now the home interface could practically be the same for all stateless session beans and message-driven beans, since all stateless session bean and message-driven bean objects are created equal. Thus, there is no need to make the bean developer provide a specific home interface for each specific stateless and message-driven bean. As for stateful session beans, their EJB objects aren't created equal; the state of a stateful session bean EJB object varies across different clients. In pre–EJB 3.0, the per-instance state of the stateful session bean was initialized by defining a special create method on the home interface such that it takes state via the method parameters from the clients and initializes the bean instance to it. In 3.0, instead of subjecting the stateful session bean provider to defining a home interface simply as a mechanism to transfer state from client to the bean instance, the bean provider can define a special method right in the bean class that would be called by the container right before invoking the first business method on the bean instance. This eliminates the need for a home interface as a factory for stateful session beans, too.

Now we come to the EJB object interface. The main purpose of the EJB object interface was to provide the client view for an EJB, meaning that the EJB object carried all the business methods that the bean wanted to expose to its local or remote clients. Depending on the clients it intends to serve, the EJB object could provide local client view, remote client view, or both. The container provided implementation for EJB object interfaces, and the bean class implemented all the EJB object's business methods implicitly by declaring and defining methods with the exact same method signatures. The container implementation of the EJB object called upon the appropriate container services before invoking the actual business method implementation on the bean class. Similarly, after invocation the container services were applied to bring a fruitful end to the invocation (by committing the current transaction, updating the cache across the cluster, and so on).

Thus, the container-generated implementation of EJB object interfaces served as a nice hook for invoking container services. However, from EJB developers' perspective, they had to write an EJB object interface containing business methods that they didn't implement directly but rather indirectly. The developers had to be extra careful in providing the implicit implementation of the EJB object interface by making sure that the signatures of business methods declared in EJB object interface exactly matched those declared in the bean class. This extra caution required on the part of the developers was not worth it. As far as providing a hook for injecting container services is concerned, it is an implementation detail of the container; it is expected that the container implementations will provide their services through one or another such hook, as long as the programming model is kept simple for the developer. Hence, in EJB 3.0, the bean provider no longer has to supply an EJB object interface and then implement it implicitly in the bean class. Instead, the bean provider has to write a simple Java interface, also known as business interface, consisting of business methods it wants to expose to the clients of the bean. The bean provider then writes a POJO that implements this business interface, and it is as simple as that. The container can internally use generated wrapper classes to intercept the calls to the bean instance and thereby provide middleware services, or it can use other design patterns to achieve this. In conclusion, how the container injects various middleware services before and after the business method invocation is a container-specific detail and need not concern the EJB developer.

The EJB 3.0 Simplified API

Now it is time to look at the new EJB 3.0 API, which offers ample simplification over the previous EJB API. Simplicity in EJB 3.0 has been achieved in various ways:

- No home and object interfaces are required.
- No component interface is required.
- Use of Java metadata annotations.
- Simplification of APIs for accessing bean's environment.

In the following sections, we go through each of these aspects of simplification of the EJB programming model.

Elimination of Home and Object Interfaces

As discussed previously, getting rid of home and object interfaces eases development on behalf of the bean provider. The new session beans put all the business methods into a business interface. Depending on whether the clients of the bean are local or remote, the bean provider can designate the business interface as a *remote business interface* or *local business interface* or both. Whereas the methods on a remote business interface can throw arbitrary application exceptions, they are not allowed to throw `java.rmi.RemoteException`. This is unlike the definition of EJB home and object interfaces for EJB 2.1 remote client view where all the methods were required to throw `java.rmi.RemoteException`. Any system-level problems, protocol or otherwise, would be encapsulated within `javax.ejb.EJBException` and returned to the client by the container. Given that `EJBException` is a subclass of `java.lang.RuntimeException`, it does not have to be listed in the throws clause of the business methods.

A message-driven bean doesn't need a business interface because there are no direct client invocations on a message-driven bean and hence there is no need to define a business interface with business methods in it. Also for the same reason, whenever an MDB runs into unexpected problems, the container will log the error and communicate it, within a `javax.ejb.EJBException`, to the underlying resource adapter instead of the client.

Elimination of Component Interface

Component interfaces in the previous versions of EJB, `javax.ejb.SessionBean` and `javax.ejb.MessageDrivenBean`, existed for a reason—they provided a way through which the container notified the bean instance of various life cycle events affecting it. A session or message-driven bean class had to implement the respective component interface in order to stay abreast of the events in its life cycle. These component interfaces carried the various life cycle methods that the bean class would implement. All that the container had to do then is call the appropriate method of the component interface to provide an opportunity to the bean instance to handle the life cycle event the way it wants. For example, the container can notify the message-driven bean instance that it is about to destroy it by invoking the `ejbDestroy()` method on the message-driven bean's corresponding bean class. Within the `ejbDestroy()` method the bean class can close an open JDBC database connection and thereby free some resources. Similarly, the container that is about to associate a client with a stateful bean instance can notify the bean instance by calling `ejbCreate()` on the bean class, and the bean class can instantiate the state of the bean instance within this method's implementation.

The issue with this mechanism is: What if the bean does not want container notifications of its life cycle events? In that case the bean still has to implement the component interfaces because that is the contractual agreement between the container and the bean instance. This enforcement on the bean provider to implement the component interface regardless of whether it is needed or not has been removed in EJB 3.0. Going forward, the bean class does not have to implement `javax.ejb.SessionBean`, in case of a session bean, or `javax.ejb.MessageDrivenBean`, in case of a message-driven bean. It will be a plain Java class, which only has to implement a business interface if the EJB is a session bean.

The question then is how can a bean class get notifications from the container if interested? There are two ways it can get that—the first is for a bean provider to write a separate class consisting of all the callback notification methods and then inform the container to treat this class as the bean's callback listener class. The second way is for the bean provider to implement notification methods right inside the bean class and designate these methods to handle appropriate events. Both these approaches require the bean to use annotations. Annotations are the biggest and most radical addition to EJB 3.0 specification. They are used not only for event notifications but also for many other purposes. The next topic focuses on annotations and their contribution in simplifying EJB 3.0 programming model.

PRE–EJB 3.0 AND EJB 3.0 COMPATIBILITY

One of the notable goals of EJB 3.0 Expert Group was to maintain compatibility, both backward and forward, between the new and the old EJB worlds. The older EJB applications can be deployed as is on an EJB 3.0 container without rewriting them, thereby accommodating forward compatibility. This is because the pre–EJB 3.0 APIs have been made available in EJB 3.0 containers. Also a bean written against EJB 3.0 APIs can service clients written to use earlier versions of EJB APIs, thereby providing backward compatibility. This is achieved by adapting the client views provided by the EJB 3.0 beans to suit the older clients.

These provisions for compatibility and portability in the EJB 3.0 specification enable four possible scenarios of deployment within an EJB 3.0 container:

- **EJB 3.0 bean with EJB 3.0 client view**
- **EJB 2.1 bean with EJB 2.1 client view**
- **EJB 3.0 bean with EJB 2.1 client view**
- **EJB 2.1 bean with EJB 3.0 client view**
- **Various combinations of the above three scenarios–for example, EJB 3.0 beans and EJB 2.1 beans deployed in the same application where EJB 2.1 clients not only make requests to EJB 2.1 beans but also to EJB 3.0 beans.**

Use of Annotations

Annotation, also known as metadata, stands for additional definition that can be attached to an element within the code to help further explain or characterize it. Annotations are used to provide additional context to the program. We in the software industry have used annotation for the longest time in the form of code comments. Comments are used to provide additional information about the code to the reviewer. At the same time, comments are ignored by the compiler/interpreter of the code. That is the way code comments, the annotations that we use to explain our code better to the readers, are designed to be processed. Annotation processing typically occurs when code consisting of annotations is compiled or interpreted by compilers, deployment tools, development tools, and so on. The outcome of annotation processing can be many different things. For example, processing annotations can result in creation of code documents (remember JavaDocs?) or the generation of other code artifacts (XDoclet) or performing various compile-time checks (C language preprocessor directives).

Java language did support annotations in the form of code comments and JavaDocs. Also, Java frameworks such as XDoclet, which used annotations to generate code artifacts and much more, came into existence over the course of time. What Java lacked though, up until Java SE 5.0 (Tiger), was a standard framework within the language platform that could be used to create and process new annotations; a facility that can be leveraged by rest of the Java language technologies as well as by custom programs. This need was addressed in J2SE 5.0 release by including JSR-175 (A Metadata Facility for the Java Programming Language) as part of the platform.

Java SE 5.0 annotations can be applied to various elements of the Java code such as methods, variables, constructors, package declarations, and so on. Annotations begin with an `@` sign followed by the annotation name which in turn is followed by annotation data (if any). Shown below is a hypothetical example of a `@Failsafe` annotation that when applied to a distributed RMI object will instruct the RMI compiler to generate the stubs and skeletons so that they can connect to a different RMI instance in the event of a failure.

```
@Failsafe
public interface SomeRMIExample extends java.rmi.Remote
{
    ...
}
```

Annotation programming is a vast subject and as such does not belong to this book on enterprise beans. What we do cover in this book are built-in annotations that are a part of EJB 3.0 and related specifications and how to use them to ease development and deployment of enterprise beans.

Annotations and Bean Development

EJB 3.0 has defined a lot of built-in annotations for use in EJB development. This changes EJB programming quite significantly in that it is now a mix of metadata tags and code constructs. The specification has also defined metadata to annotate deployment information within the code. Below is an example of a bean class that uses metadata to designate the callback listener methods for the stateful bean.

```
@Stateful
public class exampleBean implements BeanBusinessInterface
{
      @Remove
      public void removeBean()
      {
        // Close any resources that were opened to service requests.
      }
}
```

The `@Stateful` annotation indicates to the EJB compiler that the given bean is a stateful session bean and that the bean artifacts should be generated so as to suit the semantics of a stateful bean. Also, `@Remove` is another annotation used within the code, which indicates that the following method, `removeBean()`, should be called by the container when it is about to destroy the bean instance. These annotations have a special meaning to the EJB compiler. In this fashion, the annotations are used in EJB 3.0 programming.

EJB 3.0 development has been made a lot simpler as is evident from the example above. A developer can annotate the code and expect the compilers, code generators, deployment tools, or whatever is the processor working behind the scenes to take care of the appropriate semantics. Chapter 8 discusses some other nuances of using annotations in EJB 3.0, while Appendix B provides a good reference to annotation basics as well as an entire list of built-in annotations in EJB 3.0.

Annotations and Deployment Descriptors

The biggest contribution of annotations with respect to simplification is that they have made deployment descriptors redundant. EJB 3.0 annotations can be used in lieu of deployment descriptors. A deployment descriptor is an XML document consisting of information related to deployment of the bean. It specifies instructions to the container such as the kind of runtime services that would be needed by the bean for its successful execution.

Deployment descriptors were introduced for a very good reason. They enabled a mechanism through which a bean can be deployed on different EJB containers and yet can be expected to behave the same across these different containers. This is because at the time of deployment the container will read the bean's deployment descriptor and provide a standard environment for the bean's execution. The deployment descriptor thus guarantees that certain run-time aspects of the bean's execution would remain uniform as long as the bean is deployed in a standard EJB container.

The challenge that developers faced with deployment descriptors was with regard to their complexity. A deployment descriptor is XML, and XML by its very nature is prone to error when subjected to human editing. Therefore, only tools were considered capable of handling these chunks of deployment information. Most of the EJB deployment tools thus were enabled to generate deployment descriptors. Now if the bean provider wants to change the behavior of the bean, he will have no choice but to modify the deployment descriptor. For this, most of the time the bean provider will use a deployment tool GUI to change properties on the bean, which in turn will convert the bean's settings to the respective deployment descriptor XML. If the deployment tool GUI is not available, then the provider will manually edit the descriptor's XML thereby making it susceptible to syntactical errors.

To help developers who find themselves in this situation and largely to take the complexity of the deployment descriptor out of the development life cycle, the EJB Expert Group came up with the notion of defining deployment metadata so that it can replace the deployment descriptor. Deployment metadata can be embedded within the EJB code (bean class or business interface) such that at the time of deployment this metadata could be used to provide the appropriate behavior to the bean. Hence, instead of working with clumsy XML constructs, the developers can utilize easy to use Java metadata to specify the deployment configuration of their beans right in the bean class. This also helps in speeding up the development because now the developer does not have to undergo an extra step of generating a deployment descriptor.

Does this mean that deployment descriptors are out of the game in EJB 3.0? The answer is a resounding no. Deployment descriptors are very much a part of EJB 3.0. If the bean provider so desires, he can put all of the bean's configuration information in deployment descriptor or he can distribute this information across the bean class and the deployment descriptor or he can choose not to put any configuration information in the deployment descriptor and instead use deployment metadata in the bean class to specify it, and that would be fine too. So there are quite a few options available to the bean provider. In the scenario where the bean provider uses both the metadata and the deployment descriptor, the latter will always override the former if both have redundantly specified configuration information. For example, if transaction setting of a certain bean method is specified in both the bean class and the deployment descriptor, the one specified in the descriptor will always take precedence over the one specified using the metadata in the bean class. If a developer doesn't provide a deployment descriptor, at the time of deployment, a container can choose to generate a skeleton deployment descriptor.

Container Specific Deployment Descriptor

The EJB container provides a lot of container services in a standard, uniform fashion, and the bean provider asks the container to make these services available by using the metadata in the bean class or by defining a standard deployment descriptor. In addition to these standard container services, there are certain value-added services that the container can provide, such as load balancing, clustering, caching of relatively static information, and so on that are over and above the container services that are defined as part of the specification. The configuration information of these value-added services is described usually in a container-specific deployment descriptor. Hence, a typical bean deployment consists of a standard deployment descriptor, a file named `ejb-jar.xml`, and a nonstandard proprietary container-specific deployment descriptor, whose file name varies from container to container. With EJB 3.0, a container can also choose to provide respective metadata for the value-added services, which can then be used by the bean provider in the bean class.

As should be clear by now, annotations are used pervasively in EJB 3.0. And such pervasive use of deployment annotations certainly warrants a discussion on what are the pros and cons of using deployment annotations.

The Good, the Bad, and the Ugly of Deployment Annotations

Using annotations to describe the deployment configuration of the bean can be convenient and tricky at the same time. Convenient because the bean provider can place the configuration along with the bean's logic, right at the time of developing bean. Both the activities—developing the bean and describing the deployment configuration of the bean—can be accomplished at the same time and place, thereby increasing the developer productivity. Tricky because if not done properly the convenience of deployment annotations can also quickly turn into a process nightmare, and here is why.

Conventionally, EJB application life cycle is divided into various tasks, and a separate role is accorded to accomplishing each of these tasks. For instance, the role of a bean provider is to develop the bean and supply it to the application assembler who then takes the bean's Ejb-jar and assembles it with rest of the components such as other enterprise beans (supplied by other bean providers), JSP/servlets, and so on. The assembler then passes down the assembled components to the deployer who is responsible for deploying and postdeployment tuning of the components. In a given EJB project, these roles can be played by the same individual or by different people. In a scenario where the bean is developed and deployed by the same individual, using deployment metadata within the bean's code can work out fine. Because it is the same individual who is in charge of development and deployment of the bean, there is less chance of problems arising due to miscommunication and misunderstanding regarding the division of labor with respect to deployment configuration specification. However, in a scenario where the bean provider is a separate entity from the bean deployer, embedding deployment metadata within the code might lead to various issues. For one, before the deployer can generate the bean's deployment descriptor, he will now be required to go through the bean's code to make sure that the deployment descriptor does not mistakenly override the bean provider's deployment metadata–specified configuration. However, the most important issue when using deployment metadata is that each time a change in deployment is needed, the bean's code will need to be changed, leading to the recompilation and repackaging of the bean.

Our suggestion is that in projects where different individuals play the roles of bean provider and deployer, make one party responsible for specifying all the deployment configuration. If the bean provider is chosen for the job, all the deployment information should be provided as metadata within the bean class. The deployer then should be exempt from generating a deployment descriptor. And if the deployer is chosen, the bean provider should be exempt from providing deployment metadata within the bean class. In conclusion, a well-defined division of responsibilities should be done to avoid any potential chaos resulting from scattering the deployment configuration across the bean class and deployment descriptor.

Simplified Access to Environment

Accessing the environment to gain references to externally defined resources and enterprise beans, and other entries such as properties, is a chore that almost every EJB needs to perform. Up until now, an EJB had to rely solely on the JNDI APIs to get hold of these environmental entries. In EJB 3.0, other mechanisms, namely *dependency injection* and a simple `lookup()` method on the `EJBContext` interface have been added to solve the age-old problem of having to use JNDI APIs from within bean class to access the bean's dependencies.

Dependency injection is a mechanism followed by the container to inject the requested environmental entry and make it available to the bean instance before any business methods are invoked on that particular instance. The container injects these entries into the bean's variables or methods. The bean provider has to convey to the container where these dependencies should be injected at the runtime, such as in which variables or methods. The provider can use a deployment descriptor and annotations to specify this. Bean methods that are targets of dependency injection should be defined using the JavaBeans naming convention for properties in that they should follow the `setXXX()` convention.

So what happens if the dependency injection fails for some reason? If the container is not able to make available the environmental entry on which the bean is dependent for proper functioning? Well, the container will discard that bean instance and try creating the bean instance again.

EJBCONTEXT

During runtime, the bean does need to know about its environment in terms of the transaction context within which its method is being invoked, security attributes of the caller such as its security principal, and so on. The `javax.ejb.EJBContext` API is like a window for the bean to the outside world with which it is interacting, that is, the container. `EJBContext` is further subclassed into `SessionContext` and `MessageDrivenContext` for session beans and message-driven beans, respectively.

Bean instances can use dependency injection mechanism to access the `EJBContext` instance. The previous versions all the beans got access to the `EJBContext` instance as part of the mandatory implementation of the `setSessionContext()` or `setMessageDrivenContext()` methods of the `javax.ejb.SessionBean` and `javax.ejb.MessageDrivenBean` component interfaces, respectively.

The `lookup()` method of `EJBContext` interface is another alternative to the JNDI API for obtaining access to the environmental entries.

A bean can still use JNDI APIs to access the environmental dependencies, but that is done by choice and not by mandate. We will discuss dependency injection and related topics in further detail in Chapter 8.

NOTE **The examples of environmental entries typically include references to enterprise beans, Web services, connection factories, message destinations (JMS topics or queues), persistence units, persistence contexts, transaction contexts, EJB timer service, and last but not least, `EJBContext`. The container provides tools to create and initialize the environment entries. For example, a deployer will use some container-provided tool to create a message destination, say, a JMS topic. The bean can ask the container to inject this resource into a variable, say, `MyTopic`, using dependency injection, `EJBContext` lookup, or JNDI lookup.**

Packaging and Deployment of the "New" Bean

Once the bean is developed, you need to package it into an Ejb-jar file. Jar files are a convenient way of distributing Java software, and what better choice than to use them for packaging the enterprise beans? Usually, your IDE or the EJB deployment tool bundled with your container comes with a capability to package the bean's artifacts into an Ejb-jar file. Figure 3.5 shows the creation of an Ejb-jar file consisting of an EJB 3.0 bean.

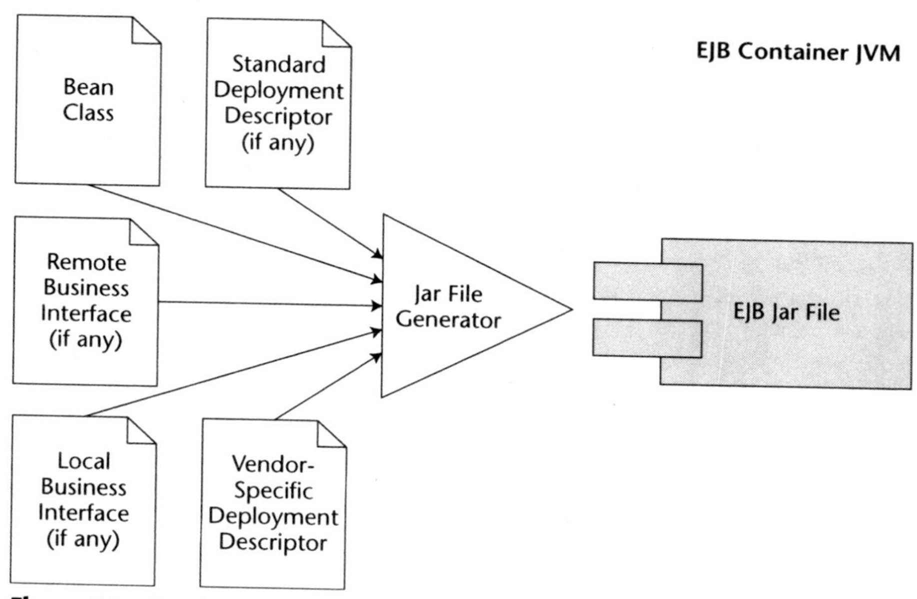

Figure 3.5 Creating an Ejb-jar file.

An Ejb-jar can contain artifacts for more than one enterprise beans. If your bean class and/or local/remote business interfaces are dependent on other user classes, then the Ejb-jar file must also contain them. Also remember that an EJB 3.0 Ejb-jar can contain pre–EJB 3.0 beans along with the new beans. This means that an Ejb-jar can contain EJB home and EJB object interfaces, old-style bean classes, and so on.

Upon creating an Ejb-jar, you will need to deploy it within the container. It is at this time that various container artifacts, such as stubs, skeletons, wrapper classes, and so on, are generated to provide an environment suitable to the bean's existence. Also during this time the container reads the deployment descriptor and/or the deployment metadata to generate the container artifacts in accordance with the services requested by the bean provider. All containers provide some kind of a deployment tool for deploying Ejb-jar within the container. Once the Ejb-jar is deployed, the deployer can then tweak and tune the beans.

Example of EJB 3.0 Bean

So far in this chapter we have explained several important aspects of EJB development and deployment and how they have been simplified a lot in EJB 3.0. However, what better way to realize the extent of simplicity than to witness the code itself?

We will undertake a very simple exercise of developing and deploying the proverbial HelloBean. It is a stateless session bean that has one method in its remote business interface, hello(), which when called returns a greeting to the client. The following are the steps involved in this exercise:

1. Write the Java code for the business interface, only making it remote in this case, and the bean class.
2. Compile the Java sources in step 1.
3. Provide a deployment descriptor.
4. Create the Ejb-jar file, containing the classes generated in step 2, using the jar utility or tools provided by your container.
5. Deploy the Ejb-jar file on the container, either using auto-deploy feature (if container supports it) or by using a container provided deployment tool.
6. Check your container to verify the EJB's deployment.
7. Write and execute a client to check the functioning of the bean.

Now let us go through the programming artifacts one by one.

The Business Interface

The business interface, Hello, is a very straightforward POJI consisting of method declaration for hello(). Source 3.1 is a listing of Hello.java.

```
package examples.session.stateless;

/**
 * This is the Hello business interface.
 */

public interface Hello {
    public String hello();
}
```

Source 3.1 Hello.java.

The Bean Class

The bean class, HelloBean, is also a straightforward POJO consisting of an implementation of hello(). In addition, it also has annotations that configures the bean appropriately. Source 3.2 shows the listing of HelloBean.java.

```
package examples.session.stateless;

import javax.ejb.Remote;
import javax.ejb.Stateless;

/**
 * Stateless session bean.
 */
@Stateless
@Remote(Hello.class)
public class HelloBean implements Hello {
     public String hello() {
         System.out.println("hello()");
         return "Hello, World!";
     }
}
```

Source 3.2 HelloBean.java.

Notice the two annotations—`@Stateless` and `@Remote`—in `HelloBean.java`. `@Stateless` annotation configures the bean as a stateless session bean, whereas `@Remote` annotation lets us configure the bean's support for remote client view via the remote business interface `Hello`. Instead of using deployment descriptor to specify these, we use annotations. Had we cared to, we could have put in much more deployment configuration information using annotations, for transaction, security, access to other resources, and so on, for our bean. In the following chapters, you will see a lot of examples where we do use metadata for this purpose, too.

The Deployment Descriptor

In this example, we do make use of deployment descriptor, although not very meaningfully. Our deployment descriptor is just a skeleton, as shown in Source 3.3.

```
<?xml version="1.0" encoding="UTF-8" ?>
 <ejb-jar  xmlns="http://java.sun.com/xml/ns/j2ee"
xmlns:xsi="http://www.w3.org/2001/XMLSchema-
instance"xsi:schemaLocation="http://java.sun.com/xml/ns/j2ee
http://java.sun.com/xml/ns/j2ee/ejb-jar_3_0.xsd"
version="3.0">
 <enterprise-beans>
 </enterprise-beans>
</ejb-jar>
```

Source 3.3 Ejb-jar.xml.

As you can see, this deployment descriptor is not used to specify any meaningful configuration. Where previously we would have declared the business interface and bean class and the like for an EJB in a deployment descriptor, now we use annotations in the bean class to do the same. In fact, we would have been able to deploy this bean even without one, but we left it here to showcase how the deployment descriptor can be rendered redundant by use of deployment annotations.

The Client

Now let us see how a Java application client of EJB 3.0 invokes the `hello()` method on the bean. Source 3.4 shows the listing of `HelloClient.java`.

```
package examples.session.stateless;

import javax.naming.Context;
import javax.naming.InitialContext;

/**
 * This class is an example of client code which invokes
 * methods on a simple, remote stateless session bean.
 */
public class HelloClient {

     public static void main(String[] args) throws Exception {
          /*
           * Obtain the JNDI initial context.
           *
           * The initial context is a starting point for
           * connecting to a JNDI tree.
           */
          Context ctx = new InitialContext();
          Hello hello = (Hello)
ctx.lookup("examples.session.stateless.Hello");

          /*
           * Call the hello() method on the bean.
           * We then print the result to the screen.
           */
          System.out.println(hello.hello());
     }
}
```

Source 3.4 HelloClient.java.

The client code is fairly simple. Although we are required to work with the JNDI interfaces given that `HelloClient` is a standalone Java client, had this been a client deployed within the container's managed environment we could have used the injection mechanism to make container inject the reference to `HelloBean`. This would have even further simplified the client code.

When one compares the code for EJB 3.0 bean to that for the EJB 2.1 bean provided in Chapter 2, one cannot help but feel awe for the extent to which the complexity of development and deployment has been reduced. We have bundled the code for this example in the code that accompanies this book.

NOTE All the code bundled with this book can be downloaded from `www.wiley.com/go/sriganesh`**. The code is configured to run on the open source Glassfish Application Server, which forms the basis of the Java EE 5 reference implementation. The code can be built and executed by running the packaged Ant scripts. Each code sample comes with a** `Readme.txt`**, describing the various steps needed to compile, package, deploy, and execute the code samples.**

Summary of Terms

For your convenience, we now list the definitions of each term we've used so far. As you read future chapters, refer to these definitions whenever you need quick clarification. You might want to bookmark this page.

The *enterprise bean instance* is a plain old Java object instance of an enterprise bean class. It contains business method implementations of the methods defined in the remote/local business interface, for session beans.

The *business interface* is a plain old Java interface that enumerates the business methods exposed by the enterprise bean. Depending on the client view supported by the bean, the business interface can be further classified into a local business interface or a remote business interface.

The *deployment descriptor* is an XML file that specifies the middleware requirements for your bean. You use the deployment descriptor to inform the container about the services you need for the bean, such as transaction services, security, and so on. Alternatively, you can specify the middleware requirements using deployment annotations within the bean class as well.

The *Ejb-jar* file is the packaging unit for an enterprise bean, consisting of all the above artifacts. An EJB 3.0 Ejb-jar file can also consist of the old-style beans, if your application uses components defined using pre–EJB 3.0 technologies.

The *vendor-specific deployment descriptor* lets you specify your bean's needs for proprietary container services such as clustering, load balancing, and so on. A vendor can alternatively provide deployment metadata for these services, which, like standard metadata, can be used within the bean class to specify the configuration for these services. The vendor-specific deployment descriptor's definition changes from vendor to vendor.

Summary

We began this chapter by providing a real-world application example that can be designed using enterprise beans, and then introduced you to the various concepts surrounding EJB development, such as containers, types of beans, the wire protocol of EJB—RMI-IIOP, and the EJB environment. We then provided a comprehensive discussion on the various new approaches adopted by the EJB Expert Group in simplifying the EJB 3.0 development and deployment. Finally, we journeyed through the development of the elementary `HelloBean` EJB.

This chapter marks an end to the first part of this book. In this part, we extensively introduced you to EJB technology. In Part I, we accomplished two objectives:

1. Established a good understanding for the core concepts of EJB architecture—such as components and component frameworks; distributed computing; middleware services; fundamental technologies such as RMI-IIOP, JNDI, and Java annotations; various roles involved in EJB application development life cycle; the service-oriented architecture and its synergy with EJB framework; the role of EJB vis-à-vis the Java EE technology, and much much more.
2. Provided a strong understanding of the encumbrances of previous versions of EJB technology and how its complexity prevented developers from achieving higher productivity. This discussion was then followed by introduction to EJB 3.0 technology and how it tries to take the complexity out of the EJB development and deployment equation. We provided examples of both, old-style EJB and the new EJB, to explain to the reader why certain decisions to change things in EJB 3.0 were made.

We begin Part II with a chapter on session beans, followed by a chapter each on session bean–based Web services, the Persistence API, and message-driven beans. Whereas Part I endeavored to set the stage right for understanding EJB technology, Part II strives to provide further details on this. We hope you enjoy the journey!

PART II The Triad of Beans and Entities

In Part II of this book, we'll focus on the development details for implementing an EJB application. We'll discuss the two types of enterprise beans: session beans (Chapter 4) and message driven beans (Chapter 7). We'll also explore their subtypes: stateless session beans, stateful session beans, and session beans as Web services (Chapter 5). Not only will we cover each of these conceptually, but we'll also write an example for each bean type. In addition, we cover in detail the new Java Persistence API defined entity programming, again with examples, in Chapter 6. We'll end Part II with a discussion in Chapter 8 of various other functionalities of EJB technology such as access to the environment, interceptors, and resource injection.

Part II is essential for those of you who are ready to go deep into EJB programming fundamentals. It provides essential groundwork for the more advanced topics such as transactions, EJB design and performance best practices, advanced persistence concepts, and so on, which are coming in Part III.

CHAPTER

4

Introduction to Session Beans

A *session bean* performs work on behalf of client code that is calling it. Session beans are reusable components that contain logic for business processes. For example, a session bean can perform price quoting, order entry, video compression, banking transactions, stock trades, database operations, complex calculations, and more.

Let's examine the characteristics of session beans in detail and then code up a stateful session bean.

Session Bean Lifetime

A key difference between session beans and other bean types is the scope of their lives. A session bean instance is a relatively short-lived object. It has roughly the lifetime equivalent of a *session* or of the client code that is calling the session bean. Session bean instances are not shared between multiple clients, and they do not represent data in a database.

For example, if the client code contacted a session bean to perform order entry logic, the EJB container is responsible for creating an instance of that session bean component. When the client later disconnects, the application server may destroy the session bean instance. From the client's point of view, the bean's life starts after the client obtains a reference, and it ends when the client's session ends. There are no guarantees about the existence of the bean instance before the client session begins or after the client session ends.

A client's session duration could be as long as a browser window is open, perhaps connecting to an e-commerce site with deployed session beans. It could also be as long as your Java applet is running, as long as a standalone application is open, or as long as another bean is using your bean.

The length of the client's *session* generally determines how long a session bean is in use—that is where the term *session bean* originated. The EJB container manages the bean's life cycle and is empowered to destroy session beans if clients time out. If your client code is using your beans for 10 minutes, your session beans might live for minutes or hours, but probably not weeks, months, or years. Typically, session beans do not survive application server crashes, nor do they survive machine crashes. They are in-memory objects that live and die with their surrounding environments.

In contrast, entity beans can live for months or even years because entity beans are *persistent objects*. Entity beans are part of a durable, permanent storage, such as a database. Entity beans can be constructed in memory from database data, and they can survive for long periods of time.

Session beans are *nonpersistent*. This means that session beans are not saved to permanent storage, whereas entity beans are. Note that session beans *can* perform database operations, but the session bean *itself* is not a persistent object.

Session Bean Subtypes

All enterprise beans hold *conversations* with clients at some level. A conversation is an interaction between a client and a bean, and it is composed of a number of method calls between the client and the bean. A conversation spans a business process for the client, such as configuring a Frame Relay switch, purchasing goods over the Internet, or entering information about a new customer.

The two subtypes of session beans are *stateless session beans* and *stateful session beans*. Each is used to model different types of these conversations.

Stateless Session Beans

Some business processes naturally lend themselves to a single request conversation. A single request business process is one that does not require state to be maintained across method invocations.

A *stateless session bean* is a bean that holds conversations that span a single method call. They are stateless because they do not hold state that would be client-visible between invocations. After each method call, the container may choose to destroy a stateless session bean, or recreate it, clearing out all information pertaining to past invocations. It also may choose to keep your instance around, perhaps reusing it for all clients who want to use the same session bean class. The exact algorithm is container-specific. The point to take away is this: Expect your bean to forget everything after each method call, and thus retain no conversational state from method to method. If your bean happens to hang around longer, then great—but that's your container's decision, and you shouldn't rely on it.

For a stateless session bean to be useful to a client, the client must pass all client data that the bean needs as parameters to business logic methods. Alternatively, the bean can retrieve the data it needs from an external source, such as a database.

NOTE ***Stateless*** **really means no *conversational* state. Stateless session beans *can* contain state that is not specific to any one client, such as a database connection factory that all clients would use. You can keep this around in a private variable. As long as you're willing to lose the data in your private variable at any time, you'll be fine.**

An example of a stateless session bean is a high-performance engine that solves complex mathematical operations on a given input, such as compression of audio or video data. The client could pass in a buffer of uncompressed data, as well as a compression factor. The bean returns a compressed buffer and is then available to service a different client. The business process spanned one method request. The bean does not retain any state from previous requests.

Another example of a stateless session bean is a credit card verification component. The verifier bean takes a credit card number, expiration date, cardholder's name, and dollar amount as input. The verifier then returns a yes or no answer, depending on whether the card holder's credit is valid. Once the bean completes this task, it is available to service a different client and retains no past knowledge from the original client.

Because stateless session beans hold no conversational state, all instances of the same stateless session bean class are equivalent and indistinguishable to a client. It does not matter who has called a stateless session bean in the past, since a stateless session bean retains no state knowledge about its history. This means that *any* stateless session bean can service *any* client request because they are all exactly the same. In fact, stateless session beans can be pooled, reused, and swapped from one client to another client on *each method call!* We show this in Figure 4.1. Instance pooling is the prime technique used by container vendors to implement efficient bean processing.

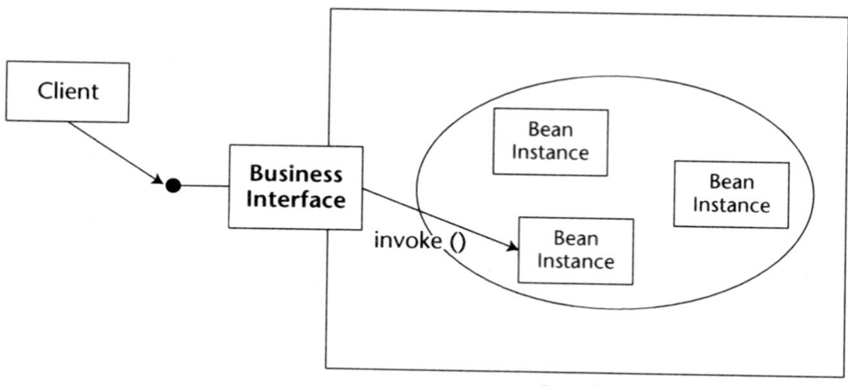

Figure 4.1 Stateless session bean pooling.

Since EJB 2.1, stateless session beans can also provide Web services interfaces to clients. We will examine this important option in detail in Chapter 5.

Stateful Session Beans

Some business processes are naturally drawn-out conversations over several requests. An example is an e-commerce Web store. As a user peruses an online e-commerce Web site, the user can add products to the online shopping cart. Each time the user adds a product, we perform another request. The consequence of such a business process is that the components must track the user's state (such as a shopping cart state) from request to request.

Another example of a drawn-out business process is a banking application. You may have code representing a bank teller who deals with a particular client for a long period of time. That teller may perform a number of banking transactions on behalf of the client, such as checking the account balance, depositing funds, and making a withdrawal.

A *stateful session bean* is a bean that is designed to service business processes that span multiple method requests or transactions. To accomplish this, stateful session beans *retain state* on behalf of an individual client. If a stateful session bean's state is changed during a method invocation, that same state will be available to that same client upon the following invocation. Stateful session beans are a little more sophisticated than their simpler stateless cousins, so let's take a closer look at them in the next section.

Special Characteristics of Stateful Session Beans

So far, we've seen session beans in general. We also coded up a simple stateless session bean to the old EJB 2.1 API in Chapter 2. Now let's look at the trickier flavor, stateful session beans.

Achieving the Effect of Pooling with Stateful Beans

With stateful session beans, pooling is not as simple as with stateless session beans. When a client invokes a method on a bean, the client is starting a *conversation* with the bean, and the conversational state stored in the bean must be available for that same client's next method request. Therefore, the container cannot easily pool beans and dynamically assign them to handle arbitrary client method requests, since each bean is storing state on behalf of a particular client. But we still need to achieve the effect of pooling for stateful session beans so that we can conserve resources and enhance the overall scalability of the system. After all, we only have a finite amount of available resources, such as memory, database connections, and socket connections. If the conversational state that the beans are holding is large, the EJB server could easily run out of resources. This was not a problem with stateless session beans because the container could pool only a few beans to service thousands of clients.

This problem should sound quite familiar to operating systems gurus. Whenever you run an application on a computer, you have only a fixed amount of physical memory in which to run. The operating system still must provide a way for many applications to run, even if the applications take up more aggregate memory than is available physically. To provide for this, operating systems use your hard disk as an extension of physical memory. This effectively extends your system's amount of *virtual memory*. When an application goes idle, its memory can be *swapped out* from physical memory and onto the hard disk. When the application becomes active again, any needed data is *swapped in* from the hard disk and into physical memory. This type of swapping happens often when switching between applications (called *context switching*).

EJB containers exploit this very paradigm to conserve stateful session bean resources. To limit the number of stateful session bean instances in memory, the container can *swap out* a stateful bean, saving its conversational state to a hard disk or other storage. This is called *passivation*. After passivating a stateful bean, the conversational state is safely stored away, allowing resources like memory to be reclaimed. When the original client invokes a method, the passivated conversational state is *swapped in* to a bean. This is called *activation*. This bean now resumes the conversation with the original client. Note that the bean that receives the activated state may not be the original bean instance. But that's all right because the new instance resumes its conversation from the point where the original instance was passivated.

Thus, EJB does indeed support the *effect* of pooling stateful session beans. Only a few instances can be in memory when there are actually many clients. But this pooling effect does not come for free—the passivation/activation steps could entail an input/output bottleneck. Contrast this to stateless session beans, which are easily pooled because there is no state to save.

How does the container decide which beans to activate and which beans to passivate? The answer is specific to each container. Most containers employ a *least recently used* (LRU) passivation strategy, which simply means to passivate the bean that has been called the least recently. This is a good algorithm because remote clients have the habit of disconnecting from the network, leaving beans stranded without a client, ready to be passivated. If a bean hasn't been invoked in a while, the container writes it to disk.

Passivation can occur at any time, as long as a bean is not involved in a method call. It's up to the container to decide when passivation makes sense. There is one exception to this rule: Any bean involved in a *transaction* (see Chapter 10) cannot be passivated until the transaction completes.

To activate beans, most containers commonly use a *just-in-time* algorithm. Just in time means that beans should be activated on demand, as client requests come in. If a client request comes in, but that client's conversation has been passivated, the container activates the bean on demand, reading the passivated state back into memory.

In general, passivation and activation are not useful for stateless session beans. Stateless beans do not have any state to passivate/activate, so the container can simply destroy stateless beans arbitrarily.

The Rules Governing Conversational State

More rigorously, the *conversational state* of a bean follows the rules laid out by *Java object serialization*. At passivation time the container uses object serialization (or an equivalent protocol) to convert the bean's conversational state to a bit-blob and write the state out to disk. This safely tucks the state away. The bean instance (which still exists) can be reassigned to a different client, and can hold a brand-new conversation with that new client.

Activation reverses the process: A serialized blob that had been written to storage is read back into memory and converted to in-memory bean data.

For every Java object that is part of a bean's conversational state, the previous algorithm is reapplied recursively on those objects. Thus, object serialization constructs an entire graph of data referred to by the main bean. Note that while your beans must follow the rules for object serialization, the EJB container itself does not necessarily need to use the default serialization protocol; it could use a custom protocol to allow for flexibility and differentiation between container vendors.

More concretely, every member variable in a bean is considered to be part of the bean's conversational state if one of the following is true:

- The member variable is a nontransient primitive type.
- The member variable is a nontransient Java object (extends `java.lang.Object`).

Your bean might also hold references to container-implemented objects. The container must preserve each of the following upon passivation/activation:

- References to other beans' local or remote business interfaces
- References to other beans' local or remote home interfaces (for code using the EJB 2.1 client view)
- References to the `SessionContext` object, the `UserTransaction`, an `EntityManager` or `EntityManagerFactory` object, or a `Timer` object (see Chapter 12)
- JNDI naming contexts

For example, let's say you have the following stateful session bean code:

```
@Stateful public class MySessionBean
{
    // State variables
    private Long myLong;
    private MySessionBeanRemoteInterface mySessionBean;
    private javax.naming.Context envContext;
    // Business methods
    ...
}
```

The container must retain the values of the preceding member variables across passivation and activation operations.

In many cases, the container will simply do this without your code having to bother, but sometimes your beans may contain state that is not covered by this contract with the container. For example, if your bean holds JDBC connections or open sockets or other nonserializable objects, then the container will not be able to properly activate and passivate the bean without a little assistance from the bean itself.

This assistance comes in the form of bean code that the container can call back during activation and passivation. The bean provider (that is, we, the developers) can provide this code as either individual callback methods in the bean, or as one or more separate callback listener classes. As you might expect by this time, we will mark the code as callback code using metadata annotations, or in the deployment descriptor files.

Activation and Passivation Callbacks

Let's now look at what actually happens to your bean during passivation and activation. When an EJB container passivates a bean, the container writes the bean's conversational state to secondary storage, such as a file or database. The container informs the bean that it's about to perform passivation by calling the bean's optional `PrePassivate` callback method. The `PrePassivate` callback is a method that is marked with the `@PrePassivate` annotation. The container uses this callback method to warn the bean that its held conversational state is about to be swapped out.

It's important that the container inform the bean using `PrePassivate` so that the bean can relinquish held resources that the container cannot handle itself. These held resources include database connections, open sockets, open files, or other resources that it doesn't make sense to save to disk or that can't be transparently saved using object serialization. The EJB container calls the `PrePassivate` method to give the bean a chance to release these resources or deal with the resources as the bean sees fit. Once the container's `PrePassivate` callback method into your bean is complete, your bean must be in a state suitable for passivation. For example:

```
@Stateful
public class MyBean  {
    @PrePassivate
    public void passivate() {
        <close socket connections, etc...>
    }
    ...
}
```

The passivation process is shown in Figure 4.2. This is a typical stateful bean passivation scenario. The client has invoked a method on a bean's business interface that does not have a bean tied to it in memory. The container's pool size of beans has been reached. Thus, the container needs to passivate a bean before handling this client's request.

Exactly the opposite process occurs during the activation process. The serialized conversational state is read back into memory, and the container reconstructs the in-memory state using object serialization or the equivalent. The container then calls the bean's optional `PostActivate` callback method. The `PostActivate` callback method gives the bean a chance to restore the open resources it released during `PrePassivate`. For example:

```
@Stateful
public class MyBean  {
    @PostActivate
    public void activate() {
        <open socket connections, etc...>
    }
    ...
}
```

The activation process is shown in Figure 4.3. This is a typical just-in-time stateful bean activation scenario. The client has invoked a method on an EJB object whose stateful bean had been passivated.

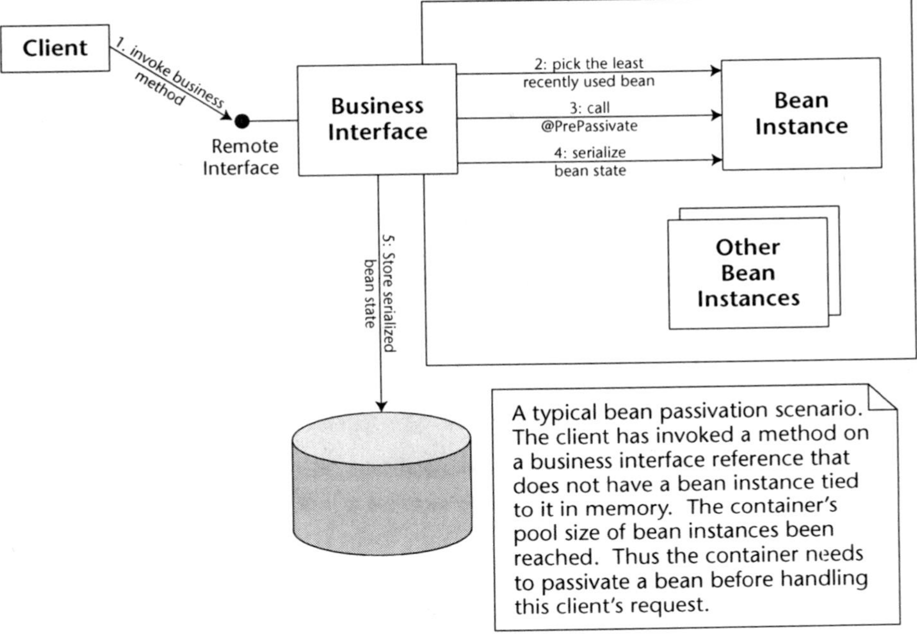
Client
1. invoke business method
Remote Interface
Business Interface
2: pick the least recently used bean
3: call @PrePassivate
4: serialize bean state
Bean Instance
Other Bean Instances
5: Store serialized bean state
A typical bean passivation scenario. The client has invoked a method on a business interface reference that does not have a bean instance tied to it in memory. The container's pool size of bean instances been reached. Thus the container needs to passivate a bean before handling this client's request.

Figure 4.2 Passivation of a stateful bean.

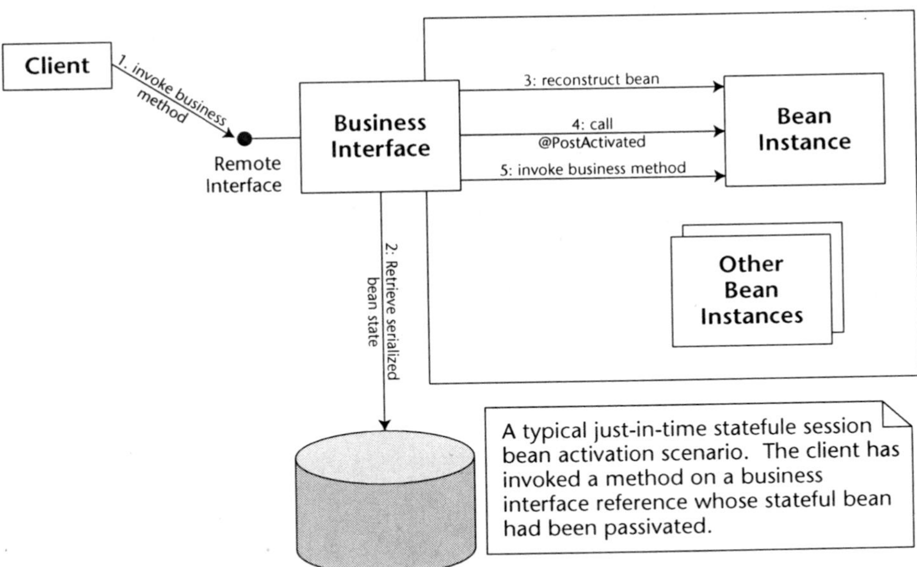
Client
1. invoke business method
Remote Interface
Business Interface
3: reconstruct bean
4: call @PostActivated
5: invoke business method
Bean Instance
Other Bean Instances
2: Retrieve serialized bean state
A typical just-in-time statefule session bean activation scenario. The client has invoked a method on a business interface reference whose stateful bean had been passivated.

Figure 4.3 Activation of a stateful bean.

The code snippets that we just saw all showed a simple method in the bean class itself. You will see an example of a separate callback listener class in the section "The Count Bean's Callback Interceptor" later in this chapter.

You don't need to worry about providing methods annotated as `PrePassivate` and `PostActivate` callbacks unless you are using open resources, such as socket connections or database connections, that must be reestablished after activation.

NOTE **The following rules apply to the life-cycle callback methods:**

- **They take the form** `public void <METHOD()>` **in the bean class.**
- **They take the form** `public void <METHOD(BeanClass bean)>` **in a callback listener class for bean class** `BeanClass`**.**
- **They must not throw application exceptions, but may throw runtime exceptions. If thrown within a transaction, it will cause the transaction to roll back.**
- **There is no dependency injection for callback listener classes.**

Summary of Callback Methods

Table 4.1 summarizes the life-cycle callbacks for session bean classes. All of these are optional, so you need to provide implementations only if your bean needs to take part in the management of its life cycle.

A Simple Stateful Session Bean

Let's put our stateful session bean knowledge to use by programming a simple stateful bean. Our bean will be a counter bean, and it will be responsible for simply counting up one by one. The current count will be stored within the bean and will increment as client requests arrive. Thus, our bean will be stateful and will hold a multimethod conversation with a particular client.

The Count Bean's Remote Interface

First let's define our bean's remote business interface. The code is shown in Source 4.1.

Table 4.1 Life-Cycle Callbacks for Session Bean Classes

ANOTATION	DESCRIPTION	TYPICAL IMPLEMENTATION (STATELESS SESSION BEANS)	TYPICAL IMPLEMENTATION (STATEFULL SESSION BEANS)
@PostConstruct	Called after the container has created a new instance of the bean class.	Perform any initialization your bean needs, such as setting member variables to the argument values passed in.	Perform any initialization your bean needs, such as setting member variables to the argument values passed in.
@PrePassivate	Called immediately before your bean is passivated (swapped out to disk because there are too many instantiated beans).	Unused because there is no conversational state. Stateless Session Beans are not passivated.	Release any resources your bean may be holding.
@PostActivate	Called immediately after your bean is activated (swapped in from disk because a client needs your bean).	Unused because there is no conversational state. Stateless session beans are not activated.	Acquire any resources your bean needs, such as those released during *PrePassivate*.
@PreDestroy	Called by the container immediately after any *@Remove* method has finished and before your bean is destroyed.	Prepare your bean for destruction. Free all resources you may have allocated.	Prepare your bean for destruction. Free all resources you may have allocated.

```
package examples.session.stateful;

/**
 * The business interface - a plain Java interface with only
 * business methods.
 */
public interface Count  {

  /**
   * Increments the counter by 1
   */
  public int count();

  /**
   * Sets the counter to val
   * @param val
   */
  public void set(int val);

  /**
   * removes the counter
   */
  public void remove();
}
```

Source 4.1 Count.java.

Our business interface defines three business methods, `count()`, `set()`, and `remove()`, which we will implement in the enterprise bean class. For those familiar with prior versions of EJB, note that the business interface is an ordinary Java interface that does not extend any EJB-specific framework interfaces. EJB3 imposes no restrictions on interface design, so our business interface could have one or more superinterfaces.

Also note that, although we intend to use the business interface remotely, the interface does not extend `java.rmi.Remote`, and that our business methods do not declare the `java.rmi.RemoteException`. We will instead declare it as a remote business interface in the implementation class `CountBean.java` below.

The Count Bean

Our bean implementation has a business method, `count()`, which is responsible for incrementing an integer member variable, called `val`. The `set()` method is used to initialize and reset the counter. The `remove()` method, finally, ends the conversation with the bean. The conversational state is the `val` member variable. Source 4.2 shows the code for our counter bean.

```
package examples.session.stateful;

import javax.ejb.*;

/**
 * A Stateful Session Bean Class that shows the basics of
 * how to write a stateful session bean.
 *
 * This Bean is initialized to some integer value. It has a
 * business method which increments the value.
 *
 * The annotations below declare that:
 * <ul>
 * <li>this is a Stateful Session Bean
 * <li>the bean's remote business interface is <code>Count</code>
 * <li>any lifecycle callbacks go to the class
 *     <code>CountCallbacks</code>
 * </ul>
 */
@Stateful
@Remote(Count.class)
@Interceptors(CountCallbacks.class)
public class CountBean implements Count {

    /** The current counter is our conversational state. */
    private int val;

    /**
     * The count() business method.
     */
    public int count() {
        System.out.println("count()");
        return ++val;
    }

    /**
     * The set() business method.
     */
    public void set(int val) {
        this.val = val;
        System.out.println("set()");
    }

    /**
     * The remove method is annotated so that the container knows
     * it can remove the bean after this method returns.
     */
    @Remove
```

Source 4.2 CountBean.java. *(continued)*

```
    public void remove() {
        System.out.println("remove()");
    }

}
```

Source 4.2 *(continued)*

Note the following about our bean:

- The bean is a plain Java class adorned with a few metadata annotations. If we had used a deployment descriptor to hold the information conveyed by these annotations, the code would contain nothing else but business method implementations.
- The bean class implements the business interface. While this is not surprising, it is not actually required: a session bean class may simply declare rather than implement its remote or local interface using the `@Remote` or `@Local` annotations (or the deployment descriptor). We recommend that you always implement the business interface for clarity and compile-time error checking. This also lets you reuse both your business interface and implementation outside of an EJB container.
- In the example, we declare `Count` as our remote business interface. Without the explicit declaration, a business interface would have been assumed to be local as long as there was only one business interface. If the bean class has more than one business interface, these interfaces all need to be explicitly declared as either remote or local.
- The `val` member variable obeys the rules for conversational state because it is serializable. Thus, it lasts across method calls and is automatically preserved during passivation/activation. Because there is no other state, there is not really any reason to implement life-cycle callbacks. We still do this, but for demonstration purposes only.
- The `@Remove` annotation tells the container that after calling `remove()` the client does not need the session bean anymore so the container may destroy the bean.

The Count Bean's Callback Interceptor

To complete our stateful bean code, we define the simple life-cycle callback interceptor class that was already declared using the `@Interceptors` annotation on the bean class. The code for our callback interceptor is in Source 4.3.

```
package examples.session.stateful;

import javax.ejb.PostActivate;
import javax.ejb.PrePassivate;
import javax.ejb.PostConstruct;
import javax.ejb.PreDestroy;

/**
 * This class is a lifecycle callback interceptor for the Count
 * bean. The callback methods simply print a message when
 * invoked by the container.
 */
public class CountCallbacks {

    /**
     * Called by the container after construction
     */
    @PostConstruct
    public void construct(InvocationContext ctx) {
        System.out.println("cb:construct()");
    }
    /**
     * Called by the container after activation
     */
    @PostActivate
    public void activate(InvocationContext ctx) {
        System.out.println("cb:activate()");
    }

    /**
     * Called by the container before passivation
     */
    @PrePassivate
    public void passivate(InvocationContext ctx) {
        System.out.println("cb:passivate()");
    }
    /**
     * Called by the container before destruction
     */
    @PreDestroy
    public void destroy(InvocationContext ctx) {
        System.out.println("cb:destroy()");
    }
}
```

Source 4.3 CountCallbacks.java.

The Count Bean's Deployment Descriptor

As an alternative to annotating the bean class, we could have relied on an XML deployment descriptor file exclusively. The deployment descriptor settings that are equivalent to the bean class annotations shown above are listed in Source 4.4.

```
<?xml version="1.0" encoding="UTF-8" ?>
<ejb-jar xmlns="http://java.sun.com/xml/ns/javaee" version="3.0"
  xmlns:xsi="http://www.w3.org/2001/XMLSchema-instance"
  xsi:schemaLocation="http://java.sun.com/xml/ns/javaee
       http://java.sun.com/xml/ns/javaee/ejb-jar_3_0.xsd">
  <description>Stateful Session Bean Example</description>
  <display-name>Stateful Session Bean Example</display-name>
 <enterprise-beans>
   <session>
     <ejb-name>CountBean</ejb-name>
     <business-remote>examples.session.stateful_dd.Count
     </business-remote>
     <ejb-class>examples.session.stateful_dd.CountBean</ejb-class>
     <session-type>Stateful</session-type>
     <transaction-type>Container</transaction-type>
   </session>
 </enterprise-beans>

 <interceptors>
   <interceptor>
       <interceptor-class>examples.session.stateful_dd.CountCallbacks
       </interceptor-class>
       <post-construct>
         <lifecycle-callback-method>construct
         </lifecycle-callback-method>
       </post-construct>
       <post-activate>
         <lifecycle-callback-method>activate</lifecycle-callback-method>
       </post-activate>
       <pre-passivate>
          <lifecycle-callback-method>passivate
          </lifecycle-callback-method>
       </pre-passivate>
    </interceptor>
  </interceptors>

  <assembly-descriptor>
    <interceptor-binding>
      <ejb-name>CountBean</ejb-name>
      <interceptor-class>examples.session.stateful_dd.CountCallbacks
      </interceptor-class>
```

Source 4.4 ejb-jar.xml. *(continued)*

```
    </interceptor-binding>
  </assembly-descriptor>
</ejb-jar>
```

Source 4.4 *(continued)*

Note that a deployment descriptor file, if present, overrides any metadata annotations on the bean class. The rationale here is that it should be possible to declare EJB properties without access to the source code.

If you need to refer to the specifics of the deployment descriptor syntax, you may need to either consult the EJB 3.0 specification itself or use the XML schema file for EJB 3 descriptors. This schema is available online at `http://java.sun.com/xml/ns/j2ee/ejb-jar_3_0.xsd`.

The Count Bean's Proprietary Descriptor and Ejb-jar File

To complete the component, we need to write any proprietary files that the application server may require and package those files and the bean together into an Ejb-jar file. These steps are similar to our Hello, World! example.

One special setting we will try to make (which is vendor-specific) is to force the container to limit the number of bean instances that it will keep active to two beans. Note that this may or may not be possible with your particular application server. We will then create three beans and observe how the container passivates instances to service requests.

To save space, in future examples we'll consider that the proprietary descriptors, the Ejb-jar file, and the deployment itself are implied steps. If you're really curious about how this is achieved, take a look at the source code accompanying the book.

The Count Bean's Client Code

Now that our bean is deployed, we can write some Java code to test our beans. Our client code performs the following steps:

1. We acquire a JNDI initial context.
2. We locate a reference to the bean's business interface using JNDI.
3. We lookup three different count beans. Thus, we are creating three different conversations and are simulating three different clients.
4. We limited the number of active bean instances in the EJB server to two beans, so during the previous step some of the three beans must have been passivated. We print out a message during the `PrePassivate` callback to illustrate this.

5. We call `count()` on each bean instance. This forces the container to activate the instances, restoring the conversations to memory once again. We print out a message during the `PostActivate` callback to illustrate this.
6. Finally, all the beans are removed.

The code appears in Source 4.5.

```
package examples.session.stateful;

import javax.naming.*;

/**
 * This class is a simple client for a stateful session bean.
 *
 * To illustrate how passivation works, configure your EJB server
 * to allow only 2 stateful session beans in memory. (Consult your
 * vendor documentation for details on how to do this.) We create
 * 3 beans in this example to see how and when beans are passivated.
 */
public class CountClient {

    public static final int noOfClients = 3;

    public static void main(String[] args) {
        try {
            /* Get a reference to the bean */
            Context ctx = new InitialContext(System.getProperties());

            /* An array to hold the Count beans */
            Count count[] = new Count[noOfClients];
            int countVal = 0;

            /* Create and count() on each member of array */
            System.out.println("Instantiating beans...");
            for (int i = 0; i < noOfClients; i++) {
                count[i] = (Count) ctx.lookup(Count.class.getName());

                /* initialize each bean to the current count value */
                count[i].set(countVal);

                /* Add 1 and print */
                countVal = count[i].count();
                System.out.println(countVal);

                /*  Sleep for 1/2 second */
                Thread.sleep(100);
```

Source 4.5 CountClient.java. *(continued)*

```
            }

            /*
             * Let's call count() on each bean to  make sure the
             * beans were passivated and activated properly.
             */
            System.out.println("Calling count() on beans...");
            for (int i = 0; i < noOfClients; i++) {

                /* Add 1 and print */
                countVal = count[i].count();
                System.out.println(countVal);

                /* let the container dispose of the bean */
                count[i].remove();

                /*  Sleep */
                Thread.sleep(50);
            }
        } catch (Exception e) {
            e.printStackTrace();
        }
    }
}
```

Source 4.5 *(continued)*

Running the Client

To run the client, you need to know the parameters your JNDI service provider uses. This should also be part of your container's documentation. See the book's accompanying source code for scripts.

Client-Side Output

After running the client, we see the following output:

```
Instantiating beans...
1
2
3
Calling count() on beans...
2
3
4
```

We first created three beans and then called `count()` on each. As expected, the beans incremented their values by one each during the second pass, so output is as expected. But were our beans really passivated and activated? Let's check the server log.

Server-Side Output

As mentioned earlier, we configured the server to only allow two bean instances to be active at a time using vendor-specific configuration means. If the container log now yields the following results:

```
cb:construct()
set()
count()
cb:construct()
set()
count()
cb:construct()
set()
count()
count()
remove()
cb:destroy()
count()
remove()
cb:destroy()
count()
remove()
cb:destroy()
```

Then, as you can see from the passivation/activation messages in the log, the container is indeed passivating and activating beans to conserve system resources. Because the client-side output is correct, each of our beans' conversational state was retained properly.

Life-Cycle Diagrams for Session Beans

Now that we've written a complete stateless session bean (in Chapter 2) and a complete stateful session bean (in this chapter), let's see what's happening behind the scenes.

Figure 4.4 shows the life cycle of a stateless session bean inside the container. Note that in this diagram, the client is not calling methods on the bean, since the client never accesses a bean directly. (The client always goes through the container.) In the diagram, the container is calling methods on the bean.

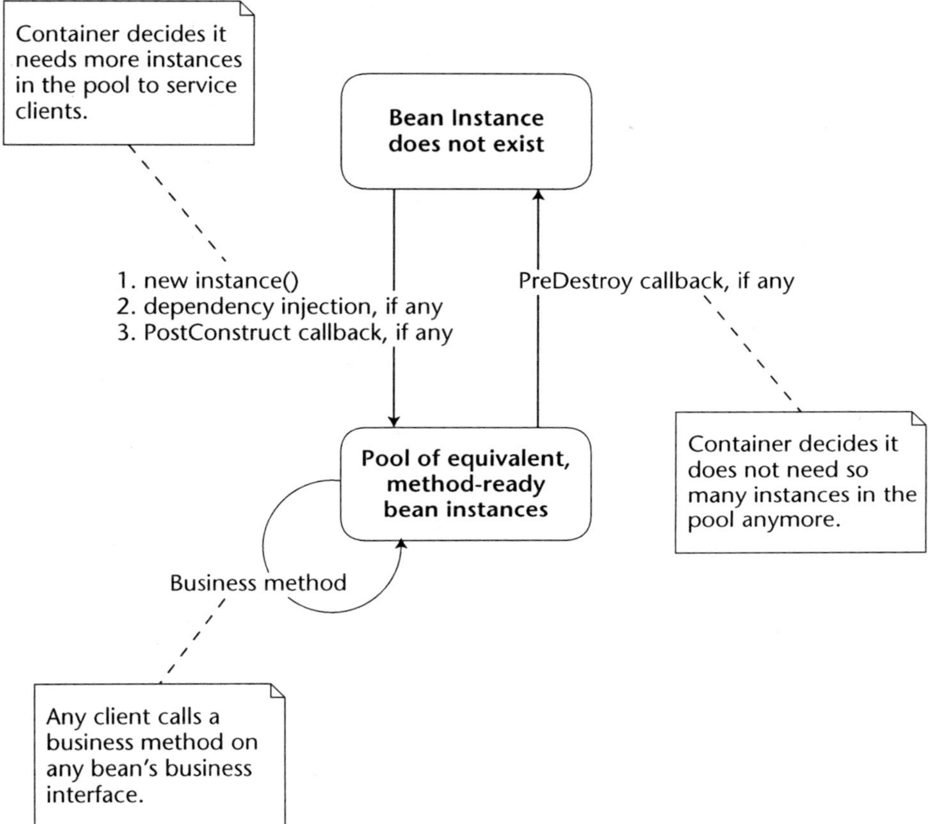

Figure 4.4 The life cycle of a stateless session bean.

Let's walk through this diagram:

1. **At first, the bean instance does not exist.** Perhaps the application server has just started up.
2. **The container decides it wants to instantiate a new bean.** When does the container decide it wants to instantiate a new bean? It depends on the container's policy for *pooling* beans. The container may decide to instantiate 10 beans all at once when the application server first starts because you told the container to do so using the vendor-specific files that you ship with your bean. Each of those beans are equivalent (because they are stateless), and they can be reused for many different clients.
3. **The container instantiates your bean.** The container calls `Class.newInstance("HelloBean.class")` on your session bean class, which is the dynamic equivalent of calling `new HelloBean()`. The container does this so that the container is not hard-coded to any

specific bean name; the container is generic and works with any bean. This action calls your bean's default constructor, which can do any necessary initialization.

4. **The container injects any required context dependencies.** Context dependencies can be declared using metadata annotations or XML descriptor files so the container knows what other objects are required by the bean class and can provide them. We'll discuss dependency injection in detail in Chapter 8.
5. **The container calls the optional `PostConstruct` callback method.** This gives the bean instance a chance to perform additional initialization. Note that because the stateless session beans' `PostConstruct` callback methods take no parameters, clients never supply any critical information that bean instances need to start up. EJB containers can exploit this and precreate instances of your session beans. In general when a client creates or destroys a bean, that action might not necessarily correspond with literally creating or destroying in-memory bean objects, because the EJB container manages their life cycles to allow for pooling between heterogeneous clients.
6. **The container can call business methods on your bean on behalf of clients.** The container can call as many business methods as it wants to call. Each business method could originate from a completely different client because all bean instances are treated exactly the same. All stateless session beans think they are in the same state after a method call; they are effectively unaware that previous method calls happened. Therefore, the container can dynamically reassign beans to client requests at the *per-method* level. A different stateless session bean can service *each* method call from a client. Of course, the actual implementation of reassigning beans to clients is container-specific.
7. **Finally, the container calls the `PreDestroy` callback methods.** When the container is about to remove your session bean instance, it calls your bean's `PreDestroy` callback methods. `PreDestroy` is a clean-up method, alerting your bean that it is about to be destroyed and allowing it to end its life gracefully. It takes no parameters. Your implementation of `PreDestroy` can prepare your bean for destruction. This means you need to free all resources you may have allocated.

Figure 4.5 shows the life cycle of a stateful session bean. Remember that in the diagram, the container (not the client) is calling methods on our bean instance.

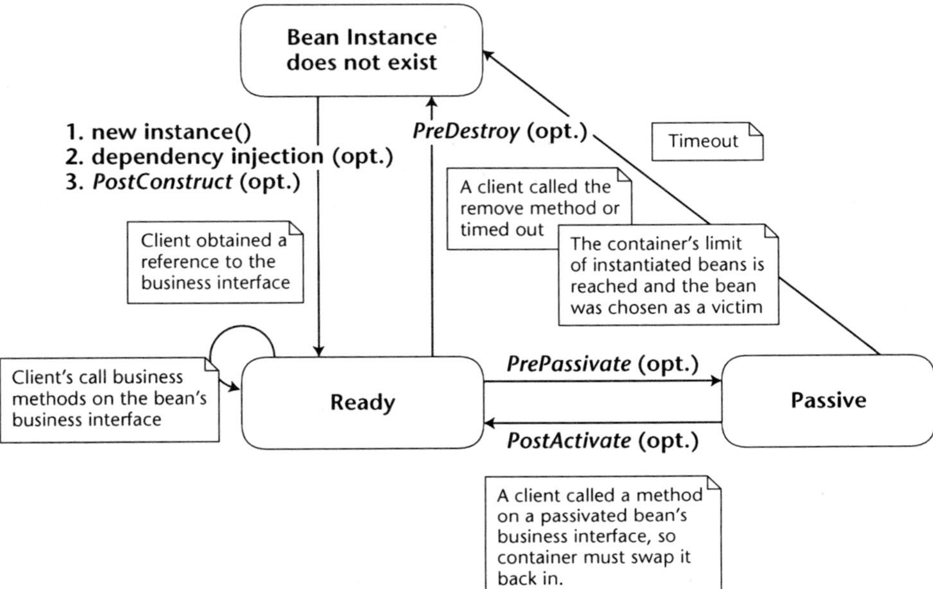

Figure 4.5 Life cycle of a stateful session bean.

The life cycle for stateful session beans is similar to that of stateless session beans. The big differences are as follows:

- There is no pool of equivalent instances because each instance contains state.
- There are transitions for passivating and activating conversational state.

DON'T RELY ON @PREDESTROY

Your container can call the `@PreDestroy` method at any time, even if the container decides that the bean's life has expired (perhaps due to a very long timeout). Note that the container may *never* call your bean's `@PreDestroy` method, for example if the container crashes or if a critical exception occurs. You must be prepared for this contingency. For example, if your bean performs shopping cart operations, it might store temporary shopping cart data in a database. Your application should provide a utility that runs periodically to remove any abandoned shopping carts from the database because otherwise the database resources associated with the abandoned shopping carts will never be freed.

Summary

In this chapter, you learned the general concepts behind session beans. You learned about achieving instance pooling with session beans, activation, and passivation. You wrote a stateful session bean that counted up and touched on session beans' life cycle.

In the next chapter, we will continue our inspection of session beans with another thrilling experience: We will let our session bean expose a Web service interface!

CHAPTER

5

Writing Session Bean Web Services

One of the most important enhancements introduced by EJB 2.1 was the support for Web services. EJB 3.0 now makes writing and using Web services both simpler and more flexible.

In this chapter, we will discuss central Web services concepts and then explain how EJB supports the writing of Web service implementations and Web services clients. We will show how EJB enables you to build Web services from stateless session beans and take a closer look at the *Java API for XML* Web services (JAX-WS) that enables you to access Web services from Java clients.

Web Services Concepts

Let's take a quick look at some fundamental concepts. As mentioned in Chapter 1, Web services are a way of building a *Service-Oriented Architecture* (SOA). SOA is an architectural approach to structuring large-scale, distributed systems that integrate heterogeneous applications behind *service* interfaces.

Figure 5.1 shows the basic model of a service lookup in a Service-Oriented Architecture as supported by Web services technologies:

- A service provider creates an abstract service definition that can *publish* in a service registry. With Web services, the description is a *Web Services*

Definition Language (WSDL) file, and the registry follows the *Universal Description, Discovery, and Integration* (UDDI) standard.

- A service requestor can *find* the service description, possibly using a set of selection criteria to query the registry.
- If a suitable description is found, the requestor can *bind* to and use the service.

You can find simple examples of Web services collected on Web sites such as `xmethods.org`, for example, a service to determine if a given Internet domain name is taken, or to convert temperature values from Fahrenheit to Celsius. More realistic Web services are built today in larger-scale, in-house architectures that interconnect existing, heterogeneous applications, for example, a billing application and a report generator.

A *service interface* is similar to an object interface, but the contract between the interface and its clients is more flexible, and the client and the service implementation are less closely coupled, than in EJB or other distribution platforms. This *looser coupling* allows client and service implementations to run on very different platforms, for example, a Microsoft .NET client could access a service running in a JavaEE application server. Also, services are generally *coarser-grained* entities than objects are. From a client perspective, their life cycles are more static because services don't just pop up and go away but stay around longer than your average object, even if services are implemented using object technology.

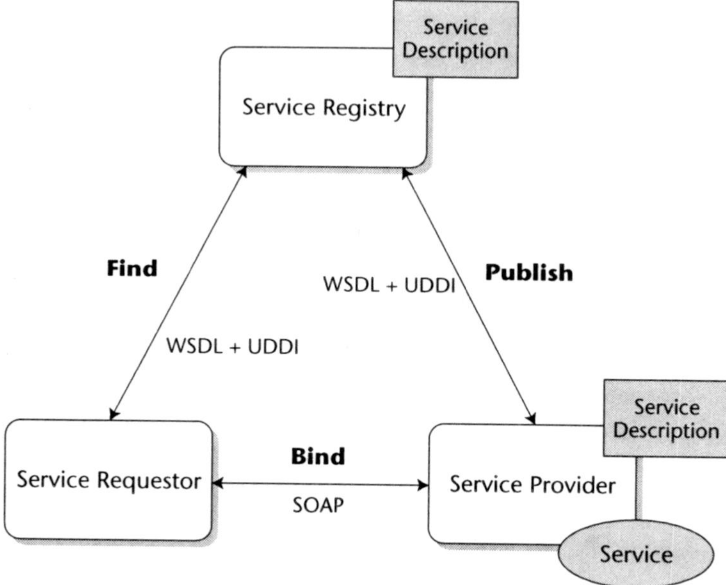

Figure 5.1 Service-Oriented Architecture with Web services.

SOAs emphasize modularity through standardized interfaces, flexibility through looser coupling, and extensibility through using XML. All of this is important in B2B scenarios, which are the primary targets of Web services. Web services are not just another RPC mechanism for your intranet applications but rather a great help in settings where no single middleware platform is applicable.

As an example, consider the B2B relationships between a car manufacturer and its suppliers. Each of these companies has its own IT infrastructure and set of applications, such as payroll, inventory, order processing, and so on. Also, each supplier builds parts for more than just a single car manufacturer, and each manufacturer buys parts from different suppliers. In a situation like this, it is highly unlikely that any of the involved parties will be able to switch to a specific middleware for the sake of the business relationship with just a single partner. For any given supplier, building a middleware X adapter (for example CORBA) to its order-processing application to interoperate with customer A, and then building another adapter Y (say, MQSeries) to interoperate with customer B, and so on is going to be too much effort and too expensive.

This is what standardization efforts in the past (such as EDI) tried but failed to tackle on a larger scale. Web services can thus be seen as a new attempt at building universally agreed-upon standards that hide the differences behind standardized interfaces. This time, the standards are going to be based on XML and on established Internet protocols.

So why do we talk about integration and interoperability so much in the context of Web services? Aren't EJBs interoperable already, thanks to the standardization of the RMI/IIOP protocol and the container and bean APIs? EJBs are interoperable in the sense of vendor and platform independence: there are Java EE/EJB products from many different vendors that run on different platforms and still talk to each other. These containers can host your beans no matter which product they were written for, so you also get portability. But there is language dependency: EJBs are coded in Java and nothing else, so you cannot create interoperable bean implementations written in different languages.

On the one hand, this is great because of Java's portability (write once run anywhere). On the other hand, portability is not always an issue, and you may actually need a specific language for your project if you wanted to leverage, say, a large amount of C++ or COBOL code for business objects that your company has investments in. With EJB, a common approach is to build wrapper beans that talk to an adapter in C++, most likely based on CORBA. Another way of putting this is to say that EJBs prescribe not only the component interfaces and client contracts but also an implementation model. With Web services, there is no single implementation framework; a contract with a Web service involves only its interface. Web services interfaces are defined in the *Web Services Description Language* (WSDL). Web services can be implemented in any language. Of course, we will be building them with EJB in this book, so they will be written in Java.

Web Services Standards

The set of de facto standards that make up Web services today can be summarized in a simple equation:

Web Services = WSDL + SOAP + UDDI

Let's take a quick look at WSDL and SOAP. We won't cover UDDI here because it is not necessarily required: Note that the actual service usage in Figure 5.1 does not depend on the existence of UDDI. The requestor may actually have known the service and its endpoint address without the registry. Also note that the registry is not simply a naming service but supports queries for services that obey a given predicate. At this stage in the life of Web services, however, it is unclear whether dynamic service lookups in UDDI registry will ever happen on a larger scale than within enterprises. It did not happen with similar concepts that were available earlier, such as CORBA Trading Service.

NOTE If you have been around in distributed computing for a while, some of the technology in the Web services arena will give you a feeling of déja vu. Figure 5.1, for example, looks a lot like the RM-ODP trader and later CORBA Trading Service. Many aspects that Web services address are not new per se but have simply not been solved on a larger scale.

WSDL

To give you a first impression of a service description in WSDL, following is the definition of a HelloWorld service like the one we used in Chapter 3.

```
<?xml version="1.0" encoding="UTF-8" standalone="yes"?>
<definitions targetNamespace="http://ws.session.examples/"
name="Greeter" xmlns:tns="http://ws.session.examples/"
xmlns:xsd="http://www.w3.org/2001/XMLSchema"
xmlns:soap="http://schemas.xmlsoap.org/wsdl/soap/"
xmlns="http://schemas.xmlsoap.org/wsdl/">
  <types>
    <xsd:schema>
      <xsd:import namespace="http://ws.session.examples/"
                  schemaLocation="Greeter_schema1.xsd"/>
    </xsd:schema>
  </types>
  <message name="hello">
    <part name="parameters" element="tns:hello"/>
  </message>
  <message name="helloResponse">
    <part name="parameters" element="tns:helloResponse"/>
  </message>
  <portType name="HelloBean">
    <operation name="hello">
```

```
      <input message="tns:hello"/>
      <output message="tns:helloResponse"/>
    </operation>
  </portType>
  <binding name="GreeterPortBinding" type="tns:HelloBean">
    <soap:binding transport="http://schemas.xmlsoap.org/soap/http"
     style="document"/>
    <operation name="hello">
      <soap:operation soapAction=""/>
      <input>
        <soap:body use="literal"/>
      </input>
      <output>
        <soap:body use="literal"/>
      </output>
    </operation>
  </binding>
  <service name="Greeter">
    <port name="GreeterPort" binding="tns:GreeterPortBinding">
      <soap:address location="http://gorilla:80/Greeter"/>
    </port>
  </service>
</definitions>
```

Some good news first before we look at the details: Relax. You don't have to write this XML document yourself. This interface description was automatically generated from an EJB using a generator tool.

A number of things are worth noting about the WSDL:

- **The number of language concepts used here is larger than in Java.** We have a *service* that provides one or more *ports* at an address. Ports represent the service interfaces and have *bindings* to protocols.
- **The service description includes an endpoint address.** The WSDL is thus like a Java interface and an object reference joined together. In other words, Web services do not have distinct identities. They are not objects and must be viewed as modules. There is no client-visible state, and you cannot compare two references for equality!
- **Operations are specified in terms of input and output messages rather than parameters and return values.** These have to be represented as elements ("parts") of input and output messages.
- **The binding for the service is a SOAP binding.** There can be other bindings in theory, but in practice SOAP is the only available option today. Also note that the `soap:binding` has an attribute `style="document"`, so there must be other possible styles. Currently, the only other style for exchanging SOAP messages is rpc-style, which simply represents the called operation slightly different in the SOAP message's body.

SOAP

The SOAP protocol defines an XML message format for Web services and their clients. Until version 1.1, SOAP was an acronym for *Simple Object Access Protocol*, but it was turned into a proper name for version 1.2 of the standard. That SOAP starts with the three letters SOA is sheer coincidence. As we just mentioned, the targets of SOAP messages (both services and clients) are not objects in the object-oriented sense, so the acronym was a misnomer anyway.

The SOAP message format is very simple. In a message exchange between a client and the Greeter service, the request message would look like this:

```
POST /Greeter HTTP/1.1
Content-Type: text/xml; charset="utf-8"
Content-Length: 398
SOAPAction: ""
Host: gorilla:8080

<?xml version="1.0" ?>
   <soapenv:Envelope
      xmlns:soapenv="http://schemas.xmlsoap.org/soap/envelope/"
      xmlns:ns1="http://ws.session.examples/">
   <soapenv:Body>
      <ns1:hello>
      </ns1:hello>
   </soapenv:Body>
</soapenv:Envelope>
```

This is an actual message as sent over the wire. As you can see, the message has two parts, an `HTTP POST` request header, and an XML document in the HTTP payload. This XML document is a SOAP envelope, which represents a request. The envelope contains a body element, which in turn contains the hello element that represents the operation call.

The reply message is just as simple:

```
HTTP/1.1 200 OK
SOAPAction: ""
Content-Type: text/xml;charset=utf-8
Transfer-Encoding: chunked

<?xml version="1.0" ?>
<soapenv:Envelope
   xmlns:soapenv="http://schemas.xmlsoap.org/soap/envelope/"
   xmlns:ns1="http://ws.session.examples/">
   <soapenv:Body>
      <ns1:helloResponse>
         <return>Hello,World!</return>
      </ns1:helloResponse>
```

```
    </soapenv:Body>
</soapenv:Envelope>
```

Again, there is the HTTP header and an XML document that contains a SOAP envelope. This time, the SOAP body represents the result of the operation call.

The two messages reproduced here serve to illustrate another key term that is often used in the context of Web services. The SOAP protocol is extremely *lightweight* in the sense that it is very simple to use and does not make many assumptions about the behavior of clients and services. The SOAP protocol is not lightweight in terms of compactness and high performance. If uncompressed, there is a large transmission overhead when compared to binary representations, for example in CORBA's IIOP protocol. The XML parsing required to marshal and unmarshal messages can also become CPU-intensive for larger messages. But this is beside the point: Web services are not designed to deliver hitherto unknown performance but to enable integration where high-performance middleware is much less useful than lightweight protocols that can be implemented easily by simple scripts. (For an interesting discussion of scripting languages as middleware, refer to Steve Vinoski's article on *Middleware Dark Matter* available at `www.iona.com/hyplan/vinoski`.)

XML Artifacts and Platform Independence

Web services help with the integration of heterogeneous, distributed systems by using standardized XML documents for many different aspects of service design, deployment, lookup, and usage that leverages a broad array of open standards and sophisticated tools that are widely available. Many of the tools, like Apache Axis SOAP, IBM WSDL4J toolkit, and JBoss Application Server, are also in the open source arena.

In a sense, the XML usage that we just looked at is perhaps the biggest technological advantage here because many of the practical virtues, like loose coupling and platform independence, follow from XML itself and the way the different XML technologies are combined. XML documents are also *self-describing* in that they contain a description of their structure in their markup tags. This does not mean that you will be able to understand arbitrary documents without any prior knowledge. What it does mean is that you can easily skip parts of a message that you are not concerned with and don't understand, and just deal with those parts that do concern you. This may sound trivial at first, but it has important consequences in that this enables the decoupling of applications and middleware.

To understand this point, recall that clients of your beans have to use a fixed component interface. If that interface changes because a parameter is added to a method signature, you will not only have to rebuild, reassemble, and redeploy your beans, but your clients will also have to be recompiled. This is not loose coupling because you cannot develop the different components of your application individually. If one piece changes, the others have to change, too. Applications are not as flexibly extensible as we would like. With IIOP-based request messages, all parties must have complete type information because they are not able to demarshal messages otherwise. There is no skipping of unknown parts of a message in IIOP. These restrictions do not exist with interfaces written in XML and with XML messages.

XML also enables you to write *extensible* specifications (after all, that's the X in XML): Data types in interface definitions can contain extensibility points from the outset. These extensibility points make use of a wildcard *any* type and, optional elements in sequences, and so on. Future versions of a service, while still servicing the clients written to the original interface, may fill in complex data records in these places for the benefit of more current client applications. If your end of the application does not rely on it, you don't need to care.

To summarize this approach more generally, you could say that Web services leave many details open for mutual agreement between the parties that will be actually involved, whereas other middleware systems, such as CORBA, have sought to define stricter, inherent semantics as part of their models. This means that to use Web services successfully in practice, you have to fill in these details. It also means that there is more room for refinement and thus wider applicability.

Implementing a Web Service

The Java EE model for Web services provides a seamless Java perspective on Web services, both for the service implementations and its clients. The model is relatively simple to use and allows you to deal with SOAP in the same way you deal with RMI or RMI/IIOP, which is to entrust all the details to the lower transport layers and happily ignore them for your business logic. The first thing to note is that your Web services, like your beans, are managed for you completely by the container.

The JSR 921 specification *Web Services for Java EE* defines the programming model for Web services. This specification uses the term *port component* for the server-side view of a Web service. A port component is a portable Java implementation of a service endpoint interface (a *port*) and comprises a Java mapping of the service interface and an implementation bean.

Port components are deployed into and live in containers. Writing a Web service using EJB requires creating one or more port components as stateless session beans. A big advantage of the way the Web services programming model is defined is that you can easily expose existing session beans as Web services. This is what we will do in the remainder of this chapter.

The concrete client and server APIs and the mapping between Java and WSDL are defined in JSR 224, Java API for XML Web Services (JAX-WS).

JAX-WS supercedes the earlier JAX-RPC standards and is not specific to Web services with EJBs, so you can implement Web services even without EJB by relying on the server-side APIs of JAX-WS.

There are basically two ways to implement a Web service:

- Start with a Java class and let the container generate the WSDL and any other required mapped XML artifacts.
- Start with a (new or preexisting) WSDL file and let development tools generate the required Java classes.

To leverage the large investments that we made in Chapter 3 and to demonstrate the simplest possible approach, we will take our HelloWorld session bean and make it available as a Web service using the "start from Java" approach.

The great news is that no additional coding is required. The only thing that our session bean is missing is a declaration as a Web service. Here's the *HelloBean*, adorned with a metadata annotation that turns it into a Web service implementation.

```
package examples.session.ws;

import javax.ejb.Stateless;
import javax.jws.WebMethod;
import javax.jws.WebService;

@Stateless
@WebService(serviceName="Greeter", portName="GreeterPort")
public class HelloBean  {

    @WebMethod
    public String hello() {
        System.out.println("hello()");
        return "Hello, World!";
    }
}
```

As you can see, the implementation has not changed. The only important changes are the `@WebService` annotation on the class and the `@WebMethod` annotation on the `hello()` method. In the example, the `@WebService` annotation has two members. The `serviceName` and `portName` members tell the container the name of the Web service and the name of the port. These names reappear in the generated WSDL file. In fact, you have already seen them in the WSDL file presented earlier in this chapter. Here is the relevant snippet again:

```
<service name="Greeter">
  <port name="GreeterPort" binding="tns:GreeterPortBinding">
    <soap:address location="http://gorilla:80/Greeter"/>
```

```
    </port>
  </service>
```

Note two things about this example. First, the `HelloBean` (also called service implementation bean) does not need to implement any specific interfaces to function as a Web service implementation. You can implement a *service endpoint interface* if you like and denote it using the `endpointInterface` member of the `@WebService` annotation, but this is not required. The client contract is defined in terms of the WSDL description that is generated from these annotations, so a separate Java interface is not necessary. If one is used, the JAX-WS specification states the following rules:

- The service endpoint interface must be a public, outer Java interface that includes a `@WebService` annotation.
- The interface may extend `java.rmi.Remote` either directly or indirectly, but need not.
- All methods are mapped to WSDL operations and may throw `java.rmi.RemoteException` but are not required to.
- The method parameters and return types must be the Java types supported by the JAX-RPC mapping.

Second, the `@WebMethod` annotation is also optional. If no such annotation is present, all methods of the service implementation bean (or the service endpoint interface, if any) will be exposed in the WSDL. If a `@WebMethod` annotation is used, then only those methods that are marked with it are exposed. The annotation types that can be used for Web services are defined in a separate specification document: JSR 181, *Web Services Metadata*. For further details on these annotations please turn to Appendix B.

After applying these annotation to declare the bean as a Web service we only need to redeploy the application, which now contains a port component. The EJB container will know how to dispatch incoming SOAP messages to the bean implementation and also how to map incoming XML data to Java. The same will happen on the way back: The container just knows how to map the Java return values back into XML, how to build a SOAP response message, and where to send it. The actual mapping rules ("binding") between XML data and Java are defined in yet another JSR, the *Java Architecture for XML Binding (JAXB)*, which is available as JSR 222.

The JAXB specification defines a mapping between a set of supported Java types and XML schema types. The Java types directly supported by JAXB are the primitive types *boolean, byte, double, float, int, long, short,* and their wrapper classes. In addition, the following nonprimitive types are directly supported by JAXB:

```
java.lang.String
java.math.BigDecimal
```

```
java.math.BigInteger
java.net.URI
java.util.Calendar
java.util.Date
javax.xml.namespace.QName
java.net.URI
javax.xml.datatype.XMLGregorianCalendar
javax.xml.datatype.Duration
java.lang.Object
java.awt.Image
javax.activation.DataHandler
javax.xml.transform.Source
java.util.UUID
```

WSDL and the XML/Java Mapping

You have seen the WSDL description of the HelloWorld Web service already. If you are building new Web services, you can start with a WSDL description of your service and write WSDL directly and then use a WSDL compiler to generate the service endpoint interface in Java. Alternatively, all Java Web services platforms and SOAP toolkits provide tools to derive WSDL descriptions automatically from Java endpoint interfaces or service implementation beans.

Packaging and Deploying a Web Service Session Bean

The packaging of a Web service implementation as a stateless session bean is an extension of the packaging for regular stateless session beans, that is, an *Ejb-jar* archive. This file contains the usual set of Java classes, plus the service endpoint interface class.

The EJB server requires extra information to be able to dispatch incoming SOAP messages to your bean. First, it needs to know the Java class that will handle these calls. As you saw, this information can be expressed using annotations. Optionally, you can provide a WSDL file. If present, the WSDL file is provided in the `META-INF` directory of the *Ejb-jar* archive.

As an alternative to using annotations, the information can be provided in an additional descriptor file, the `webservices.xml` file, which is also added to the *Ejb-jar* archive's META-INF directory. Your specific Java EE product may provide vendor-specific deployment tools to generate this file. The `webservices.xml` file for the HelloWorld service is reproduced here:

```
<?xml version="1.0" encoding="UTF-8"?>
<webservices xmlns="http://java.sun.com/xml/ns/javaee"
   xmlns:xsi="http://www.w3.org/2001/XMLSchema-instance" version="1.2"
   xsi:schemaLocation="http://java.sun.com/xml/ns/javaee
   http://www.ibm.com/webservices/xsd/javaee_web_services_1_2.xsd">
   <webservice-description>
      <display-name>Greeter</display-name>
      <webservice-description-name>Greeter
      </webservice-description-name>
      <wsdl-file>META-INF/wsdl/Greeter.wsdl</wsdl-file>
      <port-component>
         <port-component-name>HelloBean</port-component-name>
         <wsdl-port xmlns:ns1="http://ws.session.examples/">
            ns1:GreeterPort
         </wsdl-port>
         <service-endpoint-interface>
            examples.session.ws.HelloBean
         </service-endpoint-interface>
         <wsdl-service xmlns="http://ws.session.examples/">
             GreeterPort
         </wsdl-service>
         <service-impl-bean>
            <ejb-link>HelloBean</ejb-link>
         </service-impl-bean>
      </port-component>
   </webservice-description>
</webservices>
```

The `webservices.xml` file tells the container where to look for the WSDL file in the package in the `<wsdl-file>` element and defines the Web service interface and implementation package, the port component. The `<port-component>` definition lists the fully qualified Java class name of the service endpoint interface and the name of the implementation bean. The simple name is sufficient here as the container already knows the bean details from the `ejb-jar.xml` file. The port component is linked to the Web service's port using the `<wsdl-port>` element, which gives the name of the port that this port component implements.

With this, we're actually done! The container has all the information that it needs to link the abstract concept of a Web service as defined in WSDL to the port component that we have just defined by adding a service endpoint interface to the existing `HelloBean`.

Implementing a Web Service Client

Web services clients in Java EE are very similar to regular bean clients. They come in two flavors:

- Standalone JAX-WS clients without JNDI access for service lookup
- Java EE clients (both Web clients and standalone) that can access client-side JNDI contexts

Standalone clients without JNDI access, such as remote Java clients not running inside an application server, can be coded using one of two approaches. The first approach is called *proxy* and retrieves a WSDL description at runtime to generate the dynamic proxy from it. This approach relies on the client's knowledge of the service endpoint address URL and not just a symbolic lookup name as with JNDI.

The second option relies on *Dispatch* objects and is basically a dynamic invocation interface (DII) to create call objects at runtime, which allows you to build dynamic bridges and to live without any prior knowledge of a service's WSDL. We do not cover this style of programming here as it is low level and cumbersome to use, and beneficial only in limited cases. With the Dispatch approach, your client code has to create SOAP call objects (dispatch objects) and explicitly embed parameters before sending them.

The following example shows the code for a standalone, remote client to our simple HelloWorld Web service:

```
package examples.session.ws;

import java.net.URL;

import javax.xml.namespace.QName;
import javax.xml.ws.Service;

/**
 * This is an example of a standalone JAX-WS client. To compile,
 * it requires some XML artifacts to be generated from the service's
 * WSDL. This is done in the build file.
 *
 * The mapped XML classes used here are
 * 1. the HelloBean port type class (this is NOT the bean impl. class!)
 * 2. the Greeter service class
 */
public class JAXWSClient {

    static String host = "localhost";
    static String portType = "HelloBean";
    static String serviceName = "Greeter";
    static String serviceEndpointAddress =
                    "http://" + host + ":8080/" + serviceName;
    static String nameSpace = "http://ws.session.examples";

    public static void main(String[] args) throws Exception {

        URL wsdlLocation =
```

```
            new URL(serviceEndpointAddress + "/" + portType + "?WSDL");
        QName serviceNameQ = new QName( nameSpace, serviceName);

        // dynamic service usage
        Service service = Service.create(wsdlLocation, serviceNameQ);
        HelloBean firstGreeterPort = service.getPort(HelloBean.class);
        System.out.println("1: " + firstGreeterPort.hello());

        // static service usage
        Greeter greeter = new Greeter();
        HelloBean secondGreeterPort = greeter.getGreeterPort();
        System.out.println("2: " +secondGreeterPort.hello());
    }
}
```

The example shows two slightly different ways of using service proxies, where the first uses generic methods in the Service class to obtain a port object while the second uses a generated service proxy class `Greeter` with a type-specific `getGreeterPort()` method. The `Greeter class is generated from the WSDL file using vendor-specific tools.`

Java EE client code that is running in a client container, for example a servlet, can be shielded from the actual service endpoint address by using JNDI lookups instead. The client container's local JNDI context provides the binding from the service endpoint address to a service name according to the client's deployment descriptor. The exact configuration of the client container is vendor-specific.

This concludes our simple programming example for Web services in EJB. While the example itself is far from realistic or even prototypical for a Web service, it is useful to show how you can turn something into a Web service after it has been coded, and how EJB supports generating the necessary XML scaffolding without your having to worry about it. You will see another example of a Web service in action in Chapter 18.

Summary

In this chapter, we provided a basic overview of the concepts and technologies required to use and build Web services with EJB. This completes our introduction to session beans. We have covered a lot of ground, going from stateless to stateful session beans and back again to stateless beans that implement Web services.

In the next chapters, you'll learn about the more complex (and also quite interesting) entities. Turn the page and read on!

CHAPTER

6

Java Persistence: Programming with Entities

Any nontrivial enterprise application needs to handle persistent data of one kind or another. EJB has long had a component model for persistent objects, but over the years it has become apparent that these components—*entity beans*—have many practical disadvantages. With version 3.0 of the EJB specification, a completely new persistence technology can now be used. This new persistence layer has been long awaited in the industry and is called *Java Persistence*.

Java Persistence is a separate specification document of more than 220 pages and has been separated from the core EJB specification, even though it was prepared by the same expert group. It is one of the most important innovations available for EJB 3.0 and it provides a POJO programming model for persistent objects that is based on *entities*.

Entities are not an enhancement of the entity *beans* known from previous versions of EJB but rather a completely new programming concept. The new Java Persistence specification:

- Provides a standard object-relational (OR) mapping which integrates many of the concepts that were found in popular persistence frameworks such as Hibernate and JDO
- Is not tied to the Java EE container and can be tested and used in J2SE environments
- Defines a service provider interface so that different persistence providers can be used without affecting the entity code

While the older entity beans are still required to be supported by a 3.0-compliant EJB container, the new Java Persistence API is concerned *only* with entities. We concentrate on entities exclusively in this book. We recommend that you do the same and write any new code to this API. If you need to maintain legacy beans and hence need information on pre-3.0 entity beans, please refer to the third edition of this book, *Mastering Enterprise JavaBeans, Third Edition* (ISBN 0-7645-7682-8), which is freely accessible online.

In this chapter, we'll provide an overview of the most important concepts in Java Persistence. We first cover the concept of OR mapping to give you a solid foundation before we embark on the programming concepts found in Java Persistence, and on their integration in EJB 3.0. Some more advanced concepts, such as relationships and support for inheritance and polymorphism, will be covered in Chapter 9.

Object-Relational Mapping

The simplest way to persist objects in Java is to use Java's native serialization API that lets you write objects to files. For enterprise data, this is usually insufficient as data persisted in this way is not efficiently searchable, nor is concurrent access protected by transactions.

Another popular way to store Java objects is to use a traditional relational database management system (RDBMS) such as Oracle, Microsoft SQL Server, DB2, or open source alternatives such as MySQL, PostgreSQL, or Derby. Rather than serialize an object as a complete bit blob, we would decompose each object into its constituent parts and store each part separately. For example, for a bank account object, the bank account number could be stored in one relational database field and the bank account balance in another field. When you save your Java objects, you would use JDBC to *map* the object data into a relational database. When you want to load your objects from the database, you would instantiate an object from that class, read the data in from the database, and then populate that object instance's fields with the relational data read in. This is shown in Figure 6.1.

This mapping of objects to relational databases is a technology called *object-relational mapping*. It is the act of converting and unconverting in-memory objects to relational data. An object-relational (OR) mapper may map your objects to any kind of relational database schema. For example, a simple object-relational mapping engine might map a Java class to a SQL table definition. An instance of that class would map to a row in that table, while fields in that instance would map to individual cells in that row. This is shown in Figure 6.2. You'll see more advanced cases of mapping data with *relationships* to other data in Chapter 9.

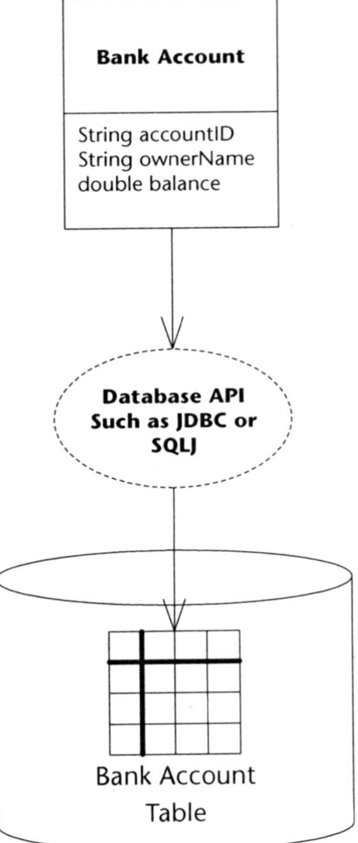

Figure 6.1 Object-relational mapping.

Object-relational mapping is a much more sophisticated mechanism of persisting objects than the simple object serialization offered by the Java language. By decomposing your Java objects as relational data, you can issue arbitrary queries for information. For example, you can search through all the database records that have an account balance entry greater than $1,000 and load only the objects that fulfill this query. More advanced queries are also possible. You can also visually inspect the database data because it is not stored as bit-blobs, which is great for debugging or auditing.

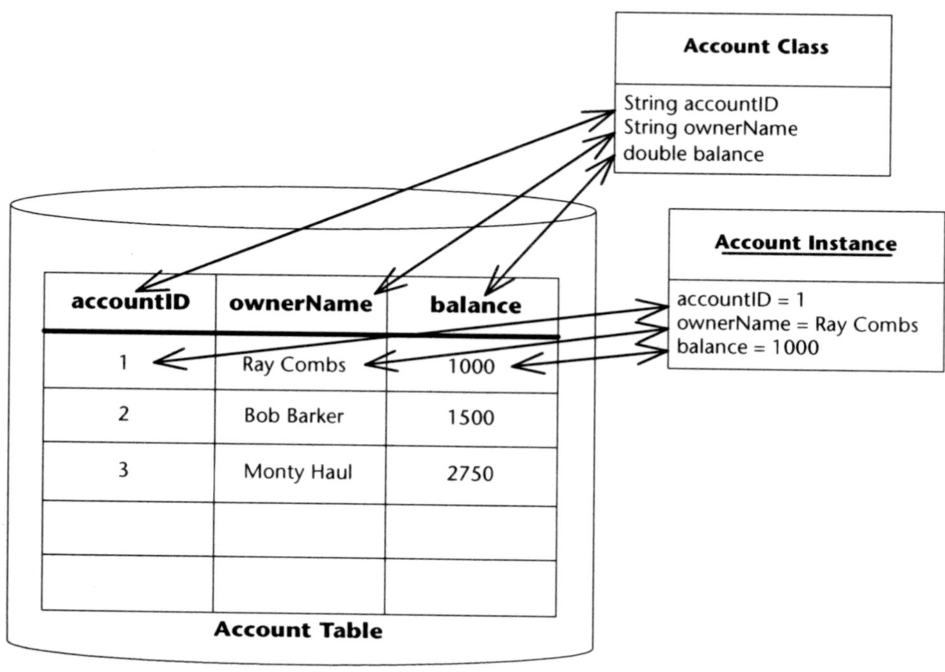

Figure 6.2 An example of object-relational mapping.

Mapping objects to relational data can be done in two ways. You can either handcraft this mapping in your code or use an object-relational mapping product, such as Oracle TopLink, or open source tools, such as Hibernate, to automate or facilitate this mapping. These tools have become increasingly popular. An automated mapper would create data definitions in the DDL (data definition language) of the target platform from either Java classes or from separate mapping description. Handcrafted mappings using a database access API such as JDBC are becoming less frequently used because the cost of developing and maintaining an object-relational mapping layer is significant.

The Sun *Java Data Objects* (JDO) specification, available as JSR 12 from the *Java Community Process* (JCP) web site at `www.jcp.org`, defines portable APIs to a persistence layer that is conceptually neutral to the database technology used to support it. It can thus be implemented by vendors of relational and object-oriented databases.

The new Java Persistence specification finally defines a standardized object-relational mapping and requires compliant products to implement it. Because it incorporates many proven concepts, there is now a broad industry consensus on a portable programming model for persistent Java objects. We will explore this standardized mapping in some detail in this chapter. The great news is that this model, by combining the best features of its predecessor products and making use of Java metadata annotations, is both flexible, powerful, and comparatively easy to use.

Now that we've set the scene for persistence mechanisms, let's take a look at how the new entity concept is used in EJB.

What Is an Entity?

In multi-tier enterprise applications you will typically find two different kinds of objects:

- **Application logic components.** These components provide methods that perform common tasks. Their tasks might include the following:
  - Computing the price of an order
  - Billing a customer's credit card
  - Computing the inverse of a matrix

  Note that these components represent actions (they're verbs). They are well suited to handling business processes.

  Session beans model these application logic components very well. They often contain interesting algorithms and logic to perform application tasks. Session beans represent work being performed for a user as a session, which includes any workflow logic.

- **Persistent data objects.** These are objects that can be rendered into persistent storage by a persistence mechanism. These kinds of objects represent *data*—simple or complex information that you'd like saved. Examples here include:
  - Bank account information, such as account number and balance
  - Human resources data, such as names, departments, and salaries of employees
  - Lead-tracking information, such as names, addresses, and phone numbers of prospective customers that you want to keep track of over time

  Note that these objects represent people, places, and things (they're nouns). They are well suited to handling long-lived business data.

Persistent objects are called *entities* in the new Java Persistence specification. Entities are plain old Java objects (POJOs) that are persisted to durable storage, such as a database or legacy system. Entities store data as fields, such as bank account numbers and bank account balances. They also have methods associated with them, such as `getAccountNumber()` and `getBalance()`. For a full discussion of when to (and when not to) use entities, see Chapter 13.

FOR THE RECORD: ENTITIES

When we talk about entities as a new concept in the rest of this chapter, we always mean new as a programming concept for persistent objects. As a term for modeling persistent data, "entity" has been used at least since 1976 when Peter Chen proposed the classic *Entity-Relationship Model* (ERM) in one of the most influential papers in computer science (Peter Chen, "The Entity-Relationship Model – Toward a Unified View of Data," *ACM Transactions on Database Systems*, Vol. 1, No. 1, March 1976).

You might question the need for such persistent data components. Why should we deal with our business data as objects, rather than deal with raw database data, such as relational rows? The answer is simple: It is handy to treat data as objects because they can be easily handled and managed and because they are represented in a compact manner. We can group related data in a unified object and factor out common attributes in an inheritance hierarchy. We associate some simple methods with that data, such as compression or other data-related activities.

Entities versus Session Beans

As already pointed out, entities are not EJBs and can be used even in J2SE environments. It is still useful to draw a quick comparison between entities and session beans to highlight some specifics. The big differences between session beans and entities are that:

- Entities have a client-visible, persistent *identity* (the primary key) that is distinct from their object reference.
- Entities have persistent, client-visible *state.*
- Entities are *not remotely accessible.*
- An entity's *lifetime* may be completely independent of an application's lifetime.

Different entities can be distinguished by comparing their identities. Clients can refer to individual entities by using that identity, pass it as a handle to other applications, and thus share common entities with other clients. All this is not possible with session beans.

On the other hand, session beans permit both local and remote clients, with the container handling remote accesses. Entities are purely local objects and cannot be directly accessed remotely.

Lifetime is another huge difference between session beans and entities. Entities can have a much longer life cycle than a client's session, perhaps years long, depending on how long the data sits in the database. In fact, the database records representing an object could have existed before its owner even decided to go with a Java-based solution, because a database structure can be language-independent. Likewise, that data may still be used when the owner of the data has long moved away from Java to what may the hottest technology in one or two decades from now. This makes sense—you definitely would want your bank account to last for a few years, regardless of technology changes at your bank.

Entities are not only longlasting; they survive critical failures, such as application servers crashing, or even databases crashing. This is because entities are just representations of data in a permanent, fault-tolerant, underlying storage. If a machine crashes, the entity can be reconstructed in memory. All we need to do is look it up again, which transparently instantiates an entity instance with fields that contain the data read in from the database.

In summary, you should think of an entity as an in-memory Java representation of persistent data that:

- Is loaded from storage and has its field populated with the stored data
- Can be modified in-memory to change the values of data
- Can be saved back, thus updating the database data

Persistence Provider

In some ways, entities are analogous to serializable Java objects. Serializable objects can be rendered into a bit-blob by the serialization mechanism and then saved in a persistent store. The mechanism to transfer entity information back and forth between the Java object and the database is implemented within your *persistence provider*. The persistence provider is typically tailored to a relational database but could also use an object database. Which particular implementation is used is transparent to the entity. In fact, the Java Persistence specification defines a *Persistence Provider* SPI to allow any conformant provider implementation to be plugged into the application runtime. In a Java EE environment, that is your container.

The persistence provider implementation worries about the proper time to load and store your data. It also automatically figures out when each of your instances needs to be refreshed, depending on the current transactional state (see Chapter 10). You don't have to worry about synchronizing your objects with the underlying database: The persistence provider black box handles it for you.

Entity Classes

Entities are similar to other EJB components in that they are implemented in a plain Java class and can have metadata annotations or an XML deployment descriptor. However, entities are not specific to EJB or even Java EE—the Java

Persistence specification defined entities specifically so that they can be used in both Java EE and J2SE environments.

It is about time we actually get to see an entity class. Source 6.1 shows a simple example.

```
package examples.entity.intro;

import java.io.Serializable;
import javax.persistence.Entity;
import javax.persistence.Id;

/**
 * This demo entity represents a Bank Account.
 * <p>
 * The entity is not a remote object and can only be accessed locally by
 * clients. However, it is made serializable so that instances can be
 * passed by value to remote clients for local inspection.
 * <p>
 * Access to persistent state is by direct field access.
 */

@Entity
public class Account implements Serializable {

    // The account number is the primary key
    @Id
    public int accountNumber;
    public String ownerName;
    public int balance;

    /**
     * Entities must have a public no-arg constructor
     */
    public Account() {
        // our own simple primary key generation
        accountNumber = (int) System.nanoTime();
    }

    /**
     * Deposit a given amount
     * @param amount
     */
    public void deposit(int amount) {
        balance += amount;
    }

    /**
     * Withdraw a given amount, or 0 if it is larger than the balance
```

Source 6.1 Account.java. *(continued)*

```
     * @param amount
     * @return The amount that was withdrawn
     */
    public int withdraw(int amount) {
        if (amount > balance) {
            return 0;
        } else {
            balance -= amount;
            return amount;
        }
    }
}
```

Source 6.1 *(continued)*

A few things are worth pointing out here:

- The entity class is a **plain Java class** that does not extend any framework classes or interfaces. It does not even have to implement `java.io.Serializable`. In the example, the class implements `Serializable` so that an entity instance can also be used as a simple data record and transferred as an argument in remote invocations. Remember that the entity itself does not provide a remote interface.
- The entity class **maps to a data definition** in a relational database schema, that is, a relational table definition. At runtime, an entity instance of that class will map to a row in that table. The Java Persistence API defines a standardized mapping from entity classes to relational database tables and allows you to control this mapping through annotations or XML descriptors.

  In the example, the standard mapper would create a table ACCOUNT with columns for all fields of the entity class.
- An entity must declare a **primary key**. We do this by marking the `accountNumber` field with the `@Id` annotation. As a consequence, the OR-mapper would define a primary key constraint for the mapped ACCOUNTNUMBER column.

  The primary key makes every entity different. In the example, if you have one million bank account entity instances, each bank account needs to have a unique ID (such as a bank account integer number) that can never be repeated in any other bank account.

  In some advanced cases, when the entity represents a complex relationship, the primary key might be an entire object. The Java Persistence API gives you the flexibility to define what your unique identifier is by including a *primary key class* with your entity. The rule is that your primary key class must be public, have a public constructor, and be serializable.

- Access to the entity's persistent state is by direct field access. An entity's state can also be accessed using JavaBean-style set and get methods. The persistence provider can determine which access style is used by looking at how annotations are applied. In Source 6.1, the `@Id` annotation is applied to a field, so we have field access.
- The entity can expose **business methods**, such as a method to decrease a bank account balance, to manipulate or access that data. Like a session bean class, an entity class can also declare some standard callback methods or a callback listener class. The persistence provider will call these methods appropriately to manage the entity. We will see examples later.

Accessing Entities in the Persistence Context

Now that we have the Java code for an entity class, how do we actually use it in an EJB environment? Since an entity cannot be accessed remotely, the only option that we have is to deploy it locally and use it from either J2SE code outside a container, or from session or message-driven beans living in an EJB container.

Either way, client code must first retrieve a particular entity instance from the *persistence context* or create one and add it to the persistence context. The persistence context is the connection between your in-memory instances and the database. It is manipulated through a new API, the `EntityManager` interface. Let's look at an example (please note that we have omitted the bean's `Bank` interface for brevity here as it does not convey any additional information):

```
package examples.entity.intro;

import java.util.List;
import javax.ejb.Stateless;
import javax.ejb.Remote;
import javax.persistence.PersistenceContext;
import javax.persistence.EntityManager;
import javax.persistence.Query;

/**
 * Stateless session bean facade for account entities,
 * remotely accessible
 */
@Stateless
```

Source 6.2 BankBean.java. *(continued)*

```
@Remote(Bank.class)
public class BankBean implements Bank {

    /** the entity manager object, injected by the container  */
    @PersistenceContext
    private EntityManager manager;

    public List<Account> listAccounts() {
        Query query = manager.createQuery("SELECT a FROM Account a");
        return query.getResultList();
    }

    public Account openAccount(String ownerName) {
        Account account = new Account();
        account.ownerName = ownerName;
        manager.persist(account);
        return account;
    }

    public int getBalance(int accountNumber) {
        Account account = manager.find(Account.class, accountNumber);
        return account.balance;
    }

    public void deposit(int accountNumber, int amount) {
        Account account = manager.find(Account.class, accountNumber);
        account.deposit(amount);
    }

    public int withdraw(int accountNumber, int amount) {
        Account account = manager.find(Account.class, accountNumber);
        return account.withdraw(amount);
    }

    public void close(int accountNumber) {
        Account account = manager.find(Account.class, accountNumber);
        manager.remove(account);
    }
}
```

Source 6.2 *(continued)*

Let's first examine the `openAccount()` method: When a new account is needed, we simply create a new instance. The new entity instance does not initially have a persistent identity and is not associated with the persistence context. At this stage, the database knows nothing about the entity, and if we quit the application at this stage, nothing will be written to the persistent storage.

To add the new entity to the persistence context we need to call the EntityManager's `persist()` method. The entity is now scheduled for synchronization with the database and will get written to disk when the transaction commits. This state in the entity's life cycle is called the *managed* state. The entity will remain in the managed state until either the persistence context ends or it is explicitly removed from that context.

In the example, we are using a stateless session bean without any additional annotations for transaction management or persistence context lifetime, so the following defaults apply:

- The persistence context lifetime has *transaction* scope, so the persistence context ends when the transaction is committed or rolls back.
- Transaction management uses *container-managed* transactions with the `required` transaction attribute (see Chapter 10 for details). This means that any business method will get invoked by the container in the context of a transaction (either an existing or a new one).

These two bullets imply that our persistence context ends when the method returns because that is when the transaction ends. At this stage, the connection between all managed entities and the entity manager is removed and the entities change to the *detached* state.

In the detached state, entity state is not synchronized with the database. So, how do we change the account so that the database is actually updated? We need to do two things: get a new persistence context, and transfer the entity to the managed state again.

PERSISTENCE CONTEXT TYPE

The persistence context that is associated with an entity manager can be one of two types, which determines the lifetime of the context. These types are *transaction-scoped* or *extended*. Within a Java EE container, the typical use for transaction-scoped persistence contexts is with stateless session beans, and extended persistence contexts are used from stateful session beans.

A transaction-scoped persistence context ends when the enclosing transaction ends. At this point, all entities in the persistence context become detached.

An extended persistence context ends when the enclosing stateful session bean is removed by the container. The entities remain managed across several invocations of the bean's business methods and can be modified even outside of transactions.

With the transaction-scoped persistence context lifetime in the example, a new persistence context is set up in the entity manager every time an entity manager operation is invoked and no persistence context exists. Our `BankBean` looks up an account entity instance each time `getBalance()`, `deposit()`, or `withdraw()` is called. This entity lookup is performed by calling the `find()` method of the `EntityManager` instance, using the entity class and the account number as arguments. Implicitly, the entity manager is associated with a new persistence context each time.

Because we do not store a reference to an entity instance anywhere but look them up each time, the entity that is found through the `EntityManager` is already in the managed state. Any changes to the internal state of the entity are synchronized with the database when the transaction is committed.

Extended Persistence Context

We will explain the entity life cycle in a little more detail in a minute, but let's first look at another example of accessing entities. In this example, we'll use a *stateful* session bean as a façade for the entity. This bean can keep the retrieved account entity around in its internal session state and thus avoid the lookup overhead on each access. Here is the example code, again omitting the bean's separate interface for brevity:

```
package examples.entity.intro;

import javax.ejb.Remote;
import javax.ejb.Stateful;
import javax.persistence.EntityManager;
import javax.persistence.PersistenceContext;
import javax.persistence.PersistenceContextType;

/**
 * Stateful session bean facade for account entities, remotely
 * accessible
 */
@Stateful
@Remote(AccountInterface.class)
public class AccountBean implements AccountInterface {

    /** The entity manager, injected by the container */
    @PersistenceContext(type=PersistenceContextType.EXTENDED,
        unitName="intro")
    private EntityManager manager;

    private Account account = null;

    public void open(int accountNumber) {
```

```
        account = manager.find(Account.class, accountNumber);
        if (account == null) {
            account = new Account();
            account.ownerName = "anonymous";
            account.accountNumber = accountNumber;
            manager.persist(account);
        }
    }

    public int getBalance() {
        if(account==null)
            throw new IllegalStateException();
        return account.balance;
    }

    public void deposit(int amount) {
        if(account==null)
            throw new IllegalStateException();
        account.deposit(amount);
    }

    public int withdraw(int amount) {
        if(account==null)
            throw new IllegalStateException();
        return account.withdraw(amount);
    }
}
```

Note the use of the `EXTENDED` persistence context type that we declared on the entity manager. Without this annotation, keeping the `account` entity instance around in the session state would be pointless: the entity would be detached every time the persistence context ends and need to be reattached (or *merged*) into a new persistence context for each new access.

With the extended persistence context type, the entity stays managed because the persistence context spans multiple transactions and ends only when the bean is removed. Hence, the individual methods in the example do not need to retrieve the account entity each time using the `EntityManager.find()` method but simply check that the account has been obtained at all in the session. If not, an `IllegalStateException` is raised.

Which kind of session bean and persistence context is more suitable depends on the expected usage of the entity data: If clients retrieve multiple entities and then interact with that same set of entities through a number of invocations, it may be better to hold onto these instances in a stateful session bean. If a single client always only accesses an entity once, then there is no need to build up client state, and a stateless session bean would be more suitable.

Packaging and Deploying Entity Classes

Entity classes are packaged and deployed in *persistence units*. A persistence unit is a logical grouping of entity classes, mapping metadata, and database-related configuration data.

A persistence unit is defined in a special descriptor file, the `persistence.xml` file, which is simply added to the `META-INF` directory of an arbitrary archive, such as an `Ejb-jar`, `.ear`, or `.war` file, or in a plain .jar file. Without a `persistence.xml` file somewhere in an application, there will be no persistence units, and without at least one persistence unit no entity manager can be obtained and used.

Here's the simplest possible example of a `persistence.xml` file:

```
<?xml version="1.0" encoding="UTF-8"?>
<persistence xmlns="http://java.sun.com/xml/ns/persistence">
    <persistence-unit name="intro"/>
</persistence>
```

At a minimum, we must provide one `persistence-unit` element together with a `name` attribute as a child of the `persistence` element. The `persistence.xml` file may contain more than one persistence unit definition, but if there is only one visible in the application, it need not be referenced explicitly in the `unitName` field of the `@PersistenceContext` annotation. If the `persistence.xml` file does not list any entity classes explicitly, all entity classes contained in the same archive as the `persistence.xml` file will be considered members of the persistence unit.

The `persistence-unit` element has a few other possible attributes and child elements. These are all optional, however, if the defaults are okay. These are:

`<description>` An optional text.

`<provider>` Fully qualified class name of the persistence provider's implementation of the SPI class `javax.persistence. spi.PersistenceProvider`. The `<provider>` element must be present in a J2SE environment, or when provider-specific behavior is required by the application.

`<transaction-type>` An attribute of the `<persistence-unit>` element. The value of this element is either `JTA` or `RESOURCE_LOCAL`. `JTA` is the default.

`<jta-data-source>`, `<non-jta-data-source>` Specifies the JNDI name of the data source that is to be used by the persistence provider. If undefined, it must be defined by the deployer, or the contained must provide a default.

`<mapping-file>` OR-mapping information for the entity classes in the persistence unit can be taken from class annotations, but it may also be specified in an XML mapping file called `orm.xml` in the same `META-INF` directory where the `persistence.xml` file is located. The `<mapping-file>` element can list one or more alternative or additional XML mapping files to be used for OR mapping.

The mapping files explicitly list entity classes. These will be available in the persistence unit.

`<jar-file>`, `<class>` These elements list the archives to search for entity classes (or the entity classes themselves) that are available in the persistence unit.

`<exclude-unlisted-classes>` If this element is present, only the entity classes or archives that are explicitly listed using the `<mapping-file>`, `<jar-file>`, or `<class>` elements will be available in the persistence unit.

`<properties>` Vendor-specific configuration properties for the persistence unit. If there are properties that are not recognized by the persistence provider, they must be ignored.

The EntityManager API

As we showed earlier in this chapter, the EntityManager is the interface that lets you access the entities in your application's persistence context. Within a persistence context, all entity identities are unique and map to a single entity instance. This section will provide more details on the EntityManager API, the entity life cycle, and query facilities.

There are two options for client code that needs to use an EntityManager:

- With a *container-managed* EntityManager, the container runtime is responsible for determining and providing the EntityManager for an application. The container injects the EntityManager, as shown in our simple example when we used the `@PersistenceContext` annotation on the `manager` field. Alternatively, an EntityManager can also be obtained from the `SessionContext` using its `lookup()` method.
- With an *application-managed* EntityManager, the application is responsible for creating an EntityManager instance itself. This is done using an `EntityManagerFactory` interface.

The complete EntityManager API provides methods for three different kinds of operations:

- Entity life-cycle management
- Database synchronization operations
- Entity lookup and queries

Let's look at each of these in turn.

Entity Life Cycle

The life of an entity instance has two main aspects: its relationship to a specific persistence context, and the synchronization of its state with the database. The EntityManager distinguishes between four states in the life cycle of an entity:

- **new.** The entity instance was created in memory, but is not yet associated with either a persistent identity in the database or a persistence context. This is the state that our Account entity was in right after creation. Changes in the entity state are not synchronized with the database at this stage.
- **managed.** The entity has a persistent identity in the database and is currently associated with a persistence context. Our Account entity was in the managed state after the `persist()` method was called. Changes to the entity will be synchronized with the database when transactions are committed or when synchronization is explicitly triggered using the `flush()` operation.
- **detached.** The entity does have a persistent identity but is not or is no longer associated with the persistence context.
- **removed.** The entity is currently associated with a persistence context but has been scheduled for removal from the database.

Figure 6.3 shows these four states and the transitions between them as EntityManager operations are called.

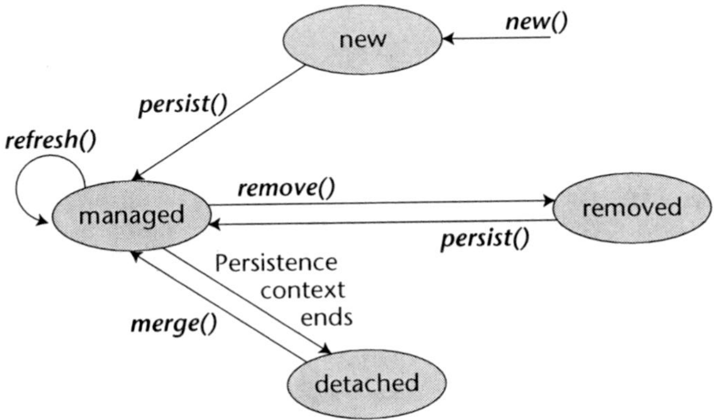

Figure 6.3 Entity life cycle.

Here's the relevant part of the EntityManager API:

```
package javax.persistence;
public interface EntityManager {
   /** Make a new instance managed and persistent. */
   public void persist(Object entity);

   /** Merge the state of the given entity into the current
       persistence context. */
   public <T> T merge(T entity);

   /** Remove the instance from the database. */
   public void remove(Object entity);

   /** Check if the instance is managed in the current persistence
       context. */
   public boolean contains(Object entity);

  // cont'd...
}
```

To destroy an entity's data in the database, the client must call `remove()`. Note that `remove()` does not mean the in-memory entity instance is actually going to be destroyed; `remove()` schedules only database data for removal. The `remove()` operation ignores entities that are new or already removed, and only works on managed entities. Calling `remove()` on a detached entity will raise an `IllegalArgumentException`. The actual deletion from the database happens when the transaction is committed, or when `flush()` is called. Database synchronization is explained in more detail below.

The `merge()` operation allows you to bring detached entities back to the persistence context. Remember that entities are detached when the persistence context ends. In the stateless session bean example, this happens whenever a business method returns. Entities also get detached when they are delivered to clients as serializable objects.

Let's quickly reexamine the first example's `openAccount()` method:

```
public Account openAccount(String ownerName) {
    Account account = new Account();
    account.ownerName = ownerName;
    manager.persist(account);
    return account;
}
```

The entity that is returned from the method is detached from the persistence context. A client of our `BankBean` could now locally change that `Account` entity, but that would not result in any database updates. To persist those changes, we would need to merge the entity back and make it managed again.

This can be done simply by allowing the client to pass that entity back, and by calling `merge()` on our entity manager.

Here's an additional business method for our `BankBean` that does just that:

```
public void update(Account detachedAccount) {
        Account managedAccount = manager.merge(detachedAccount);
}
```

Note that the `merge()` operation returns a managed entity. The entity `managedAccount` is a different entity instance than the argument `detachedAccount` in all cases where `detachedAccount` is not already a managed entity.

Life-Cycle Callbacks

Just as with EJBs, we can define life-cycle callbacks for entities that get invoked when the entity makes a transition to another life-cycle stage. Bear in mind, however, that this does not mean that entities are EJBs: These callbacks are not invoked by the EJB container but rather by the persistence provider.

The Java Persistence API specification defines the following life-cycle events for entities:

- `PrePersist`
- `PostPersist`
- `PreRemove`
- `PostRemove`
- `PreUpdate`
- `PostUpdate`
- `PostLoad`

To designate a callback method for any of the events, we simply apply the appropriate annotation to a method. For example, to react when an entity is persisted, we could use the `@PrePersist` annotation on a new method in the entity class `Account`:

```
@PrePersist
void prePersist() {
    System.out.println("prePersist called!");
}
```

Rather than annotating the entity methods with these life-cycle annotations, we can define a separate listener class for life-cycle events on `Account` entities. To declare that separate class as the entity class's listener, the following annotation would be used on the `Account` class:

```
@Entity
@EntityListeners(AccountListener.class)
public class Account ...
```

Finally, here's the `prePersist()` callback method in the `AccountListener` class:

```
    @PrePersist
    void prePersist(Account a) {
        System.out.println("pre persist " + a );
    }
```

Note the difference in the method signature: Unlike the callback method in the entity class, the callback method in the listener class takes an entity argument. When invoked, this argument will be set to the entity that triggered the life-cycle event.

Database Synchronization

Updates to local entities are generally synchronized with the underlying database at transaction commit time. However, it is sometimes important to synchronize even *before* the transaction is committed. For example, when entity state changes have been made, these might influence the result of a query in the same transaction. In this case, it may be necessary to enforce synchronization before the query is executed.

This is controlled by setting the *flush mode*. The flush mode can be set on specific methods or fields using metadata annotations, or globally on the persistence context using the `setFlushMode()` operation. The available options are `COMMIT` for synchronization at commit time only, or `AUTO` for synchronization of state at both commit time and before query execution.

The `flush()` operation enforces synchronization of the state of all entities in the persistence context but does not involve a refresh of state from the database. To refresh, the `refresh()` operation must be invoked explicitly.

Here are the relevant operations in the `EntityManager`'s interface:

```
public interface EntityManager {
   /** Synchronize the persistence context to the underlying
       database. */
   public void flush();

   /** Set the flush mode that applies to all objects contained
       in the persistence context. */
   public void setFlushMode(FlushModeType flushMode);

   /** Get the flush mode that applies to all objects contained
```

```
        in the persistence context. */
    public FlushModeType getFlushMode();

    /** Refresh the state of the instance from the database,
        overwriting changes made to the entity, if any. */
    public void refresh(Object entity);

   // to be cont'd...
}
```

Direct Entity Data Manipulation

Usually you will create, destroy, and find entity data by using the entity manager. But you can interact with entities another way, too: by directly modifying the underlying database where the data is stored. For example, if your entity instances are being mapped to a relational database, you can simply delete the rows of the database corresponding to an entity instance (see Figure 6.4). You can also create new entity data and modify existing data by directly touching the database. A situation like this might arise if you have to share the data with an existing system that touches a database directly.

This raises another important question: What happens if two applications concurrently access the same entity data?

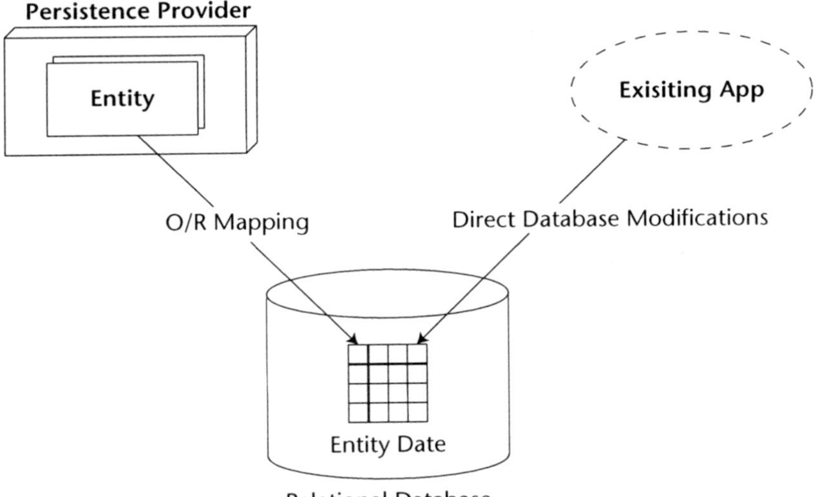

Figure 6.4 Modifying an entity's database representation directly.

Concurrent Access and Locking

Concurrent access to data in the database is always protected by *transaction isolation*, so you need not design additional concurrency controls to protect your data in your applications if transactions are used appropriately. Unless you make specific provisions, your entities will be protected by *container-managed transactions* using the isolation levels that are configured for your persistence provider and/or EJB container's transaction service.

However, it is important to understand the concurrency control requirements and semantics of your applications. We discuss transactions and their different isolation levels in detail in Chapter 10 and strongly recommend that you make yourself familiar with this subject if there is the slightest chance that your entity data may be accessed from concurrently executing transactions.

Making the right decisions and assumptions has bearings on the overall performance of your application: setting the maximum transaction isolation level (`SERIALIZABLE`) may degrade performance and even lead to deadlock situations, whereas insufficient isolation (e.g., `READ UNCOMMITTED` isolation) may lead to inconsistent data and incorrect application behavior.

The Java Persistence specification defines two important features that can be tuned for entities that are accessed concurrently:

- Optimistic locking using a *version* attribute
- Explicit read and write locks

Optimistic locking is actually a misnomer as it means that data is *not* locked for concurrency control at all. Rather, applications are free to access and update data any time. Potential write conflicts that are due to concurrent modifications of the same data are not detected until transaction commit time. At this stage, the first transaction is allowed to commit, and subsequent transactions that are in conflict with the first one are simply rolled back.

This behavior is appropriate if conflicts are rare because it imposes minimal overhead on those accesses that don't conflict, and it allows for a high degree of concurrency that will be required for scalable applications. On the downside, applications need to handle those cases where conflicts do occur. Note that optimistic locking does not rule out nonrepeatable reads. Only updates that are based on state obtained from a nonrepeatable read would be detected.

NOTE This behavior may sound familiar to you if you are using a source code version control systems like CVS or Subversion, which are based on the same principle: Let users work on their own copy of the data and write to the repository whenever they want. Conflicts are not excluded a priori by locking source files but detected later. If there are conflicts, let users deal with them, that is, manually merge conflicting regions of source code. The larger the code base and the size of your team, the more likely you are using this strategy.

The Java Persistence specification assumes that the transaction isolation level is configured no higher than READ COMMITTED by default, and that write operations to the database may be deferred until transaction commit time. In such a setting, read data is not guaranteed nor required to be consistent. (In a minute we'll discuss how you can get these consistency guarantees if you need them.) But how do you detect when a conflicting write operation is being committed, or if a detached entity is being merged back in whose persistent state was updated in the meantime? If optimistic locking is to be offered in a *portable* way, there must be a mechanism for conflict detection that is vendor-neutral.

The solution is a *version* attribute for those entities that want to use optimistic locking. This attribute is not added automatically by the persistence provider to your entity tables because you may either not care for this service, or you may prefer to obtain it in a vendor-specific way from your persistence provider. In a portable application, however, you must mark an attribute using the @Version annotation in each entity class that you wish to enable for optimistic locking control.

In the Account example, we could add the following line of code:

```
@Entity
public class Account implements Serializable {
    @Version
    public int version;
    // ...
```

The persistence provider will then check the @Version attribute to detect concurrent modifications and increment it each time an update occurs. This way, it can detect that an update is based on stale data. The type of the @Version attribute must be one of int, java.lang.Integer, short, java.lang.Short, long, java.lang.Long, java.sql.Timestamp. Note that you should never explicitly modify this attribute yourself because that might lead to undefined behavior.

As we said earlier, optimistic locking actually does not lock any data at all and only detects conflicts when data is eventually written to the database. It does not prevent nonrepeatable or phantom reads. If this is not sufficient for your application, you have two options:

- You can globally set a stricter transaction isolation level that provides stronger consistency guarantees than optimistic locking. This, however, reduces concurrency and increases the concurrency control overhead incurred by database operations
- You may use application-level locks in those places where stricter consistency is required. This option is harder to get right, but it preserves the performance and scalability advantages of optimistic locking.

The locks supported by the EntityManager API have two modes: `READ` and `WRITE`. They can be set on individual, versioned entities using the EntityManager's `lock()` method like this:

```
manager.lock(account, LockMode.WRITE);
```

Both kinds of locks, when set on an entity, prevent dirty and nonrepeatable reads of that entity's data. Figure 6.5 shows a dirty read problem:

In Figure 6.5, T2 will see an uncommitted, dirty read if the transaction isolation is `READ UNCOMMITTED` and no locks are set. T2 sees the `account.balance` value after T1 has withdrawn the amount, but before the transaction is caused to roll back by the exception, so the account balance that is printed out is $100,000 lower than its actual value. This situation would have been avoided if the account entity had first been locked by T2.

Figure 6.6 shows an unrepeatable read, again in T2.

In Figure 6.6, the number of results that the query produces in T2 is different each time. This is due to the concurrent modification in T1, which reduces the number of accounts that meet the search criterion. T2 sees these changes even if the isolation level is `READ COMMITTED` because T1 does in fact commit its changes. The only way that this problem can be prevented is if T1 first acquires a write lock on the entity.

The difference between read and write lock semantics is that calling the `EntityManager.lock(account, LockMode.WRITE)` forces an update of the version attribute for the account entity.

T1	T2
account= manager.find(Account.class, 1234);	

//update
account.withdraw(100,000);
manager.flush()	

	// find and read data
	account =
	  manager.find(Account.class, 1234);

	System.out.println(account.balance);
// trigger rollback throw new RuntimeException();	

Figure 6.5 Dirty read in transaction T2.

T1	T2
account= manager.find(Account.class, 1234);	Query query = manager.createQuery("SELECT a FROM Account a WHERE a.balance > 1000");
	System.out.println("Got" + query.getResultList().size() + " records.");
account.withdraw(100,000);	// ...
	System.out.println("Got" + query.getResultList().size() + " records.");

Figure 6.6 Unrepeatable Read in T2.

Entity Lookup and Query API

You'll rarely start your applications by creating completely new entities from scratch and feeding these into a database. In most cases, there will be preexisting data that you want to access in entities. To identify that data before we can reference it as entity instances, we need to either directly address individual data items using a primary key, or execute a query that returns a set of data based on the query conditions that we provide.

The EntityManager provides the `find()` operation to address data using primary keys. It will return a managed entity of the correct entity class when it can determine that the provided primary key belongs to that entity calls and points to a data item of that class in the database. Otherwise, it will return null.

Here's the signature of the `find()` operation. You already saw it in action in our stateless session bean example above.

```
/** Find by primary key. */
public <T> T find(Class<T> entityClass, Object primaryKey);
```

Finding a single entity by its primary key is straightforward, but in many situations we either don't know the primary key, or we need more than one result, or need to specify one or more search conditions. In all these cases, we would want to formulate a *query*. There are a number of options that we have for creating queries using the EntityManager API, but the general steps are always the same:

- Obtain an instance of `javax.persistence.Query` from the EntityManager
- Customize the query object, if necessary, by setting query parameters or an upper limit for the result set size
- Execute the query

The first step is done using the EntityManager, while the last two steps use the `Query` interface.

The EntityManager lets us choose between queries written in EJB-QL or native SQL. EJB-QL is an object query language that is syntactically very similar to SQL. It is explained in more detail in Chapter 9 and in Appendix D. For the moment, the most important difference between EJB-QL and SQL is that EJB-QL uses entities for its data model and is guaranteed to be completely portable across databases. Although an ISO standard, SQL is often not portable in practice because of the various vendor-specific extras and different SQL dialects that exist.

The two EntityManager operations for creating queries in EJB-QL or SQL are the following:

```
/** Create a Query for executing an EJB QL statement. */
public Query createQuery(String ejbqlString);

/** Create a Query for executing a native SQL statement. */
public Query createNativeQuery(String sqlString);
```

Here is an example of a simple EJB-QL query that returns all `Account` entities in the database:

```
    public List<Account> listAccounts() {
        Query query = manager.createQuery("SELECT a FROM Account a");
        return query.getResultList();
    }
```

Because native queries may return data other than entities, there are a number of overloaded variants of `createNativeQuery()` that can be used to map SQL result data to entities:

```
public Query createNativeQuery(String sqlString, Class resultClass);

public Query createNativeQuery(String sqlString,
   String resultSetMapping);
```

Named Queries

The queries that we get with these operations are called *dynamic queries* because their construction happens at runtime when the calling code is actually executed. These queries are defined by the entity provider and only used by that code. In cases where a single query is used throughout the whole persistence unit or where it must be possible for the deployer or administrator to change the query, we need to use *static* or *named queries*.

The EntityManager operation to create a query object from an external, named query string is the following:

```
/** Create a named query (in EJB QL or native SQL) */
public Query createNamedQuery(String name);
```

This operation requires that a named query already be defined, and it could be used in our *listAccounts()* method like this:

```
public List<Account> listAccounts() {
    Query query = manager.createNamedQuery("findThem");
    return query.getResultList();
}
```

In this example, the EntityManager will simply look up the definition of the query that was defined under the given name `"findThem"` and return it as a new Query object.

Finally, here's an example definition for the `"findThem"` query that was defined using the `@NamedQuery` annotation on the entity class:

```
@Entity
@NamedQuery(name="findThem", queryString="SELECT a FROM Account a")
public class Account implements Serializable {...}
```

Summary

In this chapter, we've taken the first steps toward developing with the new Java Persistence API. We started by discussing persistence mechanisms and object/relational mapping. We then looked at what an entity is (and what it is not), and explained entity classes, their annotations, persistence contexts, and deployment. We also covered entity life cycles, the EntityManager API, concurrency issues, and queries.

But there is more to come on entities. In Chapter 9, you'll learn more about advanced OR mapping, relationships, and inheritance. Chapter 10 provides more background on transactions. By the time you're through, you'll be armed to create your own entities in enterprise deployments.

CHAPTER

7

Introduction to Message-Driven Beans

In this chapter you will learn how EJB supports *messaging*, which is a lightweight vehicle for communications. Messaging is more appropriate than synchronous invocations in certain scenarios. You'll look at *message-driven beans*, special beans that can be accessed via messaging.

Specifically, you'll learn:

- How to implement messaging, including an overview of asynchronous behavior and message-oriented middleware (MOM)
- How to use the Java Message Service (JMS), the underlying MOM framework for JMS-based message-driven beans
- What the features of message-driven beans are and how message-driven beans compare with entity and session beans
- How to develop message-driven beans, including advanced topics such as gotchas and possible solutions

Motivations for Messaging

In previous chapters, you learned how to code session and entity beans—distributed components that are accessed using RMI-IIOP. RMI-IIOP is a traditional, heavyweight way to call components, and it is appropriate in most settings. However, several areas are challenging for RMI-IIOP. Here are just four examples:

Asynchrony. A typical RMI-IIOP client must wait (or block) while the server performs its processing. Only when the server completes its work does the client receive a return result, which enables it to continue processing.

Decoupling. An RMI-IIOP client has to know the individual servers it wants to use. The client directly addresses them in its communications using object references. The client and servers are closely coupled—you cannot simply remove a server from the system without directly impacting the clients.

Reliability. When an RMI-IIOP client calls the server, the latter has to be running. If the server crashes or the network crashes, data may be lost and the client cannot perform its intended operation.

Support for multiple senders and receivers. RMI-IIOP limits you to a single client talking to a single server at any given time. There is no built-in functionality for multiple clients to broadcast events to multiple servers.

Messaging is an alternative to remote method invocations (see Figure 7.1). The idea behind messaging is that a *middleman* sits between the client and the server. (As you know, a layer of indirection solves every problem in computer science.) This middleman receives messages from one or more *message producers* and broadcasts those messages to one or more *message consumers*. Because of this middleman, the producer can send a message and then continue processing. He can optionally be notified of the response later when the consumer finishes. This is called *asynchronous* programming

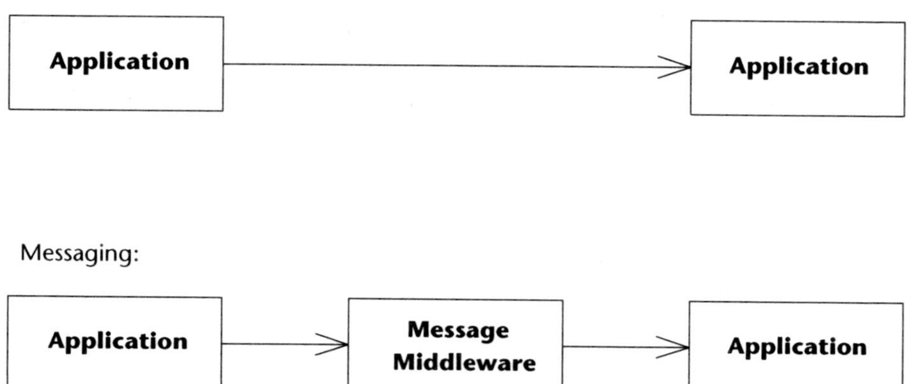

Figure 7.1 Remote method invocations versus messaging.

Messaging addresses the four previous concerns with RMI-IIOP as follows:

Nonblocking request processing. A messaging client does not need to block when executing a request. As an example, when you purchase a book using the Amazon.com's one-click order functionality, you can continue browsing the site without waiting to see if your credit card is authorized. Unless something goes wrong, Amazon.com sends you a confirmation e-mail afterward. This type of fire-and-forget system can be coded using messaging. When the user clicks to buy the book, a message is sent that results in credit card processing later. The user can continue to browse.

Decoupling. In a message-oriented middleware system, the message sender does not need to know the message receivers; it only addresses the messaging system when sending messages. Message senders are thus decoupled from consumers and continue to work regardless of changes to consumers.

Reliability. If your message-oriented middleware supports *guaranteed delivery*, you can send a message and know for sure that it will reach its destination, even if the consumer is temporarily not available. You send the message to the MOM middleman, which routes the message to the consumer when he comes back alive. With RMI-IIOP, this is not possible because there is no middleman. If the server is down, an exception is thrown.

Support for multiple senders and receivers. Most message-oriented middleware products can accept messages from many senders and broadcast them to many receivers. This enables you to have multinary communications.

Note that messaging also has many disadvantages. Performance, for one, can be slower in many circumstances due to the overhead of having the messaging middleman. For a complete comparison of when to (and when not to) use messaging, see Chapter 13.

Message-oriented middleware (MOM) is a term used to refer to any infrastructure that supports messaging. A variety of products are considered to have a MOM-based architecture. Examples include Tibco Rendezvous, IBM WebSphere MQ, BEA Tuxedo/Q, Sun Java System Messaging Server, Microsoft MSMQ, Sonic Software SonicMQ, and FioranoMQ. These products can give you a whole host of value-added services, such as guaranteed message delivery, fault tolerance, load balancing of destinations, subscriber throttling of message consumption, inactive subscribers, support for SOAP over JMS, and much, much more. By allowing the MOM server to address these infrastructure issues, you can focus on the business task at hand.

The Java Message Service (JMS)

Over the years, MOM systems have evolved in a proprietary way. Each product has its own API, which creates vendor lock-in because code is not portable to other messaging systems. It also hurts developers, because they need to relearn each messaging product's proprietary API.

The Java Message Service (JMS) is a messaging standard, designed to eliminate many of the disadvantages that MOM-based products faced over past years. JMS has two parts: an API, for which you write code to send and receive messages, and a Service Provider Interface (SPI) where you plug in JMS providers. A JMS provider knows how to talk to a specific MOM implementation. The JMS promise is that you can learn the JMS API once and reuse your messaging code with different plug-and-play MOM implementations (an idea similar to the other J2EE APIs, such as JNDI or JDBC).

Let's explore the JMS API and see how to write a simple JMS program that publishes messages.

HOW DOES GUARANTEED MESSAGE DELIVERY WORK?

With guaranteed message delivery, the MOM system persists your messages to a file, database, or other store. Your message resides in the persistent store until it's sent to a message consumer, *and* the message consumer acknowledges the consumption of the message. If the acknowledgment of a message is not received in a reasonable amount of time, the message remains on the persistent store and is redelivered.

This feature is beneficial when the message consumer is brought down on a regular basis for maintenance, and lost messages are unacceptable. This is especially true in industries such as financial services, where messages represent securities changing hands.

A variation on the guaranteed message delivery theme is certified message delivery. Certified message delivery not only ensures the delivery of a message from a producer to a consumer but also generates a consumption receipt that is delivered to the message originator, indicating a successful consumption of the message. Certified message delivery is used by producers to better manage communication with consumers.

Another variation of guaranteed message delivery is called store and forward. Store and forward enables a message producer to successfully send a message to an inactive MOM system. The producer transparently spools the message to a local store until the MOM system is reactivated, at which point the message is delivered to the MOM system and forwarded to any available consumers. Guaranteed message delivery without the store-and-forward option requires producers to send messages to active MOM systems, but consumers do not have to be active. Store and forward with guaranteed message delivery allows messages to be sent whether MOM systems or consumers are active or inactive.

Messaging Domains

When you perform messaging, you first need to decide on a messaging style or *domain*. The types of domains are:

Publish/subscribe (pub/sub). Publish/subscribe messaging is analogous to watching television: Many TV stations broadcast their signals, and many people listen to those broadcasts. Thus, with publish/subscribe, you can have *many* message producers talking to *many* message consumers. In this sense, the pub/sub domain is an implementation of a distributed event-driven processing model. Subscribers (listeners) register their interest in a particular event *topic*. Publishers (event sources) create messages (events) that are distributed to all of the subscribers (listeners). Producers aren't hard-coded to know the specific consumers interested in receiving its messages; rather, the MOM system maintains the subscriber list.

Point-to-point (PTP). Point-to-point messaging is analogous to placing an order in an online store: Some person will pick up your order, carry it out, and then delete it. Thus, with point-to-point, you can have only a single consumer for *each* message. Multiple consumers can grab messages off the queue, but any given message is consumed exactly once. In this sense, point-to-point is a special case of publish/subscribe. Multiple producers can send messages to the queue, but each message is delivered only to a single consumer. The way this works is that publishers send messages directly to the consumer or to a centralized *queue*. Messages are typically distributed off the queue in a first in, first out (FIFO) order, but this isn't ensured.

Figure 7.2 shows the difference between publish/subscribe and point-to-point.

NOTE **Another domain called request/reply is less broadly used than the others. The request/reply domain is analogous to RMI-IIOP. It requires any producer that generates a message to receive a reply message from the consumer at some later point in time. Typically, most MOM architectures implement a request/reply paradigm asynchronously using the technologies supplied in the point-to-point and publish/subscribe domains.**

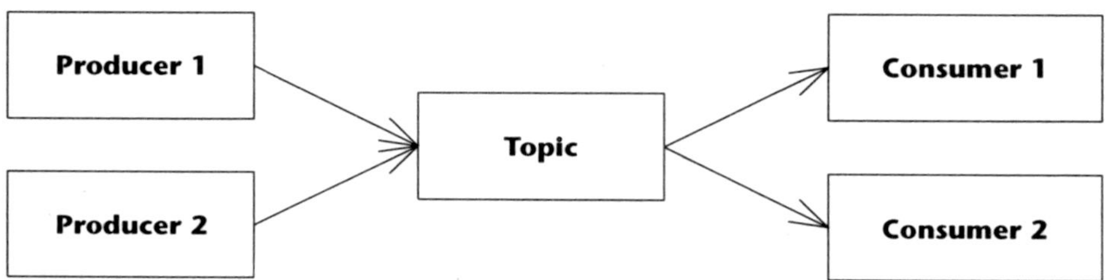

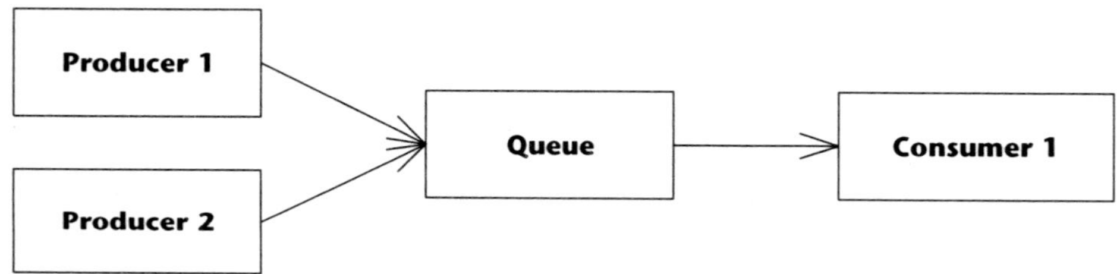

Figure 7.2 Publish/subscribe versus point-to-point.

The JMS API

Using the JMS API is more involved than RMI-IIOP: You need to become familiar with a few different interfaces to get going. Low-level topology issues, such as networking protocol, message format and structure, and server location, are mostly abstracted from the developer.

The JMS programming model is shown in Figure 7.3. It is explained in the list that follows:

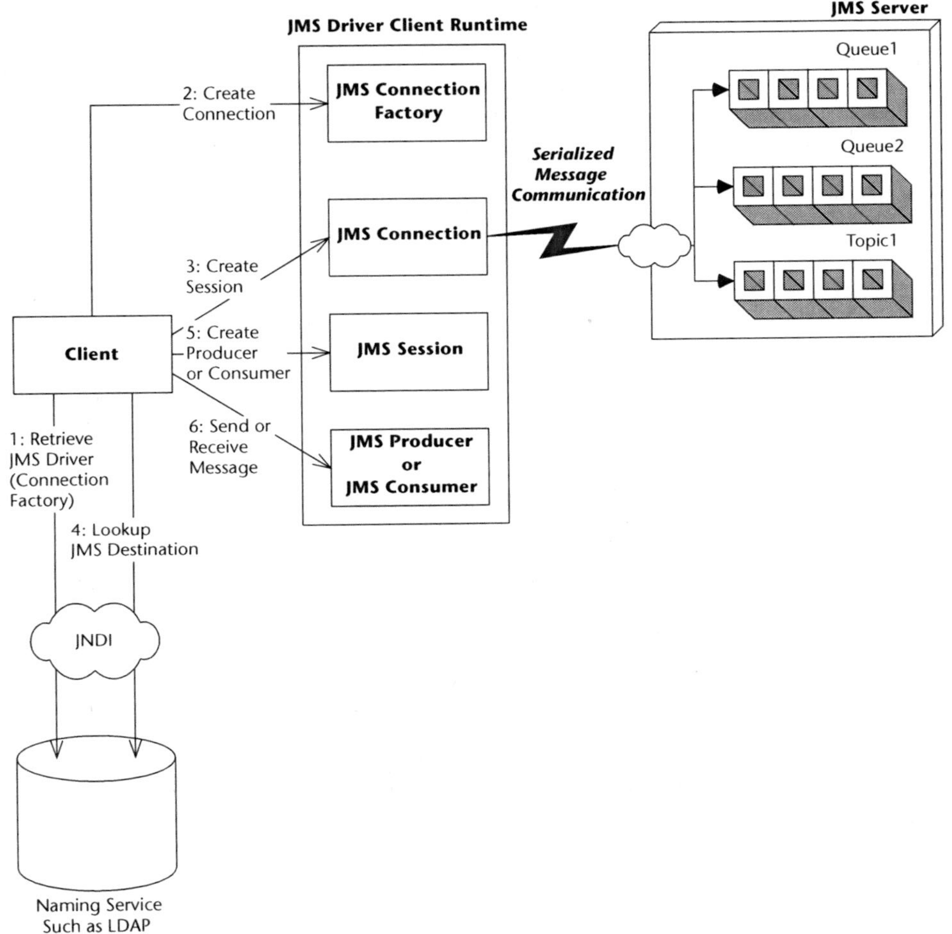

Figure 7.3 Client view of a JMS system.

1. **Locate the JMS Provider's** `ConnectionFactory` **instance.** You first need to get access to the JMS provider of the particular MOM product you're using. For this, you need to establish a connection using a `ConnectionFactory` instance. You can get hold of `ConnectionFactory` by *looking it up* in JNDI. An administrator will typically create and configure the `ConnectionFactory` for the JMS client's use.

2. **Create a JMS connection.** A JMS `Connection` is an active connection to the JMS provider, managing the low-level network communications (similar to a JDBC connection). You use the `ConnectionFactory` to get a `Connection`. If you're in a large deployment, this connection might be load balanced across a group of machines.

3. **Create a JMS session.** A JMS `Session` is a helper object that you use when sending and receiving messages. It serves as a factory for message consumers and producers, and also enables you to encapsulate your messages in transactions. You use the `Connection` to get a `Session`.

4. **Locate the JMS destination.** A JMS `Destination` is the channel to which you're sending or from which you're receiving messages. Locating the right destination is analogous to tuning into the right channel when watching television or answering the correct phone, so that you get the messages you desire. Your deployer typically sets up the destination in advance by using your JMS provider's tools, so that the destination is permanently set up. Your code looks up that destination using JNDI. This enables your programs to use the destination over and over again at runtime.

5. **Create a JMS producer or a JMS consumer.** If you want to send messages, you need to call a JMS object to pass it your messages. This object is called producer. To receive messages, you call a JMS object and ask it for a message. This object is called the `Consumer` object. You use the `Session` and `Destination` to get ahold of a producer or a consumer object.

6. **Send or receive your message.** If you're producing, you first need to put your message together. There are many different types of messages, such as text, bytes, streams, objects, and maps. After you instantiate your message, you send it using the `Producer` object. If, on the other hand, you're receiving messages, you first receive a message using the `Consumer` object, and then crack it open (depending on the message type) and see what is in it.

Everything we just learned applies to both publish/subscribe and point-to-point messaging. The words in `monofont` in the preceding process represent actual JMS interface names. There are two different flavors of those interfaces, and the flavor you use depends on if you're using publish/subscribe or point-to-point. See Table 7.1 for a list.

NOTE As you can see from Table 7.1, point-to-point has two types of message consumers: a receiver and a browser. What do you think these are for? And why does publish/subscribe have only one type of consumer?

Table 7.1 The Two Flavors of JMS Interfaces

PARENT INTERFACE	POINT-TO-POINT	PUB/SUB
ConnectionFactory	QueueConnection Factory	TopicConnection Factory
Connection	QueueConnection	TopicConnection
Destination	Queue	Topic
Session	QueueSession	TopicSession
MessageProducer	QueueSender	TopicPublisher
MessageConsumer	QueueReceiver, QueueBrowser	TopicSubscriber

As an example, the code for a client application that publishes a `TextMessage` to a topic using publish/subscribe is provided in Source 7.1.

```
package examples.messaging;

import javax.jms.*;
import javax.naming.InitialContext;

public class LogClient {

    public static void main(String[] args) throws Exception {
        // Initialize JNDI
        InitialContext ctx = new InitialContext(System.getProperties());

        // 1: Lookup connection factory
        TopicConnectionFactory factory =
            (TopicConnectionFactory) ctx.lookup
                ("jms/TopicConnectionFactory");

        // 2: Use connection factory to create JMS connection
        TopicConnection connection = factory.createTopicConnection();

        // 3: Use connection to create a session
        TopicSession session =
            connection.createTopicSession
                (false,Session.AUTO_ACKNOWLEDGE);

        // 4: Lookup destination
        Topic topic = (Topic)ctx.lookup("jms/Topic");

        // 5: Create a message publisher
```

Source 7.1 TopicClient.java. *(continued)*

```
        TopicPublisher publisher = session.createPublisher(topic);

        // 6: Create and publish a message
        TextMessage msg = session.createTextMessage();
        msg.setText("This is a test message.");
        publisher.send(msg);

        // finish
        publisher.close();
        System.out.println("Message published. Please check application
server's console to see the response from MDB.");
    }
}
```

Source 7.1 *(continued)*

Most of Source 7.1 is self-explanatory. Here are the answers to a few questions you might have:

- The parameters to `InitialContext` should be your JNDI provider information. If your JMS provider is integrated into your EJB server, the JNDI parameters should be the same as those you use when you look up an EJB. You specify this via the command line using the `-D` switch to the `java` runtime, or in a `jndi.properties` file. See the book's accompanying source code for example scripts.
- Our JNDI name for the `TopicConnectionFactory` is `jms/TopicConnectionFactory`, but it could be anything—it depends on your container's policy and also where you choose to place it using your container's tools.
- When we create a `Session`, we pass two parameters: `false`, which indicates that we don't want to use transactions (see Chapter 10 for more on transactions), and `Session.AUTO_ACKNOWLEDGE`, which indicates how we should acknowledge messages that we receive. Since our code is sending (not receiving) messages, this parameter doesn't matter. If you're curious about how message acknowledgment works, see Table 7.2 later in this chapter.

Note that this example does not illustrate point-to-point. The point-to-point code is basically the same, except we use the point-to-point interfaces listed in Table 7.1. We'll leave the point-to-point example as an exercise for you.

Note, too, that this example does not demonstrate any consumption logic. Although message consumption is an important concept, it's not relevant to our discussion, because message-driven beans effectively act as our message consumers.

SINGLE-THREADED VERSUS MULTITHREADED BEANS

One great benefit of EJB is that you don't need to write thread-safe code. You design your enterprise beans as single-threaded components and never need to worry about thread synchronization when concurrent clients access your component. In order to service concurrent client requests, your EJB container automatically instantiates multiple instances of your component.

The container's thread services can be both a benefit and a restriction. The benefit is that you don't need to worry about race conditions or deadlock in your application code. The restriction is that some problems lend themselves well to multithreaded programming, and that class of problems cannot be easily solved in an EJB environment.

So why doesn't the EJB specification allow for multithreaded beans? EJB is intended to relieve the component developers' worry about threads or thread synchronization. The EJB container handles those issues for you by load balancing client requests to multiple instances of a single-threaded component. An EJB server provides a highly scalable environment for single-threaded components.

If the EJB specification allowed for beans to control threads, a Pandora's box of problems would result. For example, an EJB container would have a *very* hard time controlling transactions if beans were randomly starting and stopping threads, especially because transaction information is often associated with a thread.

The bottom line is that EJB was not meant to be a Swiss army knife, solving every problem in existence. It was designed to assist with server-side *business problems*, which are largely single-threaded. For applications that absolutely must be multithreaded, EJB may not be the correct choice of distributed object architectures.

You should now know enough about JMS to be productive with message-driven beans. If you want to learn more about JMS, a free JMS tutorial is included in the Java EE tutorial available at `http://java.sun.com/j2ee/1.4/docs/tutorial/doc`. Rather than repeating this information, let's cover some more interesting topics—JMS-EJB integration, advanced message-driven bean topics, and gotchas.

Integrating JMS with EJB

JMS-EJB integration is a compelling idea. It allows EJB components to benefit from the value proposition of messaging, such as nonblocking clients and multinary communications.

To understand the motivations behind introducing another type of bean to consume messages in an EJB application, let us contemplate for a moment what other approaches we could have taken and whether they would have worked:

Using a Java object that receives JMS messages to call EJB components. Rather than coming up with a whole new type of bean, the Java community could have promoted the idea of a Java object that can receive messages and in turn call the appropriate EJB components, such as session beans and entity beans. The problems with this approach are:

- You'd need to write special code to register yourself as a listener for JMS messages. This is a decent amount of code (as we demonstrated previously).
- To increase the throughput of message consumption, you would have to write the multithreading logic such that you can listen to the messages in multiple threads. However, writing multithreaded applications is not a trivial task for a business application developer.
- Your Java object would need some way of starting up, since it wrapped your other EJB components. If the class ran within the container, you would need to use an EJB server-specific *startup class* to activate your Java object when the EJB server came up. This is not portable because the EJB specification does not define a standard way of activating a given logic.
- As a plain Java object, our JMS message listener wouldn't receive any services from an EJB container, such as automatic life-cycle management, clustering, pooling, and transactions. You would need to hard-code this yourself, which is difficult and error-prone.
- You would need to hard-code the JMS destination name in your Java object, which hurts reusability, or get the destination information from disk (such as with property files), which requires extra effort.

Reuse an existing type of EJB component somehow to receive JMS messages. Another option could have been to shoehorn session beans or entity beans into receiving JMS messages. Problems with this approach include:

- **Threading.** If a message arrives for a bean while it's processing other requests, how can it take that message, given that EJB does not allow components to be multithreaded?
- **Life-cycle management.** If a JMS message arrives and there are no beans, how does the container know to create a bean?

PLUGGABLE MESSAGE PROVIDERS

A message-driven bean can be defined to consume messages of a given messaging type in accordance with the message listener interface it employs, that is, JMS-based message-driven beans will implement the `javax.jms.MessageListener` interface and so on. In EJB 2.0, message-driven beans supported consumption of JMS messages only. You could not receive non-JMS messages, such as asynchronous enterprise information system–specific message. This has changed in the EJB 2.1 standard so that the message-driven bean can employ different listener interfaces to consume different message types in addition to JMS.

This is achieved with the help of Java EE Connector Architecture 1.5. The connector architecture defines message inflow contracts to enable resource adapters to asynchronously deliver messages to message endpoints residing in the application server independent of the specific messaging type or messaging semantics. So in practice, we can write resource adapters that act as message providers. Resource adapters are standard Java EE components and hence, can be plugged into any Java EE–compliant application server. As a result, resource adapters capable of delivering messages to message endpoints, such as message-driven beans, can be plugged into any Java EE–compliant application server as well. This is widely known as message provider pluggability.

For example, imagine a scenario where you want your EJB application to receive EbXML messages. Using JAX-RPC is not a choice here since it supports only SOAP 1.1 messages. Besides, JAX-RPC does not support asynchronous messaging. In this case, connector architecture–based message providers/resource adapters can be extremely handy. We can write an EbXML message provider using the connector architecture such that it provides a specific messaging listener interface, say, `com.xyz.messaging.EbXMLMessageListener`, which can be implemented by message-driven beans so as to enable their receiving EbXML messages.

This is a powerful concept—any enterprise information system can effectively send any type of messages to a message-driven bean endpoint via Java EE connector architecture-based resource adapters. All message providers from EJB 2.1 onwards, regardless of whether they consume JMS messages or not, are resource adapters based on Java EE Connector Architecture 1.5. In Chapter 15 we discuss Java EE connector architecture and provide guidance toward developing resource adapters that consume messages.

What Is a Message-Driven Bean?

A *message-driven bean* is a special EJB component that can receive JMS messages as well as other types of messages. See the sidebar "Pluggable Message Providers" to find out more about how message-driven beans can be used to consume messages other than JMS. A message-driven bean is invoked by the container upon arrival of a message at the destination or endpoint that is serviced by the message-driven bean.

A message-driven bean is decoupled from any clients that send messages to it. *A client cannot access a message-driven bean through a business interface.* In fact, a client cannot identify a message-driven bean and directly interact with it at all! The only way that clients can interact with message-driven beans is through the messaging system. You will have to use message provider–specific API, such as JMS, to send messages from clients, which in turn would be received by the message-driven beans (see Figure 7.4).

The following are some major characteristics of message-driven beans.

- **A message-driven bean does not have a remote or local business interface.** You do not call message-driven beans using an object-oriented remote method invocation interface. In fact, you don't call them at all—the container does. Message-driven beans process messages that can come from any messaging client, such as an MQSeries client, an MSMQ client, a message provider/resource adapter, or a Java EE client using the JMS API. Message-driven beans, along with appropriate message providers, can thus consume any valid message.

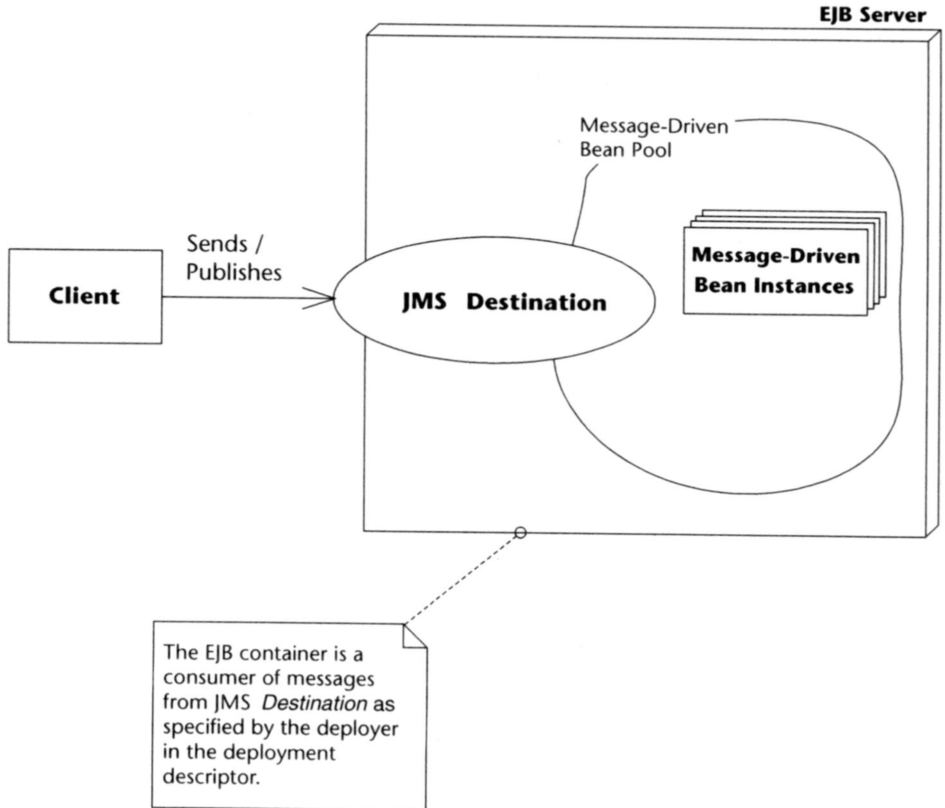

Figure 7.4 A client sending messages to JMS message-driven beans.

- **Message-driven beans support generic listener methods for message delivery.** Message-driven beans are merely receiving messages from a destination or a resource adapter and do not know anything about what's inside the messages. The listener interface implemented by message-driven beans typically has a method (or methods) called by an EJB container upon arrival of a message, or by the resource adapter (via application server). The JMS message listener interface, `javax.jms.MessageListener` has only one method, called `onMessage()`. This method accepts a JMS `Message`, which could represent anything—a `BytesMessage`, `ObjectMessage`, `TextMessage`, `StreamMessage`, or `MapMessage`. In a typical implementation of `onMessage()`, the message is cracked open at runtime and its contents are examined, perhaps with the help of a bunch of `if` statements. In formal terms, you don't get compile-time type-checking of messages that are consumed; rather, you need to use the `instanceof` operator to determine the exact type of a consumed message at runtime. This also means that you need to be careful to make sure that the message you receive is intended for you. In comparison, session or entity beans can support strongly typed business methods. Type checking can be performed at compile time to ensure that clients are properly using a given interface.
- **Message-driven bean listener method(s) generally do not have return values.** Although the EJB specification does not restrict a message-driven bean listener method from returning a value to the client, certain messaging types might not be suitable for this. For example, consider the listener interface of a messaging type that supports asynchronous messaging, such as JMS. In this case, due to the asynchronous interaction between message producers and consumers, the message producers don't wait for your message-driven bean to respond. As a result, it doesn't make sense for the `onMessage()` listener method on the `javax.jms.MessageListener` interface to return a value. The good news is that using several design patterns, it is possible to send a response to an asynchronous message producer. We discuss this later in this chapter.
- **Message-driven beans might not send exceptions back to clients.** Although EJB does not restrict message-driven bean listener interface methods from throwing application exceptions, certain messaging types might not be able to throw these exceptions to the clients. Again consider the example of a listener interface of a messaging type that supports asynchronous messaging, such as JMS. In this case, message producers won't wait for your message-driven bean to send a response because the interaction is asynchronous. Therefore clients can't receive any exceptions. All message listener interfaces, however, can generate

system exceptions regardless of the messaging semantics (synchronous versus asynchronous) because the container (rather than the client) handles system exceptions. The only exception to this rule is the `java.rmi.RemoteException`, which message-driven beans are explicitly forbidden to throw.

- **Message-driven beans are stateless.** Message-driven beans hold no conversational state and have no client-visible identity. In this sense, they are similar to stateless session beans because the container can similarly treat each message-driven bean instance as equivalent to all other instances. Thus, multiple instances of the bean can process multiple messages from a JMS destination or a resource adapter concurrently.
- **Message-driven beans are single-threaded.** A single message-driven bean can process only one message at a time. The container is responsible for serializing messages to a single message-driven bean, so there is no need for synchronization code in the bean class. It is the container's responsibility to provide concurrent message consumption by pooling multiple message-driven bean instances, but the container is not required to deliver messages to multiple concurrent beans in any specific order. Hence, applications should not rely on message order.

JMS MESSAGE-DRIVEN BEANS AND DURABLE-NONDURABLE SUBSCRIBERS

A *durable* subscription to a topic means that a JMS subscriber receives all messages, even if the subscriber is inactive. If a message is sent to a topic that has an inactive durable subscriber, the message is persisted and delivered when the durable subscriber is once again active. A *nondurable* subscription to a topic means the subscriber receives only messages that are published while the subscriber is active. Any messages delivered while the subscriber is inactive are lost. Since a JMS message-driven bean is essentially a consumer, it can register itself as a durable or nondurable subscriber to messages published to a topic. Durability allows persistent messages to be sent to a topic even though the application server hosting the JMS message-driven bean consumer has crashed. The messages will persist until the crashed application server restarts and the durable subscriber message-driven bean container positively acknowledges consumption of all of the stored messages.

Developing Message-Driven Beans

Let's now take a look at what's involved in developing message-driven beans. The subsequent sections focus on JMS message-driven beans. To a great extent, the programming model for developing other types of message-driven beans will be quite similar to that for JMS message-driven beans.

The Semantics

JMS message-driven beans are classes that implement two interfaces: `javax.jms.MessageListener` and, optionally, `javax.ejb.MessageDrivenBean`. In previous versions of the EJB spec, implementing the `MessageDrivenBean` interface was mandatory, but this requirement was relaxed in EJB 3.0. Additionally, every JMS message-driven bean implementation class must provide a no-arg constructor. Here is what the `javax.jms.MessageListener` interface looks like:

```
public interface javax.jms.MessageListener {

    public void onMessage(Message message);

}
```

And this is what the `javax.ejb.MessageDrivenBean` interface looks like:

```
public interface javax.ejb.MessageDrivenBean
 extends javax.ejb.EnterpriseBean {

 public void ejbRemove()
  throws EJBException;

 public void setMessageDrivenContext(MessageDrivenContext ctx)
  throws EJBException;
}
```

The two methods in this interface have the following semantics:

- `setMessageDrivenContext()`. The container will call this method after creating the bean instance and pass a reference to a `MessageDrivenContext` object to the bean. This interface, in turn, provides methods that allow the bean to control transactional behavior and to access the Timer Service, which we explain in Chapter 12. A message-driven bean can also acquire a reference to the `MessageDrivenContext` using dependency injection. The bean would only need to declare a dependency on the `MessageDrivenContext` by using the `@Resource` annotation.

- `ejbRemove()`. In EJB 2.1, this was a mandatory life-cycle callback method that all message-driven beans had to implement. In EJB 3.0, life-cycle callbacks are optional and can be declared using the `@PostConstruct` and `@PreDestroy` annotations. If the `ejbRemove()` method is present in a message-driven bean class, it is treated as the `@PreDestroy` callback, and no other method may be annotated with this annotation.

Given this simple description, you can see that developing JMS message-driven beans is significantly less complicated than developing session or entity beans. The number of methods that have to be implemented is less than with session or entity beans.

The life cycle of a message-driven bean is also very straightforward. Figure 7.5 illustrates the life cycle of a message-driven bean.

A message-driven bean is either in the *does not exist* state or in the *pooled* state. When a container decides to add another instance to its pool, it creates a new instance and performs any required dependency injection, such as passing its `MessageDrivenContext` object. If any `@PostConstruct` life-cycle callbacks are declared, these will then be called. Depending on its configuration parameters, the application server will likely create an initial pool of beans at startup time and then increase the size of the pool as the quantity of messages increases. A container will remove an instance from the pool and destroy it at system shutdown or when the container decides it needs to decrease the size of the pool to conserve memory. If the container decides to take an instance out of the bean pool, it calls the bean's `@PreDestroy()` method.

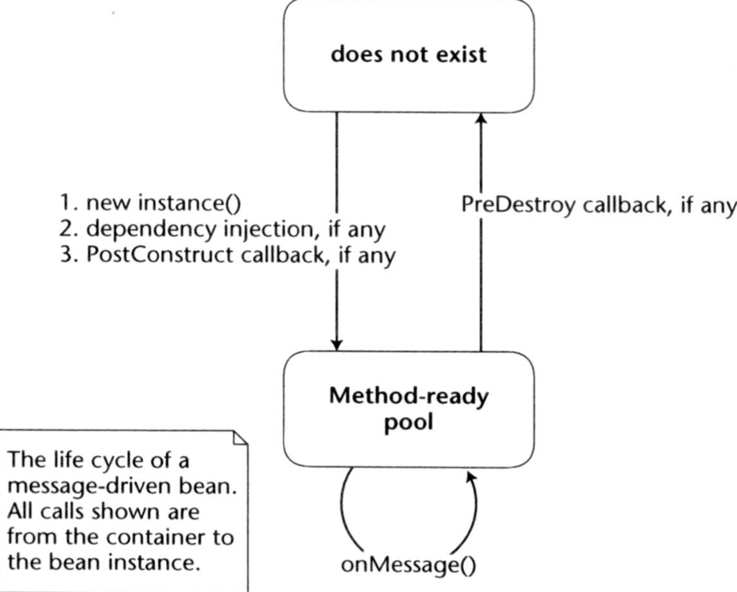

Figure 7.5 Life cycle of a message-driven bean.

A Simple Example

Let's apply our knowledge and construct a simple bean that logs text messages to the screen. In the future, you could generalize this bean and make it into a generic logging facility, where you have different log levels, depending on the urgency of the log.

This is a trivial example and not demonstrative of real-world systems. It is, however, a good template to use when writing your own beans. If you want to see a real-world message-driven bean in action that uses other EJB components, see the application example in Chapter 18, along with the book's accompanying source code. As we will see when writing this bean, the rules for writing JMS message-driven beans are simple.

The Bean Implementation Class

Since message-driven beans do not have business interfaces associated with them, we can completely skip designing a public interface to our bean. We can get right to the heart of development of this bean and write the implementation class. The code for the implementation class is shown in Source 7.2.

```
package examples.messaging;

import javax.jms.*;
import javax.ejb.*;
import javax.annotation.*;

@MessageDriven(activationConfig = {
        @ActivationConfigProperty(propertyName = "destinationType",
                propertyValue = "javax.jms.Topic")
        })
public class LogBean implements MessageListener {

    public LogBean() {
        System.out.println("LogBean created");
    }

    public void onMessage(Message msg) {
        if (msg instanceof TextMessage) {
            TextMessage tm = (TextMessage) msg;
            try {
                String text = tm.getText();
                System.out.println("Received new message : " + text);
            } catch (JMSException e) {
                e.printStackTrace();
            }
        }
```

Source 7.2 LogBean.java. *(continued)*

```
    }

    @PreDestroy
    public void remove() {
        System.out.println("LogBean destroyed.");
    }
}
```

Source 7.2 *(continued)*

This is the most basic message-driven bean. Notice the following:

- Our bean is declared as a message-driven bean with the `@MessageDriven` annotation.
- The bean is not coded for a specific queue or topic. Rather, it is associated with a specific destination at deployment time. The activation config property `"destinationType"` of the `@MessageDriven` annotation (or alternatively, the deployment descriptor) can be used to determine whether a topic or a queue is consumed. This is specified by setting the property value to either `"javax.jms.Queue"` or `"javax.jms.Topic"`.
- Our bean implements the `javax.jms.MessageListener` interface that provides the methods necessary for JMS message consumption.
- The bean is stateless and does not contain any client-specific state that spans messages. Therefore each bean is identical and has an identical initialization method—a simple constructor that takes no arguments.
- The `onMessage()` method receives a message and casts it to type `TextMessage`. `TextMessage` is a particular type of JMS message that has methods for getting and setting the text as the body of the message. After down-casting the input parameter, the method prints out the content of the message, if any exists.
- When this bean is being destroyed, there is nothing to clean up so we have a very simple `@PreDestroy` method.

NOTE A message-driven bean can register itself with the EJB Timer Service for time-based notifications by implementing the `javax.ejb.TimedObject` **interface apart from the message listener interface, or by declaring a timeout callback method with the** `@Timeout` **annotation. The container will invoke the bean instance's** `ejbTimeout()` **method or the timeout callback upon timer expiration.**

The Deployment Descriptor

As an alternative to annotating your message-driven bean, a deployment descriptor file can be packaged along with the bean class. Message-driven beans have only a couple of deployment descriptor tags applicable to them. The portion of the deployment descriptor relevant to our simple JMS message-driven bean is shown in Source 7.3.

```
<?xml version="1.0" encoding="UTF-8" ?>
<ejb-jar xmlns="http://java.sun.com/xml/ns/javaee"
xmlns:xsi="http://www.w3.org/2001/XMLSchema-instance" version="3.0"
xsi:schemaLocation="http://java.sun.com/xml/ns/javaee
http://java.sun.com/xml/ns/javaee/ejb-jar_3_0.xsd">
    <enterprise-beans>
        <!--
          For each message-driven bean that is located in an
          ejb-jar file, you have to define a <message-driven> entry
          in the deployment descriptor.
        -->
        <message-driven>
            <!-- The nickname for the bean could be used later in DD -->
            <ejb-name>LogBeanDD</ejb-name>

            <!-- The fully qualified package name of the bean class -->
            <ejb-class>examples.messaging.dd.LogBean</ejb-class>
            <messaging-type>javax.jms.MessageListener</messaging-type>

            <!-- The type of transaction supported (see Chapter 10) -->
            <transaction-type>Bean</transaction-type>

            <!-- Whether I'm listening to a topic or a queue -->
            <message-destination-type>javax.jms.Topic
            </message-destination-type>
            <!-- further details -->
            <activation-config>
              <activation-config-property>
                <activation-config-property-name>
                  destinationType
                </activation-config-property-name>
                <activation-config-property-value>
                  javax.jms.Topic
                </activation-config-property-value>
              </activation-config-property>
            </activation-config>
        </message-driven>
    </enterprise-beans>
</ejb-jar>
```

Source 7.3 ejb-jar.xml for the simple bean.

More Metadata: Activation Configuration Properties

Table 7.2 contains definitions for additional metadata unique to JMS message-driven beans. These properties can be provided either in the deployment descriptor or in the *activationConfig* part of the *@MessageDriven* annotation. Just glance over it now—it's not important to fully understand them if you're just starting to learn message-driven beans. See Appendix C for a complete deployment descriptor reference.

NOTE **EJB 2.1 introduced new *<activation-config-property>* elements in the deployment descriptors, specifically to configure message-driven beans. These elements are meant to represent operational information pertaining to message-driven beans, JMS or others, in the deployment descriptors. In the case of JMS message-driven beans, these elements are used to specify their specific operational requirements, such as type of subscription to topics, type of destination, and so on.**

As you can see, you can either use annotations or develop the corresponding deployment descriptor for JMS message-driven beans. In addition to the characteristics that are definable for all message-driven beans, application server vendors can provide value-added extensions in an application server–specific deployment descriptor. For example, an application server vendor may provide a deployment descriptor parameter that defines the maximum size of the message-driven bean pool or another parameter that defines its initial size.

A question that you may be asking now is, "Exactly how does the application server bind a JMS message-driven bean container to a specific topic or queue?" If you look closely at the deployment descriptor provided in Source 7.3, the `<message-destination-type>` tag specifies whether the bean should consume queue or topic messages; however, it never indicates which topic or queue the JMS message-driven bean container should bind to. This is done purposely to make JMS message-driven beans portable across application servers. Since the names of actual topics and queues deployed into a JMS server are application server–specific, the mapping of a bean's container to a specific JMS server destination has to be done in an application server–specific deployment descriptor. Most EJB vendors are expected to have a custom deployment descriptor that binds the bean to a specific destination.

Table 7.2 Optional Subelements for the <message-driven> Tag or the @MessageDriven Annotation

FUNCTIONALITY	DESCRIPTION	EXAMPLE

Destination type	The destination type setting advises the deployer as to whether a JMS message-driven bean will consume messages from a queue or a topic. The bean developer should provide this setting in the deployment descriptor even though deployer can override it.	`@ActivationConfigProperty( propertyName = "destinationType", propertyValue = "javax.jms.Topic")`
		
		`<activation-config-property>`
		
		`<activation-config-property-name>`
		`destinationType`
		`</activation-config-property-name>`
		`<activation-config-property-value>`
		`javax.jms.Topic`
		`</activation-config-property-value>`
		
		`</activation-config-property>`

(continued)

Table 7.2 *(continued)*

FUNCTIONALITY	DESCRIPTION	EXAMPLE
Message selector	A message selector filters, or limits, which messages are sent to your bean. Message selectors are very powerful; they increase overall performance by reducing the number of messages delivered to clients that have no interest in the message. To use message selectors, first your JMS client sets up header fields on JMS messages using the JMS API. For example, the JMS client might call message .setStringProperty("logLevel", "severe") before sending the message. When the JMS destination receives the message, the container applies the message selector criteria defined in the deployment descriptor. Only messages with headers that match the selector are delivered.	@ActivationConfigProperty(propertyName="messageSelector", propertyValue="JMSType = 'log' AND logLevel='severe' ") <activation-config-property> <activation-config-property-name> messageSelector </activation-config-property-name> <activation-config-property-value> JMSType='log' AND logLevel='severe' </activation-config-property-value> </activation-config-property> Note: You can use the more complicated SQL-like functionality here as well, such as arithmetic, logical operators (AND/OR/NOT), and more. If you use greater than (>) or less than (<) signs then you need to wrap this in a CDATA section, to avoid XML parsing confusion. See the JMS specification at http://java.sun.com/products/jms/docs.html for complete rules for message selector syntax, which is a subset of the SQL 92 standard.

Table 7.2 *(continued)*

FUNCTIONALITY	DESCRIPTION	EXAMPLE
Message acknowledgment	If you let the container handle transactions (called *container-managed transactions* described in Chapter 10), then the container delivers the message to you in a transaction. There is no need for message acknowledgment then, because if the transaction rolls back, the message is automatically put back on the queue. If you program your own transactions (called *bean-managed transactions*), the transaction occurs within your bean, and begins and ends after the message has been delivered to your bean; thus, the consumption of the message occurs outside the transaction. Therefore, if you are using bean-managed transactions, you need to tell the container to *acknowledge* messages. The *Auto-acknowledge* setting forces the container to acknowledge a message when the JMS message-driven bean's `onMessage()` method has successfully returned. The `Dups-ok-acknowledge` setting allows the container to acknowledge a message when it feels like doing so and when it finds the required resources and processing time. Since it may not acknowledge the messages fast enough, you run the risk of the JMS destination sending you a duplicate message. You should use this only if you can tolerate duplicate messages.	@ActivationConfigProperty(propertyName="acknowledgeMode", propertyValue="Auto-acknowledge") <activation-config-property> <activation-config-property-name> acknowledgeMode </activation-config-property-name> <activation-config-property-value> Auto-acknowledge </activation-config-property-value> </activation-config-property>

(continued)

Table 7.2 *(continued)*

FUNCTIONALITY	DESCRIPTION	EXAMPLE

Subscription durability	JMS message-driven beans that consume messages from topics can be either of durable type or nondurable type. We discuss durable and nondurable subscriptions in the sidebar, *"JMS Message-Driven Beans and Durable-Nondurable Subscriptions."*	`@ActivationConfigProperty(`
		` propertyName="subscriptionDurability ",`
		` propertyValue="NonDurable")`
		`<activation-config-property>`
		` <activation-config-property-name>`
		`  subscriptionDurability`
		` </activation-config-property-name>`
		` <activation-config-property-value>`
		`  NonDurable`
		` </activation-config-property-value>`
		`</activation-config-property>`

The Client Program

The client application for the simple JMS message-driven bean example is the JMS client we developed earlier in this chapter in Source 7.1. This shows you the power of message-driven beans—our client is solely a JMS client, and the application is never the wiser that a JMS message-driven bean is consuming the messages.

If you'd like to try this example yourself, see the book's accompanying source code for compilation and deployment scripts.

Advanced Concepts

So far, we have discussed the mechanics of developing JMS message-driven beans. Now let's take a closer look at the support that containers can give for JMS message-driven beans. We'll see how they might integrate with transactions, provide advanced JMS features, and behave in a clustered environment.

Transactions

JMS message-driven beans do not run in the same transaction as the producer who sends the message, because there are typically two transactions associated with every durable JMS message (one transaction for the producer to put the message on the queue and another transaction for the JMS message-driven bean to get the message off the queue). It is theoretically impossible for the JMS message-driven bean to participate in the same transaction (and hence the same unit of work) as the producer, because until the producer commits the transaction, the message wouldn't even appear on the queue!

For a complete discussion of transactions and how they apply to JMS message-driven beans, see Chapter 10.

Security

JMS message-driven beans do not receive the security identity of the producer who sends the message, because there is no standard way to stick security information into a JMS message. Therefore you cannot perform EJB security operations (described in Chapter 11) with JMS message-driven beans.

Load Balancing

Clustering message-driven beans is quite different than clustering session or entity beans (see Chapter 16). With session and entity beans, your requests are *load balanced* across a group of containers. The load-balancing algorithm *guesses* which server is the least burdened server and pushes requests out to that server. It's guessing because the client's RMI-IIOP runtime can never know for sure which server is the least burdened, because all load-balancing algorithms are approximation algorithms based on imperfect historical data. This is called a *push model* because we are pushing requests out to the server, and the server has no say about which requests it receives.

With JMS message-driven beans, producers put messages onto a destination. The messages reside in the destination until a consumer takes the messages off of the destination, or (if the messages are nondurable) the server hosting the destination crashes. This is a *pull model*, since the message resides on the destination until a consumer asks for it. The containers contend (fight) to get the next available message on the destination.

Thus, JMS message-driven beans feature an *ideal* load-balancing paradigm and distribute the load more smoothly than session or entity beans do. The server that is the least burdened and asks for a message gets the message. The trade-off for this optimal load balancing is that messaging has extra overhead because a destination "middleman" sits between the client and the server.

Duplicate Consumption in a Cluster

Since JMS topics use the publish/subscribe model, it's possible that a message sent to a JMS topic will be delivered to more than one consumer. Many containers will create a pool of many message-driven bean instances to process multiple messages concurrently, so some concern can arise around message-driven bean containers that subscribe to JMS topics.

In particular, if a JMS message-driven bean container has pooled five instances of its message-driven bean type and is subscribed to the `DogTopic`, how many consumers will consume a message sent to the `DogTopic` topic? Will the message be consumed by each JMS message-driven bean instance in the container or just once by a single JMS message-driven bean? The answer is simple: A container that subscribes to a topic consumes any given message only once. This means that for the five instances that the container created to concurrently process messages, only one of the instances will receive any particular message, freeing up the other instances to process other messages that have been sent to the `DogTopic`.

Be careful, though. *Each* container that binds to a particular topic will consume a JMS message sent to that topic. The JMS subsystem will treat each JMS message-driven bean container as a separate subscriber to the message. This means that if the same JMS message-driven bean is deployed to many containers in a cluster, then *each* deployment of the JMS message-driven bean will consume a message from the topic it subscribes to. If this is not the behavior you want, and you need to consume messages exactly once, you should consider deploying a queue instead of a topic.

For JMS message-driven beans that bind to a queue, the JMS server will deliver any message on the queue to only one consumer. Each container registers as a consumer to the queue, and the JMS server load balances messages to consumers based on availability. JMS message-driven beans that bind to queues that are deployed in a cluster are ideal for scalable processing of messages. For example, if you have two servers in your cluster and 50 messages on a queue, each server will consume on average 25 messages—as opposed to a single server responsible for consuming 50 messages.

JMS message-driven beans in a cluster are shown in Figure 7.6. Notice that many JMS message-driven beans process the same JMS message from Topic #1. Also notice that only a single bean processes any given message from Queue #1.

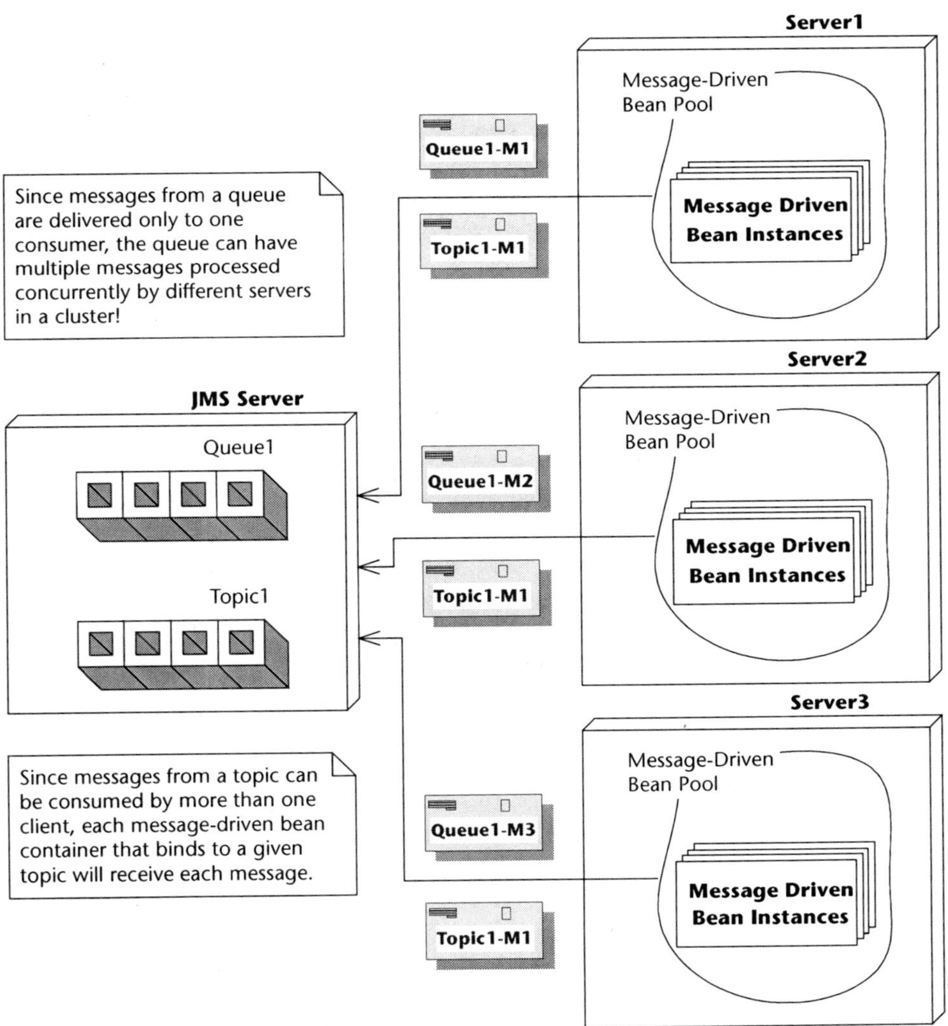

Figure 7.6 JMS message-driven beans in a cluster.

JMS Message-Driven Bean Gotchas

Although developing JMS message-driven beans is a straightforward process, many dark corners and caveats can be encountered unknowingly. In this section, we uncover some of these JMS message-driven demons and suggest solutions to help speed you on your way to successful implementation.

Message Ordering

A JMS server does not guarantee delivery of messages to a pool of JMS message-driven beans in any particular order. The container likely attempts to deliver messages in an order that doesn't impact the concurrency of message processing, but there is no guarantee as to the order that the beans actually process the message. Therefore JMS message-driven beans should be prepared to process messages that are not in sequence. For example, a message adding a second hamburger to a fast food order might be processed before the message indicating that a new fast food order with a hamburger should be created. Bean developers must take these scenarios into account and handle them appropriately.

Missed *@PreDestroy* Calls

As with session and entity beans, you are not guaranteed that the container will call your `@PreDestroy` life-cycle callback method when your bean is destroyed. In particular, if there is a system crash or a crash from within the EJB container, any active message-driven bean instances are destroyed without going through the proper life-cycle shutdown. Additionally, for any method that throws a system exception, such as `EJBException`, the callback method is not invoked. Developers should be alert to this fact and perform any relevant clean-up before throwing a system exception.

Developers should also be aware that the `@PreDestroy` life-cycle callback is invoked by the container only when the container no longer needs that instance. Many containers pool the necessary number of message-driven bean instances needed to handle concurrently multiple messages. The limits on the minimum and maximum size of the message-driven bean pool are typically set in an application server–specific deployment descriptor. A container adds and removes message-driven bean instances to and from the pool as appropriate. However, since message-driven beans are extremely lightweight objects, a container generally destroys a message-driven bean instance *only* when the EJB itself is being undeployed (the whole EJB component is being undeployed). For most systems, the only time container undeployment occurs is at system shutdown or when an administrator decides to undeploy the component. The important point here is that message-driven bean containers are rarely undeployed, and therefore message-driven instances are rarely destroyed. As a general rule of thumb, the `@PreDestroy` method is rarely invoked.

Poison Messages

When using container-managed transactions (see Chapter 10) with a JMS message-driven bean, it is easy to code yourself into a situation that causes the generation of *poison messages*. A poison message is a message that is continually retransmitted by a JMS destination to the consumer because the consumer continuously fails to acknowledge the consumption of the message. Any time your JMS message-driven bean does not acknowledge messages to the JMS destination, you have a situation with the potential to create poison messages. The diagram in Figure 7.7 shows how poison messages can inadvertently be generated.

USING QUEUES TO PARTITION BUSINESS PROCESSING IN A CLUSTER

Suppose that you have two clusters of machines: One cluster is configured for a development and test environment, and the other cluster is configured for a production environment. You need to make sure that traffic coming from test clients is sent to the development cluster, while traffic coming from real clients is sent to the production cluster.

As one solution, you could set up your JMS server with two queues: `DevelopmentQueue` and `ProductionQueue`. You could deploy a series of JSPs or front-end stateless session beans that analyze each incoming request, format it into a JMS message, and then place requests onto one of the queues. Requests that come from an internal development machine could be placed onto the `DevelopmentQueue`, and all other requests could be placed on the `ProductionQueue`.

On the back end, you could configure two clusters: One cluster has JMS message-driven beans bound to the `DevelopmentQueue`, and the other cluster has JMS message-driven beans bound to the `ProductionQueue`. The logic for each of these beans can vary based on the needs of the system. For example, the behavior of the JMS message-driven beans bound to the `DevelopmentQueue` can mimic those bound to the `ProductionQueue` but add on debugging statements. You can also tune each cluster independently, based on load to the system. Since the `ProductionQueue` will likely have more load than the `DevelopmentQueue`, you could independently grow the size of the cluster servicing the `ProductionQueue` without impacting the cluster servicing the `DevelopmentQueue`.

This illustrates a general paradigm of using queues to partition business logic processing. Rather than the servers pulling messages off a single queue, you prechoose which machines get the messages by splitting the queue into two queues. This is an artificial way to achieve controlled load balancing in a JMS system.

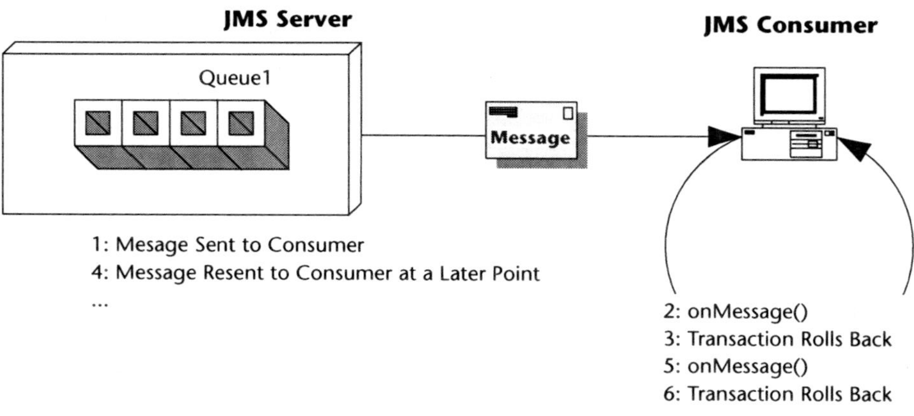

Figure 7.7 How JMS message-driven beans can cause poison messages.

For example, suppose that you have a stock-quoting JMS message-driven bean that accepts a text message, which represents the stock ticker symbol to be quoted. Your bean cracks open that message. If the string contained within the message matches a stock symbol, the bean retrieves the value of that symbol and sends a response message. Otherwise, the bean throws a system exception or calls `MessageDrivenContext.setRollbackOnly()`. This causes the transaction to be rolled back, which means the message acknowledgment will never be sent to the JMS destination. The JMS destination eventually resends the same message to the container, causing this same process to occur.

See Source 7.4 for an example of a JMS message-driven bean implementation class that will cause a poison message scenario. Note that our abuse of threading is for illustrative purposes only!

```
package examples.messaging;

import javax.jms.*;
import javax.ejb.*;
import javax.annotation.*;


@MessageDriven(activationConfig = {
  @ActivationConfigProperty(
   propertyName = "destinationType",
   propertyValue = "javax.jms.Topic") })
public class PoisonBean implements MessageListener {

    @Resource
```

Source 7.4 PoisonBean.java.

```
    private MessageDrivenContext ctx;

    public PoisonBean() {
        System.out.println("PoisonBean created");
    }

    public void onMessage(Message msg) {
        try {
            System.out.println("Received msg " + msg.getJMSMessageID());

            // Let's sleep a little bit so that we don't
            // see rapid fire resends of the message.
            Thread.sleep(3000);

            // We could either throw a system exception here or
            // manually force a rollback of the transaction.
            ctx.setRollbackOnly();
        } catch (Exception e) {
            e.printStackTrace();
        }
    }

    @PreDestroy
    public void remove() {
        System.out.println("PoisonBean destroyed.");
    }
}
```

Source 7.4 *(continued)*

You can use any of the following strategies to resolve poison messages:

- Make sure to not throw any system exceptions for any business logic-related error conditions. System exceptions like `EJBException` are intended to indicate system or container failure. If this were a session or entity bean, the ideal solution would be to generate an application exception and throw it (especially since application exceptions do not force transactions to be rolled back). However, the EJB specification discourages application exceptions from being thrown from the `onMessage()` method of a JMS message-driven bean. The ideal solution to this problem would likely involve logging the business error message and then quietly returning.
- Consider using bean-managed transactions instead of container-managed transactions. Message consumption and acknowledgment is not part of the transaction if bean-managed transactions are used. A bean-managed transaction can be rolled back and the message is acknowledged anyway.

- Some application servers enable you to configure a poison message queue. Messages that are redelivered a certain number of times are flagged as poison messages, removed from their primary queue, and placed into a poison message queue. Typically, any message that is redelivered from three to five times can be considered a poison message. You can then bind special consumers or JMS message-driven beans to the poison message queue to handle any unexpected error conditions.
- Some application servers place a retry count value as a property of any redelivered messages. Each redelivery of a message incrementally increases the retry count. Your JMS message-driven bean could check the value of a retry count (if it exists) to see if it has repeatedly consumed the same message.
- Some application server vendors provide a *redelivery delay* feature that administrators can configure to determine how long the JMS destination delays the redelivery of a message after it receives a negative acknowledgment. This way, your system doesn't grind to a halt in case of rapid-fire poison messages.

How to Return Results Back to Message Producers

The EJB specification does not outline any mechanism that allows a JMS message-driven bean to propagate a response back to the client that originally generated the message. So we need to build those facilities ourselves. Figure 7.8 shows how this could be accomplished.

Here is an explanation of Figure 7.8:

1. The client that generates a JMS message for consumption creates a *temporary destination* associated with its `Connection` object. The JMS server temporarily creates a `Topic` or `Queue` object, and that object exists for the lifetime of the `Connection` object.
2. The request message that the client sends contains extra information, so the receiving JMS message-driven bean knows how to reply correctly. Specifically, the client sticks the name of the temporary queue in the `JMSReplyTo` header field of the request message. The JMS message-driven bean can harness this field to reply on the correct queue. The client also has a unique identifier of the original message in the `JMSCorrelationID` header field of the original message. When the JMS message-driven bean replies, it embeds this original identifier, so the client knows to which original message he's receiving a reply.

3. The client creates a new `Session` object and registers a `Message Listener` object to consume messages sent to the temporary destination that was just created.
4. The client sends the message.
5. After consuming the message, the JMS message-driven bean formats a response and sends it using the `JMSReplyTo` and `JMSCorrelationID` attribute of the received message.
6. The client's `MessageListener` class asynchronously consumes the message that is sent to the temporary destination, recognizes that it is a response to the original message, and processes it.

Even though this scenario seems like a straightforward solution for responding to clients from within a JMS message-driven bean, it could potentially lead to some unexpected results. The problem arises if the *client itself* is an EJB component, such as a stateful session bean. When your stateful session bean creates the temporary destination, that temporary destination has a lifespan equal to the lifespan of the JMS connection that your bean currently holds. If your bean is *passivated* (meaning swapped out of memory), then you need to release that connection. The temporary destination then goes away, and you've lost all messages delivered to that temporary destination while you were passivated, even if you recreate the destination after you are swapped into memory again.

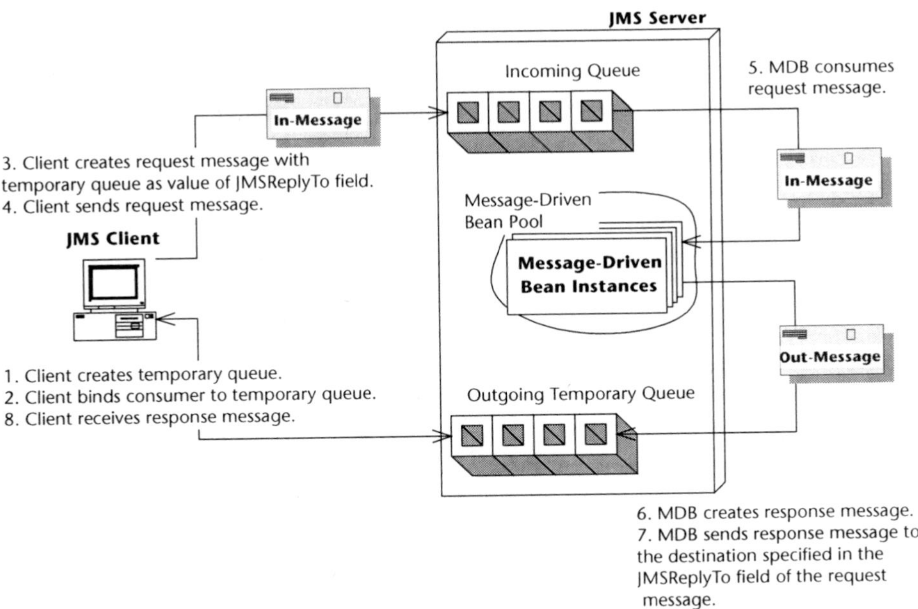

Figure 7.8 A simple JMS request/response paradigm solution.

We propose two possible solutions to this problem:

- Don't use a stateful session bean. Instead the end client, such as a servlet, application, or JSP tag library (rather than the stateful session bean), creates a temporary queue that all response messages are sent to. The stateful session bean is therefore not holding onto a connection, eliminating any danger of the destination going away because of passivation. See the book's accompanying source code for an implementation of this solution.

  The advantages of using this architecture include:

  - **Ease of implementation.** Creating temporary queues doesn't require any extra configuration from an administrator, whereas setting up a dedicated response topic requires management on the part of the administrator and your application.
  - **Security.** Since temporary queues are bound to a particular connection, malicious clients cannot bind to a temporary queue and intercept response messages.
  - **Immediate client notification.** Since the remote client creates and manages the receiving logic for the temporary queue, the client is notified immediately when a response message is generated, rather than having to wait for a middleman session bean to respond.

  The disadvantages of this architecture include:

  - **No persistent messages.** Temporary queues cannot have persistent stores associated with them and therefore cannot support guaranteed message delivery. If the system fails while a response message is located on the temporary queue, the message will be lost.
  - **Poor abstraction.** Since temporary queues are associated with a `Connection` object, a stateful session EJB cannot perform middle-tier management of the request/response process. It might be more natural to abstract away the JMS request/response logic from the client.

- A *permanent* response *topic* is configured and deployed in the JMS server. All response messages are delivered to the same response topic for all clients. Clients filter out the messages that belong to them by registering a message selector with the JMS server. Any request message that is sent has a custom application property called `ClientName=MyID` where `MyID` varies for each client. The JMS message-driven bean that consumes the request message takes the application property from the request message and inserts the same property in the response message. All response messages are sent to the same response topic irrespective of the client. Figure 7.9 illustrates this scenario, and the book's accompanying source code has its implementation.

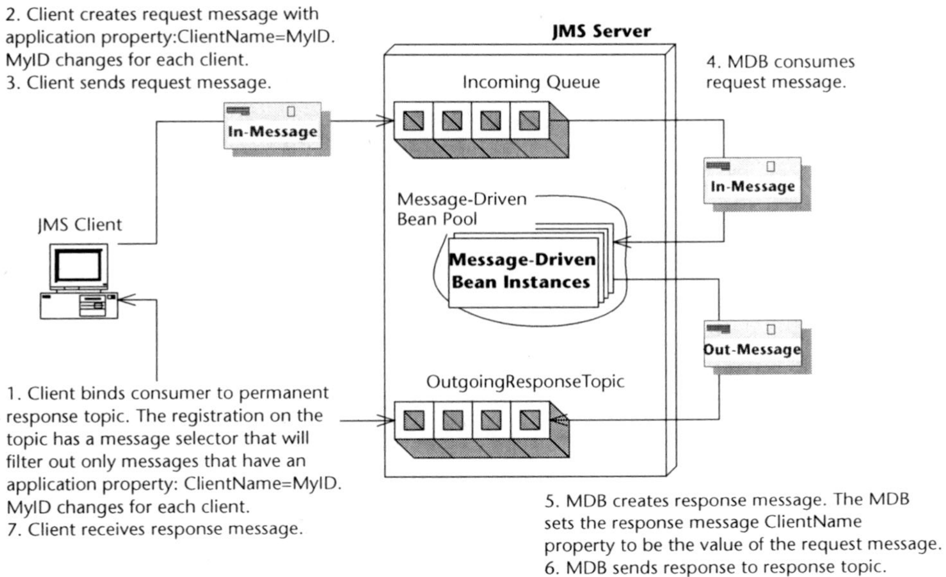
2. Client creates request message with application property:ClientName=MyID. MyID changes for each client.
3. Client sends request message.
JMS Server
4. MDB consumes request message.
Incoming Queue
In-Message
In-Message
Message-Driven Bean Pool
JMS Client
Message-Driven Bean Instances
Out-Message
OutgoingResponseTopic
1. Client binds consumer to permanent response topic. The registration on the topic has a message selector that will filter out only messages that have an application property: ClientName=MyID. MyID changes for each client.
7. Client receives response message.
5. MDB creates response message. The MDB sets the response message ClientName property to be the value of the request message.
6. MDB sends response to response topic.

Figure 7.9 Another JMS request/response paradigm solution.

The advantages of using this architecture include:

- **Better fault tolerance.** Because this architecture proposes that a permanent topic be set up for all outgoing messages, the response topic could be associated with a persistent store. All outgoing messages could then be sent persistently with guaranteed message delivery. Temporary topics and queues cannot have persistent messages delivered to them. This could be ideal for a data retrieval system. For example, suppose that you had a remote client that randomly connected to the central server requesting a download of the latest market data as it pertains to that client. The data could be anywhere from 1K to 1MB. Let's also suppose that for situations where a large amount of data needs to be retrieved for the client, you want to break up the data chunks into 100K messages. If the client needed to retrieve 1MB of data, you would need to send 10 response messages. All of the response messages could be sent with guaranteed message delivery. If the remote client application were to fail during the download process, it could easily resume from the last response message that it received instead of having to restart the entire download process.
- **Better filtering.** You can add additional filtering of response messages through the message selector that the client registers with the JMS server. In the example provided with this book, the client registers to receive messages that have an application property

`ClientName=MyID`. You could conceivably add application properties about the response message that the client filters on. These properties could be message size, message importance, and so on.

The disadvantages are as follows:

- **Lack of security.** The main disadvantage of this architecture is lack of security. Since the JMS specification does not have any security restrictions on which clients can bind which message selectors, any client can register any message selector. This presents the opportunity for a malicious client to register for consumption of response messages that are destined for another client. This malicious behavior is not possible with temporary destinations. Of course, if you're secured by a firewall, security probably isn't an issue. Also, it would take a pretty snazzy developer to actually figure out that you're sending messages and register a message listener.
- **Intermediary EJB.** This approach allows a session EJB to act as a mediator between the client and the back-end system, as mentioned in the actual description of the problem. By using an intermediary session EJB, security can be improved, because the topic that response messages are delivered to can be made available only internally by simply not exposing it to a client or blocking the message server using a firewall or other security measure. The session EJB can be coded to filter out messages based upon the logged-in user name.

An Alternative Request/Response Paradigm

If you don't feel like writing your own request/response code as we've just described, you can tap into the JMS facilities to help you. JMS has two special classes, `javax.jms.QueueRequestor` and `javax.jms.TopicRequestor`, that implement a simple request/response paradigm. You call a method called `request()` that takes as input the request message and returns the response message. This is implemented in the book's accompanying source code.

The downsides to this approach are:

- **You need to block when waiting for a response.** You can't continue processing and do other things, which is one of the major advantages of messaging in the first place.
- **You can't use transactions.** If you did, the outgoing message would be *buffered* until the transaction committed. Since the `QueueRequestor` class doesn't commit right away, but instead blocks until it receives a response message, it will block indefinitely. The outgoing request message will wait forever to be flushed from the buffer. See Chapter 10 for more on transactions.

The Future: Asynchronous Method Invocations

One of the downsides to JMS message-driven beans is that you need to learn a whole new API—JMS—to call them. This API is highly procedural in nature, because you are not invoking lots of different business methods on your JMS message-driven bean; rather, you are sending messages using the JMS API, and the server has a single method to crack the message open and then call the intended method using a giant `if` statement.

An *asynchronous method invocation* is a real method invocation executed in an asynchronous fashion. You are actually calling business methods on the server, such as `logMessage()` or `quoteStock()`. You can choose whether you want to block and wait for an asynchronous response or to return immediately and not wait for a response. Furthermore, the server can take on the context information of the client.

Asynchronous RMI and Microsoft Queued Components are asynchronous method invocation infrastructures. JAX-RPC supports one-way RPC over SOAP. CORBA also has some support for this.

We hope a future EJB specification supports asynchronous method invocations. Until then, you'll have to build such facilities on top of JMS yourself, perhaps by writing a code generator.

Summary

In this chapter, we've learned about developing JMS message-driven beans and the pitfalls associated with doing asynchronous development with EJBs. We looked at the various benefits of developing asynchronous components and how message-driven beans compare to their session and entity bean counterparts. We showed how to build a JMS message-driven bean and deploy it. Next we looked at how a JMS message-driven bean behaves in its environment, including how it interacts with transactions. Finally, we took a look at the common pitfalls of using message-driven beans and proposed some solutions.

This chapter concludes the introductory tour of the different EJB types. Beginning the next section, Chapter 8 presents additional information that you will need, such as interceptors and dependency injection.

CHAPTER

8

Adding Functionality to Your Beans

In previous chapters, you learned the fundamentals of EJB 3.0 programming. In this chapter, we'll build on that knowledge and cover a slew of essential topics, including:

- How to call beans from other beans
- Annotations
- Dependency injection
- Interceptors

These topics cover some of the major changes in the 3.0 version of the EJB specification and are constantly used across the different types of beans. Of particular importance are the use of annotation and dependency injection.

Calling Beans from Other Beans

Any nontrivial EJB object model has beans calling other beans. For example, a bank teller bean might call a bank account bean, or a customer bean might call a credit card bean. In this chapter, we'll use the following examples:

- A pricing bean that computes prices of products, using all sorts of interesting rules, such as discounts, taxes, and shipping costs

- A tax rate bean that returns a tax rate based on the state where the transaction takes place

The pricing bean calls the tax rate bean. For simplicity, we'll assume that both of these beans are stateless session beans.

Default JNDI Lookups

For your bean to call another bean, you must go through the same process that any other client would go through. Your bean would:

1. Look up the other bean's interface (either local or remote) via JNDI
2. Call business methods on the EJB object via the interface

As we mentioned earlier, to look up an EJB interface using JNDI, you first need to supply JNDI initialization parameters, such as the JNDI driver you're using, which differs from container to container. But if you're writing a bean that calls another bean, how do you know which JNDI service provider to use? After all, your beans should be container-independent. Hard-coding that JNDI information into your bean would destroy portability.

The good news is that if you're looking up a bean from another bean, you don't need to supply any JNDI initialization parameters. You simply acquire a default JNDI initial context. The container sets the default JNDI initial context before your bean ever runs. For example, the following code snippet is taken from a bean calling another bean:

```
// Obtain the DEFAULT JNDI initial context by calling the
// no-argument constructor
Context ctx = new InitialContext();

// Look up the business interface
Object result = ctx.lookup(TaxRate.class.getName());

// Convert the result to the proper type, RMI-IIOP style
TaxRate tr = (TaxRate)result;
```

The preceding code is portable because nobody ever needs to supply container-specific JNDI initialization parameters.

Notice that we looked up a bean using the remote interface `TaxRate`. We use session beans through an interface that exposes the business methods implemented in the bean class. This interface is an ordinary Java interface and as such has access to the static `class` field. Using the `class` field, we can call the `getName()` method. This returns the fully qualified name of the interface.

The EJB 3.0 specification mandates that containers bind beans to the JNDI tree by their fully qualified names at deployment time. This ensures that we can look up the beans in this very simple way.

This is vastly simplified from previous versions of the specification that relied on the `java:comp/env/ejb` JNDI context along with EJB references to look up other beans. EJB 3.0 still supports this type of reference for backward compatibility. For more information on EJB references found in the deployment descriptor, see Appendix C, available from this book's companion Web site at Wiley.com.

Another way to get a reference to beans from within other beans is to use the `@EJB` annotation. This is an even simpler approach than using a JNDI lookup. Although this is an annotation, it is used to provide references to other beans' business interfaces. Let's take a look at its use in code:

```
@EJB TaxRate tr;
```

That's it! Using the `@EJB` annotation, the container will provide a reference to the `TaxRate` business interface for the `TaxRateBean`. It is usable in the same way as in the JNDI lookup example. There are a number of elements to the `@EJB` annotation that we will look at in the next section.

One of the major strengths of EJB 3.0 is its support of intuitive defaults. This makes the job of the developer in most situations very simple and straightforward. There are times when you will need to override defaults and/or add functionality to your beans. There are a number of metadata annotations to support this, covered in the next section.

Annotations

This section looks at some key annotations that help in overriding defaults and adding functionality to your beans. First, we will look at annotations that are the same across the various types of beans. We will then discuss annotations relevant to the business interface of a bean. Finally, we will examine additional annotations for stateful session beans.

This section focuses on those annotations related to the EJB 3.0 specification. There are other annotations used for backwards compatibility with earlier releases of the specification. For a comprehensive reference, use the specification found at: `www.jcp.org/en/jsr/detail?id=220`.

Some of the annotations in this section were introduced in other chapters, but this section goes beyond the basic use of these annotations and looks at elements that can be used with the annotation to enhance or change its behavior.

Refer to Chapter 4 for an introduction to the annotations for session beans and Chapter 7 for an introduction to the annotations for message-driven beans.

Common Annotations

First, we'll take a look at annotations that apply to session beans (both stateless and stateful) and message-driven beans. The `@Stateless`, `@Stateful`, and `@MessageDriven` annotations support a number of elements:

- `name`
- `mappedName`
- `description`

By default, the `name` element of the annotation defaults to the unqualified name of the class. It can be overridden as:

```
@Stateless(name="TR")
public class TaxRateBean implements TaxRate {
...
}
```

The `mappedName` element is handled in a container specific manner. As the EJB 3.0 specification warns: *"Applications that use mappedNames may not be portable."* Here is an example:

```
@Stateful(mappedName="java:comp/env/ejb/CartBean")
public class CartBean implements Cart{
...
}
```

Here is an example of the `description` element being set:

```
@MessageDriven(description="Listens for purchase messages")
public class PurchaseMDB implements MessageListener {
...
}
```

Business Interface Annotations

By now we've now seen a number of examples where the `@Local` or `@Remote` annotation is used on an interface to indicate that it is the business interface for a session bean.

No further annotation is required if the bean class implements the business interface. The business interface does not even need to have a similar name to the bean class.

There may be other situations where the business interface name has no relation to the bean class name or where you want to use a number of interfaces for the business interface on the bean class. In this case, you will need to use elements of the `@Remote` or `@Local` annotation. Furthermore, in these cases the `@Remote` or `@Local` annotation will be defined on the bean class and not on the business interface. Let's take the case where we have a number of interfaces that we want to use to make up the business interface. Source 8.1 and 8.2 are the interface definitions. Source 8.3 is the bean class definition.

```
public interface PricerLookup {
  public double getTaxLookup(double cost, String state);
}
```

Source 8.1 PricerLookup.java.

```
public interface PricerInjection {
  Public double getTaxInjection(double cost, String state);
}
```

Source 8.2 PricerInjection.java.

```
@Stateless
@Remote({PricerLookup.class,PricerInjection.class})
public class PricerBean implements PricerLookup, PricerInjection {
  public double getTaxLookup(double cost, String state) {
    ...
  }

  public double getTaxInjection(double cost, String state) {
    ...
  }
}
```

Source 8.3 PricerBean.java.

Notice that the interfaces do not have the `@Remote` or `@Local` annotation. The `@Remote` annotation is defined on the bean class. It also includes an element that is an array of classes. The classes in this list are the interfaces that make up the business interface for this bean. When specifying the business interfaces in this way, it is not required that the bean class implement the interfaces. However, it is a good practice to explicitly implement the interfaces on the bean class. This enforces type safety in that you must provide the methods specified in the interfaces.

We will see a client example of interacting with the bean from Source 8.3 in the "Dependency Injection" section later in this chapter.

Other Stateful Annotations

As discussed in Chapter 4, the `@Remove` annotation marks a method of a stateful session bean such that when it is called the bean will be removed from the bean pool. The `@PreDestroy` life-cycle callback method (if any) will be called before the specified remove method is executed. When the remove method completes, the container will destroy the stateful session bean.

The `retainIfException` element indicates whether or not the stateful session bean will remain active if an exception is thrown in the remove method.

Let's take a look at a simple example in Source 8.4.

```
package examples.stateful;

import javax.ejb.Remove;
import javax.ejb.Stateful;
import examples.interfaces.Cart;

@Stateful
public class CartBean implements Cart {
  private int numItems;

  public void addItem() {
    numItems++;
  }

  public int getItems() {
    return numItems;
  }

  @Remove(retainIfException=false)
  public void remove1() throws Exception {
    doRemove();
  }

  @Remove(retainIfException=true)
  public void remove2() throws Exception {
    doRemove();
  }

  private void doRemove() throws Exception {
```

Source 8.4 CartBean.java. *(continued)*

```
    if (numItems > 1 && numItems < 4) {
      throw new Exception("blah");
    }
    System.out.println("Removing cart with: "+
      numItems+" items.");
  }
}
```

Source 8.4 *(continued)*

As you can see, a stateful session bean can have more than one remove method. The `remove1()` method above has the `retainIfException` set to false, while the `remove2()` method has the `retainIfException` set to `true`. Both remove methods call the private `doRemove` method. If the number of items in the "cart" is 2 or 3, an `Exception` will be thrown. This code serves no useful business purpose except to demonstrate the effects of exceptions on the removal of stateful session beans. What is the effect of this code? Let's look at some standalone client code in Source 8.5 to see what happens.

```
package examples.client;

import javax.ejb.EJBNoSuchObjectException;
import javax.naming.InitialContext;
import javax.naming.NameClassPair;
import javax.naming.NamingEnumeration;
import javax.naming.NamingException;

import examples.interfaces.Cart;

public class CartClient {
  public static void main(String[] args) {
    try {
      InitialContext ic = new InitialContext();
      for (int i=0;i<2;i++) {
        Cart cart = (Cart)ic.lookup(Cart.class.getName());
        cart.addItem();
        cart.addItem();
        System.out.println("items in the cart: "+cart.getItems());
        try {
          try {
            if (i==0) {
              cart.remove1();
            }
            else {
              cart.remove2();
            }
```

Source 8.5 CartClient.java. *(continued)*

```
            }
            catch (Exception e) {
              ;
            }
            cart.addItem();
            cart.addItem();
            cart.addItem();
            System.out.println("items in the cart: "+cart.getItems());
          }
          catch (EJBNoSuchObjectException esoe) {
            System.out.println("Cart was already removed "+
              "during iteration "+i);
          }
        }
      }
      catch (NamingException e) {
        e.printStackTrace();
      }
    }
  }
```

Source 8.5 *(continued)*

In both iterations of the loop, an exception will be thrown, since there are only two items in the cart when the `@Remove` method is called. The following lines from `CartBean` ensure this:

```
...
if (numItems > 1 && numItems < 4) {
  throw new Exception("blah");
}
...
```

THE USE OF THE BUSINESS INTERFACE

It is very important to understand the role of the business interface. This has been explained in other chapters, but it is useful to review here. The bean class implements the business interface. In object-oriented parlance, this is the "is a" type of relationship. For instance, we can say that a CartBean "is a" Cart because it implements the Cart interface. You will notice in the client code below that all interaction with the bean is done via the business interface (Cart in this case). This is how the client is kept thin—only the interface (a very small bit of code) needs to be packaged with the client.

Since the remove1 method has the retainIfException element set to false, the stateful session bean will be removed. The next call to cart.addItem will throw the runtime NoSuchEJBException Exception (which we catch in the sample code).

Since the remove2 method has the retainIfException element set to true, the stateful session bean will not be removed, and thus the next call to cart.addItem will work just fine.

The @Init annotation is used to indicate that a method corresponds to a particular create method. This is used when adapting an EJB 2.x stateful session bean for use in an EJB 3.0 container. The discussion of this annotation is outside the scope of this section. Refer to the EJB 3.0 specification at http://www.jcp.org/en/jsr/detail?id=220.

Dependency Injection

The EJB 3.0 specification introduces powerful mechanisms for obtaining references to resources and for injecting references to EJB-related objects. More technically, everything we are talking about in this section relates to injection. Injection is the technique of relying on the container (the Java EE application server) to provide handles to objects it has access to. In previous versions of the EJB specification, these resources had to be looked up using JNDI often requiring abstracted resource references and complicated initialization properties. Now, we can simply define a reference and use the objects. The container will inject the reference before any of our method calls or other initialization occurs.

Even though both resource references and resource injection are used to describe the process, both terms refer to general process of dependency injection. The major difference is that resource references use the @Resource annotation to reference objects that the container has access to but are not (necessarily) directly related to EJB. Dependency injection, on the other hand, uses other annotations to inject references to objects directly associated with EJB. Examples include @EJB and @PersistenceContext.

Resource References

The @Resource annotation is used to set up a reference to a resource in the bean's environment. For instance, the following code snippet sets up a reference to a stateful session bean's SessionContext:

```
@Resource SessionContext context;
TaxRate tr = (TaxRate)context.lookup(TaxRate.class.getName());
```

The preceding example is a good use of a resource reference, since the `SessionContext` object can do lookups in the same way that the `InitialContext` can. Take a look at this code snippet:

```
InitialContext context = new InitialContext();
TaxRate tr = (TaxRate)context.lookup(TaxRate.class.getName());
```

This code has the same result as the first example. However, instantiating the `InitialContext` object is a much more heavyweight operation than using the `SessionContext` object through the resource reference. As we saw before (and will discuss further in the injection section) an even simpler form is available:

```
@EJB TaxRate tr;
```

At times, more information is needed to get the resource reference. This information can be specified using elements of the `@Resource` annotation. For instance, when referencing a `DataSource` resource, we need to use the `name` and `type` elements:

```
@Resource(name="jdbc/__default",type=Datasource.class)
DataSource dataSource;
```

Just about any resource available to the Java EE application server is available for reference using the `@Resource` annotation. Examples include (but are not limited to): `javax.sql.DataSource`, `javax.transaction.UserTransaction`, `javax.jms.Queue`, `javax.ejb.SessionContext`, and `org.omg.CORBA.ORB`.

So far, we've looked at resource references at the field level. They can also be used at the method level for setter-based injection. Let's look at a code snippet to understand this.

```
package com.temp;

public class MyClass {
  ...
  @Resource
  private void setMyDataSource(DataSource ds) {
    myDataSource = ds;
  }
  private myDataSource;
  ...
}
```

In the preceding example, the name of the resource is inferred based on the name of the method. The name is inferred based on the reflective properties of the JavaBeans specification in conjunction with the bean class name. So the "set" is dropped and the first letter is made lowercase thus making the end of the name `myDataSource`. By default, the full name would be `java:comp/env/com.temp.MyClass/myDataSource`. The type is also inferred based on the parameter being passed into the method. The name and type can explicitly be set using the `name` and `type` elements of the `@Resource` annotation.

Resource references can even be used for environmental entries set in the deployment descriptor element: `env-entry`. For instance, if a long named timeout was specified by a bean deployer, our code could use it as follows:

```
@Resource long timeout;
```

When using resource references you need to ask yourself, "Is the object that I want to reference available to the application server?" If the answer is yes, then you should be able to use the `@Resource` annotation to inject a reference to it.

As a final note on resource references, we'll discuss the `@Resources` annotation. This annotation simply allows you to set up multiple resource references at once at the class level. Here's a sample:

```
@Resources({
  @Resource(name="datasource",type="javax.sql.DataSource.class),
  @Resource(name="queue",type="javax.jms.Queue")
})
public class X {
  ...
}
```

When using the `@Resources` or `@Resource` annotations at the class level, an entry in the bean's environment is declared, but the resource is not injected into a particular variable. It is expected that the resource would be looked up using the standard JNDI mechanism within the class. Why would you want to declare resources at the class level? Each resource may only be injected into a single field or method for a particular bean. If you need to use a resource in more than one spot in the bean class, you need to define that resource at the class level and then look it up explicitly by name.

In the next section, we will look at resource injection. We could really refer to it as *other* resource injection as the resource references we have discussed in this section use injection as well.

As described earlier in this chapter, EJB 3.0 makes it very easy to refer to other EJBs using the `@EJB` annotation. (The section "Default JNDI Lookups" provides a simple example of this annotation's use.) Here, we will look at the various elements of the `@EJB` annotation and its use when applied at the class level.

The portable elements of the `@EJB` annotation are `name`, `beanInterface`, `beanName`, and `description`. Let's take a look at an example:

```
@EJB(
  name="ejb/pricer",
  beanInterface=Pricer.class,
  beanName="pricer",
  description="This bean is used to calculate prices."
)
private Pricer pricer;
```

In the preceding example, the bean has been explicitly deployed (most likely via a deployment descriptor) using the name `java:comp/env/ejb/pricer`.

When applied at the class level, the `@EJB` annotation has the effect of binding the name in the EJB environment. Here is a code snippet:

```
@EJB(name="ejb/TaxRate", beanInterface=TaxRate.class)
@Stateless
public class PricerBean implements Pricer {
  ...
  public double getFinalPrice(double cost, String state) {
    InitialContext context = new InitialContext();
    TaxRate tr = (TaxRate)context.lookup("java:comp/env/ejb/TaxRate");
    ...
  }
  ...
}
```

One of the most powerful annotations for dependency injection in EJB 3.0 is `@PersistenceContext`. This is used to inject the `EntityManager` object, which is used synchronize entities and the database backing them. Look at Chapter 6 and Chapter 9 for more detailed information on the persistence mechanism specified for EJB 3.0. In this section, we will look at how the `EntityManager` is injected. Here is its simplest form:

```
@PersistenceContext EntityManager em;
```

Once injected, we can call methods on the `em` reference to perform persistence operations. We can also specify the name binding by using the annotation at the class level.

```
@Stateless
@PersistenceContext(name="HelloWorldEntity")
public class HelloWorldBean implements HelloWorld {
  @Resource SessionContext context;

  public void hello() {
    EntityManager em =
      (EntityManager)context.lookup("HelloWorldEntity");
    ...
  }
  ...
}
```

In this example, we are binding the name `HelloWorldEntity` in the bean's namespace. Further down, we are using that name to perform a lookup.

In the preceding examples, there was an assumption of a default *persistence unit*. As described in Chapter 6, a persistence unit is a set of classes that are mapped to a single database. Since an application server can support persistence to any number of databases, we can use the optional `unitName` element to identify the persistence unit to be used with the bean. If your application server does not have a default or if there is more than one persistence unit defined, you must supply this element. Here's what it looks like:

```
@PersistenceContext(unitName="pu1") EntityManager em;
```

In this case, a persistence unit named `pu1` was defined within the application server. We are indicating that it is this persistence unit that will be used in the bean.

Interceptors

Interceptors are methods that are invoked automatically when the business methods of a bean are invoked. Using interceptors enables a clean distinction between business logic code and meta or support code.

Interceptors can be used on session beans and message-driven beans. Interceptor methods can be defined within the bean class or in external classes. A bean class can have any number of interceptors.

The `@Interceptor` or `@Interceptors` annotation is used to indicate which external classes will be used as interceptors, while the `@AroundInvoke` annotation is used to identify a method as an interceptor. The method can either be in the bean class or in one of the named external classes.

Interceptor methods have access to information about the business method that triggered it, including method names and parameters. The interceptor method can also be used to halt processing of the business method. For instance, an interceptor might check for certain security information and, if it is not found, would halt the processing of the business method. If the interceptor does not allow the business method to proceed, all other interceptors as well as the business method will not proceed.

Interceptors are processed in the order they are specified. Interceptors defined in external classes will be executed before an interceptor defined within a bean class.

Enough background! Let's dive into some code. Sources 8.6 and 8.7 show external classes with methods used as interceptors. Source 8.8 shows a session bean that uses the external interceptors as well as an interceptor defined within the bean.

```
package examples.interceptor;

import javax.ejb.AroundInvoke;
import javax.ejb.InvocationContext;

public class LoggerInterceptor {
  @AroundInvoke
  public Object logger(InvocationContext inv) throws Exception {
    System.out.println("Intercepted call via "+
      "external class to: "+inv.getMethod().getName());
    Object[] params = inv.getParameters();
    for (int i=0;i<params.length;i++) {
      System.out.println("\tparam: "+params[i]);
    }
    return inv.proceed();
  }
}
```

Source 8.6 LoggerInterceptor.java.

AOP AND EJB

Almost everyone has heard the term AOP (Aspect Oriented Programming) by this point. AOP generally is the technique of expressing cross-cutting concerns (such as security) in a clear way so that the intent (business problem) of the underlying code remains clear.

EJBs new interceptors gives us a rudimentary AOP system in that the business code can be completely separated from the interceptor code. The interceptor code could handle the cross-cutting concerns, such as checking security. The interceptor code can influence whether or not the call to the business method will be invoked.

Common uses for interceptors are logging, performing tangential auditing functions, and security checking.

```
package examples.interceptor;

import javax.ejb.AroundInvoke;
import javax.ejb.InvocationContext;

public class AuditorInterceptor {
  @AroundInvoke
  public Object checkCost(InvocationContext inv) throws Exception {
    if (inv.getMethod().getName().startsWith("getTax")) {
      Object[] o = inv.getParameters();
      double cost = ((Double)o[0]).doubleValue();
      if (cost > 50) {
        System.out.println("Cost is > 50!");
      }
    }
    return inv.proceed();
  }
}
```

Source 8.7 AuditorInterceptor.java.

```
package examples.stateless;

import javax.annotation.EJB;
import javax.ejb.AroundInvoke;
import javax.ejb.Interceptors;
import javax.ejb.InvocationContext;
import javax.ejb.PostConstruct;
import javax.ejb.PreDestroy;
import javax.ejb.Stateless;
import javax.naming.InitialContext;
import javax.naming.NamingException;

import examples.interfaces.Pricer;
import examples.interfaces.TaxRate;

import examples.interceptor.LoggerInterceptor;
import examples.interceptor.AuditorInterceptor;

@Stateless
@Interceptors({LoggerInterceptor.class,AuditorInterceptor.class})
public class PricerBean implements Pricer {
  private TaxRate taxRate;

  @EJB
```

Source 8.8 PricerBean.java. *(continued)*

```
    private TaxRate taxRate2;

    public double getTaxLookup(double cost, String state) {
      double tax = -1;
      tax = cost * taxRate.getTaxRate(state);
      return tax;
    }

    public double getTaxInjection(double cost, String state) {
      double tax = -1;
      tax = cost * taxRate2.getTaxRate(state);
      return tax;
    }

    @PostConstruct
    public void postConstruct() {
      try {
        InitialContext ic = new InitialContext();
        taxRate = (TaxRate)ic.lookup(TaxRate.class.getName());
      }
      catch (NamingException e) {
        // some kind of appropriate handling here
      }
    }

    @PreDestroy
    public void preDestroy() {
      taxRate = null;
    }

    @AroundInvoke
    public Object logger(InvocationContext inv) throws Exception {
      System.out.println("Intercepted call via internal method to: "+
        inv.getMethod().getName());
      Object[] params = inv.getParameters();
      for (int i=0;i<params.length;i++) {
        System.out.println("\tparam: "+params[i]);
      }
      return inv.proceed();
    }
}
```

Source 8.8 *(continued)*

The `PricerBean` class incorporates a lot of the subjects that we have discussed in this chapter including beans calling other beans through injection and JNDI lookups. For now, let's focus on the interceptors.

Notice that the interceptor methods have an `InvocationContext` object passed into them. It is this object that gives us access to the method names and parameter list that triggered the interceptor. This object also allows the business method to proceed or stops it.

Notice also that the business method is solely concerned with the business at side, while the interceptors perform their own work. This separation of concerns makes the code very clear.

Finally, note that the `PricerBean` class uses the `TaxRate` interface to the `TaxRateBean`. For the purposes of this discussion, it is not necessary to display the `TaxRate` code here. Please refer to this book's Web site for all of the code used in this chapter.

Let's take a look at a client that uses the `PricerBean` and deconstruct the output from the interceptors. Source 8.9 shows the client code.

```
package examples.client;

import javax.naming.InitialContext;
import javax.naming.NamingException;

import examples.interfaces.Pricer;

public class PricerClient {
  public static void main(String[] args) {
    try {
      InitialContext ic = new InitialContext();
      Pricer pricer = (Pricer)ic.lookup(Pricer.class.getName());
      System.out.println("Tax (using lookup) on: "+
        args[0]+" for State: "+args[1]+
        " is: "+
        pricer.getTaxLookup(Double.parseDouble(args[0]),args[1]));
      System.out.println("Tax (using injection) on: "+
        args[0]+" for State: "+args[1]+
        " is: "+
        pricer.getTaxInjection(Double.parseDouble(args[0]),args[1]));
    }
    catch (NamingException e) {
      e.printStackTrace();
    }
  }
}
```

Source 8.9 PricerClient.java.

Output 8.1 shows a snippet of the log output produced by the application server when the client defined in Source 8.9 is run. The command-line parameters `85` and `ny` were used for this example.

```
A Intercepted call via external class to: getTaxLookup
A     param: 85.0
A     param: ny
B Cost is > 50!
C Intercepted call via internal method to: getTaxLookup
C     param: 85.0
C     param: ny
A Intercepted call via external class to: getTaxInjection
A     param: 85.0
A     param: ny
B Cost is > 50!
C Intercepted call via internal method to: getTaxInjection
C     param: 85.0
C     param: ny
```

Output 8.1

For clarity, the output has been grouped by letter: A, B, and C. All of the A listings are from the external interceptor: `LoggerInterceptor` defined in Source 8.6. The B listings are from the external interceptor: `AuditorInterceptor` defined in Source 8.7. The C listings are from the internal interceptor defined in the bean class: `PricerBean` defined in Source 8.8.

Notice from the client code in Source 8.9, business methods are only called twice. It is important to remember that all defined interceptors will be fired when a business method is called. Interceptors are fired in the order that they are defined with class-level external interceptor definitions taking precedence over internal interceptor definitions.

If an interceptor does not call the `proceed` method on the `InvocationContext` object, no other interceptors nor the business method itself will be executed. As such, we must take care to make the interceptor code very clear. If there is some logic branch that we take that will not call the `proceed` method, then we should give some sort of feedback, through logs or error messages, that the business method was not executed.

Summary

In this chapter, we reviewed some of the fundamental aspects of the EJB 3.0 specification that make it so powerful and easy to use.

- Beans can easily call other beans by using simplified JNDI lookups or dependency injection using the `@EJB` annotation.
- The annotations and their elements enable a very flexible and expressive environment to work with EJBs in.

- Resource and dependency injection allow us to gain access to practically any resource available to the Java EE application server.
- Interceptors enable us to execute code that is relevant but tangential in nature to our business code. This separation of concerns makes for cleaner, more understandable code. In addition, it is easy to alter the business code or the interceptor code, since they are separate. Previously, the code we now find in interceptor code would have been peppered throughout our business logic.

The common theme in all of the topics in this chapter is really leveraging the application server to do the heavy lifting. It is the application server that performs the actual injection on our behalf. The application server reads the annotations and associated elements through Java reflection. Sometimes this is done at deployment time, and sometimes it is done at runtime. We don't have to worry about it.

Through these mechanisms (and the others described throughout this book) EJB finally achieves its original goal of allowing developers to focus on the task at hand and to let the application server handle common tasks not directly related to the business problem.

In the next chapter, we will examine the advanced concepts of the new persistence layer. This is, perhaps, the most exciting aspect of EJB 3.0. The persistence layer is now greatly simplified and is modeled on other lightweight persistence layers, such as Hibernate.

Advanced Enterprise JavaBeans Concepts

If you've read to this point, you should be quite familiar with the basics of Enterprise JavaBeans development. In Part III, we raise the bar by moving on to more cutting-edge concepts. These include the following:

- **Advanced Persistence.** Chapter 9 provides an in-depth discussion on persistence topics such as inheritance, entity relationships, and EJB-QL enhancements.
- **Transactions.** Chapter 10 shows you how to harness transactions to make your EJB deployments reliable. We'll discuss transactions at a conceptual level and how to apply them to EJB. You'll also learn about the Java Transaction API (JTA).
- **EJB Security.** Chapter 11 provides an in-depth coverage of techniques and best practices surrounding EJB application security. It covers how to enable authentication and authorization declaratively and programmatically in EJB applications. Also the chapter showcases enabling JAAS-based authentication for EJB applications. In addition to these, it talks about Web services security concepts.
- **EJB Timers.** Chapter 12 focuses on building EJB applications that use the container-provided EJB Timer Service.

- **EJB Best Practices.** Chapter 13 covers a lot of best practices pertinent to EJB, such as when to use EJB, how to choose the right Web application framework when working with EJB applications that have Web clients, how to apply model-driven development or aspect-oriented programming concepts to EJB applications, and many other such guidelines.
- **EJB Performance Optimizations.** Chapter 14 covers tips and techniques for boosting EJB performance. You'll learn about best practices for boosting performance of stateless session beans, stateful session beans, and message-driven beans, as well as entities. Also, a lot of other miscellaneous design and development tips are presented in this chapter to improve the performance of your EJB applications.
- **EJB-based integration.** Chapter 15 covers various approaches to integrate disparate applications with EJB applications. Here, you will primarily learn how to use the Java EE Connector Architecture to build adapters to integrate EJB applications with the outside world.
- **Clustering.** Chapter 16 shows you how EJBs are clustered in large-scale systems. You'll learn how clustering works behind the scenes and a few strategies for how containers might achieve clustering. This is a critical topic for anyone building a system that involves several machines working together.
- **EJB-Java EE integration: Building a complete application.** Chapter 17 shows how EJB components can work together with other parts of Java EE technology stack to solve a business problem.

These are extremely interesting middleware topics; indeed, many books could be written on each subject alone. To understand these concepts, we highly recommend that you read Part I and Part II first. However, if you're already well versed in EJB, please join us to explore these advanced issues.

CHAPTER

9

Advanced Persistence Concepts

The new Java Persistence specification adds a dimension to the EJB specification that has heretofore been missing. Namely, the ability to take full advantage of object orientation while having elements of the object map persisted to the database behind the scenes.

In previous versions of EJB, in order to take advantage of container-managed persistence for entity beans, the Java code had to be written in strict conformance to the rules of the specification. These rules restricted the java code from taking advantage of the most basic features of object orientation, including inheritance and polymorphism. This barrier has been shattered by Java Persistence and entities.

Another advancement with Java Persistence is the update of the EJB Query Language (EJB-QL). This is a platform-independent query language that supports all of the modern querying capabilities, including grouping, joins, subqueries, and dynamic queries (among others). The benefit of EJB-QL, as compared to the Structured Query Language (SQL) "standard" is that it is truly platform-independent and is object-aware. This means that you reference an entity and its fields by name, rather than having to know the details of table and column names in the underlying RDBMS.

In this chapter, we will look at these advanced features of Java Persistence. We will cover inheritance, polymorphism, modeling relationships with objects, and EJB-QL enhancements.

ENTITIES VERSUS ENTITY BEANS

The EJB 3.0 specification requires that EJB container implementers still support EJB 2.1. This includes support for the previous persistence model. "entity beans" refer to objects used for persistence in previous versions of the specification. They *must* live inside the container. "Entities" refer to objects used with the new Java Persistence specification. These entities are not required to be bound to the container. Out of container and standalone EntityManagers make it possible to work with persistence in a strictly Java Standard Edition (JSE) environment.

Inheritance

Before we can jump into code, we need to talk about mapping strategies to support inheritance. As discussed in Chapter 6, we need object-relational mapping (ORM) in order to bridge the gap between inherently object-oriented technology (Java) and inherently relational technology (RDBMSs). There are a number of mapping strategies for supporting the object-oriented concept of inheritance in relational databases. These are:

- Single table per class hierarchy
- Separate table per subclass
- Single table per concrete entity class

Figure 9.1 shows a simple object model that we will use to show each of the strategies.

In this model, our root class is `RoadVehicle`. `Motorcycle` and `Car` inherit from `RoadVehicle`. `Coupe` and `Roadster` inherit from `Car`.

Sources 9.1 through 9.5 show the object model in Java. This is a straightforward inheritance chain that uses the `extends` Java keyword. We will add annotations to these classes to make them into entities and to implement each of the strategies shown above (standard setters and getters are omitted for brevity).

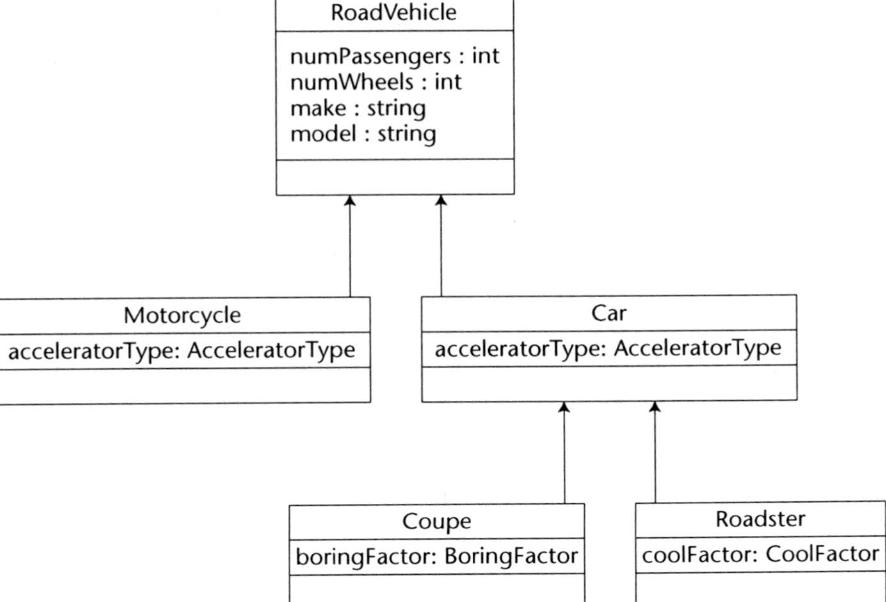

Figure 9.1 UML object model.

```
package examples.entity.single_table;

public class RoadVehicle {
    public enum AcceleratorType {PEDAL,THROTTLE};

    protected int numPassengers;
    protected int numWheels;
    protected String make;
    protected String model;

    // setters and getters go here
    ...

    public String toString() {
        return "Make: "+make+
            ", Model: "+model+
            ", Number of passengers: "+numPassengers;
    }
}
```

Source 9.1 RoadVehicle.java root class.

```
package examples.entity.single_table;

public class Motorcycle extends RoadVehicle {
    public final AcceleratorType acceleratorType =
        AcceleratorType.THROTTLE;

    public Motorcycle() {
        numWheels = 2;
        numPassengers = 2;
    }

    public String toString() {
        return "Motorcycle: "+super.toString();
    }
}
```

Source 9.2 Motorcycle.java.

```
package examples.entity.single_table;

public class Car extends RoadVehicle {
    public final AcceleratorType acceleratorType =
        AcceleratorType.PEDAL;

    public Car() {
        numWheels = 4;
    }

    public String toString() {
        return "Car: "+super.toString();
    }
}
```

Source 9.3 Car.java.

```
package examples.entity.single_table;

public class Roadster extends Car {
    public enum CoolFactor {COOL,COOLER,COOLEST};

    private CoolFactor coolFactor;

    public Roadster() {
        numPassengers = 2;
```

Source 9.4 Roadster.java. *(continued)*

```
    }

    // setters and getters go here
    ...

    public String toString() {
        return "Roadster: "+super.toString();
    }
}
```

Source 9.4 *(continued)*

```
package examples.entity.single_table;

public class Coupe extends Car {
    public enum BoringFactor {BORING,BORINGER,BORINGEST};

    private BoringFactor boringFactor;

    public Coupe() {
        numPassengers = 5;
    }

    // setters and getters go here
    ...

    public String toString() {
        return "Coupe: "+super.toString();
    }
}
```

Source 9.5 Coupe.java.

Single Table per Class Hierarchy

In this strategy, a single table is used to represent the entire class hierarchy. A *discriminator* column is used to distinguish between subclasses. The discriminator column in the database will have different values based on the Java *type* it is representing.

The advantage of this strategy is that it is very efficient and supports polymorphism (as you will see in the next section). The disadvantage is that the table must have a column representing every field of every class in the hierarchy. Not only can this produce an extremely wide table if you have a deep inheritance hierarchy, but more importantly, every field that maps to a property of a subclass must be nullable. This makes sense since a row in the table can represent many different types, it would not be possible to define all the columns as NOT NULL.

Let's see how our five listings change in order to be entities and to use the single table per class hierarchy mapping strategy. Sources 9.6 through 9.10 show this (standard setters and getters as well as imports are omitted for brevity). Significant code additions are bolded. We will discuss the code below.

```
package examples.entity.single_table;

// imports go here

@Entity(name="RoadVehicleSingle")
@Inheritance(strategy=InheritanceType.SINGLE_TABLE)
@DiscriminatorColumn(name="DISC",
    discriminatorType=DiscriminatorType.STRING)
@DiscriminatorValue("ROADVEHICLE")
public class RoadVehicle implements Serializable {
    public enum AcceleratorType {PEDAL,THROTTLE};

    @Id
    protected int id;
    protected int numPassengers;
    protected int numWheels;
    protected String make;
    protected String model;

    public RoadVehicle() {
        id = (int) System.nanoTime();
    }

    // setters and getters go here
    ...
}
```

Source 9.6 RoadVehicle with entity annotations.

```
package examples.entity.single_table;

// imports go here

@Entity
@DiscriminatorValue("MOTORCYCLE")
public class Motorcycle extends RoadVehicle implements Serializable {
    public final AcceleratorType acceleratorType =
```

Source 9.7 Motorcycle.java with entity annotations. *(continued)*

```
        AcceleratorType.THROTTLE;

    public Motorcycle() {
        super();
        numWheels = 2;
        numPassengers = 2;
    }
}
```

Source 9.7 *(continued)*

```
package examples.entity.single_table;

// imports go here

@Entity
@DiscriminatorValue("CAR")
public class Car extends RoadVehicle implements Serializable {
    public final AcceleratorType acceleratorType =
        AcceleratorType.PEDAL;

    public Car() {
        super();
        numWheels = 4;
    }
}
```

Source 9.8 Car.java with entity annotations.

```
package examples.entity.single_table;

// imports go here

@Entity
@DiscriminatorValue("ROADSTER")
public class Roadster extends Car implements Serializable {
    public enum CoolFactor {COOL,COOLER,COOLEST};

    private CoolFactor coolFactor;

    public Roadster() {
        super();
        numPassengers = 2;
```

Source 9.9 Roadster with entity annotations. *(continued)*

```
    }

    // setters and getters go here
    ...
}
```

Source 9.9 *(continued)*

```
package examples.entity.single_table;

// imports go here

@Entity
@DiscriminatorValue("COUPE")
public class Coupe extends Car implements Serializable {
    public enum BoringFactor {BORING,BORINGER,BORINGEST};

    private BoringFactor boringFactor;

    public Coupe() {
        super();
        numPassengers = 5;
    }

    // setters and getters go here
    ...
}
```

Source 9.10 Coupe with entity annotations.

Let's start our analysis of this code with Source 9.6. Our first annotation is the `@Entity` annotation. This marks this Plain Old Java Object (POJO—see the sidebar "What's in a POJO?" for more information) as an entity for the application server.

At deployment time, the annotations are inspected and appropriate action is taken. It is the `@Inheritance`, `@DiscriminatorColumn`, and `@DiscrimintaorValue` annotations that give the hints to the application server that we are setting up a hierarchy using the single-table approach. The `strategy` element of the `@Inheritance` annotation explicitly indicates which strategy we want to use: `InheritanceType.SINGLE_TABLE`, in this case. The `@DiscriminatorColumn` annotation indicates a column name and type that will be used to discriminate between types. If this is not completely clear yet, don't worry! When you see the table definition that is automatically generated for this code, it will become clearer. Our discriminator column will be named

DISC and will contain values of type String (indicated by DiscriminatorType.STRING). Finally, we indicate that for objects of type RoadVehicle that are persisted, the value put in the discriminator column should be ROADVEHICLE. This is indicated using the @DiscriminatorValue annotation.

We also added the @Id annotation, which is required for entities. We are using a simple primary key (an int in this case). The key is generated in the constructor of RoadVehicle. The implication of this is that we are going to want each of our subclasses to call super() in their constructors so that the value of id will be properly set. The bottom line is that before you persist the entity, it must have a unique ID.

Notice that for each of the other source listings (9.7–9.10) the only annotation that we added aside from the @Entity annotation, is the @DiscriminatorValue annotation. It is the discriminator value that will distinguish between types in the single table. As described previously, each subclass calls super() in its constructer to guarantee that a unique ID is created for it.

We have added implements Serializable to each of the entity classes. This is simply so that (detached) objects can be passed back from methods to a standalone client.

You should take note of the fact that we explicitly gave the entity a name using the name element of the @Entity annotation. As you will see farther down, we create another version of these classes that use the multiple table strategy. In order to distinguish between these the two entity classes named RoadVehicle, we name one RoadVehicleSingle and the other RoadVehicleJoined.

WHAT'S IN A POJO?

POJO stands for plain old Java object. It has been a long sought after goal for persistence frameworks to be able to work with plain Java objects. This goal has now finally been achieved with the EJB 3.0 persistence layer.

There have been a number of articles and comments in forums questioning whether or not entities, as described in the EJB 3.0 persistence specification, really are POJOs. After all, the entity classes need to be annotated in order to be properly identified as entities. The container picks up on these annotations in order to properly deploy the entity and to inject resources, such as the EntityManager.

EJB 3.0 entities are, in fact, POJOs. This is so because annotations, in general, are now a part of the Java language. There is nothing that would prevent a standalone program, for instance, from instantiating and using an entity object completely outside any container or managed environment.

Much has been made of the fact that now that entities are POJOs, they can be tested outside the container. While this is true and very important, it is not the whole picture. If the code relies on injected resources, the testing framework must also inject these resources, even if the injected objects are simple mockup objects for the purposes of testing.

When we package these entities into a persistence unit (as described in Chapter 6) and deploy the code to the server, a table (if it doesn't exist) is created according to the rules specified via annotations in the code. To better understand what's going on behind the scenes, let's take a look at the structure of the table that is generated. Source 9.11 shows the Data Definition Language (DDL) for the generated table.

```
CREATE TABLE ROADVEHICLE (
        ID INTEGER NOT NULL,
        DISC VARCHAR(31),
        NUMWHEELS INTEGER,
        MAKE VARCHAR(255),
        NUMPASSENGERS INTEGER,
        MODEL VARCHAR(255),
        ACCELERATORTYPE INTEGER,
        COOLFACTOR INTEGER,
        BORINGFACTOR INTEGER
    );
```

Source 9.11 DDL for table generated from entities.

Notice that *all* of the properties specified in the class hierarchy are represented in the table. We have `ID`, `NUMWHEELS`, `NUMPASSENGERS`, `MAKE`, and `MODEL` from the parent class, `RoadVehicle` (which is also the default name of the table). We have `ACCELERATORTYPE` defined in the `Motorcycle` and `Car` classes. We have `COOLFACTOR` defined in the `Roadster` class and `BORINGFACTOR` defined in the `Coupe` class. We have one extra column, named `DISC`. This is the discriminator column we defined via annotation on the `RoadVehicle` root class. This field in the database will contain different values, depending on the type of object being persisted to the database. Notice that it is only the `ID` field that is defined as `NOT NULL`. If one of the fields that mapped back to a property were defined as `NOT NULL`, we would get into trouble when persisting types that didn't have that property. For instance, if the `BORINGFACTOR` field was defined as `NOT NULL` and we were persisting a `Roadster` object, we would get an error as `Roadster` has no `BORINGFACTOR` field and thus would *want* to set the field to null.

Let's take a look at a code snippet that creates some new entities and persists those entities. We will then take a look at the database rows that result. Source 9.12 is a code snippet that we might find when creating some new entities:

```
...
    @PersistenceContext
    EntityManager em;
...
        Coupe c = new Coupe();
        c.setMake("Bob");
        c.setModel("E400");
        c.setBoringFactor(BoringFactor.BORING);
        em.persist(c);

        Roadster r = new Roadster();
        r.setMake("Mini");
        r.setModel("Cooper S");
        r.setCoolFactor(CoolFactor.COOLEST);
        em.persist(r);

        Motorcycle m = new Motorcycle();
        em.persist(m);
...
```

Source 9.12 Let's persist some entities!

Notice that we create the various objects like any other Java object. When we are ready to synchronize with the database, we use the `persist` method of the `EntityManager` interface. A reference to the `EntityManager` is injected at the start of the code snippet in Source 9.12. Table 9.1 shows the data inserted into the database after this code executes (only columns relevant to the point are shown).

See how the record representing our `Coupe` object has a `NULL` for the `CoolFactor` property (since it does not have this property) and has a `0` for the `BoringFactor` property (representing the value of `BORING` as per the code). The record representing the `Roadster` object has a value of `2` (representing the value of `COOLEST` as per the code), while it has a value of `NULL` for `BoringFactor` since `Roadster` does not have this property. The discriminator column has values as specified in the annotations for the code.

Table 9.1 Persisted Data

ID	DISC	MAKE	MODEL	COOL FACTOR	BORINGFACTOR
1818876882	COUPE	Bob	E400	NULL	0
1673414469	MOTORCYCLE	NULL	NULL	2	NULL
1673657791	ROADSTER	Mini	Cooper S	NULL	NULL

When deciding to use this strategy, you want to make sure that your class hierarchy does not contain too many properties (which would result in a very wide table) and that it is acceptable that columns in the table (potentially many of them) have NULL values.

Let's now take a look at the second strategy, the separate table per subclass.

Separate Table per Subclass

This strategy has a separate table for each subclass in the hierarchy. The layout of the table will be *only* those properties that are defined in the subclass separate from parent classes in the hierarchy.

To code this strategy in Java, we simply take away the annotations on the subclasses for discriminator (since we don't need the discriminator) and change the inheritance type in the root class. Source 9.13 shows this.

```
@Entity(name="RoadVehicleJoined")
@Table(name="ROADVEHICLEJOINED")
@Inheritance(strategy=InheritanceType.JOINED)
public class RoadVehicle {
    ...
}
```

Source 9.13 RoadVehicle with table per subclass strategy.

This time, we use the InheritanceType.JOINED to indicate the table per subclass strategy. The reason that it is referred to as joined is that in this strategy, in order to resolve all of the properties for a subclass, a join between tables must be performed. The Id from the parent object is used as the foreign key to the tables representing the subclasses. We also use the @Table annotation to specify a database table name explicitly different from the class name, in this case to differentiate the table name from that in our previous examples. By default, the container will generate the table name based on the class name. Since we already had a RoadVehicle class example with a corresponding table named ROADVEHICLE, we explicitly named the table ROADVEHICLEJOINED.

Using the exact same code from Source 9.12, let's see the tables that are generated as a result. Tables 9.2 through 9.6 show the generated tables and (relevant) values.

Each table has an ID column that is used for joining when resolving individual entities. The table representing the root of the hierarchy also has a discriminator column. By default, the column is named DTYPE and is of type DiscriminatorType.STRING. This column and its value type can be explicitly specified the same way we did for the single-table approach.

Table 9.2 ROADVEHICLEJOINED Table

ID	DTYPE	NUMWHEELS	MAKE	MODEL
1423656697	Coupe	4	Bob	E400
1425368051	Motorcycle	2	NULL	NULL
1424968207	Roadster	4	Mini	Cooper S

Table 9.3 MOTORCYCLE Table

ID	ACCELERATORTYPE
1425368051	1

Table 9.4 CAR Table

ID	ACCELERATORTYPE
1423656697	0
1424968207	0

Table 9.5 COUPE Table

ID	BORINGFACTOR
1423656697	0

Table 9.6 ROADSTER Table

ID	COOLFACTOR
1423656697	2

Let's say that we now wanted to get at all the `Roadster` entities. Behind the scenes, a query like the following might be executed:

```
SELECT
    rvj.NumWheels, rvj.Make, rvj.Model,
    c.AcceleratorType, r.CoolFactor
FROM
    ROADVEHICLEJOINED rvj, CAR c, ROADSTER r
WHERE
    rvj.Id = c.Id and c.Id = r.Id;
```

This highlights the only drawback with this strategy: Table joins must be performed in order to get at *all* of the properties of subclasses. This strategy does support polymorphism, and if your class hierarchy is not too deep, it is an excellent approach. The deeper the class hierarchy (the more subclasses), the more joins that will need to be performed. This could significantly affect performance.

Single Table per Concrete Entity Class

In this strategy, each concrete subclass has its own table. Each table has *all* of the properties found in the inheritance chain up to the parent class. Given the original source code in listings 9.1–9.5, we might expect the following layout in the generated tables, Tables 9.7–9.9.

In this strategy, each subclass has its own copy of all of the fields mapped in parent classes. This strategy does not support polymorphism well (covered in the next section).

Since the single table per concrete entity class strategy is not required to be supported by the EJB 3.0 specification, we will not go into further detail on this approach.

So far, we have been focusing on entity mapping strategies. In the next section, we will look at the other ways that entities support inheritance.

Other Modes of Inheritance

In a nutshell, the following general rules apply to inheritance with entities:

- Entities can extend non-entity classes
- Non-entity classes can extend entity classes
- Abstract classes can be entities
- An entity class can inherit from another entity class (as we saw above)

In order for an entity to extend a non-entity class, the `@MappedSuperclass` annotation is used. The superclass will not have any database tables directly associated with it, regardless of the mapping strategy used. You would want to use a mapped superclass in situations where a number of entities inherit from it. Source 9.14 shows this in action.

```
...
@MappedSuperclass
public class RoadVehicle {
    public enum AcceleratorType {PEDAL,THROTTLE};

    @Id
    protected int id;
    protected int numPassengers;
    protected int numWheels;
```

Source 9.14 Mapped superclass example. *(continued)*

Table 9.7 Database Table Layout Mapped for Roadster.java

ID	NUMPASSENGERS	NUMWHEELS	MAKE	MODEL	ACCELERATORTYPE	COOLFACTOR

Table 9.8 Database Table Layout Mapped for Coupe.java

ID	NUMPASSENGERS	NUMWHEELS	MAKE	MODEL	ACCELERATORTYPE	BORINGFACTOR

Table 9.9 Database Table Layout Mapped for Motorcycle.java

ID	NUMPASSENGERS	NUMWHEELS	MAKE	MODEL	ACCELERATORTYPE

```
    protected String make;
    protected String model;
    ...
}
...

@Entity
public class Motorcycle extends RoadVehicle {
    public final AcceleratorType ac = AcceleratorType.THROTTLE ;
    ...
}
...

@Entity
public class Car extends RoadVehicle {
    public final AcceleratorType ac = AcceleratorType.PEDAL;
    ...
}
...
```

Source 9.14 *(continued)*

The preceding example is very similar to what we have seen before. The difference is that this time, while we have maintained the inheritance hierarchy in Java, the table mappings will be different. Even if we use the `JOINED` strategy, `RoadVehicle` will never have its own table. It is not an entity by itself.

There is no problem with an entity class inheriting from a non-entity class that is not annotated as a mapped superclass. But none of the properties of the superclass will be persisted to the database. You may want to do this in a situation where there are transient properties in the superclass that you explicitly don't want to be persisted to the database.

Abstract classes can be entities. The only difference between abstract entities and concrete entities is that they cannot be instantiated. This, of course, is the same rule that applies to Java in general. Abstract entities can be mapped to the database and can be the target of queries.

In the next section, we will look at the polymorphic behavior of entities. The lack of support for polymorphism in previous versions of EJB has been one of the most bitter complaints of the specification. EJB 3.0's support for polymorphism marks a big leap forward in its maturity.

Polymorphism

Polymorphism with EJB 3.0 functions in exactly the same way we are used to with regular Java. Once a table mapping strategy has been selected, we can employ polymorphic behavior over a collection of entities. This can be done through an EJB-QL query, for instance (a more detailed discussion of EJB-QL queries follows later in this chapter, in the "EJB-QL Enhancements" section). Source 9.15 shows a code snippet that performs the query. Source 9.16 shows a client that interacts with the collection returned from the query.

```
...
@Stateless
public class RoadVehicleStatelessBean implements RoadVehicleStateless {
    @PersistenceContext(unitName="pu1")
    EntityManager em;

    public void doSomeStuff() {
        Coupe c = new Coupe();
        c.setMake("Bob");
        c.setModel("E400");
        c.setBoringFactor(BoringFactor.BORING);
        em.persist(c);

        Roadster r = new Roadster();
        r.setMake("Mini");
        r.setModel("Cooper S");
        r.setCoolFactor(CoolFactor.COOLEST);
        em.persist(r);

        Motorcycle m = new Motorcycle();
        em.persist(m);
    }

    public List getAllRoadVehicles() {
        Query q = em.createQuery(
            "SELECT r FROM RoadVehicleSingle r");
        return q.getResultList();
    }
    ...
}
...
```

Source 9.15 RoadVehicleStatelessBean.java.

```
...
public class RoadVehicleClient {
    public static void main(String[] args) {
        InitialContext ic;
        try {
            ic = new InitialContext();
            String name =
```

Source 9.16 RoadVehicleClient.java. *(continued)*

```
                RoadVehicleStateless.class.getName();
            RoadVehicleStateless rvs =
                (RoadVehicleStateless)ic.lookup(name);

            rvs.doSomeStuff();

            for (Object o : rvs.getAllRoadVehicles()) {
                System.out.println("RoadVehicle: "+o);
            }
        }
        catch (NamingException e) {
            e.printStackTrace();
        }
    }
}
```

Source 9.16 *(continued)*

The query in Source 9.15 will return a List of all `RoadVehicles`. The persistence layer will automatically handle searching the database for any data that maps to objects in the `RoadVehicle` hierarchy. In the `for` loop highlighted in Source 9.16, we iterate over this collection and pass the retrieved object in to the `System.out.println()` method. This causes the `toString()` method to be executed for each object in the list. If you reexamine the code in Sources 9.1 to 9.5, you will see that each class in the `RoadVehicle` hierarchy (including `RoadVehicle` itself) has its own implementation of the `toString()` method. We can see the polymorphic behavior in action in Output 9.1.

```
RoadVehicle: Coupe: Car:
    Make: Bob, Model: E400, Number of passengers: 5
RoadVehicle: Motorcycle:
    Make: null, Model: null, Number of passengers: 2
RoadVehicle: Roadster: Car:
    Make: Mini, Model: Cooper S, Number of passengers: 2
```

Output 9.1 Polymorphic behavior with entities.

In this case, the list returned from the query had three `RoadVehicle` elements: a `Coupe`, a `Motorcycle`, and a `Roadster`. The query was not explicit. Rather, it requested a list of all `RoadVehicle` entities. Since each of the subclasses is an entity, their data was added to the list. Calling `o.toString()` in the for loop exercised the polymorphic behavior and the individual object's `toString()` method was executed.

In the next section, we will look at the new annotations to support relationships between entities. While previous versions of the specification supported relationships between entities, the EJB 3.0 specification greatly simplifies marking these classes as participating in a relationship through annotation.

Relationships

Support for relationships has been around since the EJB 2.x specifications. EJB 3.0 significantly simplifies working with related entities through the use of annotation. First, let's review the matrix of entity relationships.

Relationship Types

Coming from the relational database world, the following are the possible relationships with a brief description of how each works.

- **One-to-one.** There is exactly one record related to another record. An example of this is the relationship between a Person and their home Address.
- **One-to-many.** A particular record is related to many other records. An example of this is the relationship between a Manager and his or her Employees. We can say, "one Manager has many Employees."
- **Many-to-one.** Many records are related to one particular record. An example of this is the relationship between Bank Accounts and a Person. There may be many Accounts belonging to one Person.
- **Many-to-many.** Many records are related to many other records. An example of this is the relationship between a Subscriber and an E-mail list. Each Subscriber can be subscribed to many E-mail lists. And, each E-mail list can have many Subscribers.

Relationships are also said to have directionality. They can be unidirectional or bidirectional. In a unidirectional relationship only the *owning* side of the relationship is aware of it. In a bidirectional relationship, both sides of the relationship are aware of it. For instance, if a one-to-one relationship between a Person and a Toothbrush is unidirectional, then given a Person we can get to the related Toothbrush. But, given a Toothbrush we can not get to the related Person. If the relationship were bidirectional, then given a Toothbrush, we could also get to the related Person.

So, with four relationship types and two types of directionality, we have a total of eight combinations, right? Wrong! There are actually only seven. This is because a bidirectional one-to-many relationship is equivalent to a bidirectional many-to-one relationship. Let's examine this in more detail. Suppose that we have a bidirectional one-to-many relationship between a Customer and some Orders. Given a particular Person, we can get to all of their Orders. An Order is related to a particular Customer. In a collection of these Orders, all of them relate back to the same person. Let's use the same example with a many-to-one bidirectional relationship. Given a collection of Orders, we can relate them back to a Customer. And, given a Customer, we can get to all of his or her Orders. It is the same relationship.

We will now look at code examples for each of the relationship types.

One-to-One

In a one-to-one relationship, each constituent can have at most one relationship with the other constituent. Examples of one-to-one relationships include:

- Person:Address
- Car:Windshield
- Order:Shipment

One-to-one relationships are typically set up by a *foreign key* relationship in the database. Figure 9.2 shows a possible database setup.

In Figure 9.2, the order has a relationship with a shipment. The order table has a foreign key, which is the shipment table's primary key. This foreign key is the link between the two tables. Note that this isn't the only way to set up a one-to-one relationship. In this figure, the relationship is unidirectional. If we wanted it to be bidirectional, the Shipment table would have a foreign key link back to the Order table.

OrderPK	OrderName	Shipment ForeignPK
12345	Software Order	10101

ShipmentPK	City	ZipCode
10101	Austin	78727

Figure 9.2 A possible one-to-one database schema.

Let's take a look at some code implementing the relationship shown in Figure 9.2. Sources 9.17 and 9.18 show two entities: Order and Shipment.

```
...
@Entity(name="OrderUni")
public class Order implements Serializable {
    private int id;
    private String orderName;
    private Shipment shipment;

    public Order() {
        id = (int)System.nanoTime();
    }

    @Id
    public int getId() {
        return id;
    }

    public void setId(int id) {
        this.id = id;
    }

    ...
    // other setters and getters go here
    ...

    @OneToOne(cascade={CascadeType.PERSIST})
    public Shipment getShipment() {
        return shipment;
    }

    public void setShipment(Shipment shipment) {
        this.shipment = shipment;
    }
}
```

Source 9.17 Order.java.

```
...
@Entity(name="ShipmentUni")
public class Shipment implements Serializable {
    private int id;
    private String city;
    private String zipcode;

    public Shipment() {
```

Source 9.18 Shipment.java. *(continued)*

```
        id = (int)System.nanoTime();
    }

    @Id
    public int getId() {
        return id;
    }

    public void setId(int id) {
        this.id = id;
    }

    ...
    // other setters and getters go here
    ...
}
```

Source 9.18 *(continued)*

In both sources, the entities are explicitly named. This is because these examples are repeated in a separate package to show bidirectional behavior (we look at the bidirectional example below). We name the entities to avoid naming conflicts. Each source also implements `Serializable`. This is so that these objects can be returned to a standalone client.

The `Order.java` class is a simple POJO. It has a reference to a `Shipment` object. In order to give the hint to the application server that we want to establish a one-to-one relationship between `Order` and `Shipment`, we use the `@OneToOne` annotation on the getter for the `Shipment` property. That's it (see the sidebar "To Cascade or Not to Cascade" for an explanation of the `cascade` element). The `Shipment.java` requires no other annotation as this is a unidirectional relationship.

Source 9.19 shows a code snippet from a stateless session bean with a method that persists an `Order` entity and a method that retrieves all of the `Order` entities. Source 9.20 shows a code snippet from a client that outputs the Order information as well as the related Shipment information.

```
...
@Stateless
public class OrderShipmentUniBean implements OrderShipment {
    @PersistenceContext
    EntityManager em;

    public void doSomeStuff() {
```

Source 9.19 OrderShipmentUniBean.java snippet. *(continued)*

```
        Shipment s = new Shipment();
        s.setCity("Austin");
        s.setZipcode("78727");

        Order o = new Order();
        o.setOrderName("Software Order");
        o.setShipment(s);

        em.persist(o);
    }

    public List getOrders() {
        Query q = em.createQuery("SELECT o FROM OrderUni o");
        return q.getResultList();
    }
}
```

Source 9.19 *(continued)*

TO CASCADE OR NOT TO CASCADE

In Source 9.17, you are introduced to the cascade element. This element is available to all of the relationship annotations. In order to provide the proper persistence behavior for related objects, we need to give hints to the application server on how to handle them. The cascade element indicates what types of persistence operations should be cascaded to the related entity or entities.

The cascade element takes an array of values from the enumeration `CascadeType`**. Valid values are:** `PERSIST`**,** `MERGE`**,** `REMOVE`**,** `REFRESH`**, and** `ALL`**. Specifying** `cascade={CascadeType.ALL}` **is equivalent to specifying** `cascade={CascadeType.PERSIST, CascadeType.MERGE, CascadeType.REMOVE, CascadeType.REFRESH}`**. By default, there is no cascade. In the example in Source 9.17, we indicate that persist operations on the** `Order` **entity should be cascaded to the related** `Shipment` **entity. If an** `Order` **entity were removed from the database using the** `EntityManager`**'s** `remove` **method, the operation would *not* cascade to the related** `Shipment` **entity.**

Generally speaking, we will want persistence operations to cascade to related entities. However, this is not a universal rule. For instance, suppose that you have an entity tracking transaction history. Just because you remove a particular record, you don't want a related transaction history record to automatically be removed because of your cascade settings.

You will have to decide on an entity-by-entity basis what the most appropriate cascade settings should be.

```
...
InitialContext ic = new InitialContext();
OrderShipment os =
    (OrderShipment)ic.lookup(OrderShipment.class.getName());

os.doSomeStuff();

System.out.println("Unidirectional One-To-One client\n");

for (Object o : os.getOrders()) {
    Order order = (Order)o;
    System.out.println("Order "+order.getId()+": "+
        order.getOrderName());
    System.out.println("\tShipment details: "+
        order.getShipment().getCity()+" "+
        order.getShipment().getZipcode());
}
...
```

Source 9.20 OrderShipmentClient.java snippet.

In Source 9.19, we create `Shipment` and `Order` objects. Notice how the `setShipment` method on the `Order` object is called. The very next line persists the `Order` to the database. Because of our cascade element settings in the `@OneToOne` annotation on `Order`, the related `Shipment` object is also persisted to the database. Tables 9.10 and 9.11 show the database table definitions automatically generated for these entities.

The foreign key column SHIPMENT_ID is automatically generated by the application server. There are rules for the naming of this column outlined in the JSR 220: Java Persistence API part of the EJB 3.0 specification. In this case, the name is formed from the relationship property found in `Order.java` (namely `shipment`), followed by an underscore (_), followed by the name of the primary key in the related entity.

To finish up this section, let's take a look at a bidirectional version of this same example. The `Order.java` code found in Source 9.17 stays the same (with the exception that the entity name is changed to `OrderBid` in order to avoid naming conflicts). Source 9.21 shows the `Shipment.java` code annotated to support a bidirectional relationship.

Table 9.10 Database Table Layout Mapped for Order.java

ID	ORDERNAME	SHIPMENT_ID

Table 9.11 Database Table Layout Mapped for Shipment.java.

ID	CITY	ZIPCODE

```
...
@Entity(name="ShipmentBid")
public class Shipment implements Serializable {
    private int id;
    private String city;
    private String zipcode;
    private Order order;

    public Shipment() {
        id = (int)System.nanoTime();
    }

    @Id
    public int getId() {
        return id;
    }

    public void setId(int id) {
        this.id = id;
    }

    ...
    // other setters and getters go here
    ...

    @OneToOne(mappedBy="shipment")
    public Order getOrder() {
        return order;
    }

    public void setOrder(Order order) {
        this.order = order;
    }
}
```

Source 9.21 Shipment.java (bidirectional version).

In this version of the code, we add an `Order` property along with the standard getter and setter code. We also add the `@OneToOne` annotation. We use the `mappedBy` element of the `@OneToOne` annotation to indicate that the shipment property from the `Order` entity is used in the database mapping. That is, the target side of a one-to-one relationship needs to know the property from the owner side of the relationship in order to make it bidirectional.

Source 9.22 shows code added to our stateless session bean from Source 9.19. Source 9.23 shows code added to our client from Source 9.20.

```
...
public List getShipments() {
    Query q = em.createQuery("SELECT s FROM ShipmentBid s");
    return q.getResultList();
}
...
```

Source 9.22 Snippet added to OrderShipmentBidBean.java.

```
...
for (Object o : os.getShipments()) {
    Shipment shipment = (Shipment)o;
    System.out.println("Shipment: "+
        shipment.getCity()+" "+
        shipment.getZipcode());
    System.out.println("\tOrder details: "+
        shipment.getOrder().getOrderName());
}
...
```

Source 9.23 Snippet added to OrderShipmentClient.java.

In Source 9.22, we can see that this time we are querying on the `Shipment` side of the relationship. In Source 9.23, we get a hold of the order that is related to the shipment through the bidirectional relationship.

Interestingly, the resultant table layout is exactly the same as in the unidirectional example. This highlights the fact that the underlying database table layout is not always an exact match to the properties in the class definitions. In this case, it is not necessary to have a separate ORDER_ID column in the SHIPMENTBID table because it is a one-to-one relationship. This means that there should only be one ORDERBID record for a SHIPMENTBID record. A simple query will get hold of the ORDERBID record that is related to a given SHIPMENTBID record. It might look something like this:

```
SELECT
    o.Id, o.OrderName
FROM
    ORDERBID o, SHIPMENTBID s
WHERE
    s.Id = 646590264 and s.Id = o.Shipment_Id;
```

Let's now take a look at the next relationship type, one-to-many. Note that in this section we will cover many-to-one relationships as well, since they are functionally equivalent from a database perspective.

One-to-Many

A one-to-many relationship is one of the more common relationships you'll see in your object model. This is because one-to-one relationships are often combined into a single data object, instead of having a relationship between two separate data objects. Examples of one-to-many relationships include:

- Order:LineItems
- Customer:Orders
- Company:Employees

One-to-many relationships are also typically set up by a foreign key relationship in the database. In a unidirectional one-to-many relationship, the application server automatically generates a *join table*. The join table has two foreign key columns. The first foreign key column references the "one" side of the relationship, while the second foreign key column references the "many" side of the relationship. There is unique constraint placed on the second foreign key column. This ensures that the "many" side of the relationship can't be repeated. See the "Join Table Generation Rules" sidebar in the "Many-to-Many" section for more information on join table generation rules. Figure 9.3 shows this database layout.

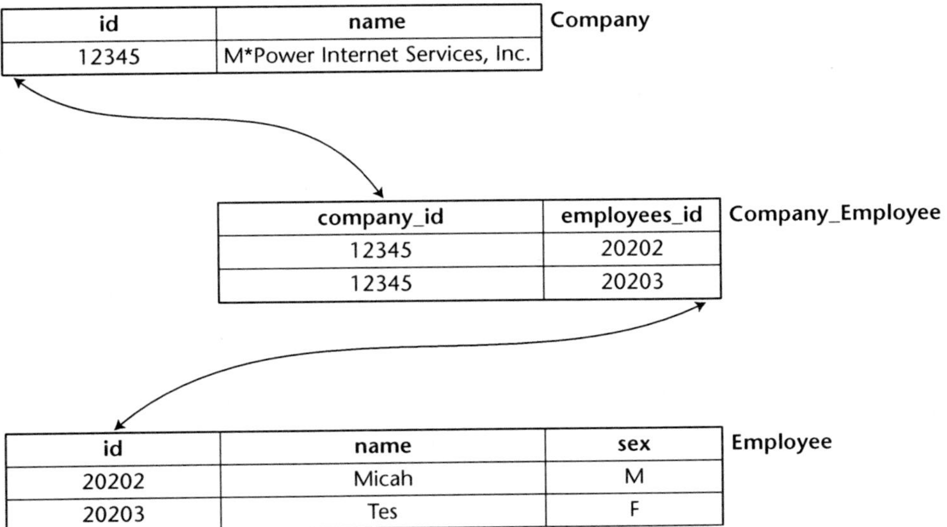

Company

id	name
12345	M*Power Internet Services, Inc.

Company_Employee

company_id	employees_id
12345	20202
12345	20203

Employee

id	name	sex
20202	Micah	M
20203	Tes	F

Figure 9.3 Unidirectional one-to-many relationship with join table.

Let's take a look at a unidirectional one-to-many example using the layout from Figure 9.3. Sources 9.24 and 9.25 show the code for our two entities involved in the unidirectional one-to-many relationship.

```
...
@Entity(name="CompanyOMUni")
public class Company implements Serializable {
    private int id;
    private String name;
    private Collection<Employee> employees;

    ...
    // other getters and setters go here
    // including the Id
    ...

    @OneToMany(cascade={CascadeType.ALL},fetch=FetchType.EAGER)
    public Collection<Employee> getEmployees() {
        return employees;
    }

    public void setEmployees(Collection<Employee> employees) {
        this.employees = employees;
    }
}
```

Source 9.24 Company.java.

```
...
@Entity(name="EmployeeOMUni")
public class Employee implements Serializable {
    private int id;
    private String name;
    private char sex;

    ...
    // other getters and setters go here
    // including the Id
    ...
}
```

Source 9.25 Employee.java.

In Source 9.24, we indicate the one-to-many on the `getEmployees` method. In this example, we use the `fetch` element of the `@OneToMany` annotation. The reason is that we will be returning the entities (detached) to a standalone client. The default behavior is to use lazy fetching (`FetchType.LAZY`), which fills in related entities only as needed. Lazy fetching is an important tool to improve performance on the server side. However, we must use eager fetching because the returned collection will become detached when sent back to the standalone client. Source 9.26 shows a code snippet from a stateless session bean and Source 9.27 shows a snippet from a standalone client that interacts with the stateless session bean.

LAZY AND EAGER FETCHING

Understanding the difference between lazy and eager loading, and when to use them, is critical to dealing with relationships efficiently.

Lazy loading will retrieve related entities only *as needed*, while eager loading attempts to retrieve all related entities at once.

The type of loading is marked using the `fetch` element to one of the relationship types, as in Source 9.24.

Eager loading is generally less efficient because the entire relationship map is retrieved. For instance, take the example where we have multiple customers, each of whom can have many orders, where each order can have many line items. If our fetch type is eager among all of these relationships, then a simple query of customers would produce a huge object map, including all of the orders for each customer with each order including all of the line items for that order. Marking everything as `FetchType.EAGER` often leads to poor performance.

If you are operating on a set of managed entities within an existing persistence context, then lazy loading is usually more efficient. In most cases, behind the scenes, related entities will be loaded as needed. In the customers example, if we wanted to query the list of customers for the purpose of retrieving each of their e-mail addresses, lazy loading would ensure that the related orders (and the orders' line items) were not retrieved because they would not be needed (referenced) in such a query.

A more granular level of loading can be achieved by using lazy loading in conjunction with *fetch joins*. Fetch joins are described in more detail in the "Join Operations" section. For now, we'll just state that a fetch join allows for eager loading on a case-by-case basis through a specific query. That is, if the query doesn't explicitly specify a fetch join, then the query will return results using lazy loading. If a fetch join is specified in the query, those entities involved in the join will be eagerly loaded.

```
...
@Stateless
public class CompanyEmployeeOMUniBean implements CompanyEmployeeOM {
    @PersistenceContext
    EntityManager em;

    public void doSomeStuff() {
        Company c = new Company();
        c.setName("M*Power Internet Services, Inc.");

        Collection<Employee> employees = new ArrayList<Employee>();
        Employee e = new Employee();
        e.setName("Micah Silverman");
        e.setSex('M');
        employees.add(e);

        e = new Employee();
        e.setName("Tes Silverman");
        e.setSex('F');
        employees.add(e);

        c.setEmployees(employees);
        em.persist(c);

        c = new Company();
        c.setName("Sun Microsystems");

        employees = new ArrayList<Employee>();
        e = new Employee();
        e.setName("Rima Patel");
        e.setSex('F');
        employees.add(e);

        e = new Employee();
        e.setName("James Gosling");
        e.setSex('M');
        employees.add(e);

        c.setEmployees(employees);
        em.persist(c);
    }

    public List getCompanies() {
        Query q = em.createQuery("SELECT c FROM CompanyOMUni c");
        return q.getResultList();
    }
}
```

Source 9.26 CompanyEmployeeOMUniBean.java.

```
...
    InitialContext ic = new InitialContext();
    CompanyEmployeeOM ceom = (CompanyEmployeeOM)ic.lookup(
        CompanyEmployeeOM.class.getName());

    ceom.doSomeStuff();

    for (Object o : ceom.getCompanies()) {
        Company c = (Company)o;
        System.out.println("Here are the employees for company: "+
            c.getName());
        for (Employee e : c.getEmployees()) {
            System.out.println("\tName: "+
                e.getName()+", Sex: "+e.getSex());
        }
        System.out.println();
    }
...
```

Source 9.27 CompanyEmployeeClient.java.

In Source 9.26, we set up two `Company` entities in the `doSomeStuff` method. Each `Company` entity has two `Employees` associated with it. Just before we persist the company to the database, we call the `setEmployees` method and pass in the `Employees` collection. Since we have a cascade setting of `CascadeType.ALL` defined on the `@OneToMany` annotation, the related `Employees` entities will be persisted as well. Source 9.27 is a snippet from a standalone client. The `getCompanies` method returns all the `Company` entities based on the query from Source 9.26. We iterate over these `Company` entities, and for each one get the collection of related `Employees`.

The bidirectional version of this code requires some more annotation, but results in an underlying database model that does not require a join table.

In Figure 9.4, each employee has a foreign key, which is the company table's primary key. Thus, the employees are pointing back to their company. This may seem backward if we want to get from the company to the employees. It works, however, because the database doesn't care—it is a flat structure without a sense of direction. You can still construct queries that get from the company to employees.

CompanyPK	Name
12345	The Middleware Company

EmployeePK	Name	Sex	Company
20202	Ed	M	12345
20203	Floyd	M	12345

Figure 9.4 A one-to-many database schema.

Let's see how the code changes to be bidirectional. Source 9.28 shows a snippet from `Company.java`.

```
...
@Entity(name="CompanyOMBid")
public class Company implements Serializable {
    private int id;
    private String name;
    private Collection<Employee> employees;

    ...

    @OneToMany(cascade={CascadeType.ALL},
        fetch=FetchType.EAGER,
        mappedBy="company")
    public Collection<Employee> getEmployees() {
        return employees;
    }

    public void setEmployees(Collection<Employee> employees) {
        this.employees = employees;
    }
...
```

Source 9.28 Company.java bidirectional annotation.

The only change to our code is to add the `mappedBy` element to the `@OneToMany` annotation. This indicates the property from the target entity that will participate in the relationship. Source 9.29 shows the bidirectional version of the `Employee,java` code.

```
...
@Entity(name="EmployeeOMBid")
public class Employee implements Serializable {
    private int id;
    private String name;
    private char sex;
    private Company company;

    ...

    @ManyToOne
    public Company getCompany() {
        return company;
    }

    public void setCompany(Company company) {
        this.company = company;
    }
}
...
```

Source 9.29 Employee.java with bidirectional annotation.

You will notice that we added a `Company` property to the `Employee` class. This enables the reference from `Employee` to `Company` without the need for a join table. The `@ManyToOne` annotation is used to identify the relationship from `Employee` back to `Company`.

Let's take a look at the stateless session bean code for the bidirectional example. Source 9.30 shows the `CompanyEmployeeOMBidBean.java` code.

```
...
@Stateless
public class CompanyEmployeeOMBidBean implements CompanyEmployeeOM {
    @PersistenceContext
    EntityManager em;

    public void doSomeStuff() {
        Company c = new Company();
        c.setName("M*Power Internet Services, Inc.");

        Collection<Employee> employees = new ArrayList<Employee>();
        Employee e = new Employee();
        e.setName("Micah Silverman");
        e.setSex('M');
        e.setCompany(c);
```

Source 9.30 CompanyEmployeeOMBidBean.java. *(continued)*

```
        employees.add(e);

        e = new Employee();
        e.setName("Tes Silverman");
        e.setSex('F');
        e.setCompany(c);
        employees.add(e);

        c.setEmployees(employees);
        em.persist(c);

        ...
        // the other Company and Employee code
        // comes after this
        ...
    }
    ...
}
```

Source 9.30 *(continued)*

This code is the same as before, except that now we must explicitly set the `Company` reference for each `Employee` entity.

For the final part of this section, we'll focus on the unidirectional many-to-one relationship. In this example, we have many `Employees` that all have the same (one) business `Address`. Source 9.31 shows the `Employee` class, and Source 9.32 shows the `BusinessAddress` class.

```
...
@Entity
public class Employee implements Serializable {
    private int id;
    private String name;
    private BusinessAddress address;

    public Employee() {
        id = (int)System.nanoTime();
    }

    @Id
    public int getId() {
        return id;
    }

    public void setId(int id) {
```

Source 9.31 Employee.java. *(continued)*

```
        this.id = id;
    }

    public String getName() {
        return name;
    }

    public void setName(String name) {
        this.name = name;
    }

    @ManyToOne(cascade={CascadeType.ALL})
    public BusinessAddress getAddress() {
        return address;
    }

    public void setAddress(BusinessAddress address) {
        this.address = address;
    }
}
```

Source 9.31 *(continued)*

```
...
@Entity
public class BusinessAddress implements Serializable {
    private int id;
    private String city;
    private String zipcode;

    ...
    // setters and getters go here
    ...
}
```

Source 9.32 BusinessAddress.java.

The owner side of the unidirectional relationship, the Employee entity, has the @ManyToOne annotation. Since it is a unidirectional relationship, no other annotation is required on the target side of the relationship, the BusinessAddress entity.

To close the relationship section of this chapter, we will examine the many-to-many relationship.

Many-to-Many

Many-to-many relationships are not as common as one-to-many relationship but are still important. Examples of many-to-many relationships include:

- Student:Course
- Investor:MutualFund
- Stock:Portfolio

Many-to-many relationships are typically set up by a *join* table in the database. As you saw in the unidirectional one-to-many example, a join table contains foreign keys to the two other tables. Figure 9.5 shows a possible database setup.

We're going to first look at the unidirectional implementation of the many-to-many Student/Course example. Source 9.33 shows the `Student` entity code, and Source 9.34 shows the `Course` entity code.

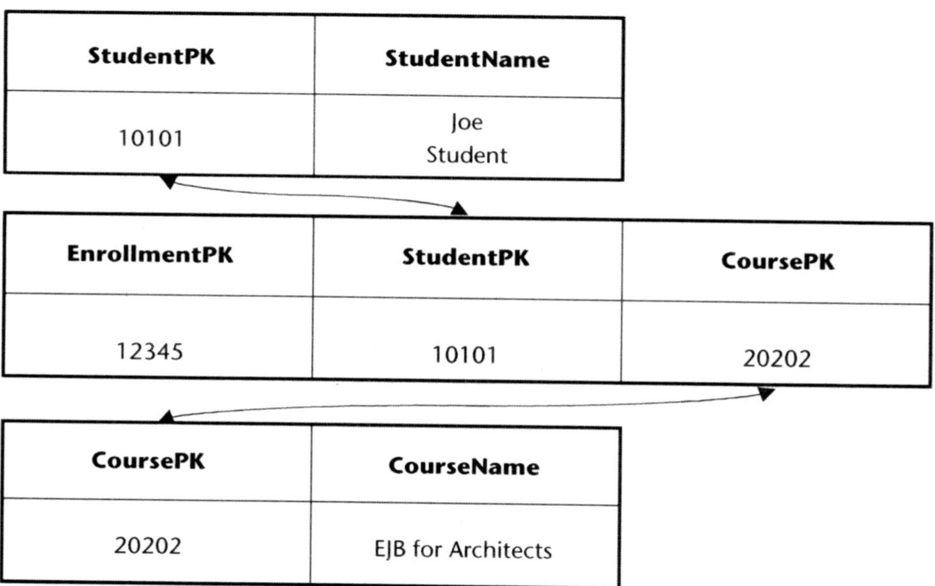

Figure 9.5 A possible many-to-many database schema.

```
...
@Entity(name="StudentUni")
public class Student implements Serializable {
    private int id;
    private String name;
    private Collection<Course> courses = new ArrayList<Course>();

    public Student() {
        id = (int)System.nanoTime();
    }

    @Id
    public int getId() {
        return id;
    }

    ...
    //other setters and getters go here
    ...

    @ManyToMany(cascade={CascadeType.ALL},fetch=FetchType.EAGER)
    @JoinTable(name="STUDENTUNI_COURSEUNI")
    public Collection<Course> getCourses() {
        return courses;
    }

    public void setCourses(Collection<Course> courses) {
        this.courses = courses;
    }
}
```

Source 9.33 Student.java.

```
...
@Entity(name="CourseUni")
public class Course implements Serializable {
    private int id;
    private String courseName;
    private Collection<Student> students = new ArrayList<Student>();

    ...
    //setters and getters go here
    ...
}
```

Source 9.34 Course.java.

First, notice that each entity uses the `name` element of the `@Entity` annotation. This has nothing to do with the many-to-many nature of them, but since further along we will use this same example in a bidirectional configuration, we want to distinguish between the entity names. This will have the effect of auto-creating database tables with the same entity name (more on this later). As before, each of the entities implements the `Serializable` interface so that they can be returned to a standalone client.

The `Student` entity has a collection of `Course` entities. This collection is initialized when a new `Student` entity is created. You will see a little farther down why we initialize the collection this way.

The `Student` entity also has the `@ManyToMany` annotation. This gives the hint to the container to generate the appropriate tables, including a join table to model the relationship. In this example, we also specify the `@JoinTable` annotation. This is done because the default behavior of the join table generation is to use the names of the entities involved with an underscore (_) in between (see the "Lazy and Eager Fetching" sidebar in the "One-to-Many" section). Thus, without the `@JoinTable` annotation, the generated join table would be named STUDENT_COURSE. Since we will have similar entities defined for the bidirectional example, we want to explicitly name the join table so that there is no naming conflict.

The `Course` entity has no further annotation, since this is a unidirectional relationship.

JOIN TABLE GENERATION RULES

The EJB 3.0 specification defines specific rules to auto-generating join tables and the columns of join tables. These rules take effect if not overridden by annotations (see Appendix B for a full treatment of all the EJB 3.0 annotations).

The rules for generating a join table are:

1. **The name of the join table will be the name of the owning entity, followed by an underscore (_), followed by the name of the target entity.**
2. **The name of the first column in the join table will be the property name, followed by an underscore, followed by the primary key name in the owner entity.**
3. **The name of the second column in the join table will be the property name, followed by an underscore, followed by the primary key name in the target entity.**
4. **The types of the columns in the join table will match the primary key types of the tables that will be referenced by it.**

In the Student/Course many-to-many example (without any overriding annotation), the join table would be named STUDENT_COURSE. This first column would be named STUDENTS_ID, and the second column would be named COURSES_ID.

Let's take a look at these entities in action. Source 9.35 shows a stateless session bean used to interact with the entities. Source 9.36 shows code for a standalone client.

```
...
@Stateless
public class StudentCourseUniBean implements StudentCourse {
    @PersistenceContext
    EntityManager em;

    public void doSomeStuff() {
        Course c1 = new Course();
        c1.setCourseName("EJB 3.0 101");

        Course c2 = new Course();
        c2.setCourseName("EJB 3.0 202");

        Student s1 = new Student();
        s1.setName("Micah");

        s1.getCourses().add(c1);

        c1.getStudents().add(s1);

        Student s2 = new Student();
        s2.setName("Tes");

        s2.getCourses().add(c1);
        s2.getCourses().add(c2);

        c1.getStudents().add(s2);
        c2.getStudents().add(s2);

        em.persist(s1);
        em.persist(s2);
    }

    public List<Student> getAllStudents() {
        Query q = em.createQuery("SELECT s FROM StudentUni s");
        return q.getResultList();
    }
}
```

Source 9.35 StudentCourseUniBean.java stateless session bean.

```
...
    InitialContext ic = new InitialContext();
    StudentCourse sc = (StudentCourse)ic.lookup(
        StudentCourse.class.getName());

    sc.doSomeStuff();

    for (Student s : sc.getAllStudents()) {
        System.out.println("Student: "+s.getName());
        for (Course c : s.getCourses()) {
            System.out.println("\tCourse: "+c.getCourseName());
        }
    }
...
```

Source 9.36 StudentCourseClient.java code snippet.

In the `doSomeStuff` method of Source 9.35, we create two `Course` entities. We then create a `Student` entity. The first bolded line of code shows how we use methods to manage the Collection of `Courses`. We first call the `getCourses` method, which returns the Collection. We then call its add method to add the course to the Collection. This highlights why we initialize the Collection in Source 9.33 and Source 9.34. The first `Student` is taking one `Course` and the second `Student` is taking two `Courses`.

We perform the same collection operations with the `Course` entity in order to register `Students`. The first `Course` has two students, and the second `Course` has one `Student`. Output 9.2 shows the output from the standalone client code above.

```
Student: Micah
        Course: EJB 3.0 101
Student: Tes
        Course: EJB 3.0 101
        Course: EJB 3.0 202
```

Output 9.2 Output from standalone client.

Since this is a unidirectional many-to-many relationship with `Student` being the "owner," we iterate over the list of all `Students` and show the `Courses` that each student has.

The bidirectional version of this code is more interesting and more powerful, since we can get at the data from both sides. Given a `Student`, we can see all the `Courses` she is taking, and given a `Course`, we can see all the `Students` enrolled in that course.

Let's take a look at the differences in the code when we make it bidirectional. The only changes to `Student.java` are the entity name (StudentBid) and the join table name (STUDENTBID_COURSEBID). Other than that, the code is exactly the same. Source 9.37 shows the changes to `Course.java` to enable a bidirectional relationship.

```
...
@Entity(name="CourseBid")
public class Course implements Serializable {
    private int id;
    private String courseName;
    private Collection<Student> students = new ArrayList<Student>();

    ...
    //getters and setters go here
    ...

    @ManyToMany(cascade={CascadeType.ALL},
        fetch=FetchType.EAGER,mappedBy="courses")
    public Collection<Student> getStudents() {
        return students;
    }

    public void setStudents(Collection<Student> students) {
        this.students = students;
    }
}
```

Source 9.37 Course.java bidirectional.

In this version of the code, the `@ManyToMany` annotation is used and the `mappedBy` element is used to indicate which property of the "owner" entity is used in the mapping. When using a many-to-many bidirectional relationship either side can be the owner.

Source 9.38 shows a snippet from the stateless session bean. The only change is the addition of a method to return all of the `Course` entities.

```
...
    public List getAllCourses() {
        Query q = em.createQuery("SELECT c FROM CourseBid c");
        return q.getResultList();
    }
...
```

Source 9.38 StudentCourseBidBean.java snippet

Source 9.39 shows the bidirectional many-to-many entities in action.

```
...
    InitialContext ic = new InitialContext();
    StudentCourse sc = (StudentCourse)ic.lookup(
        StudentCourse.class.getName());

    sc.doSomeStuff();

    for (Object o : sc.getAllStudents()) {
        Student s = (Student)o;
        System.out.println("Student: "+s.getName());
        for (Object o1 : s.getCourses()) {
            Course c = (Course)o1;
            System.out.println("\tCourse: "+c.getCourseName());
        }
    }
    System.out.println();
    for (Object o : sc.getAllCourses()) {
        Course c = (Course)o;
        System.out.println("Course: "+c.getCourseName());
        for (Object o1 : c.getStudents()) {
            Student s = (Student)o1;
            System.out.println("\tStudent: "+s.getName());
        }
    }
...
```

Source 9.39 Standalone client.

In this version of the standalone client, we still iterate over all of the `Students` and show the Collection of `Courses` for each `Student`. We also iterate over all of the `Courses` and show the Collection of `Students` for each `Course`.

Output 9.3 shows the output from the standalone client.

```
Student: Micah
        Course: EJB 3.0 101
Student: Tes
        Course: EJB 3.0 101
        Course: EJB 3.0 202

Course: EJB 3.0 202
        Student: Tes
Course: EJB 3.0 101
        Student: Tes
        Student: Micah
```

Output 9.3 Output from standalone client.

We have covered a huge amount of ground in this section. The way that the new Java Persistence specification handles the various types of relationships makes bridging the gap between Java objects and relational databases more straightforward than it has ever been.

There are many more annotations that offer a finer grain of control than we covered in this section. Using these annotations, we have total control over the mapping process, including table names and column names. This is extremely important when dealing with legacy databases, where we may not be able to use the defaults of table generation. See Appendix B for a more thorough discussion of available annotations.

In the next section you look at enhancements to the standardized query language for EJB 3.0.

EJB-QL Enhancements

In this section, we will focus on enhancements to EJB-QL for EJB 3.0. EJB-QL was introduced in Chapter 6. (For more information on EJB-QL, see Appendix D, available from this book's companion Web site.)

EJB-QL has been enhanced from the EJB 2.1 specification to include operations and modes common to those familiar with relational databases. These enhancements include:

- Bulk updates
- Bulk deletes
- `JOIN` operations
- `GROUP BY` clause
- `HAVING` clause
- Projection
- Subqueries
- Dynamic queries
- Named parameters
- Constructing new objects in `SELECT` statements

We will look at each of these in turn.

Bulk Updates and Deletes

Bulk updates and deletes are a common operation when working with a relational database. As you might guess (or already know), the idea is to remove a number of entities at once (which in turn removes a number of rows from the database all at once) or to update a number of entities at once (which, in turn, updates a number of rows from the database all at once). There are a few rules that apply to these operations:

1. The operation applies to the specified entity and *all* subclasses of the entity.
2. The operation does not cascade to any related entities.
3. The new value specified in a bulk update must be the right type for the update field in the database.
4. Bulk updates occur directly in the database. This means that optimistic locking checks are bypassed and the value of the version column (if it exists) is not automatically updated.
5. The persistence context is *not* synchronized with the result of the operation.

The first three items are fairly intuitive. It is critical to understand the implications of the last two items. Because of the way that bulk updates and deletes are handled, they should be performed either at the beginning of a transaction or should be performed in a separate transaction. Doing otherwise could result in an invalid or inconsistent state between entities in the current persistence context and the database.

Let's look at a few examples. We'll examine the bulk operations on a previous example involving inheritance. Recall our `RoadVehicle` entity from the beginning of the chapter. In particular, we'll focus on the single-table inheritance example, although everything we cover here would work for the table per subclass method as well. We're going to add a few methods to the stateless session bean (and its corresponding business interface) in order to perform some bulk update and delete operations. Source 9.40 shows these methods.

```
...
    public void deleteAll(String type) {
        Query q = em.createQuery("DELETE FROM "+type);
        q.executeUpdate();
    }

    public void updateAll(String type) {
        Query q = em.createQuery("UPDATE "+type+
            " r SET r.numPassengers = 1");
        q.executeUpdate();
    }
...
```

Source 9.40 RoadVehicleStatelessBean.java snippet.

Both the `deleteAll` and `updateAll` methods take a `type` parameter. We will see this in action in a moment. Source 9.41 shows a standalone client to exercise all the methods of our stateless session bean, which in turn works with our entities.

```
...
public class RoadVehicleClient {
    public static void main(String[] args) {
        String action = "insert";
        String type = "RoadVehicleSingle";

        if (args.length>0) {
            if (args[0].startsWith("update")) {
                action="update";
            }
            else if (args[0].startsWith("delete")) {
                action="delete";
            }

            if (args.length == 2) {
                type = args[1];
            }
        }

        InitialContext ic;
        try {
            ic = new InitialContext();
            RoadVehicleStateless rvs =
                (RoadVehicleStateless)ic.lookup(
                RoadVehicleStateless.class.getName());

            if (action.equals("insert")) {
                System.out.println("Inserting...");
                rvs.doSomeStuff();
            }
            else if (action.equals("update")) {
                System.out.println("Updating "+type+"...");
                rvs.updateAll(type);
            }
            else if (action.equals("delete")) {
                System.out.println("Deleting "+type+"...");
                rvs.deleteAll(type);
            }

            System.out.println(
                "Here is the list of all RoadVehicles:\n");
            for (Object o : rvs.getAllRoadVehicles()) {
                System.out.println("RoadVehicle: "+o);
```

Source 9.41 RoadVehicleClient.java. *(continued)*

```
            }
        }
        catch (NamingException e) {
            e.printStackTrace();
        }
    }
}
```

Source 9.41 *(continued)*

This client takes an optional action parameter and an optional type parameter. By default the action will be insert and the type will be `RoadVehicleSingle`. We perform the indicated action and then call the `getAllRoadVehicles` method. This conforms to our rules above in that we are performing a bulk update or delete before we retrieve a collection of `RoadVehicle` entities.

The type parameter only applies for the update and delete actions. By specifying a valid entity type, the bulk operation will be performed only on that type. Output 9.4 shows the result of performing an insert and Output 9.5 shows the result of a subsequent update using the default parameters. Note: Extra whitespace and formatting have been added for readability.

```
Inserting...
Here is the list of all RoadVehicles:

RoadVehicle: Coupe: Car:
    Make: Bob, Model: E400, Number of passengers: 5
RoadVehicle: Motorcycle:
    Make: null, Model: null, Number of passengers: 2
RoadVehicle: Roadster: Car:
    Make: Mini, Model: Cooper S, Number of passengers: 2
```

Output 9.4 Create some entities and persist to the database.

```
Updating RoadVehicleSingle...
Here is the list of all RoadVehicles:

RoadVehicle: Coupe: Car:
    Make: Bob, Model: E400, Number of passengers: 1
RoadVehicle: Motorcycle:
    Make: null, Model: null, Number of passengers: 1
RoadVehicle: Roadster: Car:
    Make: Mini, Model: Cooper S, Number of passengers: 1
```

Output 9.5 Bulk update.

After the bulk update operation is performed (per the code in Source 9.40) you can see that all the values for the number of passengers have been changed to 1.

Given the same setup as in Output 9.4, let's do the bulk update again, only this time we will perform the update only for the `Car` entities (named `CarSingle`). Output 9.6 shows this.

```
Updating CarSingle...
Here is the list of all RoadVehicles:

RoadVehicle: Coupe: Car:
    Make: Bob, Model: E400, Number of passengers: 1
RoadVehicle: Motorcycle:
    Make: null, Model: null, Number of passengers: 2
RoadVehicle: Roadster: Car:
    Make: Mini, Model: Cooper S, Number of passengers: 1
```

Output 9.6 Bulk update only for CarSingle.

Notice that only those entities of type `Car` (`Coupe` and `Roadster`) have had their number of passengers updated. This is a powerful example of object relational mapping in action.

Let's do a bulk delete. Output 9.7 shows the result of a bulk delete where the passed in type is `CarSingle`.

```
Deleting CarSingle...
Here is the list of all RoadVehicles:

RoadVehicle: Motorcycle:
    Make: null, Model: null, Number of passengers: 2
```

Output 9.7 Bulk delete only for CarSingle.

Notice that all of the `Car` entities have been deleted. In the next section, we will look at EJB-QL enhancements for `JOIN` operations.

JOIN Operations

Joins are a very common operation in the relational database world. A table will have a foreign key that corresponds to the primary key in another table. This process is critical to having *normalized* databases. A normalized database is one in which, to the greatest extent possible, data is not repeated across tables.

Join operations are performed to identify *which* data should be selected. An *inner* join (the default) will only select records when the join condition is satisfied. For instance, the following query will select companies that have at least one associated employee:

```
SELECT c FROM CompanyOMUni c JOIN c.employees e
```

A *left join* (synonymous with the term *left outer join*) will retrieve entities where matching values from the join condition may be absent. The following query will select companies even if there are not associated employees:

```
SELECT c FROM CompanyOMUni LEFT JOIN c.employees e
```

A *fetch join* enables the prefetching of related entities specified in a query. Fetch joins take precedence over `FetchTypes` specified in relationships (see the "Lazy and Eager Fetching" sidebar in the "One-to-Many" section). Let's say that you have customers, each of whom may have made any number of orders (one-to-many relationship). Let's also say that lazy loading was specified for the orders when querying customers. Why would you want the orders to be "lazy loaded"? If you were performing a query just to get a list of customers to get their contact information, it would be a much more efficient query if all of the associated orders were not fetched as part of that query. Now, though, let's say we *do* want to perform a query that will prefetch all the orders as well as the customers. We might have an EJB-QL query that looks like this:

```
SELECT c from Customer c LEFT JOIN FETCH c.orders
```

Using the fetch join above, all orders for each customer would be prefetched which (in this use case) would make getting at this information much more efficient.

GROUP BY and HAVING clauses

The `GROUP BY` and `HAVING` clauses are also very common to relational databases. They are new, however, to EJB-QL. `GROUP BY` allows the results to be grouped according to a set of properties. For instance, if we wanted to know how many female and male employees there were in the database, we might have the following query:

```
SELECT
    e.sex, count(e)
FROM
    EmployeeOMBid e
GROUP BY
    e.sex
```

This will give us the information across the entire collection of employees. The HAVING clause allows us to further filter the results. For instance, if we just wanted to see the number of female employees, we would add a HAVING clause to our query:

```
SELECT
    e.sex, count(e)
FROM
    EmployeeOMBid e
GROUP BY
    e.sex
HAVING
    e.sex = 'F'
```

The following rules apply to the use of these clauses:

- Any argument that appears in the SELECT clause that is not an aggregation function (such as SUM, AVG, etc.) must appear in the GROUP BY clause.
- The HAVING clause must specify conditions on the GROUP BY arguments or by other aggregation functions (such as SUM, AVG, and so on).
- The use of HAVING in the absence of GROUP BY is not required to be supported by implementations of the EJB 3.0 specification and, therefore, should not be used.

Projection

Projections allow us to write a query over a (potentially large) set of entities, but only return certain attributes from the entities. This optimization allows for more efficient querying if the entire entity or set of entities is not required to be returned. Take the following query, for instance:

```
SELECT
    e.name,c.name
FROM
    EmployeeOMBid e, CompanyOMBid c
WHERE
    e.company = c
```

In this case, we are querying over the EmployeeOMBid entity and the CompanyOMBid entity, but we are only interested in the Employee name and the Company name attributes. This query would return a Vector containing an array of type Object for each element. In this case, each Object array in the Vector would contain two elements: a String for the employee name and a String for the company name.

Fun with Queries

EJB-QL now supports many common query operations from the relational database world, including dynamic queries (with named parameters), subqueries, and named queries. We will look at each of these in turn.

Dynamic Queries and Named Parameters

Elements of a query, and even the entire query itself, can be processed at runtime. Let's look at a simple example in the following snippet, Source 9.42.

```
...
@PersistenceContext
EntityManager manager;
...
public List findByName(String name) {
    return manager.createQuery("SELECT e FROM Employee e "+
        "WHERE e.name LIKE :empName")
        .setParameter("empName", name)
        .listResults();
}
...
```

Source 9.42 Dynamic query with named parameter.

In the preceding example, the named parameter `:empName` is replaced at runtime through the `setParameter` method of the Query class (returned by the `createQuery` method).

Subqueries

Subqueries allow us to perform complete queries as part (or all) of a `WHERE` clause. Note, that deep subqueries can affect performance. Often, subqueries can be optimized as joins. Let's look at an example where we select only companies that have at least one employee.

```
SELECT
    c
FROM
    CompanyOMBid c
WHERE
    (SELECT COUNT(e) FROM c.employees e) > 0
```

We can see that the left side of the `WHERE` expression is a fully contained query.

Named queries allow us to reference a query much in the same way that we use variables in programming. Refer to Chapter 6 for more information about named queries.

Object Construction in SELECT Statements

One of the most exciting and convenient enhancements to EJB-QL is the ability to instantiate an object to be used as the target of a query operation. This is commonly used in queries using projection (as explained above). Source 9.43 shows a simple Java Bean. Source 9.44 shows this bean being used in a query.

```
public class CompanyEmployeeInfo {
    private String companyName;
    private String employeeName;

    public CompanyEmployeeInfo(String cName, String eName) {
        companyName = cName;
        employeeName = eName;
    }

    ...
    // setters and getters go here
    ...
}
```

Source 9.43 CompanyEmployeeInfo.java.

```
...
@PersistenceContext
EntityManager manager;
...
public List getSomeInfo() {
    return
    manager.createQuery(
    "SELECT "+
    "NEW examples.entity.relation.bid.one_to_many."+
    "CompanyEmployeeInfo(c.name, e.name) "+
    "FROM EmployeeOMBid e JOIN e.company c")
    .getResultList();
}
...
```

Source 9.44 Constructor in query code snippet.

Note that the highlighted lines are split for readability. The `getSomeInfo` method returns a Collection of `CompanyEmployeeInfo` objects because of the constructor in the `SELECT` clause. The fully qualified name of the class must be supplied.

Summary

Whew! In this chapter, we covered some of the most exciting material in the EJB 3.0 specification. The ability to handle inheritance in a standard object-oriented way and still easily map to a relational database is a big advancement in the technology. The ability to model standard relationships found in databases in our Java objects using annotations is another big advancement in the technology.

EJB-QL creates a true standard for querying that is database-platform-independent and is fully object-aware. We query against objects, not database tables (although we can use native queries when absolutely necessary).

Persistence and associated persistence operations are the most powerful and the easiest to work with in this version of the specification. EJB has now (finally) achieved its original intended goal of being able to take advantage of common cross-cutting services provided by an application server, while being able to handle long-term persistence in a straightforward way.

In the next chapter, we will jump into transactions. Transactions enable us to group multiple operations into a single unit. Either the whole group of operations succeeds or, if something fails along the way, the whole group fails. So read on to learn all there is to know about EJB 3.0 transactions.

CHAPTER

10

Transactions

Many middleware services are needed for secure, scalable, and reliable server-side development. This includes resource pooling services, security services, remoting services, persistence services, and more.

A key service required for robust server-side development is *transactions*. Transactions, when used properly, can make your mission-critical operations run predictably in an enterprise environment. Transactions are an advanced programming paradigm that enables you to write robust code. Transactions are also very useful constructs when performing persistent operations such as updates to a database.

In the past, transactions have been difficult to use because developers needed to code directly to a transaction API. With EJB, you can gain the benefits of transactions without writing any transaction code.

In this chapter, we'll discuss some of the problems that transactions solve. We'll also discuss how transactions work and show how they're used in EJB. Because transactions are at the very core of EJB and are somewhat difficult to understand, we'll provide extensive background on the subject. To explain transactions properly, we'll occasionally get a bit theoretical. If the theory presented in this chapter piques your interest, many tomes written on transactions are available for further reading. See the book's accompanying Web site, `www.wiley.com/go/sriganesh`, for links to more information.

Motivation for Transactions

We begin our discussion with a few motivational problems that transactions address.

Atomic Operations

Imagine that you would like to perform multiple discrete operations yet have them execute as one contiguous, large, *atomic* operation. Take the classic bank account example. When you transfer money from one bank account to another, you want to withdraw funds from one account and deposit those funds into the other account. Ideally, both operations will succeed. But if an error occurs, you would like *both* operations to always fail; otherwise, you'll have incorrect funds in one of the accounts. You never want one operation to succeed and the other to fail, because both operations are part of a single atomic transaction.

One simplistic way to handle this is to perform exception handling. You could use exceptions to write a banking module to transfer funds from one account to another, as in the following pseudo-code:

```
try {
     // Withdraw funds from account 1
}
catch (Exception e) {
     // If an error occurred, do not proceed.
return;
}
try {
     // Otherwise, deposit funds into account 2
}
catch (Exception e) {
     // If an error occurred, do not proceed,
     // and redeposit the funds back into account 1.
return;
}
```

This code tries to withdraw funds from account 1. If a problem occurs, the application exits and no permanent operations occur. Otherwise, we try to deposit the funds into account 2. If a problem occurs here, we redeposit the money back into account 1 and exit the application.

There are many problems with this approach:

- The code is bulky and unwieldy.
- We need to consider every possible problem that might occur at every step and code error-handling routines to consider how to roll back our changes.
- Error handling gets out of control if we perform more complex processes than a simple withdrawal and deposit. It is easy to imagine, for example, a 10-step process that updates several financial records. We'd need to code error-handling routines for each step. In the case of a problem, we need to code facilities to undo each operation. This gets tricky and error-prone to write.
- Testing this code is yet another challenge. You would have to simulate logical problems as well as failures at many different levels.

Ideally, we would like a way to perform *both* operations in a single, large, atomic operation, with a guarantee that both operations either always succeed or always fail.

Network or Machine Failure

Let's extend our classic bank account example and assume that our bank account logic is distributed across a multi-tier deployment. This may be necessary to achieve necessary scalability, and modularization. In a multitier deployment, any client code that wants to use our bank account application must do so across the network via a remote method invocation (see Figure 10.1).

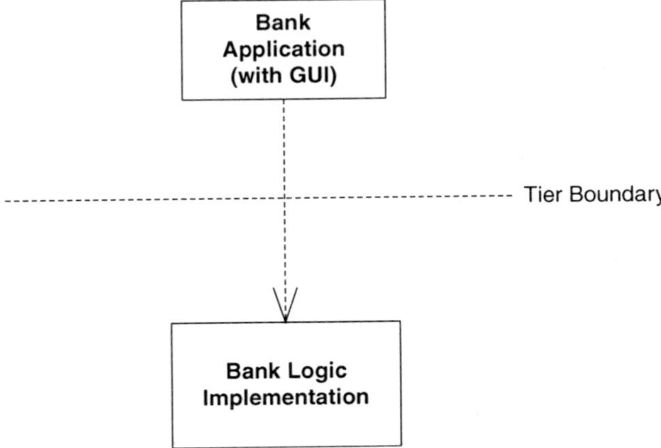

Figure 10.1 A distributed banking application.

Distributing our application across the network introduces failure and reliability concerns. For example, what happens if the network crashes during a banking operation? Typically, an exception (such as a Java RMI `RemoteException`) is generated and thrown back to the client code—but this exception is quite ambiguous. The network may have failed *before* money was withdrawn from an account. It's also possible that the network failed *after* we withdrew the money. There's no way to distinguish between these two cases—all the client code sees is a network failure exception. Thus, we can never know for sure how much money is in the bank account.

The network may not be the only source of problems. In dealing with bank account data, we're dealing with persistent information residing in a database. It's entirely possible that the database itself could crash. The machine on which the database is deployed could also crash. If a crash occurs during a database write, the database could be in an inconsistent, corrupted state.

None of these situations is acceptable for a mission-critical enterprise application. Big iron systems, such as mainframes or mid-frames, do offer preventive measures, such as system component redundancy and hot swapping of failed components to handle system crashes more graciously. But in reality, nothing is perfect. Machines, processes, and networks will always fail. There needs to be a recovery process to handle these crashes. Simple exception handling such as `RemoteException` is not sufficient for enterprise-class deployments.

Multiple Users Sharing Data

In any enterprise-level distributed system, you will see the familiar pattern of multiple clients connecting to multiple application servers, with those application servers maintaining some persistent data in a database. Let's assume that these application servers all share the same database, as in Figure 10.2. Because each server is tied to the same database image, servers could potentially be modifying the *same* set of data records within that database.

For example, you might have written an application to maintain your company's catalog of products in a database. Your catalog may contain product information that spans more than one database record. Information about a single product could span several database records or even tables.

Several people in your organization may need to use your catalog application simultaneously. But if two users modify the same product data simultaneously, their operations may become interleaved. Therefore, your database may contain product data that's been partially supplied by one user and partially supplied by another user. This is essentially corrupted data, and it is not acceptable in any serious deployment. Having the wrong data in a bank account could result in loss of millions of dollars to a bank or the bank's customers.

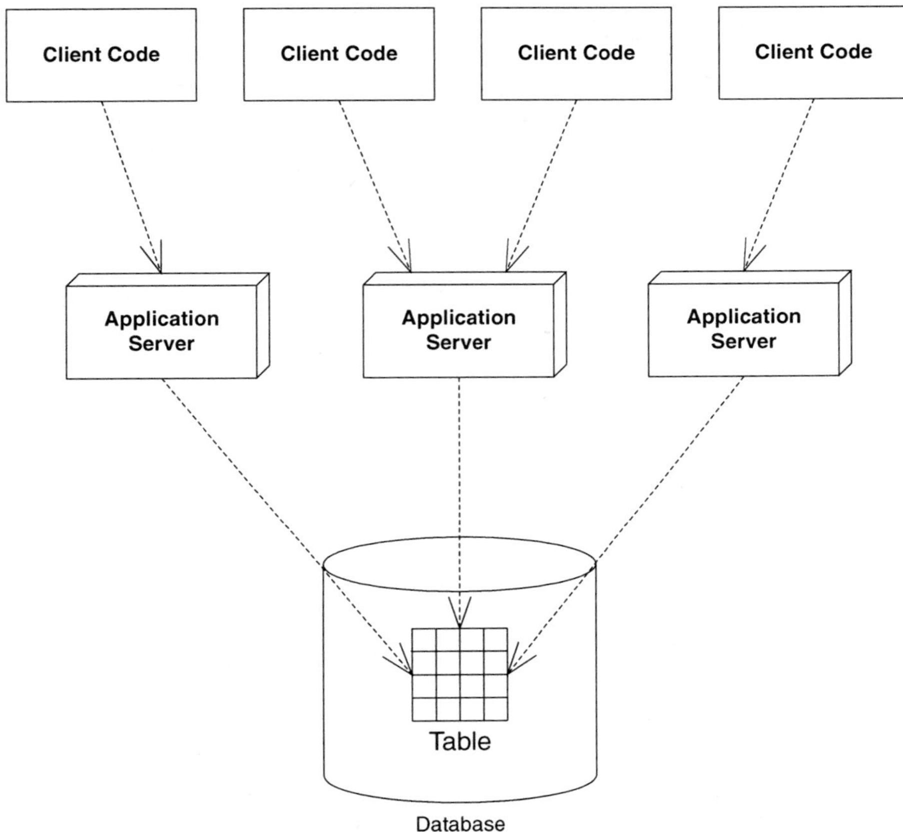

Figure 10.2 Application servers tied to a single database.

Thus, there needs to be a mechanism to deal with multiple users concurrently modifying data. We must guarantee data integrity even when many users concurrently update the data.

Benefits of Transactions

The problems raised in the previous sections can lead to catastrophic errors. You can avoid these problems by properly using *transactions*.

A transaction is a series of operations that appear to execute as one large, atomic operation. Transactions guarantee an all-or-nothing value proposition: Either all of your operations will succeed or none of them will. Transactions account for network or machine failure in a graceful, reliable way. Transactions allow multiple users to share the same data and guarantee that any set of data they update will be completely and wholly written, with no interleaving of updates from other clients.

By using transactions properly, you can force multi-user interactions with databases (or other resources) to occur independently. For example, two clients reading and writing from the same database will be mutually exclusive if transactions are properly used. The database system automatically performs the necessary concurrency control (that is, locking) on the database to keep client threads from affecting each other.

Transactions offer far more than simply letting simultaneous users use the same persistent stores. By having your operations run within a transaction, you are effectively performing an advanced form of concurrency control and exception handling.

The ACID Properties

When you properly use transactions, your operations will always execute with a suite of four guarantees. These four guarantees are well known as the *ACID properties* of transactions. The word ACID stands for *atomicity, consistency, isolation,* and *durability*. The following list explains each property.

TRANSACTION VOCABULARY

Before we get into the specifics of transactions, let's establish a vocabulary. There are several types of participants in a transaction: *transactional objects, transaction managers, resources,* and *resource managers*. Let's take a look at each of these parties in more detail.

A transactional object (or transactional component) **is an application component, such as a banking component, that is involved in a transaction. This could be an enterprise bean, a Microsoft .NET–managed component, a CORBA component, and so on. These components perform operations that need to execute in a robust fashion, like database interactions.**

A transaction manager **is responsible for managing the transactional operations of the transactional components. It manages the entire overhead of a transaction, running behind the scenes to coordinate things (similar to the way a conductor coordinates a symphony).**

A resource **is persistent storage from which you read or write. A resource could be a database, a message queue, or other storage.**

A resource manager **manages a resource. An example of a resource manager is a driver for a relational database, object database, message queue, or other store. Resource managers are responsible for managing all state that is permanent. The most popular interface for communication between resource managers and the transaction manager is the *X/Open XA* resource manager interface. Most database drivers support this interface. Supporting this interface will allow the resource manager to participate in transactions managed by a third party such as an EJB transaction manager.**

- **Atomicity** guarantees that many operations are bundled together and appear as one contiguous *unit of work*. In our banking example, when you transfer money from one bank account to another, you want to add funds to one account and remove funds from the other account, and you want both operations to occur or neither operation to occur. Atomicity guarantees that operations performed within a transaction undergo an *all-or-nothing paradigm*—either all the database updates are performed or nothing happens if an error occurs at any time. Many different parties can participate in a transaction, such as an enterprise bean, a CORBA object, a servlet, and a database driver. These transaction participants can force the transaction to result in *nothing* due to any malfunction. This is similar to a voting scheme: Each transaction participant votes on whether the transaction should be successful, and if any of the participants votes no, the transaction fails. If a transaction fails, all the partial database updates are automatically undone. In this way, you can think of transactions as a robust way of performing error handling.
- **Consistency** guarantees that a transaction leaves the system's state to be *consistent* after a transaction completes. What is a consistent system state? A bank system state could be consistent if the rule *bank account balances must always be positive* is always followed. This is an example of an invariant set of rules that define a consistent system state. During the course of a transaction, these rules may be violated, resulting in a temporarily inconsistent state. For example, your enterprise bean component may temporarily make your account balance negative during a withdrawal. When the transaction completes, the state is consistent once again; that is, your bean never leaves your account at a negative balance. And even though your state can be made inconsistent temporarily, this is not a problem. Remember that transactions execute *atomically* as one contiguous unit of work (from the atomicity property discussed previously). Thus, to a third party, it appears that the system's state is always consistent. Atomicity helps enforce that the system *always* appears to be consistent.
- **Isolation** protects concurrently executing transactions without seeing each other's incomplete results. Isolation allows multiple transactions to read or write to a database without knowing about each other because each transaction is isolated from the others. This is useful for multiple clients modifying a database at once. It appears to each client that he or she is the only client modifying the database at that time. The transaction system achieves isolation by using low-level synchronization protocols on the underlying database data. This synchronization isolates the work of one transaction from that of another. During a transaction, locks on data are automatically assigned as necessary. If

one transaction holds a lock on data, the lock prevents other concurrent transactions from interacting with that data until the lock is released. For example, if you write bank account data to a database, the transaction may obtain locks on the bank account record or table. The locks guarantee that, while the transaction is occurring, no other concurrent updates can interfere. This enables many users to modify the same set of database records simultaneously without concern for the interleaving of database operations.

- **Durability** guarantees that updates to managed resources, such as database records, survive failures. Some examples of failures are machines crashing, networks crashing, hard disks crashing, and power failures. Recoverable resources keep a transactional log for exactly this purpose. If the resource crashes, the permanent data can be reconstructed by reapplying the steps in the log.

Transactional Models

Now that you've seen the transaction value proposition, let's explore how transactions work. We begin by taking a look at *transactional models*, which are the different ways you can perform transactions.

There are many different models for performing transactions. Each model adds its own complexity and features to your transactions. The two most popular models are *flat transactions* and *nested transactions*.

NOTE To use a particular transaction model, your underlying transaction manager must support it. The EJB-defined transaction manager does not support nested transactions; it requires support for only flat transactions. Nested transactions are a good way to solve a host of transactional problems. Even though most of the transactionally aware applications can get around fine with flat transactions, nested transactions provide an elegant solution in many cases. To avoid the additional burden of having to implement nested transactions that most of the business applications might not even end up using, The EJB Expert Group did not mandate support for nested transactions.

Flat Transactions

A *flat transaction* is the simplest transactional model to understand. A flat transaction is a series of operations that are performed atomically as a single *unit of work*. After a flat transaction begins, your application can perform any number of operations. Some may be persistent operations, and some may not. When you decide to end the transaction, there is always a binary result: either success or failure. A successful transaction is *committed*, while a failed transaction is *aborted*. When a transaction is committed, all persistent operations become permanent changes; that is, all updates to resources, such as databases, are made durable in permanent storage only if the transaction ends with a *commit*. If the transaction is aborted, none of the resource updates are made durable, and thus all changes are *rolled back*. When a transaction aborts, all persistent operations that your application may have performed are automatically undone by the underlying system. Your application can also be notified in case of an abort, so that your application can undo in-memory changes that occurred during the transaction.

This is the *all-or-nothing* proposition we described earlier. The flat transaction process is outlined in Figure 10.3.

A transaction might abort for many reasons. Many components can be involved in a transaction, and any one component could suffer a problem that would cause an abort. These problems include the following:

- **Invalid parameters passed to one of the components.** For instance, a banking component may be called with a null argument when it was expecting a bank account ID string.
- **An invariant system state was violated.** For example, if an ongoing transactional operation can cause the bank account to reach a negative balance, your banking component can force the transaction to abort, undoing all associated bank account operations.
- **Hardware or software failure.** If the database that your component is using crashes, the transaction is rolled back and all permanent changes are undone. Similarly, if there is a software failure (such as a JVM crash) the transaction is rolled back.

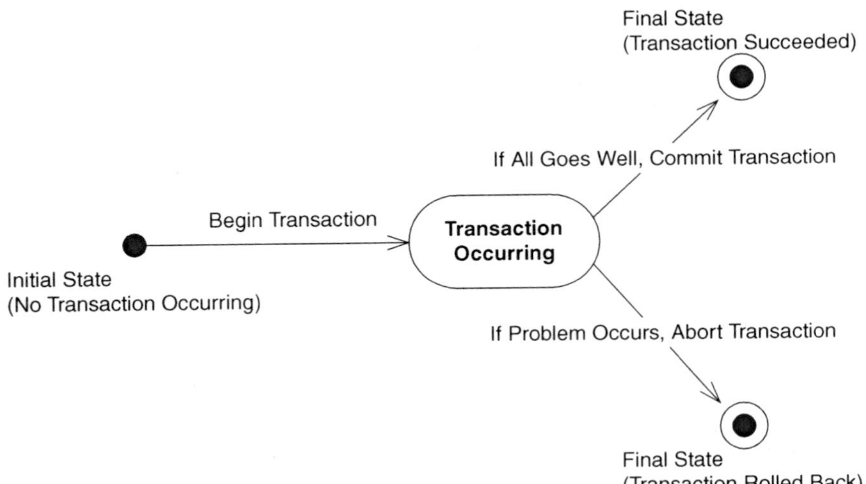

Figure 10.3 The flat transaction.

Any of these problems can cause a transaction to abort. But when an abort occurs, how is the transactional state rolled back? That is the topic of the next section.

How Transactional State Is Rolled Back

Let's assume that you're performing a flat transaction that includes operations on physical, persistent resources, such as databases. After the transaction begins, one of your business components requests a connection to a database. This database connection is automatically enlisted in the transaction in which your component is involved. Next, your component performs some persistent operations, such as database updates. But when this happens, your database's resource manager does not permanently apply the updates to the database—your persistent operations are not yet durable and permanent. The resource manager waits until a *commit* statement has been issued. A commit is issued only when the transaction is complete, meaning when all your business components have finished performing all of the operations under that transaction. If the resource is told to commit, it persists the data permanently. If the transaction aborts, the data is not persisted at all.

The take-away point from this discussion is that if there's an *abort*, the resource (such as a database) does not make your database updates permanent. Your components don't have any *undo* logic for permanent data inside of them; rather, the underlying system does it for you behind the scenes. Your components control the transaction and tell the transaction to abort, but the persistent state rollback is performed for you automatically. Thus, when your business components perform operations under a transaction, each component should perform all persistent operations assuming that the transaction will complete properly.

Now that you've seen flat transactions, let's take a quick look at nested transactions.

Nested Transactions

We begin our discussion of nested transactions with a motivational example. Let's say you need to write an application that can plan trips for a travel agency. You need to code your application to plan trips around the world, and your application must purchase the necessary travel tickets for the trip. Consider that your application performs the following operations:

1. Your application purchases a train ticket from Boston, USA, to New York, USA.

2. Your application purchases a plane ticket from New York, USA, to London, England.

3. Your application purchases a balloon ride ticket from London, England, to Paris, France.
4. Your application finds out that there are no outgoing flights from France.

This is the famous *trip-planning problem*. If this sequence of bookings were performed under a flat transaction, your application would have only one option: to roll back the entire transaction. Thus, because there are no outgoing flights from France, your application has to rollback all the work done as part of the bookings made from Boston to New York, New York to London, and London to Paris! But it may be possible to use another means of transportation out of France, which might allow you to salvage the bookings for the other segments. Thus, a flat transaction is insufficient. The all-or-nothing proposition is inefficient for such scenarios, and we need a more comprehensive transactional model.

A nested transaction solves this problem. A *nested transaction* enables you to embed atomic units of work within other units of work. The unit of work that is nested within another unit of work can roll back without forcing the entire transaction to roll back. Therefore, the larger unit can attempt to retry the embedded unit of work. If the embedded unit can be made to succeed, the larger unit can succeed. If the embedded unit of work cannot be made to work, it will ultimately force the entire unit to fail.

You can think of a nested transaction as a *tree* of transactions, all spawning off one *root-* or *top-level transaction*. The root transaction is the *main* transaction: In the trip-planning example, the root transaction is the overall process of booking tickets around the world. Every other transaction in the tree is called a *subtransaction*. The subtransactions can be flat or nested transactions (see Figure 10.4).

What's special about nested transactions is that subtransactions can independently roll back without affecting higher transactions in the tree. That's a very powerful idea, and it solves our trip-planning problem: If each individual booking is a nested transaction, we can roll back any one booking without canceling all our other reservations. But in the end, if the nested transaction cannot be committed, the entire transaction will fail.

Other Transactional Models

This concludes our discussion of transactional models. There are other models as well, such as *chained transactions* and *sagas*, but we will not address these subjects here because the EJB specification does not support them. And because the EJB specification does not currently mandate support for nested transactions, for the rest of this chapter we'll assume that our transactions are flat.

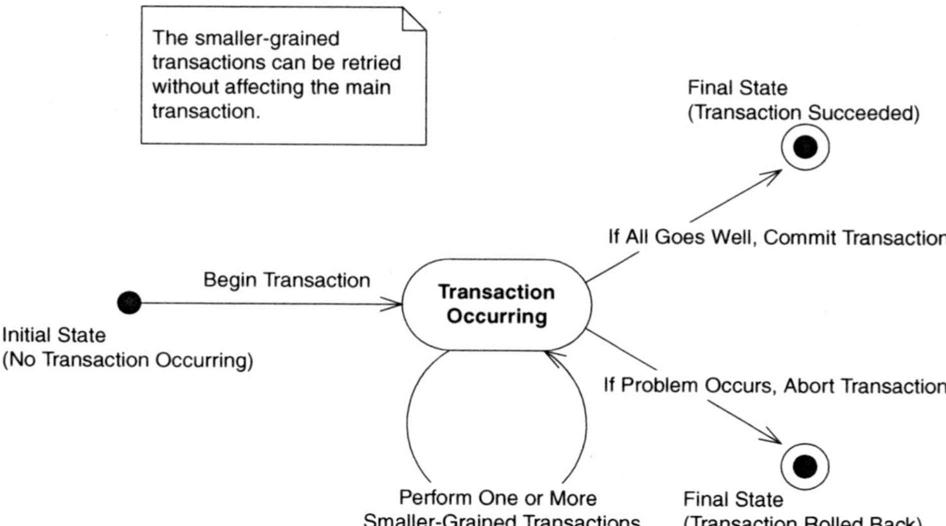

Figure 10.4 The nested transaction.

Distributed Transactions

Now that we've concluded our discussion of various transaction models, we'll shift gears a bit and talk about *distributed transactions*, which are transactions spanning multiple tiers of deployments and potentially involving multiple types of resources.

The most basic transaction occurs when components deployed on a single application server make changes to data on a single resource (a database, say). Depending on the functionality of your application server's transaction service, you may be able to perform *distributed transactions* as well. Distributed transactions obey the same rules as simple transactions (also known as *local transactions*), that is if a component on one machine aborts the transaction, the entire transaction is aborted. But with distributed transactions, you can have many different types of resources coordinating in a single transaction across the network. Here are some possible scenarios where distributed transactions are applicable:

- You have multiple application servers coordinating in the same transaction.
- You have updates to different databases in the same transaction.
- You are trying to perform a database update and send or receive a JMS message from a message queue in the same transaction.

- You are connecting to a legacy system as well as one or more other types of resources (such as databases, message queues, or other legacy systems) in the same transaction.

Each of these scenarios requires collaboration of one or more types of resource managers across multiple processes, potentially across a network, to solve a business problem. Distributed transactions come to your aid here. They allow multiple transaction participants to collaborate under one transactional hood.

The two-phase commit protocol is one of the widely implemented technologies for supporting distributed transactions. In the next section, we discuss the two-phase commit protocol, also known as 2PC.

Durability and the Two-Phase Commit Protocol

One important ACID property is durability. Durability guarantees that all resource updates that are committed are made permanent. Durability is easy to implement if you are manipulating the state of just one resource. But what if multiple resource managers are involved? If one of your resources undergoes a catastrophic failure, such as a database crash, you need to have a recovery mechanism. How do transactions accomplish this?

One way would be to log all database operations before they actually happen, allowing you to recover from a crash by consulting the log and reapplying the updates. This is exactly how transactions guarantee durability under the two-phase commit protocol. In this protocol, the transactions complete in two *phases*.

- **Phase One** begins by sending a *before commit* message to all resources involved in the transaction. At this time, the resources involved in a transaction have a final chance to abort the transaction. If any resource involved decides to abort, the entire transaction is cancelled and no resource updates are performed. Otherwise, the transaction proceeds on course and cannot be stopped, unless a catastrophic failure occurs. To prevent catastrophic failures, all resource updates are written to a transactional log or journal. This journal is persisted by all 2PC-enabled resource managers, so that it survives crashes and can be consulted after a crash to reapply all resource updates.
- **Phase Two** occurs only if Phase One completed without an abort. At this time, all of the resource managers perform the actual data updates.

If any participant votes that the transaction should abort, all participants must be rolled back.

In the distributed two-phase commit, there is one master transaction manager called the *distributed transaction coordinator*. The transaction coordinator runs the show and coordinates operations among the other transaction managers across the network. The following steps occur in a distributed two-phase commit transaction:

1. The transaction coordinator sends a *prepare to commit* message to each transaction manager involved.
2. Each transaction manager may propagate this message to the resource managers that are tied to that transaction manager.
3. Each transaction manager reports back to the transaction coordinator. If everyone agrees to commit, the commit operation that's about to happen is logged in case of a crash.
4. Finally, the transaction coordinator tells each transaction manager to commit. Each transaction manager, in turn, calls each resource manager, which makes all resource updates permanent and durable. If anything goes wrong, the log entry can be used to reapply this last step.

This flow is shown in Figure 10.5.

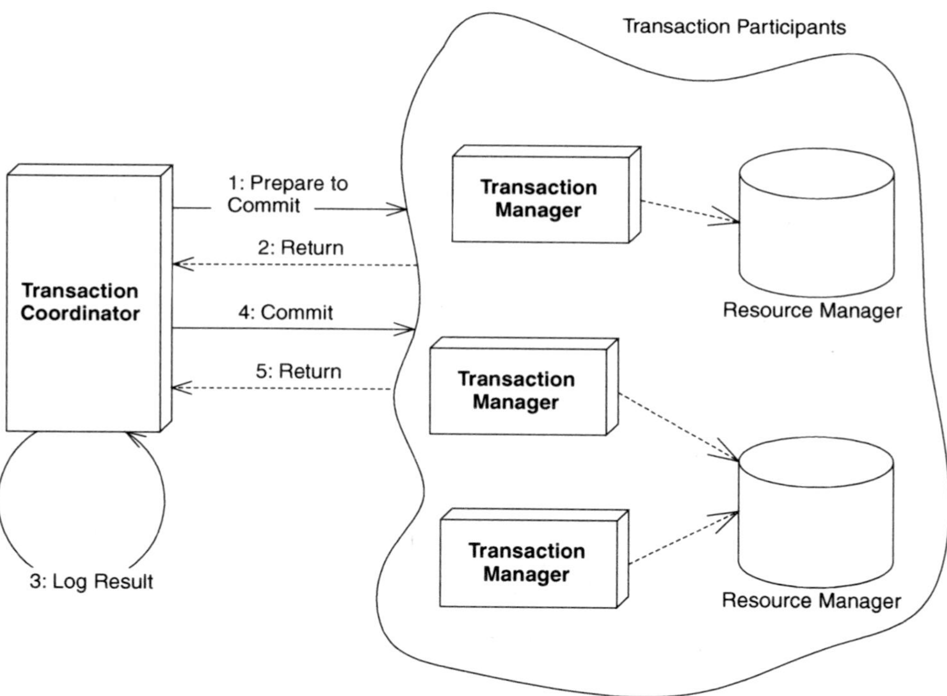

Figure 10.5 A distributed transaction accomplished using two-phase commit protocol.

The Transactional Communications Protocol and Transaction Contexts

A distributed two-phase commit transaction complicates matters, because the transaction managers must all agree on a standard mechanism of communicating. Remember that each of the participants in a distributed transaction may have been written by a different vendor, as is the case in a deployment with heterogeneous application servers. The communication mechanism used is called the *transactional communications protocol*. An example of such a protocol is the *Internet Inter-ORB Protocol* (IIOP), which we describe in Appendix A.

The most important piece of information sent over the transactional communications protocol is the *transaction context*. A transaction context is an object that holds information about the system's current transactional state. It is passed around among parties involved in transactions. By querying the transaction context, you can gain insight into whether you're in a transaction, what stage of a transaction you are at, and other useful data. For any component to be involved in a transaction, the current thread in which the component is executing must have a transaction context associated with it.

Java Transaction Service and Java Transaction API

The Enterprise JavaBeans Expert Group chose to reuse a lot of work that went into CORBA while defining the EJB container's support for transaction services. When we described the ACID properties earlier in this chapter, we mentioned that many parties, such as an enterprise bean and a database driver, could participate in a transaction. This is really an extension to the basic ACID properties, and it's the primary reason that Object Management Group (OMG) developed a standardized Object Transaction Service (OTS) as an optional CORBA service. OTS provides various improvements on many earlier transaction systems that didn't support multiple parties participating in a transaction.

OTS and Java Transaction Service

OTS is a suite of well-defined interfaces that specify how transactions can run behind the scenes—interfaces that the transaction manager, resource manager, and transactional objects use to collaborate. OTS is composed of two parts: `CosTransactions` and `CosTSPortability`.

- **The `CosTransactions` interfaces** are the basic interfaces that transactional objects or components, resources, resource managers, and transaction managers use to interoperate. These interfaces ensure that any combination of these parties is possible.

- **The `CosTSPortability` interface** offers a portable way to perform transactions with many participants.

In the EJB world, *Java Transaction Service* is the technology that provides Java binding to CORBA's OTS services at a very low level. Only system developers are interested in working with JTS at this level. Most of us, business application programmers, deal with JTS through the Java Transaction API.

The Java Transaction API

The *Java Transaction API* (JTA) defines the core of transaction support in EJB. It defines interfaces between a transaction manager and other parties, namely, application programs such as enterprise beans, resource managers, and application servers. JTA can be based upon the low-level JTS; the communication between transaction manager that implements JTA and JTS takes place through proprietary interfaces.

In this last case, we don't care about the lack of standardization for dealing with disparate JTS interfaces, since we will never work with JTS directly. We work only with JTA. So integration between JTS and JTA is not our concern. Non-EJB applications can use the JTA as well—for example, a standalone client application can call your beans within a transaction boundary that it marks using the JTA APIs.

JTA consists of three sets of interfaces:

- The `javax.transaction.xa.XAResource` interface that JTA uses to communicate with X/Open XA–enabled resource managers.
- The `javax.transaction.TransactionManager` interface that JTA uses to communicate with the application servers.
- And finally, the `javax.transaction.UserTransaction` interface, which can be used by beans and other application programs to work with the EJB transactions.

Figure 10.6 further clarifies the relationship of transaction manager, which implements JTA, with the rest of the parties in a distributed transactional system.

One of the things OTS defines is Communications Resource Manager (CRM), which is shown in Figure 10.6. CRM supports propagation of transaction contexts among other things. The EJB specification does not mandate the support for JTS, and hence, the support for CRM cannot be taken for granted in your EJB container. This has some implications on interoperability of distributed transactions across multiple application servers. Let us see how exactly does JTS support affect the distributed transaction interoperability in the next section.

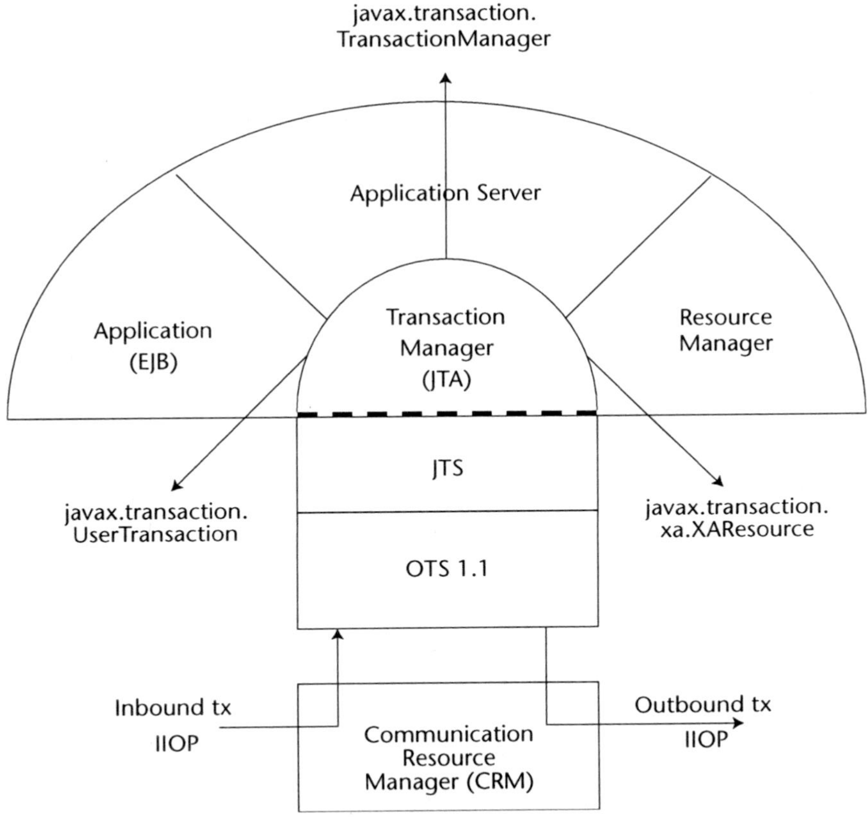

Figure 10.6 JTA: The glue between application program, application server, resource manager, and JTS.

JTS and Distributed Transaction Interoperability across Application Servers

The EJB specification suggests, but does not require, that application server vendors support on-the-wire transaction context interoperability. If an application server does support interoperable transactions, EJB requires that it leverage the transaction context propagation facilities built into CORBA OTS and IIOP. Application servers that use these technologies should be interoperable and run in a distributed two-phase commit transaction.

Since the EJB specification does not require this level of interoperability, application servers from different vendors cannot be guaranteed to work together and participate in a distributed two-phase commit transaction, because they may not be able to communicate in an interoperable way. Thus, it is important to understand which communication protocol your application server uses. If you want to perform a distributed two-phase commit transaction across multiple application servers, all the application servers must support OTS to facilitate interoperable propagation of transaction context.

Enterprise JavaBeans Transactions

Let's apply what we've learned so far about transactions to the EJB world.

Enterprise beans can be transactional in nature. This means they can fully leverage the ACID properties to perform reliable, robust server-side operations. Thus, enterprise beans are ideal modules for performing mission-critical tasks.

Underlying Transaction System Abstraction

In EJB, your code never gets directly involved with the low-level transaction system. Your enterprise beans never interact with a transaction manager or a resource manager. You write your application logic at a much higher level, without regard for the specific underlying transaction system. The low-level transaction system is totally abstracted out by the EJB container, which runs behind the scenes. Your bean components are responsible for simply voting on whether a transaction should commit or abort. If things run smoothly, you should commit; otherwise, abort.

Container-Managed, Bean-Managed, and Client-Controlled Transactions

Throughout this chapter, we've said that once a transaction begins, it ends with either commit or abort. The key pieces of information we're lacking are *who* begins a transaction, *who* issues either a commit or abort, and *when* each of these steps occurs. This is called *demarcating transactional boundaries*. In the EJB world, you can demarcate the transactions yourselves or let the container do that for you or rely upon your clients to demarcate them. Depending on who demarcates the transactional boundaries, the transaction management style is called bean-managed, container-managed, or client-controlled, respectively. When using bean-managed transactions, the bean provider is responsible for programming transaction logic into the application code. That is, *you* are responsible for issuing a *begin* statement and either a *commit* or an *abort* statement.

For example, an EJB banking application might have an enterprise bean that acts as a bank teller. A teller bean would expose a method to transfer funds from one bank account to another. With bean-managed transactions, the teller bean is responsible for issuing a *begin* statement to start the transaction, performing the transfer of funds, and issuing either a *commit* or *abort* statement. This is the traditional way to program transactions, and it is shown in Figure 10.7.

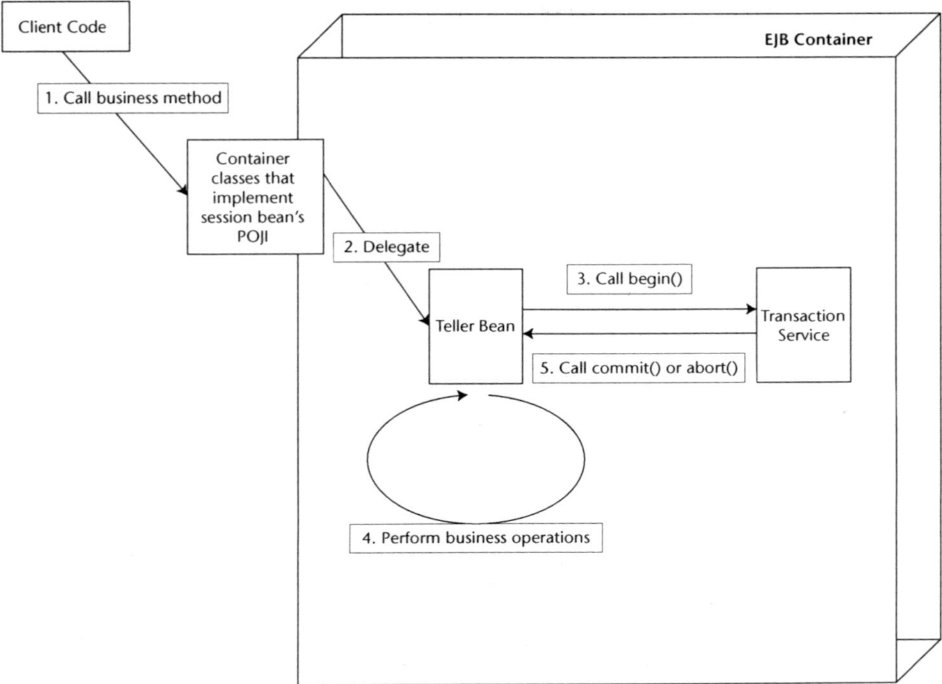

Figure 10.7 Bean-managed transactions.

Container-Managed Transactions

Container-managed transactions allow for components to *automatically* be enlisted in transactions. That is, your enterprise beans never explicitly issue a *begin*, *commit*, or *abort* statement. The EJB container performs it for you. The container demarcates the transaction boundaries based on the transactional behavior specified by the bean provider.

Let's take our bank teller example again, and assume some client code has called our teller bean to transfer funds from one account to another. With container-managed transactions, the EJB container starts a transaction automatically on behalf of your bean. That is, the container issues the *begin* statement to the underlying transaction system to start the transaction. The container then delegates the invocation to your enterprise bean, which performs operations in the scope of that transaction. Your bean can do anything it wants to, such as perform logic, write to a database, send an asynchronous message, or call other enterprise beans. If a problem occurs, the bean can signal to the container that the transaction must abort. When the bean is done, it returns control to the container. The container then issues either a *commit* or *abort* statement to the underlying transaction system, depending on the success of the operation(s). This is a very simple model, and it is shown in Figure 10.8.

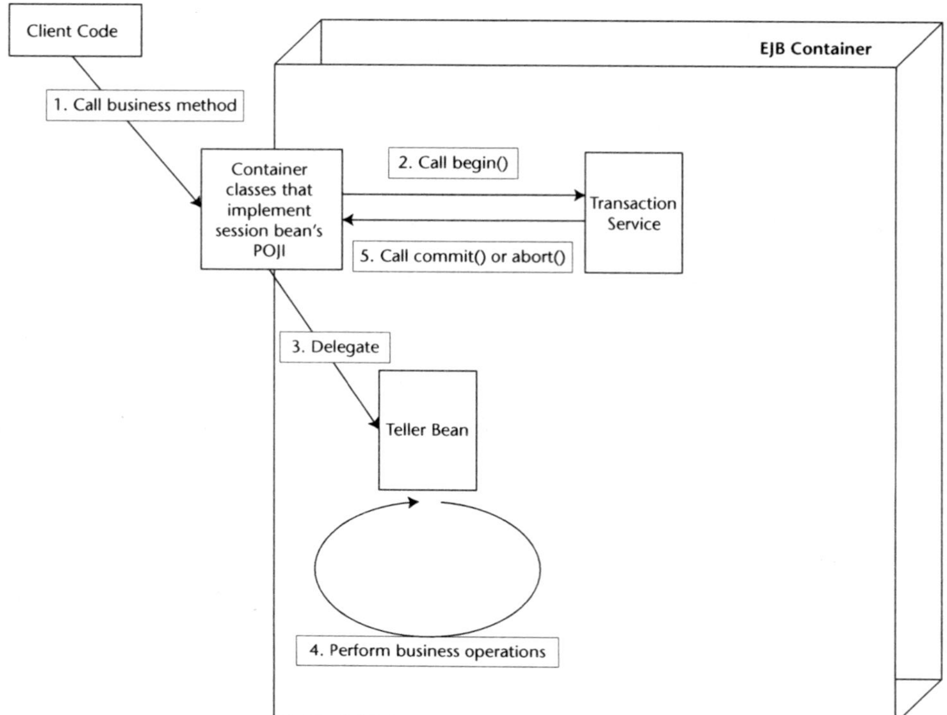

Figure 10.8 Container-managed transactions.

EJB container-managed transactions add huge value to your deployments because your beans may not need to interact with any transaction API. In essence, your bean code and your client are not even really aware of transactions happening around them.

So how do you instruct the container about whether your bean is using container-managed or bean-managed transactions? In EJB 3.0, you can specify your enterprise bean's transaction management style either by using `@TransactionManagement` annotation or through the deployment descriptor.

If neither the bean provider nor the deployer specifies transaction management, then the default is assumed to be container-managed.

Client-Controlled Transactions

The final way to perform transactions is to write code to start and end the transaction from the client code outside of your bean. For example, if you have a servlet, JSP tag library, standalone application, applet, CORBA client, or other enterprise bean as a client of your beans, you can begin and end the transaction in that caller. This is shown in Figure 10.9.

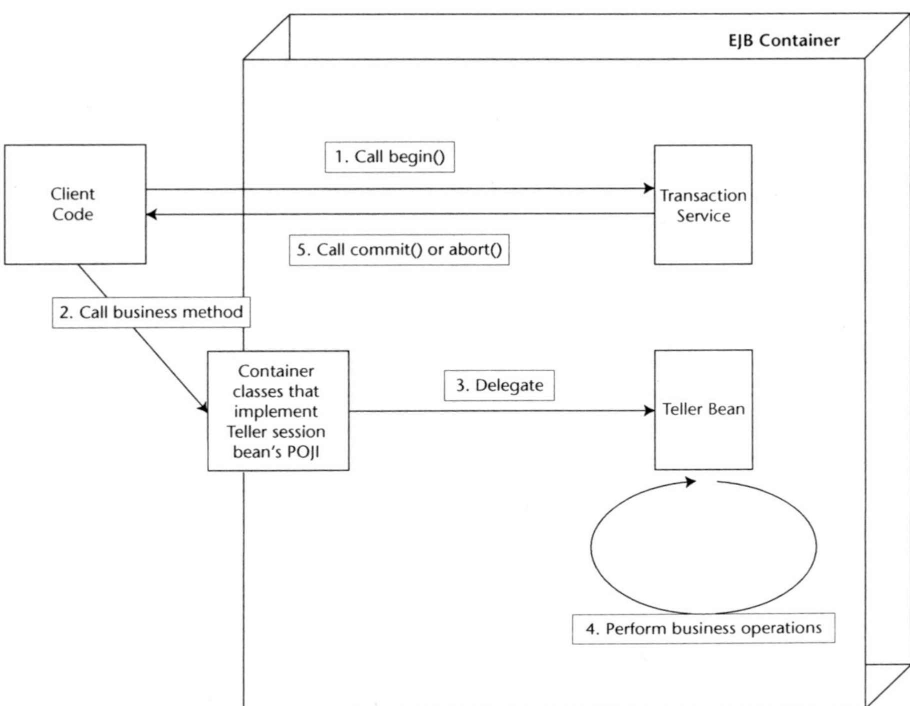

Figure 10.9 Client-controlled transactions.

Note that the enterprise bean the client calls still need to specify whether they support container-managed or bean-managed transactions.

Choosing a Transaction Style

One question that developers often ask is "Should I use declarative, programmatic, or client-controlled transactions?"

The benefit of bean-managed transactions is that you, as a developer, have full control over transactional boundaries. For instance, you can use bean-managed transactions to run a series of mini-transactions within a bean's method. In comparison, with container-managed or client-controlled transactions, your entire bean method must either run under a transaction or not run under a transaction.

The benefit of container-managed transactions is that they are simpler. You don't need to write transactional logic into your bean class, which saves coding time. Also, by having transactions configured at the level of bean, you keep client code from misusing your beans under inappropriate transaction settings. This reduces a great number of headaches for a component provider.

To understand the benefit of client-initiated transactions, consider the following scenario in which we *don't* use client-initiated transactions. Imagine that a nontransactional remote client calls an enterprise bean that performs its own transactions (either bean-managed or container-managed). The bean succeeds in the transaction, but the network or application server crashes before the result is returned to a remote client. The remote client would receive a Java RMI `RemoteException` indicating a network error but would not know whether the transaction that took place in the enterprise bean was a success or a failure. The remote client would then have to write code to check the state of the resources to find out whether they were updated successfully by the transaction. This code places an additional burden on the application developer.

With client-initiated transactions, you do not need to worry about this scenario, because the transaction is demarcated from within the client code. If anything goes wrong, the client will know about it. The downside to client-initiated transactions is that, for distributed applications, there may be a greater chance of client-controlled transaction rollbacks because the transactions are occurring over a network and, hence, network failures can cause the transaction to roll back more often. Because of this, use client-transactions sparingly—especially if the network connectivity between client and the bean is intermittent.

Container-Managed Transactions

Let's now assume that we are using container-managed transactions and understand how to implement them. Although we're not writing any code that starts and stops transactions, we still need to provide instructions to the container for how we'd like our transactions to operate. For example, how can we choose whether a bean always runs in a transaction, or whether a bean never runs in a transaction?

A *transaction attribute* is a setting that you give to a bean to control how your bean is enlisted in container-managed transactions. You can specify a different transaction attribute on each bean in your system, no matter how many beans are working together.

The transaction attribute can be specified either using `@TransactionAttribute` annotation or in the bean's deployment descriptor. The container knows how transactions should be handled for a bean from its transaction attribute. You must specify transaction attributes on all business methods for your beans.

EJB Transaction Attribute Values

Every enterprise bean must have a transaction attribute setting. The following subsections explain the possible values for the transaction attributes.

Required

You should use the `Required` mode if you want your bean to *always* run in a transaction. If a transaction is already running, your bean joins in on that transaction. If no transaction is running, the EJB container starts one for you.

For example, say you write a credit card component that performs operations on credit cards, such as charging a credit card or refunding money on a credit card. Let's assume that you ship the component with the `Required` transaction attribute. You then deploy that component for two customers.

- **Customer 1** deploys the component in its customer service center, using the component to refund money when an angry customer calls. The customer writes some code to call your bean as necessary. When the client code calls your bean method, the container automatically starts a transaction by calling `begin` and then delegating the call to your bean. When your method completes, the container issues either a `commit` or `abort` statement, depending on whether a problem occurred.
- **Customer 2** uses the billing component as part of a complete workflow solution. The customer wants to use the credit card component to charge a user's credit card when a user purchases a product from a Web site. The customer then wants to submit an order to manufacture that product, which is handled by a separate component. Thus, the customer has two separate components running but both of them run under the same transaction. If the credit card cannot be charged, the customer doesn't want the order to be submitted. If the order cannot be submitted, the customer doesn't want the credit card charged. Therefore, the customer produces his or her own workflow bean, which first calls the credit card–charging bean and then calls the bean to generate a manufacturing order. The workflow bean is deployed with `Required`, so a transaction automatically starts up. Because your credit card bean is also deployed with `Required`, you *join* that transaction, rather than start your own transaction. If the order submission component is also deployed with `Required`, it joins the transaction as well. The container commits or aborts the transaction when the workflow bean is done.

Thus, `Required` is a flexible transaction attribute that enables you to start your own transaction or join existing ones, depending on the scenario.

RequiresNew

You should use the `RequiresNew` attribute if you always want a *new* transaction to begin when your bean is called. If a transaction is already under way when your bean is called, that transaction is suspended during the bean invocation. The container then launches a new transaction and delegates the call to the bean. The bean performs its operations and eventually completes. The container then commits or aborts the transaction and finally resumes the old transaction. Of course, if no transaction is running when your bean is called, there is nothing to suspend or resume.

`RequiresNew` is useful if your bean needs the ACID properties of transactions but wants to run as a single unit of work without allowing other external logic to also run in its transaction.

Supports

When a bean is called with `Supports`, it runs in a transaction only if the client had one running already. If the client does not have a transaction, the bean runs with no transaction at all.

`Supports` is similar in nature to `Required`, with the one exception: `Required` enforces the starting of a new transaction if one is not running already. Because `Supports` will sometimes not run within a transaction, you should be careful when using this attribute. Mission-critical operations should be encapsulated with a stricter transaction attribute (like `Required`).

Mandatory

`Mandatory` mandates that a transaction *must be already running* when your bean method is called. If a transaction isn't running, the `javax.ejb.EJBTransactionRequiredException` exception is thrown back to the caller.

`Mandatory` is a safe transaction attribute to use. It guarantees that your bean should run in a transaction. There is no way that your bean can be called if a transaction isn't already running. However, `Mandatory` relies on a third party to start the transaction before your bean is called. The container will *not* automatically start a transaction; rather, an exception will be thrown back to the caller. This is the chief difference between `Mandatory` and `Supports`. `Mandatory` is useful if your component is designed to run within a larger system, such as a workflow system, where your bean is only part of a larger suite of operations, and you want to mandate that the larger operations start a transaction before calling your bean.

NotSupported

If you set your bean to use `NotSupported`, then your bean *cannot* be involved in a transaction at all. For example, assume that we have two enterprise beans, A and B. Let's assume bean A begins a transaction and then calls bean B. If bean B is using the `NotSupported` attribute, the transaction that A started is suspended. None of B's operations are transactional, such as reads/writes to databases. When B completes, A's transaction is resumed.

You should use `NotSupported` if you are certain that your bean operations do not need the ACID properties. This should be used only if your beans are performing non–mission-critical operations, where you are not worried about isolating your bean's operations from other concurrent operations. An example here is an enterprise bean that performs rough reporting. If you have an e-commerce portal, you might write a bean that routinely reports a rough average number of online purchases per hour by scanning a database. Because this is not a critical operation and you don't need exact figures, `NotSupported` is an ideal, low-overhead mode to use.

Never

The `Never` transaction attribute means that your bean cannot be involved in a transaction. Furthermore, if the client calls your bean in a transaction, the container throws `javax.ejb.EJBException` back to the client.

This transaction attribute is useful when you want to make sure all clients that call your bean do not use transactions. This can help reduce errors in client code, because a client will not be able to call your bean erroneously in a transaction and expect your bean to participate in the ACID properties with other transaction participants. If you are developing a system that is not transactional in nature and would like to enforce that behavior, consider using the `Never` attribute.

Transaction Attribute Summary

Table 10.1 is a summary of the effects of each transaction attribute. In the chart, T1 and T2 are two different transactions. T1 is a transaction passed with the client request, and T2 is a secondary transaction initiated by the container.

Table 10.1 is important because you need to understand how various transaction attributes will affect the length and scope of your transaction.

Table 10.1 The Effects of Transaction Attributes

TRANSACTION ATTRIBUTE	CLIENT'S TRANSACTION	BEAN'S TRANSACTION
`Required`	None	T2
	T1	T1
`RequiresNew`	None	T2
	T1	T2
`Supports`	None	None
	T1	T1
`Mandatory`	None	Error
	T1	T1
`NotSupported`	none	None
	T1	None
`Never`	none	None
	T1	Error

Container-Managed Transaction Example

Let us consider an example to better understand container-managed transactions. Let's say that you want to perform a transfer between two bank accounts. To achieve this, you might have a bank teller session bean that calls into two bank account entities. If you deploy the teller bean with say `Required` transaction attribute, all three of them—the bean as well as the bank account entities—will be involved in a single transaction such that changes made to one bank account will be made durable only if the changes made to the other bank account succeed. Since, at the time of persistence context creation of the account entities, the teller bean's transaction is active, both the bank account entities are enlisted in the Teller's active transaction. This scenario is illustrated in Figure 10.10.

Let us now take a look at the teller bean class that uses container-managed transactions. We use annotations in the bean class to specify the transaction management style as well as transaction attribute applicable to one of its methods, `transferFunds()`. Source 10.1 shows source for `TellerBean`.

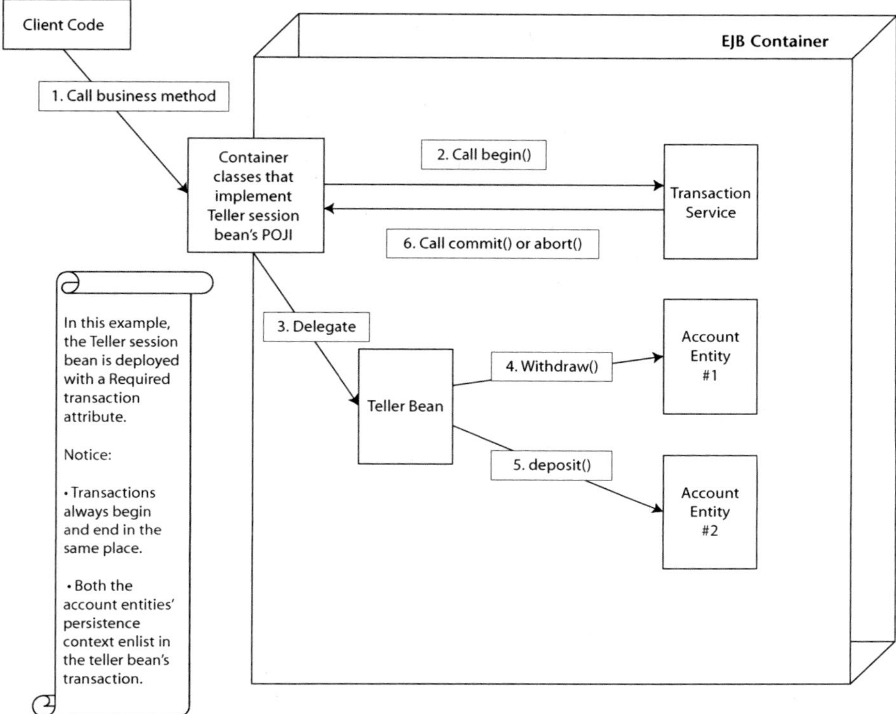

Figure 10.10 Using transaction attributes to control transactional boundaries.

```
import javax.ejb.*;
import javax.annotation.Resource;
import javax.persistence.PersistenceContext;
import javax.persistence.EntityManager;

@Stateless()
@TransactionManagement(javax.ejb.TransactionManagementType.CONTAINER)
public class TellerBean implements Teller {
    @PersistenceContext private EntityManager em;
    @Resource private SessionContext ctx;

    @TransactionAttribute(javax.ejb.TransactionAttributeType.REQUIRED)
    public void transferFunds(float amount, String fromAccount, String
                              toAccount)
    {
        // Lookup for accts with the provided account IDs

        BankAccount acct1 = em.find(BankAccount.class, fromAccount);
```

Source 10.1 Specifying transaction attributes using annotations. *(continued)*

```
        BankAccount acct2 = em.find(BankAccount.class, toAccount);

        if (acct1.balance < amount)
            ctx.setRollbackOnly();

        acct1.withdraw(amount);
        acct2.deposit(amount);

        em.persist(acct1);
        em.persist(acct2);
    }
}
```

Source 10.1 *(continued)*

As can be seen in Source 10.1, the bean provider doesn't have to worry about beginning or committing the transaction; the container begins the transaction before calling the `transferFunds()` method, and commits or rolls back the transaction once the method ends. Also notice a small rule that we have set in our method—if the balance of the withdrawal account is less than the amount that is being withdrawn, it should mark the transaction for rollback by calling the `setRollbackOnly()` method on the bean's context object. This will ensure that the container never commits the transaction under such a condition.

Another way to specify the transactional behavior for the teller bean is by using deployment descriptors. Once again note that if transactional attributes are specified in both the bean class through annotations as well as in the deployment descriptor, the deployment descriptor configuration always take precedence. Source 10.2 shows the listing of deployment descriptor for the teller bean containing transaction attribute settings.

```
<?xml version="1.0" encoding="UTF-8"?>
<ejb-jar xmlns="http://java.sun.com/xml/ns/javaee"
xmlns:xsi="http://www.w3.org/2001/XMLSchema-instance" full="false"
version="3.0" xsi:schemaLocation="http://java.sun.com/xml/ns/javaee
http://java.sun.com/xml/ns/javaee/ejb-jar_3_0.xsd">
  <enterprise-beans>
    <session>
      <display-name>TellerBean</display-name>
      <ejb-name>TellerBean</ejb-name>
      <business-remote>Teller</business-remote>
      <ejb-class>TellerBean</ejb-class>
      <session-type>Stateless</session-type>
      <transaction-type>Container</transaction-type>
      <security-identity>
        <use-caller-identity/>
```

Source 10.2 Specifying transaction attribute using deployment descriptor. *(continued)*

```
      </security-identity>
    </session>
  </enterprise-beans>

  <assembly-descriptor>
    <container-transaction>
      <method>
        <ejb-name>TellerBean</ejb-name>
        <method-name>transferFunds</method-name>
      </method>
      <trans-attribute>Required</trans-attribute>
    </container-transaction>
  </assembly-descriptor>
</ejb-jar>
```

Source 10.2 *(continued)*

Thus we created a transaction spanning one session bean and two entities by merely using transaction attributes.

DOOMED TRANSACTIONS

Dooming a transaction **means to force a transaction to abort. You may need to doom a transaction if something goes wrong, such as a database being unavailable or the client sending you bad parameters. The question is how do you doom a transaction that the container started? The answer to this lies in using the** `setRollbackOnly()` **method of the** `EJBContext` **interface. When you call this method, you essentially are declaring that the container should never commit the given transaction.**

Dooming transactions brings up an interesting side discussion. Imagine that you have 10 beans in a chain executing in the same transaction, and bean 2 decides to doom the transaction by calling `setRollbackOnly()`**. Why should beans 3 through 10 perform their work if the transaction is doomed to failure anyway? After all, those beans might be performing CPU- or database-intensive operations, all of which will be wasted away when the transaction aborts. The solution to avoiding this unnecessary work lies in your beans** ***detecting*** **whether the active transaction is doomed, and if it is, then just not performing the work. Your bean can detect whether the transaction is marked for rollback by calling the** `getRollbackOnly()` **method on bean's context. If this method returns** `true`**, then that means the transaction is set for rollback.**

In general, it is a good practice to check for a transaction's status at various points in your code if a lot of intensive work is happening within a single transaction in your bean. In our example, we can improve the implementation of the `transferFunds()` **method further by checking the status of the active transaction by calling** `getRollbackOnly()` **right before we make** `persist()` **calls on bank account entities.**

Applicability of Transaction Attributes to Various Beans

Finally, you should note that not all transaction attributes are available for use on all beans. Table 10.2 shows permissible transaction attributes for session beans and message-driven beans.

Table 10.2 provides the following important information about the support of transactions in various types of beans:

- Stateless session beans support all transactional attributes.
- A method on a Web service endpoint interface for a stateless session bean cannot support the `Mandatory` attribute. This is so because there is not yet a way to propagate a transaction context within the SOAP protocol that can then be translated to IIOP transaction context for invocations of a stateless session bean's Web service endpoint interface business methods.
- Stateful session beans that implement the `javax.ejb.Session Synchronization` interface should not specify the `Supports`, `NotSupported`, and `Never` transaction attributes. Implementing the `SessionSynchronization` interface is a mechanism for a stateful session bean to find out about the life cycle of the transaction in which it participates. In essence, a stateful bean must have the ability to participate in transactions whenever it implements the `Session Synchronization` interface to fulfill the latter's purpose. Note that we will discuss `SessionSynchronization` later in this chapter.
- A message-driven bean's client does not call a message-driven bean directly; rather, message-driven beans read messages off a message queue in transactions separate from the client's transaction. There is no client, and therefore transaction attributes that deal with the notion of a client's transaction make no sense for message-drivenbeans—namely `Never`, `Supports`, `RequiresNew`, and `Mandatory`.

A client does not call a message-driven bean directly; rather, message-driven beans read messages off a message queue in transactions separate from the client's transaction. There is no client, and therefore transaction attributes that deal with the notion of a client's transaction make no sense for message-driven beans.

Table 10.2 Permissible Transaction Attributes for Session and Message-driven beans

TRANSACTION ATTRIBUTE	STATELESS SESSION BEAN	STATELESS SESSION BEAN WEB SERVICE ENDPOINT METHOD	STATEFUL SESSION BEAN (IMPLEMENTS SESSION SYNCHRO-NIZATION)	MESSAGE-DRIVEN BEAN
`Required`	Yes	Yes	Yes	Yes
`RequiresNew`	Yes	Yes	Yes	No
`Mandatory`	Yes	No	Yes	No
`Supports`	Yes	Yes	No	No
`NotSupported`	Yes	Yes	No	Yes
`Never`	Yes	Yes	No	No

TRANSACTIONS AND JMS MESSAGE-DRIVEN BEANS

When using JMS message-drivenbeans, your choice of transaction style has a big impact on your bean. As we know now, only the `Required` and `NotSupported` transaction attributes can be applied to the JMS message-driven bean listener method `onMessage()`.

If you use container-managed transactions, your JMS message-driven bean will read a message off the destination in the same transaction as it performs its business logic. If something goes wrong, the transaction will roll back and the message acknowledgment will occur.

If you use bean-managed transactions, the transaction begins ***after*** your JMS message-driven bean receives the message. You can then use the `acknowledgeMode` property of the `@MessageDriven` annotation or deployment descriptor ***acknowledgment modes*** to instruct the container about when to acknowledge messages (see Chapter 7).

If you don't support transactions at all, the container will acknowledge the message at some later time, perhaps when your bean's method completes. The timing is not guaranteed, however.

So which style do you use? If you don't use container-managed transactions, you can't cause the JMS messages to stay on the original destination if something goes wrong, because your bean has no way to indicate that a problem has occurred.

In general, we recommend using container-managed transactions with JMS message-driven beans. If you want to perform many smaller transactions, consider breaking up your JMS message-driven bean into several other beans, with each bean having a granularity of a single transaction, and call these beans from this overarching MDB.

(continued)

TRANSACTIONS AND JMS MESSAGE-DRIVEN BEANS *(continued)*

Note that there is a huge caveat with using container-managed transactions with JMS message-driven beans in a certain scenario. Let's say you have an EJB component (any type of component) that sends *and then* receives a message all within one big container-managed transaction. In this case, the send operation will never get its message on the queue, because the transaction doesn't commit until after the receive operation ends. Thus, you'll be waiting for the receive operation to complete forever. This is called the *infinite block* problem, also known as the *halting problem* in computer science.

An easy solution to this problem is, after sending the request message, you can call `commit()` **on the JMS *Session*, which is your JMS transaction helper object. This causes the outgoing message buffer to be flushed. Hence, the receive operation does not have to wait forever for the transaction to commit to get a message.**

Bean-Managed Transactions

Next let's discuss how a bean provider can control bean-managed transactions programmatically in EJB. Programmatically demarcating transactions allow for more transaction control than container-managed transactions do, but they are trickier to use. To control transaction boundaries yourself, you must use the JTA interface `javax.transaction.UserTransaction`.

EJB AND ENTITIES: HOW THEY WORK TOGETHER IN A TRANSACTION

As we know already, persistence API supports both JTA and local transactions at the entity manager's level. The type of transactions supported by the entity manager is specified when the underlying entity manager factory is created. When Persistence API is used within a managed environment such as a Java EE/EJB container, it is required to support both JTA as well as local transactions. The JTA transaction always begins and ends externally to the JTA entity manager. Beans and container, in case of bean-managed and container-managed transactions, respectively, will begin and end the JTA transactions; they make entities a part of their active transactions by enlisting the entity manager's persistence context.

The entity manager, therefore, only participates in an already active JTA transaction; it does not actually begin or commit a JTA transaction on its own. Hence, there is no mechanism to specify the transactional behavior of the entities. Their transactional behavior is completely dependent on the caller. This is just as well—entities are concerned with providing persistence, and not with transaction processing. Transaction processing is left up to the EJB layer. Entities play to the tune of beans when it comes to transactions.

When an entity manager is invoked from within an already active JTA transaction in a managed environment, a new persistence context is created if one doesn't exist already. The persistence context ends when the JTA transaction completes and all entities that were managed by entity manager are detached. This is what we term as *transaction-scoped persistence context.* Then there is the notion of an *extended persistence context*, wherein the entities don't detach even after the JTA transactions are committed. The idea is to use extended persistence contexts in scenarios where stateful conversations take place, such as when we use entities from within stateful session bean. We do not want the persistence context to be created each time a transaction is committed on a container-managed stateful session bean. Hence, we specify an extended persistence context when we first get hold of an entity manager. The extended persistence context is destroyed only when the entity manager closes.

We discuss transactions as they pertain to entities in Chapter 6 as well.

The javax.transaction.UserTransaction Interface

The `javax.transaction.UserTransaction` interface enables you to programmatically control transactions. Here is what the `javax.transaction.UserTransaction` interface looks like:

```
public interface javax.transaction.UserTransaction
    public void begin();
    public void commit();
    public int getStatus();
    public void rollback();
    public void setRollbackOnly();
    public void setTransactionTimeout(int);
}
```

As you can see, six methods are exposed by the `UserTransaction` interface. Three of them—`begin`, `commit`, and `rollback`—are used to begin a new transaction, commit a transaction permanently, and roll back a transaction if some problem occurred, respectively. These methods are explained in Table 10.3.

> **TRANSACTIONS AND JAVA EE CONNECTORS**
>
> **The Java EE Connector Architecture defines a standard contract between Resource Adapters (RA) and application servers such that RA can leverage the container services for supporting transactions. This standard contract enables an application server to provide the infrastructure and runtime environment for transaction management of RA components. RA can support either a local transaction, which is managed internally by the resource manager, or it can support a distributed transaction, whose coordination does involve external transaction managers. If RA supports local transactions, the client component, such as an EJB, will have to acquire the common client interface API object, such as `javax.resource.cci.LocalTransaction` or an equivalent from the resource adapter to demarcate the transactions. If RA supports distributed transactions, the container will automatically enlist the client in the transaction context, if the client wants to work within a distributed transaction.Java EE Connector Architecture 1.5 supports the inflow of transactions from Enterprise Information System (EIS) to the Java EE environment. This is a powerful concept because it enables the Java EE applications to participate in transactions initiated by backend EIS. For example, you can make your stateless session bean participate in a transaction that was initiated in the Tuxedo environment, given that the underlying RA supports this contract. Chapter 15 explains Java EE Connector Architecture in more details.**

Table 10.3 The *javax.transaction.UserTransaction* Methods for Transactional Boundary Interaction

METHOD	DESCRIPTION
`begin()`	Begins a new transaction. This transaction becomes associated with the current thread.
`commit()`	Runs the two-phase commit protocol on an existing transaction associated with the current thread. Each resource manager will make its updates durable.
`getStatus()`	Retrieves the status of the transaction associated with this thread.
`Rollback()`	Forces a rollback of the transaction associated with the current thread.
`setRollbackOnly()`	Calls this to force the current transaction to roll back. This will eventually force the transaction to abort.
`setTransactionTimeout(int)`	The transaction timeout is the maximum amount of time that a transaction can run before it's aborted. This is useful for avoiding deadlock situations, when precious resources are being held by a transaction that is currently running.

JTA also defines a number of constants that indicate the current status of a transaction. You will be returned one of these constants when you call the `UserTransaction.getStatus()` method:

```
public interface javax.transaction.Status {
    public static final int STATUS_ACTIVE;
    public static final int STATUS_NO_TRANSACTION;
    public static final int STATUS_MARKED_ROLLBACK;
    public static final int STATUS_PREPARING;
    public static final int STATUS_PREPARED;
    public static final int STATUS_COMMITTING;
    public static final int STATUS_COMMITTED;
    public static final int STATUS_ROLLING_BACK;
    public static final int STATUS_ROLLEDBACK;
    public static final int STATUS_UNKNOWN;
}
```

Table 10.4 explains the values of those constants.

Table 10.4 The *javax.transaction.Status* Constants for Transactional Status

CONSTANT	MEANING
`STATUS_ACTIVE`	A transaction is currently active.
`STATUS_NO_TRANSACTION`	No transaction is active.
`STATUS_MARKED_ROLLBACK`	The current transaction will eventually abort because it's been marked for rollback. This could be because some party called `UserTransaction.setRollbackOnly()`.
`STATUS_PREPARING`	The current transaction is preparing to be committed (during Phase One of the two-phase commit protocol).
`STATUS_PREPARED`	The current transaction has been prepared to be committed (Phase One is complete).
`STATUS_COMMITTING`	The current transaction is in the process of being committed right now (during Phase Two).
`STATUS_COMMITTED`	The current transaction has been committed (Phase Two is complete).
`STATUS_ROLLING_BACK`	The current transaction is in the process of rolling back.
`STATUS_ROLLEDBACK`	The current transaction has been rolled back.
`STATUS_UNKNOWN`	The status of the current transaction cannot be determined.

Bean-Managed Transaction Example

We now show you how to write an enterprise bean that uses bean-managed transactions. To do this, we'll use the same teller bean example that was illustrated in Figure 10.10. The `transferFunds()` method of the teller bean needs to use transactions to make sure that the updates to the bank account entities are done as part of the same transaction. Let us see how we do this by using `javax.transaction.UserTransaction` methods. Source 10.3 shows the `TellerBean` code, which now manages its own transaction boundaries.

```
import javax.ejb.*;
import javax.annotation.Resource;
import javax.persistence.PersistenceContext;
import javax.persistence.EntityManager;
import javax.transaction.UserTransaction;

@Stateless()
@TransactionManagement(javax.ejb.TransactionManagementType.BEAN)
public class TellerBean implements Teller {
    @PersistenceContext private EntityManager em;
    @Resource private javax.transaction.UserTransaction userTx;

    public void transferFunds(float amount, String fromAccount, String
                             toAccount)
    {
        // Lookup for accts with the provided account Ids
        try {
            userTx.begin();

            BankAccount acct1 = em.find(BankAccount.class, fromAccount);
            BankAccount acct2 = em.find(BankAccount.class, toAccount);

            if (acct1.balance < amount)
                userTx.rollback();

            acct1.withdraw(amount);
            acct2.deposit(amount);

            em.persist(acct1);
            em.persist(acct2);

            userTx.commit();
        } catch (Exception e) {
            System.out.println("Exception occurred during transfer of
                               funds." + e.getMessage());
        }
    }
}
```

Source 10.3 The transferFunds() method implementation using UserTransaction.

In Source 10.3, first notice that we used annotation to specify the transaction management style, that is bean-managed, for our teller bean. Since we are planning to control the transaction boundaries ourselves in the code, we first retrieve the `UserTransaction` JTA object from the bean's context. Then, rather than relying on the EJB container to *begin* and *commit* transactions, we perform these steps ourselves. Also notice that if the bank account from which the money is being withdrawn does not meet the specific balance condition, we roll back the transaction, thereby dooming it right away.

NOTE When using programmatic transactions, always try to complete your transactions in the same method in which you began them. Doing otherwise results in spaghetti code where it is difficult to track the transactions; the performance decreases because the transaction is held open longer, and the behavior of your system may be odd. See the EJB specification for more details about what the container will do if your transaction is left open.

Client-Controlled Transactions

The last way you can control transactions is from client code (by *client* we mean anything that calls your beans, even other enterprise beans). You use the Java Transaction API (JTA) to control transactions from client code. You can get hold of the JTA `UserTransaction` interface either by using resource injection or by looking it up in the JNDI registry.

When you demarcate transactional boundaries in client code, you should be *very* careful. Always strive to keep your transactions as short in duration as possible. Longer-lived transactions result in multi-user performance grinding to a halt. If you need a long transaction (that lasts for minutes, hours, or days) use a distributed locking mechanism, such as the CORBA locking service. No distributed locking service equivalent currently exists in the Java Enterprise Edition.

Transactional Isolation

Now that we understand how to apply transactions to EJB applications in various ways, let's further discuss the advanced concepts behind the *I* in ACID: *isolation*. Isolation is the guarantee that concurrent users are isolated from one another, even if they are touching the same database data. Isolation is important to understand because it does not come for free. As we'll see, you can control how isolated your transactions are from one another. Choosing the right level of isolation is critical for the robustness and scalability of your deployment.

The underlying transaction system achieves isolation by performing *concurrency control* behind the scenes. We elaborate on this concept in the following section.

The Need for Concurrency Control

Let's begin our isolation discussion with a motivational example. Imagine that there are two instances of the same component executing concurrently, perhaps in two different processes or two different threads. Let's assume that the component wants to update a shared database through an entity. Each of the instances of the component performs the following steps:

1. Read an integer *X* from a database.
2. Add 10 to X.
3. Write the new value of *X* to the database.

If each of these three steps executes together in an atomic operation, everything is fine. Neither instance can interfere with the other instance's operations. Remember, though, that the thread-scheduling algorithm being used in the background does not guarantee this. If two instances are executing these three operations, the operations could be interleaved. The following order of operations is possible:

1. Instance A reads integer *X* from the database. The database now contains $X = 0$.
2. Instance B reads integer *X* from the database. The database now contains $X = 0$.
3. Instance A adds 10 to its copy of *X* and persists it to the database. The database now contains $X = 10$.
4. Instance B adds 10 to its copy of *X* and persists it to the database. The database now contains $X = 10$.

What happened here? Due to the interleaving of database operations, instance B is working with a stale copy of X: the copy before instance A performed a write. Thus, instance A's operations have been lost! This famous problem is known as a *lost update*. It is a very serious situation—instance B has been working with stale data and has overwritten instance A's write. How can transactions avoid this scenario?

The solution to this problem is to use *locking* on the database to prevent the two components from reading data. By locking the data your transaction is using, you guarantee that your transaction and only your transaction has access to that data until you release that lock. This prevents the interleaving of sensitive data operations.

In our scenario, if our component acquired an exclusive lock before the transaction began and released that lock after the transaction, then no interleaving would be possible.

1. Request a lock on *X*.
2. Read an integer *X* from a database.
3. Add 10 to *X*.
4. Write the new value of *X* to the database.
5. Release the lock on *X*.

If another component ran concurrently with ours, that component would have to wait until we relinquished our lock, which would give that component our fresh copy of *X*. We explore locking further in the "Isolation and Locking" sidebar.

ISOLATION AND LOCKING

During a transaction, a number of *locks* are acquired on the resource being updated. These locks are used to ensure isolation: Multiple clients all updating the same data set cannot interfere with each other. The locks are implicitly retrieved when you interact with resource managers—you do not have to worry about obtaining them yourself.

By intelligently acquiring locks on the resource being used, transactions guarantee a special property: *serializability*. Serializability means that a suite of concurrently executing transactions behaves as if the transactions were executing one after another (nonconcurrently). This is guaranteed no matter how scheduling of the transactions is performed.

The problem with locking is that it physically locks out other concurrent transactions from performing their database updates until you release your locks. This can lead to major performance problems. In addition, a *deadlock* scenario (not specific to databases, by the way) can arise. Deadlock causes the entire system to screech to a dead stop. An example of deadlock occurs when two concurrent transactions are both waiting for each other to release a lock.

To improve performance, transactions distinguish between two main types of locks: *read locks* and *write locks*. Read locks are nonexclusive, in that any number of concurrent transactions can acquire a read lock. In comparison, write locks are exclusive—only one transaction can hold a write lock at any time.

Locking exists in many circles: databases, version control systems, and the Java language itself (through the *synchronized* keyword). The problems experienced in locking are common to all arenas. EJB abstracts concurrency control away from application developers via *isolation levels*.

If you would like more details about locking and transactions, check out *Principles of Databases Systems* by Jeffrey D. Ullman (Computer Science Press, 1980). This classic, theoretical book on databases forms the basis for many database systems today.

Isolation Levels

You can control how isolated the transactions that your EJB components perform on various resources are from one another by using various levels of isolation. You can enforce strict isolation or allow relaxed isolation. If you have very strict isolation, you can rest assured that each concurrent transaction will be isolated from all other transactions. But sometimes enforcing strict isolation is a hindrance rather than a benefit. Because isolation is achieved by acquiring locks on underlying resources, the locks can result in unacceptable performance degradation.

Thus, you need to be smart about how much isolation you really need. *Isolation levels* give you a choice over how much isolation you want and allow you to specify concurrency control at a very high level. If you specify a very strict isolation level, then your transactions will be perfectly isolated from one another, at the expense of performance. If you specify a very loose isolation level, your transactions will not be isolated, but you will achieve higher concurrent transaction performance.

There are four transaction isolation levels:

- **The** `READ UNCOMMITTED` **mode** does not offer any isolation guarantees but offers the highest performance.
- **The** `READ COMMITTED` **mode** solves the *dirty read* problem.
- **The** `REPEATABLE READ` **mode** solves the previous problem as well as the *unrepeatable read* problem.
- **The** `SERIALIZABLE` **mode** solves the previous problems as well as the *phantom* problem.

It's important to understand why *dirty reads*, *unrepeatable reads*, and *phantoms* occur, or you won't be able to use transactions properly.

The Dirty Read Problem

A dirty read occurs when your application reads data from a database that has not been committed to the resource yet. Consider two instances of the same component performing the following:

1. You read integer X from the database. The database now contains $X = 0$.
2. You add 10 to X and save it to the database. The database now contains $X = 10$. You have not issued a *commit* statement yet, however, so your database update has not been made permanent.
3. Another application reads integer X from the database. The value it reads in is $X = 10$.

4. You *abort* your transaction, which restores the database to $X = 0$.
5. The other application adds 10 to X and saves it to the database. The database now contains $X = 20$.

The problem here is the other application reads your update before you committed. Because you aborted, the database data has erroneously been set to 20; your database update has been added in despite the abort! This problem of reading uncommitted data is a *dirty read*. (The word *dirty* occurs in many areas of computer science, such as caching algorithms. A dirty cache is a cache that is out of sync with the main source.)

READ UNCOMMITTED

Dirty reads can occur if you use the weakest isolation level, called `READ UNCOMMITTED`. With this isolation level, if your transaction is executing concurrently with another transaction, and the other transaction writes some data to the database *without* committing, your transaction will read that data in. This occurs regardless of the isolation level being used by the other transaction.

`READ UNCOMMITTED` experiences the other transactional problems as well: unrepeatable reads and phantoms. We'll describe those problems in the pages to come.

When to Use READ UNCOMMITTED

This isolation level is dangerous to use in mission-critical systems with shared data being updated by concurrent transactions. It is inappropriate to use this mode in sensitive calculations, such as in banking transactions while you are updating the balances on accounts, say. For those scenarios, it's better to go with one of the stricter isolation levels.

This level is most appropriate if you know beforehand that an instance of your component will be running only when there are no other concurrent transactions. Because there are no other transactions to be isolated from, this isolation level is adequate. But for most applications that use transactions, this isolation level is insufficient.

The advantage of this isolation level is performance. The underlying transaction system doesn't have to acquire any locks on shared data in this mode. This reduces the amount of time that you need to wait before executing, and it also reduces the time concurrent transactions waste waiting for you to finish.

READ COMMITTED

The `READ COMMITTED` isolation level is very similar to `READ UNCOMMITTED`. The chief difference is that your code will read committed data only when running in `READ COMMITTED` mode. When you execute with this isolation level, you will *not* read data that has been written but is uncommitted. This isolation level thus solves the dirty read problem.

Note that this isolation level does not protect against the more advanced transactional problems, such as unrepeatable reads and phantoms.

When to Use READ COMMITTED

This isolation level offers a step up in robustness from the `READ UNCOMMITTED` mode. You aren't going to be reading in data that has just been written but is uncommitted, which means that any data you read is going to be consistent data.

One great use for this mode is for programs that read data from a database to report values of the data. Because reporting tools aren't in general mission-critical, taking a snapshot of committed data in a database makes sense.

When you run in `READ COMMITTED` mode, the underlying concurrency control system needs to acquire additional locking. This makes performance slower than with `READ UNCOMMITTED`. `READ COMMITTED` is the default isolation level for most databases, such as Oracle or Microsoft SQL Server.

The Unrepeatable Read Problem

Our next concurrency control problem is an *unrepeatable read*. Unrepeatable reads occur when a component reads some data from a database, but upon rereading the data, the data has been changed. This can arise when another concurrently executing transaction modifies the data being read. For example:

1. You read a data set *X* from the database.
2. Another application overwrites data set *X* with new values.
3. You reread the data set *X* from the database. The values have magically changed.

Again, by using transactional locks to lock out those other transactions from modifying the data, we can guarantee that unrepeatable reads will never occur.

REPEATABLE READ

`REPEATABLE READ` guarantees yet another property on top of `READ COMMITTED`: Whenever you read committed data from a database, you will be able to reread the same data again at a later time, and the data will have the same values as the first time. Hence, your database reads are *repeatable*. In contrast, if you are using the `READ COMMITTED` mode or a weaker mode, another concurrent transaction may commit data between your reads.

When to Use REPEATABLE READ

Use REPEATABLE READ when you need to update one or more data elements in a resource, such as one or more records in a relational database. You want to read each of the rows that you're modifying and then be able to update each row, knowing that none of the rows are being modified by other concurrent transactions. If you choose to reread any of the rows at any time later in the transaction, you'd be guaranteed that the rows still have the same data that they did at the beginning of the transaction.

The Phantom Problem

Finally, we have the phantom problem. A phantom is a *new* set of data that magically appears in a database between two read operations. For example:

1. Your application queries the database using some criteria and retrieves a data set.
2. Another application inserts new data that would satisfy your query.
3. You perform the query again, and *new* sets of data have magically appeared.

The difference between the unrepeatable read problem and the phantom problem is that unrepeatable reads occur when existing data is changed, whereas phantoms occur when *new* data that didn't exist before is inserted. For example, if your transaction reads a relational record, and a concurrent transaction commits a new record to the database, a new *phantom record* appears that wasn't there before.

SERIALIZABLE

You can easily avoid phantoms (as well as the other problems described earlier) by using the strictest isolation level: SERIALIZABLE. SERIALIZABLE guarantees that transactions execute serially with respect to each other, and it enforces the isolation ACID property to its fullest. This means that each transaction truly appears to be independent of the others.

When to Use SERIALIZABLE

Use SERIALIZABLE for mission-critical systems that absolutely must have perfect transactional isolation. You are guaranteed that no data will be read that has been uncommitted. You'll be able to reread the same data again and again. And mysterious committed data will not show up in your database while you're operating due to concurrent transactions.

Use this isolation level with care because serializability does have its cost. If all of your operations execute in SERIALIZABLE mode, you will quickly see how fast your database performance grinds to a halt. However, because transactional errors can be very difficult to detect, due to scheduling of processes, variable throughput, and other issues, we subscribe to the view that it's better to be safe than sorry.

Transaction Isolation Summary

The various isolation levels and their effects are summarized in Table 10.5.

Using Various Isolation Levels in EJB Applications

EJB does not provide a way to specify isolation levels directly, in that the specification doesn't provide an API, an annotation or a deployment descriptor setting through which we can set isolation level directly on our beans. Instead, we specify the isolation levels on the resource API itself. For example, if our resource happens to be a database, then we use the JDBC API, specifically, `Connection.setIsolationLevel()`, to set the isolation level. Bottom line—isolation levels are always set on the resource API, however, the isolation level in use has a deep impact on the performance of your EJB applications.

Now if you're using different resource managers within a single transaction, each resource manager can have a different isolation level, yet all run together under a single transaction. At the same time, access to a particular resource manager under a given transaction should always occur under the same isolation level.

Table 10.5 The Isolation Levels

ISOLATION LEVEL	DIRTY READS?	UNREPEATABLE READS?	PHANTOM READS?
READ UNCOMMITTED	Yes	Yes	Yes
READ COMMITTED	No	Yes	Yes
REPEATABLE READ	No	No	Yes
SERIALIZABLE	No	No	No

WHY DOESN'T EJB ALLOW ISOLATION LEVEL SETTINGS?

As we now know, the EJB standard does not deal with isolation levels directly, and rightly so. EJB is a component specification. It defines the behavior and contracts of a business component with clients and middleware infrastructure (containers) such that the component can be rendered as various middleware services properly. EJBs therefore are transactional components that interact with resource managers, such as the JDBC resource manager or JMS resource manager, via JTS, as part of a transaction. They are not, hence, resource components in themselves. Since isolation levels are very specific to the behavior and capabilities of the underlying resources, they should therefore be specified at the resource API levels.

In fact, when EJB was first introduced, it did have a way to specify isolation levels at the component level. Later on the EJB Expert Group realized that this was a wrong place to specify isolation level. Besides, vendors found that implementing isolation levels at the component level was way too clumsy. Hence, the next revision to the specification got rid of component-level isolation setting and suggested that isolation level be set at the individual resource level, through the usage of the respective resource APIs or some other means of configuration.

Pessimistic and Optimistic Concurrency Control

The two basic object concurrency control strategies that EJBs may follow, pessimistic and optimistic, are summarized in Table 10.6. Pessimistic concurrency control is the algorithm we've been assuming throughout this chapter—you acquire a lock for the data for the duration of the transaction, ensuring that nobody messes with your data.

Table 10.6 Comparing Pessimistic and Optimistic Concurrency Control Strategies

STRATEGY	ADVANTAGES	DISADVANTAGES
Pessimistic–Your EJB locks the source data for the entire time it needs the data, not allowing anything greater (at least anything greater than read/view access) to potentially update the data systems until it completes its transaction.	* Brute force approach * Provides reliable access to data * Suitable for small-scale systems * Suitable for systems simultaneous access where concurrent access is rare	* Does not scale well because it blocks simultaneous access to common resources

With optimistic concurrency control, your EJB component does not hold the lock for the duration of the transaction. Instead, you *hope* everything will be okay. Then if the database detects a collision, the transaction is rolled back. The basic assumption behind optimistic concurrency is that because it is unlikely that separate users will access the same object simultaneously, it is better to handle the occasional collision than to limit the request-handling throughput of your system.

Designing Transactional Conversations in EJB

In this chapter, we've seen that a transactional abort entails an automatic rollback of database updates that were performed during the transaction. But database updates are only half of the picture. Your application code needs to consider the impacts of a failed transaction as well.

When a transaction aborts, your application code has several choices. You can abort your business process and throw an exception back to the client, or you can attempt to retry the transaction several times. But unfortunately, your application cannot sit in a loop retrying transactions forever, because that would yield horrible performance for concurrent threads of execution. If the transaction cannot eventually be made to succeed, you should consider aborting your business process.

For a stateless session bean, aborting a business process is a simple task—simply throw an exception back to the client. But for a stateful session bean, things are a bit trickier. Stateful session beans represent business processes that span multiple method calls and hence have in-memory *conversational state*. Tossing away that conversation and throwing an exception to the client could entail a significant amount of lost work.

Fortunately, a well-designed stateful session bean can salvage its conversations in the case of failed transactions. The key is to design your beans to be aware of changes to conversational state and to be smart enough to undo any of those changes if a transactional abort occurs.

Because this process is highly application-specific, your application server cannot automate this task for you. Your application server *can* aid you in determining when a transaction failed, enabling you to take application-specific steps. If your session bean needs to be alerted to transaction status (such as failed transactions), your enterprise bean class can implement an optional interface called `javax.ejb.SessionSynchronization`, shown in the following code:

```
public interface javax.ejb.SessionSynchronization
{
    public void afterBegin();
    public void beforeCompletion();
    public void afterCompletion(boolean);
}
```

You should implement this interface in your enterprise bean class and define your own implementations of each of these methods. The container will call your methods automatically at the appropriate times during transactions, alerting you to important transactional events. This adds to the existing arsenal of alerts that your session beans receive already—life-cycle alerts via `PostConstruct` and `PreDestroy` methods, passivation alerts via `PrePassivate` and `PostActivate` methods, and now transactional alerts via `afterBegin()`, `beforeCompletion()`, and `afterCompletion()`.

Here's what each of the `SessionSynchronization` methods do:

- `afterBegin()` is called by the container directly after a transaction begins.
- `beforeCompletion()` is called by the container right before a transaction completes.
- `afterCompletion()` is called by the container directly after a transaction completes.

The key method that is most important for rolling back conversations is `afterCompletion()`. The container calls your `afterCompletion()` method when a transaction completes in either a commit *or* an abort. You can figure out whether a commit or an abort happened by the Boolean parameter that gets passed to you in `afterCompletion()`: `true` indicates a successful commit, `false` indicates an abort. If an abort happened, you should roll back your conversational state to preserve your session bean's conversation.

Source 10.4 shows `afterCompletion()` method in action:

```
import javax.ejb.*;

@Stateful
@Remote(examples.Count.class)
public class CountBean implements examples.Count,
SessionSynchronization{
    private int val;
    private int oldVal;

    public int count() {
```

Source 10.4 Using SessionSynchronization to manage transactional conversations in stateful session beans. *(continued)*

```
            System.out.println("count()");
            return ++val;
    }

    public void set(int val)  {
            this.val = val;
            System.out.println("set()");
    }

    @PostConstruct
    public void construct(examples.Count bean)
    {
           this.val = val;
           this.oldVal = val;
    }

    @Remove
    public void remove() {
           System.out.println("remove()");
    }

    public void afterBegin(){}

    public void beforeCompletion(){}

    public void afterCompletion(boolean b){
            if (b==false)
                  val = oldVal;
    }
}
```

Source 10.4 *(continued)*

This is the same count bean that you saw in Chapter 4. The conversational state is *val,* an integer that increases incrementally whenever `count()` is called. We also keep a backup copy of `val`, called `oldVal`, which we revert to in case of a transactional rollback. Here is what's going on:

1. When the bean is first initialized in the `PostConstruct` method `construct()`, or when a transaction first begins in `afterBegin()`, `val` and `oldVal` are set to the same value.
2. One or more `count()` business methods are called, incrementing `val`.
3. If the transaction fails, the `afterCompletion()` method is called when the transaction completes. If the transaction failed (that is, if a `false` value was passed into `afterCompletion()`), we roll back the conversational state by reverting back to `oldVal`.

Note that for this to work, we must make `count()` transactional using either annotations or deployment descriptor. We will use one of the transaction attributes discussed earlier in this chapter to achieve that.

`SessionSynchronization` is also useful when your stateful session bean caches database data in memory during a transaction. You can use `SessionSynchronization` to track when to cache and when not to cache data as follows:

- When the container calls `afterBegin()`, the transaction has just started. You should read in any database data you want to cache in your stateful session bean.
- When the container calls `beforeCompletion()`, the transaction has ended. Write out any database data you've cached.

NOTE **You can implement `SessionSynchronization` *only* if you're using a stateful session bean with container-managed transactions. If your bean is using bean-managed transactions, you are already in control of the transaction because you issue the `begin()`, `commit()`, and `abort()` statements. Stateless session beans do not hold conversations and hence do not need these callbacks.**

Summary

Whew! That's a lot of information to digest. You may want to reread this chapter later to make sure you've grasped all the concepts.

In this chapter, we discussed transactions and how they can make a server-side deployment robust. We saw the virtues of transactions, which are called the ACID properties. We looked at different transactional models, including flat and nested transactions, followed by a discussion on distributed transactions and two-phase commit protocol. We also provided notes on Java Transaction API, the underpinning that provides support of transactions on EJB platform, and Java Transaction Service, the Java binding to the robust CORBA OTS.

We then applied this transactional knowledge to EJB. We discussed how container-managed, bean-managed, and client-controlled transactions are useful in EJB and learned how to code with each model. We also threw in a lot of information about how EJB transactions work in unison with entities, Java EE connectors, and JMS resources. We looked at transaction isolation levels and understood the problems that each level solves. Finally, we covered how to write transactional conversations to manage state according to the outcome of the transactions in stateful session beans.

Reading this chapter will prove well worth the effort, because now you have a wealth of knowledge about the importance and usefulness of transactions in EJB. You should definitely refer this chapter frequently when you're creating transactional beans.

CHAPTER

11

Security

This chapter introduces and explains EJB security in detail. Let's start with a fundamental observation: When building systems based on enterprise middleware, you typically want to integrate important business resources. Because *important* also means *critical*, security can be one of the most important aspects of your EJB application architecture. To build a secure system, you need to make informed and *balanced* decisions about placing security controls. Without understanding the fundamental risks in your application and its environment, you won't be able to make these decisions. Balancing your decisions is important because security comes at a price, such as increased cost or complexity; reduced performance, maintainability, or functionality; and so on.

An introduction to important security concepts is given in the introductory section. We will then take a look at Web application security in Java EE as a prelude to introducing the two basic security approaches in EJB—declarative and programmatic security. We provide information on security interoperability aspects that are important for applications that span different EJB vendors' platforms and communicate across individual networks. Finally, we explain the latest and greatest in security technology for Web services.

Introduction

Security is often a nebulous thing. It can be difficult and costly, and dealing with it is often avoided until very late in a project. In large-scale projects involving enterprise middleware like EJB, however, the risks of a badly or altogether unprotected infrastructure can be enormous. For example, losing the customer data in your enterprise database because someone drilled a hole into the back end with an unprotected EJB application can put you out of business very quickly.

Being secure means that no harmful events can happen to you and your assets (data, processes, infrastructure, whatever). What makes security sometimes hard to grasp is that it spans a wide variety of technologies, such as networks, operating systems, databases, application servers, EJBs, and so on. Moreover, security is not confined to information technology but also involves physical controls like door locks and alarms. It also depends to a great degree on appropriate human behavior, such as correct operations, proper monitoring of systems, swift responses to alarms, and users not sharing passwords or keys with others. Security books abound with anecdotes about successful social engineering attacks, where attackers simply exploited people's good will and trust in others. To complete the story, it can sometimes be very hard to say exactly (and completely) what must be considered secure or insecure. This last issue is the domain of security policy design. In a broader sense, then, security is the process that aims at securing systems rather than the idealized state of absolute security itself.

NOTE **One word of caution before we start getting into details: don't roll your own security systems! Don't start designing new exciting crypto algorithms, authentication protocols, or access control systems. This is a discipline that takes years of experience, and you need to understand the faults and sidetracks taken in the past in order to avoid repeating them. At best, it is a waste of time and money. At worst, the false sense of security created by homegrown technology will cloud up the enormous risks created by the subtle or not so subtle design flaws in your protections.**

For further reading on EJB and enterprise security with many more details than we are able to cover in this one chapter, please refer to *Enterprise Security with EJB and CORBA* by Bret Hartman et al. (John Wiley & Sons, 2001; ISBN: 0471401315). For in-depth treatment of security as an engineering discipline, we recommend Ross Anderson's *Security Engineering* (John Wiley & Sons, 2001; ISBN 0471389226).

Violations, Vulnerabilities, and Risk

Let's quickly define a handful of terms that we need on the following pages. Feel free to jump ahead and skip this and the following section if you are familiar with these terms. The events that you would like to avoid are often called security breaches or *violations*, for example an intruder reading files that you would prefer to remain confidential. A security violation is possible if there are no safeguards that protect against them, in other words no file system protection. Alternatively, violations are possible if the system has weaknesses that allow users to circumvent security, for example, where a user can obtain another user's privileges and thus get access. Both these deficiencies are called *vulnerabilities*, which can be exploited by those who find them. Another example of a vulnerable system is one that has its default administrator password unchanged after installation and is thus open to anyone who can read the installation documentation, or a program using libraries that are ridden with buffer overflow bugs.

Because the list of potential vulnerabilities is open-ended and increases with every piece of hardware or software that is added to a system, complete protection is not a realistic goal. Also, it may be very expensive to protect even against all known vulnerabilities. As there is no perfect security anyway, it has become common practice to try to *reduce the overall risks* to an acceptable level instead. To reduce risks, however, we first need to know them, meaning that we need to perform a *risk assessment* before we can decide how much and what needs to be done.

In the simplest definition, risk is a product of two factors: *probability of the occurrence* of a violation and the *estimated damage* caused by this event. This may sound a bit like insurance business, and in fact it is very similar. The probability of occurrence is a function of your system's vulnerabilities and the attacker's resources, and the potential damage is a function of the value of your assets. In other words, if you have a complex system with weak protections and a resourceful enemy, then the probability of a successful attack is high. Don't let this turn your hair gray yet; given our definition of risk, we may not have to worry about this: If the system is just a gaming console that does not represent any business value (and the resourceful attackers are students doing an internship at your company), then the actual risk is low!

Controls

By eliminating or reducing the vulnerabilities in your systems, risks are reduced, ideally down to zero. (The obvious other measure, reducing the value of your assets, is not a desirable option in most cases.) This is done by placing security *controls* in the right places.

ATTACKER MODEL

As we saw, risk assessment should include a model of your potential adversary, such as foreign intelligence services, determined criminals, or bored high-school students. The motivation for defining who to defend against is that the different levels of skills, determination, and resources that are associated with the different model attackers shed a different light on the concept of vulnerability. A password that is hard to crack for some people using their limited attacker toolbox and computing resources may be very easy to crack for others using offline attacks with terabytes of precomputed passwords that are indexed for faster lookup. A bored teenager will not be sufficiently motivated to spend more than the weekend to analyze messages encrypted with even low-grade cryptography, but a foreign intelligence service may be. Defining your model attacker is a more precise way of estimating your vulnerabilities by establishing additional context.

As you saw, it is important to understand the risks in a system before you start setting up arbitrary controls. Without such an understanding, you may be spending an enormous amount of time and resources protecting against relatively harmless events that may not be more than a nuisance—while not paying attention to the others that will ruin your company. For example, the actual risk associated with an attacker observing the `update()` method calls in an MVC pattern may not even warrant the use of SSL/TLS protection, with the associated performance hit at connection setup time and the administrative overhead of distributing credentials such as public key certificates.

The term *control* is generally translated to one or more of the following, canonic security functions:

- **Authentication.** Verifying the authenticity of user information. In most cases, this means verifying that the other side is who it claims to be. The authenticated entity is called *principal*. Authentication can mean checking a provided user ID and password against a database, or it can involve verifying a digital signature on a public key certificate to establish trust in the holder of that key.
- **Authorization.** Controlling principals' accesses to resources. This usually involves checking access privileges to find out who is authorized.
- **Data integrity protection.** Preventing, or at least detecting, modifications of data. Data integrity mishaps can be prevented by controlling all write accesses to that data. When data is communicated over an open transport channel, such as a WLAN, access to that data cannot be prevented at all times. In these cases, integrity protection usually means applying a cryptographic hash and later recomputing that hash to determine whether the data has been modified in transit.

- **Data confidentiality protection.** Preventing unauthorized disclosure of information. As with data integrity, data confidentiality can be protected by controlling read access to data, or by encrypting the data on the wire so that it can be read only by receivers with the correct cryptographic keys.

To conclude this introductory section before taking a dive into the security technologies that are relevant for EJB, let's take a minute to think about the security of the EJB infrastructure itself. This chapter is about protecting applications using EJB security, but this obviously hinges on the security of the system that provides it, meaning your application server. We need not go as far as looking for programming errors in the software; all the security that we are about to introduce now can be turned off again, just like that, if administrator access is not adequately controlled. This means that choosing a good password and protecting it is a prerequisite for any higher-level security. Protecting the application server is necessarily a product-specific task, and you should take the time to consult your product documentation to find out what needs to be done.

In addition, consider the security of the services that the EJB container provides to applications and that may be externally accessible. Most importantly, this means the *Java Naming and Directory Service* (JNDI). Can anyone other than your expected clients connect to your container's JNDI contexts, for example by using RMI over IIOP (RMI/IIOP) applications? With most application servers, this is possible by default. If there is no protection for the JNDI, then your application may think it is retrieving a particular bean reference, but in fact it is receiving an object reference to a carefully crafted *man-in-the-middle* bean at *hacker.org* that was skillfully bound to the very name of the bean that you expected to use. This bean can then intercept and inspect any application traffic and may actually forward it to the appropriate server so that its existence can remain concealed for a while. Rebinding a name in JNDI is simple, so you must make sure that only trusted clients may bind or rebind names.

Web Application Security

In Java EE applications with a Web tier, the first point of interaction with a client is the Web container and the JSP files or servlets it hosts, as shown Figure 11.1. Clients send HyperText Transfer Protocol (HTTP) requests, and the servlets, JSP or JSF files would call bean instances in the EJB containers using RMI-IIOP or SOAP.

Web application security is not covered by the EJB specifications but rather by the *Java Servlet Specification* and the *Java EE 5 Platform Specification*. The general security concepts used by Java EE for both servlets and EJB are very similar, but if you are building complex Web applications, we recommend that you consult the *Java Servlet Specification* that is available at http://java.sun.com/products/servlet.

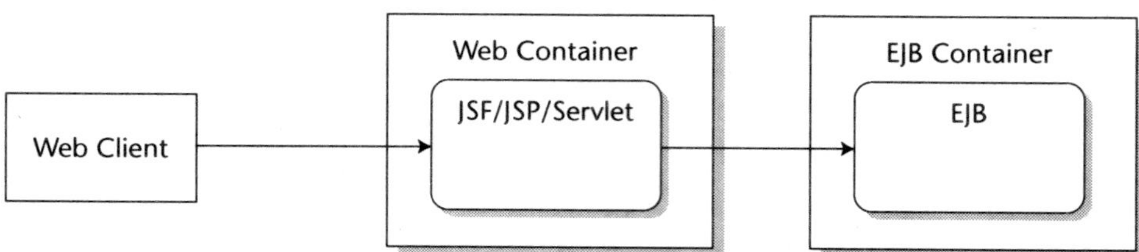

Figure 11.1 Web applications.

Authentication in Web Applications

Web applications are accessed by sending HTTP request messages to the servlet container. The servlet specification does not define any additional authentication mechanisms beyond the ones that are available in HTTP, so the actual authentication is done by the general Web server component.

Authentication requirements for Web applications can be specified in the Web application's deployment descriptor (the `web.xml` file). This file is found underneath the (required) WEB-INF folder within the Web application.

The supported mechanisms are:

- **HTTP Basic and Digest authentication.** A user ID and password mechanism, where both the user name and password are transmitted in a special header field of the HTTP request. With basic authentication, the password is transmitted in base64 encoding, but unencrypted. This is insecure and only appropriate in combination with SSL (HTTPS), or in relatively trusted environments. With digest authentication, the password is transmitted in encrypted form. Digest authentication is not in widespread use, and hence not required to be available in all products.
- **Form-based authentication.** Another form of user ID and password authentication. The user information is sent in the request message body as part of HTML form input data. Like basic authentication, this data is unprotected unless additional mechanisms (HTTPS) are used.
- **HTTPS Client authentication.** A strong authentication mechanism based on public key certificates exchanged in the Secure Socket Layer (SSL/TLS) underneath HTTP. HTTPS client authentication requires clients to provide a public key certificate in X.509 format. When client authentication is required, the SSL layer performs a handshake procedure as part of the connection establishment process. In this process, the SSL layer will transmit the client's public key certificate and use the corresponding private key to prove possession of the public key. These keys may reside in a Java keystore file at the client.

Authentication requirements for Web applications are specified in the Web application's deployment descriptor using the `login-config` element. To require HTTP basic authentication for a servlet, the `login-config` element would look like this, where `realm-name` refers to an authentication realm (a set of users) that is known to the servlet container:

```
<login-config>
  <auth-method>BASIC</auth-method>
  <realm-name>basic-file</realm-name>
</login-config>
```

Other valid content for the `login-config` element is `DIGEST`, `FORM`, or `CLIENT-CERT`, as in the following example:

```
<login-config>
  <auth-method>CLIENT-CERT</auth-method>
  <realm-name>basic-file</realm-name>
</login-config>
```

Authorization

There are two options for authorization checking for a Java EE Web application:

- **Declarative security.** The servlet container checks access to Web resources based on access rules in deployment descriptors.
- **Programmatic security.** The servlet performs its own access checks based on internal state, hard-coded access rules, and the authentication information provided by the container. The security context API provided by the servlet container is similar to the one provided by EJB containers, which we explain later in this section. Servlets can use the `isUserinRole` and the `getUserPrincipal` methods to make authorization decisions. Refer to the servlet specification for details.

To specify access rules declaratively, the servlet specification uses the `security-constraint` element of the deployment descriptor, which defines constraints for a collection of Web resources. Here is an example:

```
<security-constraint>
  <web-resource-collection>
    <web-resource-name>basic security test</web-resource-name>
    <url-pattern>/*</url-pattern>
  </web-resource-collection>
```

```
    <auth-constraint>
      <role-name>staffmember</role-name>
    </auth-constraint>
  </security-constraint>
```

The preceding descriptor snippet specifies that all HTTP requests that apply to the URL pattern /*, in other words to all URLs in the Web application, are to be constrained to the listed role staffmember, meaning that only users who are members of that role are allowed access. An auth-constraint with empty content would be taken as denial. How users are mapped to roles is vendor-specific. Typically, application servers will use an additional descriptor file with a role-mapping element for this purpose.

Confidentiality and Integrity

Confidentiality and integrity protection for Web applications is based entirely on secure transport, meaning on HTTPS. A Web application's requirements are again expressed in the deployment descriptor, as in the following example:

```
<security-constraint>
   <web-resource-collection>
      <web-resource-name>wholesale</web-resource-name>
      <url-pattern>/acme/wholesale/*</url-pattern>
      <http-method>GET</http-method>
      <http-method>POST</http-method>
   </web-resource-collection>
   <auth-constraint>
      <role-name>CONTRACTOR</role-name>
   </auth-constraint>
   <user-data-constraint>
      <transport-guarantee>CONFIDENTIAL</transport-guarantee>
   </user-data-constraint>
</security-constraint>
```

Here, the user-data-constraint contains a transport-guarantee element that requires confidentiality protection from the transport layer. Other values for the transport-guarantee are INTEGRAL and NONE, where NONE means that no requirements exist. Note that CONFIDENTIAL implies INTEGRAL because any encrypted data is implicitly protected against modifications: Modified encrypted data simply does not correctly decrypt on the receiver side.

The confidentiality and integrity protections for Web applications are relatively coarse-grained in that there is no way for the deployment descriptor to express requirements on the cryptographic strength of the protection through the choice of SSL/TLS cipher suite. When you deploy a Web application, you must trust the container that its provision of a `CONFIDENTIAL` transport is confidential enough.

Understanding EJB Security

There are two security measures that clients must pass when you add security to an EJB system: authentication and authorization. Authentication must be performed before any EJB method is called. Authorization, on the other hand, occurs at the beginning of each EJB method call.

Authentication in EJB

Since EJB 2.0, authentication is now portable and robust. You can call authentication logic through the *Java Authentication and Authorization Service* (JAAS), an integral part of Java since Java 2 SDK v1.4. Let's now take a mini-tutorial of JAAS and see how it can be used in an EJB environment.

We will see below that the authorization piece on EJB methods is easily achieved via security annotations.

JAAS Overview

JAAS is a portable interface that enables you to authenticate and authorize users in Java. In a nutshell, it allows you to log in to a system without knowing about the underlying security system being used. Behind the scenes in JAAS, the implementation (such as an application server) then determines if your credentials are authentic. Moreover, JAAS enables you to write your own customized authentication modules that can then be plugged in without the need to change client code.

The power of JAAS lies in its ability to use almost any underlying security system. Some application servers allow you to set up user names and passwords in the application server's properties, which the application server reads in at runtime. More advanced servers support complex integration with existing security systems, such as a list of user names and passwords stored in an LDAP server, database, or custom security system. Other systems support certificate-based authentication. Regardless, the integration is performed behind the scenes by the container and does not affect your application code.

There are two likely candidate scenarios for use when you may want to utilize JAAS from your code, shown in Figure 11.2.

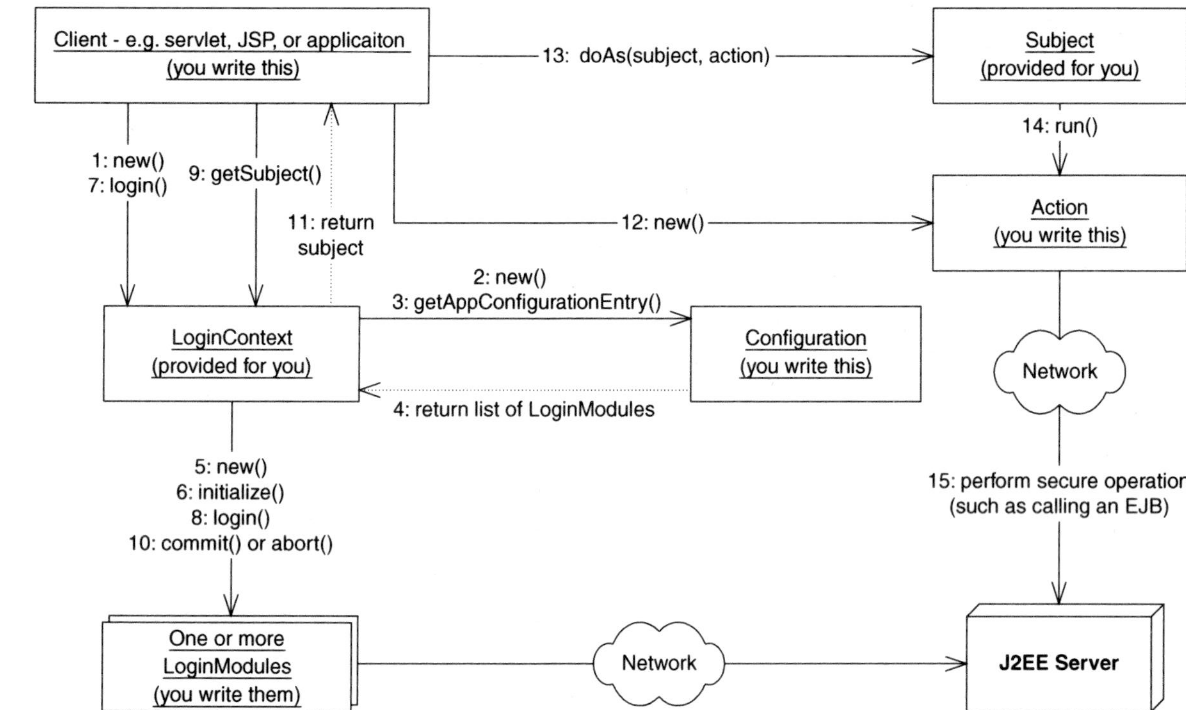

Figure 11.2 JAAS overview.

- When you have a standalone application connecting to a remote EJB system, the user would supply credentials to the application (or perhaps the application would retrieve the credentials from a file or other system). The standalone application would then use the JAAS API to authenticate the user prior to calling the EJB components residing within the application server. The application server would verify the user's credentials. Once the user has been authenticated via JAAS, the client can call EJB methods securely, and the user's security identity will be propagated to the server upon method invocations.
- When you have a Web browser client connecting to a servlet or JSP layer, the Web browser user supplies credentials to a servlet/JSP layer, and the servlet or JSP layer can use JAAS to authenticate the user. The Web browser could supply the credentials in one of the four ways that we discussed in the section on Web application security. To recap, these are:
  - Basic authentication
  - Form-based authentication
  - Digest authentication
  - Certificate authentication

As with standalone applications, once the user has been authenticated via JAAS, the client can call EJB methods securely, and the user's security identity will be propagated to the server upon method invocations.

The JAAS Architecture

JAAS has a flexible design, but can be surprisingly complicated for what you think would be a simple function. We have distilled JAAS down into a simple procedure to make it easier for you to understand.

Figure 11.3 shows the basics of a JAAS authentication procedure.

The JAAS authentication procedure breaks down as follows (follow along with the picture as we review each step):

1. The client instantiates a new login context. This is a container-provided class. It's responsible for coordinating the authentication process.
2. The login context retrieves a configuration object. The configuration object knows about the type of authentication you want to achieve by consulting a configuration file that lists the login modules. For example, your configuration object might know that you want to perform both password-based authentication and certificate-based authentication.
3. The login context asks the configuration object for the list of authentication mechanisms to use (such as password-based and certificate-based).

4. The configuration object returns a list of authentication mechanisms. Each one is called a login module. A login module knows how to contact a specific security provider and authenticate in some proprietary way.
5. The login context instantiates your login modules. You can have many login modules if you want to authenticate across several different security providers. In the example we're about to show, we will use only one login module, and it will know how to authenticate using a user name and password combination to a Java EE server.
6. The login context initializes the login modules.
7. The client code tries to log in by calling the `login()` method on the login context.
8. The login context delegates the `login()` call to the login modules, since only the login modules know how to perform the actual authentication.
9. The login modules (written by you) authenticate you using a proprietary means. In the example we're about to show, the user name and password login module will perform a local authentication only that always succeeds because the authentication data is not checked on the client side at all. After the login succeeds, the login module is told to `commit()`. It can also `abort()` if the login process fails. This is not a very critical step to understand—read the JAAS docs if you're curious, to understand more.
10. Authentication information is kept in a subject. You can use this subject to perform secure operations or just have it sit in the context.
11. Your client code calls remote operations (such as in an EJB component) and the logged-in security context is automatically propagated along with the method call. If you are curious: for RMI/IIOP clients the machinery to pass this context is based on the CSIv2 standard that we will explain later in this chapter. The EJB server can now perform the actual authentication using the authentication data that is passed in the security context. The server can then perform authorization based on the authenticated client identity.

NOTE What's neat about JAAS is that the login modules are separate from the configuration, which means that you can chain together different login modules in interesting combinations by specifying different configurations in the local configuration file. Another thing to note in the sequence outlined above is that the authentication may succeed on the client side but fail on the server side. If the password is incorrect, this will result in the server rejecting the invocation with a `NO_PERMISSION` **exception.**

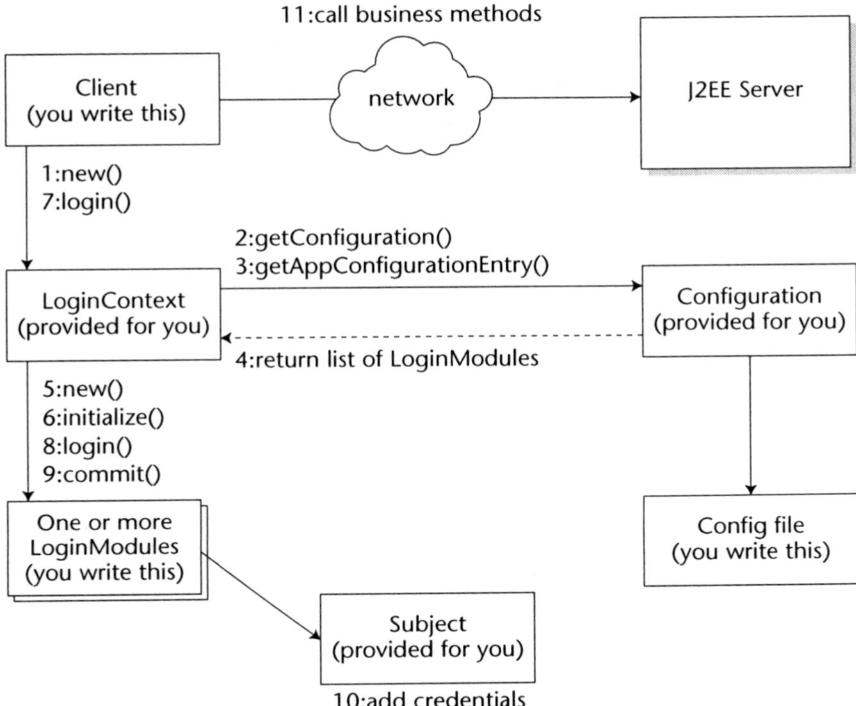

Figure 11.3 JAAS authentication in detail.

JAAS Sample Code

Let's show a simple JAAS example. The code will authenticate and then call a "Hello, World" method on a bean. If the password is right, then the invocation succeeds. If not, then the server throws an exception. The example shows both the use of the JAAS client API and how a custom `LoginModule` is plugged in.

The code is in Source 11.1 through 11.3 and is fairly self-documenting. By reviewing Figure 11.3, this sample code, and the process we laid out earlier, you should be able to get a feeling for what this code is doing. Note in Source 11.1 that if authorization fails on the method call, an `EJBException` is propagated back to the client. We will look at authorization in more detail in the next section.

```
package examples.security;

import java.util.*;
import javax.security.auth.*;
```

Source 11.1 HelloClient.java. *(continued)*

```
import javax.security.auth.login.*;
import javax.naming.*;

/**
 * A client program that uses JAAS to authenticate
 */
public class HelloClient
{
    public static void main(String[] args)
    {
        try
        {
            /* Authenticate via JAAS */
            LoginContext loginContext =
                new LoginContext("HelloClient", new CallbackHandler());
            loginContext.login();

            /* Get a bean */
            Context ctx = new InitialContext();
            Object obj = ctx.lookup(Hello.class.getName());
            Hello hello = (Hello)obj;

            /*
            Call a business method, propagating the security context
            */
            String result;
            try {
                result = hello.hello();
            }
            catch (javax.ejb.EJBException e) {
                result = e.getCausedByException().getMessage();
            }

            /* Print the return result from the business logic */
            System.out.println(result);
        }
        catch (Exception e)
        {
            e.printStackTrace();
        }
    }
}
```

Source 11.1 *(continued)*

```
package examples.security;

import java.util.*;
import java.io.IOException;

import javax.security.auth.*;
import javax.security.auth.callback.*;
import javax.security.auth.login.*;
import javax.security.auth.spi.*;

javax.resource.spi.security.PasswordCredential;

/**
 * A login module that performs password authentication.
 *
 * The purpose of this class is to actually use a callback handler
 * to collect authentication information and add it to the subject
 */

public class PasswordLoginModule
    implements LoginModule
{
    private Subject subject;
    /**
    the callback handler is the mechanism to
    collect authentication data
    */
    private
    javax.security.auth.callback.CallbackHandler callbackHandler;

    /** credentials: username and password */
    private String username;
    private char[] password;

    /**
     * Initializes us with a particular subject to which we will later
     * add the collected password data.
     */

    public void initialize(Subject subject,
      javax.security.auth.callback.CallbackHandler callbackHandler,
      Map sharedState,
      Map options)
    {
        this.subject = subject;
        this.callbackHandler = callbackHandler;
    }

    /**
```

Source 11.2 PasswordLoginModule.java. *(continued)*

```
    * Authenticate the user by prompting for a user name and password.
    * It is called when the client tries to log in.
    *
    * @return    true in all cases since this <code>LoginModule</code>
    *            should not be ignored.
    * @exception FailedLoginException if the authentication fails.
    * @exception LoginException if this <code>LoginModule</code>
    * is unable to perform the authentication.
    */

   public boolean login()
       throws LoginException
   {
       // prompt for a username and password
       if (callbackHandler == null)
       {
           throw new LoginException("Error: No CallbackHandler "+
             "available to collect authentication information");
       }

       // set up a name callback and a password callback
       Callback[] callbacks = new Callback[2];
       callbacks[0] = new NameCallback("username: ");
       callbacks[1] = new PasswordCallback("password: ", false);

       try
       {
           // let handler handle these
           callbackHandler.handle(callbacks);

           // get authentication data
           username = ((NameCallback)callbacks[0]).getName();
           if(username == null)
           {
               throw new LoginException("No user specified");
           }

           char[] tmpPassword =
             ((PasswordCallback)callbacks[1]).getPassword();

           if (tmpPassword == null)
           {
               // treat null password as an empty password
               tmpPassword = new char[0];
           }
           password = new char[tmpPassword.length];
           System.arraycopy(
             tmpPassword, 0, password, 0,
             tmpPassword.length
```

Source 11.2 *(continued)*

```
            );
            ((PasswordCallback)callbacks[1]).clearPassword();
        }
        catch (java.io.IOException ioe)
        {
            throw new LoginException(ioe.toString());
        }
        catch (UnsupportedCallbackException uce)
        {
            throw new LoginException("Error: No Callback available "+
              "to collect authentication data :"  +
              uce.getCallback().toString());
        }
        catch( Exception e )
        {
            e.printStackTrace();
        }

        // The client side login module will always succeed. The
        // actual login will take place on the server side when the
        // security context is passed.
        return true;
    }

    /**
     * This method is called if the overall authentication succeeds
     * after potentially many login modules had their way. In our
     * simple case, we always succeed. The important part here is
     * adding the newly authenticated principal to the security
     * context.
     *
     * @return true if this method executes properly
     */

    public boolean commit()
        throws LoginException
    {
        // add the user name and password as credentials to the
        // security context, i.e., the Subject
        PasswordCredential pc =
            new PasswordCredential(username,password);

        subject.getPrivateCredentials().add(pc);

        username = null;
        password = null;
        return true;
```

Source 11.2 *(continued)*

```
    }

    /**
     * This method is called if the overall authentication failed
     * (even if this particular login module succeeded).  This cannot
     * happen in our simple examples.
     *
     * @return true if this method executes properly
     */

    public boolean abort()
        throws LoginException
    {
        return true;
    }

    /**
     * Log out the user and clean up.
     *
     * @return true if this method executes properly
     */
    public boolean logout()
        throws LoginException
    {
        username = null;
        password = null;
        return true;
    }
}
```

Source 11.2 *(continued)*

```
package examples.security;

import java.io.*;
import java.util.*;
import javax.security.auth.login.*;
import javax.security.auth.*;
import javax.security.auth.callback.*;

/**
 * Implements the CallbackHandler that gathers uid/pw input from
 * System.in.
 */
public class CallbackHandler
    implements javax.security.auth.callback.CallbackHandler
```

Source 11.3 CallbackHandler.java/

```
{
    /**
     * @param callbacks an array of <code>Callback</code> objects
     *
     * @exception java.io.IOException
     * @exception UnsupportedCallbackException if the
     * <code>callbacks</code> parameter contains unknown
     * callback objects
     */
    public void handle(Callback[] callbacks)
        throws IOException, UnsupportedCallbackException
    {
      for (int i = 0; i < callbacks.length; i++) {
          if (callbacks[i] instanceof NameCallback) {
            // prompt user for name
            NameCallback nc = (NameCallback)callbacks[i];
            System.out.print(nc.getPrompt());
            String name = (new BufferedReader(
              new InputStreamReader(System.in))).readLine();
            nc.setName(name);
          }
          else if (callbacks[i] instanceof PasswordCallback) {
             // prompt user for password
            PasswordCallback pc = (PasswordCallback)callbacks[i];
            System.out.print(pc.getPrompt());
            String pwLine = (new BufferedReader(
              new InputStreamReader(System.in))).readLine();
            pc.setPassword( pwLine.toCharArray());
          }
          else {
            throw new UnsupportedCallbackException(
              callbacks[i], "Unrecognized Callback");
          }
      }
    }
}
```

Source 11.3 *(continued)*

Finally, here is the content of a client-side configuration file that specifies that the `PasswordLoginModule` is used both as the default login module and for applications that provide the name "HelloClient" as the parameter to the `LoginContext` constructor.

```
certificate {
  com.sun.enterprise.security.auth.login.ClientCertificateLoginModule
     required debug=false;
```

```
};

default {
   examples.security.PasswordLoginModule required debug=false;
};

HelloClient {
   examples.security.PasswordLoginModule required debug=false;
};
```

The java system property `java.security.auth.login.config` is used to reference the resource containing the above configuration information. For instance, if the above configuration information were contained in a file named `client.conf`, you might have the following on your java command line:

```
java -Djava.security.auth.login.config=client.config ...
```

You will also need to specify security permissions in order to execute the code in Sources 11.1 to 11.3. In particular, this code from Source 11.1 creates a login context:

```
            LoginContext loginContext =
                new LoginContext("HelloClient", new CallbackHandler());
```

The code from Source 11.2 also uses private credentials, as in:

```
subject.getPrivateCredentials().add(pc);
```

The code snippets above will necessitate the following policies (respectively) being set:

```
    permission javax.security.auth.AuthPermission
        createLoginContext.SecurityExampleClient";
    permission javax.security.auth.AuthPermission
        "modifyPrivateCredentials";
```

For a complete discussion of security and policy files, browse to: `http://java.sun.com/j2se/1.5.0/docs/guide/security/PolicyFiles.html`. Setting the policy file is also done through a system property. If the above permissions were set in a file named `client.policy`, you might have the following on your `java` command line:

```
java -Djava.security.policy=client.policy ...
```

Authorization in EJB

After the client has been authenticated, it must pass an authorization test to call methods on your beans. The EJB container enforces authorization by defining *security policies* for your beans. Again, there are two ways to perform authorization with EJB:

- **With *programmatic authorization*, you hard-code security checks into your bean code.** Your business logic is interlaced with security checks.
- **With *declarative authorization*, the container performs all authorization checks for you.** You declare how you'd like authorization to be achieved through the deployment descriptor, and the container *generates* all necessary security checks. You are effectively delegating authorization to the EJB container.

Security Roles

Regardless of whether you're performing programmatic or declarative authorization, you need to understand the concept of *security roles*. A security role is a collection of client identities. For a client to be authorized to perform an operation, its security identity must be in the correct security role for that operation. The EJB deployer is responsible for associating the identities with the correct security roles *after* you write your beans.

The advantage to using security roles is that you do not hard-code specific identities into your beans. This is necessary when you are developing beans for deployment in a wide variety of security environments, because each environment will have its own list of identities. This also enables you to modify access control without recompiling your bean code.

Specifying security roles in EJB is application server-specific but should not affect the portability of your code. Table 11.1 shows some sample mappings.

Table 11.1 Sample Security Roles

SECURITY ROLE	VALID IDENTITIES
Employees	EmployeeA, EmployeeB
Managers	ManagerA
Administrators	AdminA

Performing Programmatic Authorization

Let's discuss how to authorize programmatically. Then we'll see how to authorize declaratively and compare the two approaches.

Step 1: Write the Programmatic Security Logic

To perform explicit security authorization checks in your enterprise beans, you must first get information about who is calling your bean's method. You can get this information by querying the container through the EJB context object.

The EJB context object has the following relevant security methods:

```
public interface javax.ejb.EJBContext
{
    ...
    public java.security.Principal getCallerPrincipal();
    public boolean isCallerInRole(String roleName);
    ...
}
```

`isCallerInRole(String role)` checks whether the current caller is in a particular security role. When you call this method, you pass the security role that you want the caller compared against. For example:

```
@Stateless
public class EmployeeManagementBean {

        @EJB private SessionContext ctx;

...

    public void modifyEmployee(String employeeID)
        throws SecurityException
    {
        /*
         * If the caller is not in the 'administrators'
         * security role, throw an exception.
         */
        if (!ctx.isCallerInRole("administrators")) {
            throw new SecurityException(...);
        }

        // else, allow the administrator to modify the
        // employee records
        // ...
    }
}
```

The preceding code demonstrates how to perform different actions based on the security role of the client. Only if the caller is in the *administrators* role (defined in Table 11.1, and setup using your container's tools) does the caller have administrator access.

The other programmatic security method, `getCallerPrincipal()`, retrieves the current caller's security principal. You can use that principal for many purposes, such as retrieving the caller's distinguished name from it to use this name in a database query. This might be handy if you're storing your security information in a database. Here is sample code that uses `getCallerPrincipal()`:

```
import java.security.Principal;

...

@Stateless
public class EmployeeManagementBean {

    @EJB private SessionContext ctx;

...

   public void modifyEmployee() {
       Principal id = ctx.getCallerPrincipal();
       String name = id.getName();
       // Query a database based on the name
       // to determine if the user is authorized
   }
}
```

Step 2: Declare the Abstract Security Roles Your Bean Uses

Next you must declare all the security roles that your bean code uses, such as an *administrators* role. This can now be done via annotations on the code. The deployment descriptor entries from the EJB 2.1 specification are still supported in the EJB 3.0 specification. Declaring security roles signals to others (like application assemblers and deployers) that your bean makes the security check `isCallerInRole (administrators)`. This is important information for the deployer, because he or she needs to fulfill that role. Source 11.4 demonstrates the annotation approach.

```
@Stateless
@DeclareRoles({"administrators"})
public class EmployeeManagementBean {
    ...
}
```

Source 11.4 Declaring a bean's required security roles via annotation.

Source 11.5 shows the deployment descriptor version. This accomplishes the exact same declaration as onSource 11.4.

```
...
<enterprise-beans>

    <session>

        <ejb-name>EmployeeManagement</ejb-name>
        ...

        <!--
        This declares that our bean code relies on
        the administrators role; we must declare it here
        to inform the application assembler and deployer.
        -->
        <security-role-ref>

            <description>
            This security role should be assigned to the
            administrators who are responsible for
            modifying employees.
            </description>

            <role-name>administrators</role-name>

        </security-role-ref>

        ...
    </session>

    ...

</enterprise-beans>
...
```

Source 11.5 Declaring a bean's required security roles.

Step 3: Map Abstract Roles to Actual Roles

Once you've written your bean, you can ship it, build it into an application, or make it part of your company's internal library of beans. The consumer of your bean might be combining beans from all sorts of sources, and each source may have declared security roles a bit differently. For example, we used the string `administrators` in our previous bean, but another bean provider might use the string `sysadmins` or have completely different security roles.

The deployer of your bean is responsible for generating the *real* security roles that the final application will use (see Source 11.6).

```
. . .
<enterprise-beans>

    <session>

        <ejb-name>EmployeeManagement</ejb-name>
        ...

        <security-role-ref>

            <description>
            This security role should be assigned to the
            administrators who are responsible for
            modifying employees.
            </description>

            <role-name>administrators</role-name>
            <!--
            Here we link what we call "administrators" above, to
            a real security-role, called "admins", defined below
            -->
            <role-link>admins</role-link>

        </security-role-ref>

        . . .
    </session>

    <assembly-descriptor>

        . . .

        <!--
        This is an example of a real security role.
        -->
        <security-role>

            <description>
            This role is for personnel authorized to perform
            employee administration.
            </description>

            <role-name>admins</role-name>
```

Source 11.6 Mapping abstract roles to actual roles. *(continued)*

```
        </security-role>

        . . .

    </assembly-descriptor>

  </enterprise-beans>
  . . .
```

Source 11.6 *(continued)*

Once you've completed your application, you can deploy it in a wide variety of scenarios. For example, if you write a banking application, you could deploy that same application at different branches of that bank, because you haven't hard-coded any specific principals into your application. The deployer of your application is responsible for mapping principals to the roles you've declared using proprietary container APIs and tools.

Performing Declarative Authorization

Now that you've seen programmatic authorization, let's move on to declarative authorization. The primary difference between the two models is that with declarative authorization, you *declare* your bean's authorization requirements in your deployment descriptor. The container enforces these requirements at runtime.

Step 1: Declare Method Permissions

You first need to declare permissions on the bean methods that you want to secure. The container takes these instructions and *generates* security checks in your EJB objects. This can be done via annotations or via the deployment descriptor. Source 11.7 shows the annotation version and Source 11.8 shows the equivalent deployment descriptor.

```
import javax.annotation.security.*;
...
@Stateless
//default role allowed will be administrators
@RolesAllowed({"administrators"})
public class EmployeeManagementBean implements EmployeeManagement {
    ...
    //overrides default role allowed of administrators.
    //only managers can call this method.
```

Source 11.7 Declaring a bean's security policy via annotations. *(continued)*

```
    @RolesAllowed({"managers"})
    public void modifySubordinate() {
        ...
    }

    //overrides default role allowed of administrators.
    //only managers can call this method.
    @RolesAllowed({"managers"})
    public void modifySelf() {
        ...
    }

    //overrides default role allowed of administrators.
    //only employees can call this method.
    @RolesAllowed({"employees"})
    public void modifySelf(String name) {
        ...
    }

    //overrides default role allowed of administrators.
    //anyone can call this method.
    @PermitAll
    public String getMyName() {
        ...
    }

    //no override. Only administrators can call this method
    public Collection getAllEmployees() {
        ...
    }

    //no one can call this method
    @DenyAll
    public void modify401kPlan() {
        ...
    }
    ...
}
```

Source 11.7 *(continued)*

There a few items we should note from Source 11.7. The `@RolesAllowed` annotation can be used at the type level or at the method level. Using it at the type level sets the default roles allowed for the entire bean. If no other security annotations are present on a method, then that method's roles allowed will be what were specified at the type level.

However, `@RolesAllowed` specified at the method level take precedence (or override) `@RolesAllowed` specified at the type level. The other security annotations @PermitAll and @DenyAll applied to a method also take precedence over @RolesAllowed at the type level.

Denying access to a method is useful when you are using a third-party bean and you do not want anyone to be able to use certain methods. You often will not have access to source code in this situation, so the @DenyAll annotation is not terribly useful here. Refer to the <exclude-list> element in the deployment descriptor in Source 11.8.

```
. . .

<assembly-descriptor>

    . . .

    <!--
    You can set permissions on the entire bean.

    Example: Allow role "administrators"
    to call every method on the bean class.
    -->
    <method-permission>
        <role-name>administrators</role-name>

        <method>
            <ejb-name>EmployeeManagement</ejb-name>
            <method-name>*</method-name>
        </method>
    </method-permission>

    <!--
    You can set permissions on a method level.

    Example: Allow role "managers" to call method
             "modifySubordinate()" and "modifySelf()".
    -->
    <method-permission>
        <role-name>managers</role-name>

        <method>
            <ejb-name>EmployeeManagement</ejb-name>
            <method-name>modifySubordinate</method-name>
        </method>

        <method>
            <ejb-name>EmployeeManagement</ejb-name>
            <method-name>modifySelf</method-name>
        </method>
```

Source 11.8 Declaring a bean's security policies in the deployment descriptor. *(continued)*

```
    </method-permission>

    <!--
    If you have multiple methods with the same name
    but that take different parameters, you can even set
    permissions that distinguish between the two.

    Example: allow role "employees" to call method
             "modifySelf(String)" but not "modifySelf(Int)"
    -->
    <method-permission>
        <role-name>employees</role-name>

        <method>
            <ejb-name>EmployeeManagement</ejb-name>
            <method-name>modifySelf</method-name>
            <method-params>String</method-params>
        </method>
    </method-permission>

    <!--
    This is the list of methods that we don't want
    ANYONE to call.  Useful if you receive a bean
    from someone with methods that you don't need.
    -->
    <exclude-list>
        <description>
             We don't have a 401k plan, so we don't
             support this method.
        </description>
        <method>
            <ejb-name>EmployeeManagement</ejb-name>
            <method-name>modify401kPlan</method-name>
            <method-params>String</method-params>
        </method>
    </exclude-list>

    . . .

</assembly-descriptor>
. . .
```

Source 11.8 *(continued)*

Once defined, the EJB container automatically performs these security checks on your bean's methods at runtime and throws a `java.rmi.AccessException` exception back to the client code if the client identity is not authenticated or authorized.

Step 2: Declare Security Roles

Declaring security roles is a process similar to programmatic security. We need to define our security roles and (optionally) describe each so the deployer can understand them. Source 11.9 has the annotated version, and Source 11.10 shows the descriptor.

```
@Stateless
@DeclareRoles({"administrators","managers","employees"})
public class EmployeeManagementBean {
    ...
}
```

Source 11.9 Declaring security roles via annotations.

```
<assembly-descriptor>

    . . .

    <security-role>
        <description>
        System administrators
        </description>
        <role-name>administrators</role-name>
    </security-role>

    <security-role>
        <description>
        Employees that manage a group
        </description>
        <role-name>managers</role-name>
    </security-role>

    <security-role>
        <description>
        Employees that don't manage anyone
        </description>
        <role-name>employees</role-name>
    </security-role>

   . . .

</assembly-descriptor>
```

Source 11.10 Declaring security roles for the deployer.

The deployer reads in Source 11.10 and, using the container's tools, maps these roles to principals, as shown in Table 11.1.

If annotations were used, the bean is interrogated at deployment time and the mapping is done automatically.

Declarative or Programmatic?

As with persistence and transactions, security is a middleware service that you should strive to externalize from your beans. By using declarative security, you decouple your beans' business purpose from specific security policies, thus enabling others to modify security rules without modifying bean code. No security role strings are hard-coded in your bean logic, keeping your code simple.

In the ideal world, we'd code all our beans with declarative security. But unfortunately, the EJB specification does not provide adequate facilities for this; specifically, there is no portable way to declaratively perform *instance-level authorization or condition-based authorization*. This is best illustrated with an example.

Let's say that you have an enterprise bean that models a bank account. The caller of the enterprise bean is a bank account manager who wants to withdraw or deposit into that bank account. But this bank account manager is responsible only for bank accounts with balances below $1,000, and we don't want him modifying bank accounts with larger balances. Declarative authorization has no way to declare in your deployment descriptor that bank account managers can modify only certain bean instances. You can specify security roles only on the enterprise bean class, and those security rules apply for all instances of that class. Thus, you would need to create separate methods for each security role, as we did in Sources 11.7 and 11.8. This gets hairy and makes your bean's interface dependent on security roles. For these situations, you should resort to programmatic security.

Security Propagation

Behind the scenes, all security checks are made possible due to *security contexts*. Security contexts encapsulate the current caller's security state. You never see security contexts in your application code, because the container uses them behind the scenes. When you call a method in EJB, the container can propagate your security information by implicitly passing your security context within the stubs and skeletons.

For example, let's say that a client is authenticated and has associated security credentials. That client calls bean A, which calls bean B. Should the client's security credentials be sent to bean B, or should bean B receive a different principal? By controlling security context propagation, you can specify the exact semantics of credentials streaming from method to method in a distributed system.

You can control the way that security information is propagated via annotation or in your deployment descriptor. The general rule is that if there is no explicit specification, either by descriptor or annotation, the caller principal is propagated. The design of EJB 3.0 recognizes this rule by having the @RunAs annotation. This annotation is applied at the class level. The parameter it takes is the role name that will be used to run as rather than the client's credentials. The snippet below shows the annotation.

```
@RunAs("admins")
@Stateless
public class EmployeeManagementBean {
    ...
}
```

Here is a deployment descriptor snippet that accomplishes the same thing as the annotation:

```
...
<enterprise-beans>
      ...
      <session>
            <ejb-name>EmployeeManagement</ejb-name>
            ...
            <security-identity>
                  <run-as>
                        <role-name>admins</role-name>
                  </run-as>
            </security-identity>
            ...
      </session>

<assembly-descriptor>
      . . .
      <security-role>
             <description>
             This role is for personnel authorized
             to perform employee administration.
             </description>

             <role-name>admins</role-name>
       </security-role>
       . . .
</assembly-descriptor>
</enterprise-beans>
```

The EJB container is responsible for intercepting all method calls and ensuring that your bean is running in the propagation settings you specify. It does this by generating code that executes at the point of interception (inside the EJB objects).

Secure Interoperability

Secure interoperability means that EJB containers from different vendors cooperate in protecting EJB invocations that originate in one vendor's product and target EJBs in another. The most important functionality that EJB containers must agree on here is the authentication of principals on one end of the invocation and the propagation of the principal information to the other. In addition, there must be consensus about how confidentiality and integrity protections should be applied on the wire.

For this to happen, any security information that needs to be exchanged must be standardized. Otherwise, one vendor's product would not be able to understand the information sent by its colleague on the other end of the wire.

The general protocol that the EJB specification requires for interoperability is RMI-IIOP. For the additional, security-related interoperability, the EJB specification leverages two more protocols that were originally designed for CORBA:

- IIOP/SSL (IIOP over SSL) for authentication, integrity, and confidentiality
- CSIv2 (*Common Secure Interoperability version 2*), for additional authentication capabilities and principal propagation.

You will probably not need to deal with the internal details of either IIOP/SSL or CSIv2 directly in development, but if you are curious about what is under the hood, then the rest of this section provides the background information. Also, when you are responsible for managing large-scale EJB server architectures that involve interoperating with external clients or servers, you should be aware of the trust relationships that must be established to allow for principal delegation across platforms.

IIOP/SSL

The first part of interoperable security—integrity and confidentiality protections—is actually simple thanks to SSL/TLS, which takes care of all the details of setting up secure transports between endpoints. For deployers, there is nothing left to do but provide proper credentials that SSL/TLS can use during its initial handshake. This is far from trivial, but since credentials are necessary anyway, this adds little complexity.

Internally, the hosting EJB container's CORBA Object Request Broker (ORB) is equipped to insert SSL-level transport information into `EJBObject` references. For IIOP/SSL, these references take the format of the CORBA *Interoperable Object References* (IORs), and SSL/TLS-related information is stored in the IOR as *tagged components*. The receiving container's ORB recognizes the IOR and its tagged components and hence knows how to let the SSL/TLS layer open transport connections.

CSIv2

SSL/TLS is not a silver bullet for all your security problems. It does offer interoperable, standardized means for mutual authentication between communicating peers, but it requires public key certificates in X.509 format to do this. While this is a proven mechanism, it requires some form of certificate management infrastructure. Mapping other client authentication mechanisms, such as Kerberos, is hard, and propagating principal information from clients a few hosts up in the invocation chain is not supported at all. Moreover, SSL/TLS is heavyweight in the sense that the initial handshake required to set up a secure transport adds a significant overhead. In some cases you may want to authenticate a client but don't actually care for the additional integrity and confidentiality protection of SSL.

Common Secure Interoperability version 2 (CSIv2) was specified for CORBA by the Object Management Group (OMG) in 1999 as a successor to earlier secure interoperability protocols. CSIv2 was designed to be used together with transport-level SSL security and to complement it. The *Security Attribute Service* (SAS) protocol in CSIv2 defines additional client authentication functionality that is independent of SSL/TLS and can be used with Kerberos or UserID/Password schemes. Target authentication is not supported in the SAS protocol, so if *mutual* authentication is required, the SAS protocol must be combined with the transport-level target authentication offered by SSL/TLS.

Additionally, the CSI protocol supports *identity assertions* as a means of principal propagation. An identity assertion is sent by the calling client to tell the receiver that it should not consider the client identity (which was established on the transport layer or by the authentication process) for making authorization decisions, but the asserted *identity* instead. An asserted identity is much like a `run-as` statement or a `set-uid` bit in the UNIX file system—with one important difference: It is the client who wants to define a different identity for its own actions.

With identity assertions, a single method call may have as many as three different identities associated with it: the transport-level identity as established by SSL, an additional client identity established through the SAS client authentication, and the asserted identity. Note that any or all of these may be missing. Figure 11.4 illustrates these layers.

What are these many identities good for? An asserted identity is useful when the client is acting on behalf of another principal who should be held responsible, especially when the client cannot reuse the principal's credentials to impersonate it when talking to the target. For example, the client may be a remote servlet container (running in vendor X's application server) calling an

EJB container (a product by vendor Y) on a different network, as shown in Figure 11.5. The Web container did authenticate the Web user by using SSL client authentication and established a principal identity. It cannot itself authenticate as the principal to the EJB container, however. Because it does not have access to the client's required private keys, it can authenticate only itself. However, access control and auditing should use the actual user ID, not the servlet container's identity, so the Web container needs to assert the client identity.

Security Attribute Layer	**Identity Assertion**
Client Authentication Layer	**Client Authentication**
Transport Layer (SSL/TLS)	**Client Authentication** **Message Protection** **Target Authentication**

Figure 11.4 Layers in CSIv2.

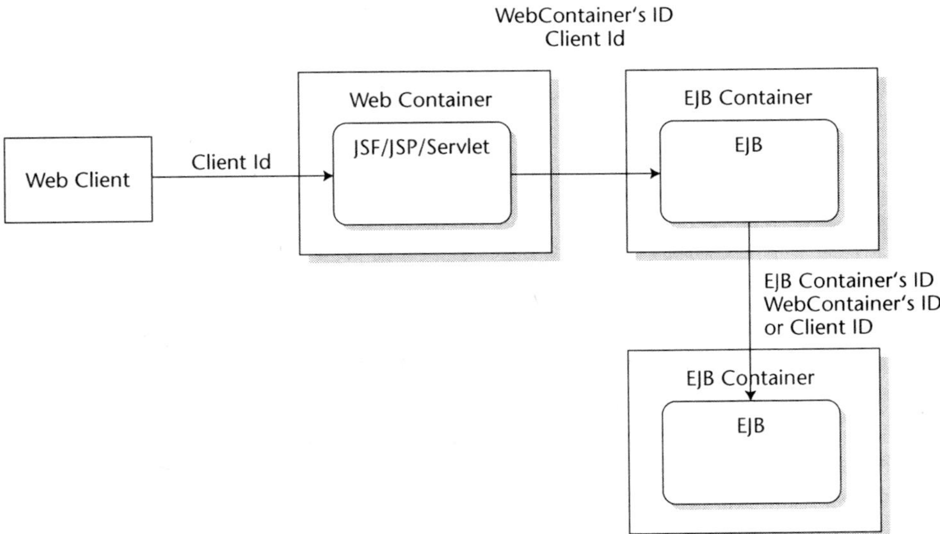

Figure 11.5 Identity assertion in a call chain.

Obviously, accepting an asserted identity that arrives in the security context of a method call is a matter of trust. Trust here means trusting that the JSP files and servlets did not cheat when inserting the identity assertion, and trusting that an attacker did not penetrate the Web container host. Looking closer, we find that this trust actually extends to all predecessors in the call chain, which the target has no secure way of identifying. This is also called *transitive trust*. The EJB specification simply states that identity assertions should be accepted only from containers with predefined trust, which in most practical settings means that containers authenticate each other using public key certificates on the transport layer that were distributed beforehand. A receiving container can then simply accept identities that the sending container asserts.

Note that the problem with transitive trust still exists: The whole trust chain is only as strong as its weakest link. Effectively, this means that deployers should take considerable care when exchanging public key certificates and marking them as trustworthy.

Because no tight control of principal propagation can be enforced by the technology alone, there must be organizational frameworks to support cooperation and trust establishment.

Web Services Security

You may be wondering why, after so much security coverage, there is a need for an extra section on security for Web services. The simple reason is that Web services are not just an implementation approach for stateless session beans: They need to interoperate with other, potentially non-EJB Web services, say, in the .NET world. It follows that there must again be secure interoperability.

The standards that we mention here have been incorporated into the Java EE 5 specification.

NOTE **Sun has decided to drop the number "2" from all of its platforms and specifications. This is, in part, because as Java has matured, the "2" (as in J2SE and J2EE) has become a bit dated. The J2EE (Java 2 Enterprise Edition) will now be referred to as the Java EE (Java Enterprise Edition). Likewise, the developer tools will drop the "2." So, the J2SDK (Java 2 Software Development Kit) will henceforth be referred to as the JDK (Java Development Kit). JDK is actually what it was called prior to the emergence of the Java 2 Platform. To make matters a little more interesting (this is a polite way of saying confusing), Sun refers to the version numbers for specifications differently from the version numbers for its tools. For instance, the developer toolset for the latest release is JDK 1.5, while the specification it is based on is the Java SE 5.0.**

The Java Specification Requests (JSRs) included here have been released. Most modern application servers already come equipped with some Web services security mechanisms and prestandard APIs to the functionality described here. The remainder of this section is intended to provide you with an overview of the relevant standards and concepts so that you will be able to use them successfully.

The basic security functionality that must be provided in a standardized fashion should by now sound familiar to you: authentication, authorization, integrity, and confidentiality. Interestingly, the Web services security standards go well beyond the traditional approaches in a number of respects. The most important goal that the technologies we are about to meet aim for is true *end-to-end security* for the messages sent to and received from Web services, such as SOAP messages.

End-to-End Security

Let's consider the scenario where a client uses a Web Service, which behind the scenes delegates some of the functionality to other Web services, which may do the same with still other services. The original client has no way of knowing who will see which parts of the original request message, nor does it know who will actually create which parts of the result. (See Figure 11.6.)

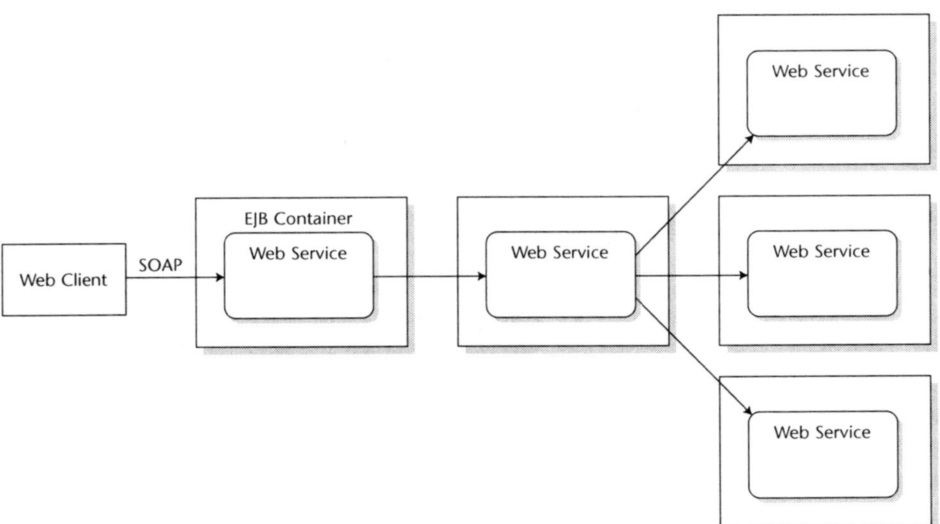

Figure 11.6 End-to-end security.

This functional abstraction is fundamental for making large-scale architectures possible, but from a security standpoint it means that you have to trust a potentially unlimited number of unknown parties to play fair. This may be okay within your own local network where you trust all servers and services, including their administrators, but it is certainly not acceptable in cross-enterprise applications with third- and fourth-party involvement. You don't want records of the hardware that you order to be compiled (and the records potentially disclosed), and you don't want the project schedules and design studies that you exchange with a business partner getting fiddled with.

This is where end-to-end security comes into play. It means control over the security of your messages from the point at which you send them until they reach their final destination, regardless of the number and kind of intermediaries that may get a chance to see your messages. Contrast this with the notion of transitive trust in EJB that we had to accept earlier: With transitive trust, anybody that your partner trusts is implicitly trusted by you, too. Regardless of whether you actually trust them or if you even know they exist.

End-to-end security is not possible with a point-to-point technology like SSL/TLS. It is possible to build a long channel out of several short ones, but each hop in such a chain of connections terminates one SSL/TLS connection and starts a new one. When SOAP messages and other EJB requests travel through multiple intermediate hops before they reach their final target, the messages are protected *between* hops but unprotected *within* each hop. All you can do with point-to-point security is trust that the software in those hops doesn't read or modify your messages where it shouldn't.

Enter two security standards that can protect XML documents (and thus also SOAP messages) independently of the transport layer and in true end-to-end fashion: XML Digital Signature and XML Encryption.

XML Digital Signature and XML Encryption

The names of these two standards certainly imply heavy-duty cryptography but don't worry: there are no new algorithms or protocols that we need to discuss here. Both standards rely on traditional cryptography and don't add any of their own. In fact, these two standards, issued by the World Wide Web Consortium (W3C), simply define XML syntax for encrypted or signed data. The data that is either signed or encrypted can be anything, including, of course, XML content, but it may also be other documents, or even arbitrary binary data.

As an example, consider the following SOAP message that contains a message body with a single, encrypted data element, the operation. The binary, encrypted data content of the inner `CipherValue` has been base64-encoded, the outer `EncryptedData` element describes the encryption algorithm (triple DES) that was used to create the `CipherValue`. Note that the receiver must know the symmetric key that was used to encrypt the message; otherwise, he won't be able to decrypt it. We'll discuss in the next section how information about the key (or even the key itself) can be sent in the message.

```
<soapenv:Envelope
xmlns:soapenv="http://schemas.xmlsoap.org/soap/envelope/">
  <soapenv:Header>
....
  </soapenv:Header>
  <soapenv:Body>
    <EncryptedData xmlns="http://www.w3.org/2001/04/xmlenc#"
      Id="#xdn_id0" Type="http://www.w3.org/2001/04/xmlenc#Element">
      <EncryptionMethod
Algorithm="http://www.w3.org/2001/04/xmlenc#tripledes-cbc"/>
      <CipherData>
        <CipherValue>Vy58P2KaKedALCyZt23Hoi7TSK8ZiZvygWorXUX
        Q56EmS1z5LVp8frzQvivk2iIrrYQI8DSbIG+ywfNnZfoVC0QiTbWE29
       HztGTRUhAE2f/VbRzpMisxe2+/Xc7EZXfurZOVFNR2NjW+Ayiuqd
       W5OxkZi7la6tmQefFFYUSAzsUA6p0nabXOVsNCds8Y7pdZXeJtH+
       lnMpfSCFNbS7R4GhFsZBjNL5Hxqb1vUZlgwcP9Lh6ua1yqi2DgUKvtI1/p
       thPNA/QYj3VfEZzk1sit/A==</CipherValue>
      </CipherData>
    </EncryptedData>
  </soapenv:Body>
</soapenv:Envelope>
```

XML digital signatures can cover data that is completely external to the transmitted document. For example, it may be a signature value over the content of a remote Web site or over a Microsoft Word document in a knowledge base somewhere. An XML message may even contain a signature over parts of itself. The added value here is that this signature data can now be transported within XML documents without having the receiver's XML parser complain about unexpected, non-XML data. To give you an impression, here's an example of an XML digital signature that was taken from another SOAP message.

```
  <Signature xmlns="http://www.w3.org/2000/09/xmldsig#">
    <SignedInfo>
      <CanonicalizationMethod
       Algorithm="http://www.w3.org/TR/2001/REC-xml-c14n-20010315"/>
      <SignatureMethod Algorithm="http://www.w3.org/2000/09/xmldsig#rsa-sha1"/>
      <Reference>
        <Transforms>
          <Transform Algorithm="http://www.w3.org/TR/1999/REC-xpath-19991116">
            <XPath
              xmlns:soap="http://schemas.xmlsoap.org/soap/envelope/">
              ancestor-or-self::soap:Envelope[1] and ancestor-or-self::
soap:Body[1]
```

```
            </XPath>
          </Transform>
          <Transform
            Algorithm="http://www.w3.org/TR/2001/REC-xml-c14n-20010315"/>
        </Transforms>
        <DigestMethod Algorithm="http://www.w3.org/2000/09/xmldsig#sha1"/>
        <DigestValue>/VYLngXLqJP//BWhmGxVysqlrxw=</DigestValue>
      </Reference>
    </SignedInfo>
    <SignatureValue>J+L8HqI7Q+/u0zuDWZeg5zKkiHRvQqCMZ1FkmGn8x+x8KPNqu/j
RpbEvacA1MjIIY00snVIti2yIgDHtfhNTQDa5GludCINbT5sEYeGYjVQwv8nFtwCMX+EmDXig/
        E2JHbQEDT4E02/1MrMV7Mk2cUorqk7bHuEG4wwIGdzqEIk=
    </SignatureValue>
    <KeyInfo>
      <X509Data>
        <X509Certificate>...</X509Certificate>
      </X509Data>
    </KeyInfo>
  </Signature>
```

The `Signature` element has three main elements: the `SignedInfo` that describes the signed data, the `SignatureValue` (a base64 encoding of an encrypted hash value), and the `KeyInfo`, that describes which key was used to create the signature. The `SignedInfo` describes the data that is signed. In this case, it is a SOAP message header body, which is referred to using an XML path expression (XPath). This data was then transformed using a canonicalization algorithm before actually applying the signature algorithm (RSA-SHA1) to the message digest, which was computed using the SHA1 hash algorithm. Canonicalization is necessary for all XML content before signing because XML documents may undergo a number of changes (such as adding or removing whitespace in some places) during transport or other processing that do not change the document structure or content and thus should not cause the signature to break. To allow for these XML modifications, the sender first constructs the canonical form of an XML document and only then applies the signature. The receiver also first constructs the canonical form of the document he just received and then compares the outcome of another signature computation with the signature value that was received.

The two standards discussed in this section support some very important security features:

- **With XML Digital Signature and XML Encryption** it is possible to send encrypted XML documents through untrusted channels. Only legitimate receivers that possess the necessary cryptographic keys will be able to decrypt the encrypted parts, and any in-transit modifications of signed parts of the message will be detected by the recipients.

- **With transport-independent protections** it is now possible to persist the signature, meaning that we can store the signature with the message, for example as a signed receipt. This is not possible with SSL/TLS: as soon as the message leaves the secure transport, the signature is gone, so SSL/TLS is not a good tool for application-level cryptography.
- **With the granularity of XML digital signature and XML encryption** it is possible to encrypt or sign only selected parts of a message. With SSL/TLS, in contrast, messages were always signed and/or encrypted completely. It would not be possible to create a controlled document-based workflow where some parts of a message are designed for modifications by processors at different stages in the workflow, whereas others remain locked.

SAML

The acronym SAML means *Security Assertion Markup Language*, and this is an open standard ratified by the OASIS consortium. OASIS is short for *Organization for the Advancement of Structured Information Standards* and is a large industry consortium comparable to the OMG. OASIS is also responsible for WS-Security (see the following section). The two main application areas for SAML are interoperability between security products and single sign-on (SSO). SAML has two main parts: the XML syntax for security assertions, and a simple request/response protocol for requesting assertions from SAML *authorities*. We only cover the assertion syntax here.

Assertion is another word for a security token. Assertions are used by entities that need security information in order to enforce security. In SAML speak, these entities are *policy enforcement points*. The creator or issuer of a SAML assertion is called a SAML *authority*. Obviously, there is no need for SAML if the enforcement point creates all security tokens internally and for its own use and, therefore, does not need any external information. But if the enforcer is not in a position to authenticate the actual caller of a request and still needs to make an authorization decision, then a SAML assertion made earlier by an authentication service would help a lot. Sounds a lot like principal propagation, doesn't it? Yes, you may think of SAML as the CSIv2 of the Web services world.

Now for a quick summary of the remaining SAML concepts: An SAML assertion expresses statements by the *issuer* about the *subject* of the assertion, such as "subject S is authenticated (by me)," or "subject S is authorized for actions A and B (by me)," or even "subject S has attribute R," where R may be a role membership. Here is an example of an authentication assertion:

```
<Assertion xmlns="urn:oasis:names:tc:SAML:1.0:assertion"
  MajorVersion="1" MinorVersion="0" AssertionID="4711"
  Issuer="MySecuritySoftware"
  IssueInstant="2003-08-19T14:54:43">
    <Conditions NotBefore="2003-08-19T14:54:43"
                NotOnOrAfter="2003-08-19T15:04:43"/>
    <AuthenticationStatement
       AuthenticationMethod="urn:oasis:names:tc:SAML:1.0:am:unspecified"
       AuthenticationInstant="2003-08-19T14:54:43">
        <Subject>
            <NameIdentifier>Bart</NameIdentifier>
        </Subject>
    </AuthenticationStatement>
</Assertion>
```

The main part of the assertion is the `AuthenticationStatement` element, which states that someone named `Bart` was authenticated at a specific point in time using an unspecified mechanism. The outer `Assertion` element comprises further details, such as a validity condition (`NotBefore` and `NotOnOrAfter`), information about the issuer and issue instant, an assertion ID, and the SAML version used.

These assertions are made not just by anybody but by authorities that someone inspecting an assertion would trust. In the previous assertion, all we know about the issuer is that she calls herself `MySecuritySoftware`. In an untrusted environment, an assertion would normally be digitally signed by the authority so that trust in the assertion could be established. In the example, this step was skipped to reduce overhead because, presumably, the enforcement point axiomatically trusts the issuer, and forgery of assertions was assumed not to be possible.

WS-Security

WS-Security is another specification ratified by the OASIS consortium. It describes how encryption and signatures should be used on SOAP messages to enable end-to-end security, and defines a SOAP security header element. Moreover, it defines a couple of security tokens, such as a user name and password token, an X.509 token, and a binary token format that can be used to transmit Kerberos tickets. As a standard, it is comparatively short and straightforward, at least when compared to the EJB specification or CORBA.

The new security header was defined because the authors of the specification knew that message-oriented, end-to-end security cannot rely on sessions between peers along the way. The security header was, therefore, designed to contain the complete security information about the message in the message. In other words, the message is its own security context!

Here is an example of a SOAP message with this new WS-Security header element. In fact, this example contains the security information necessary to decrypt the encrypted message shown in the previous section, an encrypted key (a session key). Note how the `EncryptedKey` element's child `ReferenceList` refers to the encrypted data in the SOAP body using a URI reference to the `Id` attribute:

```
<soapenv:Envelope>
  <soapenv:Header>
    <wsse:Security xmlns:wsse="http://www.docs.oasis-open.org/wss/2004/
01/oasis-200401-wss-wssecurity-secext-1.0.xsd">
      <EncryptedKey xmlns="http://www.w3.org/2001/04/xmlenc#">
        <EncryptionMethod
          Algorithm="http://www.w3.org/2001/04/xmlenc#rsa-oaep-mgf1p"/>
        <KeyInfo/>
        <CipherData>
          <CipherValue>
jQEtmEsQ9CUUT0CuUM6yKKcpBbGV4psNdYN2o+eaXyAc2D1JM3Zz0xHqKoRURwy2y13nGv3q
zrjbPO55uyTn0KBG6jZRoFi6zsAdw1bJc0qBzDE3ca5LuLTKZ/PEqvtIptmgQefv80bgXXQj
mFTuyOEkOxLLv6uoobDxb29Lkf0=
          </CipherValue>
        </CipherData>
        <ReferenceList>
          <DataReference URI="#xdn_id0"/>
        </ReferenceList>
      </EncryptedKey>
    </wsse:Security>
  </soapenv:Header>
  <soapenv:Body>
    <EncryptedData Id="#xdn_id0">
 ....
```

Figure 11.7 illustrates how the different standards can be combined to send a SAML assertion, which is an authentication assertion, with a SOAP message. The SOAP header contains a WS-Security header, which in turn contains the SAML assertion. To prevent any modifications while in transit and to bind the assertion to the message, an XML digital signature is used, which is also contained in the security header. This signature not only guarantees integrity but also serves to authenticate the SAML assertion in the context of the message: without such a signature, the assertion could have been obtained by someone eavesdropping on the message traffic and then attached to his or her own messages.

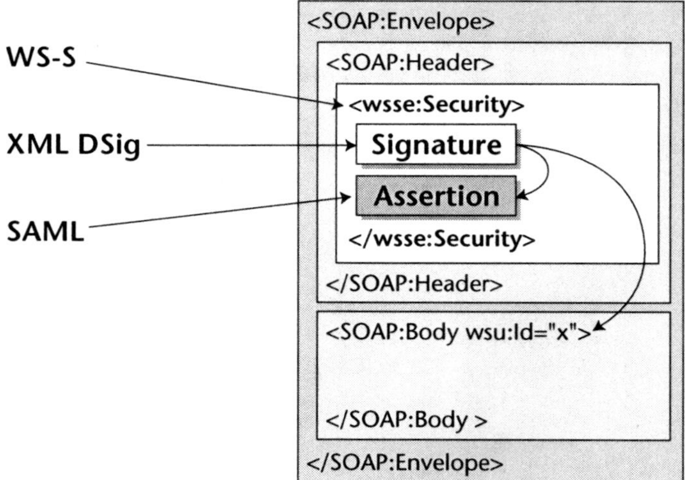

Figure 11.7 Standards in concert.

Summary

For all practical purposes, security should be seen as a trade-off between risks and cost. This chapter has described the most important security standards relevant in the EJB world, including the Java EE view on Web Application security. You have encountered both declarative and programmatic security in EJB, and the security interoperability protocol CSIv2. Moreover, we have presented some important standards in the Web services security world that have become standardized APIs.

CHAPTER

12

EJB Timers

Until EJB 2.1came along, the Enterprise JavaBeans standard lacked a decent scheduling mechanism. EJB 2.1 addressed this requirement by introducing the EJB Timer Service. In this chapter, in addition to examining how to use the EJB Timer Service with different types of beans, you will see how the EJB 3.0 programming model further simplifies development and deployment of timer-enabled beans. We also provide an example to walk you through a typical EJB timer development.

Scheduling

Scheduling functionality is required in many business applications. Various scenarios involving scheduling ensure that certain code is executed at a given point in time. For instance, imagine a system that handles huge loads during the peak hours and during the off hours wants to run maintenance chores such as cleaning the file system of temporary files, generating the activity reports, cleaning the databases, preparing audit reports of access from various parties to its subsystems, and so on. These tasks can be carried out automatically by scheduling them to run during off hours. This way your IT systems will not be hard pressed for resources during peak traffic hours and also at the same time can be utilized to perform routine maintenance tasks and all around use its resources better.

In many other similar situations scheduling can help—workflows are another example. Simply put, a workflow is a set of activities, each of which is scheduled to run at a specific time or when a conditional criteria is met. For example, consider a reservation workflow rule that ensures that if a customer does not guarantee a reservation with a credit card within 24 hours, the reservation is cancelled and an e-mail notification is sent to the customer's travel agent and also possibly to the customer. There are numerous ways in which scheduling can help you implement such use cases.

Scheduling techniques have been around for many years in the computer science world. UNIX-based operating systems have supported job-scheduling mechanisms through system services such as *Cron* for a long time. Cron is basically a daemon that uses the system clock to facilitate the scheduling of jobs for execution at any given time of day. Scheduled jobs, or Cron jobs as they might be called, are UNIX commands or scripts that you want to run on a particular schedule. These jobs are maintained in Cron tables. Authorized UNIX users create/edit these Cron tables, which are then read by the Cron daemon *almost* every minute to start these jobs. The Cron table is an ASCII text file consisting of entries for Cron jobs; each entry specifies a UNIX command to execute and its scheduled time of execution in terms of hours and minutes, day of week, day of month, and month. Another variant of the Cron service is the *At* utility. While Cron enables you to schedule a repetitive task, At lets you schedule a one-time task for execution. UNIX also supports another form of scheduling through its *Batch* utility. Batch executes a set of tasks instead of a single task; however, it is similar to At in that it executes only once.

Windows-based operating systems support a similar kind of functionality through the *At* utility, which basically takes the information about the command or batch program to execute, time to execute, and other such parameters, and schedules the job for execution. Linux too offers system-level scheduling capabilities quite similar to those of UNIX.

Hence, all the operating-system environments today support sophisticated scheduling mechanisms. It should come as no surprise that developers would want similar scheduling functionality in their programming platforms to be able to exploit scheduling techniques in different applications—EJB developers are no different.

EJB and Scheduling

If you think scheduling operating system commands and programs is powerful, think how powerful it would be to be able to schedule execution of parts of your code or methods on your components. Yes, that is what scheduling with EJB should allow us to do. EJB containers should let us schedule a given method to run at a particular point in time so that the container can call back that method once the scheduled time has elapsed. This capability can open a whole new world of possibilities with EJB.

THE JAVA PLATFORM AND SCHEDULING

The Java language platform has been providing basic scheduling capabilities since J2SE 1.3 via the `java.util.Timer` and `java.util.TimerTask` APIs. Together, these are termed the Java Timer APIs. Java Timer APIs provide a programming model in which your schedulable task, in other words the worker class, will extend the `TimerTask` abstract class. `TimerTask` implements `Runnable` and it represents a Java class that can be scheduled to run once or repeatedly by a timer. Thus, the action you need to perform when the timer calls your class should be put in the `run()` method of your `TimerTask` implementation.

The `Timer` object provides methods that you can use to schedule `TimerTask` objects for future execution in a background thread. Corresponding to each `Timer` object is a single background thread that is used to execute all the timer's tasks sequentially. Thus, if you used the same `Timer` object to schedule multiple timer tasks and if a certain timer task takes longer than expected to complete, the subsequent timer task will be held up until the previous one completes.

The `Timer` object, and hence the corresponding background thread, is kept alive by the JVM as long as there is an outstanding task to complete. Once all the tasks associated with the given `Timer` object are done executing, the JVM will kill the thread and release the `Timer` object in the subsequent garbage collection cycle. By default, your application could be held up as long as the timer is alive. This means that if you have a repeated timer task, your application can theoretically keep running forever. To get around this, you can create a `Timer` object that uses a daemon thread so that it does not keep the application from terminating.

An important point to understand about scheduling on the Java platform is that due to the inherent nature of Java, it is impossible to guarantee that the timer will execute a given timer task at exactly the specified moment. In other words, Java does not provide us with a consistently met real-time guarantee, the main reason for this is that the implementation of thread scheduling, on which job scheduling is dependent, is inconsistent across various JVMs. The `Timer` object schedules tasks via the `Object.wait()` mechanism, and so the exact moment at which the JVM wakes up the timer task objects is dependent on JVM's thread scheduling policy and such factors. Garbage collection is yet another factor that further makes job scheduling on the Java platform nondeterministic.

Thus, the Java Timer API is more than enough for simple scheduling activities for nonmanaged Java applications. If you need more sophisticated functionality, you can use scheduling frameworks, such as Quartz, to meet those needs. There is also another timer API in Java: the JMX (Java Management Extensions) timer API. However, it is very tightly coupled with the JMX framework and hence is not suitable for generic purposes.

The EJB Timer Service

EJB 2.1 introduced support for scheduling through the container-managed EJB Timer Service. Developers interact with the EJB Timer Service through various Timer Service APIs. These APIs can be used for creating timers for specified dates and periods. You can also create timers scheduled to expire at recurring intervals. As soon as the date or period specified for the timer is reached/ elapsed, the timer expires and the container notifies your bean of the timer expiration by calling a timeout callback method on the EJB. This callback method will implement the logic that you want to execute upon timer expiration(s). Figure 12.1 illustrates the high-level interaction between the Timer Service and an EJB interested in receiving timer notifications.

Enterprise beans interested in receiving timer notifications will register themselves with the Timer Service. Stateless session beans, entity beans, and message-driven beans can all receive timed notifications from the container. Timers cannot be created for stateful session beans and Java Persistence entities; however, future versions of EJB might support timers for these as well.

NOTE **As with the rest of this book, this chapter does not discuss the applicability of timers to entity beans, since there is nothing to add there. You can refer to the previous edition of this book if you need more information on implementing timers for entity beans.**

Timer Service API

The Timer Service API consists of four interfaces—`javax.ejb.TimedObject`, `javax.ejb.Timer`, `javax.ejb.TimerHandle`, and `javax.ejb.TimerService`. The following sections provide an overview of each of these interfaces.

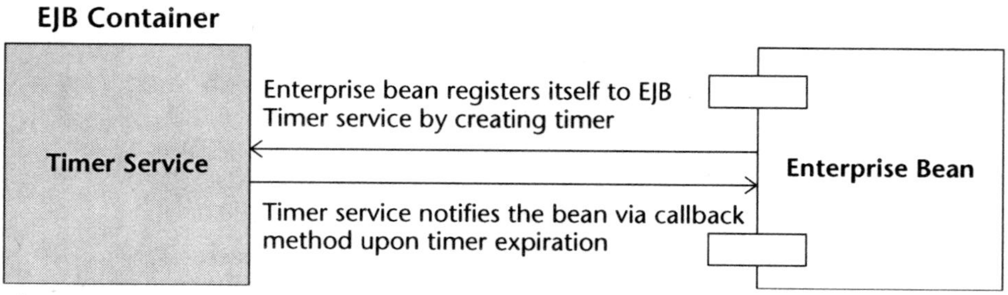

Figure 12.1 Interaction between the Timer Service and EJB.

javax.ejb.TimerService

This interface provides enterprise bean components with access to the container's Timer Service. It provides various `createTimer()` methods to create timers and thereby register with the container Timer Service for timer notifications. Using these `createTimer()` methods, you can create mainly four types of timers, depending on your needs.

- Recurrent expiration timers whose first expiration occurs at a given point in time as specified by the `Date` argument to `createTimer()` method. Subsequent timer expirations occur at interval durations specified in milliseconds.
- One-time expiration timers whose first and only expiration occurs at a given point in time as specified by the `Date` argument to `createTimer()` method.
- Recurrent expiration timers whose first expiration occurs after the specified number of milliseconds has elapsed. Subsequent timer expirations occur at interval durations specified in milliseconds.
- One-time expiration timers, whose first and only expiration occurs after the specified number of milliseconds has elapsed.

Apart from various methods for creating timers, `TimerService` has made available a `getTimers()` method, which retrieves all the timers associated with the given bean.

Source 12.1 shows the definition of the `TimerService` interface.

```
public interface javax.ejb.TimerService {
    public Timer createTimer(long duration, Serializable info)
            throws IllegalArgumentException, IllegalStateException,
            EJBException;
    public Timer createTimer(long initialDuration, long
            intervalDuration, Serializable info) throws
            IllegalArgumentException, IllegalStateException,
            EJBException;
    public Timer createTimer(Date expiration, Serializable info)
            throws IllegalArgumentException, IllegalStateException,
            EJBException;
    public Timer createTimer(Date initialExpiration, long
            intervalDuration, Serializable info) throws
            IllegalArgumentException, IllegalStateException,
            EJBException;
    public Collection getTimers() throws IllegalStateException,
            EJBException;
}
```

Source 12.1 The javax.ejb.TimerService interface.

javax.ejb.Timer

This interface represents a timer instance that was created through `TimerService`. Its methods provide information about the timer, such as the point in time when the next timer expiration is scheduled, the number of milliseconds that will elapse before the next scheduled timer expiration, and so on.

Also, this interface provides access to the timer information class through the `getInfo()` method. The timer information class has to be a `Serializable` instance, and it can be used as a means to provide application-specific information corresponding to the timer, such as the actions a bean will take upon timer expiration. This information class is written by the application provider and is passed as an argument to the respective `createTimer()` method in `TimerService`. If you do not want to provide a timer information object, pass null while creating the timer.

Finally, the `getHandle()` method retrieves the `Serializable` handle to the timer. This handle can be persisted and retrieved at a later time to obtain a reference to the timer instance.

Source 12.2 shows the definition of the `Timer` interface.

```
public interface javax.ejb.Timer {
     public void cancel() throws IllegalStateException,
              NoSuchObjectLocalException, EJBException;
     public long getTimeRemaining() throws IllegalStateException,
              NoSuchObjectLocalException, EJBException;
     public Date getNextTimeout() throws IllegalStateException,
              NoSuchObjectLocalException, EJBException;
     public Serializable getInfo() throws IllegalStateException,
              NoSuchObjectLocalException, EJBException;
     public TimerHandle getHandle() throws IllegalStateException,
              NoSuchObjectLocalException, EJBException;
}
```

Source 12.2 The javax.ejb.Timer interface.

javax.ejb.TimedObject

This interface contains a single method: `ejbTimeout()`. The container calls this callback method to notify the EJB of timer expiration. A bean class that implements this interface will receive timer notification from the container via invocation of the `ejbTimeout()` method. This timeout callback method, therefore, should contain the logic that you want to execute upon receiving timer notifications.

Source 12.3 shows the definition of the `TimedObject` interface.

```
public interface javax.ejb.TimedObject {
    public void ejbTimeout(Timer timer);
}
```

Source 12.3 The javax.ejb.TimedObject interface.

So this is one way of implementing timeout callback methods. Another way is by declaring a method as the timeout callback method, either in the bean class via the `@Timeout` annotation or in the deployment descriptor. The container will call this method upon timer expiration, just as it would call the `ejbTimeout()` method had you implemented the `javax.ejb.TimedObject` interface.

The container passes a corresponding instance of *Timer* associated with the bean in its invocations to timeout callback methods.

javax.ejb.TimerHandle

This interface contains a single method, `getTimer()`, which retrieves the reference to `Timer` represented by the given handle. The method throws `NoSuchObjectException` if invoked for a timer that has already expired or has been cancelled.

Source 12.4 shows the definition of the `TimerHandle` interface.

```
public interface javax.ejb.TimerHandle extends Serializable {
    public Timer getTimer() throws IllegalStateException,
           NoSuchObjectException, EJBException;
}
```

Source 12.4 The javax.ejb.TimerHandle interface.

NOTE Durations in the timer API are specified in milliseconds, taking into consideration that the rest of the J2SE APIs use millisecond as the unit of time. However, do not expect the timers to expire with millisecond precision given the incapability of the Java platform to support true real-time predictability.

Interaction between the EJB and the Timer Service

It is clear that `TimerService` is the top-level API that allows you to create timers. The question is—how to get access to a `TimerService` instance? You can get hold of the `TimerService` instance through `EJBContext`. The `EJBContext` interface has the `getTimerService()` method, which can be called from any business method of your stateless session bean or message-driven bean. Another way to get access to the Timer Service is to look up the `TimerService` object in the JNDI. And yet another way, in EJB 3.0 applications, is to obtain the `TimerService` object via dependency injection.

NOTE **What happens if you create a timer from one of your EJB methods without implementing the `TimedObject` interface for that EJB? Check it out.**

Figure 12.2 shows the sequence diagram of interaction between EJB and the Timer Service.

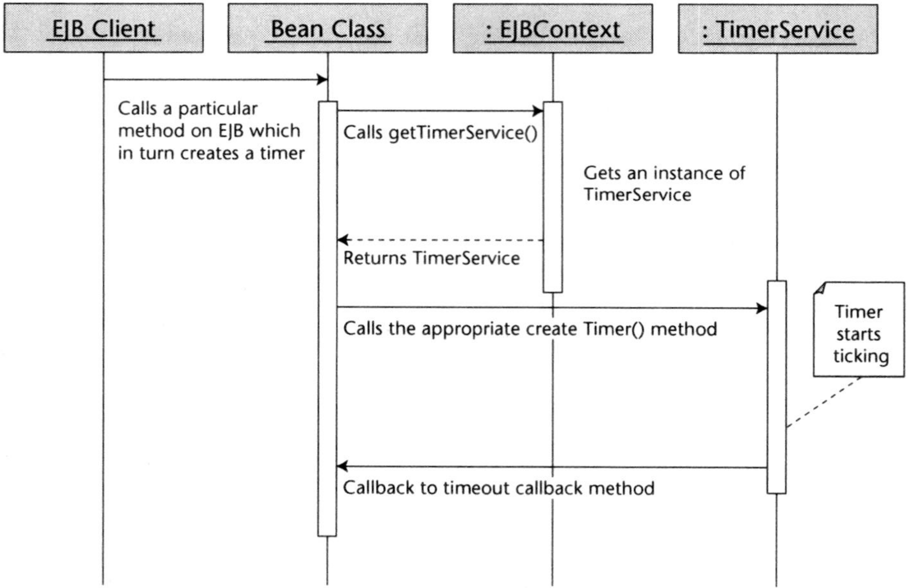

Figure 12.2 Sequence diagram of interaction between EJB and the Timer Service.

TIMERS AND TRANSACTIONS

The creation of timers is supported within transactions.

Therefore, if an enterprise bean method that creates the timer is executed as part of a transaction and if that transaction is rolled back, the timer creation is rolled back too. Similarly, if an enterprise bean method cancels the timer by calling `cancel()` on the `Timer` interface within a transaction and if that transaction is rolled back, the container rolls back the timer cancellation as well. The container restores the duration of the timer to the duration it would have had, had it not been rolled back.

The timeout callback method can also be called within a transaction and typically has transaction attributes of `REQUIRES` or `REQUIRES_NEW`. Hence, if the transaction rolls back, the container will call the timeout callback method again.

Timer Example: CleanDayLimitOrdersBean

Let us now examine the code for stateless session bean timers. The message-driven bean timers are written exactly the same way as stateless session bean timers are. To understand this example, consider an online securities trading system. The system allows the customer to place *limit* orders for a given security, say for example equities, such that the buy or sell transaction for the given security can be limited to occurring anytime during a day or anytime during the trading week or anytime until the end of the current month and so on as long as the buy/sell criteria specified by the customer is met. Limit orders are supported by most of the contemporary online securities trading systems. Now not all limit orders are executed, since the criteria, mainly the price criteria, set by the customer may not be met during the specified limit period. Obviously, such limit orders should be removed upon expiration of limit periods.

Our example bean, `CleanDayLimitOrdersBean`, demonstrates an elegant way of cleaning the trading database by removing all the limit orders that were not executed during the limit period. In our scenario, a client application, `CleanDayLimitOrdersClient`, will invoke the `cleanPeriodicallyDayLimitOrders()` method on `CleanDayLimitOrdersBean`. `cleanPeriodicallyDayLimitOrders()` creates a recurrent expiration timer based on the current date such that at the end of every trading day a timer expires and the container invokes the timeout callback method `handleTimeout()`. Notice that the `CleanDayLimitOrdersBean` does not implement a `javax.ejb.TimedObject` interface. Instead, it implements the timeout logic in the `handleTimeout()` method and marks it with the `@Timeout` annotation. Basically, we are using the annotated method to implement the callback timeout logic. For now, we are least concerned with the database logic and hence, this example code does not elaborate the database part.

Note that the source files for this example are available on the book's accompanying Web site wiley.com/go/sriganesh.

The CleanDayLimitOrders Business Interface

First, let us define our bean's business interface. The code is shown in Source 12.5. The remote interface defines a single business method, cleanPeriodicallyDayLimitOrders(), which we will implement in the enterprise bean class.

```
package examples.timer;
import javax.ejb.Remote;

@Remote
public interface CleanDayLimitOrders {
    public void cleanPeriodicallyDayLimitOrders();
}
```

Source 12.5 The examples.CleanDayLimitOrders interface.

The CleanDayLimitOrdersBean Class

Our bean class has one business method, cleanPeriodicallyDayLimit Orders(), which is responsible for cleaning the trading system database of expired day limit orders. The implementation of this method makes use of java.util.TimeZone and java.util.Calendar types to manipulate the time. It does various calculations to arrive at the number of milliseconds that should expire until the market closes on the current day. This example takes into consideration the U.S. exchanges' market close time, which is 4 PM Eastern Standard Time. Finally the method creates a recurrent expiration timer, whose subsequent expirations occur at an interval of 86,400,000 milliseconds (24 hours). The idea is that once the first timer is fired off sometime after 4 PM Eastern Standard Time, the subsequent timers will fire off exactly 24 hours after that instant.

Also the bean class does not implement the TimedObject interface. Instead, it uses annotation to mark a method as the timeout method, thereby letting the container know that it is interested in receiving the timer notifications and that the timeout method, handleTimeout(), should be invoked to send the notification callbacks.

Source 12.6 shows the CleanDayLimitOrdersBean.java code.

```
package examples.timer;

import javax.ejb.*;
import javax.annotation.Resource;

import java.util.Calendar;
import java.util.TimeZone;
import java.util.SimpleTimeZone;
import java.util.GregorianCalendar;
import java.util.Date;

@Stateless
public class CleanDayLimitOrdersBean implements CleanDayLimitOrders {

    @Resource private SessionContext ctx;

    public void cleanPeriodicallyDayLimitOrders()
    {
      // Get hold of the eastern time zone assuming that the
      // securities are being traded on NYSE and NASDAQ exchanges.
      String[] timezoneIDs = TimeZone.getAvailableIDs (-5 * 60 * 60 *
      1000);

      SimpleTimeZone est = new SimpleTimeZone (-5 * 60 * 60 * 1000,
      timezoneIDs[0]);

      // Provide the rules for start and end days of daylight savings
      // time.
      est.setStartRule (Calendar.APRIL, 1, Calendar.SUNDAY, 2 * 60 * 60
      * 1000);
      est.setEndRule (Calendar.OCTOBER, -1, Calendar.SUNDAY, 2 * 60 * 60
      * 1000);

      // Get hold of a calendar instance for the eastern time zone.
      Calendar cal = new GregorianCalendar(est);

      // Set the calendar to the current time.
      cal.setTime (new Date ());

      // Calculate the difference between now and market close i.e. 4 PM
      // Eastern.
      int hourofday = cal.get (cal.HOUR_OF_DAY);
      int minuteofhour = cal.get (cal.MINUTE);

      // If this method is invoked after the market close, then set the
      // timer expiration immediately, i.e. start=0. Otherwise,
      // calculate the milliseconds that needs to elapse until first
      // timer expiration.
      long start = 0;
```

Source 12.6 The examples.CleanDayLimitOrdersBean class. *(continued)*

```
        if (hourofday < 16)
        {
          int hourdiff = 16 - hourofday - 1;
          int mindiff = 60 - minuteofhour;

          start = (hourdiff * 60 * 60 * 1000) + (mindiff * 60 * 1000);
        }

        // Finally, get hold of the Timer Service instance
        // from EJBContext object and create the recurrent expiration
        // timer.
        TimerService timerService = ctx.getTimerService();
        Timer timer = timerService.createTimer(start, 86400000, null);

        System.out.println("CleanDayLimitOrdersBean: Timer created to
        first expire after " + start + " milliseconds.");
      }

      @Timeout
      public void handleTimeout(Timer timer)
      {
        System.out.println("CleanDayLimitOrdersBean: handleTimeout
        called.");

        // Put here the code for cleaning the database of day limit orders
        // that have not been executed.
      }
    }
```

Source 12.6 *(continued)*

When trying this example, you might want to provide smaller values for both start and interval periods to immediately see the timer expiration results. That's it—our `CleanDayLimitOrders` EJB is all set to receive timeout callbacks from the container.

The CleanDayLimitOrders EJB Deployment Descriptor

We can deploy our bean without the deployment descriptor. However, if you wanted to specify the timeout callback method within the deployment descriptor, Source 12.7 shows what your deployment descriptor should look like.

```
<?xml version="1.0" encoding="UTF-8"?>
<ejb-jar xmlns="http://java.sun.com/xml/ns/javaee"
xmlns:xsi="http://www.w3.org/2001/XMLSchema-instance" full="false"
version="3.0" xsi:schemaLocation="http://java.sun.com/xml/ns/javaee
http://java.sun.com/xml/ns/javaee/ejb-jar_3_0.xsd">
  <enterprise-beans>
    <session>
      <display-name>CleanDayLimitOrdersBean</display-name>
      <ejb-name>CleanDayLimitOrdersBean</ejb-name>
      <business-remote>examples.timer.CleanDayLimitOrders</business-
      remote>
      <ejb-class>examples.timer.CleanDayLimitOrdersBean</ejb-class>
      <session-type>Stateless</session-type>
      <timeout-method>
         <method-name>handleTimeout</method-name>
         <method-params>
             <method-param>javax.ejb.Timer</method-param>
         </method-params>
      </timeout-method>
      <transaction-type>Container</transaction-type>
      <security-identity>
        <use-caller-identity/>
      </security-identity>
    </session>
  </enterprise-beans>
</ejb-jar>
```

Source 12.7 The ejb-jar.xml file.

The CleanDayLimitOrders EJB Client

Now that the bean is ready, we need to write the client. The client runs in the Java EE application client container. The Java EE application client container can perform dependency injection of resources in a Java application the same way that an EJB container does dependency injection of resources in an EJB application. Therefore, notice that our client does not use JNDI APIs to get a reference to `CleanDayLimitOrders`; instead, it injects the reference to the `CleanDayLimitOrders` EJB using `@EJB` annotation. The client then invokes the `cleanPeriodicallyDayLimitOrders()` method on this reference. Source 12.8 shows the code for `CleanDayLimitOrdersClient.java`.

```
package examples.timer;

import javax.ejb.EJB;

public class CleanDayLimitOrdersClient {
    @EJB
    private static CleanDayLimitOrders cleanDayLimitOrders;

    public static void main(String[] args) {
        try {
            cleanDayLimitOrders.cleanPeriodicallyDayLimitOrders();

            System.out.println ("cleanPeriodicallyDayLimitOrders()
            returned successfully. Take a look at the application
            server log or console for messages from bean.");
        } catch (Exception ex) {
            System.err.println("Caught an unexpected exception!");
            ex.printStackTrace();
        }
    }
}
```

Source 12.8 The examples.CleanDayLimitOrdersClient class.

Running the Client

To run the client, look at the Ant scripts bundled along with this example. The following is the client-side output you will get upon running `CleanDayLimitOrdersClient`.

```
C:\MEJB4.0\src\examples\timer>asant run_client_in_appcontainer
Buildfile: build.xml
build_cpath:
init_common:
setup_env:
run_client_in_appcontainer:
     [exec] cleanPeriodicallyDayLimitOrders() returned successfully.
Take a look at the application server log or console for messages from
bean.
```

On the application server console or in the application server log file, you should see the following output. Make sure to run your application server in verbose mode to be able to see this output on the server console.

```
[#|2006-03-21T15:58:11.927-0500|INFO|sun-appserver-pe9.0|javax.enterprise
.system.stream.out|_ThreadID=11;_ThreadName=p: thread-pool-1; w:
3;|CleanDayLimitOrdersBean: Timer created to first expire after 120000
milliseconds.|#]
[#|2006-03-21T16:00:11.929-0500|INFO|sun-appserver-pe9.0|javax.enterprise
.system.stream.out|_ThreadID=11;_ThreadName=p: thread-pool-1; w:
3;|CleanDayLimitOrdersBean: handleTimeout called.|#]
```

Take a close look at the highlighted portions. You'll notice that our timer was first created at around 3:58 PM Eastern Standard Time, and the first timer was fired at 4:00:11 PM Eastern Standard Time. You should continue to get these notifications for as long as the enterprise bean is deployed and its respective Java EE application is running. Of course, the application server has to be running in order to receive these notifications.

Finally note that this output is for an EJB deployed on the reference implementation of Java EE 5.

NOTE We can generalize `CleanDayLimitOrders EJB` further so that it can clean the end-of-week or end-of-month limit orders as well. For this, we can create multiple timers associated with the bean in a way that each of these timers expires at a different interval.

Now that you know how to develop EJB timers, let us take a look at some of the strengths and shortcomings of the EJB Timer Service.

Strengths and Limitations of EJB Timer Service

The EJB Timer Service has some obvious strengths with respect to other scheduling utilities and frameworks, in that:

- Scheduling semantics provided by the EJB Timer Service are platform-independent. You can use platform-specific utilities such as Cron or At to schedule calls to an EJB client, which in turn calls a certain EJB method, and this will work just fine. However, there is a caveat to this approach. What do you do if your client needs to run on a different platform? You will now have to learn and work with the scheduling semantics of the new platform, which again may or may not satisfy your requirements.
- The EJB Timer Service lets you schedule the timers programmatically. Consider a scenario in which EJB wants to create timers based on a certain request from a client. Without having a framework API, such as the one provided by the EJB Timer Service, it is hard to achieve this—more so if you use platform-specific utilities for scheduling calls to EJB methods, because then your EJB will require a way to schedule *platform* timers from within the EJB environment.

- Finally, the EJB Timer Service provides a standard interface to scheduling functionality as opposed to frameworks such as Flux or Quartz. This gives you one less thing to worry about when your application is required to support multiple Java EE–platform products.

On the other hand, there is a lot of scope for the EJB Timer Service to improve further. Currently, it lacks two features:

- Support for declaration of timer intervals in the deployment descriptors is not available today. As a result, the developer has to embed the timer expiration period and the subsequent expiration interval information in the EJB bean class. This restricts the ability of the developer to declaratively provide timer-related information at the time of deployment.
- There is not much flexibility in the way the timers can be specified today. Consider our example. Since the only unit of time that the timer APIs accept is milliseconds, we had to write the logic for converting the hours and minutes into milliseconds in order to create the timer for the `CleanDayLimitOrders` EJB. Had the timer API given a provision for creating timers wherein the periods could be specified in terms of hours, days, or months, it would have been much more powerful and simpler to use.

  Also, we cannot create timers that expire on given days of the week but not on other days. Again, consider `CleanDayLimitOrders` EJB. Here, we actually want a timer that would expire after 4 PM Eastern Standard Time every day from Monday through Friday. We do not want our timer to expire on Saturdays and Sundays. However, because there is no mechanism to specify this level of finer-grained scheduling information, we will have to add this logic in our code. Our implementation does not have this, but a real trading system should have the logic in place to avoid hitting the database when the timer expiration occurs on Saturdays, Sundays, and other nontrading days (such as public holidays).

Our hope is that in the subsequent EJB specifications, these features will be added.

Summary

In this chapter, we provided a complete overview of using the EJB Timer Service. You learned that although the EJB Timer Service is simple to use and very helpful for implementing certain scenarios, it has some shortcomings, which should be addressed in the upcoming EJB specifications.

In the next chapter, we discuss an advanced and very interesting topic—EJB best practices. So sit up straight and read on!

CHAPTER

13

EJB Best Practices

In this chapter, we will discuss best practices in terms of design, development, building, testing, and working with EJB. These guidelines will help in resolving some of the dilemmas you face in real-world EJB projects. By being aware of these best practices, you will avoid common pitfalls that others have experienced when building EJB systems.

Note that persistence-related best practices and various performance optimizations are covered in Chapter 9 and Chapter 14, respectively.

Let us begin now with various design, development, testing, debugging, and deployment strategies.

NOTE We do not discuss lower-level EJB design patterns in this chapter, since there are many resources in terms of books, papers, and so on that already focus on that. Besides, discussing lower-level EJB design patterns itself warrants a whole book. Our recommendation is that you read *EJB Design Patterns* (ISBN: 0-471-20831-0) published by John Wiley & Sons as a guide for EJB design patterns.

When to Use EJB

The cost of not making a correct go or no-go decision for EJB can be very high. It can range from a project getting delayed to a project getting scrapped. Hence, we would like to take a few moments to address this very crucial design point in the very beginning.

In our opinion, you should think of using EJB in the following design situations:

- **Remoting is required.** Gone are the days when everybody used to think of distributed systems as a panacea. Modeling an application's functionality into various tiers composed of reusable components is surely a way to achieve a clean and manageable design. However, deploying these components on separate boxes just for the heck of it does not necessarily result in the best systems. Do not confuse the need for componentization with the distribution of these components on multiple systems. Both are quite different and both have different costs associated with them.

  With that said, once you determine the need for distributed components in your application, consider EJB as your first alternative. Their sole purpose is to provide a programming model to build managed and distributed components on the Java platform.

- **Distributed transactions are required.** Transaction semantics are beautifully defined by the EJB standard. A protocol as complicated as the two-phase commit—one of the most widely used distributed transactions protocols in enterprise applications today—is neatly supported by the EJB architecture. Although, nonstandard frameworks such as Spring and Hibernate do support distributed transactions, the level of support of these in EJB containers is one of the best. It probably has to do with maturity gained by EJB server vendors on account of implementing distributed transactions for years. Hence, for large-scale distributed transactional systems, leveraging EJB makes a lot of sense.

NOTE One of the common complaints against the EJB transaction model is its lack of support for nested transactions and long-running transactions. Well, this will not remain the case for long. JSR 095 (Java EE Activity Service for Extended Transactions) defines a low-level framework for creating various transaction models. At the time of this writing, JSR 095 is in the proposed final draft stage. Hopefully, it shall become part of Java EE 1.5 platform.

- **Component-security is required.** EJB architecture defines a standard fine-grained security model for the components. Although, EJB architecture does not provide support for fancy security schemes, such as single sign-on or biometric authentication, as yet, it does provide a basic framework for authentication and access control that is more than enough to meet security needs of 85 percent of enterprise applications. So if you have a requirement for access control at the application-component level (and not just at the Web level), then you should consider using EJB.
- **Persistence is required.** Much has been said—both, good and bad—about the persistence functionality as defined by the EJB standard. With EJB 3.0, the persistence model is a whole new ball game. It incorporates the best of what has been learned from lightweight approaches, such as Hibernate, into a mature standard. EJB persistence is now based on plain old Java objects (POJOs). It can be used outside the container. It supports declarative relationships and true object orientation (such as polymorphism). Early benchmarks show that common design patterns for persistence perform twice as fast compared to EJB 2.1 (for further details, see `http://java.sys-con.com/read/131767_2.htm`). The persistence model is now easily understood and, thus, if persistence is a requirement for your project, you should strongly consider using EJB. (Chapters 6 and 9 cover the EJB 3.0 persistence model in detail.)
- **Integration with legacy applications is required.** More recently, this has become one of the main selling points of EJB architecture. EJB provides multiple elegant models through Java EE Connector Architecture, EJB Web services, and JMS for integrating with legacy/nonlegacy applications deployed on heterogeneous platforms. Thus, if your application requires integration with another application, you should consider using the EJB framework for this integration. Chapter 18 covers these EJB integration programming models and related best practices in depth.
- **Scalability is required.** EJB technology was designed with scalability in mind. The idea is to make scaling up of applications seamless, for example without rearchitecting and reprogramming, so that it simply becomes a matter of throwing more hardware at an application. Java EE enables you to scale your EJB and Web tiers separately. Remoting allows you to keep both of these tiers on separate boxes and scale these boxes as needed. For example, in an application that involves a simple Web interface but complex middle-tier processing, throwing more resources at systems on which an EJB application is deployed just makes more sense.

In conclusion, if you are going to need transactions, remoting, security, persistence, application integration, and other such infrastructure-oriented facilities in your application, consider leveraging the time-tested EJB framework in your project. Working with EJB can get complex if not done right. However, there are thousands of ways to deal with this complexity. However, creating your own framework is definitely not one of them.

IS USING A POJO + FRAMEWORK COMBINATION ALWAYS A GOOD IDEA?

The recent wave in enterprise Java computing is to replace all or some parts of the EJB framework with popular open source frameworks, such as Spring, Hibernate, and so on, that have grown from the wider Java community. The Spring framework (`springframework.org`) is a Java EE framework. Spring applications can be built using EJB or POJOs. In case you choose POJOs, Spring can provide declarative local transactions for POJOs without relying on the EJB container. Similarly, Spring supports data access via JDBC and O/R mapping frameworks such as Hibernate, as well as dependency injection. Thus, Spring is unique in the sense that it makes using heavyweight EJB containers a matter of choice and not necessity in some respects. It provides a lightweight framework alternative for writing business tier objects.

Hibernate (`hibernate.org`) is another popular O/R framework whose biggest value proposition is ease of use. It is a POJO-driven lightweight transactional persistence and data access framework. One of the interesting features it provides is the modeling of inheritance relationships of data.

Like always, we would like to maintain that just as EJB is not a sure-shot way of building robust and scalable applications, using POJO frameworks is not a sure-shot way of simplifying business tier development and deployment. Think of using POJOs only when the architectural benefits are substantial. Note that ease of development is not always equipped with highly transactional enterprise functionality. For instance, if distributed transactions are a must for your application, Spring + POJOs would not work.

The safest route is to stick to EJBs and trust the Java Community Process (JCP) to evolve the standard, and evolve it they will. Now that EJB 3.0 supports POJOs and can model inheritance relationships of data (having embraced the Hibernate model), the decision on when to use EJB has been simplified. Dependency injection is another feature, which although present in Spring, is now being supported in EJB 3.0 via annotations. Many people turned to Hibernate and Spring because of their flexibility and accessibility, but now EJB 3.0 offers many of the same features with the benefit of being backed by major industry Java vendors.

How to Choose a Web Application Framework to Work with EJB

Model 2 Web application frameworks have very much become a part of infrastructure software these days and rightly so. Working with such frameworks guarantees a lot of functionality related to localization, error handling, validation of form data, and so on out of the box. Many of these functions would otherwise need to be coded when working with raw Web components, such as servlets and Java Server Pages (JSP).

You can choose from dozens of Web application frameworks, both open source and closed source. Choosing a Web application framework is an important decision for you as an architect. Here are some of the factors that you should consider when deciding on a Web application framework for your EJB project:

- **Integration with EJB technology.** In EJB projects, one of the obvious considerations for your Web application framework is how well it integrates with EJB technology. EJB integration basically implies the support for EJB design patterns, EJB entity beans handling, and so on from within the framework components. For instance, the Struts community has made it quite simple to work with EJB via the StrutsEJB project (`http://strutsejb.dev.java.net`). The StrutsEJB project provides base classes and patterns (mainly Service Locator, Business Delegate, DTO, and Session Façade patterns) to build a Struts Web application that uses EJB in the business tier. The Java Server Faces (JSF) technology offers a server-side component framework for user interfaces (the view). It includes APIs for UI components, state management, input validation, and handling events (among other things). There are many in the Java community who would like to see the EJB and JSF specifications merged. As of this writing, the effort to merge the specifications has not gained any traction, but there are many examples of using JSF and EJB together. For more information, browse to the JSF homepage at `http://java.sun.com/j2ee/javaserverfaces`.
- **Tools support.** Tools enable rapid application development (RAD) thereby increasing productivity. Most of the framework communities and vendors provide some kind of IDE plug-in technology-based tools to help in development. However, usually this plug-in support is limited to one or two IDE at most. So if you are using an IDE that the plug-in doesn't support, you might have no tools available for the framework.

  For instance, although Tapestry is a powerful framework, Spindle, a plug-in that provides IDE support for Tapestry, is available only for the

Eclipse IDE. As a result, developers of projects that use other IDEs, such as NetBeans, have to develop and deploy the framework components manually.

On the other hand, mature frameworks, such as Struts, have good tools support in the form of IDE plug-ins (Struts Console plug-in for NetBeans, Eclipse and Struts Tools for IBM WSAD, and so on) and standalone GUI tools (Struts Console and Struts Studio).

- **Small-device support.** Generating content in a markup language so that it can be rendered on small devices is a very real requirement of today's business applications. If your application falls in this category, then you should select an application framework that provides a comparatively painless way of generating markup content for small device browsers. Most of the device browsers today support WML, HDML, cHTML, or XHTML markup languages. Frameworks, such as Cocoon, SOFIA, and Struts, provide tag libraries for generating device markups, such as WML, HDML, and XHTML.

NOTE If your candidate framework does not provide a tag library for the needed markup language, then you should think about developing a new tag library. Developing a tag library is a nontrivial task and, hence, should be considered only when other options are not available.

- **Standards support.** View technology leveraged by these Web application frameworks should be standards-based simply because you do not want to trade innovation from the wider JCP community for innovation from your specific Web application framework community. Although, all the Web application frameworks are based on standards, watch out for those proprietary hooks.
- **Learning curve and availability of expertise.** If you are planning on using your existing staff for application development, then you should consider the learning curve required for them, in order to develop efficiently using the candidate Web application framework. Make sure that proper help and documentation is available for the candidate framework, regardless of whether it is open or closed sourced, to speed up the learning process. On the other hand, if you are planning to hire new people for your project, then select a framework that is popular and widely used so that finding the right talent is possible.
- **Open source versus closed source.** At the end of the day, if most of your requirements in the areas mentioned previously are met by a given application framework, we'd like to say it does not matter

whether it is closed source or open source. However, in the real world, both cost and a sense of control over your own destiny are important concerns. We have witnessed quite a few projects where open source Web application frameworks were chosen because they were "good enough" and were "free." In some other projects, open source Web application frameworks were chosen simply because their source was made available for tweaking; whereas in a select few cases, customers went for closed source application frameworks from vendors because of a well-defined product support model.

Whatever your reasons might be for choosing an open or closed source Web application framework, we recommend that you select a framework that meets most of the criteria given in this section.

Applying Model Driven Development in EJB Projects

Model Driven Development (MDD) is becoming more and more popular within the developer community lately because of its promise of increased productivity over the traditional code-centric development approach. MDD is a development methodology wherein a model is at the core of development. In this context, the model typically represents an entity in the problem domain and applicable business logic that needs to be performed on this domain entity. For example, in a typical order-processing system, a customer model will represent appropriate data attributes and business operations applicable to a customer entity. Thus, if such an order processing system is developed using the MDD paradigm, a given MDD tool will take the customer model as input and generate application code from it, thereby establishing a close link between the model and its system implementation.

Here is an obvious question: "What is the difference between the modeling tools such as Together or Rational Rose and MDD tools?" After all, modeling tools have been generating skeleton implementation code from models for years.

Well, the difference is in how far the tool can take you with a model. Any modeling tool these days can generate Java classes from a corresponding UML class diagram. However, is that enough? No. Because even after the tool generates a Java class, we are still required to write code for utilizing persistence, security, logging, transactions, and other such services of the underlying EJB/JDO/JDBC/XYZ framework. Similarly, we still need to write code for accessing other services, implemented as POJOs, EJB, or Web services, from our Java class.

On the other hand, an MDD tool will generate most of these relevant artifacts from a given model and also potentially adhere to the industry best practices of the underlying platform, say Java, Java EE, or .NET. Thus, MDD tools translate the domain model to code not just based on technical specifications but also based on best practices and design patterns. For example, application code generated by Compuware OptimalJ or open source AndroMDA MDD tools can implement the core Java EE design patterns, such as Command, DAO, and so on, with discretion from the architect, of course. Thus, MDD tools are capable of generating highly functional and high-quality code.

NOTE **As of this writing these tools support the J2EE specifications. Be on the lookout for new versions supporting the Java EE 5 specification.**

Evidently tools play a crucial role in the MDD paradigm. We believe that a natural evolution for modeling tools today would be toward supporting MDD. Now, MDD tools can be categorized as follows:

- **Tools that follow standards.** Tools such as Compuware OptimalJ, Infer-Data Model Component Compiler (MCC), Interactive Objects ArcStyler, and open source tools, such as AndroMDA and OpenMDX, and so on, support Model Driven Architecture (MDA), an OMG vendor-neutral standard of building platform-independent models for consumption by MDD tools. MDA makes extensive use of UML and XMI (XML Metadata Interchange) to achieve its goal of platform independence.
- **Tools that do not follow standards.** Tools such as IBM Rational Rapid Developer (RRD) do not support any specific standard for MDD, but rather follow their own paradigm. For example, RRD is based on proprietary MDD methodology named Architectured Rapid Application Development (ARAD).

Here are some suggestions for those considering MDD for EJB projects:

- **Begin with a proof of concept.** Start by developing a small application using both traditional code-centric and MDD approaches to verify whether MDD does in fact bring productivity gains to your team. Also, in our opinion, it is easier to apply the MDD approach to new application development than to existing application development or maintenance. This is so because, at present, not many tools provide a sound strategy for migrating existing applications developed using a code-centric approach to MDD.
- **Consider using standards-based tools.** Using tools that follow standards, such as MDA, protects you from vendor lock-in. A healthy ecosystem of tools around a given standard enables migration of platform-independent domain models from one tool to another in future.

- **Consider MDD tool integration with an existing infrastructure.** Consider how well your candidate MDD tool integrates with the existing platform infrastructure products used in your shop. For instance, if you're using JBoss, an obvious question should be whether MDD would generate packaging and deployment artifacts specific to JBoss.

  Similarly, not all MDD tools (for example, OpenMDX) provide modeling facilities. As a result, you will have to make sure that the MDD tool you choose integrates with your existing modeling tool.

Applying Extreme Programming in EJB Projects

Extreme Programming (XP) is a software engineering discipline whose core practices revolve around an underlying assumption: Change in requirements, and hence software design, will inevitably occur during the course of software development. As almost all software development methodology pundits agree, XP's underlying assumption is not far from reality. After all, how many projects have you worked on where the design was frozen before writing a single line of code so that it never had to change? None.

This pragmatic approach that XP takes makes it extremely alluring to architects and development team leaders. There are almost a dozen practices defined by the original thinker of XP, Kent Beck. However, we do not think that you need to understand and implement all of them in your EJB projects as long as you follow a couple of core practices strictly.

NOTE **One of the great advantages of using XP is the availability of a wide variety of tools that can be used for functions ranging from unit testing XP code to managing XP projects to continually integrating components developed using XP methodology. Even better, most of these tools are highly functional, time tested, and open source.**

In our opinion, here is how the core principles of XP should be followed in EJB projects:

- **Iterative development.** In iterative development, the development team is given a certain target to meet per iteration. These iterations can last one week, two weeks, or more; whatever seems reasonable to code your requirements. Each such successful iteration will lead the system toward its final form. You will need to divide your EJB projects into such iterations. What has worked very well for us in the past is subdividing a given iteration into three subphases.
- **EJB subphase.** This is when we develop, build, and deploy the EJB—session beans, message-driven beans, or entities—on development systems.

- **Testing subphase.** This is when we build the unit test clients that follow simple test cases such as checking the getters/setters, mocking the calls to beans, checking whether the data in the database gets added/updated/deleted properly. Various strategies for unit testing EJB are discussed in the best practice section titled "How to Test EJB." It is useful to note here, though, that EJB 3.0 has greatly enhanced the ability to unit test using standard tools, such as JUnit. Since beans and entities are now POJOs, testing outside the container (necessary for using JUnit) is very straightforward. We will discuss this further in the next sections.
- **User subphase.** In this phase, we present the work we have done in the given iteration to the actual users. These users might be people from other business units who in turn will be using your application, or from your customer. The clients define various acceptance tests that they would use in this subphase to make sure that their requirements, defined during the iteration planning, are met.

  An important factor for the success of iterative development is setting and meeting deadlines. To meet deadlines, you should refrain from adding new functionality in the middle of the iteration. The idea is to keep your iterations short and yet meaningful.
- **Continuous integration.** Continuous integration is about keeping various application components in sync with each other so that the system is fully integrated most of the time. The motivation behind this practice is to avoid integration nightmares, which usually arise when you take a piecemeal approach to application development and do not stop to check that various pieces work with each other. Frequently checking that the different parts of application fit nicely leads to fewer surprises during the testing subphase. Continuous integration is achieved by typically building the system at least once a day; however, the exact period between consequent builds will mostly depend on how long your iteration is. But the idea is not to defer integration of application components until last moment.
- **Refactoring.** Refactoring is a process of continuously improving the design of existing code without affecting the code behavior. Refactoring usually involves the restructuring of code so as to remove the redundant code, reduce coupling in the code, introduce better naming conventions in the code, or organize the code more cohesively and consistently.

  An example of a good refactoring candidate is an EJB application where one EJB, say `SavingsBean`, has a method named calculateInterest() that accepts parameters in this order: accountId and interestRate. While another EJB, say Mortgage-Bean, has a method named calculateMortgage() that accepts parameters in this order: interestRate and accountId. Here, one of the bean methods takes the accountId parameter first; whereas the other bean method takes interestRate first. This is a clear example of inconsistency in code design and hence, a good candidate for refactoring.

Thus, each cycle of refactoring transforms your code into a more evolved structure. A good practice to follow is to keep the changes during refactoring small and have multiple refactoring cycles. Each refactoring cycle should be followed by continuous integration and then testing to ensure that your code evolution has not introduced any new bugs.

Martin Fowler's book *Refactoring: Improving the Design of Existing Code* (ISBN: 0201485672) is a good resource in that it discusses various techniques for code refactoring so that the underlying behavior is retained. Also http://industriallogic.com/xp/refactoring/catalog.html maintains a catalog of patterns to be used during code design to achieve maximum refactoring. Most of the J2EE/EJB IDEs these days support refactoring transformations of code. Some tools such as Eclipse also enable you to preview the changes resulting from a refactoring action before actually carrying them out. They also can let you know the potential problems refactoring might lead to in the functioning of your code.

- **Test-driven development.** XP focuses largely on testing and thereby requires obtaining feedback from customers at various logical points (end of iteration cycles) in the development life cycle. Also XP-style test-driven development encourages doing a lot of unit testing of new or modified code. A typical XP project will maintain a set of unit test cases that a developer will run whenever new or modified code is released. Quite a lot of emphasis is put on the automation of these tests to make XP even more efficient. We talk about EJB testing best practices in the next section.

XP development, thus, is lightweight and flexible as compared to more formal development methodologies such as Rational Unified Process or even some of the obsolete development models such as the waterfall model. We think that applying XP to your EJB projects can provide good benefits regardless of the project complexity given that core principles of XP are followed strictly.

Testing EJB

Of the three types of testing—code testing, regression and functional testing, and load testing—we will focus on the techniques for code testing using unit tests because that is an area where you can automate a lot and thereby make code testing easier and more efficient. Code testing is about ensuring that the given code behaves the way a developer intended it to behave; a code unit test is a piece of code that checks the behavior of the target code. Whereas code unit testing leads to acceptance of a piece of code, functional unit testing leads to acceptance of a subsystem of the application. The quality assurance team does functional testing at the use-case level, and it is often composed of customers.

EJB Unit Testing

You can write code unit tests for your EJB to see if your beans are doing the *right* things. For example a code unit test for an account entity can determine whether instantiation and field population is inserting the account data in the database properly. Similarly, a code unit test for a mortgage session bean might check whether its `calculateMortgage()` method is calculating the mortgage payment right. Thus, a code unit test is always about testing the piece of code and its localized behavior. Another important reason to unit test your EJB code is that it helps you catch the inconsistencies and difficulties in using the EJB interfaces early on.

One of the major advancements of EJB 3.0 is that beans and entities can now be tested in the same way as plain Java classes. The tricky thing, however, is to deal with resource injection in unit tests. For entities, you can use an out-of-container `EntityManager`. For the bean types, it may be necessary to perform mockup routines to populate variables that would be injected by the container (we'll cover mockups later in this chapter). With the advent of Application Client Container (ACC), it is even easier to run standalone unit tests. Our unit tests might encompass deployment and probably redeployment of EJB. The good news is that we can automate deployment. However testing EJB as a standalone component might not make much sense in certain scenarios. For example, consider a design in which a stateless session bean is acting as a façade to other session beans and entity beans. In that case, you should also deploy these other beans in order to unit test the façade stateless session beans. Similarly for entity beans that have relationships with other entity beans, you have to ready all the relationship beans to unit test the original entity bean.

You will need to deploy and redeploy various beans during the testing process. These days, most Java EE application servers support some form of autodeployment, which has made deployment must less of a pain than in the past. With Glassfish and JBoss, for instance, you can drop a properly prepared

.ear file into the right folder and the server will automatically deploy (or redeploy) it. Still, it is best to automate the deployment process for your beans. Pretty much all EJB servers provide command-line tools for deploying EJB. You can use these tools in combination with Ant scripts to automate the deployment. You can also automate redeployment (if necessary) as a two-step process: undeploy the existing EJB and deploy the newer version again.

Use Frameworks for EJB Unit Testing

Using a framework will greatly help reduce the effort involved in unit testing. Let us see some of the commonly used frameworks for EJB unit testing.

The JUnit Framework

A unit test framework such as JUnit will make it easier to create unit tests by extending unit test cases from the framework base classes. JUnit also provides the facility to create a test suite made up of tests that you want to run. Hence, you can combine several unit tests in a test suite to enable regression testing. Graphical test runners based on Swing are made available by JUnit. Test runners are responsible for running JUnit tests and collecting, summarizing, and formatting their results.

JUnit also integrates with Ant so that you can run various tests as part of the build process. For this you will have to insert the `<junit>` Ant task in the Ant script. The `<junit>` Ant task can also create a file consisting of the status of each test. This integration with Ant is very useful because you can bundle not just the test cases but also the configuration needed to run them as part of your Ant scripts. Another benefit of using JUnit and Ant together is that it enables the generation of HTML test reports by using the `<junitreport>` task. This task uses XSLT technology to transform XML test results to HTML.

JUnit is a widely adopted framework with great support tools. It integrates with IDEs such as Eclipse, Netbeans, Oracle JDeveloper, IntelliJ IDEA, Borland JBuilder, and so on. Also, several modeling tools such as Borland TogetherJ support the generation of test cases based on JUnit framework.

Another test framework of interest could be Apache Cactus. Cactus is an extension of JUnit, and it specifically caters to testing enterprise Java applications. You can unit test EJB using classic JUnit framework itself; however, you should use Cactus if your EJB clients also run in a Java EE environment, as is the case when servlets or JSP use your beans. This is a requirement for more than half of the EJB applications and Cactus comes in handy for testing such applications because it unit tests these client Java EE components as well, apart from EJB. With Cactus you get an end-to-end framework for unit testing EJB applications with a Web front end. Cactus allows for writing three types of test case classes based on the `ServletTestCase`, `JspTestCase`, and `FilterTestCase` classes also known as redirectors. Hence, your test case classes will extend any one of these, depending on which client model you use, and get a reference to your EJB, call the method on it, and assert the test results.

Like the `<junit>` Ant task, the `<cactus>` Ant task provides Cactus integration with Ant. In fact, `<cactus>` extends the `<junit>` task to enable in-container testing. It deploys the .war/.ear file containing Cactus classes and related deployment information into the target container, starts the container if it is not started, and runs the Cactus tests. It supports most of the Web and EJB containers including Apache Tomcat, JBoss, Orion, Resin, and WebLogic. Also if your container is not supported explicitly by Cactus, then you can use a generic Cactus container, which lets you specify Ant targets to be executed to start up and shut down your container.

Mock Object Frameworks

Using mock objects could be another approach to unit testing EJB. A mock is a dummy placeholder object instead of a real object that:

- Acts as a false implementation of an interface or a class mimicking the external behavior of their true implementation.
- Observes how other objects interact with its methods and compares this with preset expectations. If a discrepancy occurs, the mock object interrupts the test and reports about it.

Expectations, a term often used in the mock object world, consists of a set of conditions that we want our code to meet. For example, we might *expect* our code to close a database connection after using it. A mock object can be told to expect conditions such as these so that it can let us know when our expectations are not met.

You should use mock objects when unit testing complex logic that has dependencies on other objects and you want to test the interaction among these objects. The mock object will show you whether the tested code calls the right methods on the mocked object with the correct parameters. There are a number of mock object–based unit testing frameworks such as MockObjects. There are also quite a few mock object code generation utilities such as MockMaker and XDoclet (which now incorporates the original MockDoclet templates). Both these code generation tools rely on the `doclet` tags embedded within the Javadocs of the class being mocked, which are referred to as *target objects*. These `doclet` tags are read during the preprocessing in order to generate mocks. It is a good idea to use mock object code generation utilities when the target object has a frequently changing API. Another genre of mock object code generation consists of utilities such as EasyMock and jMock (previously Dynamocks). Both of them use the dynamic proxy approach to generate mock objects. Hence, you can generate mock objects only for target objects that implement interfaces using these utilities unless you apply patches to enable mock object code generation for target objects that do not implement interfaces. Of all the above-mentioned tools, XDoclet and EasyMock are most up to date. Mocking objects is a good solution to unit testing although it cannot and should not be used for integration tests, since during integration tests you are supposed to test your entire application end to end.

Thus, by using such frameworks developers can test their EJB code and make design changes, if necessary, before the code moves to QA.

Implementing Client-Side Callback Functionality in EJB

Imagine a scenario wherein an EJB has to place a callback to the client. How would you implement this scenario? There is no provision for implementing a client-side callback in the EJB standard. As a result, developers find themselves in a tough spot when faced with this requirement. The three viable strategies for implementing client-side callbacks in EJB are presented in the following sections. Note that all these strategies have their own pros and cons and should be applied under specific situations.

JMS

In this strategy, the client uses JMS temporary destinations (queue or topic, depending on your need) to receive callback notifications from EJB server components. The reason we want to a use temporary JMS destination for each client is that we do not want multiple clients popping messages from the same JMS destination; we want EJB server components to have unique `ReplyTo` addresses for all our clients.

Before calling a given method on EJB, the client will create a temporary JMS destination from which it will later receive messages. The client passes the JNDI name of the temporary JMS destination to the bean during the method call. The client starts listening, on a separate thread, to the temporary destination that it created earlier. On the EJB side, the bean will send a JMS message when it needs to call back the client. The client JMS listener receives the message and notifies the application upon receipt. Finally, the client deletes the temporary destination and closes the JMS connection.

As far as we know, this is the simplest way to achieve client-side callback functionality in EJB today. However, creating a temporary destination for each client does consume resources. You should do enough load testing to ensure that this model scales up to your needs.

Remote Method Invocation

This strategy is particularly useful with application clients. The idea here is to create RMI remote object on the client side that implements the `java.rmi.Remote` interface and registers it with the EJB. After registering this remote object, the client can continue doing its work, until the server calls a method on the registered RMI Remote object.

Implementing this strategy is fairly straightforward. You will need to provide the callback object stubs to the EJB.

Web Service

This strategy is useful in order to make callbacks happen across the firewalls or when the client is a Java EE Web application. Here, the client implements a JAX-RPC service endpoint to which the EJB will send a SOAP message in case of a callback. The bean will use Dynamic Invocation Interface (DII) to keep the callback Web service client code generic. On the client side, you can use either a document model or RPC model for implementing such a callback Web service.

One of the major drawbacks associated with this strategy used to be the lack of reliability. The SOAP message sent by the bean might never reach the client-side callback Web service, because SOAP over HTTP was inherently unreliable. Now that OASIS has finalized the Web services Reliable Messaging standard (`http://oasis-open.org/committees/tc_home.php?wg_abbrev=wsrm`), this is a much more viable solution.

Choosing between Servlets and Stateless Session Beans as Service Endpoints

Java EE Web services are based on three main technologies: JAX-RPC, servlet, and stateless session beans. As you know by now, a Java EE Web service endpoint can be implemented either as a stateless session bean or as a servlet. So then, which component model should you use for your Web services, a servlet or stateless session bean? Here are some guidelines that should help you in choosing between the two.

Use a servlet as Web service endpoint if:

- The business logic of the service is within a Web tier, because in this case the endpoint and Web service's business implementation will reside in the same tier.
- You need a lightweight Web service container viz. servlet container.
- You need to execute some logic that resides on the Web tier before invoking Web services.

- You do not mind writing logic for synchronizing multithreaded access to your service. This is required, since the servlet container does not synchronize concurrent requests to the servlet instance and, hence, in this case, to your Web service endpoint.

Use a stateless session bean as Web service endpoint if:

- The business logic of the service is within an EJB tier, because in this case both the endpoint and the Web service's business implementation will reside in the same tier.
- You need the Web service implementation to avail themselves of the transaction- and component-level security services from the container.
- Before invoking Web services, you need to execute some logic that resides on the EJB tier.
- You want the container to take care of synchronizing concurrent access to your service.

Considering the Use of Aspect-Oriented Programming Techniques in EJB Projects

There has been a lot of discussion lately about using aspect-oriented programming, or AOP, with EJB. Here are some of the concepts that are worth understanding about AOP before we continue our discussion of when you should use AOP in EJB projects.

Aspect-Oriented Programming

AOP techniques are not new. They have been around for close to a decade; in fact, Microsoft Transaction Server is one of the early implementations that employed AOP techniques followed by EJB servers.

So what is AOP? Obviously, *aspect* forms the core of AOP. Aspects are *reusable* services that are quintessentially cross-cutting services of your application. In the context of a business application, services that provide user authentication, user authorization, logging of access to the system, and persistence of application data are examples of cross-cutting services or *concerns* for a business application developer—*concerns* because a developer cannot write robust applications without taking care of them. Hence, AOP can be defined as a programming platform that facilitates the development of *aspects* to mitigate *concerns* so that aspects can be *reused* by all the living objects within a given environment. Note the emphasis placed on reuse here.

With this in mind, come back to the EJB world and think about whether it uses AOP techniques or not—of course, it does. All the services that our beans get are aspects; for example, persistence, life-cycle management, transaction management, security, and dozens of other things are concerns that we, the business application developers, care about. EJB containers implement these cross-cutting concerns and provide reusable aspects so that all the beans deployed within the container can offload these concerns on the container aspects. So yes, it is very much an aspects-oriented implementation.

However, here is the caveat: The EJB programming model does not allow you to develop new aspects to take care of concerns that are not supported by the EJB container, not today at least. Therefore EJB, and Java EE for that matter, is not an AOP platform even though EJB technology uses AOP techniques.

When to Use AOP in EJB Applications

In order to use AOP in EJB, you will need to use tools such as AspectJ, Spring AOP, or tools provided by your application server. Quite a few application server vendors such as the JBoss Group and IBM already support or have declared the intent to support AOP in their products. The only thing you have to be wary of when going the AOP route is that standard Java platform does not provide inherent support in terms of APIs and compilers for AOP, and that you are embedding AOP in your application at the risk of losing portability.

We present some of the scenarios here to consider use of AOP with EJB.

Support Custom Concerns

The EJB container does provide implementation of some of the very common infrastructure areas such as transaction management, security, persistence, and so on. However, EJB designers have kept the implementation of these aspects transparent to the EJB developers. This means that developers cannot customize the behavior of aspects beyond what annotations and deployment descriptor configuration parameters allow nor can they create new aspects using EJB programming model. As a result, if you want to support a concern that is cutting across your application components but is not provided by the EJB container, then you need more than EJB can provide, and you should use AOP for developing aspects to address your concerns.

Are Interceptors AOP?

The short answer to the question "Are interceptors AOP?" is that the new support for interceptors in EJB 3.0 is AOP-*like*. It does work in a cross-cutting way in that the interceptor will be automatically executed whenever a business method is called. However, with AOP the code that might trigger an aspect to execute is generally not aware of the aspect. With EJB, the bean must "know" its interceptors by using the `@Interceptor` or `@Interceptors` annotations. Since the interceptor method can be defined within the bean class, this makes the bean class itself the "aspect," which is also antithetical to AOP.

Supply Aspects to the World Outside the EJB Container

Almost all of us have worked in EJB projects where we had to use POJOs in order to get around constraints imposed by the EJB standard—for example, to do things like access file systems or read/write static fields. We might also end up reusing these POJOs outside the EJB container, for example, in a Web application or a Swing application. In this scenario, it might be better to write reusable aspects to address concerns relevant to your POJOs. For example, consider a POJO that reads and writes to a file. Here, you might need to log the timestamp of the last updating of the file. In which case, you would create an aspect to address the logging concern. This way you can use the Logging aspect no matter whether your POJO is being used within an EJB container or within a Web container or in a vanilla Java Swing application.

NOTE **A word of caution: Do not use aspects for the sake of it. Especially, do not replace EJB services with your aspects, unless you are sure of what you are doing. After all, EJB vendors have prewritten these aspects to keep you out of implementing them mainly because implementing them is a humongous task. And finally, do not think that AOP is going to replace OOP (object-oriented programming)!**

IS AOP DIFFERENT THAN OOP?

We see this question many times and the simple answer to it is—yes. One of the common traits of both OOP and AOP platforms is their support for reusability. However, OOP instills reusability via inheritance. This means that in order to reuse the behavior encapsulated in an object, say A, some object B will have to *inherit* A. Inheritance is the key word here. B is able to reuse A's behavior only if it expects to build a longlasting relationship with A, such as a parent-child relationship. This works well if B does not mind A's sub-imposed behavior as a side effect of reuse and direct effect of inheritance.

However, OOP does not work when behavior needs to be reused horizontally, owing to the behavior's cross-cutting nature. Now why would you need to reuse behavior horizontally? Because you do not want your business object, for example a `ShoppingCart`, to inherit the behavior pertaining to transactions, since these behaviors are unrelated; you do not want an apple to inherit grape-like qualities; rather you want to mix apples and grapes to prepare a margarita. This is where AOP comes into picture.

AOP and OOP are not competing but complementary technologies. Consider, for example, an EJB server where cross-cutting aspects are provided to your object-oriented beans. In conclusion, OOP and AOP coexist.

Reflection, Dynamic Proxy, and EJB

When you call an EJB, you write code that essentially takes the binding information of the EJB object in JNDI or obtains a reference to an EJBObject via injection, and invokes methods on an EJB object. This style of invocation is usually referred to as *static* invocation, where the information about the interface and methods to invoke on its object are known at the compile time. Although there are advantages to other styles of invocation models, such as dynamic proxy and dynamic invocation interface (DII), EJB programming APIs support only static invocation.

In the dynamic proxy approach, a proxy class implements a list of interfaces specified by the client at runtime. Hence, this approach provides a type-safe invocation on interfaces wherein proxy is generated dynamically during runtime rather than at compile time. Any method invocation on an instance of a dynamic proxy object, for example, the `java.lang.reflect.Proxy` object, is dispatched to a single method, `invoke()`, in the instance's invocation handler object; `invoke()` accepts method information via the `java.lang.reflect.Method` object as well as method arguments via an object array. Dynamic proxy invocation is slightly different from reflective invocation in that the former provides a generic API for implementing methods of a class manufactured at runtime, whereas the latter provides a generic API for dynamic invocation of *already* implemented methods. Combining dynamic proxies with reflective invocation leads to a powerful generic object that is capable of intercepting methods from the clients on *any* server object.

Hence, you may want to use dynamic proxies for EJB method invocation in order to:

- Dynamically invoke methods on EJB in scenarios where the client does not have a priori knowledge of interfaces implemented by EJB.
- Write interceptors that can provide additional services during invocation such as security services, logging services, and so on.

Before making a decision to invoke your EJB using dynamic proxies, always remember that reflective invocation is slower than direct method invocation even with all the reflection-oriented performance enhancements in JDK 1.5. Besides this, debugging dynamic proxy stack trace is generally trickier than static invocation stack.

Deploying EJB Applications to Various Application Servers

Deploying EJB applications can be trickier than you think, especially when you are trying to package EJB applications to be deployed on multiple application servers. Multiple application server deployment is a common requirement for commercial applications written using the EJB framework. In spite of the standardization of most of the EJB application metadata in the form of deployment descriptors or annotations, a lot of deployment information still remains in application server specific deployment descriptors. A good example of this is the security role mapping information used to map roles defined in EJBs to actual roles in the application server. This information is normally kept in a deployment descriptor specific to the target application server.

Thus, in situations where you are required to automate deployment of your EJB applications on multiple application servers, an obvious choice is to use the open source XDoclet framework. XDoclet is a powerful, attribute-oriented, open source code generation engine. Using XDoclet, a developer can generate practically anything—XML descriptors, such as deployment descriptors, source code and so on—by inserting attributes (metadata) within the JavaDoc for their source. For instance, while generating code for EJB, it can generate code for value classes, primary key classes, and a struts action form based on entities. Finally, when the XDoclet engine parses the source file, it generates the code necessary for supporting the semantics of attributes. Note that apart from generating code for standard frameworks such as EJB, Servlet, JDO, and others, XDoclet is also capable of generating code for nonstandard but popular frameworks such as Hibernate, Castor, and Struts.

XDoclet can generate server-specific deployment descriptors, apart from standard deployment descriptors, for all major application servers, including JBoss, IBM WebSphere, BEA WebLogic, Sun Java System Application Server (Glassfish), Pramati, and so on, with the help of their respective attributes. Also, integration of XDoclet with Ant through `ejbdoclet` tasks makes it an even more powerful framework for deployments.

ATTRIBUTE-ORIENTED PROGRAMMING

Attribute-oriented programming is a technique that revolves around the notion of using attributes a.k.a. metadata a.k.a. annotations within the source to instruct the underlying framework to perform a certain action upon encountering an attribute while parsing the source. This "action" might be about generating programming artifacts—for example, skeleton code for EJB bean classes—or might be about providing cross-cutting functionality—for example, security or logging—at a certain juncture in the source.

With the final release of JSR 175, which provides a metadata facility for the Java language, XDoclet has been relegated to the task of generating server specific deployment descriptors and other types of meta-information not addressed by annotations. XDoclet is not generally needed to generate Java code anymore.

THE JAVA EE DEPLOYMENT API

The Java EE Deployment API (JSR-88) aims to address the problem of Java EE application deployment on multiple Java EE application servers rather interestingly. It defines an API, and the deployment of the API, which should be implemented by all application servers so that tools can use this API to send Java EE application deployment and undeployment requests to the application server. The Deployment API standard is part of Java EE 5 platform. Therefore, all Java EE 5 application servers will have to implement such a *Deployment* service.

This facility provides the utmost benefit to tools vendors. Tool vendors will not have to write proprietary plug-ins for automating deployment tasks for application servers they support. This will increase productivity and lessen product development cost for tools vendors. It benefits the application developers as well. They no longer have to worry about their IDE's integration with their application server. They can take it for granted.

So then, does the Java EE Deployment API eliminate the need for XDoclet-like frameworks? Not, exactly. If you are in the business of selling packaged applications, your setup application has to be able to deploy Java EE components to the customer's application server naturally without using tools. In this case you have two options: either build your own client that uses Java EE deployment service of your customer's application server or simply use XDoclet. Obviously, using XDoclet and the like in such scenarios will provide an easier solution for automated deployment than using the Java EE Deployment API will, simply because the former comes in ready to go, whereas you will have to write a client for the latter.

Debugging EJB

As EJB technology is evolving quickly, the containers are evolving as well. The containers or their tools often have small oddities. In addition, users may introduce bugs that are difficult to debug. How do you debug with EJB?

Unfortunately, true debugging is a problem with EJB. Because your beans run under the hood of a container, you'd have to load the container itself into a debugger. But for some containers, this is impossible because you don't have access to the container's source code or the source code has been obfuscated. For these situations, you may need to use the tried-and-true debugging method of logging.

An even more serious debugging problem occurs if exceptions are being thrown from the EJB container rather than from your beans. This can happen for a number of reasons:

- **Your EJB container's generated classes are incorrect**, because your interfaces, classes, or deployment descriptor haven't fully complied with the EJB specification. Your EJB container's tools should ship with compliance checkers to help resolve this. But know that not everything can be checked. Often because of user error, your deployment descriptor will not match your interfaces. This type of problem is extremely difficult to target, especially if your container tools crash!

- **Your EJB container has a real bug.** This is a definite possibility that you must be prepared to encounter. In the future, however, this should not happen very often because EJB containers that comply with Java EE must test their implementations against the Sun Microsystems Java EE Compatibility Toolkit (Java EE TCK).
- **A user error occurs within the EJB container.** Probably the most frustrating part of an application is doing the database work. Punctuation errors or misspellings are tough to debug when performing EJB QL. This is because your JDBC queries are not compiled—they are interpreted at runtime, so you don't get the nifty things like type checking that the Java language gives you. You are basically at the mercy of the EJB QL engine (and the underlying JDBC driver). It may or may not give you useful error description. For example, let's say that you're modeling a product, and you use the word `desc` rather than *description* to describe your products. Unfortunately, the keyword `desc` is a SQL reserved keyword. This means that your JDBC driver will throw an exception when trying to execute any database updates that involved the word `desc`. These exceptions might be cryptic at best, depending on your JDBC driver. And when you try to figure out why JDBC code is acting up, you will run into a roadblock: The JDBC code won't be available because your bean does not perform its own data access! What do you do in this situation?

When you're faced with grim situations like these, contacting your EJB vendor is probably not going to be very helpful. If you are operating with a deadline, it may be too late by the time your vendor comes up with a solution. If you could only somehow get access to the JDBC code, you could try the query yourself using the database's tools.

You can try several options here:

- Some EJB containers support IDE debugging environments, allowing you to step through your code in real time to pinpoint problems. This is something you should look for when choosing a container.
- Check your database's log file to view a snapshot of what is really happening.
- Your EJB container tools may have an option to keep generated Java files, rather than to delete them when compiling them into classes. For example, you can do this with BEA WebLogic with the `keepgenerated` option to its EJB compiler tool. This is analogous to the way you can use the `keepgenerated` option to keep generated proxies with Java RMI's *rmic* compiler.

- As a last resort, you may have to decompile the offending classes to see what's going on. A good decompiler is *Jad* by Pavel Kouznetsov (see the book's accompanying Web site `wiley.com/compbooks` for a link). Of course, decompiling may be illegal, depending on your container's licensing agreement.

The ability to debug EJBs has advanced greatly with EJB 3.0. EJBs can now be tested out of container in standard ways, such as by using JUnit. This will still require some care in that you have to handle injected resources. This can be accomplished with an out-of-container persistence manager or through the use of mock objects.

Most application servers that support EJB 3.0 will also have a debugging service that will allow you to connect on a port remotely for the purposes of debugging. Within your IDE, you will be able to set breakpoints in your bean implementation code and, once connected to the remote debugging service, processing will stop at these breakpoints. This can come in very handy for debugging a server instance running on your development machine or even for debugging a remote machine to which your EJBs have been deployed.

Inheritance and Code Reuse in EJB

Our next best practice addresses the challenge of developing reusable components. This may be important, for example, if you're developing beans to be reused by other business units within your organization or if you are shipping a product assembled as EJB components and your customers want to customize your product. There can be many such situations.

First, let's do a reality check—don't believe anyone who tells you that enterprise beans are reusable by definition because that is *not true*, at least not today. You need to design your beans correctly if you want them to be reusable. You need to consider the different applications, domains, and users of your enterprise beans, and you need to develop your beans with as much flexibility as possible. Developing a truly reusable set of beans will likely require many iterations of feedback from customers using your beans in real-world situations.

Roughly speaking, bean reusability can be at three different levels:

- **Reuse as given.** The application assembler uses the acquired bean *as is* to build an application. The bean functionality cannot be tailored to fit the application. Most projects will have a difficult time reusing these components because of their inflexibility.
- **Reuse by customization.** The application assembler configures the acquired bean by modifying the bean properties to fit the specific needs of the application. Bean customization typically occurs at deployment time. To allow for a more flexible maintenance environment, some bean providers allow runtime bean customization.

- **Reuse by extension (subclass).** This is the kind of reuse that is not possible, not in a straightforward way, in EJB simply because EJB does not support component-level inheritance. By component-level inheritance, we mean extending EJB component A to enable its reuse by another EJB component B. This level of reusability is generally more powerful but not available in EJB. Hence, you will have to use a technique to enable reuse by extension of EJB components—put all the bean logic in a POJO and make your bean class inherit this POJO. The ability for a bean to implement more than one business interface does improve the flexibility for reuse of the bean. For instance, you may have a bean that has some methods that should only be used in by a particular role and others that could be used by everyone. Aside from the security you can place on the bean, described in Chapter 11, you might have multiple interfaces defined. One interface would have the methods that would be used only by the particular role, while the other interface would include those methods intended for use by everyone. Clients could then perform a lookup or use injection (if running within an application client container) on one or both of the interfaces, depending on its intended use. In the case of entities, this issue has been specifically addressed in EJB 3.0. Inheritance (and the various approaches to inheritance) is explained in detail in Chapter 9.

The more reusability levels that a bean can provide, the more useful a bean becomes. By leveraging prebuilt beans, organizations can potentially lessen the development time of building enterprise applications.

Many organizations have tried—and failed—to truly reuse components. Because of this, it is a perfectly valid strategy to not attempt *true* reuse at all. Rather, you can shoot for a *copy-and-paste reuse* strategy, which means to make the source code for components available in a registry to other team members or other teams. They can take your components' code and change it as necessary to fit their business problem. While this may not be true reuse, it still offers some benefits.

Writing Singletons in EJB

A *singleton* is a very useful design pattern in software engineering. In a nutshell, a singleton is a single instantiation of a class with one global point of access. You would normally create a singleton in Java by using the *static* keyword when defining a class. However, one restriction of EJB is that you cannot use static fields in your beans. This precludes the use of the singleton design pattern. But if you still have to use a singleton, then here are a couple of strategies:

- **Limit the pool size.** If your EJB product lets you finely tune the EJB bean instance pool, then you can limit the size of the bean instances to 1, by setting both the initial and maximum size to 1. This is not truly a singleton, although it simulates singleton behavior, because although the container guarantees that at any given point in time there will only be one instance of bean in the pool, it does not guarantee that it will always be the same bean instance in the pool. The container might destroy the bean instance if it remains inactive for a certain period of time.
- **Use RMI-IIOP and JNDI.** You can use JNDI to store arbitrary objects to simulate the singleton pattern. If all your objects know of a single, well-known place in a JNDI tree where a particular object is stored, they can effectively treat the object as a single instance. You can perform this by binding an RMI-IIOP stub to a JNDI tree. Any client code that accessed the JNDI tree would get a copy of that remote stub, and each copy would point back to the same RMI-IIOP server object. The downside to this pattern is you are leaving the EJB sandbox and downgrading to vanilla RMI-IIOP, and thus you lose all the services provided by EJB.

When to Use XML with EJB

XML has become the de facto standard in a number of arenas, including descriptors and for protocol communication between potentially disparate platforms. We should discuss the appropriateness of XML in an EJB deployment. XML is useful in the following scenarios:

- **For data-driven integration.** If you have a large number of legacy systems, or even if you have one big hairy legacy system, you'll need a way to view the data that you send and receive from the legacy system. XML can help you here. Rather than sending and receiving data in proprietary structures that the legacy system might understand, you can invent an XML façade to the legacy systems. The façade takes XML input from your EJB components and maps that XML to the proprietary structures that the legacy system supports. When the legacy system returns data to your EJB application, the XML façade transforms the legacy data into XML data that your EJB application can understand.
- **As a document persistence mechanism.** If you are persisting large documents (news reports, articles, books, and so on), representing those documents using XML may be appropriate. This will help to translate the XML documents into various markups supported by client devices.
- **As a Web service interface.** As described in Chapter 5, EJB components can also be accessed as a Web service, in which case XML becomes the on-the-wire data format sent between Web services.

The one important scenario that XML is not useful for is as an on-the-wire format for communication *between* EJB components.

The idea is that rather than application components sending proprietary data to each other, components could interoperate by passing XML documents as parameters. Because the data is formatted in XML, each component could inspect the XML document to determine what data it received.

Although several Java EE-based workflow solutions use this approach, XML is often inappropriate for EJB-EJB communications because of performance issues. It makes less sense now to use XML for this type of communication, since you can use resource injection and let the container handle giving you a reference to another EJB. Parsing XML documents takes time, and sending XML documents over the wire takes even longer. For high-performance enterprise applications, using XML at runtime for routine operations is costly. The performance barrier is slowly becoming less important, however, as XML parsers become higher performing and as people begin to use several techniques, such as XML compression, before sending XML documents over the wire. However, it still remains the bottleneck in many systems.

Another important reason not to use XML is because it's often simply not needed. Assuming that a single organization writes all your EJB applications, there is less need for data mapping between these various systems, since you control the object model.

When to Use Messaging versus RMI-IIOP

Another hot topic when designing an EJB object model is choosing when (and when not) to use messaging, rather than RMI-IIOP.

The following advantages of messaging provide reasons why you might want to use it:

- **Database performance.** If you are going to perform relational database work, such as persisting an order to a database, it may be advantageous to use messaging. Sending a message to a secondary message queue to be processed later relieves stress on your primary database during peak hours. In the wee hours of the morning, when site traffic is low, you can process messages off the message queue and insert the orders into the database. Note that this works only if the user doesn't need immediate confirmation that his operation was a success. It would not work, for example, when checking the validity of a credit card.
- **Quick responses.** A client may not want to block and wait for a response that it knows does not exist. For methods that return *void,* the only possible return values are nothing or an exception. If a client never expects to receive an exception, why should it block for a response? Messaging allows clients to process other items when they would otherwise be blocking for the method to return.

- **Smoother load balancing.** In Chapter 7, we discuss how message-driven beans distribute loads more smoothly than session or entity beans do. With session and entity beans, a load-balancing algorithm makes an educated *guess* about which server is the least burdened. With messaging, the server that is the least burdened will *ask* for a message and get the message for processing. This also aids in upgrading your systems in terms of capacity because all you need to do is detect when your queue size reaches a threshold. When the queue size reaches threshold value, it indicates that the number of consumers is not enough to meet the messaging load and that you need to add new machines.
- **Request prioritization.** Asynchronous servers can queue, prioritize, and process messages in a different order than that in which they arrive into the system. Some messaging systems allow message queues to be prioritized to order messages based upon business rules. For example, in a military battle tank, if all requests for the system sent to a centralized dispatch queue are made asynchronously, disaster could result if a fire control message was queued up behind 100 communication messages that had to be processed first. In a military system, it would be advantageous to process any fire control and safety messages before communication messages. A prioritized queue would allow for the reordering of messages on the queue to account for the urgency of fire control in a battle tank.
- **Rapid integration of disparate systems.** Many legacy systems are based on message-oriented middleware and can easily interact with your Java EE system through messaging. Messaging provides a rapid development environment for systems that have distributed nodes that perform business processing and must communicate with one another.
- **Loosely coupled systems.** Messaging enables loose coupling between applications. Applications do not need to know about each other at compile time. This empowers you to have *dynamic consumption* of applications and services, which may be useful in a rapidly changing, service-oriented business environment.
- **Geographically disperse systems.** Messaging is very useful when you have applications communicating over the Internet or a wide area network. The network is slow and unreliable, and RMI-IIOP is not intended for such broad-range communications. Messaging along with guaranteed message delivery adds an element of safety to your transactions.
- **Parallel processing.** Messaging is a way to perform pseudo-threading in an EJB deployment. You can launch a series of messages and continue processing, which is the distributed equivalent of launching threads.

- **Reliability.** Messaging can be used even if a server is down. System-level problems (such as a database crashes) typically do not affect the success of the operation, because when you're using *guaranteed message delivery* the message remains on the queue until the system-level problem is resolved. Even if the message queue fails, message producers can spool messages and send them when the queue comes back up (called *store and forward*). If you combine guaranteed message delivery with store-and-forward methodology, the system will not lose any requests unless a complete system failure happens at all tiers (extremely unlikely).
- **Many-to-many communications.** If you have several parties communicating together, messaging is appropriate since it enables many producers and many consumers to collaborate, whereas RMI-IIOP is a single-source, single-sink request model.

The following are scenarios in which you *might not* want to use messaging:

- **When you're not sure if the operation will succeed.** RMI-IIOP systems can throw exceptions, whereas message-driven beans cannot.
- **When you need a return result.** RMI-IIOP systems can return a result immediately because the request is executed immediately. Not so for messaging. You can return results eventually with messaging, but it's clunky—you need to send a separate return message and have the original client listen for it.
- **When you need an operation to be part of a larger transaction.** When you put a message onto a destination, the receiving message-driven bean does not act upon that message until a future transaction. This is inappropriate when you need the operation to be part of a single, atomic transaction that involves other operations. For example, if you're performing a bank account transfer, it would be a bad idea to deposit money into one bank account using RMI-IIOP and then withdraw money using messaging, because the deposit and withdrawal operations will not occur as part of a single transaction, and hence, the failure in the latter will not roll back the former.
- **When you need to propagate the client's security identity to the server.** Since messaging does not propagate the client's security identity to the receiving message-driven bean, you cannot easily secure your business operations.
- **When you are concerned about request performance.** Messaging is inherently slower than RMI-IIOP because there's a middleman (the JMS destination) sitting between the sender and the receiver.

- **When you want a strongly typed, OO system.** You send messages using a messaging API such as JMS. This is a flat API and is not object-oriented. If you want to perform different operations, the server needs to crack open the message or filter it somehow. In comparison, RMI-IIOP allows you to call different business methods, depending on the business operation you want to perform. This is much more intuitive. It's also easier to perform compile-time semantic checking.
- **When you want a tighter, more straightforward system.** Synchronous development tends to be more straightforward than messaging is. You have great freedom when sending data types, and the amount of code you need to write is minimal compared to messaging. Debugging is also much more straightforward. When using services that are completely synchronous, each client thread of control has a single execution path that can be traced from the client to the server, and vice versa. The effort to trace any bugs in the system is thus minimal.

Summary

We covered so many best practices in this chapter—and we aren't even half-done with best practices yet! We will talk about performance-related best practices and tuning tips in Chapter 14. Also, we have woven the discussion of best practices related to integration to and from the EJB world in Chapter 15. So there is a lot more to come.

CHAPTER

14

EJB Performance Optimizations

In this chapter, we will discuss *EJB best practices*—tried-and-true approaches relevant to EJB performance optimization. By being aware of these best practices, you will be able to architect for good performance right from the beginning so that you will not be required to retrofit your design and code to achieve the performance numbers during load/performance testing.

Let's begin now with our collection of best practices, optimizations, tips, and techniques for performance.

NOTE This chapter does *not* cover low-level EJB design patterns. We started to put those together but realized that those patterns deserved a book of their own. That's what gave birth to Floyd Marinescu's book *EJB Design Patterns*, published by John Wiley & Sons and a companion to this book.

It Pays to Be Proactive!

The most important requirement for building highly optimized applications is to specify clearly performance requirements right in the design stages. Defining performance requirements basically means outlining your performance needs from various points of views: determining user experience under varying loads, the percentage of the system resources used, the allocation of system resources to achieve the desired performance, and so on. Many times we see these requirements defined after the system is developed and is about to be deployed—most often, on the night of load testing. QA calls the development manager to discuss a JVM "out-of-memory" error with a concurrent load of 20 users! And more often than not, the crash takes place because some developer forgot to release a Java container object, such as a collection, containing hundreds of instances of data transfer objects returned from a stateful session bean, after displaying its contents to the client.

To avoid this nightmare, we suggest the following:

- **Be proactive in defining your performance expectations.** This is the only way you will know what you want from your application and, hence, how you should plan, design, and develop your application right from the start.
- **Design applications with performance in mind.** The most effective way to do this is by making use of the right architecture and design patterns, which are not anti-performance. Hire architects with sound knowledge of these patterns and their implications on performance (and simplicity and code maintenance). If you do not have this expertise in-house then hire competent consultants for architecting and designing your applications. The investment required to put in place a performance-friendly skeleton of your application at the architecture level would pay you back later.
- **Be proactive in educating your developers to write optimized code.** Even though you might have the best software architects or consultants in the world to design your application, if the developers implementing the design do not understand how to write optimized code, the cost you incurred in hiring these architects will be in vain. Therefore, we suggest conducting regular code reviews and finding coding bottlenecks.
- **Master the science of tuning.** The first step toward mastering tuning is to understand that tuning can and should be done at multiple levels to achieve the highest levels of performance. In a typical Java EE enterprise application, you can ideally tune all the layers right from the network communications and operating system level to JVM to Java EE application server to your application code to your database to your cluster. Thus, the scope for tuning is much wider. If your performance requirements are extremely stringent, we suggest that you tune all the layers of this stack. For most of the business applications, however, we have observed that tuning Java EE application server (both Web/EJB containers), the JVM used by the application server and Java application (in case of a Swing client), and the database is sufficient for a tuning exercise. You can actually define a tuning methodology so that everyone becomes aware of all the steps involved in tuning all new development your organization.

With this in mind, let us see which best practices and optimizations lead us toward better EJB performance.

The Stateful versus Stateless Debate from a Performance Point of View

There's been a lot of fuss over statelessness. The limitations of statelessness are often exaggerated, as are its benefits. Many statelessness proponents blindly declare that statelessness leads to increased scalability, while stateful backers argue about having to rearchitect entire systems to accommodate statelessness. What's the real story?

Designed right, statelessness has two virtues:

- With stateless beans, the EJB container is able to easily pool and reuse beans, allowing a few beans to service many clients. While the same paradigm applies to stateful beans, if the server is out of memory or has reached its bean instance limit, then the bean state may be passivated and activated between method calls, possibly resulting in I/O bottlenecks. So one practical virtue of statelessness is the ability to easily pool and reuse components with little or no overhead.
- Because a stateful session bean caches a client conversation in memory, a bean failure may entail losing your conversation. This can have severe repercussions if you don't write your beans with this in mind or if you don't use an EJB container that provides stateful recovery. In a stateless model, the request could be transparently rerouted to a different component because any component can service the client's needs.

The largest drawback to statelessness is that you need to push client-specific data into the stateless bean for each method invocation. Most stateless session beans need to receive some information that is specific to a certain client, such as a bank account number for a banking bean. This information must be resupplied to stateless beans each time a client request arrives because the bean cannot hold any state on behalf of a particular client.

One way to supply the bean with client-specific data is to pass the data as parameters into the bean's methods. This can lead to performance degradation, however, especially if the data being passed is large. This also clogs the network, reducing available bandwidth for other processes.

Another way to get client-specific data to a stateless bean is for the bean to store data persistently on behalf of a client. The client then does not need to pass the entire state in a method invocation but simply needs to supply an identifier to retrieve the data from persistent storage. Using stateless beans in conjunction with entities can achieve this: The entity would contain the information about client state. In prior versions of EJB, this approach had its own performance issues because of the general performance of entity beans. Much of the performance concerns around entity beans have been alleviated with EJB 3.0 persistence and entities. Early EJB 3.0 performance experiments showed that the performance using the session façade (stateless session bean acting as a façade to interact with an entity) was nearly double that of EJB 2.1. We'll cover this in more detail in the session façade section below. The trade-off here is, again, performance; storing conversations persistently could lead to storage I/O bottlenecks, rather than network I/O bottlenecks.

Yet another way to work around the limitations of statelessness is for a bean to store client-specific data in a directory structure using JNDI. The client could later pass the bean an identifier for locating the data in the directory structure. This is quite similar to storing data in a database. The big difference is that a JNDI implementation could be an in-memory implementation such as the one from the SourceForge.net Tyrex project `http://sourceforge.net/projects/tyrex`—an effect similar to a shared property manager, familiar to COM+ readers. If client data is stored in memory, there is no database hit.

When choosing between the stateful and stateless approaches, you should ask if the business process spans multiple invocations, requiring a conversation. Since most business processes are stateful anyway, you quite probably need to retain state on behalf of clients. So the guideline to follow is if you are short of resources on the server, choose stateless session beans and maintain the conversation in a database or an in-memory directory. If you have enough resources on the server system so that you do not need to passivate or activate the stateful bean instances frequently under average to high loads, then go for stateful session beans.

Note that if you are going to maintain state, and if you're building a Web-based system, you may be able to achieve what you need with a servlet's `HttpSession` object, which is the Web server equivalent to a stateful session bean and is easier to work with because it does not require custom coding. We have found that a stateful session bean should be used rather than an `HttpSession` object in the following situations:

- You need a stateful object that's transactionally aware. Your session bean can achieve this by implementing `SessionSynchronization`, described in Chapter 10.
- You have both Web-based and non-Web-based clients accessing your EJB layer, and both need state.
- You are using a stateful session bean to temporarily store state for a business process that occurs within a single HTTP request and involves multiple beans. To understand this point, consider that you are going through a big chain of beans, and a bean deep in the chain needs to access state. You could marshal the state in the parameter list of each bean method (ugly and could be a performance problem if you're using remote interfaces). The better solution is to use a stateful session bean and just pass the object reference through the stack of bean calls.

WHAT IF MY STATEFUL BEAN DIES?

Bean failure is an important factor to consider. Because a stateful session bean caches a client conversation in memory, a bean failure may entail losing your conversation. This was not a problem with statelessness—there was no conversation to be lost. Unless you are using an EJB product that routinely checkpoints (that is, persists) your conversations, your conversations will be lost if an application server fails.

Losing a conversation can have a devastating impact. If you have large conversations that span time, you've lost important work. And the more stateful session beans that you use in tandem, the larger the existing network of interconnected objects that each rely on the other's stability. Many EJB servers today do offer stateful recovery of Enterprise Java Beans. However, if yours does not then your code will need to be able to handle the failover gracefully. Here are some of the guidelines you can use while designing your stateful beans to enable them to handle stateful recovery:

- Keep your conversations short.
- If the performance is feasible, consider checkpointing stateful conversations yourself to minimize the impacts of bean failure (such as by using entities).
- Write smart client code that anticipates a bean failure and reestablishes the conversational state with a fresh stateful session bean.

In summary, most sophisticated deployments are likely to have a complex and interesting combination of the stateless and stateful paradigm. Use the paradigm that's most appropriate for your business problem. If you are on the fence about stateful versus stateless, you may find that stateful session beans are not your primary issue—until you test your code, you're just shooting in the dark. It would help to do a proof of concept for stateful session beans. However, shooting down stateful session beans blindly is not advisable. Don't forget that they exist for a good reason—to take the load of managing client-related state off your shoulders and thereby make your life easier.

How to Guarantee a Response Time with Capacity Planning

Many types of business problems are trivial, such as basic Web sites or non-mission-critical applications. But then there are those that *must not fail* and must *guarantee* a certain response time. For example, a trading application needs to guarantee a response time because stock market conditions might change if the trade is delayed. For those serious deployments, capacity planning is essential for your deployment.

The specific amount of hardware that you'll need for your deployment varies greatly depending on the profile of your application, your anticipated user load, your performance requirements, and the EJB server you choose. Most of the major EJB server vendors have strategies for capacity planning that they can share with you.

One strategy, however, works with all EJB server vendors. The idea is to *throttle*, or limit, the amount of work any given EJB server instance can process at any one time. Why would you ever want to limit the amount of work a machine can handle? A machine can only guarantee a response time for the clients it serves and be reliable if it isn't using up every last bit of system resources it has at its disposal. For example, if your EJB server runs out of memory, it either starts swapping your beans out to disk because of passivation/activation or it uses virtual memory and uses the hard disk as swap space. Either way, the response time and reliability of your box is jeopardized. You want to prevent this from happening at all costs by limiting the amount of traffic your server can handle at once.

You can throttle (or limit) the amount of traffic your machine can handle using a variety of means. One is by limiting the *thread pool* of your EJB server. By setting an upper bound on the number of threads that can execute concurrently, you effectively limit the number of users that can be processed at any given time. Another possibility is to limit the *bean instance pool*. This lets you control how many EJB components can be instantiated at once, which is great for allowing more requests to execute with lightweight beans and fewer requests to execute with heavyweight beans.

Once you've throttled your machine and tested it to make sure it's throttled correctly, you need to devise a strategy to add more machines to the deployment in case your clusterwide capacity limit is reached. An easy way to do this is to have a standby machine that is unused under normal circumstances. When you detect that the limit is reached (such as by observing message queue growth, indicating that your servers cannot consume items off the request queue fast enough), the standby machine kicks in and takes over the excess load. A system administrator can then be paged to purchase a new standby machine.

This algorithm guarantees a response time because each individual server cannot exceed its limit, and there's always an extra box waiting if traffic increases.

Use Session Façade for Better Performance

Consider the following scenarios:

- A bank teller component performs the business process of banking operations, but the data used by the teller is the bank account data.

- An order entry component performs the business process of submitting new orders for products, such as submitting an order for a new computer to be delivered to a customer. But the data generated by the order entry component is the order itself, which contains a number of order line items describing each part ordered.
- A stock portfolio manager component performs the business process of updating a stock portfolio, such as buying and selling shares of stock. But the data manipulated by the portfolio manager is the portfolio itself, which might contain other data such as account and stock information.

In each of these scenarios, business process components are manipulating data in some underlying data storage, such as a relational database. The business process components map very well to session beans, and the data components map very well to entities. The session beans use entities to represent their data, similarly to the way a bank teller uses a bank account. Thus, a great EJB design strategy is to wrap entities with session beans. This design pattern is generally referred to as session façade.

Another benefit of this approach is performance. In prior versions of EJB, accessing an entity bean directly over the network was expensive, due to:

- The stub
- The skeleton
- Marshaling/demarshaling
- The network call
- The EJB object interceptor

With EJB 3.0, there is no such thing as a remote interface to entities. If you have a standalone client, you *must* use some sort of remote object to access your entities. A great way to do this is by using the remote interface to a session bean which interacts with entities. The only other way would be to use an out of container `EntityManager`. The session beans perform bulk create, read, update, delete (CRUD) operations on behalf of remote clients. The session bean also serves as a transactional façade, enforcing the fact that transactions occur on the server, rather than involving a remote client. This makes entities into an implementation detail of session beans. The entities are never seen by the external client; rather, entities just happen to be the way that the session bean performs persistence.

A final benefit of this approach is that your entities typically achieve a high level of reuse. For instance, consider an order entry system, where you have an order submission session bean that performs operations on an order entity. In the next generation of your application, you may want an order fulfillment session bean, an order reporting session bean, and so on. That same order entity can be reused for each of these session beans. This approach enables you to fine-tune and change your session bean business processes over time as user requirements change.

Thus, in practice you can expect the reuse of entities to be high. Session beans model a current business process, which can be tweaked and tuned with different algorithms and approaches. Entities, on the other hand, define your core business. Data such as purchase orders, customers, and bank accounts do not change very much over time.

There are also a few caveats about this approach:

- You can also wrap entities with other entities, if you have a complex object model with relationships (refer to Chapter 9 for more on this).
- The value of session beans as a network performance optimization goes away if you do not have remote clients. This could occur, for example, if you deploy an entire Java EE application into a single process, with servlets and JSPs calling EJB components in-process. However, the session façade could still be used for proper design considerations and to isolate your deployment from any particular multi-tier configuration. Note that what we've presented here are merely guidelines, not hard-and-fast rules.

Choosing between Local Interfaces and Remote Interfaces

Local interfaces, a feature since EJB 2.0, enable you to access your EJB components without incurring network traffic. They also allow you to pass nonserializable parameters around, which is handy. So what is the value of a remote interface? Well, there really isn't a value, unless:

- You need to access your system remotely (say from a remote Web tier or standalone client).
- You are trying to test EJB components individually and need to access them from a standalone client to perform the testing.
- You need to allow your containers more choices for workload distribution and failover in a clustered server environment.

For optimal performance, we recommend that you build your system using all local interfaces, and then have one or more session bean wrappers with remote interfaces, exposing the system to remote clients.

In previous versions of EJB, your client code would be different depending on how you were accessing a bean (remote or local). One of the benefits of EJB 3.0 is that your code no longer has to be different depending on the access type. The only difference now would be the annotation used: `@Remote` or `@Local`.

It is still a good idea to decide whether the clients of your beans are going to be local or remote *before you start coding*. For example, if you're building a Web-based system, decide whether your system will be a complete Java EE application in a single process, or whether your Web tier will be split off from your EJB tier into a separate process. We discuss the trade-offs of these approaches in Chapter 16.

As a final note, if you are connecting to your EJB deployment from a very distant client (such as an applet or application that gets downloaded by remote users), consider exposing your EJB system as an XML-based Web service, rather than a remote interface. This will be slower than a straight RMI/IIOP call, but is more appropriate for WAN clients. In corporate environments, which are strictly controlled by internal firewalls, it is often easier to get HTTP traffic (such as that for a Web service) approved than to get RMI/IIOP traffic approved.

Partitioning Your Resources

When programming with EJB, we've found it very handy to separate the kinds of resources your beans use into two categories: *bean-specific resources* and *bean-independent resources*.

- **Bean-specific resources** are resources that your bean uses that are tied to a specific data instance in an underlying storage. For example, a socket connection is a bean-specific resource if that socket is used only when particular bank account data is loaded. That is, the socket is used only when your bean instance is bound to a particular EJB object. Such a resource should be acquired when a bean instance is created in the `@PostConstruct` method or when activated in `@PostActivate` method and released when the instance is removed in the `@PreDestory` or `@Remove` methods or passivated in the `@PrePassviate` method.
- **Bean-independent resources** are resources that can be used over and over again, no matter what underlying data your instance represents. For example, a socket connection is a bean-independent resource if your bean can reuse that socket no matter what bank account your bean represents (that is, no matter what EJB object your bean instance is assigned to). Global resources like these should be acquired when your bean is first created, and they can be used across the board as your bean is assigned to different EJB objects. They can also be acquired during the life-cycle methods as indicated in the bean-specific resources section. In this case, though, the resource is presumed to be available as opposed to having to create it. In the case of a socket, for instance, you would expect to obtain a handle to an already established socket as opposed to having to instantiate and connect the socket.

Because acquiring and releasing resources may be costly operations, categorizing your resources as outlined is a vital step. Of course, the stingiest way to handle resources is to acquire them on a *just-in-time* basis and release them directly after use. For example, you could acquire a database connection only when you're about to use it and release it when you're done. Then there would be no resources to acquire or release during activation or passivation. In this case, the assumption is that your container pools the resource in question. If not, just-in-time acquisition of resource might prove expensive because every time you request to acquire a resource, its handle is actually being created and every time you request to release the resource, the underlying object is actually being destroyed. To get around this, you will need to write your own implementation that can pool the resource in question. You will then need to use this pool manager abstraction to acquire or release the resource. The slight disadvantage to just-in-time resource acquisition or release is that you need to code requests to acquire or release resources over and over again in your bean.

Tuning Stateless Session Beans

Taking into consideration the life cycle of stateless session beans, as discussed in Chapter 4, these tuning techniques should be examined closely to achieve best performance:

- **Tune pool size.** The pool size-related settings are made available by your EJB server vendor, and hence, you will need to specify them in the vendor-specific deployment descriptor. It controls the number of stateless session bean instances in the pool. Some products will enable you to specify a range for pool size. In this case, mostly, you would also be able to specify the resize quantity of your pool. When the server runs out of pooled bean instances to service further client requests, the resize quantity will specify the number of new instances a server should create at one time, until the maximum of the pool size range is reached.

  For example, suppose that the range for pool size is `initial=50` and `maximum=100`, and the resize quantity is `10`. Now, if at a given point in time all 50 instances are busy servicing client requests, then when the 51st request comes for that stateless session bean, the EJB container will create 10 more instances of the bean, make available one of these newly created instances to the client, and pool the remaining 9 instances for future requests. This resizing of the pool will continue happening until the maximum pool size range is reached, that is 100. So then what happens when at a given point in time all 100 instances are servicing requests? The 101st client request will have to wait for one of the previous 100 clients to release the bean so that the container can make this underlying bean instance available to our 101st client. The client request thus will have to be queued by the container.

Also some containers will provide you with a pool idle timeout setting. It basically specifies the maximum time that a stateless session bean is allowed to be idle in the pool before removing it from the pool. The pool resize quantity setting will play a role here, too. It will specify the number of beans that the server will destroy once they have reached idle time limit. Hence, an increase or decrease in the maximum limit of the pool size should mean an appropriate change in the resize quantity too to maintain a good balance.

Make sure that you set the initial and maximum values for the pool size so that they are representative of the normal and peak loads on your system. Setting a very large initial or maximum value is an inefficient use of system resources for an application that does not have much concurrent load under normal and peak conditions, respectively. Also this will cause large garbage collection pauses. At the same time, setting a very small initial or maximum value compared to the typical loads is going to cause a lot of object creation and object destruction.

- **Efficient resource caching.** As discussed earlier, it is a good practice to cache bean-independent resources and release the cache in the bean life cycle. However, if you cache a resource, such as a database, connection in the previous methods within a stateless session bean deployment with large pool size and heavy concurrent client access, chances are that container will run out of free connection instances in the connection pool very soon; the container might need to queue the request for connection resource. To avoid this, it is better to obtain connection resources from the connection pool *just-in-time* in such situations.

Tuning Stateful Session Beans

Taking into consideration the life cycle of stateful session beans as discussed in Chapter 4, these tuning techniques should be examined closely to achieve best performance:

- **Tune pool size.** Stateful session beans are not pooled in the traditional sense. Some vendors will create a pool of instantiated, but empty and unassigned, bean objects. The instantiation of objects is a fairly heavyweight process, so having this available pool is useful. When a client performs a lookup or injects a reference, the container can take one of these instantiated objects, initialize it, and bind it to the client. If your vendor supports this type of pooling, there will be a way to tune the size of this pool.

- **Tune cache size.** The stateful session bean life cycle is defined by the EJB standard is such a way that stateful session beans are cached but not pooled in the same way as stateless beans. Beans are cached when the number of concurrent users requesting the services of stateful session bean exceeds that of the maximum allowable number of stateful session bean instances. During caching, the state of the bean is stored in the disk (a.k.a. passivation) for later use by its client, and the bean instance is made available for use to another client. The cache and other stateful session bean–related tuning settings are EJB server–specific, and so they will go in the vendor-specific deployment descriptor. Most of the vendors allow you to specify the maximum cache size for stateful session beans.

  Some vendors will allow you to specify a cache resize quantity that works similarly to the pool resize quantity for stateless session beans. The container can use a variety of algorithms to select beans for passivation, and if the container is good enough, it will let you choose the algorithm for passivation. These algorithms could be the least recently used (LRU); first in, first out (FIFO); or not recently used (NRU) techniques.

  The cache idle timeout setting will let you specify the time interval after which an idle bean will be passivated. Some containers will also let you specify the removal timeout value, which sets the time interval after which the passivated state of the bean is removed from the disk, thereby freeing the disk resources. A good coding practice is for your client code to explicitly remove the bean instance by having an `@Remove` method. This way the state, on behalf of your client, will not unnecessarily be maintained on the server until the container passivates it and finally removes it.

  Again, tune the cache, taking into consideration the number of concurrent users that will access your stateful session bean under typical and peak conditions. Setting a large maximum value for cache size in comparison to the typical loads and peak loads of concurrent users, respectively, will lead to inefficient usage of memory resources, whereas setting a small maximum value for cache size will lead to a lot of passivation and activation of bean instances and, hence, serialization and deserialization, thereby straining on the CPU cycles and disk I/O.

- **Control serialization.** Serialization consumes CPU cycles and I/O resources. More serialization leads to more consumption of resources. The same is the case for deserialization, which takes place during the activation of stateful session beans. It is a good practice to keep the amount of serialization and deserialization to a minimum. One way to achieve this is by explicitly instructing the container to not serialize the state that you will not need after activation. You can do so by marking such objects as *transient* in your stateful session bean class.

Tuning Entities

Taking into consideration the life cycle of entities as discussed in Chapter 6, the following tuning techniques and best practices should be examined closely to achieve best performance:

- **Tune pool size.** The entity life cycle, as defined by EJB standard, is such that entities are pooled as well as cached. The pooling of entities is quite similar to that of stateless session beans. Most of the EJB servers have a provision to specify vendor-specific pool settings, such as initial pool size (also known as steady pool size in some products), maximum pool size, pool resize quantity, and pool idle timeout. The best practices for tuning the entity pool are the same as those discussed previously for stateless session beans.
- **Tune cache size.** The caching of entities is similar to the caching of stateful session beans in that the tuning settings for stateful session beans and entity beans for a given vendor are the same. Most of the EJB servers will provide some common cache-tuning options such as maximum cache size, cache resize quantity, cache idle timeout, removal timeout, and so on. Apart from the best practices for tuning the cache that we discussed for stateful session beans, you should also:
  - **Provide a bigger cache** for entities that are used a lot, and provide a smaller cache for entities that are not used very much.
  - **Keep the maximum** limit of the pool size the same as the maximum cache size, because while associating data with the entity instance, the container brings the entity instance from the pool. Hence, having a pool smaller than cache can lead to a situation where clients are waiting for the container to get hold of the entity, which in turn is waiting for the entity pool queue, in its turn, to get hold of an instance.

NOTE While tuning the entity pool and cache, always keep in mind that in most of the deployments the number of entities is mostly going to be larger than the number of session beans, taking into consideration finder methods that return large numbers of entity stubs. Hence, pool and cache sizes of entities are usually much larger than those for stateless and stateful session beans.

- **Use lazy loading.** If you do not need all the data of your entity the first time you access it, choose to lazy load the unneeded data upon request from the client. This can be done using the `@Basic` annotation with the `fetch=lazy` element or with the relational annotations using their `fetch` element. This will optimize memory consumption on your system as well as the use of network bandwidth.

Lazy loading helps a lot when accessing relationship data. For example, you can load the data for an Employee:Paychecks one-to-many relationship only when the client actually wants the paycheck information of that given employee and not when a client is just interested in getting the basic employee information. You do have to depend on the container to enable lazy loading of relationship data.

Remember though that there is always a trade-off when using lazy loading for core entity data—your entity can end up accessing the database quite a number of times if the client requests data chosen for lazy loading often. To get around this issue, you need to closely observe the way client applications use your entity and then select the less frequently requested data for lazy loading.

NOTE **As per the EJB 3.0 specification, using the `fetch=lazy` element is only a *hint* to the container to use lazy loading. The implementation, at its discretion, can load eagerly even if you have specified lazy loading. Since the specification clearly leaves the implementation of lazy loading to the vendor, you must find out how your particular vendor handles it.**

- **Choose the right semantics for transactions.** Be sure that the transactions that run on the server are as short as possible, and encapsulate all the entity operations you'd like to have participating in that transaction. This is important because the synchronization with underlying database occurs at the beginning and end of transactions. If you have a transaction occurring for each entity get/set operation, you are performing database hits on each method call. The best way to perform transactions with entities is to wrap all your entity calls within a session bean method and mark that session bean method as transactional. Here you will also have to mark the entity methods with the transaction attribute of `REQUIRED`. This creates a transaction in the session bean that encapsulates all entities in the same transaction.
- **Choose the right transaction isolation level.** Isolation levels are explained with a lot of detail in Chapter 10. In short, isolation levels help maintain integrity of concurrently accessed data. You should choose an optimum isolation level for your application. Isolation levels are typically set at the database connection (or connection pool) level using vendor-specific APIs or descriptors (and not in your deployment descriptors or `persistence.xml` file). Hence, the chosen isolation level will apply for all database access—from a single bean, multiple beans, one Java EE application, or multiple Java EE applications—via that connection pool. Some of the best practices for selecting the right isolation level are:

- Use the lowest possible isolation level, for example READ_UNCOMMITTED for beans that represent operations on data that is not critical from a data integrity standpoint. If you do not care about reading uncommitted data or others updating the rows that you are reading or inserting new data into the data set you are accessing, go for this isolation level.
- Use READ_COMMITTED for applications that intend to always read the data that is committed. However, your applications still have to be prepared to live with unrepeatable read and phantom read problems.
- Use REPEATABLE_READ for applications that intend to always read and reread the same data. However, your applications still can get newly created rows when they try to reread the same data. Understand that your database achieves this behavior by locking the rows you are reading so that nobody else can update these rows. However, other users can still read your data.
- Use SERIALIZABLE for applications that want to hold exclusive access to data. The cost of using this isolation mode is that all requests to read and modify this data will be serialized by your database. Hence, others will have to wait to read/update the data that you are accessing. You should only use this isolation level in cases that warrant for single user data access.
- Finally set transaction isolation levels only when you are fully aware of your application's semantics. Also note that not all databases support all the transaction isolation levels.

- **Use JDBC access when retrieving very large amounts of data.** Entities work very well when working with small to medium-sized data sets. When working with larger data sets, for example, working in use cases where a single SELECT statement is going to retrieve thousands of records, it may turn out better not to use entities. Code such data access by using JDBC from session beans. You can use a Data Access Object (DAO) abstraction in between to place all the JDBC code. Again, using JDBC has another benefit. If you were to use JDBC 3.0, you could make use of a CachedRowSet implementation to get disconnected rowset functionality. This boosts performance by not maintaining a connection to the database while you are traversing the large set of data.
- **Choose the optimal database driver—Entity Manger—for accessing data.** This applies also when working directly with data from session beans or other Java EE components. Know the differences between the four types of JDBC drivers. Most importantly, avoid using type 1 JDBC drivers a.k.a. JDBC-ODBC drivers. They tend to give the least performance because of the fact that all the JDBC calls are translated twice—JDBC to ODBC and ODBC to database-specific calls. Use type 1 drivers

only when your database does not support a JDBC driver, which is an unlikely situation. Today, you can find various types of JDBC drivers for almost all major databases. Another criterion for selecting JDBC driver is to get a driver that supports the latest JDBC standard. This is because with each version of the JDBC standard, the sophistication of its SPI keeps increasing, thereby providing better performing data access to the database. For example, all JDBC 2.0 and above drivers provide connection pooling support. Hence, if you are using a driver earlier than 2.0 you will not gain the performance enhancement due to connection pooling. Another example—JDBC 3.0 driver supports `PreparedStatement` object pooling. Anybody who has worked with JDBC would know that prepared statements are precompiled SQL statements, so they boost performance dramatically, especially when the same precompiled SQL is used multiple times. However, creating the `PreparedStatement` object imposes some overhead. To avoid incurring this overhead each time you use the prepared statement, you can pool it using a JDBC 3.0 driver.

- **Choose the right *Statement* interface.** JDBC provides three main types of statement abstractions: `Statement`, `PreparedStatement`, and `CallableStatement`. `Statement` is to execute SQL statements with no input and output parameters. `PreparedStatement` should be used when you want precompilation of SQL statement that accept input parameters. `CallableStatement` should be used when you need precompilation of SQL statements that support both input and output parameters. You should use `CallableStatement` for most of your stored procedures.

Tuning Message-Driven Beans

Now let us examine some best practices and techniques to boost message-driven bean performance:

- **Tune pool size.** MDB is essentially a stateless session bean whose `onMessage()` method is invoked by the container upon arrival of a message. Hence, to reduce the overhead of creation (and the release) of MDB bean instances upon each message arrival, the container pools them. The pool tuning settings are pretty much the same as stateless session bean. A container can let you specify one or all of the initial pool size, maximum pool size, resize quantity, and pool idle timeout settings.

  Use these settings to match the message-processing loads under typical and peak conditions. For better throughput under high-traffic conditions, maintain a large pool of MDB bean instances. Needless to say, these settings go into the vendor-specific deployment descriptor.

- **JMS-specific tuning.** If your MDB consumes JMS messages, one important type of performance tuning you can do is to select the right acknowledgment mode. You can set the acknowledgment mode using annotation or in the deployment descriptor. Chapter 7 discusses the various acknowledgment modes in detail. Use `Auto_acknowledge` mode when you do not want to receive duplicates and thereby avoid inefficient use of network bandwidth. Note that here the JMS engine makes sending the acknowledgment a top priority. Hence, throughput might suffer in scenarios where a lot of JMS messages arrive and need to be processed by the MDB. On the other hand, if you want your JMS engine to leave everything in order to send acknowledgment, you should consider `Dups_ok_acknowledge` mode.

Tuning Java Virtual Machine

Don't ignore the impact of a nicely tuned JVM on which your EJB server is running. Each application server comes with a different JVM and hence, different tuning parameters. However, some of the settings remain common across most of the JVMs. In our experience, 95 percent of the JVM tuning exercise involves tuning the garbage collector. The garbage collector is a piece of code within the JVM that releases the memory claimed by objects whose references have gone out of scope or for objects whose references are explicitly set to null. Understand that you have no control over when the garbage collector runs—it will run when the JVM thinks it should and when your underlying OS schedules the GC thread to run. There are two things you should do to work well with the JVM: Make your code JVM friendly, and use JVM proprietary switches to further tune the garbage collector and set the heap space–related settings. Let us examine both of these:

- **Write JVM friendly code.** This entails writing Java code that releases objects in a timely manner by setting their references to null. By setting the references to null, you are declaring to the JVM that you no longer need the object and so the garbage collector should reclaim its memory allocated in the JVM heap space. Also, you should refrain from implementing `final()` methods on your Java objects, because finalizers might not be called before the object reference goes out of scope and hence, the object might never get garbage collected (because the finalizer hasn't been executed).

  Also, do not use `System.gc()` if you can avoid it, because it does not guarantee that the garbage collector would be executed upon your request. If you understand the semantics of `System.gc()`, you know that it is basically meant to *request* the JVM to run the garbage collector and thereby reclaim the memory; at the end of the call, however, your request may or may not have been granted; it all depends on whether JVM thinks that it is time to run the garbage collector. We are amazed to see developers with many years of Java experience putting `System.gc()` calls all over in their code.

Yet another example of writing JVM-friendly code is the use of weak references when writing implementations for caching or similar functionality. Weak references allow your code to maintain references to an object in a way that does not prevent the object from being garbage collected if need be. You can also receive notifications when an object to which you hold a weak reference is about to be garbage collected. Thus, if the JVM is running very low on memory, your weak reference to the live object will not stop the JVM from garbage collecting the object.

These are just a few examples of writing JVM-friendly code. If you read some of the classic Java performance books, you can find many more techniques.

- **Tune the JVM via switches.** Each JVM implementation, and there are about a dozen of them, provides vendor-specific switches to further tune the virtual machine. To effectively use these switches though, you will need to understand the implementation of the JVM. For example, all recent Sun JVMs support a technology, called HotSpot, which employs a concept termed *generational garbage collection* to effectively garbage collect the memory without introducing huge garbage collector caused pauses in the application. Ultimately, the goal of garbage collection is to reduce those inevitable system pauses during the period when the garbage collector is running. So in order to efficiently work with a Sun JVM, you should understand how generational garbage collection works, various algorithms for garbage collection supported by the Sun JVM, when to use which algorithm for garbage collection, and so on. The same holds true for most of the other JVMs. For example, BEA WebLogic products use the BEA JRockit JVM. Thus, if you are a BEA shop, you should understand how JRockit works in order to be able to tune it properly.

  Most of the JVM implementations also allow setting the heap memory size available to the virtual machine. The heap requirements for server applications obviously would be more than that of client applications. You should tune the heap size so that it is not too small or too large for your application. A small JVM heap would cause the JVM to run garbage collection more frequently thereby introducing unexpected pauses, albeit short, in your application. On the other hand, a large JVM heap will not cause frequent garbage collection but whenever garbage collection happens it takes a good while for it to scour through the large heap space and reclaim the memory, thereby introducing a longer pause.

Bottom line—thou must know thy JVM!

Miscellaneous Tuning Tips

Now let us see some other miscellaneous tips to further help your optimization exercises:

- **Send output** to a good logging/tracing system, such as a logging message-driven bean. This enables you to understand the methods that are causing bottlenecks, such as repeated loads or stores.
- **Use a performance-profiling tool**, OptimizeIt or JProbe, to identify bottlenecks. If your program is hanging on the JDBC driver, chances are the database is your bottleneck.
- **Tune the JDBC connection pool** using various options provided by your persistence provider. Most persistence providers will let you specify initial pool size, maximum pool size, pool resize quantity, maximum wait time the caller will have to wait before getting a connection timeout, idle timeout period, transaction isolation level, and so on. A larger connection pool will provide more connections to fulfill requests although it would consume more resources in the persistence provider and also on the database server. On the other hand, a smaller connection pool will provide a fewer number of connections to fulfill requests, but it also consumes fewer resources on database and EJB servers. Also some EJB servers can enable you to specify a connection validation option, which, if set to true, essentially checks whether the connection instance is a valid instance, at the time of the request. Remember that setting this option to true will add some latency during the initial connection establishment.
- **Avoid putting unnecessary** directories in the `CLASSPATH`. This will improve the class-loading time.
- **Utilize the RMI-IIOP** protocol specific–tuning settings. Also, many servers provide a means to tune the thread pool of server. You can use these settings to have better control on the overall number of threads in your EJB server.

DON'T FORGET TO TUNE THE WEB SERVER

Most of the time, EJBs sits behind Web applications. Hence, it is important to tune the Web applications accessing your EJB application, since an underperforming Web application can lead to bad user experience as well. Although Web application–tuning entails a lot more details, following are some of the common and useful tips that you should use to boost performance:

- **Explicitly turn HTTP session support off for stateless Web applications. Session management does add to overhead, so you should turn it off when not using it. Use the JSP directive** `<%page session="false"%>` **to turn session off. Also don't store very large objects in HTTP session. Also release sessions when you are done using them by calling** `HTTPSession.invalidate()`.
- **Set optimal values for various HTTP keep-alive settings. The HTTP 1.1 protocol refers to the keep-alive connections as persistent connections. Keep-alive connections are essentially long-lived connections that allow multiple requests to be sent over the same TCP connection. In some cases, enabling keep-alive connections has produced a good reduction in latency.**
- **Turn off JSP recompilation, especially if your JSPs are not changing frequently.**
- **Use JSP and servlet caching techniques made available by your Web server. Also cache servlet instance independent resources in** `Servlet.init()` **method for efficient utilization of resources.**
- **Don't use the single-thread model for servlets, because they have been deprecated. This means that all servlets are designed to be multithreaded. Hence, you should carefully avoid using class-level shared variables. If you do have to, synchronize the access to these class-level object references for ascertaining integrity.**

Choosing the Right EJB Server

Finally, you need to choose an EJB server that offers the best performance numbers and optimization techniques. The following list details the criteria through which you should evaluate the performance and tuning support provided by your EJB server:

- **Persistence Management.** Make sure that persistence optimizations, such as lazy loading, entity failover recovery, various pooling and caching strategies, and so on are supported by your EJB server.

- **Load balancing and clustering.** Most of the EJB servers provide clustering support for session beans and entity beans, whereas only some servers provide clustering and stateful recovery for stateful beans and entity beans. Also, not every application server provides load balancing, especially for message-driven beans. This could be an important consideration for high-throughput message consumption as well as failover support for message-driven beans.
- **Throttling of resources.** Throttling capabilities can help a great deal during capacity planning. Most of the high-traffic deployments do throttle resources. If you are one of such deployments, check with the vendors about whether their product provides throttling support. The more types of resources you throttle, the better tuning you will have.
- **Various types of tuning facilities.** Tuning options for various types of beans are not the only thing you should seek. You should make sure that your vendor provides comprehensive tuning options for your Web server (if you are using a Web server from the same vendor), thread management, CPUs, resources such as connection pools, JMS connections, topics/queues, IIOP tuning, JVM tuning, and so on.

Summary

In this chapter, we reviewed a series of performance optimizations and best practices for working on an EJB project. We hope that you refer back to these strategies while working with EJB—after all, an ounce of prevention is worth a pound of cure.

CHAPTER 15

EJB Integration

In this chapter, we will begin our journey into the world of EJB integration. If you are faced with a situation where you are required to integrate EJB applications with those running on other platforms or legacy applications, this chapter will provide you with a lot of helpful information. Specifically, you'll learn about the following:

- Introduction to integration, including an overview of various styles of integration
- Various approaches to integrate EJB with non-EJB applications
- Java EE connector architecture by example
- Best practices for integrating EJB applications

Why Does Integration Matter?

Integrating applications, services, and data is absolutely critical for streamlining and automating business processes. These processes might run throughout your company or be used by your business partners, suppliers, and customers. Companies with integrated business processes are quick to respond to fluctuating business conditions as compared to those lacking integrated business processes. Also, if the industry you are in is hit by a consolidation wave, it is quite possible for your company to participate in mergers and acquisitions. With every merger or acquisition comes the huge challenge of integrating enterprise applications as part of business processes, mostly electronic, of the two companies. Although, this integration is gradual, it provides a definite value to your company.

Apart from the business imperatives, there are many technical reasons why businesses should take integration seriously. A typical enterprise IT today comprises anywhere from dozens to hundreds of applications. These applications might have been acquired from outside or built in-house. Many times these applications would be developed using legacy technologies or deployed on legacy platforms. It is not uncommon to find an enterprise with silos of applications mostly written using different architectures and potentially maintaining their own instances of domain data. Some of the clear-cut benefits of integrating these isolated silos of applications across your IT are:

- Integration eliminates the need to build new applications and services every time a new business requirement has to be met. Thereby, it maximizes the use of current IT assets and provides a better return on IT investments.
- Integration makes it possible to optimize resources in terms of storage and processing by taking redundancy out of data and business functions.
- Integration brings together the entire enterprise from back-end transaction processing to front-end customer service. This ultimately increases the value of IT to a business.

These benefits are the core reasons why integration does matter to a CIO and, hence, to us.

Integration Styles

Depending on whether it is being done within or across the enterprise boundary, integration solutions can be categorized as intra-enterprise or inter-enterprise. Integration solutions can be further classified into the following two groups:

- **Application integration** focuses on establishing connectivity between applications. This style forms the basis for enterprise application integration (EAI) solutions. This connectivity can be established through messaging systems such as message-oriented middleware (MOM) or RPC communications such as IIOP, sockets, SOAP RPC, and so on.
- **Business process integration** automates business processes by coordinating and controlling activities that span multiple systems. Process integration middleware can reuse various applications, which in turn implement process activities and can also support long-running

transactions. Traditionally, this style of integration has been achieved using business process management systems (BPMS) from vendors such as Vitria, SeeBeyond (now Sun Microsystems), Intalio, TIBCO, IBM, Microsoft, BEA, Oracle, and so on. Also some BPM vendors provide BPM products that focus exclusively on the target industries. Recently, this area has seen a lot of standardization in terms of how the processes are described and how their activities are executed/coordinated. OMG BPML, W3C WS-Choreography, OASIS WS-BPEL, and OASIS ebXML BPSS (ebBP) are just a few examples of such standards.

Thus, process integration can be viewed as a business logic layer that determines *what* needs to be done at a given point in a process, while application integration can be viewed as a technology layer that determines *how* it gets done. Usually, business process integration is done with the help of business analysts, as opposed to application integration that is done by software architects. As technologists we are best served by focusing on the *how* part of integration, that is application integration.

EJB and Integration

Presently, EJB applications have three technology choices for application integration:

- **JMS and JMS-based message-driven beans** are a foremost technology choice for communicating with message-oriented middleware systems from EJB platform.
- **Java Web services** is another approach of integrating EJB applications, especially with a target platform such as Microsoft .NET, which is also Web services–aware.
- **Java EE Connector Architecture** is a full-fledged enterprise integration framework for building adapters or connectors that can integrate EJB applications with the outside non-Java world.

We already discussed JMS-based message-driven beans and Java Web services in Chapters 7 and 5, respectively. In this chapter, we will focus on learning Java EE Connector Architecture and see how it addresses the integration problem.

NOTE We have seen many people use JCA to refer to Java EE Connector Architecture. We will not do so, however, and for a very good reason—doing so creates confusion with another critical Java technology, Java Cryptography Architecture. Many Java developers refer to latter as JCA. Due to the fact that Java Cryptography Architecture was developed before Java EE Connector Architecture, we will allow the cryptography crowd the benefit of using the JCA acronym.

Java EE Connector Architecture

Java EE Connector Architecture is a standard framework for supporting enterprise application integration for Java platform. Connector architecture defines the notion of a resource adapter (RA) that can be plugged into any Java EE-compliant application server to enable Java EE applications to communicate with the enterprise information system (EIS). The connector specification thus defines a component model for developing and deploying resource adapters.

Why Java EE Connectors?

Even before Java EE Connector Architecture existed, it was possible to communicate with native applications via Java Native Interfaces (JNI). Socket communication presented yet another alternative of integrating with non-Java applications. And don't forget IIOP—using RMI-IIOP it is possible to communicate with any CORBA-IIOP application. So why do we need Java EE connectors?

To understand this, let us first understand various problems of integration in a connectorless world.

NOTE **An EIS encompasses all those systems that provide information infrastructure for an enterprise. These EISs provide a well-defined set of information services to their clients through various interfaces. Examples of EISs include ERP systems, transaction-processing systems, and database systems. More recently, the term EIS is also used to refer to custom IT applications.**

Integrating Java EE Platform with Non-IIOP World

The two most common ways to integrate with non-IIOP applications from the Java platform are to use JNI or sockets. However, if you want to integrate a Java EE application with non-IIOP application you cannot use either of these mechanisms, since using both JNI and sockets (server sockets, more specifically) is tabooed in Java EE for security reasons. A safe, robust framework that provides integration with the non-IIOP world of applications is needed. Java EE Connector Architecture is an answer to this need.

The M x N Integration Problem

Prior to Java EE connectors no standard mechanism of integrating Java EE applications with heterogeneous non-Java EE, non-IIOP EIS existed. To integrate Java EE applications with an EIS, most EIS vendors and application server vendors had to provide nonstandard proprietary solutions. For example, if you had to integrate your Java EE order management application with a SAP inventory management application you had to use proprietary integration adapters to make your application server communicate with SAP. These nonstandard adapters could have been provided by your application server vendor or by your EIS vendor, which was SAP in this case. Similarly, if you wanted your Java EE applications to integrate with any other EISs, you needed specific adapters that allowed your application server to talk to your EIS.

This presented a big challenge for the vendors of application servers and EISs—they were required to support and maintain M x N number of proprietary integration solutions to make M number of application servers communicate with N number of EISs. This M x N problem, described in Figure 15.1, was the main motivation for these vendors to create Java EE connector technology that enables building standard adapters (a.k.a. resource adapters/connectors) for specific EISs so that these adapters can plug into any Java EE complaint application server and communicate with the EIS.

Hence, the M x N problem is now reduced to 1 x N problem, where N adapters are needed to integrate with N number of EISs from *any* Java EE environment, as shown in Figure 15.2.

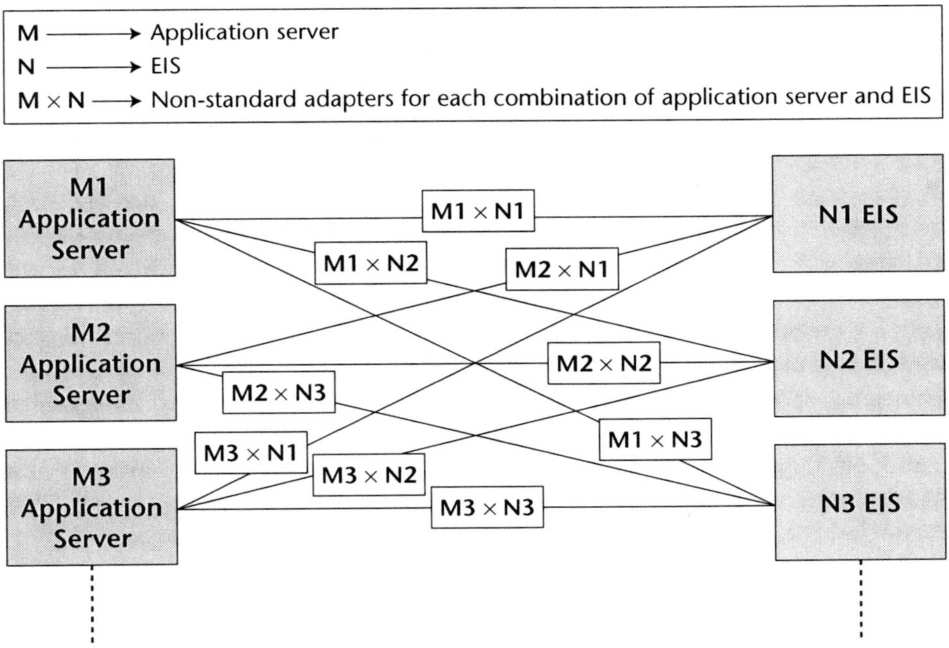

Figure 15.1 The M x N integration problem.

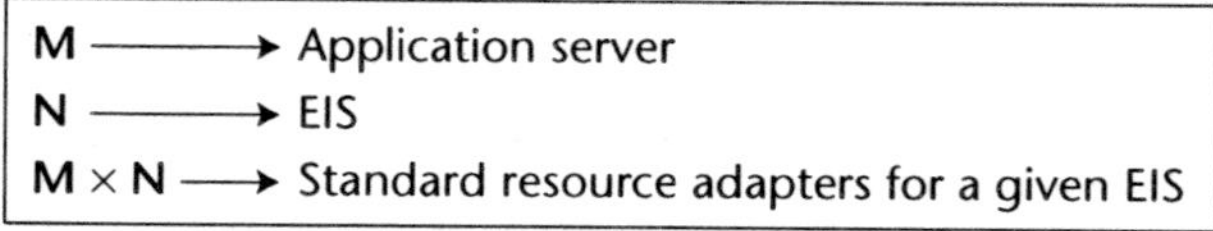

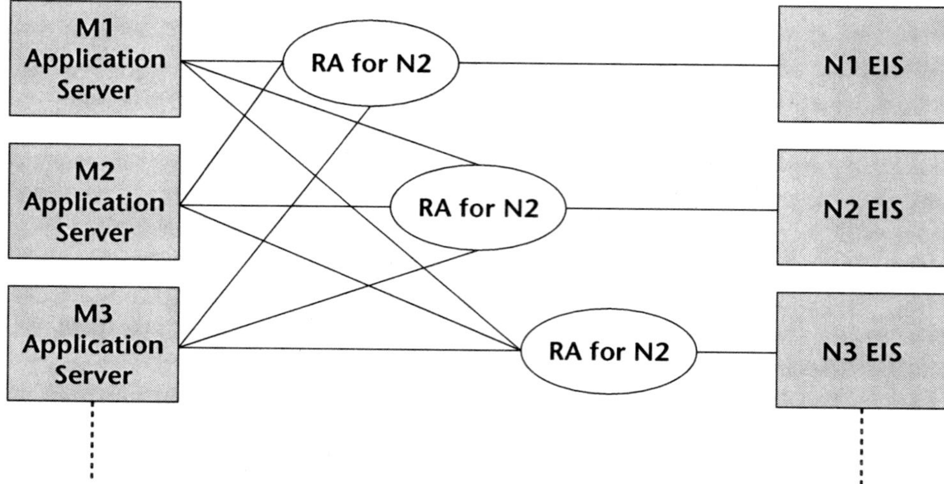

Figure 15.2 Reduction of M x N integration problem to 1 x N.

The Infrastructure Services Problem

Another challenge when building integration solutions is to enable support for infrastructure services—such as resource pooling (for threads, connections, and so on), transaction management, security, life cyclemanagement, and so on—required for transactional, robust, and secure integration. Without a standard framework that provides these services, an integration solution developer is responsible for writing logic for these services. It usually takes experts to write these services, plus it requires a longer cycle of solution development, debugging, deployment, and testing. This makes high-quality integration with underlying EIS very difficult to achieve.

Java EE Connector Architecture solves this problem too—it extends the infrastructure services provided by the container to the resource adapters. This means that the Java EE container will provide connection pooling, transaction management, security, and so on to the deployed RA. It provides these services through well-defined system contracts. The RA will need to implement these contracts in order for the container to provide the system services.

Thus, the application server and resource adapter keep the system-level details related to the interaction with the underlying EIS transparent from the application component. This is one of the main reasons for using resource adapters—it keeps the components free from the complexity of having to deal with transactions, security, connections, multithreading, and other such infrastructure details, while communicating with the EIS. This is what we call "integration made simple"!

Resource Adapter Interaction with Java EE Components

When deployed in a managed environment by way of an application server, the RA accepts requests from various Java EE components, such as servlets, JSPs, and EJBs; translates those requests into EIS-specific calls; and sends those requests to the EIS. The response that it receives from the EIS is forwarded to the client Java EE components. Application components thus interact with the RA through its client contracts. The RA can support client contracts in one of the following ways:

- **Common Client Interfaces (CCI)** is a standard set of APIs for interacting with *any* EIS through its respective RA. CCI provides a mechanism for accessing a heterogeneous EIS using the same interface. CCI support is optional although recommended for the RA provider. In particular, providers that expect their RA to be used by third-party tools should support CCI to enable tools to communicate with them through the standard CCI.
- **EIS-specific client interfaces** can be supported by the RA provider to make it easier for application components to work with the underlying EIS by using APIs attuned to the EIS's inner workings. Most of the EISs have EIS-specific client APIs. For example, the JDBC API is the client API for communicating with an RDBMS EIS.

Figure 15.3 shows this interaction between various Java EE components, the RA, and the EIS.

JAVA EE CONNECTORS AND NONMANAGED ENVIRONMENTS

Standalone Java applications run in a nonmanaged environment, since there is no container to provide them with *managed* services such as transactions, security, life cycle management, resource pooling, and so on.

Java EE Connector Architecture supports nonmanaged environments. This enables Java applications to access the underlying EIS through an RA. In a nonmanaged scenario, the application client directly uses the RA library. RAs that support nonmanaged access should expose the low-level APIs for transaction, security, and connection management. The application client will interact with the RA and use its low-level APIs. This model is similar to using a resource adapter such as a JDBC driver in a nonmanaged environment.

Since this chapter is on EJB integration, we will discuss connectors only in the context of managed environment.

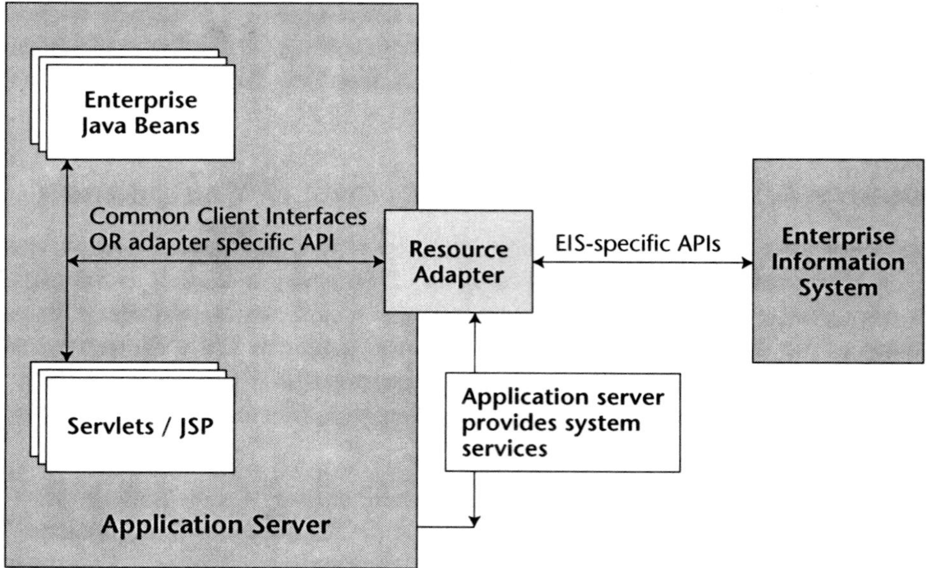

Figure 15.3 Interaction between the Java EE connector, RA, and EIS.

Resource Adapter Interaction with Application Server

To interact with the application server and avail various container services, the RA provider can choose to implement the following system contracts:

- **The connection management contract** enables application components to connect to the EIS so that the application server can pool these connections. Essentially, by implementing this contract your components can connect to the resource adapter, which in turn will establish the connection to the underlying EIS.
- **The transaction management contract** allows transactional access to the EIS from your application components. It enables the application server to leverage the transaction manager for managing global transactions across multiple resource managers, including the EIS resource manager. Also, the RA can support local transactions, which do not require coordination from a transaction manager through this contract.
- **The security contract** enables secure access to the EIS from the application component.

- **The life cyclemanagement contract** was introduced in Java EE Connector Architecture 1.5. It allows the application server to manage life cycle functions, such as bootstrapping the RA upon application server startup or RA deployment, and shutting down the RA upon application server shutdown or undeployment, on behalf of a resource adapter. The application server will notify the RA instance of these bootstrapping/shutdown events.
- **The work management contract** was introduced in Java EE Connector Architecture 1.5. By implementing this contract, the RA can submit the *work* it needs to perform to the application server, which in turn will spawn a new thread or retrieve a worker thread from its thread pool to execute RA-delegated work. This contract thus enables the RA to increase throughput of handling requests from application components without having to spawn or manage threads directly.
- **The transaction inflow contract**, also introduced in Java EE Connector Architecture 1.5, allows the RA to propagate the transaction context imported from the EIS to the application server. This contract supplements the transaction management contract, which allowed the RA to propagate the transaction context from application server to the underlying EIS. Through this contract, the RA can notify the application server of transaction completion and crash recovery calls initiated by the EIS thereby helping the application server coordinate transactions at its end.
- **The message inflow contract**, introduced in Java EE Connector Architecture 1.5, allows the RA to asynchronously deliver messages to message endpoints residing in the application server independent of the messaging semantics, style, and infrastructure used to deliver messages. This contract also serves as a standard message provider pluggability contract that allows a wide range of messaging providers to be plugged into any compatible Java EE application server via a resource adapter.

THE IMPORTANCE OF CONNECTORS IN JAVA EE

J2EE 1.4 onwards, the application of RA had been extended further in that the RA could now be used to provide connectivity for all kinds of EIS applications. Regardless of whether a standard connectivity solution to the EIS from the Java platform exists, vendors are encouraged to provide connectivity to their EIS through the RA. Hence, we will eventually see vendors providing an RA for connecting to all kinds of EISs—RDBMS, MOM systems, and enterprise applications such as SAP, Siebel, PeopleSoft, and so on.

(continued)

THE IMPORTANCE OF CONNECTORS IN JAVA EE *(continued)*

This is a step in a good direction because:

- **The whole industry can now unify around a single architecture for connectivity regardless of the type of underlying EIS. This will enable tool vendors and system integrators to provide out-of-the-box integration solutions, which in turn will reduce the cost of building integration solutions on Java EE platform.**
- **The industry will not have to spend time defining connectivity per EIS. Connector architecture eliminates the need to define Service Provider Interfaces (SPI) for different EIS connectivity providers. As a result, the Java community is not required anymore to create standard SPIs for writing JMS message providers or JDBC providers in the future. Rather, the vendors will leverage SPIs defined by Java EE connector architecture to interact with the Java EE application server and its container services.**

The fact that vendors are building and shipping RAs for connecting to all kinds of EISs—including databases, messaging systems, and enterprise applications—establishes connector architecture as the predominant framework in the Java EE integration space.

The Java EE Connector API

The Connector API consists of six packages—`javax.resource`, `javax.resource.cci`, `javax.resource.spi`, `javax.resource.spi.endpoint`, `javax.resource.spi.security`, and `javax.resource.spi.work`. We will take a look at each of these packages and their main interfaces and classes. This overview of connector APIs followed by the description of how RAs should implement various system contracts should help you understand the connector architecture.

The javax.resource Package

Table 15.1 discusses the main members of this top-level connector API package.

Table 15.1 The javax.resource Package Members

PACKAGE MEMBERS	DESCRIPTION
`javax.resource.Referenceable`	The implementation class of the RA's connection factory is required to implement `Referenceable` interface to enable its registration in the JNDI namespace.
`javax.resource.ResourceException`	This is the root interface of the connector exception hierarchy.
`javax.resource.NotSupportedException`	This class extends `ResourceException` and is thrown to indicate that the RA did not support a particular operation.

The javax.resource.cci Package

This package comprises the APIs that should be implemented by an RA that supports CCI. Table 15.2 discusses the main members of this package.

The javax.resource.spi Package

This package consists of APIs corresponding to various system contracts. An RA should implement APIs for system contracts that it chooses to support with the help of the application server. Table 15.3 discusses the main members of this package.

Note once again that the RA should implement only system contracts that are needed. For instance, if the RA does not need help for managing outgoing connections to the EIS, it does not have to implement the various `javax.resource.spi` APIs for connection management. Similarly, if the RA does not need help managing its life cycle, it does not need to implement the `javax.resource.ResourceAdapter` interface.

Table 15.2 The javax.resource.cci Package Members

PACKAGE MEMBERS	DESCRIPTION
`javax.resource.cci.Connection`	This interface represents a handle that is used by the client to access the underlying physical connection represented by a `ManagedConnection` instance.
`javax.resource.cci.ConnectionFactory`	Represents a factory interface that is used to obtain the `Connection` handle via `getConnection()` method. The client looks up an instance of `ConnectionFactory` registered with JNDI during deployment. The `ConnectionFactory` implementation class is required to implement `Referenceable` so that it can support registration to JNDI.
`javax.resource.cci.ConnectionMetaData`	The client can use this interface to get specific information, such as product name and version, about the underlying EIS. Also, `ConnectionMetaData` provides a user name corresponding to the resource principal under whose security context the given connection to the EIS has been established. An instance of `ConnectionMetaData` could be obtained through the `getMetaData()` method on the `Connection` interface.
`javax.resource.cci.ConnectionSpec`	If supported by the RA, the client can use this interface to pass the connection request–specific properties to `ConnectionFactory`. `ConnectionSpec` is a marker interface, and the RA should implement this interface as a JavaBean with getters/setters for each connection property. The specification defines standard connection properties, such as `UserName` and `Password`. However, the RA is not required to implement getters/setters for these standard properties if it is not relevant to the underlying EIS.

Table 15.2 *(continued)*

PACKAGE MEMBERS	DESCRIPTION
@TX:`javax.resource.cci.Interaction`	`Interaction` is a representation of the client's interaction with the EIS in terms of executing various functions or procedures on the EIS. The client obtains the `Interaction` instance through the `createInteraction()` method on `Connection`. There are two methods the client can use to interact with the EIS: `execute (InteractionSpec ispec, Record input)` executes the EIS function as specified by the `InteractionSpec` instance and produces the output `Record`, which carries the resulting return value. `execute (InteractionSpec ispec, Record input, Record output)` executes the EIS function as specified by the `InteractionSpec` instance and updates the output `Record` with the resulting return value.
`javax.resource.cci.InteractionSpec`	This interface represents properties required for driving interaction with the EIS. RA is required to implement `InteractionSpec` as a JavaBean with getters/setters for each of the properties. Connector specification defines the following three standard interaction properties: `FunctionName` corresponds to the name of the EIS function that the given interaction will execute.`InteractionVerb` specifies the mode of interaction with EIS. The standard interaction verbs are `SYNC_SEND`, `SYNC_SEND_RECEIVE`, and `SYNC_RECEIVE`. `SYNC_SEND` specifies that the execution of an `Interaction` will perform only send operation and not the receive operation. `SYNC_SEND_RECEIVE` specifies that the execution will perform both synchronous send and receive operations. `SYNC_RECEIVE` specifies that the execution will perform only synchronous receive operations. The last mode is used by an application component to perform a synchronous callback to EIS. Note that CCI does not support asynchronous delivery of messages to the application components. The message inflow system contract should be used for the same, as we will see later in this chapter. `ExecutionTimeout` specifies the number of milliseconds an `Interaction` will wait for an EIS to execute the specified function. RA is not required to support a standard property if that property does not apply to the underlying EIS. Also, the RA can support additional `InteractionSpec` properties if they are relevant to the EIS.

(continued)

Table 15.2 *(continued)*

PACKAGE MEMBERS	DESCRIPTION
`javax.resource.cci.Record`	This interface represents input or output to the `execute()` methods on `Interaction` object. This is the base interface for `javax.resource.cci.MappedRecord`, `javax.resource.cci.IndexedRecord`, and `javax.resource.cci.Resultset` types of records.
`javax.resource.cci.MappedRecord`	`MappedRecord` represents input or output in the form of a key-value-pair-based collection. Naturally, it extends `java.util.Map`, apart from `javax.resource.cci.Record` interface, to provide this functionality.
`javax.resource.cci.IndexedRecord`	`IndexedRecord` represents input or output in the form of an ordered and indexed collection. It extends the `java.util.List` interface, apart from `javax.resource.cci.Record`, to enable this searchable and indexed collection of record elements.
`javax.resource.cci.ResultSet`	This interface represents tabular data that is retrieved from EIS as a result of executing a function on EIS. It extends `java.sql.ResultSet`, apart from the `javax.resource.cci.Record` interface, to provide this functionality. Thus, a CCI `Resultset` has capabilities similar to JDBC `ResultSet` in that it can be scrollable and updatable, can support various Java types and concurrency modes, and so on.
`javax.resource.cci.ResultSetInfo`	The client application component can get information about the various facilities provided for `ResultSet` by the EIS through this interface. `ResultSetInfo` supports methods such as `supportsResultSetType()`, `supportsResultTypeConcurrency()`, and so on, to provide this information. The client can get hold of the `ResultSetInfo` instance through the `getResultSetInfo()` method on `Connection`.

Table 15.2 *(continued)*

PACKAGE MEMBERS	DESCRIPTION
`javax.resource.cci.RecordFactory`	This factory interface allows the clients to create instances of `MappedRecord` and `IndexedRecord`. Note that it is not used for creating `ResultSet` records. The client component gets a hold of the `RecordFactory` instance through `getRecordFactory()` method on `ConnectionFactory`.
`javax.resource.cci.LocalTransaction`	This represents the transaction demarcation interface to be used by client application components for managing local transactions at the EIS level. If the RA supports local transactions, it should implement this interface. The client can get hold of the `LocalTransaction` instance through the `getLocalTransaction()` method on the `Connection` object. If the RA's CCI implementation does not support local transactions, `getLocalTransaction()` should throw `javax.resource.NotSupportedException`.
`javax.resource.cci.MessageListener`	This CCI interface represents a request/response message listener that should be implemented by message endpoints (such as message-driven beans) to enable the EIS to communicate with them through the `onMessage()` method.
`javax.resource.cci .ResourceAdapterMetaData`	This interface provides information about the capabilities of the RA. The client gets hold of its instance through the `getMetaData()` method on `ConnectionFactory`.

Note that the RA is only supposed to implement the type of record that it deems fit for the underlying EIS.

Table 15.3 The javax.resource.spi Package Members

PACKAGE MEMBERS	DESCRIPTION
`javax.resource.spi.ConnectionManager`	The `allocateConnection()` method on `ConnectionManager` provides a hook to the application server so that it can provide *generic* quality of services such as security, connection pooling, transaction management, logging, and so on, while establishing a connection to the EIS.
`javax.resource.spi.ManagedConnection`	This interface represents a physical connection to the underlying EIS.
`javax.resource.spi.ManagedConnectionFactory`	This acts as a factory for `ManagedConnection`. It also provides methods for matching and creating `ManagedConnection` instances, thereby supporting connection pooling. The `ManagedConnectionFactory` instance can support various standard and nonstandard connection properties. However, it must support these connection properties through JavaBean-style getters/setters.
`javax.resource.spi.ManagedConnectionMetaData`	This interface provides information about the underlying EIS instance. An application server uses `ManagedConnectionMetaData` to get runtime information about the connected EIS instance such as the user associated with the `ManagedConnection` instance, the maximum limit of active connections that an EIS can support, and the EIS's product name and version. The application server gets this metadata instance through the `getMetaData()` method on `ManagedConnection`.
`javax.resource.spi.ConnectionEventListener`	This interface, implemented by the application server, is used by the `ManagedConnection` implementation to send connection events to the application server. The application server registers an instance of `ConnectionEventListener` with `ManagedConnection` through the `addConnectionEventListener()` method on `ManagedConnection`. The application server uses these event notifications to manage connection pools, local transactions, and perform clean-up, and so on.

Table 15.3 *(continued)*

PACKAGE MEMBERS	DESCRIPTION
`javax.resource.spi.ConnectionRequestInfo`	RA implements this interface to support its own connection request–specific properties. The application server passes these properties to a resource adapter via the `createManagedConnection()` and `matchManagedConnection()` methods on `ManagedConnectionFactory` so that RA can use this additional per-request information to do connection creation and matching.
`javax.resource.spi.ResourceAdapter`	This interface represents an RA instance. It contains various operations for life-cycle management and message endpoint setup, provided that the RA supports life-cycle management and the message inflow system contract. If the RA does not support these contracts, it does not have to implement this interface.
`javax.resource.spi.BootstrapContext`	The `BootstrapContext` instance is passed by the application server to the RA that implements the life-cycle system contract through the `start()` method on `ResourceAdapter`. It allows the RA to use various application server–provided facilities such as the timer service and work manager. Also, it provides an instance of `XATerminator` through the `getXATerminator()` method.
`javax.resource.spi.XATerminator`	The application server implements this interface as part of the transaction inflow system contract. The RA uses the `XATerminator` instance to flow in transaction completion and crash recovery calls from an EIS. `XATerminator` provides methods such as `commit()`, `prepare()`, `forget()`, `recover()`, and `rollback()` to communicate with the application server's transaction manager about the state of the incoming global transaction.

(continued)

Table 15.3 *(continued)*

PACKAGE MEMBERS	DESCRIPTION
javax.resource.spi.LocalTransaction	The RA implements the LocalTransaction interface to support transactions local to EIS. The RA provides access to its LocalTransaction instance through the getLocalTransaction() method on ManagedConnection. The getLocalTransaction() method on the Connection interface implementation will call the getLocalTransaction() method on ManagedConnection to ultimately provide an instance of javax.resource.cci.LocalTransaction to the client application component.
javax.resource.spi.ResourceAdapterAssociation	The RA implements this interface to associate the ResourceAdapter object with other objects such as ManagedConnectionFactory and ActivationSpec. It has getResourceAdapter() and setResourceAdapter() methods that can be used for this purpose.
javax.resource.spi.ActivationSpec	The RA that supports message inflow contract should implement this interface as a JavaBean. The ActivationSpec instance can provide connectivity information to enable inbound messaging.

The javax.resource.spi.endpoint Package

This package consists of APIs pertaining to message inflow system contract. Table 15.4 discusses the main members of this package.

The javax.resource.spi.security Package

This package contains APIs for security system contract. Table 15.5 discusses members of this package.

Table 15.4 The javax.resource.spi.endpoint Package Members

PACKAGE MEMBERS	DESCRIPTION
`javax.resource.spi .endpoint.MessageEndpoint`	The application server implements this interface. The RA calls various methods on this interface to notify the application server that it is about to deliver a message or that it just delivered a message. The application server uses these notifications to start or stop transactions, provided that message delivery is transactional, that is, the `onMessage()` method on the message listener interface implemented by MDB is marked as transactional (container managed).
`javax.resource.spi .MessageEndpointFactory`	When the RA supports message inflow contract it uses an instance of `MessageEndpointFactory` to obtain message endpoint instances for delivering messages. Also, the RA can use this interface to find out if message deliveries to a target method on message listener interface implemented by a given message endpoint is transactional or not. Like `MessageEndpoint`, the application server also implements `MessageEndpointFactory`.

Table 15.5 The javax.resource.spi.security Package Members

PACKAGE MEMBERS	DESCRIPTION
`javax.resource.spi. security.PasswordCredential`	This class acts as a holder of the user name and password security token. This class enables the application server to pass user's security credentials to the RA.

The RA uses other interfaces and classes as well for implementing security system contract. These are discussed later in this chapter.

The javax.resource.spi.work Package

This package contains APIs for work management system contract. Table 15.6 discusses main members of this package.

Table 15.6 The javax.resource.spi.work Package Members

PACKAGE MEMBERS	DESCRIPTION
`javax.resource.spi .work.WorkManager`	The application server implements this top-level interface for the work management contract. The RA gets a hold of `WorkManager` by calling `getWorkManager()` on `BootstrapContext`. It provides methods used by the RA for submitting `Work` instances for processing.
`javax.resource.spi .work.Work`	The `Work` interface is implemented by the RA and it represents the logic, such as delivering incoming messages to message endpoints in the application server that the RA wants the application server to execute on a different thread.
`javax.resource.spi .work.WorkListener`	The RA can implement this interface if it wants to be notified by the application server of various stages, such as work accepted, work completed, work rejected, and so on, in the work-processing life cycle. The RA supplies the `WorkListener` instance to the application server via various work submission methods such as `scheduleWork()`, `startWork()`, or `doWork()` on `WorkManager`.
`javax.resource.spi .work.WorkListener`	The RA can implement this interface if it wants to be notified by the application server of various stages, such as work accepted, work completed, work rejected, and so on, in the work-processing life cycle. The RA supplies the `WorkListener` instance to the application server via various work submission methods such as `scheduleWork()`, `startWork()`, or `doWork()` on `WorkManager`.

Table 15.6 *(continued)*

PACKAGE MEMBERS	DESCRIPTION
`javax.resource.spi .work.ExecutionContext`	This class models an execution context associated with a given `Work` instance such as transactions, security, and so on. The RA can extend this class and override methods of interest to further tune the execution context to the EIS.
`javax.resource.spi .work.WorkEvent`	This class represents the various events that occur during `Work` processing. The application server constructs the `WorkEvent` instance and passes it to the RA via `WorkListener`.

System Contracts

Now that you know connector APIs, let's look at how the RA implements system contracts so as to enable the application server to provide it with various services. This understanding will prove instrumental when developing an RA for your own EIS.

Life Cycle Management

By implementing life cycle management contract, the RA enables the application server to manage its life cycle in terms of:

- **Bootstrapping an RA instance** during RA deployment or application server startup. During bootstrapping, the application server makes facilities such as the timer service and work manager available to the RA.
- **Notifying the RA instance** during its deployment, application server startup, undeployment, and application server shutdown events.

Figure 15.4 shows the object diagram for life cyclemanagement.

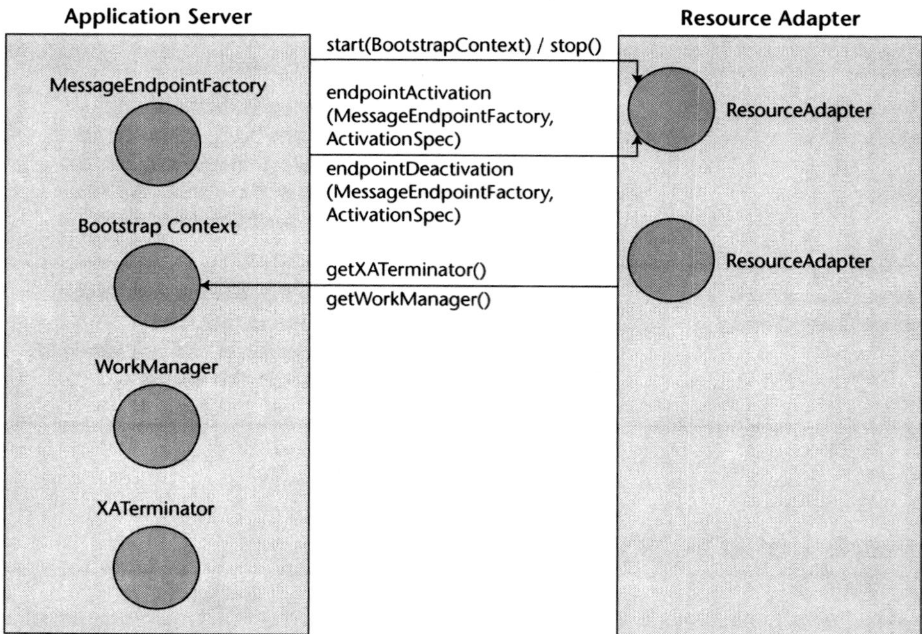

Figure 15.4 Life cycle management object diagram.

Some of the important implementation details for this contract are:

- The RA implements the `ResourceAdapter` interface to receive its life cycle related notifications from application server.
- If the RA supports inbound communication from the EIS in the form of message or transaction inflow, this occurs within the context of a `ResourceAdapter` thread.
- The application server calls the `start()` method on `ResourceAdapter` during, which it passes `BootstrapContext` instance. The RA saves this `BootstrapContext` instance for later use. The RA can also perform other initialization routines in `start()`, such as setting up `Work` instances to be executed on multiple threads or preparing to listen incoming messages from the EIS.
- The application server calls the `stop()` method on `ResourceAdapter` in which the RA should release its resources.

Connection Management

By implementing a connection management contract, the RA enables the application server to manage connections and provide quality of service on its behalf. The RA provides connection and connection factory interfaces. A connection factory acts as a factory for EIS instances. For example, `java.sql.DataSource` and `java.sql.Connection` act as connection factory and connection interfaces for JDBC databases. If an EIS does not have an EIS-specific API, then it can provide implementations of `javax.resource.cci.ConnectionFactory` and `javax.resource.cci.Connection`.

The various steps involved during connection management are:

1. When the RA is deployed or the application server is started, an instance of `ManagedConnectionFactory` is created. The application server calls various setters on `ManagedConnectionFactory` instance to set the RA-specific connection properties, if they were provided during RA deployment. For example, if your RA needs to know the EIS URL in order to connect to it, you can provide an `Eis_Url` connection property during RA deployment and implement the respective getter/setter methods for this property in `ManagedConnectionFactory` implementation.
2. The deployer then creates a connection pool for the given RA, using the vendor-provided administration tools.
3. When a client application component attempts to create a connection to the EIS for the first time after pool creation or after the application server has been started, the application server creates `ManagedConnection` instances by calling `createManagedConnection()` on the `ManagedConnectionFactory` object. The deployer can specify the number of managed connection instances required in the connection pool during the pool creation.
4. The application component then looks up the EIS connection factory in the JNDI namespace. The application server either returns an instance of an EIS-specific connection factory (such as `javax.sql.DataSource`) or CCI connection factory (`javax.resource.cci.ConnectionFactory`). The application server does this by calling the `createConnectionFactory()` method on the `ManagedConnectionFactory` instance.
5. Once the client gets the connection factory instance, it calls an appropriate method to get a hold of the connection instance. In case of an RA supporting CCI, this would mean calling the `getConnection()` method on the `ConnectionFactory` instance.

6. The connection factory implementation delegates the request for a connection to the `javax.resource.spi.ConnectionManager` instance by calling its `allocateConnection()` method. As already noted, `allocateConnection()` provides a hook to the application server for it to provide services such as connection pooling, security, transactions, logging, and so on.
7. Upon receiving the request for a connection from the connection factory, the `ConnectionManager` instance calls `matchManagedConnection()` on the `ManagedConnectionFactory` instance, passing it a set of all the unused `ManagedConnection` instances in the pool.
8. If the `matchManagedConnection()` method determines that a `ManagedConnection` could be used, it returns it to the application server. This determination is done by matching the connection request properties provided by the client application component, through the `javax.resource.cci.ConnectionRequestInfo` object, with that of the `ManagedConnection` instance.
9. If the `matchManagedConnection()` method does not find a usable instance of `ManagedConnection`, the application server creates a new instance of `ManagedConnection`.
10. The application server calls `getConnection()` on the `ManagedConnection` instance and returns the connection handle corresponding to `ManagedConnection` (`javax.resource.cci.Connection` in case of CCI) to the client.
11. Once the application component gets a connection handle, it starts interacting with the EIS using the appropriate client-side APIs. An application component working with a CCI-enabled RA uses the `javax.resource.cci.Interaction` object to do this. It gets hold of the `Interaction` object by calling the `createInteraction()` method on the `Connection` instance.
12. The client application component uses one of the `execute()` methods on `Interaction` to execute an EIS function. The semantics of the EIS function call such as function name, execution timeout, and so on, are provided through the `InteractionSpec` instance. The input and output to the EIS function is provided in terms of `javax.resource.cci.Record` instances.
13. Once the EIS function is executed and the application component receives the resultant output, it can close the connection to the EIS by calling `close()` on `Connection` instance.

14. By calling the `close()` method, the application server is notified that the managed connection corresponding to the given connection handle is finished servicing the client and that it can be placed back into the pool. At this time, the application server can also call `destroy()` on `ManagedConnection` if it created a new instance of `ManagedConnection` just to satisfy this specific client request. This happens when the application server has had to create a new `ManagedConnection` instance in spite of reaching the maximum limit of connections in the pool to satisfy a client request.
15. Finally, when the application server is about to shut down or when the connection pool is undeployed (using the vendor-provided administration tools), the application server will call `destroy()` on each instance of `ManagedConnection` in the pool.

Figure 15.5 shows the interaction between various objects upon receiving connection request from the client application component.

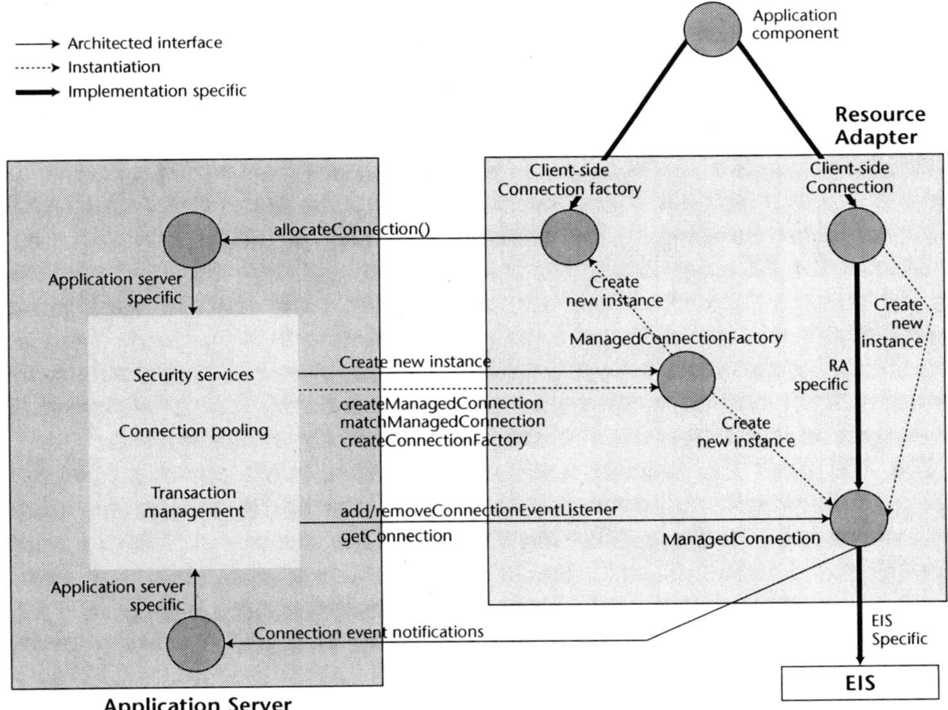

Figure 15.5 Connection management object diagram.

Security Management

The security management contract is an extension of the connection management contract, meaning that the RA will have to implement the connection management contract to provide security connectivity to and from the EIS. Connector security architecture extends the security model for Java EE applications, specifically authentication and authorization, to EIS sign-on. The connector architecture specification does not mandate that application servers support specific authentication mechanisms. The Java EE reference implementation, however, supports Kerberos v5 and basic password authentication mechanisms.

EIS sign-on can be done programmatically or declaratively. The former is known as component-managed sign-on and the latter is known as container-managed sign-on.

Container-Managed Sign-On

In container-managed sign-on, the application server is configured to manage EIS sign-on. When the client application component calls `getConnection()` on `javax.resource.cci.ConnectionFactory` or an equivalent method of the RA client API, it is not required to pass any security information. When the `getConnection()` method invokes the `allocateConnection()` method on `ConnectionManager`, it gives the application server a chance to provide security services. This is when the application server creates the JAAS `Subject` corresponding to the authenticated user. It passes this `Subject` instance to the RA when calling the `createManagedConnection()` method on the `ManagedConnectionFactory` instance. Note that an application server might map the caller principal (principal associated with the application component's security context) to the resource principal (principal under whose security context a connection to EIS is established) or might provide other specific security services before passing the `Subject` to the RA.

The RA uses the security credential(s) information presented within `Subject` to establish a connection to the EIS. Depending on authentication mechanism used by the application server and RA, the credentials can be of type `javax.resource.spi.security.PasswordCredential` or `org.ietf.jgss.GSSCredential`. Thus, in container-managed sign-on, the RA is driven by the application server in that it acts based on the security information passed down by the container.

The sequence diagram in Figure 15.6 demonstrates container-managed EIS sign-on.

Refer to Chapter 11 for more on EJB security and JAAS.

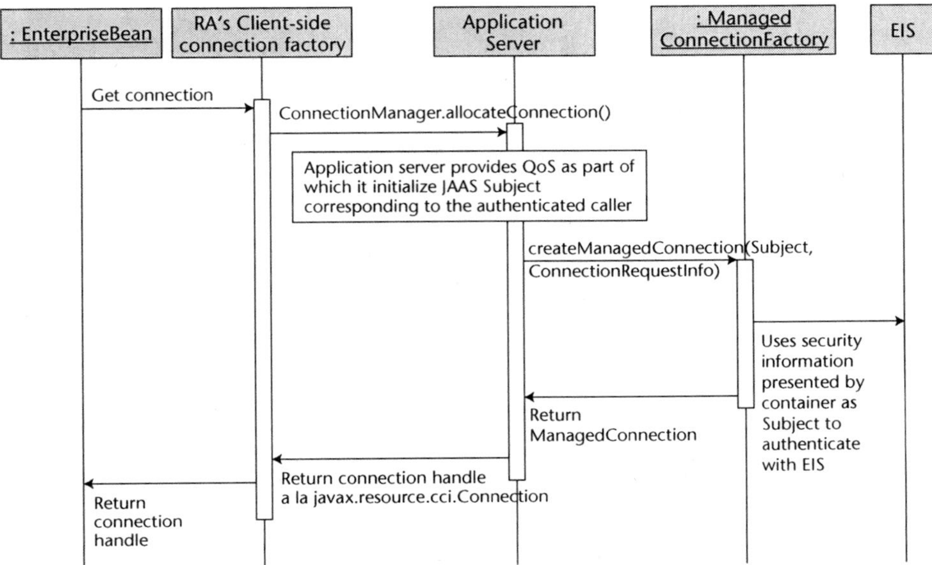

Figure 15.6 Container-managed EIS sign-on.

Component-Managed Sign-On

This type of sign-on requires the client application component to provide security information explicitly through `ConnectionSpec` in `getConnection()` or an equivalent method of the RA client API. The `getConnection()` method on the connection factory instance invokes the `allocateConnection()` method on the `ConnectionManager` instance and passes this security information via the `ConnectionRequestInfo` object. The security information passed this way is opaque to the application server. Hence, when the application server calls `createManagedConnection()` on the `ManagedConnectionFactory` instance, it passes it a null `Subject` instance. However, the security information passed by the client application component is maintained intact in the `ConnectionRequestInfo` object passed to `createManagedConnection()`. The RA uses the security information presented within the `ConnectionRequestInfo` JavaBean to establish a connection to the EIS. Thus in component-managed sign-on, the RA is driven by the client application component in that it acts based on the security information provided by the component.

The sequence diagram in Figure 15.7 demonstrates container-managed EIS sign-on.

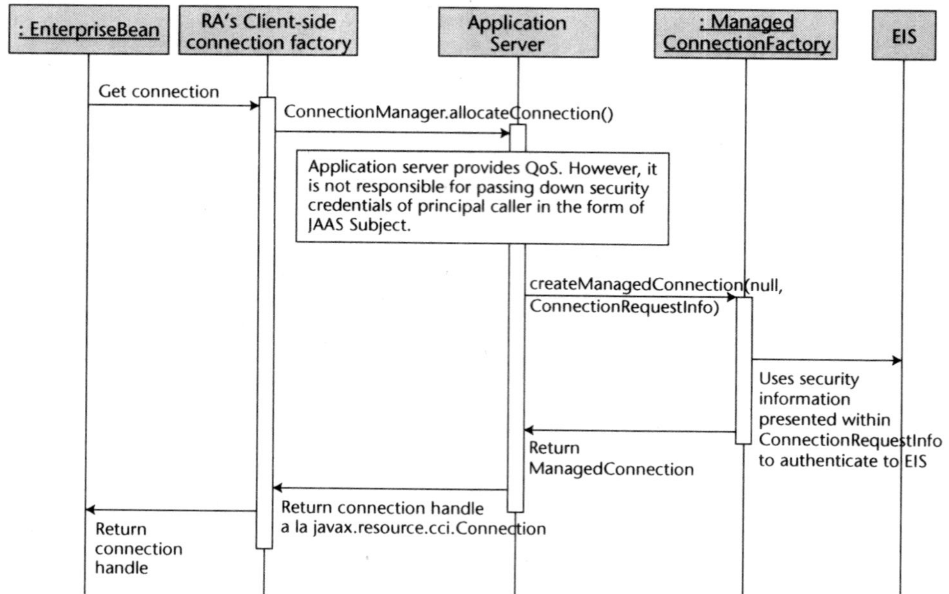

Figure 15.7 Component-managed EIS sign-on.

Transaction Management

The transaction management contract is layered on top of connection management. To support outbound transaction propagation, the RA has to support outbound connections to the EIS. The RA can support either local transactions or global transactions through the transaction management system contracts. A local transaction is managed internally in the EIS and RA, without any help from external transaction managers such as the one provided by the Transaction Service. Global transactions, on the other hand, are controlled and coordinated by an external transaction manager.

Local Transaction Management Contract

A local transaction management contract requires the RA to implement the `javax.resource.spi.LocalTransaction` interface. The `LocalTransaction` implementation will work with the low-level EIS APIs to signal its resource manager about the transaction begin, commit, and rollback events.

The application server uses the instance of `LocalTransaction` to transparently manage local transactions in case of container-demarcated transactions. The application server gets a hold of the `LocalTransaction` instance by calling `getLocalTransaction()` on `ManagedConnection`. Figure 15.8 shows how local transaction management is done for a container-managed transaction.

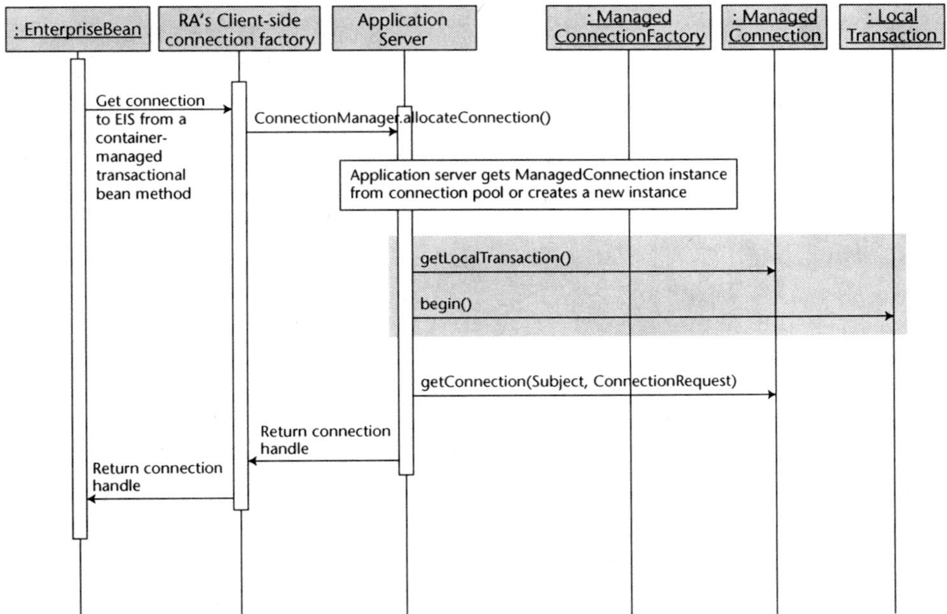

Figure 15.8 Local transaction management for a container-managed transaction.

If the client application component chooses to demarcate transactions using an RA-supported client transaction demarcation API (such as `javax.resource.cci.LocalTransaction`), then the RA will be responsible for notifying the application server of the transaction events such as begin, commit, and rollback. The RA does this by calling the `localTransactionStarted()`, `localTransactionCommitted()`, and `localTransactionRolledback()` methods on `javax.resource.spi.ConnectionEventListener`. Figure 15.9 shows how local transaction management is done for a client-demarcated transaction.

Global Transaction Management Contract

A global transaction management contract requires the RA to provide an implementation for the `javax.transaction.xa.XAResource` interface. The `XAResource` implementation will use low-level libraries to communicate with the EIS resource manager. Implementing `XAResource` will enable the EIS resource manager to participate in transactions that are controlled and coordinated by the application server's transaction manager. The transaction manager communicates transaction association, completion, and recovery signals to the EIS resource manager via `XAResource`.

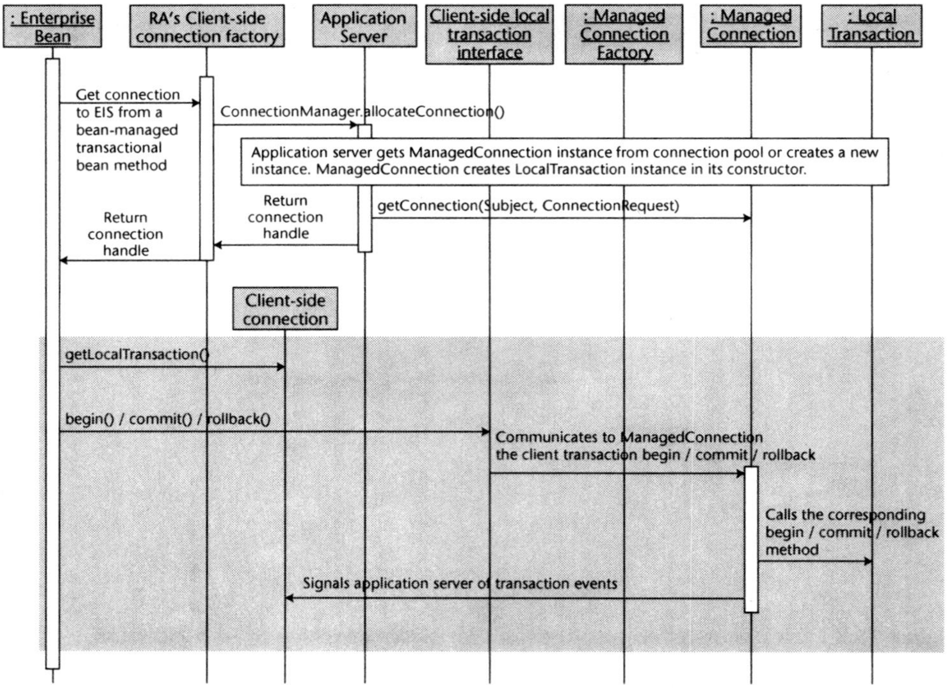

Figure 15.9 Local transaction management for client-demarcated transaction.

The application server gets the `XAResource` instance by calling the `getXAResource()` method on `ManagedConnection`. The application server gets the `XAResource` instance when it has to enlist the EIS resource manager in a global transaction. Subsequently, when the client application component closes the connection, the application server performs transactional clean-up by de-listing the `XAResource` corresponding to `ManagedConnection` from the transaction manager.

The object interaction diagrams of enlisting and delisting `XAResource` are shown in Figures 15.10 and 15.11.

Work Management

Sometimes, you need your RA to multithread. However, in a managed environment creating and executing threads is not encouraged, mainly because the application server will not have control over such threads and, therefore, will not be able to manage them. To prevent the RA from creating and managing threads directly, the connector architecture provides a mechanism through which the RA can delegate thread management to the application server and consequently get its work done on multiple threads.

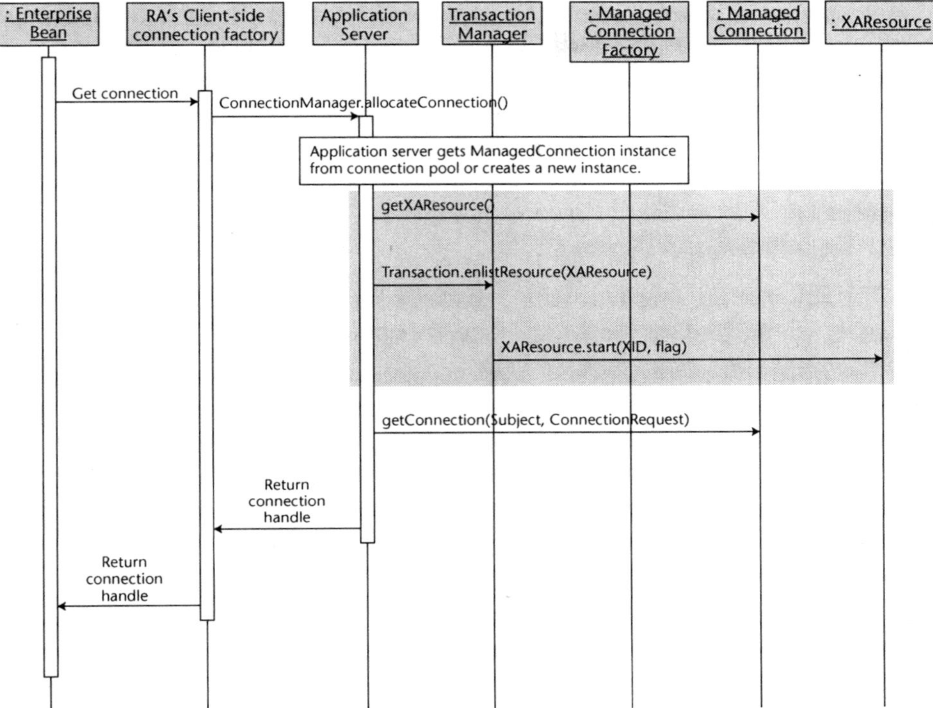

Figure 15.10 Enlisting EIS resource manager with transaction manager.

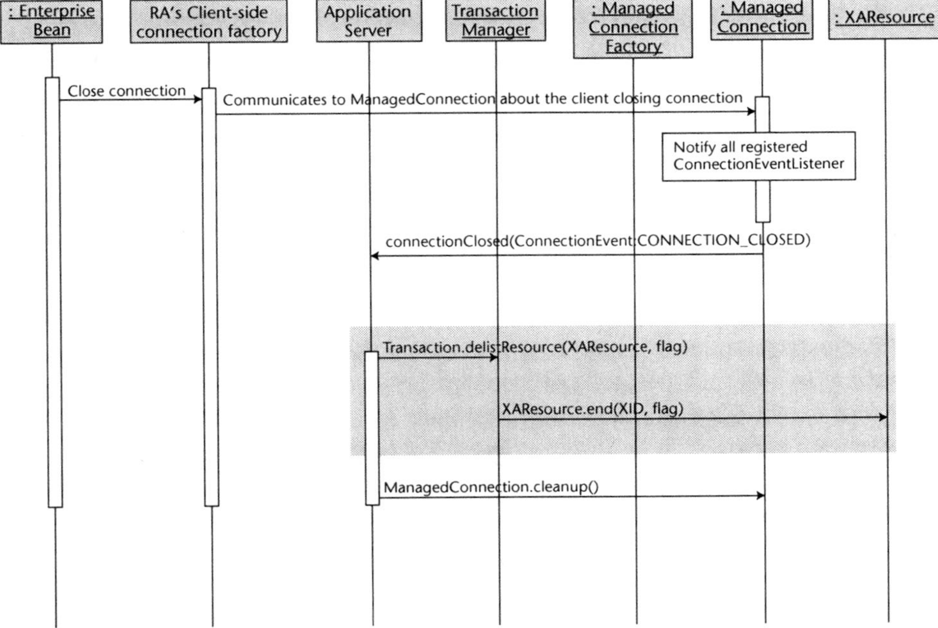

Figure 15.11 Delisting EIS resource manager with transaction manager.

Under the work management contract, the RA creates Work instances, representing units of work that the RA wants to execute on different threads, and submits them to the application server. The application server uses the threads from its pool to execute these submitted Work instances. Work instances can be executed on separately executing threads, since they implement Runnable.

Figure 15.12 shows the interaction among various objects during work management.

Note the following in Figure 15.12:

- The RA gets the WorkManager instance by calling the getWorkManager() method on the BootstrapContext object.
- The RA implements units of work as instances of Runnable and submits them for execution on different threads to the application server through the doWork(), startWork(), or scheduleWork() methods. The doWork() method blocks the current thread until the Work instance completes execution; the startWork() method blocks until the Work instance starts execution, and the scheduleWork() method accepts the Work instance for processing and returns immediately.
- After accepting Work for processing, the WorkManager dispatches a thread that calls the run() method to begin execution of Work. The Work execution completes when run() returns. The WorkManager can call release() to request Work instance to complete execution as soon as it can.
- Additionally, the RA can provide ExecutionContext within which the Work instance will be executed, when submitting work.
- Also, the RA can provide a WorkListener object to the work submission methods so that the application server can call the RA to notify it of various work execution relatedevents such as work acceptance, work rejection, and so on.

Message Inflow

The message inflow contract allows the RA to asynchronously deliver messages to message endpoints, such as message-drivenbeans, residing within the application server independent of messaging semantics. This contract supplements the connection management contract in that, just like the connection management contract, it is implemented for outbound communication from the RA to the EIS; the message inflow contract is implemented for receiving inbound messages sent from the EIS to the application server endpoints.

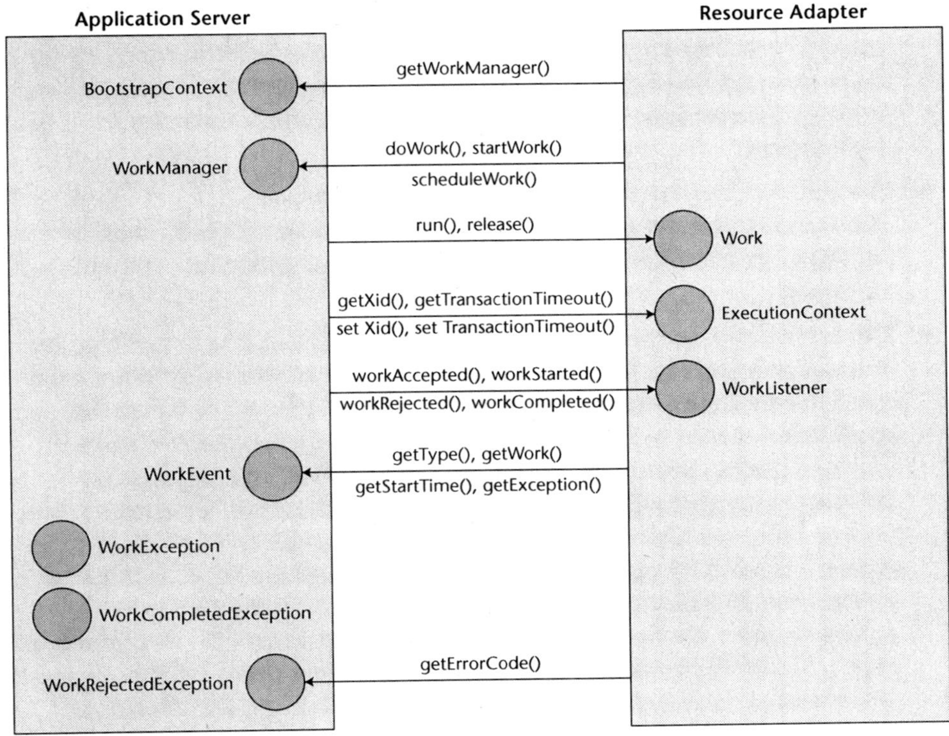

Figure 15.12 Work management object diagram.

Considering message-oriented middleware (MOM) systems as a category of EIS, inbound communication from such MOM systems to the application server endpoints can be facilitated by implementing the message inflow contract. Hence, from J2EE 1.4 onwards, all JMS and non-JMS messaging providers were implemented as RAs, which in turn implemented the message inflow contract.

Some of the important implementation details for this contract are:

- The RA implements the `javax.resource.spi.ActivationSpec` JavaBean and supplies its class to the application server during its deployment. `ActivationSpec` is opaque to the application server and is used by the RA to establish subscriptions to the requested data from the EIS.
- The RA provides a message listener interface, akin to `javax.jms.MessageListener`, and a message interface, akin to `javax.jms.Message`. The message listener interface will be implemented by message endpoints similar to the way that JMS MDB implements `javax.jms.MessageListener`. Also, the message listener

interface should have a public method, akin to `onMessage()` of the `javax.jms.MessageListener` interface, that can be invoked by the RA to deliver messages to the endpoint. The deployer will specify the message listener interface class associated with the RA during its deployment.

- The RA also implements the `javax.resource.spi.ResourceAdapter` interface to facilitate message inflow by implementing the `endpointActivation()` and `endpointDeactivation()` methods.
- The application server calls the `endpointActivation()` method on `ResourceAdapter` to notify the RA when the message endpoint interested in consuming messages from the RA is deployed or when the application server with such a deployed message endpoint is started. The application server passes `javax.resource.spi.endpoint.MessageEndpointFactory` and `ActivationSpec` instances when calling `endpointActivation()`. The `MessageEndpointFactory` instance is used by the RA to create a `MessageEndpoint` instance later when it has to deliver a message to the endpoint by invoking its `onMessage()` method. `ActivationSpec` represents the deployment properties of the message endpoint. The deployer provides these properties during message endpoint deployment. The application server creates the `ActivationSpec` JavaBean instance and instantiates its properties with values supplied by the deployer. The RA uses the information in the `ActivationSpec` JavaBean to establish subscription to the requested data from the EIS.
- The application server calls the `endpointDeactivation()` method on `ResourceAdapter` to notify the RA when the message endpoint interested in consuming messages from the RA is undeployed or when the application server with such a deployed message endpoint is being shut down. The application server passes `MessageEndpointFactory` and `ActivationSpec` instances when calling `endpointDeactivation()`. The RA uses `MessageEndpointFactory` to retrieve the underlying endpoint consumer and remove it from its list of active message endpoints.

Figure 15.13 shows the object diagram of message inflow contract.

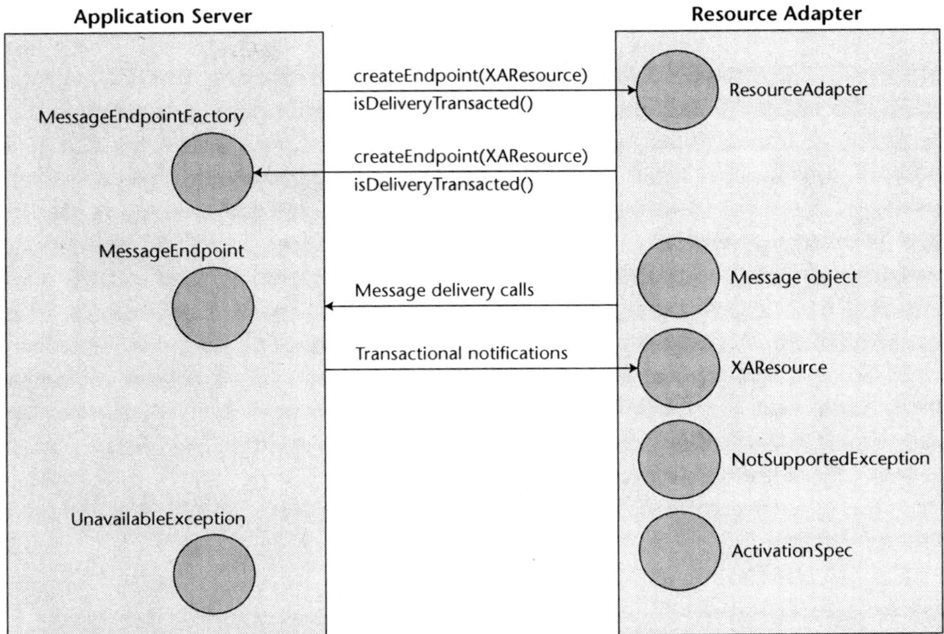

Figure 15.13 Message inflow object diagram.

Connector Example: OutboundLoanRA

Okay! So we are halfway through our journey of learning about the Java EE Connector Architecture. The remaining half will be more exciting than the previous half because we will now deep dive into developing and deploying our own connector, `OutboundLoanRA`. As is obvious from the name, our RA supports outbound communication from the application server to the EIS. RA development tends to be more complex than that of other Java EE components, since the RA developer is responsible for implementing not just client contracts but also system contracts. To keep the complexity manageable, we will implement only the connection management system contract in `OutboundLoanRA`. Even then, you should find this example helpful given that most of the connectors support outbound communication to the EIS, and hence, connection management. Connection management is the most commonly implemented contract.

`OutboundLoanRA` supports client contracts in the form of CCI.

Example Architecture

OutboundLoanRA provides an elegant way of integrating our EJB application, LoanApplication, with our legacy application LoanApp.dll. LoanApp.dll is a Windows DLL written in Visual C++. LoanApp.dll is a backend application that provides typical loan-processing functionality. LoanApplication leverages LoanApp.dll for loan processing. A standalone Java application is a client to our LoanApplication EJB application, consisting of LoanRatesEJB. A real-world loan-processing application provides way more functionality, however, for our example we will assume that the loan-processing application, LoanApp.dll, implements just one function: getHomeEquityLoanRate(). It basically returns the rate of interest on home equity loans as a float. Internally, OutboundLoanRA uses the JavaLoanApp class, which in turn uses JNI to communicate with the native C++ DLL.

Figure 15.14 shows architecture for our example.

We will examine each of these architectural components in detail in the subsequent sections.

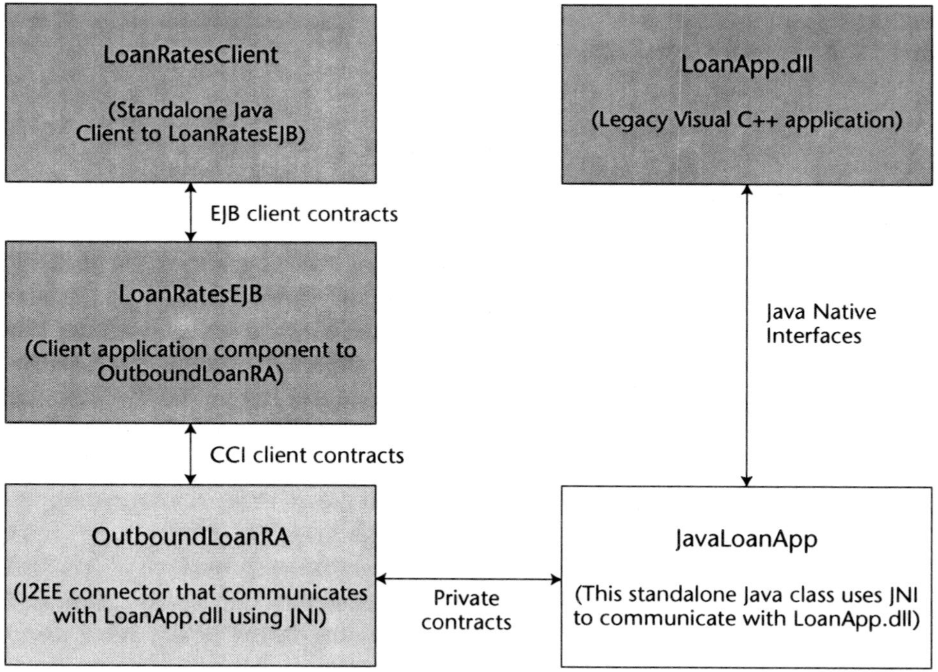

Figure 15.14 Example architecture.

NOTE All the source files and setup details for this example are available on the book's accompanying Web site: wiley.com/go/sriganesh.

JavaLoanApp.java

This is a POJO that uses JNI to communicate with LoanApp.dll. Here, getHomeEquityLoanRate() is declared as a native function. Source 15.1 shows JavaLoanApp.java code.

```
package examples.jni;

public class JavaLoanApp
{
     public JavaLoanApp(String libPath) {
          System.load(libPath);
     }

     // Native method declaration
     public native float getHomeEquityLoanRate();
}
```

Source 15.1 The examples.jni.JavaLoanApp class.

Once we compile the source using a conventional javac compiler, we will need to generate a header file containing the JNI function definition so that it can be included by the C++ LoanApp.dll application. We can use the javah utility that ships with JDK for this. Source 15.2 shows the generated examples_jni_JavaLoanApp.h containing the JNI exported function Java_examples_jni_JavaLoanApp_getHomeEquityLoanRate().

```
/* DO NOT EDIT THIS FILE - it is machine generated */
#include <jni.h>
/* Header for class examples_jni_JavaLoanApp */

#ifndef _Included_examples_jni_JavaLoanApp
#define _Included_examples_jni_JavaLoanApp
#ifdef __cplusplus
extern "C" {
#endif
/*
 * Class:     examples_jni_JavaLoanApp
 * Method:    getHomeEquityLoanRate
 * Signature: ()F
```

Source 15.2 The examples_jni_JavaLoanApp.h header file. *(continued)*

```
 */

/* JNI export function definition (generated by javah utility)
 */
JNIEXPORT jfloat JNICALL
Java_examples_jni_JavaLoanApp_getHomeEquityLoanRate
     (JNIEnv *, jobject);
#ifdef __cplusplus
}
#endif
#endif
```

Source 15.2 *(continued)*

LoanApp.dll

The source code of interest in `LoanApp.dll` is `LoanApp.h`. It implements the JNI exported function, `Java_examples_jni_JavaLoanApp_getHomeEquityLoanRate()`. We have kept the JNI function definition very simple—it always returns 5.64 percent as the home equity loan rate. Source 15.3 shows `LoanApp.h`. Note how we included the `javah` generated `examples_jni_JavaLoanApp.h` header file.

```
// LoanApp.h : main header file for the LoanApp DLL
#pragma once

#ifndef __AFXWIN_H__
     #error include 'stdafx.h' before including this file for PCH
#endif

#include "resource.h"            // main symbols

// CLoanAppApp

#include "examples_jni_JavaLoanApp.h"

class CLoanAppApp : public CWinApp
{
public:
     CLoanAppApp();

// Overrides
public:
```

Source 15.3 The LoanApp.h header file.

```
    virtual BOOL InitInstance();

    DECLARE_MESSAGE_MAP()
};

/* A very simplistic implementation of JNI exported function
 */
JNIEXPORT jfloat JNICALL
Java_examples_jni_JavaLoanApp_getHomeEquityLoanRate(JNIEnv *, jobject) {
    return 5.64;
};
```

Source 15.3 *(continued)*

OutboundLoanRA

Now that we have skimmed through the implementations of `JavaLoanApp` and `LoanApp.dll`, let us examine the source code for `OutboundLoanRA`. We will examine the client contracts first, followed by the system contracts.

OutboundLoanRA Client Contracts

As noted earlier, `OutboundLoanRA` supports client contracts through CCI. We have implemented `javax.resource.cci.ConnectionFactory`, `javax.resource.cci.Connection`, `javax.resource.cci.ConnectionMetaData`, `javax.resource.cci.ConnectionSpec`, `javax.resource.cci.Interaction`, `javax.resource.cci.MappedRecord`, `javax.resource.cci.RecordFactory`, and `javax.resource.cci.ResourceAdapterMetaData` client contracts for this example.

ConnectionFactoryImpl.java

Source 15.4 shows `ConnectionFactoryImpl.java`, which implements the `javax.resource.cci.ConnectionFactory` client contract.

```
package examples.integration.out_loan_ra;

import java.io.*;

import javax.resource.Referenceable;
import javax.resource.*;
import javax.resource.spi.*;
import javax.naming.Reference;
```

Source 15.4 The ConnectionFactoryImpl class. *(continued)*

```
import javax.resource.cci.*;

public class ConnectionFactoryImpl implements ConnectionFactory,
Serializable, Referenceable {

     private ManagedConnectionFactory manConnFactory;
     private ConnectionManager connManager;
     private Reference ref;

     // ManagedConnectionFactory implementation creates
     // ConnectionFactory instance by calling this constructor. During
     // construction it also passes an instance of ConnectionManager
     // which ConnectionFactoryImpl will use to call
     // allocateConnection() method on ConnectionManager later when
     // client component invokes getConnection() on ConnectionFactory.
     public ConnectionFactoryImpl(ManagedConnectionFactory
     manConnFactory, ConnectionManager connManager) {
          System.out.println("ConnectionFactoryImpl
          (ManagedConnectionFactory manConnFactory, ConnectionManager
          connManager) called");
          this.manConnFactory = manConnFactory;
          this.connManager = connManager;
     }

     // Client component calls this definition of getConnection() when
     // container manages EIS sign-on.
     public javax.resource.cci.Connection getConnection() throws
     ResourceException {
          System.out.println("ConnectionFactoryImpl.getConnection()
          called");

          javax.resource.cci.Connection conn = null;
          conn = (javax.resource.cci.Connection)
          connManager.allocateConnection(manConnFactory, null);

          return conn;
     }

     // Client component can call this method to pass ConnectionSpec
     // containing RA specific security and connection information.
     public javax.resource.cci.Connection getConnection
     (ConnectionSpec cSpec) throws ResourceException {
          System.out.println("ConnectionFactoryImpl.getConnection
          (ConnectionSpec cSpec) called");

          javax.resource.cci.Connection conn = null;
          ConnectionRequestInfo connRequestInfo =
          new ConnectionRequestInfoImpl();
          conn = (javax.resource.cci.Connection)
```

Source 15.4 *(continued)*

```
            connManager.allocateConnection(manConnFactory,
            connRequestInfo);

            return conn;
        }

        public ResourceAdapterMetaData getMetaData() throws
        ResourceException {
            return new ResourceAdapterMetaDataImpl();
        }

        public RecordFactory getRecordFactory() throws ResourceException {
            return new RecordFactoryImpl();
        }

        public void setReference(Reference ref) {
            this.ref = ref;
        }

        public Reference getReference() {
            return ref;
        }
}
```

Source 15.4 *(continued)*

Note the following about `ConnectionFactoryImpl`:

- Our class implements `Referenceable` so that the connection factory can be registered with JNDI.
- The application server creates an instance of `ConnectionFactory` using a constructor, during which it passes an instance of `Managed ConnectionFactory` for creating physical connections to the EIS.
- One implementation of the `getConnection()` method does not take any arguments and calls `allocateConnection()` on `Connection Manager`, passing it a reference to `ManagedConnectionFactory` and a null `ConnectionRequestInfo` object.
- The other implementation of the `getConnection()` method takes a single argument, a `ConnectionSpec` instance. `ConnectionSpec` is used by an application component to pass connection request–specific properties. However, since we do not have any connection request–specific properties our `ConnectionSpec` is practically empty. If we had connection request–specific properties (such as user name, password, port number, and so on), the `getConnection()` implementation would be required to populate `ConnectionRequestInfo` with these

ConnectionSpec properties. Since we do not have any connection request properties, we simply create the ConnectionRequestInfo object and pass it as an argument to allocateConnection() on ConnectionManager.

- The getMetaData() method returns an instance of the ResourceAdapterMetaData, and getRecordFactory() method returns an instance of RecordFactory.

ConnectionImpl.java

Source 15.5 shows ConnectionImpl.java, which implements the javax .resource.cci.Connection client contract.

```
package examples.integration.out_loan_ra;

import java.util.*;

import javax.resource.cci.*;
import javax.resource.ResourceException;
import javax.resource.spi.ConnectionEvent;
import javax.resource.spi.IllegalStateException;
import javax.resource.spi.*;
import javax.resource.NotSupportedException;

public class ConnectionImpl implements javax.resource.cci.Connection {

     private ManagedConnectionImpl manConn;

     // RA creates an instance of Connection using this constructor from
     // getConnection() method of ManagedConnection.
     ConnectionImpl(ManagedConnectionImpl manConn) {
          System.out.println("ConnectionImpl(ManagedConnectionImpl)
          called");

          this.manConn = manConn;
     }

     public Interaction createInteraction() throws ResourceException {
          return new InteractionImpl(this);
     }

     public javax.resource.cci.LocalTransaction getLocalTransaction()
     throws ResourceException {
          throw new NotSupportedException("Local transactions are not
          supported.");
```

Source 15.5 The ConnectionImpl class.

```
    }

    public ResultSetInfo getResultSetInfo() throws ResourceException {
        throw new NotSupportedException("ResultSet records are not
        supported.");
    }

    // This method called by client component should be used to signal
    // to the underlying physical connection of client's intent to
    // close the connection. How client-side connection handle signals
    // these (and other events such as  transaction begin, commit, and
    // rollback in case of client-demarcated local
    // transactions), is left up to RA to decide. In our implementation
    // we make our ManagedConnection implementation provide a private
    // contract method named sendEvent() that our ConnectionImpl will
    // call to signal it of various connection-
    // related events. Since this is a Connection.close() method imple-
    // mentation, we will signal a CONNECTION_CLOSED event.
    public void close() throws ResourceException {
        System.out.println("ConnectionImpl.close() called");

        if (manConn == null)
            return;

        manConn.sendEvent(ConnectionEvent.CONNECTION_CLOSED, null,
        this);
        manConn = null;
    }

    public ConnectionMetaData getMetaData() throws ResourceException {
        return new ConnectionMetaDataImpl(manConn);
    }
}
```

Source 15.5 *(continued)*

Note the following about our implementation:

- It throws `javax.resource.NotSupportedException` if someone tries to call the `getLocalTransaction()` and `getResultSetInfo()` methods. It does so because it does not implement the transaction management system contract and it does not support `ResultSet` type of `Record`.
- In the implementation for `close()`, it sends a `CONNECTION_CLOSED` event notification to `ManagedConnection`. The application server uses this event notification to either destroy the underlying `ManagedConnection` or to put the `ManagedConnection` instance back into the pool.

ConnectionMetaDataImpl.java

Source 15.6 shows `ConnectionMetaDataImpl.java`, which implements the `javax.resource.cci.ConnectionMetaData` client contract. `ConnectionMetaDataImpl` simply provides information about the underlying EIS connected through the given `Connection` handle.

```
package examples.integration.out_loan_ra;

import javax.resource.ResourceException;
import javax.resource.cci.*;
import javax.resource.spi.*;

public class ConnectionMetaDataImpl implements ConnectionMetaData {

    private ManagedConnectionImpl manConn;

    public ConnectionMetaDataImpl (ManagedConnectionImpl manConn) {
        this.manConn = manConn;
    }

    public String getEISProductName() throws ResourceException {
        return "Loan Application DLL";
    }

    public String getEISProductVersion() throws ResourceException {
        return "1.0";
    }

    public String getUserName() throws ResourceException {
        return null;
    }
}
```

Source 15.6 The ConnectionMetaDataImpl class.

ConnectionSpecImpl.java

Source 15.7 shows `ConnectionSpecImpl.java`, which implements the `javax.resource.cci.ConnectionSpec` client contract. This is the minimal implementation of `ConnectionSpec`, given that we do not support any connection request–specific properties. If we did support connection request–specific properties, then we would have to provide getters and setters for those properties.

```
package examples.integration.out_loan_ra;

import javax.resource.cci.*;

public class ConnectionSpecImpl implements ConnectionSpec {

    public ConnectionSpecImpl() {
    }
}
```

Source 15.7 The ConnectionSpecImpl class.

InteractionImpl.java

Source 15.8 shows `InteractionImpl.java`, which implements the `javax.resource.cci.Interaction` client contract.

```
package examples.integration.out_loan_ra;

import examples.jni.JavaLoanApp;

import java.util.*;
import javax.resource.ResourceException;
import javax.resource.spi.ConnectionEvent;
import javax.resource.spi.IllegalStateException;
import javax.resource.cci.*;
import java.lang.reflect.*;
import java.lang.*;

public class InteractionImpl implements Interaction {

    Connection conn = null;

    public InteractionImpl(Connection conn) {
        System.out.println("InteractionImpl(Connection conn) called");
        this.conn = conn;
    }

    public javax.resource.cci.Connection getConnection() {
        return conn;
    }

    public void close() throws ResourceException {
        conn = null;
    }

    public boolean execute (InteractionSpec iSpec, Record in, Record out)
```

Source 15.8 The InteractionImpl class. *(continued)*

```
throws ResourceException {
     System.out.println ("InteractionImpl.execute(InteractionSpec iSpec,
     Record in, Record out) called");

     out = exec((MappedRecord)in,(MappedRecord)out);

     if (out != null) {
          return true;
     } else {
          return false;
     }
}

public Record execute (InteractionSpec iSpec, Record in) throws
ResourceException
{
     System.out.println ("InteractionImpl.execute(InteractionSpec iSpec,
     Record in) called");

     MappedRecord out = new MappedRecordImpl();
     return exec((MappedRecord)in, out);
}

Record exec(MappedRecord in, MappedRecord out) throws ResourceException {
     try {
          System.out.println("InteractionImpl.exec(MappedRecord in,
          MappedRecord out) called");

          Set keys = in.keySet();
          Iterator iterator = keys.iterator();
          while (iterator.hasNext()) {
               String key = (String)iterator.next();
               if (key.equalsIgnoreCase("HomeEquityRate")) {
                    JavaLoanApp jlaObj = new
                    JavaLoanApp("C:\\LoanApp.dll");
                    float equityRate = jlaObj.getHomeEquityLoanRate();
                    System.out.println ("JNI Call Returned: " +
                    equityRate);
                    out.put(key, new Float(equityRate));
               }
          }
          return out;
     }
     catch(Exception e) {
          throw new ResourceException(e.getMessage());
     }
}

public ResourceWarning getWarnings() throws ResourceException {
     return null;
```

Source 15.8 *(continued)*

```
    }

    public void clearWarnings() throws ResourceException {
    }
}
```

Source 15.8 *(continued)*

This is the crux of `OutboundLoanRA`. `InteractionImpl` contains the logic required for communicating with the EIS. It is `InteractionImpl` that creates an instance of `JavaLoanApp` and calls its native method. Note the following about our implementation:

- We support both the `execute()` methods; the one that takes input and output records as well as the one which takes only input and returns output record.
- Both the `execute()` methods call the `exec()` method, which in turn takes the input `Record`, gets the name of the EIS function to execute, instantiates `JavaLoanApp`, and finally calls the `getHomeEquityLoanRate()` native method on `JavaLoanApp`. The result of this invocation is put into the output `Record` and returned to the client application component, which is `LoanRatesEJB` in this case.

MappedRecordImpl.java

Source 15.9 shows `MappedRecordImpl.java`, which implements the `javax.resource.cci.MappedRecord` client contract. `MappedRecordImpl` implements both the `java.util.Map` and `javax.resource.cci.Record` interfaces. Evidently implementing `MappedRecord` is fairly simple.

```
package examples.integration.out_loan_ra;

import java.util.*;

public class MappedRecordImpl implements javax.resource.cci.MappedRecord
{

    private String recordName;
    private String recordDescription;
    private HashMap mappedRecord;

    public MappedRecordImpl() {
        mappedRecord = new HashMap();
```

Source 15.9 The MappedRecordImpl class. *(continued)*

```
    }

    public MappedRecordImpl (String recordName) {
        mappedRecord = new HashMap();
        this.recordName = recordName;
    }

    public String getRecordName() {
        return this.recordName;
    }

    public void setRecordName(String recordName) {
        this.recordName = recordName;
    }

    public String getRecordShortDescription() {
        return recordDescription;
    }

    public void setRecordShortDescription(String recordDescription) {
        this.recordDescription = recordDescription;
    }

    public boolean equals(Object object) {
        if(!(object instanceof MappedRecordImpl))
            return false;

        MappedRecordImpl mappedRecordObject =
        (MappedRecordImpl)object;

        return (recordName == mappedRecordObject.recordName) &&
        mappedRecord.equals(mappedRecordObject.mappedRecord);
    }

    public int hashCode() {
        return (new String("MappedRecordImpl")).hashCode();
    }

    public Object clone() throws CloneNotSupportedException {
        return this.clone();
    }

    public void clear() {
        mappedRecord.clear();
    }

    public boolean containsKey(Object key) {
```

Source 15.9 *(continued)*

```
        return mappedRecord.containsKey(key);
    }

    public boolean containsValue(Object value) {
        return mappedRecord.containsValue(value);
    }

    public Set entrySet() {
        return mappedRecord.entrySet();
    }

    public Object get(Object object) {
        return mappedRecord.get(object);
    }

    public boolean isEmpty(){
        return mappedRecord.isEmpty();
    }

    public Set keySet(){
        return mappedRecord.keySet();
    }

    public Object put(Object key, Object value) {
        return mappedRecord.put(key, value);
    }

    public void putAll(Map map) {
        mappedRecord.putAll (map);
    }

    public Object remove(Object object) {
        return mappedRecord.remove(object);
    }

    public int size() {
        return mappedRecord.size();
    }

    public Collection values() {
        return mappedRecord.values();
    }
}
```

Source 15.9 *(continued)*

RecordFactoryImpl.java

Source 15.10 shows `RecordFactoryImpl.java`, which implements the `javax.resource.cci.RecordFactory` client contract. Since `OutboundLoanRA` supports only the `MappedRecord` client contract, we throw `NotSupportedException` if somebody tries to create an indexed record.

```
package examples.integration.out_loan_ra;

import javax.resource.cci.*;
import java.util.Map;
import java.util.Collection;
import javax.resource.ResourceException;
import javax.resource.NotSupportedException;

public class RecordFactoryImpl implements
javax.resource.cci.RecordFactory{

      public MappedRecord createMappedRecord(String recordName) throws
      ResourceException {
            return new MappedRecordImpl(recordName);
      }

      public IndexedRecord createIndexedRecord(String recordName) throws
      ResourceException {
            throw new NotSupportedException("IndexedRecords are not
            supported.");
      }
}
```

Source 15.10 The RecordFactoryImpl class.

ResourceAdapterMetaDataImpl.java

Source 15.11 shows `ResourceAdapterMetaDataImpl.java`. In our implementation of the `javax.resource.cci.ResourceAdapterMetaData` client contract, we provide not only general information about the RA but also information about specific capabilities of the RA such as the system contracts it supports.

```
package examples.integration.out_loan_ra;

import java.io.*;

import javax.resource.Referenceable;
import javax.resource.*;
```

Source 15.11 The ResourceAdapterMetaData class. *(continued)*

```
import javax.resource.spi.*;
import javax.naming.Reference;
import javax.resource.cci.*;

public class ResourceAdapterMetaDataImpl implements
ResourceAdapterMetaData {

     private String adapterName;
     private String adapterShortDescription;
     private String adapterVendorName;
     private String adapterVersion;
     private String[] interactionSpecsSupported;
     private String specVersion;
     private boolean supportsExecuteWithInputAndOutputRecord;
     private boolean supportsExecuteWithInputRecordOnly;
     private boolean supportsLocalTransactionDemarcation;

     // Additional properties
     private boolean supportsGlobalTransactions;
     private boolean supportsLifecycleManagement;
     private boolean supportsMessageInflow;
     private boolean supportsTransactionInflow;
     private boolean supportsConnectionManagement;
     private boolean supportsSecurityManagement;

     public ResourceAdapterMetaDataImpl() {
          adapterName = "Loan Application Resource Adapter";
          adapterShortDescription = "Loan Application Resource Adapter
          provides connectivity to Loan Application DLL";
          adapterVendorName = "Connectors Inc.";
          adapterVersion = "1.0";
          interactionSpecsSupported[0] = "InteractionImpl";
          specVersion = "1.5";
          supportsExecuteWithInputAndOutputRecord = true;
          supportsExecuteWithInputRecordOnly = true;
          supportsLocalTransactionDemarcation = false;
          supportsGlobalTransactions = false;
          supportsLifecycleManagement = false;
          supportsMessageInflow = false;
          supportsTransactionInflow = false;
          supportsConnectionManagement = true;
          supportsSecurityManagement = false;
     }

     public String getAdapterName() {
          return adapterName;
     }

     public String getAdapterShortDescription() {
```

Source 15.11 *(continued)*

```
        return adapterShortDescription;
    }

    public String getAdapterVendorName() {
        return adapterVendorName;
    }

    public String getAdapterVersion() {
        return adapterVersion;
    }

    public String[] getInteractionSpecsSupported() {
        return interactionSpecsSupported;
    }

    public String getSpecVersion() {
        return specVersion;
    }

    public boolean supportsExecuteWithInputAndOutputRecord() {
        return supportsExecuteWithInputAndOutputRecord;
    }

    public boolean supportsExecuteWithInputRecordOnly() {
        return supportsExecuteWithInputRecordOnly;
    }

    public boolean supportsLocalTransactionDemarcation() {
        return supportsLocalTransactionDemarcation;
    }

    public boolean supportsGlobalTransactions() {
        return supportsGlobalTransactions;
    }

    public boolean supportsLifecycleManagement() {
        return supportsLifecycleManagement;
    }

    public boolean supportsMessageInflow() {
        return supportsMessageInflow;
    }

    public boolean supportsTransactionInflow() {
        return supportsTransactionInflow;
    }

    public boolean supportsConnectionManagement() {
        return supportsConnectionManagement;
```

Source 15.11 *(continued)*

```
    }

    public boolean supportsSecurityManagement() {
        return supportsSecurityManagement;
    }
}
```

Source 15.11 *(continued)*

OutboundLoanRA System Contracts

Now let's examine the connection management–related system contracts for `OutboundLoanRA`. We implemented `javax.resource.spi.ManagedConnectionFactory`, `javax.resource.spi.ManagedConnection`, `javax.resource.spi.ConnectionRequestInfo`, and `javax.resource.spi.ManagedConnectionMetaData` system contracts for this example.

ManagedConnectionFactoryImpl.java

Source 15.12 shows `ManagedConnectionFactoryImpl.java`, which implements the `javax.resource.spi.ManagedConnectionFactory` system contract.

```
package examples.integration.out_loan_ra;

import java.io.*;
import java.util.*;

import javax.resource.*;
import javax.resource.spi.*;
import javax.resource.spi.security.PasswordCredential;
import javax.resource.spi.SecurityException;
import javax.security.auth.Subject;
import javax.naming.Context;
import javax.naming.InitialContext;

public class ManagedConnectionFactoryImpl implements ManagedConnectionFactory,
Serializable {

    private PrintWriter manConnLogWriter;

    public ManagedConnectionFactoryImpl() {
        System.out.println("ManagedConnectionFactoryImpl() called");
    }

    // This method is called by application server and is a hook for RA to
```

Source 15.12 The ManagedConnectionFactoryImpl class. *(continued)*

```
// to create the client-side connection factory interface instance.
// Application server passes an instance of ConnectionManager to this
// method, which is passed forward to the client-side connection factory
// instance. The connection factory instance on the client-side will use
// ConnectionManager to call allocateConnection().
public Object createConnectionFactory(ConnectionManager connManager) throws
ResourceException {
     System.out.println
     ("ManagedConnectionFactoryImpl.createConnectionFactory
     (ConnectionManager) called");

     return new ConnectionFactoryImpl(this, connManager);
}

// This method will never be called in a managed environment because
// in a managed environment application server is required to provide
// an implementation of ConnectionManager such that its
// allocateConnection() method provides all the QoS necessary. Hence,
// application server will never call this version of
// createConnectionFactory(). This method is part of
// ManagedConnectionFactory interface only to accommodate non-managed
// environments.
public Object createConnectionFactory() throws ResourceException {
     throw new ResourceException ("How can you call this method in a
     managed environment?");
}

// This method is called by application server to create an instance of
// ManagedConnection. It passes an instance of Subject representing
// authenticated user's principal in case of container-managed EIS sign-on.
// In case of component-managed EIS sign-on, application component can pass
// connection request properties including username/password (or other form
// of security credential information) through ConnectionSpec JavaBean
// when it calls getConnection() on ConnectionFactory. ConnectionFactory
// implementation will take ConnectionSpec property information and
// populate ConnectionRequestInfo JavaBean, and pass it down to application
// server as an argument to allocateConnection() on ConnectionManager. When
// application server calls createManagedConnection(), it passes this very
// instance of ConnectionRequestInfo so that ManagedConnectionFactory can
// get access to connection request properties, including security
// information.
public ManagedConnection createManagedConnection (Subject subject,
ConnectionRequestInfo connRequestInfo) {
     System.out.println
     ("ManagedConnectionFactoryImpl.createManagedConnection
     (Subject, ConnectionRequestInfo) called");

     return new ManagedConnectionImpl (this);
```

Source 15.12 *(continued)*

```
}

// This method is called by application server and is a hook for RA to
// implement the connection matching logic. If the EIS connection have
// connection properties, then the match logic should also compare the
// property values of ConnectionRequestInfo structure with those of
// the available connections to determine the correct match.
public ManagedConnection matchManagedConnections(Set connSet, Subject
subject, ConnectionRequestInfo connRequestInfo) throws ResourceException {
      System.out.println
      ("ManagedConnectionFactoryImpl.matchManagedConnections
      (Set, Subject, ConnectionRequestInfo) called");

      Iterator iterator = connSet.iterator();
      while (iterator.hasNext()) {
            Object object = iterator.next();
            if (object instanceof ManagedConnectionImpl) {
                  ManagedConnectionImpl manConn = (ManagedConnectionImpl)
                  object;
                  ManagedConnectionFactory manConnFactory =
                  manConn.getManagedConnectionFactory();

                  if (manConnFactory.equals(this)) {
                        System.out.println("From ManagedConnectionFactoryImpl.
                        matchManagedConnections() -> Connection matched");
                        return manConn;
                  }
            }
      }
      System.out.println("From ManagedConnectionFactoryImpl.
      matchManagedConnections() -> Connection did not match");

      return null;
}

public void setLogWriter(PrintWriter manConnLogWriter) {
      this.manConnLogWriter = manConnLogWriter;
}

public PrintWriter getLogWriter() {
      return manConnLogWriter;
}

public boolean equals(Object object) {
      if (object == null) return false;
      if (object instanceof ManagedConnectionFactoryImpl) {
           return true;
      } else {
           return false;
      }
```

Source 15.12 *(continued)*

```
    }

    public int hashCode() {
        return (new String("ManagedConnectionFactoryImpl")).hashCode();
    }
}
```

Source 15.12 *(continued)*

Note the following about our implementation:

- In the `createManagedConnection()` method, had we implemented the security system contract, we would have been required to get the caller principal credentials from the `Subject`, in case of container-managed EIS sign-on, or from the `ConnectionRequestInfo` JavaBean, in case of component-managed EIS sign-on.
- Had we used connection request–specific properties, in `matchManagedConnection()` method, we would have been required to match the properties as well as determine the matching connection from the pool.

ManagedConnectionImpl.java

Source 15.13 shows `ManagedConnectionImpl.java`, which implements the `javax.resource.spi.ManagedConnection` system contract.

```
package examples.integration.out_loan_ra;

import java.io.*;
import java.util.*;

import javax.resource.*;
import javax.resource.spi.*;
import javax.resource.spi.security.PasswordCredential;
import javax.resource.spi.IllegalStateException;
import javax.resource.spi.SecurityException;
import javax.resource.NotSupportedException;
import javax.security.auth.Subject;
import javax.transaction.xa.XAResource;

public class ManagedConnectionImpl implements ManagedConnection {

    private ConnectionEventListener connEventListener;
    private ManagedConnectionFactory manConnFactory;
    private boolean isDestroyed;
```

Source 15.13 The ManagedConnectionImpl class. *(continued)*

```
private PrintWriter manConnLogWriter;

// This method is called by createManagedConnection() of
// ManagedConnectionFactory.
ManagedConnectionImpl (ManagedConnectionFactory manConnFactory) {
     System.out.println("ManagedConnectionImpl(ManagedConnectionFactory)
     called");

     this.manConnFactory = manConnFactory;
}

// This method is called by application server to obtain the client-side
// connection handle for this physical connection. If you want to share
// a physical connection to the EIS among various clients, you can use
// caller security information represented in Subject or
// ConnectionRequestInfoobjects to authenticate each client that shares
// this physical connection to the backend EIS.
public Object getConnection(Subject subject, ConnectionRequestInfo
connectionRequestInfo) throws ResourceException {
     System.out.println("ManagedConnectionImpl.getConnection(Subject,
     ConnectionRequestInfo) called");

     ConnectionImpl conn = new ConnectionImpl(this);
     return conn;
}

// This method is called by application server to explicitly destroy the
// physical connection to the EIS.
public void destroy() throws ResourceException {
     System.out.println("ManagedConnectionImpl.destroy() called");

     isDestroyed=true;
     cleanup();
}

// The cleanup method is called by application server when it has to
// put the ManagedConnection instance back in pool. In this method's
// implementation you should release all the client-specific associated
// with ManagedConnection instance.
public void cleanup() throws ResourceException {
     System.out.println("ManagedConnectionImpl.cleanup() called");
}

// RA should implement this method if it supports physical connection
// sharing such that it can associate a different client-side connection
// handle with the Managedconnection instance. Application server will
// call this method based on its criteria of connection sharing.
public void associateConnection(Object connection) throws
ResourceException {
     throw new NotSupportedException
     ("ManagedConnectionImpl.associateConnection() not supported.");
```

Source 15.13 *(continued)*

```
}

 // Application server calls this method to associate
 // ConnectionEventListener object with this managed connection.
 public void addConnectionEventListener(ConnectionEventListener
 connEventListener){
      System.out.println("ManagedConnectionImpl.addConnectionEventListener
      (ConnectionEventListener) called");

      this.connEventListener = connEventListener;
}

public void removeConnectionEventListener (ConnectionEventListener
connEventListener) {}

public XAResource getXAResource() throws ResourceException {
      throw new NotSupportedException("Global transactions are not
      supported");
}

public LocalTransaction getLocalTransaction() throws ResourceException {
      throw new NotSupportedException("Local transactions are not
      supported");
}

public ManagedConnectionMetaData getMetaData() throws ResourceException {
      if (isDestroyed)
            throw new ResourceException ("Managed connection has already
            been closed.");

      return new ManagedConnectionMetaDataImpl (this);
}

public void setLogWriter(PrintWriter manConnLogWriter) {
      this.manConnLogWriter = manConnLogWriter;
}

public PrintWriter getLogWriter() {
      return manConnLogWriter;
}

// This method is implemented as part of private contract between RA and
// the client-side connection API, so that client-side connection can
// communicate with ManagedConnection instance various connection related
// events such as connection close, transaction begin / commit / rollback,
// and so on. Once we determine the type of client-side connection event,
// we call the appropriate method on ConnectionEventListener object to
// provide a hook to application server to add its own container services.
void sendEvent(int eventType, Exception e, Object connHandle) {
      System.out.println("ManagedConnectionImpl.sendEvent(int, e,
```

Source 15.13 *(continued)*

```
            connHandle) called");

            ConnectionEvent connEvent = null;
            if (e == null)
                connEvent = new ConnectionEvent(this, eventType);
            else
                connEvent = new ConnectionEvent(this, eventType, e);

            connEvent.setConnectionHandle(connHandle);
            switch (connEvent.getId()) {
                case ConnectionEvent.CONNECTION_CLOSED:
                     this.connEventListener.connectionClosed(connEvent);
                     break;
                case ConnectionEvent.LOCAL_TRANSACTION_STARTED:
                     this.connEventListener.localTransactionStarted(connEvent);
                     break;
                case ConnectionEvent.LOCAL_TRANSACTION_COMMITTED:
                     this.connEventListener.localTransactionCommitted(connEvent);
                     break;
                case ConnectionEvent.LOCAL_TRANSACTION_ROLLEDBACK:
                     this.connEventListener.localTransactionRolledback
                    (connEvent);
                     break;
                case ConnectionEvent.CONNECTION_ERROR_OCCURRED:
                     this.connEventListener.connectionErrorOccurred(connEvent);
                     break;
                default:
                     throw new IllegalArgumentException("Unsupported event: " +
                     connEvent.getId());
            }
        }

        ManagedConnectionFactory getManagedConnectionFactory() {
            return manConnFactory;
        }
    }
```

Source 15.13 *(continued)*

Note the following about our implementation of `ManagedConnection`:

- The application server registers a `ConnectionEventListener` with the `ManagedConnection` instance. We maintain this `ConnectionEventListener` for later use.
- We implement a `sendEvent()` method so that the client contract's connection implementation, `ConnectionImpl`, can notify the underlying managed connection instance when it is about to close the connection, and other such events. The `sendEvent()` method, in

turn, calls the appropriate event notification method such as `connectionClosed()`, `connectionErrorOccured()`, and so on, on the `ConnectionEventListener` object.

- Since we do not support transaction management system contract, calls to the `getXAResource()` or `getLocalTransaction()` methods throw `NotSupportedException`.
- We do not support the sharing of `ManagedConnection` instances among connection handles and, therefore, the `associateConnection()` implementation throws `NotSupportedException`.

ConnectionRequestInfoImpl.java

Source 15.14 shows `ConnectionRequestInfoImpl.java`, which implements the `javax.resource.spi.ConnectionRequestInfo` system contract. As can be seen, `ConnectionRequestInfoImpl` is a very simple implementation of `ConnectionRequestInfo`, since the RA does not have any connection request–specific properties.

```
package examples.integration.out_loan_ra;

import javax.resource.spi.ConnectionRequestInfo;

public class ConnectionRequestInfoImpl implements ConnectionRequestInfo
{
    public ConnectionRequestInfoImpl() {}

    public boolean equals(Object object) {
         if (object == null) return false;
         if (object instanceof ConnectionRequestInfoImpl) {
              return true;
         } else {
              return false;
         }
    }

    public int hashCode() {
         return (new String("ConnectionRequestInfoImpl")).hashCode();
    }
}
```

Source 15.14 The ConnectionRequestInfoImpl class.

ManagedConnectionMetaDataImpl.java

`ManagedConnectionMetaDataImpl` implements the `javax.resource.spi.ManagedConnectionMetaData` system contract. Since its implementation is quite similar to that of `ConnectionMetaData`, we will skip listing its source code.

Deploying OutboundLoanRA

During RA deployment, the deployer will specify the interface and implementation classes for various client and system contracts supported by the RA.

- **If the RA supports the connection management system contract**, then the deployer will have to provide interface and implementation classes for connection factory and connection. In our case, these will be `javax.resource.cci.ConnectionFactory/example.out_loan_ra.ConnectionFactoryImpl` and `javax.resource.cci.Connection/example_out_loan_ra.ConnectionImpl`, respectively. Also, the deployer will have to provide the implementation class for `ManagedConnectionFactory`, which is `ManagedConnectionFactoryImpl` in our case.

  If RA supports configuration properties for connection factories, that will be specified during deployment. In our case, we do not have any connection factory configuration properties.
- **If RA supports transaction management system contract**, the deployer will have to specify whether it supports local or global transactions.
- **If RA supports security management system contract**, you can also specify the authentication mechanism used during deployment.
- **If RA supports the message inflow contract**, the deployer will need to provide the message listener interface class and activation specification JavaBean class.
- **If RA supports message inflow or life cycle contract**, the deployer will need to specify the `ResourceAdapter` implementation class.

Apart from bundling the system and client contract classes, the deployer will also bundle the libraries that the RA uses to handle communication with EIS. For our example, this would be the `JavaLoanApp` Java class. Hence, we also bundle the `JavaLoanApp` class with `OutboundLoanRA`.

Also, if your RA loads native libraries or does socket communication, or any such activity that warrants explicit permissions, you must set the right runtime permissions for the application server's JVM instance. Since `OutboundLoanRA` uses a Java class that loads the system library, we will have to explicitly permit the underlying JVM instance to do so. One of the ways to achieve this is by directly modifying the `java.policy` file in `<JDK_HOME>/jre/lib/security` folder to grant runtime permission to load native libraries.

Once the RA is deployed, the deployer will create a connection pool and associate it with the RA's connection factory. The deployer will use vendor-provided administration tools for creating a connection pool. Finally, the deployer will bind the connection pool to JNDI so that client application components can retrieve the underlying connection factory instance from JNDI and create the connection to the EIS.

OutboundLoanRA Deployment Descriptor

Source 15.15 shows the standard deployment descriptor for `OutboundLoanRA`.

```
<?xml version='1.0' encoding='UTF-8'?> <connector
     xmlns="http://java.sun.com/xml/ns/j2ee"        version="1.5"
     xmlns:xsi="http://www.w3.org/2001/XMLSchema-instance"
     xsi:schemaLocation="http://java.sun.com/xml/ns/j2ee
     http://java.sun.com/xml/ns/j2ee/connector_1_5.xsd">

  <display-name>OutboundLoanRA</display-name>
  <vendor-name>Vendor Name</vendor-name>
  <eis-type>EIS Type</eis-type>
  <resourceadapter-version>1.5</resourceadapter-version>
  <license><license-required>false</license-required></license>
  <resourceadapter>
    <outbound-resourceadapter>
      <connection-definition>
        <managedconnectionfactory-class>
          examples.integration.out_loan_ra.ManagedConnectionFactoryImpl
        </managedconnectionfactory-class>
        <connectionfactory-interface>
          javax.resource.cci.ConnectionFactory
        </connectionfactory-interface>
        <connectionfactory-impl-class>
          examples.integration.out_loan_ra.ConnectionFactoryImpl
        </connectionfactory-impl-class>
        <connection-interface>
          javax.resource.cci.Connection
        </connection-interface>
        <connection-impl-class>
          examples.integration.out_loan_ra.ConnectionImpl
        </connection-impl-class>
      </connection-definition>
      <transaction-support>LocalTransaction</transaction-support>
      <reauthentication-support>false</reauthentication-support>
    </outbound-resourceadapter>
  </resourceadapter>
</connector>
```

Source 15.15 The ra.xml file.

Now that we have developed and deployed the RA as well as the RA connection pool and the JNDI resources associated with it, the RA is all set to receive requests from client application components, such as `LoanRatesEJB`.

LoanRatesEJB

`LoanRatesEJB` is a stateless session bean that uses `OutboundLoanRA` to communicate with the back-end loan processing application, `LoanApp.dll`.

Developing LoanRatesEJB

LoanRatesEJB's business interface has a single method, `getHomeEquityRate()`. The `getHomeEquityRate()` method implementation uses the CCI client contracts supported by `OutboundLoanRA`. Source 15.16 is a listing of the `LoanRatesEJB` bean class, `LoanRatesBean.java`.

```
package examples.integration.loanratesejb;

import javax.resource.cci.*;

import javax.ejb.Stateless;
import javax.ejb.Remote;
import javax.ejb.TransactionManagement;
import javax.ejb.TransactionManagementType;
import javax.annotation.*;

@Stateless
@Remote(LoanRates.class)
@TransactionManagement(TransactionManagementType.BEAN)
public class LoanRatesBean implements LoanRates{

    @Resource (name="OutboundLoanJNDIName")
    public javax.resource.cci.ConnectionFactory connFactory;

    public float getHomeEquityRate() {
        float retVal=0;

        System.out.println("LoanRatesBean.getHomeEquityRate()
        called");

        try {
            javax.resource.cci.Connection myCon =
            connFactory.getConnection();
            javax.resource.cci.Interaction interaction =
            myCon.createInteraction();
            javax.resource.cci.MappedRecord recordIn =
```

Source 15.16 The LoanRatesBean class. *(continued)*

```
                connFactory.getRecordFactory().createMappedRecord("");

                recordIn.put("HomeEquityRate","");

                javax.resource.cci.MappedRecord recordOut =
                (javax.resource.cci.MappedRecord) interaction.execute
                (null, (javax.resource.cci.Record)recordIn);

                myCon.close();

                Object result = recordOut.get("HomeEquityRate");
                retVal = ((Float)result).floatValue();

            } catch(Exception e) {

                e.printStackTrace();
            }

            return retVal;
        }
    }
```

Source 15.16 *(continued)*

Note that we are using the `@Resource` annotation to get hold of the resource connection factory via the resource injection mechanism. We have no use for a deployment descriptor in this example, since all the deployment information is supplied in the bean class, using annotations.

LoanRatesClient

`LoanRatesClient` standalone Java application is a client to `LoanRatesEJB`. Like a typical EJB client, it looks up the EJB business interface object and invokes the `getHomeEquityRate()` method once it has reference to the business interface object. Source 15.17 shows `LoanRatesClient.java`.

```
package examples.integration.loanratesejb;

import javax.naming.Context;
```

Source 15.17 The LoanRatesClient class.

```
import javax.naming.InitialContext;

public class LoanRatesClient {

    public static void main(String[] args) throws Exception{

                Context ctx = new InitialContext();

                LoanRates loanRates = (LoanRates)
                ctx.lookup("examples.integration.loanratesejb.LoanRates");

                System.out.println("getHomeEquityRate() returned: " +
                loanRates.getHomeEquityRate() + ". Take a look at
                application server log or console for messages from
                LoanRatesEJB and OutboundLoanRA.");
    }
}
```

Source 15.17 *(continued)*

Running the Client

To run the client, look at the Ant scripts bundled along with this example. The following is the client-side output you would get upon running the LoanRatesClient.

```
C:\MEJB4.0\src\examples\integration>asant run_client
Buildfile: build.xml

build_cpath:

init_common:

setup_env:

run_client:
     [java] Mar 24, 2006 3:32:14 PM
com.sun.corba.ee.spi.logging.LogWrapperBasedoLog
     [java] INFO: "IOP00710299: (INTERNAL) Successfully created IIOP
listener on the specified host/port: all interfaces/2090"
     [java] getHomeEquityRate() returned: 5.64. Take a look at
application server log or console for messages from LoanRatesEJB and
OutboundLoanRA.

BUILD SUCCESSFUL
Total time: 6 seconds
```

On the application server side, you can find out about the goings on by running your application server in verbose mode or by looking into the `server.log` file. For Java EE 5 reference implementation, you can find this file under the `<Java EE 5 Install Directory>/domains/domain1/logs` directory. Note that this output is for Java EE 5 reference implementation.

```
[#|2006-03-24T15:32:16.346-0500|INFO|sun-appserver-pe9.0|javax
.enterprise.system.stream.out|_ThreadID=17;_ThreadName=p: thread-pool-1;
w: 12;|LoanRatesBean.getHomeEquityRate() called|#]

[#|2006-03-24T15:32:16.346-0500|INFO|sun-appserver-pe9.0|javax
.enterprise.system.stream.out|_ThreadID=17;_ThreadName=p: thread-pool-1;
w: 12;|ConnectionFactoryImpl.getConnection() called|#]

[#|2006-03-24T15:32:16.366-0500|INFO|sun-appserver-pe9.0|javax
.enterprise.system.stream.out|_ThreadID=17;_ThreadName=p: thread-pool-1;
w: 12;|ManagedConnectionFactoryImpl.createManagedConnection (Subject,
ConnectionRequestInfo) called|#]

[#|2006-03-24T15:32:16.366-0500|INFO|sun-appserver-pe9.0|javax
.enterprise.system.stream.out|_ThreadID=17;_ThreadName=p: thread-pool-1;
w: 12;|ManagedConnectionImpl(ManagedConnectionFactory) called|#]

[#|2006-03-24T15:32:16.376-0500|INFO|sun-appserver-pe9.0|javax
.enterprise.system.stream.out|_ThreadID=17;_ThreadName=p: thread-pool-1;
w: 12;|ManagedConnectionImpl.addConnectionEventListener
(ConnectionEventListener) called|#]

[#|2006-03-24T15:32:16.386-0500|INFO|sun-appserver-pe9.0|javax
.enterprise.system.stream.out|_ThreadID=17;_ThreadName=p: thread-pool-1;
w: 12;|ManagedConnectionFactoryImpl.createManagedConnection (Subject,
ConnectionRequestInfo) called|#]

[#|2006-03-24T15:32:16.386-0500|INFO|sun-appserver-pe9.0|javax
.enterprise.system.stream.out|_ThreadID=17;_ThreadName=p: thread-pool-1;
w: 12;|ManagedConnectionImpl(ManagedConnectionFactory) called|#]

[#|2006-03-24T15:32:16.386-0500|INFO|sun-appserver-pe9.0|javax
.enterprise.system.stream.out|_ThreadID=17;_ThreadName=p: thread-pool-1;
w: 12;|ManagedConnectionImpl.addConnectionEventListener
(ConnectionEventListener) called|#]

[#|2006-03-24T15:32:16.386-0500|INFO|sun-appserver-pe9.0|javax
.enterprise.system.stream.out|_ThreadID=17;_ThreadName=p: thread-pool-1;
w: 12;|ManagedConnectionFactoryImpl.createManagedConnection (Subject,
ConnectionRequestInfo) called|#]

[#|2006-03-24T15:32:16.386-0500|INFO|sun-appserver-pe9.0|javax
.enterprise.system.stream.out|_ThreadID=17;_ThreadName=p: thread-pool-1;
```

```
w: 12;|ManagedConnectionImpl(ManagedConnectionFactory) called|#]

[#|2006-03-24T15:32:16.386-0500|INFO|sun-appserver-
pe9.0|javax.enterprise.system.stream.out|_ThreadID=17;_ThreadName=p:
thread-pool-1; w:
12;|ManagedConnectionImpl.addConnectionEventListener(ConnectionEventList
ener) called|#]

[#|2006-03-24T15:32:16.386-0500|INFO|sun-appserver-
pe9.0|javax.enterprise.system.stream.out|_ThreadID=17;_ThreadName=p:
thread-pool-1; w:
12;|ManagedConnectionFactoryImpl.createManagedConnection (Subject,
ConnectionRequestInfo) called|#]

[#|2006-03-24T15:32:16.386-0500|INFO|sun-appserver-
pe9.0|javax.enterprise.system.stream.out|_ThreadID=17;_ThreadName=p:
thread-pool-1; w: 12;|ManagedConnectionImpl(ManagedConnectionFactory)
called|#]

[#|2006-03-24T15:32:16.386-0500|INFO|sun-appserver-
pe9.0|javax.enterprise.system.stream.out|_ThreadID=17;_ThreadName=p:
thread-pool-1; w:
12;|ManagedConnectionImpl.addConnectionEventListener(ConnectionEventList
ener) called|#]

[#|2006-03-24T15:32:16.386-0500|INFO|sun-appserver-
pe9.0|javax.enterprise.system.stream.out|_ThreadID=17;_ThreadName=p:
thread-pool-1; w:
12;|ManagedConnectionFactoryImpl.createManagedConnection (Subject,
ConnectionRequestInfo) called|#]

[#|2006-03-24T15:32:16.386-0500|INFO|sun-appserver-
pe9.0|javax.enterprise.system.stream.out|_ThreadID=17;_ThreadName=p:
thread-pool-1; w: 12;|ManagedConnectionImpl(ManagedConnectionFactory)
called|#]

[#|2006-03-24T15:32:16.386-0500|INFO|sun-appserver-
pe9.0|javax.enterprise.system.stream.out|_ThreadID=17;_ThreadName=p:
thread-pool-1; w:
12;|ManagedConnectionImpl.addConnectionEventListener(ConnectionEventList
ener) called|#]

[#|2006-03-24T15:32:16.386-0500|INFO|sun-appserver-
pe9.0|javax.enterprise.system.stream.out|_ThreadID=17;_ThreadName=p:
thread-pool-1; w:
12;|ManagedConnectionFactoryImpl.createManagedConnection (Subject,
ConnectionRequestInfo) called|#]

[#|2006-03-24T15:32:16.386-0500|INFO|sun-appserver-pe9.0|javax
.enterprise.system.stream.out|_ThreadID=17;_ThreadName=p: thread-pool-1;
```

```
w: 12;|ManagedConnectionImpl(ManagedConnectionFactory) called|#]

[#|2006-03-24T15:32:16.386-0500|INFO|sun-appserver-pe9.0|javax
.enterprise.system.stream.out|_ThreadID=17;_ThreadName=p: thread-pool-1;
w: 12;|ManagedConnectionImpl.addConnectionEventListener
(ConnectionEventListener) called|#]

[#|2006-03-24T15:32:16.386-0500|INFO|sun-appserver-pe9.0|javax
.enterprise.system.stream.out|_ThreadID=17;_ThreadName=p: thread-pool-1;
w: 12;|ManagedConnectionFactoryImpl.createManagedConnection (Subject,
ConnectionRequestInfo) called|#]

[#|2006-03-24T15:32:16.386-0500|INFO|sun-appserver-pe9.0|javax
.enterprise.system.stream.out|_ThreadID=17;_ThreadName=p: thread-pool-1;
w: 12;|ManagedConnectionImpl(ManagedConnectionFactory) called|#]

[#|2006-03-24T15:32:16.386-0500|INFO|sun-appserver-pe9.0|javax
.enterprise.system.stream.out|_ThreadID=17;_ThreadName=p: thread-pool-1;
w: 12;|ManagedConnectionImpl.addConnectionEventListener
(ConnectionEventListener) called|#]

[#|2006-03-24T15:32:16.386-0500|INFO|sun-appserver-pe9.0|javax
.enterprise.system.stream.out|_ThreadID=17;_ThreadName=p: thread-pool-1;
w: 12;|ManagedConnectionFactoryImpl.createManagedConnection (Subject,
ConnectionRequestInfo) called|#]

[#|2006-03-24T15:32:16.397-0500|INFO|sun-appserver-pe9.0|javax
.enterprise.system.stream.out|_ThreadID=17;_ThreadName=p: thread-pool-1;
w: 12;|ManagedConnectionImpl(ManagedConnectionFactory) called|#]

[#|2006-03-24T15:32:16.397-0500|INFO|sun-appserver-pe9.0|javax
.enterprise.system.stream.out|_ThreadID=17;_ThreadName=p: thread-pool-1;
w: 12;|ManagedConnectionImpl.addConnectionEventListener
(ConnectionEventListener) called|#]

[#|2006-03-24T15:32:16.397-0500|INFO|sun-appserver-pe9.0|javax
.enterprise.system.stream.out|_ThreadID=17;_ThreadName=p: thread-pool-1;
w: 12;|ManagedConnectionFactoryImpl.matchManagedConnections(Set,
Subject, ConnectionRequestInfo) called|#]

[#|2006-03-24T15:32:16.397-0500|INFO|sun-appserver-pe9.0|javax
.enterprise.system.stream.out|_ThreadID=17;_ThreadName=p: thread-pool-1;
w: 12;|From ManagedConnectionFactoryImpl.matchManagedConnections() ->
Connection matched|#]

[#|2006-03-24T15:32:16.397-0500|INFO|sun-appserver-pe9.0|javax
.enterprise.system.stream.out|_ThreadID=17;_ThreadName=p: thread-pool-1;
```

```
w: 12;|ManagedConnectionImpl.getConnection(Subject,
ConnectionRequestInfo) called|#]

[#|2006-03-24T15:32:16.417-0500|INFO|sun-appserver-pe9.0|javax
.enterprise.system.stream.out|_ThreadID=17;_ThreadName=p: thread-pool-1;
w: 12;|ConnectionImpl(ManagedConnectionImpl) called|#]

[#|2006-03-24T15:32:16.427-0500|INFO|sun-appserver-pe9.0|javax
.enterprise.system.stream.out|_ThreadID=17;_ThreadName=p: thread-pool-1;
w: 12;|InteractionImpl(Connection conn) called|#]

[#|2006-03-24T15:32:16.437-0500|INFO|sun-appserver-pe9.0|javax
.enterprise.system.stream.out|_ThreadID=17;_ThreadName=p: thread-pool-1;
w: 12;|InteractionImpl.execute(InteractionSpec iSpec, Record in)
called|#]

[#|2006-03-24T15:32:16.437-0500|INFO|sun-appserver-pe9.0|javax
.enterprise.system.stream.out|_ThreadID=17;_ThreadName=p: thread-pool-1;
w: 12;|InteractionImpl.exec(MappedRecord in, MappedRecord out) called|#]

[#|2006-03-24T15:32:16.467-0500|INFO|sun-appserver-pe9.0|javax
.enterprise.system.stream.out|_ThreadID=17;_ThreadName=p: thread-pool-1;
w: 12;|JNI Call Returned: 5.64|#]

[#|2006-03-24T15:32:16.467-0500|INFO|sun-appserver-pe9.0|javax
.enterprise.system.stream.out|_ThreadID=17;_ThreadName=p: thread-pool-1;
w: 12;|ConnectionImpl.close() called|#]

[#|2006-03-24T15:32:16.467-0500|INFO|sun-appserver-pe9.0|javax
.enterprise.system.stream.out|_ThreadID=17;_ThreadName=p: thread-pool-1;
w: 12;|ManagedConnectionImpl.sendEvent(int, e, connHandle) called|#]

[#|2006-03-24T15:32:16.467-0500|INFO|sun-appserver-pe9.0|javax
.enterprise.system.stream.out|_ThreadID=17;_ThreadName=p: thread-pool-1;
w: 12;|ManagedConnectionImpl.cleanup() called|#]
```

Carefully study the output above. This will further clear up the sequence of interactions among various objects in our integration solution. Take a look at the highlighted portions in the text. As you can see, the container creates eight instances of `ManagedConnection the first time you run` `LoanRatesClient`. These instances are maintained in the pool to service subsequent requests. Obviously, the next time you run `LoanRatesClient`, the instances will not be created again. Instead, a `ManagedConnection` instance from the pool will be assigned to service the request. You can change the size of the resource adapter's connection pool by modifying the vendor specific deployment descriptor. For Java EE 5 reference implementation, this file is `sun-ra.xml`.

Extending OutboundLoanRA

Before ending our discussion of the example application, let's briefly go through possible extensions to OutboundLoanRA.

Implementing additional system contracts can certainly augment the current capabilities of OutboundLoanRA. A good starting point for this exercise will be to add security management. Try component-managed EIS sign-on. LoanApp.dll currently does not authenticate access. However, you can improve LoanApp.dll by adding a signOn() native method. The signOn() method implementation could be as simple as logging the user name/password security credentials received from the client. At the RA end, you will be required to implement the ConnectionSpec and ConnectionRequestInfo JavaBeans so that they reflect the user name/password connection properties.

Another possible extension could be to augment the current outbound connection management contract of OutboundLoanRA with the inbound messaging contract. Imagine a scenario in which a user submits a loan application to our loan-processing application. Since it can take days to make a decision on loan application, we want our loan application to send a message to the RA when the loan approval decision is ready. This could be done very simply: The loan application can create a simple text file containing the loan approval decision, in a file system location that is continuously monitored by the RA. The RA will pick up the loan approval decision's text file, parse it, and create an examples.integration.out_loan_ra.LoanApprovalMessage instance. Finally, it sends this message to the endpoint that implements examples.integration.out_loan_ra.LoanApprovalMessageListener within application server. You can extend this one step further by allowing the RA to do file system monitoring with the help of a Work instance!

Integration Best Practice: When to Use Which Technology

Now that you know all the technologies for integrating EJB applications, the question is how to decide which one to use in a given scenario. The following guidelines should help you determine the right technology for your application integration problem on the EJB platform.

When to Use JMS and JMS-Based MDB

Java Message Service is a Java abstraction to MOM systems. All application servers support a JMS service that listens to a messaging provider (an RA, actually) and delivers messages from the messaging provider to JMS messaging endpoints a.k.a. JMS-based MDB. Decoupled communication along with reliable and asynchronous messaging forms the basis of this approach.

Use JMS and JMS-based MDB for application integration when:

- You are integrating Java application endpoints; for example, consider a scenario where a Java application wants to integrate with your EJB application in an asynchronous yet reliable manner. Here, your Java application can simply create and send a JMS message to the MDB, and it is all set.
- You are integrating non-real-time applications—for example, processing inventory and shipping or communication with suppliers.
- You need reliability and transaction support for integrating application endpoints.

The only disadvantage to this approach is that because JMS does not define a wire protocol, out-of-the-box integration across various JMS products is difficult and almost impossible without using MOM bridges. As a result, if your scenario involves using different JMS products, this approach might not work without using a bridge to translate your JMS product's protocol to that of the target application endpoint's JMS product protocol.

When to Use Java EE Connectors

Use Java EE connectors for application integration when:

- You want to integrate with back-end EIS applications without modifying them.
- Quality of service is a prerequisite for integration. For example, if you need transactional and secure access to the EIS, connectors can be the way to go. If you want the application server to pool your outbound connections, connector architecture can enable that. Again, if you want the application server to host message endpoints so that they can consume messages from your EIS, connector architecture is the answer.
- You are integrating with a widely used EIS because you are likely to find off-the-shelf connectors for most of these. This greatly reduces the time it takes to integrate with the EIS.

When to Use Java Web Services

Web services are becoming a predominant choice for application integration, both within and outside the enterprise boundaries. The main reason behind this is the ubiquitous support for Web services protocols found in most of the modern programming platforms and languages. The interoperability guidelines from organizations such as Web Services Interoperability (WS-I) further increase the applicability of Web services in integration space.

Think of using Web services when:

- You need to quickly integrate application endpoints.
- The target applications for integration exist on disparate platforms.
- The target application endpoints are deployed behind the demilitarized zone (DMZ), thereby requiring access through the firewalls.

Web services provide a quick fix to the integration problem. However, they are far from providing a robust solution for integration because of the lack of quality of service support in the Web services protocols. The good news is that industry is working hard to define security, transactions, and other such semantics for Web services.

Summary

In this chapter, we introduced integration and presented an overview of various styles of integration. You learned how Java EE connectors provide an excellent framework for integrating EJB with non-IIOP applications. You then learned various best practices related to choosing appropriate technology for application integration on the EJB platform.

In the next chapter, you learn about various clustering techniques you can implement in the enterprise Java applications.

CHAPTER

16

Clustering

In this chapter, we'll talk about *clustering* technology, which addresses many of the challenges faced by large, high-capacity systems. This chapter first explores many issues relating to EJB and large systems. After providing you with a broad understanding of these issues we'll look at solutions.

Specifically, we'll cover the following topics:

- Approaches and characteristics of large-scale systems with Java EE application servers
- How clustering addresses the requirements of large-scale systems
- Approaches to instrumenting clustered EJBs
- Issues related to designing clustered EJB systems
- Issues that impact EJB performance in a clustered system

Overview of Large-Scale Systems

The number of systems being developed is rapidly increasing year after year. Some of these systems are small, targeted at a specific, well-defined user group that is understood when development of the system begins. Other systems are large, targeted at a diverse, massive user group that evolves over time. Given the variety of systems that can be designed, what makes a system large-scale? And, more importantly, how can EJB technology operate in a large-scale system?

This section discusses some of the principles behind large systems and defines terminology that will be used throughout the chapter.

What Is a Large-Scale System?

Unfortunately, there is no complete computer science definition of a large-scale system. Since requirements for systems vary wildly, what may be considered large for one project is insignificant for another project. For example, we will not consider system size in terms of function points, number of components or interfaces, or lines of code. Rather, our focus here is on operational characteristics. Let's just enumerate the most important and obvious ones.

A large-scale system typically:

- Has many users, potentially in many different places
- Is long-running, that is, required to be "always up"
- Processes large numbers of transactions per second
- May see increases in both its user population and system load
- Represents considerable business value
- Is operated and managed by multiple persons

For example, think of a worldwide online store that needs to accommodate a growing number of customers and transactions, or an air traffic control system that needs to handle more flights every year.

Essential requirements on large-scale systems are often summarized by the following three properties (collectively called RAS):

- **Reliability** gauges whether the system performs consistently as expected. A completely reliable system works 100% of the time according to its specification. In theory, this means it has no errors in any of its components that would impact its functionality or performance. This is a little too ambitious for any practical system, so you should think of a reliable system as one that can perform predictably even in the presence of faults. Fault tolerance is one aspect of a reliable system.
- **Availability** measures the percentage of time that your system is available for use by its clients. Availability is not related to the effectiveness of servicing those requests; rather, it focuses on whether the services are accessible at all. A system may be unavailable for a variety of reasons, such as network blockage, network latency, maintenance downtimes, or total system failure.

A popular way of saying how available a system is to its clients is to count the number of nines in the percentage figure: A system has an availability of five nines if it is available 99.999 percent of the time, whereas four nines means 99.99 percent of the time. With four nines, a system is unavailable no more than 52 minutes throughout the year (considering 24-hour operations). This time is reduced to just 5 minutes with five nines. How many restarts of your application server can you perform in this time?

- **Serviceability** measures how manageable your system is. System management occurs at a variety of levels, including runtime monitoring, configuration, maintenance, upgrades, and so on. Indirectly, high serviceability can improve availability: If it is easy to upgrade a running system to a new software version with fewer bugs and security holes, then there is a better chance that administrators will actually upgrade it even before an outage occurs. Consequently, that system will be more available.

Another requirement for large systems that is not explicitly covered by RAS is *scalability*.

- **Scalability** measures how easily a system can be adapted to increasing load, typically by adding extra resources such as CPUs, memory, communication lines, and so on. It is highly unlikely that system designers can estimate the exact load that a long-running system may need to handle, say, three years after its installation, so being able to scale it is an essential requirement.

NOTE **Many organizations fail to estimate the load that their systems will require and so design their system with only small-scale characteristics in mind. While current project schedules may not leave room for planning far into the future, we recommend that you always assume that you will need a large-scale system eventually. With this in mind, you should anticipate ways of scaling up the system and always have a path to follow if your user load increases, due to future business forces that may be out of your control.**

Clustering addresses many of the issues faced by large-scale systems at the same time. A cluster is a loosely coupled group of servers that provide unified services to their clients. Clients that use services deployed into a cluster are typically unaware that their requests are being serviced by a cluster and typically have no control over deciding which servers in the cluster process their requests. Requests are transparently directed to a node in the cluster that can handle the request. The client's view of the cluster is a single, simple system, not a group of collaborating servers. This is often referred to as a *single-system view* or *single-system image*. Servers in a cluster may operate on one or more computers, each of which may have one or more processors. These computers are also called *nodes*.

Clustering can be a very involved technology, potentially encompassing group communication and replication protocols, and network components such as load balancers and traffic redirectors at different layers in the protocol stack. Most commercial and open source Java EE application servers support some form of clustering, but how it is set up and used is highly vendor-dependent because clustering features are out of scope of the Java EE specifications proper.

Figure 16.1 shows a cluster with a client that is unaware of the cluster and addresses it as if it were a single server. The request is delivered to one of the servers in the cluster. The figure does not depict how the request is actually routed, or if any load balancing or replication is performed in the cluster.

The principle behind clustering is that of *redundancy*. If you have many redundant copies of a resource you can spread the load between them. At the same time, redundant resources enable you to lose one or more and still be able to operate. Clustering is the prime technology used to provide redundancy. With this in mind, let's reexamine the RAS and scalability requirements and see how they are impacted by clustering.

- **Reliability.** For every component added to a system, the number of scenarios that can cause a disruption in reliable service increases. This makes reliability of the overall system harder to ensure. Adding *redundant* components that remove single points of failure, however, can improve reliability because it allows failures to be masked.
- **Availability.** If the probability of a single server being unavailable is $1/m$, the probability that the server will be available is $1 - 1/m$. If there are n application servers in a cluster, the probability that all of them are unavailable at the same time is $(1 - 1/m)n$. The value of $(1 - 1/m)n$ decreases as n increases. If these servers are truly redundant, then the overall availability is $1 - (1 - 1/m)n$, implying that a cluster will always be more available than a single server.

  The calculation that we just sketched assumes that one server in the cluster is as good as any other, and that any server can take over processing from a failing partner in the cluster at any time. We will explain some of this in a little more detail later in this chapter.
- **Serviceability.** The principle of serviceability states that two application servers are more complex to service than a single application server. This implies that a cluster is inherently more difficult to service than a nonclustered system. (This holds true even when you consider that a

cluster may provide you with a chance for hot upgrades that a single server may not have at all. In this case, your cluster is still more complex to service, but you gain availability.)

- **Scalability.** The principle of scalability states that a system that lets you add more resources than another system, and lets you do this more cost-effectively, is more scalable. This is one of the strong points of clustering: First, it is cheaper to build (and extend!) a cluster using standard hardware than to rely on multiprocessor machines. This may not be immediately obvious considering that multiprocessors PCs are inexpensive these days, but these do not normally go beyond 4 CPUs. If your load increases beyond that point, clustering becomes the cheaper option. Second, extending a cluster by adding extra servers can be done during operation and hence is less disruptive than plugging in another CPU board. In both situations, a cluster is more scalable.

  Note that for a cluster to scale well, there must be a way to actually share the load. Nothing would be gained if we added resources that did not get used. Hence, a load-balancing mechanism must be employed to actually distribute the load between the servers in the cluster.

An important take-away point of the preceding discussion is that a cluster does not optimize all four requirements and is clearly not the optimal choice under all circumstances. As we saw, *increasing the availability of a system impacts its serviceability.* It is important to appreciate that there is no such thing as a perfect system. Any system that has a high level of availability will likely not have a high level of serviceability. You just need to be aware of the trade-offs.

Load Balancing and Failover

As we saw, the main application areas for clustering are scalability and high availability.

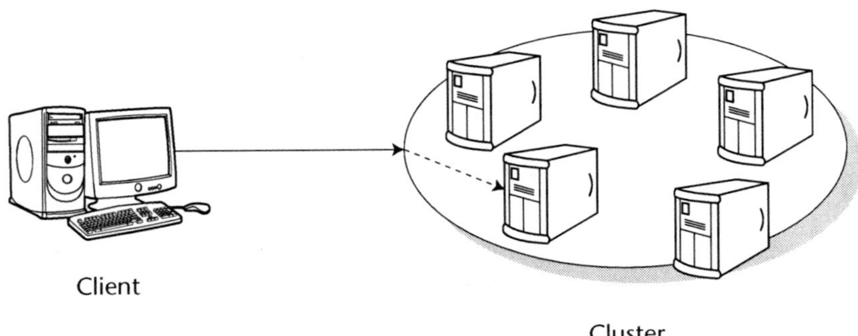

Figure 16.1 Cluster.

For a cluster to enhance scalability, it must provide some form of load balancing so that the additional resources provided by the cluster are utilized. Load balancing means distributing the requests among cluster nodes to optimize the performance of the whole system. Figure 16.2 illustrates a cluster with a load balancer that distributes requests from different clients to different nodes in the cluster.

The algorithm that the load balancer uses to decide which target node to pick for a request can be systematic (such as plain or weighted round robin) or random. Alternatively, the load balancer could try to monitor the load on the different nodes in the cluster and pick a node that appears less loaded than the others. Available load balancers range from dedicated hardware appliances to software plug-in modules for Web or application servers.

Java EE load balancing can occur in different either the Web or the EJB tiers, or even in both tiers. We will take a closer look at load balancing different EJBs later in this chapter. An important feature for Web load balancers is *session stickiness*. Session stickiness means that all requests in a client's session are directed to the same server. In many Web applications, session state needs to be kept between invocations from a client. If the client's next request went to a different server, that session state would simply be missing, and the application could not function correctly.

Note that a pure load-balancing cluster does not make any provisions to deal with failure: when the server that a client interacts with fails, the client will notice that and may need to start over. While this sounds unattractive at first, it means load balancing can be simple and efficient, especially if no application state is shared between the nodes in the cluster.

For a cluster to provide higher availability to clients than a single server, the cluster must be able to failover from a primary server to another, secondary server when failures occur. This is shown in Figure 16.3, where a *dispatcher* or *traffic redirector* component forwards requests to servers and detects failures.

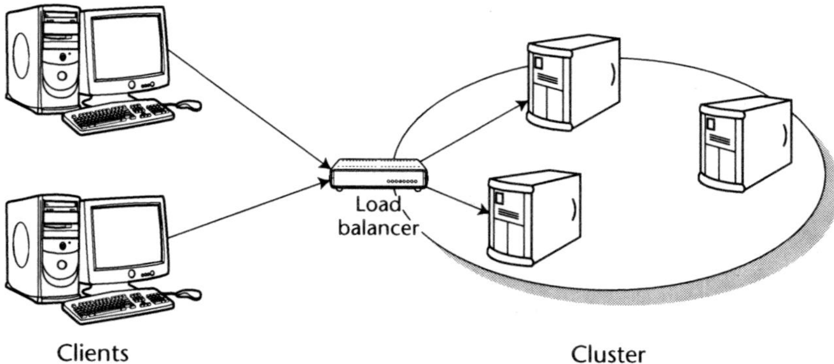

Figure 16.2 Load-balancing cluster.

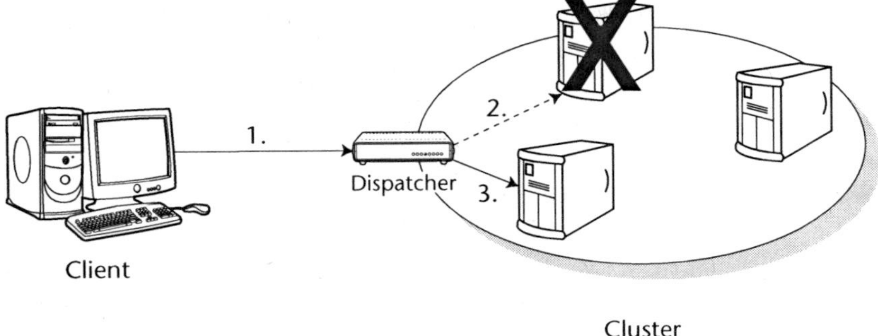

Figure 16.3 Failover in a cluster.

Here, the dispatcher finds that the primary server cannot be reached in step 2, possibly due to a machine failure or network problems. Transparently to the client, the request is redirected to another, secondary server.

Failover in either the Web or the EJB tier can take on one of two forms:

- **Request-level failover.** Request-level failover occurs when a request that is directed to one node for servicing cannot be serviced and is subsequently redirected to another node.
- **Session failover.** If session state is shared between clients and servers, request-level failover may not be sufficient to continue operations. In this case, the session state must also be reconstructed at the server node.

For failover to work seamlessly, the client needs to see the same application state and perhaps even session state after failover. This implies that this state is somehow made available in the cluster. The mechanism that is used to make this happen is *replication,* that is, primary servers backup their application state and session state during normal operation by copying it somewhere, for example to a central database, to one or more secondary servers, or even to all servers in the cluster. Existing approaches differ in exactly where and how servers perform replication. A typical approach is to rely on group communication protocols based on IP multicast internally. Note that replication is required repeatedly to keep backups in synch with the primary server's session.

The load-balancing and failover concepts that we just discussed were presented separately for clarity. In practice, you will find that clusters frequently offer both functions at the same time and in the same components. For example, the dispatcher will often also be able to offer load-balancing functionality. However, we encourage you to also examine your clustering requirements separately and choose the right size of the solution for your needs. High availability based on replication is technically challenging and requires runtime operations that can cause significant processing overhead and network traffic.

NOTE **Load balancing and failover logic doesn't exist for local interfaces. Remember that local interfaces do not receive traffic from the network. Parameters must be marshaled by reference rather than by value serialization. If the client is local to the bean, then any failure of either component will likely cause the other to fail, too. Nothing can be done to save such a situation. Thus, our discussion applies only to remote clients.**

Clustering with Collocated or Distributed Java EE Containers

Before going into the details of clustering technologies, let's look at the different choices you have for setting up servers in a Java EE system.

Java EE servers contain a Web container and an EJB container. This means that in a Web-based system, the following configurations are possible:

- **A collocated architecture** runs the Web server components (servlets and JSP files) and application server components (EJBs) on the same machine.
- **A distributed architecture** separates the Web server components and application server components on different physical machines.

The differences between clustering the two architectures and the request flows are shown in Figures 16.4 and 16.5.

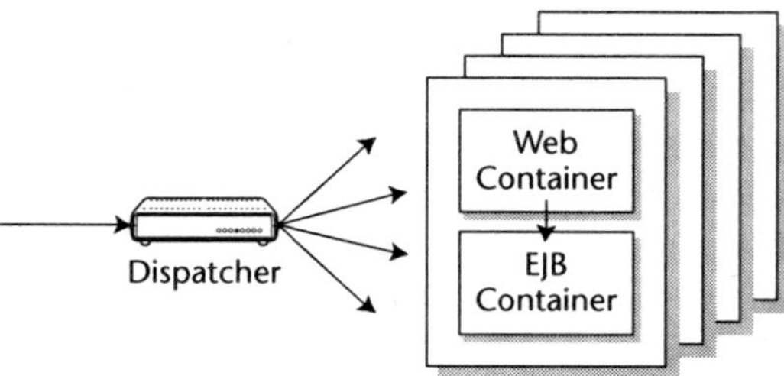

Figure 16.4 Clustered servers with collocated containers.

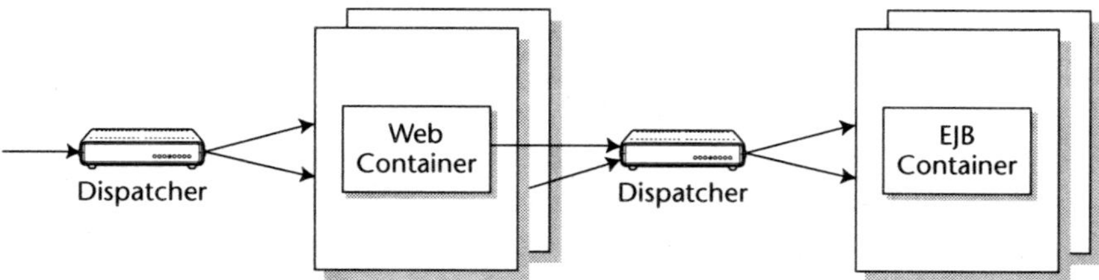

Figure 16.5 Clustered servers with distributed containers.

The collocated versus distributed server debate is important as the chosen architecture has many ramifications for clustering. A distributed architecture is invariably more complex to set up and maintain because distribution introduces new classes of problems such as increased latency and additional failure modes. It can also give more flexibility in certain areas, such as scalability and security, as we discuss below. Whether this flexibility is worth the added complexity must be carefully evaluated. A collocated architecture is sufficient and simpler to operate in many situations—and hence recommended whenever applicable.

The pros and cons of collocated and distributed servers are listed in Table 16.1.

Table 16.1 Clustering Collocated versus Distributed Containers

FEATURE	COLLOCATED	DISTRIBUTED	WINNER?
Reliability	High, because there is no remote interprocess communication. Everything is in a single process, so there are few factors that can cause unpredictable behavior.	Low, because there are more machines involved with a single request. Hence, there are more factors that can cause unpredictable behavior, such as network connections.	Collocated
Availability	High, because any machine can failover to any other machine. When the whole cluster fails, the entire site is down.	Higher than no cluster at all, but lower than in the collocated setting, because there are typically fewer machines that can provide for failover in a given tier (assuming we have the same absolute number of machines as in the collocated case). Because we actually have a cluster for each tier, failure of a complete cluster for one tier may still leave the other tier intact.	Collocated

(continued)

Table 16-1 *(continued)*

FEATURE	COLLOCATED	DISTRIBUTED	WINNER?
Serviceability	High, because each box is identical (simpler), and there is no network connection between the Web servers to bother with.	Low, because the Web server cluster must be maintained differently than the application server cluster. There is also a network connection between the tiers.	Collocated
Network efficiency	The Web server components can call EJB local interfaces. Local communication means no sockets to traverse between the Web servers and application servers.	The Web server components must call the EJB remote interfaces, which means more marshaling overhead. Remote interprocess communication between Web servers and application servers slows things down significantly.	Collocated
Efficient use of hardware	High, because a Java EE server can be used for whatever purposes it is needed at a given point in time (Web server tasks or application server tasks).	Low, because you need to predetermine how many machines to devote to Web server tasks, and how many machines to devote to application server tasks. This may not be exactly optimal, and your load characteristics may change over time.	Collocated
Security	You cannot place a firewall between your Web server and application server. Therefore, your EJB components are more exposed than in the distributed case.	You can place a firewall between the Web servers and application servers to further restrict accesses from Web components to EJBs.	Distributed

Table 16-1 *(continued)*

FEATURE	COLLOCATED	DISTRIBUTED	WINNER?
Serving quick static data, or simple Web requests that do not involve EJB components	If the application servers are overloaded, static data (such as HTML and images) are served up slowly because the Web servers are competing for hardware resources with the application servers.	If the application servers are overloaded, static data (such as HTML and images) can be served up quickly because the Web servers are dedicated.	Distributed
Conflicts over ownership and management responsibility	High because the Web team and EJB team use the same boxes, which could mean conflicts if you're in a political environment.	Low, because the Web team and EJB team use different boxes. They don't interfere with each other as much.	Distributed
Load balancing	You need to set up a separate load-balancing box (dispatcher) in front of the Java EE *servers.*	You need to set up a separate load-balancing box (dispatcher) in front of the *Web servers and optionally the EJB servers.*	Equal

To determine which architecture is most appropriate you have to consider a large number of factors. We generally favor the collocated approach because it is simpler. However, the arguments for a distributed server architecture tend to become more important the larger your system is.

- **Static data.** Static data can be served faster in a distributed architecture, but this is not an issue for companies that actually run a separate Web server box just for static data. That static Web page server could also make use of a Storage Area Network (SAN), a network of hard drives to increase throughput.
- **Scalability.** The separation between Web and EJB servers enables you to fine-tune each set of servers separately and more precisely to the actual requirements of the applications. For example, you may have applications that use servlets and JSP files only sparingly but create significant load on EJB servers so that adding to the number of EJB servers more directly enhances the overall performance. This argument tends

to be less important in smaller systems where the differences among the interaction patterns between clients and Web components and EJBs may not be significant.

- **Security.** The fact that you can have a firewall in distributed server systems (between the Web servers and application servers) is important. It may seem difficult to create a malicious RMI-IIOP request that targets exposed EJBs, but it really is not that difficult for anyone who understands the protocols. Hence, your beans should never be directly reachable without first passing through security controls. A firewall is a necessary first line of defense at the perimeter, but it is not sufficient. (See Chapter 11 for details on additional security controls.) Moreover, a separation of the Web and EJB servers reduces the chance that an attacker can exploit weaknesses, such as buffer overflows, in server implementations and thereby gain control of the entire server machine. Such vulnerabilities are frequently found in Web Server implementations. The captured server would then be used to stage additional attacks, for example on your databases, because internal firewalls allow traffic from the server. Again, these considerations become more important the larger your system is, as the business value of your assets tends to increase as well.

NOTE **Remember that we recommended you always keep the option of scaling your systems up, so when choosing the collocated approach, you should be prepared to switch to a distributed architecture later when it becomes necessary.**

Instrumenting Clustered EJBs

Although the actual technology that your Java EE server uses is proprietary, most application servers have similar approaches to clustering. Let's look at the possible options that application server vendors have for clustering EJBs of all types. We'll then look at the specifics of clustering stateless session, stateful session, entity, and message-driven beans.

How EJBs Can Be Clustered

There are many places in the system where vendors can provide *clustering logic* (such as load balancing or failover logic):

- **JNDI.** A vendor could provide load-balancing logic in the JNDI contexts that are used to locate objects. The JNDI context could have several equivalent objects for a given name and spread traffic across numerous machines. Some vendors let you deploy an application to all machines in the cluster at the same time.

- **Container.** A vendor could provide clustering logic directly within the container. The containers would communicate with one another behind the scenes using an interserver communication protocol. This protocol could be used to exchange state or perform other clustering operations. For example, if a ShoppingCart stateful session bean container has filled up its cache and is constantly activating and passivating EJBs to and from secondary storage, it might be advantageous for the container to send all `create()` invocations to another container in a different server that hasn't reached its cache limit. When the container's burden has been reduced, it can continue servicing new requests.
- **Smart stub.** This is the first object accessed by remote clients and runs locally on a client's virtual machine. Since stub code is generated by a vendor tool, the underlying logic in a stub can be vendor-specific so that the stub knows about multiple equivalent copies of the target. Vendors can instrument method-level load balancing and failover schemes directly in a smart stub. Every `create()`, `find()`, and business method invocation can have its request load balanced to a different server in the cluster; it doesn't matter which machine handles each request.

NOTE **The most common scenario is for stubs to be generated at development time through a utility, such as a vendor-specific EJB compiler. This isn't the only option, however. Some application servers can use interception technology, such as the JDK 1.3 Proxy class, to automatically generate remote stub logic dynamically at runtime. The JBoss application server is an example of a server that has an EJB container using this approach.**

Whether an application server uses interception technology or creates custom classes for the stubs and skeletons does not alter the places where cluster-based logic can be inserted. In the following discussions, we continue to reference stubs or containers irrespective of how or when these pieces are generated.

One potential drawback of vendor-specific logic on the client side is the loss of portability: When moving clients to a different vendor's products, even standalone RMI-IIOP clients need to be redeployed using the new vendor's tools. Porting applications to a different server creates significant amount of work on the server side anyway, however, so this issue is a comparatively minor one.

The different options that are available to developers and vendors provide a vast array of configurations with which clusterable EJB may be instrumented. By now, you must be thinking, "How do I know what to use, when, and where?" The answer lies within the capabilities of any single application server. The rest of this chapter discusses the various issues that application server vendors face when attempting to provide a clusterable infrastructure for stateless session beans, stateful session beans, entities, and message-driven EJBs.

The Concept of Idempotence

An *idempotent* (pronounced *'i-dim-po-tent*, not *i-'dimp-uh-tent*) method is one that can be called repeatedly with the *same* arguments and achieves the *same* results each time. For example, HTTP `GET` requests are assumed to be idempotent, which means that any sequence of accesses to the same resource using `GET` yields the same results.

An idempotent method in a distributed system can be called repeatedly without worry of altering the system so that it becomes unusable or provides errant results. Generally, any methods that alter a persistent store based on its current state are not idempotent, since two invocations of the same method will alter the persistent store twice. For example, if a sequencer is stored in a database and `m1()` increments the sequencer, two calls to `m1()` will leave the sequencer at a different value than if `m1()` was invoked only once. An idempotent method leaves the value in the persistent store the same no matter how many invocations of `m1()` occur. A `reset()` method that sets the sequencer value to `0` can be called multiple times and will always leave the value in the persistent store at `0`.

Remote clients that witness a failure situation of a server-side service are faced with a perplexing problem: Exactly how far did the request make it before the system failed? A failed request could have occurred at one of three points:

- After the request has been initiated but *before* the method invocation on the server has begun to execute. Failover of the request to another server should always occur in this scenario.
- After the method invocation on the server has begun to execute, but before the method has completed. Failover of the request to another server should occur only if the method is idempotent.
- After the method invocation on the server has completed but before the response has been successfully transmitted to the remote client. Failover of the request to another server should occur only if the method is idempotent.

Why is this important? A remote stub that witnesses a server failure *never* knows which of the three points of execution the request was in when the failure occurred. Even though failures of requests that haven't even begun method execution should always failover, a client can never determine when a failed request is in this category.

Thus, remote stubs can automatically failover only requests that were sent to methods flagged as idempotent. In comparison, failover of nonidempotent methods must occur programmatically by the client that originated the request.

Some EJB servers give you the ability to mark an EJB component's method as idempotent or nonidempotent using proprietary annotations or container descriptors. There is no standard EJB annotation for this purpose, however.

NOTE You might think that all methods that are marked to require a new transaction are idempotent. After all, if failure happens, the transaction will roll back, and all transactional state changes (such as transactional JDBC operations) will be undone. So why can't the stub failover to another bean to retry the operation?

The answer is that container-managed transactions have an inherent flaw, which we first discussed in Chapter 12. What if the transaction commits on the server, and the network crashes on the return trip to the stub? The stub would then not know whether the server's transaction succeeded and would not be able to failover.

Stateless Session Bean Clustering

Now, let's take a look at how we can cluster each type of EJB component. We begin with stateless session beans.

Load Balancing

All Java object instances of a stateless session bean class are considered identical. There is no way to tell them apart, since they do not hold state. Therefore all method invocations on a remote stub can be load balanced. Some EJB servers also give you flexibility here and allow you to *pin* stubs so that they direct requests to a single server only. Some vendors even allow you to configure subsets of methods on a single stub to be pinned or load balanced. This flexibility in load balancing stateless session bean instances is what drives the perception that stateless session EJBs are the most scalable types of synchronous EJB components.

Failover

For stateless session beans, automatic failover can always occur.

Automatic failover on *remote stubs* can occur only if the called method is idempotent. If your method is nonidempotent, or if your vendor does not support automatic failover, you might be able to failover *manually* by writing code to retry the method. You need to be careful, however, and factor business rules and other logic into the decision as to whether a failover request should be made.

For example, the following pseudo-code manually fails over any method invocation that is not automatically done so by the remote stub.

```
InitialContext ctx = null;
SomeRemoteStub remote = null;

try {
  ctx = ...;

  // Loop until create() completes successfully
  boolean createSuccessful = false;
  while (createSuccessful == false) {

    try {

      remote = ctx.lookup(..);

    }  catch (RemoteException re) {
      // Handle remote exception here.
      // If fail over should occur, call continue;

    }  catch (Exception e) {
      // Handle system exception here.
      // If fail over should occur, call continue;
      continue;

    }

    // If processing gets here, then no failure condition detected.
    createSuccessful = true;

  }

  boolean answerIsFound = false;
  while (answerIsFound == false) {

    try {

      remote.method(...);

    }  catch (ApplicationException ae) {
      // Handle application exception here.
      // If fail over should occur, call continue.

    }  catch (RemoteException re) {
      // Handle server-side exception here.
      // If fail over should occur, call continue.

    }  catch (Exception e) {
      // Failure condition detected.
```

```
            // If fail over should occur, call continue.
            continue;

          }

          // If processing gets here, then no failure condition detected.
          answerIsFound = true;

        } // while
      } catch (Exception e) { }
```

If we wanted it to do so, our EJB component could also assist with this failover decision by checking the system state before continuing.

Stateful Session Bean Clustering

Stateful session beans are clustered a bit differently than their stateless cousins. The major EJB server vendors support *replication* of state. It works like this: When a stateful session bean is created, the state must be copied to another machine. The backup copy isn't used unless the primary fails. The bean is routinely synchronized with its backup to ensure that both locations are current. If the container ever has a system failure and loses the primary bean instance, the remote stub of the bean fails over invocations to another machine. That other machine can use the backup state and continue processing. A new backup is then nominated, and the state begins to replicate to that new backup. This all occurs magically behind the scenes after you configure your EJB server to replicate state, using your EJB server's proprietary annotations or descriptors, or administrative console.

NOTE Stateful replication should be used with caution. It will limit your performance. Instead, you may want to consider placing critical, transactional, and persistent data in a database via session beans entities. Stateful session beans should be used for session-oriented (conversational) data that would not adversely impact the system if the data were lost.

Replication of stateful data typically occurs at one of two points:

- **At the end of every method.** This is not ideal, since unnecessary replication of unmodified data can frequently occur.
- **After the commit of a transaction.** For reasons touched upon in Chapter 10, this is ideal. Transactions give you an all-or-nothing failover paradigm. By replicating on transactional boundaries, your stateful session bean state remains consistent in time with other changes to your system state.

Most EJB servers perform stateful failover in one of two ways:

- **In-memory replication.** The state could be replicated in-memory across the cluster. In-memory replication is fast. The downside is that most EJB servers limit the replication to only two machines, since memory then becomes a scarce resource.
- **Persistent storage to a shared hard drive or database.** This approach is slower than in-memory replication, but every server in the cluster has access to the persistent state of the replicated bean.

Load Balancing

Remote stubs cannot load balance as easily. Your client requests can be sent only to the server that has your state. Note that if your stateful session bean is *replicated* across multiple servers, a remote stub could conceivably load balance different requests to different servers. This wouldn't be ideal, however, since most vendors have a designated *primary* object that requests are sent to first. The effort involved with load balancing requests in this scenario outweighs any benefits.

Failover

You might think that failover can always occur with stateful session beans if the state is replicated across a cluster. After all, if something goes wrong, we can always failover to the replica.

However, this is *not* the case. If your bean is in the *middle of a method call*, we still need to worry about idempotency. Your bean might be modifying the state elsewhere, such as calling a legacy system using the Java EE Connector Architecture. Your stub can failover to a backup only if the method is idempotent. The only time your EJB server can disregard idempotency is when your container crashes when nobody was calling it, either between method calls or between transactions, depending on how often you replicate.

For stateful session beans, automatic failover on a *remote stub* can occur only if your methods are idempotent. Most methods are not idempotent, such as a `create()` method or a `set()` method. However, stateful session beans *can* have some idempotent methods! Any method that does not alter the state of the system or always leaves the state stored in the stateful session EJB at the same value is an idempotent method. For example, if a stateful session EJB had a series of `get()` accessor methods to retrieve the values of state stored in the server, these `get()` accessor methods would be idempotent.

If your method is not idempotent, or if your container does not support replication, you can manually failover, similarly to our approach to stateless session beans.

Entity Clustering

Now that we've seen session beans, let's see how entities are clustered. Note that dealing with these issues is in the domain of the persistence provider and the database, so there is no need for you to write code for any of the concepts mentioned here. You can consider the following as background material.

Load Balancing

With the new Java persistence API entities can only be accessed remotely through a session bean façade. Therefore, all accesses to entities occur over local interfaces by in-process session beans, rather than remote clients. Thus, the need for separate load-balancing entities goes away.

Failover

Since you can only access entities using local interfaces, failover makes little sense.

NOTE Entities don't have the same replication needs as stateful session beans. This is because entities are routinely synchronized with a database via its store and load operations. Thus, an entity *is* backed up on a regular basis by design. From this perspective, you can think of an entity as a stateful session bean that is always replicated by the container on transactional boundaries through store and load operations. Those automatic load and store operations are the most important differences between stateful session beans and entities.

Caching

Because entities are basically Java objects that represent database data, they are in themselves a middle tier cache for that database. It is a tricky and technically complicated task for an application server's persistence provider to support this cache well. It is also a common misperception that caching always improves the performance of a system. Caching makes a system perform better only when the average overhead associated with updating the cache is less than the overhead that would be needed to access individual instances repeatedly between cache updates. Since the amount of synchronization needed to manage a cache in a cluster is high, a cache generally needs to be accessed three or four times between updates for the benefits of having the cache to outweigh not having it.

Persistence providers provide many different types of caching algorithms. Each of these algorithms has the same principle behind it: to reduce the frequency of database load and store operations, which are normally called on transactional boundaries.

You set up these caches using proprietary container tools, or annotations or descriptors. No Java coding should be required.

Read-Only Caches

A *read-only cache* contains a bunch of read-only entities. This is a very useful cache because most enterprise data *is* read-only. This type of caching has enormous benefits.

Since read-only entities never change, their store methods are never called, and they are never called with a transactional context. If your entity class methods are participating in a read-only cache, they need to have `Never` or `Not Supported` as their transactional attribute.

Read-only caches implement an *invalidation strategy* that determines when the data in the read-only instance is no longer valid and should be reloaded from the persistent store. Common algorithms include:

- **Timeout.** Every *X* seconds, the cache is invalidated and the read-only entity is reloaded immediately or upon the next method invocation. You set the time-out interval based on your tolerance for witnessing stale data.
- **Systemwide notification.** When someone changes entities in a read/write cache, the container invalidates those entity that also reside in a read-only cache elsewhere.

It doesn't take long for you to perform operations on a read-only entity . The lock on the entity bean needs to be held just long enough to perform the method call that gets you the data you need. Thus, each server's read-only cache typically keeps a single entity instance in memory for each primary key. This saves overhead involved with creating multiple instances and managing the concurrent access.

Distributed Shared Object Caches

A *distributed shared object cache* is an advanced EJB server feature that few vendors provide today. It is a clusterwide cache for read/write data. This immediately introduces an obvious problem: *cache consistency*. How does the container stay in sync with the database? What if someone updates the database behind your back? You'll need to refresh your cache.

A distributed shared object cache could theoretically detect collisions at the database level. This might be detected through database triggers, although this gets very hairy. The idea is that when someone updates the database behind your back, a trigger is fired. The cache is notified by this trigger and updates its contents so that read-only clients can access the latest data. Because each of the servers receives the notification, updating of the data can occur concurrently across the cluster.

A distributed shared object cache also needs to stay in sync with other caches in the cluster. It needs to replicate itself to other nodes on regular intervals, similar to the concept of stateful session bean replication. It also needs to implement a distributed *lock manager* that locks objects in memory, similar to how a database locks database rows. Additionally, if an unreliable messaging infrastructure, such as IP multicast, is used to send notification messages between servers, a system runs the risk of having two caches trying to lock the same data concurrently; their notification messages might cross in midair! An algorithm that allows the pausing of other systems during the period where critical events and notification messages are generated needs to be implemented. As you can see, this convergence of state across multiple nodes is very difficult to implement.

Read-Mostly Caches

Some application servers provide an exciting *read-mostly* algorithm. This powerful idea allows you to have read-only entity beans that are also updated every now and then, without having the burden of a true distributed shared object cache. The idea is that for any given entity class, some instances will be read-only, and some will not be cached at all (read/write).

- **When you perform a read operation**, you use a cached, read-only entity for performance.
- **When you perform a write operation**, you use a regular, uncached entity. When you modify a regular entity and a transaction completes, all of the read-only entity caches are invalidated. When the read-only entities are next used, they need to be reloaded from the database.

This *read-mostly* pattern has some interesting characteristics:

- **Each cache uses a different JNDI name.** For example, a read-only cache might have RO appended to the JNDI name, while a read/write cache might have RW appended to the JNDI name. This is somewhat annoying.
- **This pattern requires only the use of a read-only cache,** which almost all application servers have. You don't need to deal with the complexity of a true distributed shared object cache.

When using a read-mostly algorithm, be sure that your container uses a reliable communications protocol when invalidating the read-only cache. If a message is accidentally lost, you could be working with stale data.

Message-Driven Bean Clustering

Message-driven beans behave differently than session beans and entities do and thus have different implications in a cluster. Since message-driven beans do not have remote interfaces, they don't have any remote stubs or skeletons that can perform load balancing and failover logic on their behalf.

Message-driven beans are consumers of messages; they behave in a pull scenario grasping for messages to consume, rather than a push scenario in which a remote client sends invocations directly to the consumer. See Chapter 9 for a full discussion of this behavior.

Message-driven bean clustering is really about JMS clustering. A message-driven bean is dependent upon the clusterable features of the JMS server and destinations that it binds itself to. Message-driven beans achieve load balancing by having multiple EJB servers of the same type bound to a single JMS queue for message consumption. If four messages arrive concurrently at the queue and four containers of the same message-driven bean type are bound to the destination, each container is delivered one of the messages for consumption. Each container consumes its message concurrently, achieving a pseudo-load-balancing effect.

Failover of message-driven beans is integrated into the very nature of the beans themselves. Failover occurs any time a message that is being processed is acknowledged as *unsuccessful* to the JMS server. An unacknowledged message is placed back on the destination for reconsumption. The message-driven bean that consumes the message a second (or third, fourth, and so on) time need not be the one that consumed it the first time.

In some advanced JMS server implementations, JMS destination replication allows nonpersistent messages to be replicated across servers in a cluster. Message-driven beans that bind to a replicated destination detect any server failures and automatically rebind themselves as a consumer to the server hosting the replicated destination.

Other EJB Clustering Issues

This final section discusses some miscellaneous issues about J2EE clustering that can impact the behavior of a system.

First Contact

When a client wants to use an EJB component, whether it is a session or message-driven bean, the client must always first connect to the JNDI tree:

- Clients that want to use a session bean look up their stub.
- Clients that want to send a JMS message to be consumed by a message-driven bean must look up a JMS `ConnectionFactory` and `Destination` object.

Since all EJB clients use JNDI, naming server clustering ultimately has an impact on the behavior of EJB components in a cluster, too. What kind of clustering enhancements can be made to naming servers, and how does this impact EJBs? There are two types of clustered naming servers:

- **Centralized.** The naming server is hosted on a single server. All EJB servers register their same EJB components on the single naming server, and all clients look up EJB components on the single naming server. The naming server can even distribute clients to the identical servers in the cluster.
- **Shared, replicated.** Each node in a cluster hosts its own JNDI naming server that contains replicated objects hosted on other servers in the cluster. The naming servers replicate their contents—including stubs, JDBC `DataSource` objects, JMS `ConnectionFactory` object, JMS `Destination` objects—to the other naming servers in the cluster. Thus, every naming server has a copy of every other naming server's objects in the tree. If a server in the cluster crashes, all of the other naming servers that are still active merely have to remove from their naming server the objects hosted on the other machine.

Initial Access Logic

When an application server provides a *centralized naming server,* the logic that clients use to get access to the cluster is simple: They hard-code the DNS name or IP address of the centralized naming server into all of their `InitialContext` creation calls.

But what about Java EE vendors that support a shared, replicated naming server? Clients can connect to any server in the cluster and make a request for a service hosted anywhere else in the cluster. Architects have a variety of options available to them.

- **DNS load balancing.** This allows multiple IP addresses to be bound to a single name in a network's *Domain Name Service* (DNS). Clients that ask for an `InitialContext` pass in a DNS name in the URL of the naming server. Every translation of the DNS name results in the generation of a different IP address, which is part of a round-robin list for that name in the DNS server. Using this technique, every client `InitialContext` request is transparently directed to a different server. Networks support this feature or they do not—it is *not* dependent upon the capabilities of your application server. Generally, this is a low-level technique that can cause difficult-to-solve network problems and needs to be well understood and implemented. We do not recommend it for your average network.
- **Software proxies.** Software proxies maintain open connections to a *list of servers* that are preconfigured in a descriptor file. Software proxies can maintain keep-alive TCP/IP connections with each of the servers to provide better performance instead of attempting to reconnect every request. These software proxies immediately detect any server crash or unresponsiveness because their link is immediately lost. Software proxies can also support a wider range of load-balancing algorithms, including round-robin, random, and weight-based algorithms.
- **Hardware proxies.** Hardware proxies have capabilities similar to software proxies but often can outperform their software counterparts. Hardware proxies can also double as firewalls and gateways.

Summary

In this chapter, we discussed the major challenges and solutions for working with EJB in a clustered system. We also discussed the major characteristics that large systems exhibit and how clustering addresses the issues that arise in these systems. We then presented the concepts of load balancing and failover and compared the collocated and distributed approaches to clustering. We analyzed the type-specific behavior that can be exhibited by stateless session beans, stateful session beans, entities, and message-driven beans in a cluster. And finally, we discussed cluster deployments of EJB, clustered naming servers, and initial access logic to naming servers. So pat yourself on the back! You've just learned a great deal about clustering.

CHAPTER

17

EJB-Java EE Integration: Building a Complete Application

In this chapter, we will show you how to design and build a complete EJB/ Java EE system. In particular, you'll learn how to use entities, session beans, and message-driven beans *together*, and how to call EJB components from Java servlets and Java Server Pages (JSP). We will also expose a stateless session bean as a Web service for integration with other applications.

We will first provide motivation for our deployment by describing the business problem. We'll then design the example system. The complete source code is available on the book's accompanying Web site at `www.wiley.com/go/sriganesh`. The code is fully commented and ready to run. As we go through the design, we will point out implementation alternatives that you can use for your own experiments.

If you have read previous editions of this book, you may want to compare the EJB 3.0 design of this application with that of the previous editions. What you will find is that EJB 3.0 lets you build the entire application a lot easier and much closer to the actual domain model. The large amounts of infrastructure code that earlier EJB versions required you to write have simply vanished.

The Business Problem

Jasmine's Computer Parts, Inc. is a fictitious manufacturing company that makes a wide variety of computer equipment, including motherboards, processors, and memory. Jasmine, the company's owner, has been selling her products using direct mail catalogs, as well as a network of distributors and resellers.

Jasmine wants to lower the cost of doing business by selling her computer parts directly to the end customer through a Web-based sales model. Jasmine has given us a high-level description of the functionality of the e-commerce solution. She'd like the following features in the system we provide for her:

- **User authentication.** Registered users would first log in to the Web site to access the complete catalog. Only registered users should be able to browse and purchase from her online store.
- **An online catalog.** Users should be able to browse her complete product line on the Web and view details of each product.
- **Shopping cart functionality.** While browsing the catalog, a user should be able to choose the products he or she wants. The user should be able to perform standard shopping cart operations, such as viewing the current shopping cart or changing quantities of items already picked out.
- **Specialized pricing functionality.** Users who order items in bulk should get a percentage discount. For example, if I order five memory modules, I get a 10 percent discount on that memory. In addition, registered users who frequent the store should get additional discounts.
- **Order generation.** Once the user is happy with his or her selections and has committed to ordering the products, a permanent order should be generated. A separate fulfillment application (which we won't write) would use the data in the orders to manufacture the products and ship them. The user would be able to return to the Web site later to view the status of current orders.
- **Billing functionality.** Once the user has placed the order, we should bill it to him or her. If the user does not have enough funds to pay, the order should be cancelled.
- **E-mail confirmation.** After the order has been placed and the credit card debited, a confirmation e-mail should be sent to the user.

This is definitely going to be a full-featured deployment!

A Preview of the Final Web Site

To give Jasmine an idea of what the final product should be like, our sales team has put together a series of screenshots. The screenshots show what the e-commerce system will look like when an end user hits the Web site. These example screens do not yet contain any artwork or corporate design items because we focus on functionality here.

Figure 17.1 shows a user logging into the system initially. Our authentication will be through login names and passwords.

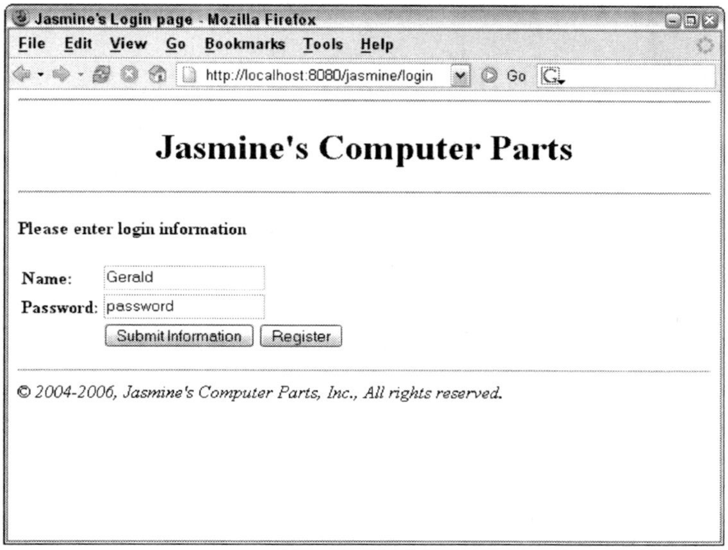

Jasmine's Login page - Mozilla Firefox
File Edit View Go Bookmarks Tools Help
http://localhost:8080/jasmine/login Go

Jasmine's Computer Parts

Please enter login information

Name: Gerald
Password: password
Submit Information Register

© 2004-2006, Jasmine's Computer Parts, Inc., All rights reserved.

Figure 17.1 A user logging into Jasmine's Computer Parts.

After the user has been recognized, he or she is presented with a Web storefront. The Web storefront is the main page for Jasmine's online store (see Figure 17.2). From the Web storefront, the user can jump to the catalog of products that Jasmine offers (see Figure 17.3). A user who wants to view details about a product can check out the product detail screen (see Figure 17.4). The user can also add the product to the current shopping cart—a temporary selection of products that the user has made but has not committed to purchasing yet.

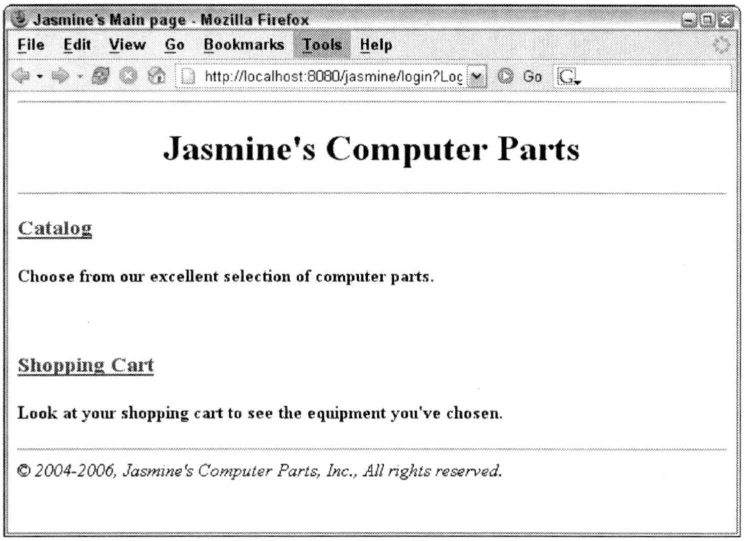

Jasmine's Main page - Mozilla Firefox
File Edit View Go Bookmarks Tools Help
http://localhost:8080/jasmine/login?Loc Go

Jasmine's Computer Parts

Catalog

Choose from our excellent selection of computer parts.

Shopping Cart

Look at your shopping cart to see the equipment you've chosen.

© 2004-2006, Jasmine's Computer Parts, Inc., All rights reserved.

Figure 17.2 The Web storefront for the online store.

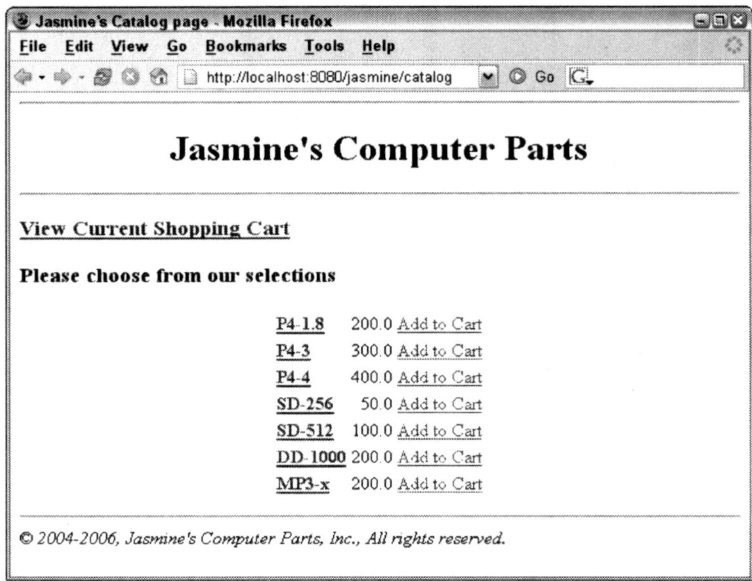

Figure 17.3 Browsing the online catalog.

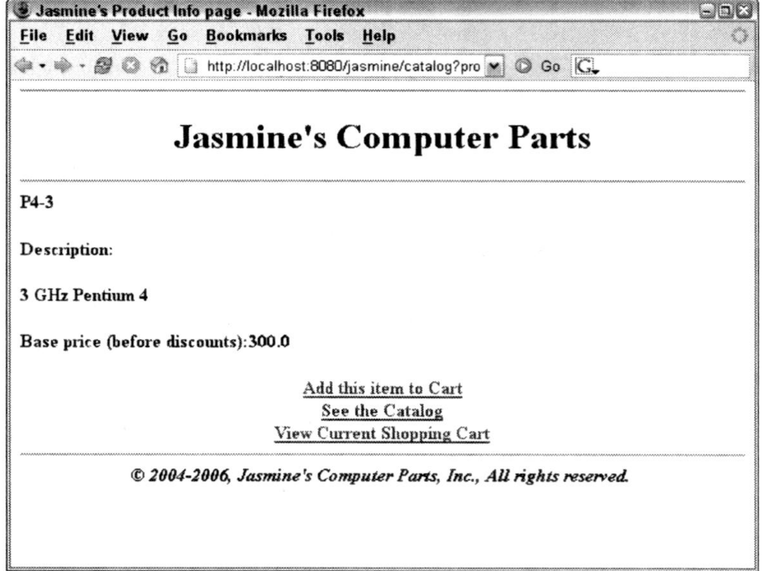

Figure 17.4 Viewing a particular product.

Once the user has made product choices, the user can view a cart for the current selections (and make any last-minute changes), as shown in Figure 17.5. When the user clicks the button to purchase the selection, he or she is billed and a new order is generated. Finally, the user is given the order number for future reference (see Figure 17.6).

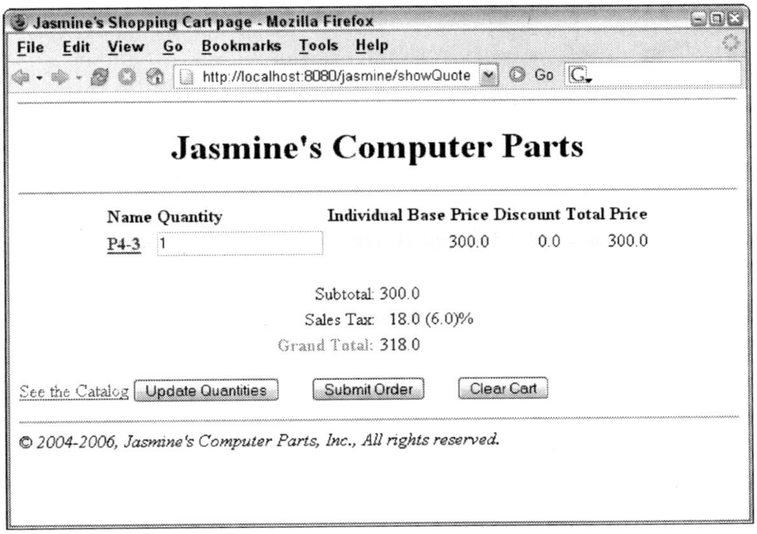

Figure 17.5 Viewing and modifying a cart.

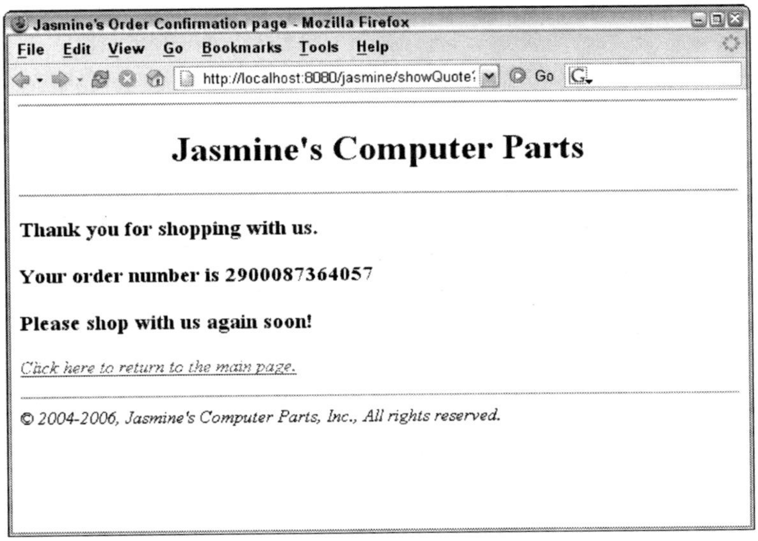

Figure 17.6 Making a purchase.

Scoping the Technical Requirements

While meeting Jasmine's requirements, we'd like to develop an extensible infrastructure that she can add to in the future. That means making the right abstractions to loosen the coupling between our components. Ideally, Jasmine should be able to plug in a different implementation of any part of the system with very few modifications.

Our deployment will be partitioned into three tiers:

- **The presentation tier** involves one or more Web servers, each responsible for interacting with the end user. The presentation tier displays the requested information in HTML to the end user; it also reads in and interprets the user's selections and makes invocations to the business tier's EJB components. The implementation of the presentation tier uses *servlets* and *JSP technology*.
- **The business logic tier** consists of multiple EJB components running under the hood of an EJB container or server. These reusable components are independent of any user interface logic. We should be able to, for example, take the business tier and port it to a different presentation tier (such as a disconnected salesforce's laptop) with no modifications. The business tier is made up of session beans, and message-driven beans that realize the business logic. Entities implement the data access layer. To allow Jasmine to integrate the pricing functionality with other applications, we will additionally expose this bean as a Web service.
- **The data tier** is where our permanent data stores reside. The databases aggregate all persistent information related to the e-commerce site. Jasmine has relational databases already in place, so we need to map any persistent data to relational tables.

The Business Logic Tier

Let's begin by designing the entity classes that we need to handle Jasmine's persistent data. After that, we will look at the session and message-driven beans that we want to build.

Persistent Data: Entities

For discussing her business domain with Jasmine and for determining which entity classes we will need to develop, we created a simple Unified Modeling Language (UML) class diagram that will be the basis for our design. Let's take a quick tour through the central classes in Figure 17.7. Except for the cart and the catalog class, all classes in the diagram represent nonvolatile, persistent data. These will be our entity classes.

Customer

First, we need to represent information about Jasmine's customers. A customer represents an end user—perhaps an individual or a corporation that purchases goods from our Web site. Our customer abstraction contains the following data:

- The customer's name (also used as the customer's login name for our Web site)
- The customer's address
- The customer's password (used to verify the customer's identity)
- Personal discount information for the customer

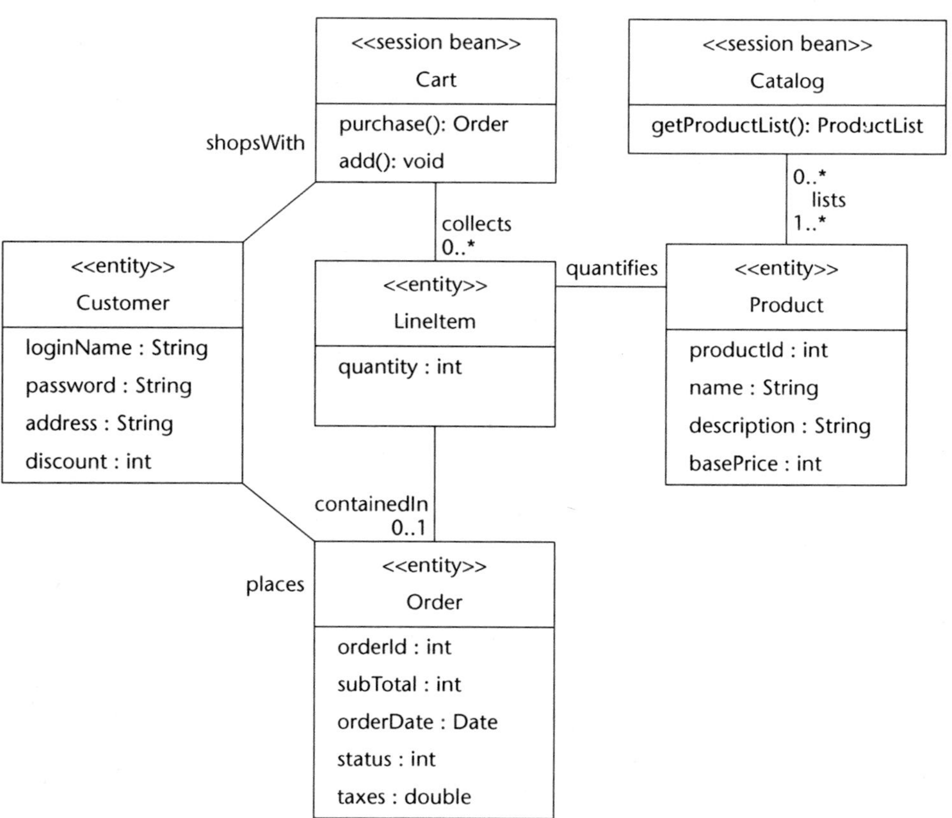

Figure 17.7 The UML class diagram.

NOTE New customers, products, and so on can be added to the system in many ways. Jasmine could have users log in through a separate Web site and input their name, address information, password, and other profile data. We could also develop a custom maintenance tool (standalone or Web-based) for adding new products. To keep this example simple, we'll manually insert direct database data, but feel free to extend this for your purposes.

In each shopping session, a `Customer` uses a single `Cart` object to collect his or her shopping items. The cart is not a persistent object and will be modeled as a stateful session bean. It's in the diagram only to represent the relationship between customers and line items. It will be explained in more detail in the next section. Suffice it to say here that the `purchase()` operation creates an `Order` object from the cart's contents when the customer's selection is complete.

Order

Next, we need to model a permanent order for goods. We'll define an order class in the diagram for this purpose. An order is a shopping cart that has been converted into a work request. An order represents a real business action that needs to take place, such as the production of goods. Generating an order and billing a customer go hand in hand.

An order contains the following information:

- The ID of this order (which the user can use to check on order status)
- The customer for which this order is generated (used for shipping address information)
- The products and quantities that should be ordered (as with carts, best represented as separate information; contained in line items, described shortly)
- The subtotal and taxes on the order
- The date the order was placed
- The order status

Orders are permanent, persistent objects. You want an order's state to be around even if your deployment crashes for any reason because an order means money. Therefore, orders are best depicted as entities. In comparison, carts are not permanent—they represent temporary interactions with the customer. You don't want to write a cart's data to a database during a customer interaction, but you do want to keep track of the user's information—hence the stateful session bean is best applied for carts.

Line Item

For convenience of manipulation, we break up our notion of an order into individual line items, where each line item represents data pertaining to a single product the user has ordered. An order has a one-to-many relationship with its constituent line items. Our line item abstraction contains the following data:

- The ID of this order line item
- The product that this order line item represents (used by manufacturing to reveal which product to make)
- The quantity of the product that should be manufactured

Because order line items are permanent, persistent objects, they are represented as entities. At first, you might think a line item is too small and fine-grained to be an entity and might better be represented as Java classes for performance. However, with EJB local interfaces and by properly tweaking your EJB server, it is possible to have both fine-grained and large-grained entities. Chapter 14 has more detail about how to optimize such entities for performance.

Line items will be part of persistent orders, but they also serve as simple data objects in carts. Since carts are session beans and not persistent, we will not persist line items before an order is actually generated. Until then, we will just pass them around as plain, serializable Java objects.

Products and Catalog

At some stage we need to model the products that Jasmine is selling. A product could be a motherboard, a monitor, or any other component. Products should be persistent parts of the deployment that last forever. Our product abstractions should represent the following data:

- The unique product ID
- The product name
- A description of the product
- The base price of the product (indicating the price of the product, with no discounts or taxes applied)

Jasmine should be able to add and delete products from the system using a separate tool that connects to the database; we don't provide this functionality in our Web shop. Because products are permanent, persistent parts of the system, they are best modeled as entities. The product entity should have methods to get and set the above fields. We also have a catalog session bean that functions as a façade for this entity bean, serving as a transactional networked façade.

NOTE **Rather than entity classes, we could have used Java classes to represent the entities in our system, such as products, customers, and so on. However, many of these nouns (especially products) are prime candidates to be cached by the container. This means that by going with entities, our performance would actually improve. Because we are using local interfaces, the access time is comparable to a local object access.**

Business Logic: Session and Message-Driven Beans

You have seen the central entities that make up our domain model, but so far there has not been much activity in our Web shop.

The entity classes just explained should not directly contain any of this business logic because Jasmine should be able to reuse our entity access layer in future applications, such as inventory or marketing tools. Also, these entities cannot be accessed from outside the container. Hence, we develop a number of EJBs that implement the application's business logic and provide access to entity data. Figure 17.8 depicts the beans in our business logic tier.

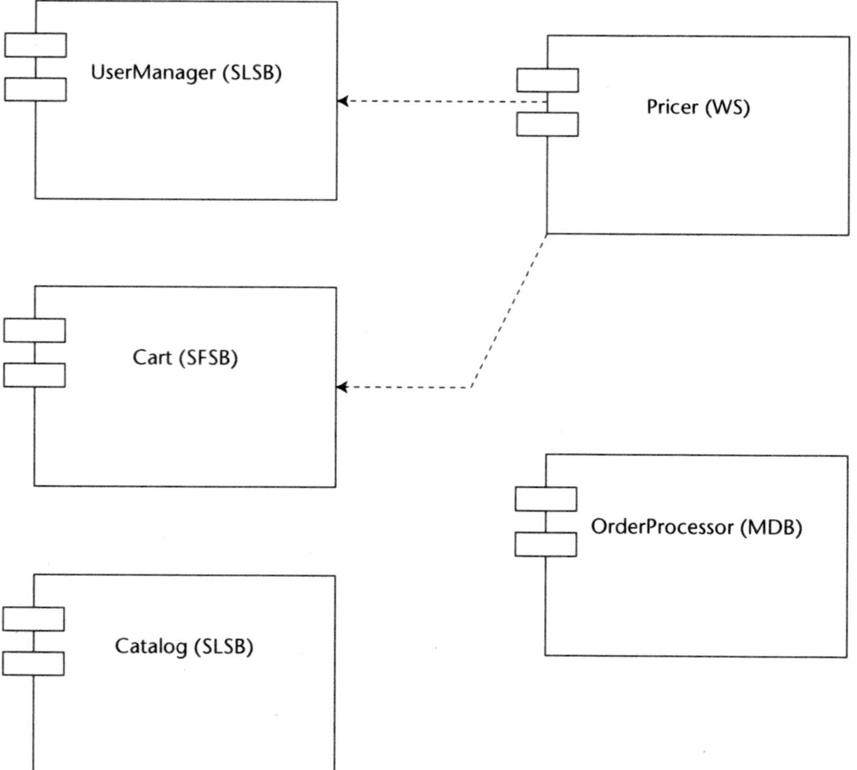

Figure 17.8 The major EJB components in our system.

The central actual shopping functionality that our Web shop provides is built around the shopping cart session bean, with which users interact. The business function of calculating the prices for carts by adding up the individual items and applying personal and bulk discounts is modeled in a separate Pricer session bean. Let's now take a closer look at each of the beans in turn.

Carts

We need to keep track of the selections a customer has made while navigating our catalog by modeling a shopping cart. Each customer who has logged in should have his or her own temporary and separate cart in which to work. Therefore, our carts need to hold client-specific state in them. They should not be persistent, because the user can always cancel the cart.

This naturally lends itself to the stateful session bean paradigm. Each cart stateful session bean holds conversational state about the user's current cart. It enables us to treat the entire cart as one coarse-grained object. A new cart needs to be generated every time a user logs in. Each cart bean contains the following information:

- The customer we authenticated at the login screen. We need to store customer information so that we know who to bill, what discounts to apply, and where to ship the manufactured products.
- The products and quantities that the customer currently has selected. We can reuse the `LineItem` entity class here that we introduced earlier, which does just the right thing. When the cart is transformed into an order, these line items are persisted and stored together with the order.
- The subtotal for the cart, taking into account all the prices of the products the user wants as well as any discounts the user gets.
- The taxes charged. This is added to the subtotal for the final grand total.

In addition to this data, the cart beans will be smart and will know how to generate permanent orders from themselves. We describe orders a bit later.

NOTE When making shopping cartlike functionality, you have several choices. You can use session beans (as we are) for temporary shopping carts. You can also use servlets or JSP session objects, which is appropriate if your shopping cart is primitive in functionality and shouldn't be reused for other graphical user interfaces.

A final choice is to use entities and to keep the shopping cart data in the database. The entity approach is appropriate for persistent shopping carts, where you'd like the user to retrieve the shopping cart when returning later. This might be useful if it requires complex configuration to get an item into a shopping cart, such as custom configuring a laptop computer. The downside to the entity approach is that you need to write a shopping cart cleaning program that routinely sweeps abandoned shopping carts from the database.

Pricer

Because Jasmine wants customized pricing, we need the concept of a pricer—a component that takes a cart as input and calculates the price of that cart based on a set of pricing rules. A pricing rule might be, "Customer X gets a 5 percent discount" (a frequent-buyer discount) or "If you purchase 10 motherboards, you get a 15 percent discount" (a bulk discount). These pricing rules could be read in from a database or set via EJB environment properties (see Chapter 10). The implementation on the companion Web site uses this latter approach. It is a useful exercise to move the frequent buyer discount information to the customers database instead.

Our pricer takes a cart as input and computes the subtotal (before taxes) of that cart. It figures out the subtotal by computing a discount for each cart line item in that bean and subtracting the discounts from the total price.

Our pricer works on any cart and holds no client-specific state. Once the pricer has computed a price on a cart, it is available to perform another computation on a different cart. It is also not a persistent object—it would not make sense to save a price, because a pricer simply performs logic and holds no state. This means that our pricer fits into the EJB world best as a stateless session bean.

Finally, Jasmine considers reusing the pricing logic in other applications, such as her mail order processing system and even considers making it available to external applications. Consequently, we need to plan in advance for integrating this component with other, potentially non-EJB systems. We, therefore, expose the pricer stateless session bean as a Web service to allow for easy integration.

Order Processor

The last challenge we face is how to *generate* orders in our system. We'd like for the user to continue browsing the Web site when he has placed the order, rather than waiting to see if his credit card is approved. This is similar to the Amazon.com one-click functionality. We'd also like to e-mail the user afterward, indicating whether the order was successfully placed.

The best paradigm to achieve this is messaging. When the user wants to order the shopping cart, we could send a JMS message containing the shopping cart reference. Then later, the message will be processed off the queue by an *order processor* message-driven bean. This order processor is responsible for querying the shopping cart, checking the user's credit card, checking inventory, e-mailing the user a confirmation, and creating the order (entity bean).

The challenge of sending data through JMS is that we cannot marshal EJB stubs in a JMS message. Thus, we couldn't send a shopping cart stub as a serialized bit-blob in a JMS message. This is a fundamental problem with message-driven beans: It's very challenging to send data into a message-driven bean that comes from another bean.

One option is to use *EJB object handles*, which are serializable stubs. However, this might not work either, since the stateful session bean cart might time out before the JMS message was processed.

Another option is to create a custom, serializable representation of the shopping cart, perhaps by using serializable Java objects. The problem here is that we'd need to create all these extra Java classes, which is very annoying. Alternatively, we could create the order and transmit that as a serializable object, which is simple if we let the entity class `Order` implement `java.io.Serializable`.

The best solution for us is to submit the order *before* sending a JMS message. We then mark the order status as *unverified*. The order processor receives the primary key of the order, retrieves the order entity from the database, checks the credit card, sends the confirmation e-mail, and then changes the order status to *submitted*.

Our notion of an order can be easily extended to include order status, such as *Manufacturing* or *Shipping* and other order fulfillment information. It would also be interesting to e-mail the order status to the end user at regular intervals using the `JavaMail` API. Since we do not fulfill orders, we leave this as an exercise to the reader.

The Presentation Tier

Our next task is to design our presentation tier, which displays the graphical user interface to the end user. For our presentation tier, we will use a few Java servlets and JSP files to interact with a client over HTTP. The following sections contain a brief introduction to servlets and JSP technologies. You can safely skip this if you are already familiar with these technologies.

What Are Servlets?

A *servlet* is a Java object that runs within a Web container and reacts to HyperText Transfer Protocol (HTTP) requests by sending HTTP responses. Requests contain data that the client wants to send to the server. A *response* is data that the server wants to return to the client to answer the request. A servlet is a Java object that takes a request as input, parses its data, performs some logic, and issues a response back to the client (see Figure 17.9).

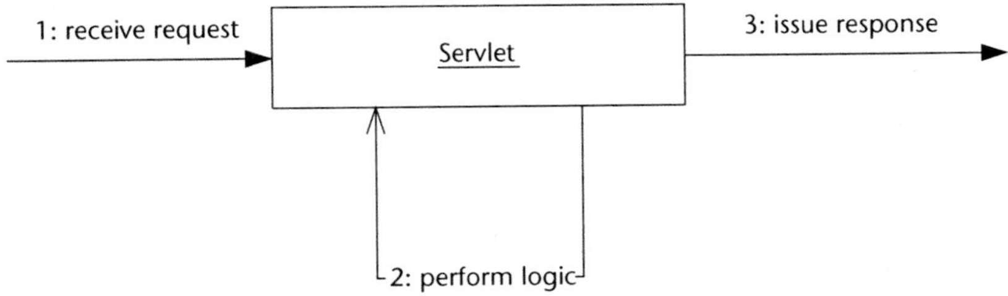

Figure 17.9 The basic servlet paradigm.

Figure 17.10 illustrates an HTTP servlet running inside a Java EE server, and Source 17.1 shows an example of an HTTP servlet.

```
import javax.servlet.*;
import javax.servlet.http.*;
import java.io.*;

public class HelloWorld extends HttpServlet
{
  public void service(HttpServletRequest req, HttpServletResponse rsp)
      throws ServletException, IOException
  {
      PrintWriter out = rsp.getWriter();
      out.println("<H1>Hello World</H1>");
  }
}
```

Source 17.1 A sample HTTP servlet.

As you can see, HTTP servlets are very straightforward. They have a simple method called `service()` that responds to HTTP requests. In that method, we write some HTML back to the browser. If properly configured, the Java EE server will pool and reuse this servlet to service many HTTP requests at once.

We can also do trickier things—respond differently to different types of HTTP requests, maintain user sessions, read input parameters from Web forms (using the `HttpServletRequest` object), and call EJB components.

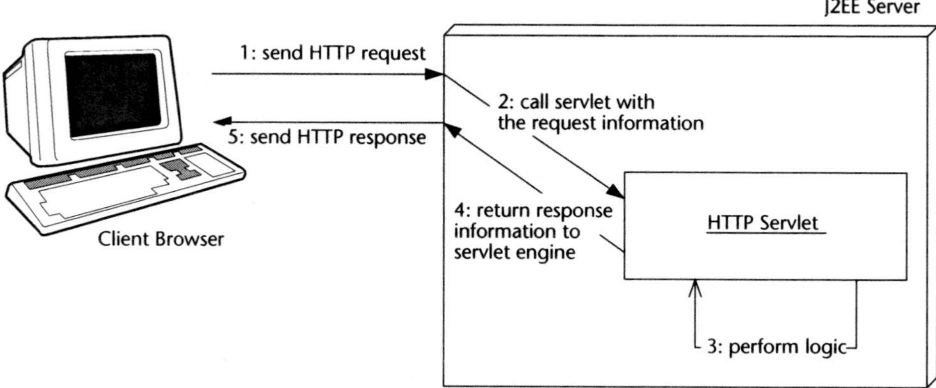

Figure 17.10 HTTP servlets.

The great thing about servlets is that they are written in Java and, therefore, can be debugged just like any other Java code. The downside to servlets is that they require Java knowledge. It is, therefore, inappropriate to use servlets to write large amounts of HTML back to the user, because that HTML is interlaced with Java code, as you saw in Source 17.1. This makes it very challenging for Web designers to get involved with your deployment.

What Are Java Server Pages?

A Java Server Page (JSP) is a flat file that is translated at runtime into a servlet. JSP files are generally useful for presentation-oriented tasks, such as HTML rendering. You don't need to know Java to write a JSP file, which makes JSP files ideal for Web designers. A sample JSP is shown in Source 17.2.

```
<!doctype html public "-//w3c/dtd HTML 4.0//en">
<html>
<body>
<H1>Hello World</H1>
</body>
</html>
```

Source 17.2 A sample JSP.

As you can see, this just looks like HTML and is easily maintained by a graphic designer. You can do fancy things as well, such as interlacing Java code with JSP, managing user sessions, and so on. Just about anything you can do in a servlet can be done with JSP. The difference is that a JSP file is a flat file that is translated into a servlet later. The code in Source 17.2 would be translated into a servlet with `out.println()` statements for the HTML code.

How Do I Combine Servlets, JSP, and EJB Components?

You have several choices when architecting your Web-based system. Here are just a few examples.

- **The JSP files can have embedded Java code that calls EJB components.** For example, we could interlace the following code into a JSP file:

  ```
  <html>
  <H1>About to call EJB...</H1>
  <%
  ```

```
javax.naming.Context ctx = new javax.naming.InitialContext();
C cObj = (C)ctx.lookup(C.class.getName());
...
%>
</html>
```

When this JSP is translated into a servlet, the Java code would be inserted into the generated servlet. This is a bad idea, because the JSP files cannot be easily maintained by a graphic designer due to the large amount of Java code in the JSP file.

- **The JSP files can communicate with EJB components via custom tags.** You can design custom JSP tags that know how to interact with EJB components, called *JSP tag libraries*. Tag libraries are appealing because once you've designed them, graphic designers can call EJB components by using familiar tag-style editing rather than writing Java code. The tags then call Java code that understands how to invoke EJB components.
- **Servlets can call EJB components and then call JSP files.** You can write one or more Java servlets that understand how to call EJB components and pass their results to JSP files. This is a Model-View-Controller (MVC) paradigm, because the EJB layer is the model, the JSP files are the view, and the servlet(s) are the controller—they understand which EJB components to call and then which JSP files to call (see Figure 17.11). The advantage of this paradigm is that it pushes most of the Java code into servlets and EJB components. The JSP files have almost no Java code in them at all and can be maintained by graphic designers.
- **You can go with an off-the-shelf Web framework.** Several off-the-shelf Web frameworks aid in building Web-based systems, such as Jakarta Struts.

JSP Files in Our E-Commerce Deployment

We will choose an MVC paradigm for our e-commerce deployment. We will have servlets that perform the controller processing, call our EJB components, and select the appropriate JSP file based on the results of the EJB layer processing.

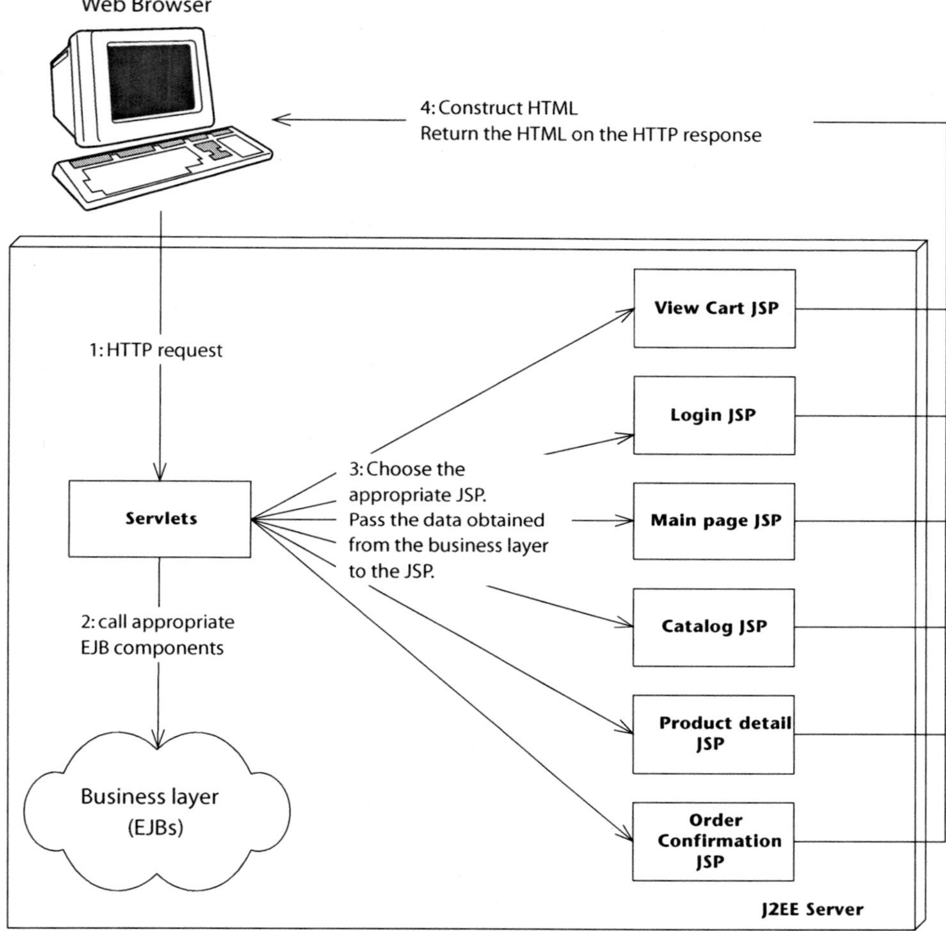

Figure 17.11 The EJB-JSP-Servlet Model-View-Controller paradigm.

To fulfill Jasmine's requirements, we'll define the following servlets and JSP files:

- **A login page.** The login page will be the first page that the user deals with when going to Jasmine's Web site. It is responsible for reading in the user's name and then retrieving the appropriate customer entity bean that matches that name. It compares the user's submitted password with the permanent password stored with the customer entity bean. If the passwords match, a new cart stateful session bean is created for this customer. The customer information is stored in the cart so the cart contains the user's billing and shipping information. If the passwords don't match, an error is displayed and the user is given another chance to enter a password.

- **A Web storefront page.** The user who gets through the login page is redirected to the Web storefront, which is the main page for Jasmine's store. This is the main navigation page for Jasmine's store. It links to the catalog page and the view cart page.
- **A catalog page.** To start adding products to the cart, the user can browse the list of available products by going to the catalog page. The user can also view details of a particular product, in which case we direct the user to the product detail page.
- **A product detail page.** When the user wants information about a particular product in the catalog, the product detail page shows that information. From this screen, the user can add the product to his or her cart.
- **A view cart page.** This page enables the user to view and modify the shopping cart. This means deleting items or changing quantities. Every time the user changes something, we recalculate the price of the cart by calling the pricer stateless session bean.
- **An order confirmation page.** Finally, when the user is happy, he or she can convert the cart stateful session into an order entity bean. The user is then shown his or her order number, which is extracted from the order bean. We then send a JMS message to the `OrderProcessor` bean, which asynchronously processes the order.

This completes the design for our presentation tier. The flow of control for our pages is depicted in Figure 17.12. Note that the JSP files do not directly call each other: Servlets receive all requests, call the appropriate EJB components, and route the results to the appropriate JSP file for the HTML to be rendered.

Once we've developed the application, we need to package and deploy it. A Java EE application is packaged this way:

- **An Ejb-jar file (.jar)** contains EJB components.
- **A Web archive file (.war)** contains Web components, such as servlets, JSP files, HTML, images, and JSP tag libraries.
- **An enterprise archive file (.ear)** is a Java EE application that contains a .jar file and a .war file. This is the unit of deployment you care most about, because it represents a Java EE application.

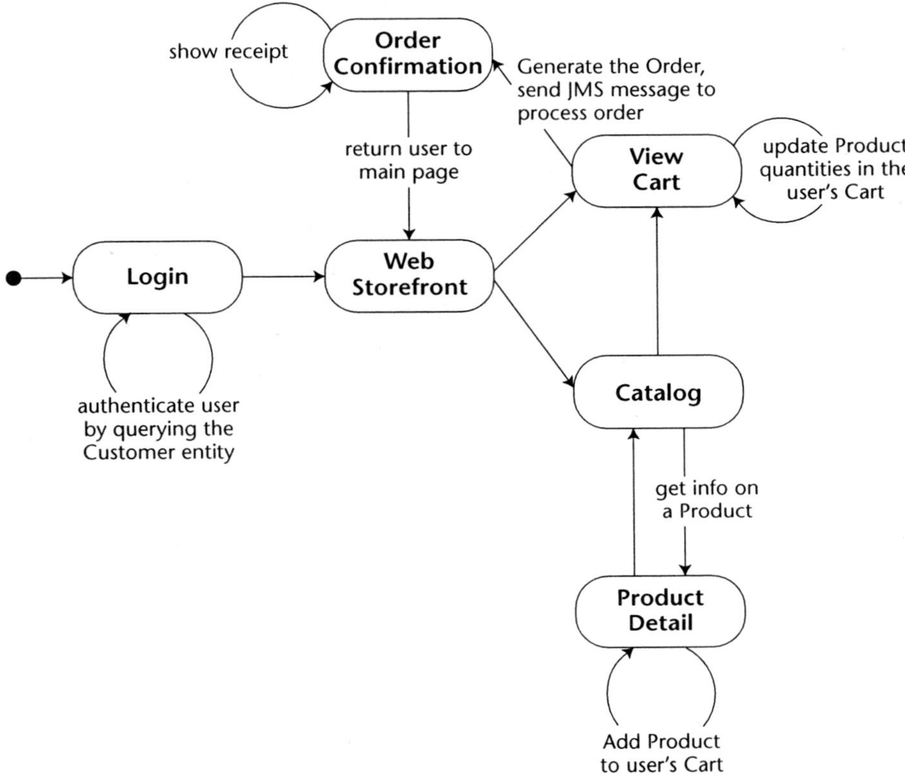

Figure 17.12 State diagram for our Web shop.

Each of these files follows the ZIP rules for compression. The idea is that you first create the Ejb-jar file, then the Web archive, and then zip them up together into an enterprise archive. You deploy the enterprise archive into your application server using its tools, or perhaps by copying it into the appropriate folder. For code examples of how to build and deploy these archives, see the book's accompanying source code.

Example Code

Before concluding this chapter, let's look at an example of a servlet calling EJB components and then calling a JSP file, so that you can grasp how this MVC paradigm is achieved. As a final piece of code, we will also look at the pricer Web service and bean interfaces.

We'll take the example of logging into our site. Source 17.3 shows the login JSP code.

```
<%--
 This JSP displays a login screen.  When the user fills out the login
 screen, it will submit it to the Login Servlet, which will verify the
 user's credentials by calling EJB components.

 If the verification is unsuccessful, the login servlet will return
 the user to this page to reenter his credentials.

 If the verification is successful, Jasmine's main page will be
displayed.
--%>

<html>
<head>
 <title>Jasmine's Login page </title>
</head>

<body>

<%-- Include the title, which is "Jasmine's Computer Parts"--%>
<jsp:include page="title.jsp" />

<%-- Indicate the error page to use if an error occurs --%>
<jsp:directive.page errorPage="error.jsp" />

<%-- Display the login form --%>
<h4>Please enter login information</h4>
<p>
<form action="/jasmine/login" method="get">
 <table>
  <tr>
   <td><b>Name:</b></td>
   <td>
    <input type="text" name="Login" size="19"/>
   </td>
  </tr>
  <tr>
   <td><b>Password:</b></td>
   <td>
    <input type="text" name="Password" size="19"/>
   </td>
  </tr>
  <tr>
   <td></td>
```

Source 17.3 The login JSP. *(continued)*

```
    <td>
      <input type="submit" value="Submit Information"/>
      <input type="submit" value="Register"/>
    </td>
   </tr>
  </table>
</form>

<%
  // get whether the person logged in successfully
  Boolean failed = (Boolean) request.getAttribute("loginFailed");
  if (failed != null) {
    if (failed.booleanValue() == true) {
%>
    <p>
    <strong>Could not log in!  Please try again.</strong>
    <p>
<%
    }
  }
%>

<%-- Include the page footer --%>
<jsp:include page="footer.jsp" />

</body>
</html>
```

Source 17.3 *(continued)*

Source 17.4 shows the login servlet.

The login servlet is self-documenting. It cracks open the request, figures out which EJB components to call, and selects the appropriate JSP file.

```
package examples.shop.web.servlet;

import java.io.IOException;

import javax.naming.Context;
import javax.naming.InitialContext;
import javax.servlet.RequestDispatcher;
import javax.servlet.ServletConfig;
import javax.servlet.ServletException;
import javax.servlet.http.HttpServlet;
```

Source 17.4 The login servlet. *(continued)*

```
import javax.servlet.http.HttpServletRequest;
import javax.servlet.http.HttpServletResponse;
import javax.servlet.http.HttpSession;

import examples.shop.logic.Cart;
import examples.shop.logic.UserManager;

/**
 * This is the very first servlet the client deals with. It's a login
 * authentication servlet and asks the user for his name and password,
 * and passes it to the UserManager stateless session bean for
 * verification.
 *
 * If the user authenticates properly, a reference to a new Cart is
 * saved in his HttpSession object, and the user can begin to add items
 * to his cart and shop around.
 */
public class LoginServlet extends HttpServlet {

    /** the user manager used to authenticate the user */
    UserManager userManager;

    /** the user's cart object */
    Cart cart;

    /**
     * The servlet engine calls this method once to initialize a servlet
     * instance.
     */
    public void init(ServletConfig config) throws ServletException {
        super.init(config);
        try {
            /*
             * Get the initial context using the above startup params.
             */
            Context ctx = new InitialContext();
            userManager = (UserManager) ctx.lookup(UserManager.class
                    .getName());
            cart = (Cart) ctx.lookup(Cart.class.getName());

        } catch (Exception e) {
            log(e);
            throw new ServletException(e.toString());
        }
    }

    /**
```

Source 17.4 *(continued)*

```
     * The servlet engine calls this method when the user's desktop
     * browser sends an HTTP request.
     */
    public void service(HttpServletRequest request,
                        HttpServletResponse response)
            throws ServletException, IOException {
        /*
         * Set up the user's HttpSession
         */
        HttpSession session = request.getSession(true);

        System.out.println(request.getAttributeNames().toString());
        /*
         * Retrieve the login name/password from the URL string.
         */
        String loginName = request.getParameter("Login");
        String password = request.getParameter("Password");
        boolean isLogin = false;

        /*
         * If user has not tried to log in yet, present him with the
         * login screen.
         */
        if ((loginName == null) || (password == null)) {
            writeForm(request, response, false);
            return;
        } else {
            /*
             * Otherwise, the user has been to this screen already, and
             * has entered some information. Verify that information.
             */
            try {
                isLogin = userManager.validateUser(loginName, password);
            } catch (Exception e) {
                writeForm(request, response, true);
                e.printStackTrace();
                return;
            }
            /*
             * If the passwords match, make a new Cart Session Bean,
             * and add it to the user's HttpSession object. When the
             * user navigates to other servlets, the other servlets can
             * access the HttpSession to get the user's Cart.
             */
```

Source 17.4 *(continued)*

```
            if (isLogin) {
                try {
                    cart.setOwner(loginName);
                    cart.clear();
                    session.setAttribute("cart", cart);

                    /*
                     * Call the main page
                     */
                    RequestDispatcher disp = this.getServletContext()
                            .getRequestDispatcher("/wsf.jsp");
                    disp.forward(request, response);

                    return;
                } catch (Exception e) {
                    log(e);
                    throw new ServletException(e.toString());
                }
            } else
                writeForm(request, response, true);
        }

        /*
         * If there was no match, the user is not authenticated. Present
         * another login screen to him, with an error message indicating
         * that he is not authenticated.
         */
        writeForm(request, response, true);
    }

    /**
     * Writes the login screen (private use only)
     *
     * @param showError
     *          true means show an error b/c client was not
     *          authenticated last time.
     */
    private void writeForm(HttpServletRequest request,
            HttpServletResponse response, boolean showError)
            throws ServletException, IOException {

        /*
         * Set a variable indicating whether or not we failed to log in.
         * The JSP will read this variable.
         */
        request.setAttribute("loginFailed", new Boolean(showError));

        /*
         * Forward the request to the login JSP
```

Source 17.4 *(continued)*

```
        */
        RequestDispatcher disp =
            this.getServletContext().getRequestDispatcher(
                "/login.jsp");
        disp.forward(request, response);
    }

    private void log(Exception e) {
        e.printStackTrace();
    }

    public String getServletInfo() {
        return "The Login servlet verifies a user.";
    }
}
```

Source 17.4 *(continued)*

As a final code example, let's look at the interface that the Pricer component exposes, in Source 17.5.

```
package examples.shop.logic;

import java.util.List;
import examples.shop.impl.entity.LineItem;

/**
 * These are the business logic methods exposed publicly by the
 * Pricer component, a function that computes a price for a
 * given user and base price.
 */

public interface Pricer {
    /**
     * Computes the price of a set of goods
     */

    public double priceSubtotal(String user, List<LineItem> items);

    public double priceTaxes(double subtotal);

    /**
     * @return the applicable tax rate
```

Source 17.5 The Pricer Web service interface. *(continued)*

```
     */
    double getTaxRate();

    /**
     * @return the current discount rate for buying lots of items
     */
    double getBulkDiscountRate();

    /**
     * @return the discount rate for a given user in percent
     */
    double getPersonalDiscountRate(String userName);

    /**
     * This method computes the applicable discount in absolute
     * figure, based on bulk and personal discounts that may apply.
     *
     * @param quantity the number of items that a user intends to buy
     * @param basePrice the overall, non-discounted volume of the
     *        purchase (individual price times quantity)
     * @param the user name
     * @return the subTotal for the line item after applying any
     *         applicable discounts, excluding taxes
     */
    double getDiscount(int quantity, double basePrice, String user);

}
```

Source 17.5 *(continued)*

In the same manner as in Chapter 5, we can let the application server tools generate a WSDL file from the Java session bean class, and then generate SOAP stubs and a JAX-RPC mapping file from the WSDL. The pricer bean exposes and implements a regular business interface in Source 17.6. The rationale here is that other applications at Jasmine's, such as a mail order application, do not use the shopping cart abstraction that our Web shop uses. These applications do need the discount calculation operations, however. Source 17.6 shows the stateless session bean implementation of the Web service.

```
package examples.shop.impl.session;

import java.util.Iterator;
import java.util.List;

import javax.annotation.Resource;
import javax.ejb.EJB;
```

Source 17.6 The Pricer Web service. *(continued)*

```
import javax.ejb.Remote;
import javax.ejb.Stateless;
import javax.jws.WebService;

import examples.shop.impl.entity.Customer;
import examples.shop.impl.entity.LineItem;
import examples.shop.logic.Pricer;
import examples.shop.logic.UserManager;

/**
 * Stateless Session Bean that computes prices based
 * upon a set of pricing rules.  The pricing rules are
 * deployed with the bean as environment properties.
 */
@Stateless
@Remote(Pricer.class)
@WebService(serviceName="PricerService", portName="PricerPort")
public class PricerBean implements Pricer {

    @Resource(name="taxRate")
    public int taxRate = 0;

    @Resource(name="bulkDiscountRate")
    public int bulkDiscountRate = 0;

    @EJB
    UserManager userManager;

    public PricerBean() {
    }

    /**
     * bulk discounts apply to quantities of BULK or more items
     */
    private static final int BULK = 5;

    /**
     * This method computes the applicable discount in absolute
     * figures, based on bulk and personal discounts that may apply.
     *
     * @param quantity the number of items that a user intends to buy
     * @param basePrice the overall, non-discounted volume of the
     *        purchase (individual price times quantity)
     * @param the user name
     * @return the subTotal for the line item after applying any
     *         applicable discounts, excluding taxes
     */
```

Source 17.6 *(continued)*

```
    public double getDiscount(int quantity, double basePrice,
                              String user) {
        double discountRate = getPersonalDiscountRate(user);
        if (quantity >= BULK) {
            discountRate += getBulkDiscountRate();
            System.out.println("Using getBulkDiscountRate " +
                getBulkDiscountRate());
        }

        /*
         * Calculate the discount in absolute figures
         */
        return basePrice * (discountRate / 100);
    }

    /**
     * A bulk discount applies to quantities of more than 5 pieces.
     * @return the bulk discount rate int percent
     */
    public double getBulkDiscountRate() {
        return this.bulkDiscountRate;
    }

    /**
     * Customers with certain names get discounts.  The discount rules
     * are stored in the environment properties that the bean is
     * deployed with.
     */
    public double getPersonalDiscountRate(String userName) {
        /*
         * Get the name of this customer.
         */
        Customer user = userManager.getUser(userName);
        if( user != null)
            return user.getDiscount();
        else
            return 0;
    }

    /**
     * Computes the subtotal price for a set of products the customer
     * is interested in.  The subtotal takes into account the price of
     * each product the customer wants, the quantity of each product,
     * and any personal discounts the customer gets.  However, the
     * subtotal ignores taxes.
     *
```

Source 17.6 *(continued)*

```
     * @param quote All the data needed to compute the
     * subtotal is in this parameter.
     */
    public double priceSubtotal(String user, List<LineItem> items) {
        System.out.println("PricerBean.priceSubtotal() called");

        /*
         * Compute the subtotal
         */
        double subTotal = 0;

            for(Iterator<LineItem> iter = items.iterator();
                  iter.hasNext(); ) {
                LineItem item = iter.next();
                item.setDiscount(
                    getDiscount(item.getQuantity(),
                                item.basePrice(),user));

                /*
                 * Add the price to the subtotal.
                 */
                subTotal += (item.basePrice() - item.getDiscount());
            }

        return subTotal;
    }

    /**
     * Computes the taxes on a quote.
     */
    public double priceTaxes(double subtotal) {
        System.out.println("PricerBean.priceTaxes() called, taxes: " +
            getTaxRate());
        return (getTaxRate() / 100) * subtotal;
    }

    /**
     * @return the applicable tax rate
     */
    public double getTaxRate() {
        return taxRate;
    }
}
```

Source 17.6 *(continued)*

If you're curious to see how the other use cases are implemented, see the book's accompanying source code. And as a reminder, this is just one of many ways to implement a Web architecture.

NOTE As an alternative, we could have also chosen a single-servlet architecture with only one servlet and many JSP files. This single servlet would call Java classes, and each Java class would represent a Web use case and understand the EJB components to call. For example, we could have a Java class that understood how to verify login credentials. The advantage of this paradigm is we could reuse these Web use-case classes in several pages, and our servlet layer would be completely decoupled from our EJB components.

Summary

In this chapter, we've painted a picture of how our e-commerce system should behave. Now that we've made the proper abstractions, our components should fall into place easily. By performing this high-level analysis, we can be confident that our final product will be extensible and reusable for some time to come.

We strongly encourage you to compile and run the example code that we have provided for you. You can use this code as the basis for doing your own experiments with a shopping-style application and for exploring other options. Some of the directions that we encourage you to take with the example is to play with global distributed transactions, devise your own graphic design for the JSP files, let the `OrderProcessor` send e-mail notifications to customers, and perhaps try a different, non-JMS messaging style for the `OrderProcessor` message-driven bean.

APPENDIX

A

RMI-IIOP and JNDI Tutorial

For more technological background on EJB, this appendix explains the technologies that EJB depends upon—Java RMI-IIOP and the Java Naming and Directory Interface (JNDI). RMI-IIOP is the networking protocol used in EJB and is key to interoperability with non-EJB applications, such as legacy applications written in C++ or COBOL. JNDI is how beans (and their clients) look up other beans and external resources by name when dependency injection is not available or sufficient.

The goal of this appendix is to teach you enough about RMI-IIOP and JNDI to be productive in an EJB environment. This tutorial will cover the basics, but is by no means a complete RMI-IIOP and JNDI tutorial, and for good reason—most organizations will not need to use these technologies beyond the extent we describe in this appendix, and your reading time is valuable.

Readers who want to learn more about RMI-IIOP and JNDI should consult the following references:

- **The RMI-IIOP and JNDI tutorials.** These are available for free on the Sun Microsystems Web site at `http://java.sun.com`.
- **The RMI-IIOP and JNDI specifications.** The specifications define the core of RMI-IIOP and JNDI. They are a bit more technical but should not be tough to understand after reading this appendix. They are also downloadable from `http://java.sun.com`.

Java RMI-IIOP

Java RMI (which stands for Java Remote Method Invocation) is a mechanism for performing simple but powerful networking. Using RMI you can write distributed objects in Java, enabling objects to communicate in memory, across Java Virtual Machines and physical devices.

Java RMI-IIOP (which stands for Java RMI over the Internet Inter-ORB Protocol) is J2EE's de facto mechanism for providing networking services relying on the CORBA network protocol IIOP. The main advantage of IIOP over plain RMI's native transport protocol JRMP (Java Remote Method Protocol) is that IIOP lets your code interoperate remotely with any application on any platform that uses CORBA. It is also more mature than JRMP.

NOTE **RMI-JRMP has some interesting features not available in RMI-IIOP, such as distributed garbage collection, object activation, and downloadable class files. Because of the importance of CORBA interoperability, EJB and J2EE mandate that you use RMI-IIOP, not RMI-JRMP, so we focus on this RMI variant exclusively. Note that whenever we refer to RMI in the following, we always mean RMI-IIOP.**

The fundamental concepts of remote invocations that we explain here apply to both RMI-JRMP and RMI-IIOP, but keep in mind that only RMI-IIOP provides CORBA interoperability. We also provide a short survey of the CORBA compatibility features of RMI-IIOP later in this chapter.

Remote Method Invocations

A *remote procedure call (RPC)* is a procedural invocation from a process on one machine to a process on another machine. RPCs enable traditional procedures to reside on multiple machines yet still remain in communication. They provide a simple way to perform cross-process or cross-machine networking.

A *remote method invocation (RMI)* in Java takes the RPC concept one step further and allows for distributed *object* communications. RMI enables you to invoke not procedures, but methods, on objects remotely. You can build your networked code as full objects. This yields the benefits of object-oriented programming, such as inheritance, encapsulation, and polymorphism.

Remote method invocations are by no means a simple mechanism. These are just some of the issues that arise:

- **Marshaling and unmarshaling.** RMIs (as well as RPCs) enable you to pass parameters, including Java primitives and Java objects, over the network. But what if the target machine represents data differently than the way you represent data? For example, what happens if one machine uses a different binary standard to represent numbers? The problem becomes even more apparent when you start talking about objects. What happens if you send an object reference over the wire? That pointer is not usable on the other machine because that machine's memory layout is completely different from yours. *Marshaling* and *unmarshaling* is the process of massaging parameters so that they are usable on the machine on which they are invoked remotely. It is the packaging and unpackaging of parameters so that they are usable in two heterogeneous environments. As you will see, this is taken care of for you by Java and RMI-IIOP.

- **Parameter passing semantics.** There are two major ways to pass parameters when calling a method: *pass-by-value* and *pass-by-reference* (see Figure A.1). When you use the pass-by-value parameter, you pass a copy of your data so that the target method is using a copy, rather than the original data. Any changes to the argument are reflected only in the copy, not the original. Pass-by-reference, on the other hand, does not make a copy. With pass-by-reference, any modifications to parameters made by the remote host affect the original data. The flexibility of both the pass-by-reference and pass-by-value models is advantageous, and RMI supports both. You'll see how in the following pages.
- **Network or machine instability.** With a single JVM application, a crash of the JVM brings the entire application down. But consider a distributed object application, which has many JVMs working together to solve a business problem. In this scenario, a crash of a single JVM should not cause the distributed object system to grind to a halt. To enforce this, remote method invocations need a standardized way of handling a JVM crash, a machine crash, or network instability. When some code performs a remote invocation, the code should be informed of any problems encountered during the operation. RMI performs this for you, abstracting out any JVM, machine, or network problems from your code.

As you can see, there's a lot involved in performing remote invocations. RMI handles many of these nasty networking issues for you.

J2EE-compliant servers are required to ship RMI-IIOP implementations to enable you to perform networking. Your RMI code is then portable to any hardware or operating system on which these implementations execute. Better still, RMI-IIOP lets you even communicate with non-EJB, non-Java applications written in any language such as banking applications written in C++ or COBOL. Contrast this with proprietary, platform-dependent RPC libraries, and you can see some real value in RMI-IIOP.

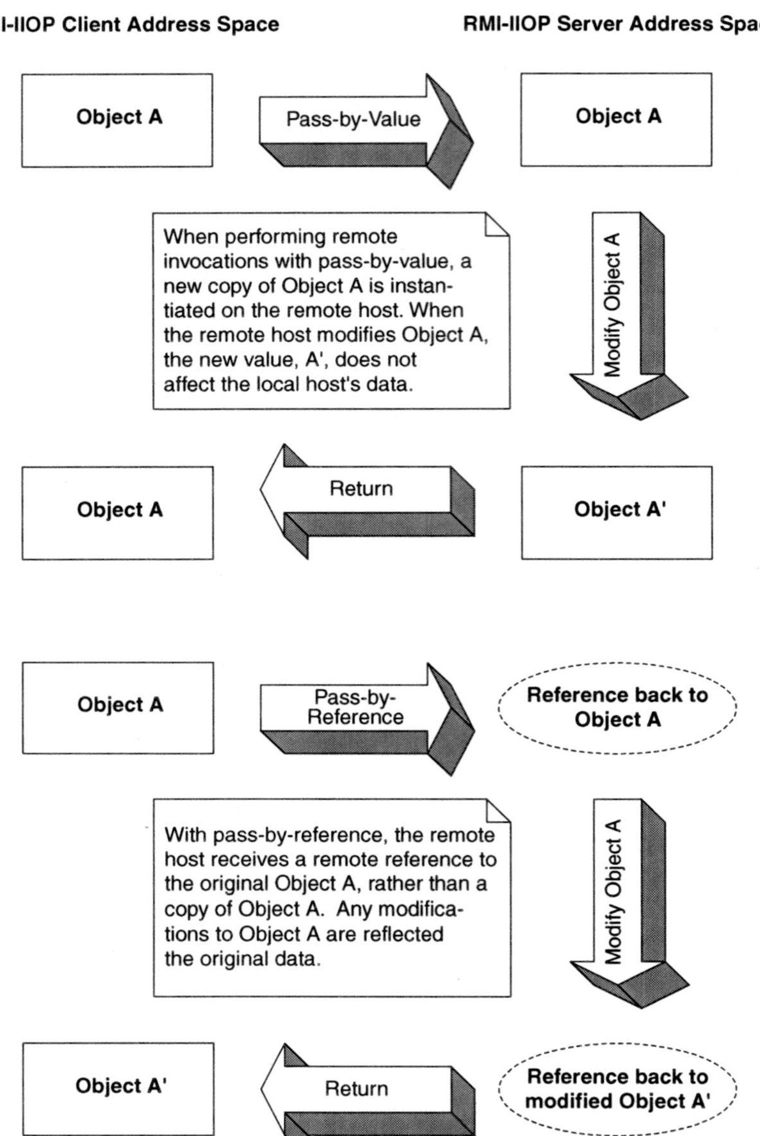

Figure A.1 Pass-by-value versus pass-by-reference.

The Remote Interface

We begin our exploration of RMI by reviewing one of object-oriented design's great programming practices—the separation of the interface of code from its implementation.

- **The interface** defines the exposed information about an object, such as the names of its methods and what parameters those methods take. It's what the client works with. The interface masks the implementation from the viewpoint of clients of the object, so clients deal only with the end result: the methods the object exposes.
- **The implementation** is the core programming logic that an object provides. It has some very specific algorithms, logic, and data.

By separating interface from implementation, you can vary an object's proprietary logic without changing any client code. For example, you can plug in a different algorithm that performs the same task more efficiently.

RMI makes extensive use of this concept. All networking code you write is applied to interfaces, *not* implementations. In fact, you *must* use this paradigm in RMI—you do not have a choice. It is impossible to perform a remote invocation directly on an object implementation because the RMI networking service layer needs to get involved to contact the remote object.

Therefore, when using RMI, you must build a custom interface, called a *remote interface*. This remote interface *extends* the interface `java.rmi.Remote`. Your interface provides all methods that your remote object exposes.

We'll now begin to build a simple example illustrating the basics of RMI. In this example, a remote object exposes one method: `generate()`. The `generate()` method returns a new, unique long number each time it's called. This is useful, for example, when generating primary keys for data, such as entity beans (discussed in Chapter 6).

Source A.1 is a valid remote interface.

```
package examples.jndi;

import java.rmi.Remote;
import java.rmi.RemoteException;

/**
 * The remote interface for the remote object. Clients use it
 * for all operations on the remote object.
 */
public interface PrimaryKeyGenerator extends Remote {
    public long generate() throws RemoteException;
}
```

Source A.1 primaryKeyGenerator.java.

Client code that wants to call methods on your remote object must operate on `PrimaryKeyGenerator`. Notice that each method must also declare a `java.rmi.RemoteException`. A `RemoteException` is thrown when there is a problem with the network, such as a machine crashing or the network dying.

NOTE With RMI, you can never fully separate your application from the network. At some point, you'll need to deal with remote exceptions being thrown due to networking issues. Some may consider this a limitation of RMI because the network is not entirely transparent: Remote exceptions force you to differentiate a local method from a remote method. But in some ways, this is an advantage of RMI as well. Interlacing your code with remote exceptions forces you to think about the network and encourages distributed object developers to consider issues such as invocation latency, the network failing, the size of parameters going across the network, and more.

The Remote Object Implementation

Remote objects are networked object implementations that can be called by code in another JVM. They *implement* a remote interface and thus expose methods that can be invoked by remote clients.

The physical locations of remote objects and the clients that invoke them are not important. For example, it is possible for a client running in the same address space as a remote object to invoke a method on that object. It's also possible for a client across the Internet to do the same thing. To the remote object, both invocations appear to be the same.

To make your object available as a remote object and allow remote hosts to invoke its methods, your remote class must perform *one* of the following steps:

- **Extend the class** `javax.rmi.PortableRemoteObject` . `PortableRemoteObject` is a base class from which you can derive your remote objects. When your remote object is constructed, it automatically calls the `PortableRemoteObject` constructor, which makes the object available to be called remotely.
- **Manually export your objects as remote objects.** Perhaps your remote object class needs to inherit implementation from another custom class. In this case, because Java does not allow for multiple implementation inheritance, you cannot extend `PortableRemoteObject`. Therefore, you must manually export your object so that it is available to be invoked on by remote hosts. To export your object, call `javax.rmi.PortableRemoteObject.exportObject()`.

Now let's create the remote object class. This class implements the `PrimaryKeyGenerator` interface, and it is shown in Source A.2.

```
package examples.jndi;

import java.rmi.RemoteException;
import javax.rmi.PortableRemoteObject;

/**
 * The implementation of a remote object which generates primary keys
 */
public class PrimaryKeyGeneratorImpl
    extends PortableRemoteObject
    implements PrimaryKeyGenerator {

    private static long i = System.currentTimeMillis();

    public PrimaryKeyGeneratorImpl() throws Exception, RemoteException {
        /*
         * Since we extend PortableRemoteObject, the super
         * class will export our remote object here.
         */
        super();
    }

    /**
     * Generates a unique primary key
     */
    public synchronized long generate() throws RemoteException {
        return i++;
    }
}
```

Source A.2 PrimaryKeyGeneratorImpl.java.

Extending `javax.rmi.PortableRemoteObject` makes the object available to be called remotely. Once the remote object's constructor is complete, this object is available forever for any virtual machine to invoke on; that is, until someone calls `unexportObject()`.

ISSUES WITH OUR PRIMARY KEY GENERATION ALGORITHM

Our primary key generation algorithm is to simply increment a number each time someone calls our server. This generator overcomes two common challenges when writing an RMI implementation:

- **Threading. RMI-IIOP allows many clients to connect to a server at once. Thus, our remote object implementation may have many threads running inside of it. But when generating primary keys, we never want to generate a duplicate key because our keys are not unique and thus would not be good candidates to use in a database. Therefore, it is important to have the synchronized block around the `generate()` method, so that only one client can generate a primary key at a time.**
- ***JVM crashes.* We must protect against a JVM crash (or hardware failure). Thus, we initialize our generator to the current time (the number of milliseconds that have elapsed since 1970). This is to ensure that our primary key generator increases monotonically (that is, primary keys are always going up in value) in case of a JVM crash. Note that we haven't considered daylight savings time resulting in duplicate keys. If we were to use this code in production, we would need to account for that.**

If you need to generate primary keys in production, see the companion book to this book, Floyd Marinescu's *EJB Design Patterns* (ISBN 0-4712-0831-0), published by John Wiley & Sons.

Stubs and Skeletons

Now that we've seen the server code, let's look at the architecture for networking in RMI. One of the benefits of RMI is an almost illusionary, transparent networking. You can invoke methods on remote objects just as you would invoke a method on any other Java object. In fact, RMI completely masks whether the object you're invoking on is local or remote. This is called *local/remote transparency*.

Local/remote transparency is not as easy as it sounds. To mask that you're invoking an object residing on a remote host, RMI needs some way to simulate a local object that you can invoke on. This local object is called a *stub*. It is responsible for accepting method calls locally and *delegating* those method calls to their actual object implementations, which are possibly located across the network. This effectively makes every remote invocation appear to be a local invocation. You can think of a stub as a placeholder for an object that knows how to look over the network for the real object. Because you invoke methods on local stubs, all the nasty networking issues are hidden.

Stubs are only half of the picture. We'd like the remote objects themselves—the objects that are being invoked from remote hosts—not to worry about networking issues as well. Just as a client invokes methods on a stub that is local to that client, your remote object needs to accept calls from a *skeleton* that is local to that remote object. Skeletons are responsible for receiving calls over the network (perhaps from a stub) and delegating those calls to the remote object implementation (see Figure A.2).

RMI-IIOP provides a means to *generate* the needed stubs and skeletons, thus relieving you of the networking burden. Typically, this is achieved through command-line tools. The core J2SE includes a tool called *rmic* (which stands for the RMI compiler) to generate stub and skeleton classes. As you can see from Figure A.2, you must deploy the stub on the client machine and the skeleton on the server machine.

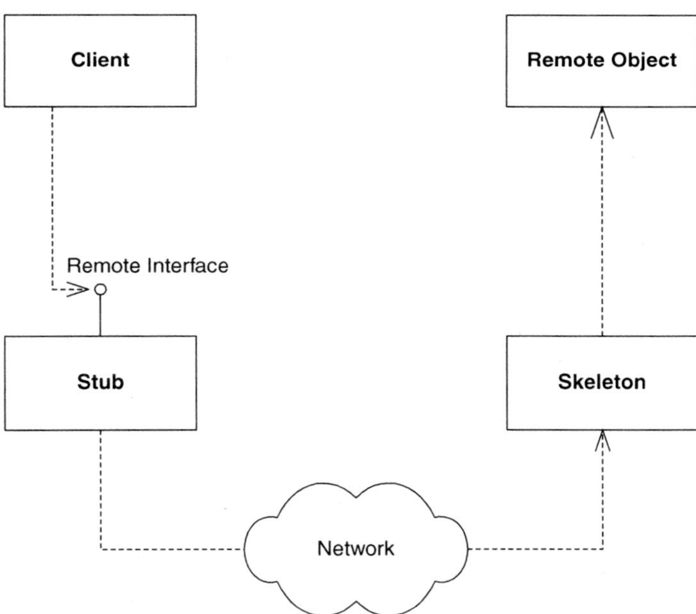

Figure A.2 Stubs and skeletons.

Object Serialization and Parameter Passing

One of the more interesting responsibilities of stubs and skeletons is to handle your parameters. The following section discusses how parameters are passed in Java RMI. We also explore the role of *object serialization* in parameter passing.

Passing by Value

When invoking a method using RMI-IIOP, all parameters to the remote method are passed *by value*. This means that when a client calls a server, all parameters are copied from one machine to the other.

Passing objects by value is very different from passing objects in the Java programming language. When you call a method in Java and pass an object as a parameter, that object is passed *by reference*. More specifically, the reference to the object is copied, but the actual object's data is not.

There's a big problem with passing by value. If you're trying to pass an object over the network and that object contains references to other objects, how are those references resolved on the target machine? A memory address on one machine does not map to the same memory address on another machine. Also, the referenced object may not even exist on the target machine. How do you get around this?

Object Serialization

Java introduces the concept of *object serialization* to handle this problem. *Serialization* is the conversion of a Java object into a bit-blob representation of that object. You can send bit-blobs anywhere. For example, you can use object serialization as an instant file format for your objects and save them to your hard disk. RMI also uses object serialization to send parameters over the network. When you're ready to use the object again, you must deserialize the bit-blob back into a Java object. Then it's magically usable again.

The Java language handles the low-level details of serialization. In most cases, you don't need to worry about any of it. To tell Java that your object is serializable, your object must implement the `java.lang.Serializable` interface. That's all there is to it: Take this one simple step, and let Java handle the rest. `java.lang.Serializable` defines no methods at all—it's simply a *marker interface* that identifies your object as something that can be serialized and deserialized.

You can provide your own custom serialization by implementing the `writeObject()` method on your object, or provide custom deserialization by implementing `readObject()`. This might be useful if you'd like to perform some sort of compression on your data before your object is converted into a bit-blob and decompression after the bit-blob is restored to an object.

Figure A.3 shows the serialization/deserialization API, where `writeObject()` is responsible for saving the state of the class, and `readObject()` is responsible for restoring the state of the class. These two methods will be called automatically when an object instance is being serialized or deserialized. If you choose not to define these methods, then the default serialization mechanisms will be applied. The default mechanisms are good enough for most situations.

Rules for Serialization

Java serialization has the following rules for member variables held in serialized objects:

- Any basic primitive type (`int`, `char`, and so on) is serializable and will be serialized with the object, unless marked with the `transient` keyword. If serialized, the values of these types are available again after deserialization.
- Java objects can be included with the serialized bit-blob or not; it's your choice. The way you make your choice is as follows:
  - Objects marked with the `transient` keyword are not serialized with the object and are not available when deserialized.
  - Any object that is not marked with the `transient` keyword must implement `java.lang.Serializable`. These objects are converted to the bit-blob format along with the original object. If your Java objects aren't transient and don't implement `java.lang.Serializable`, a `NotSerializable` exception is thrown when `writeObject()` is called.

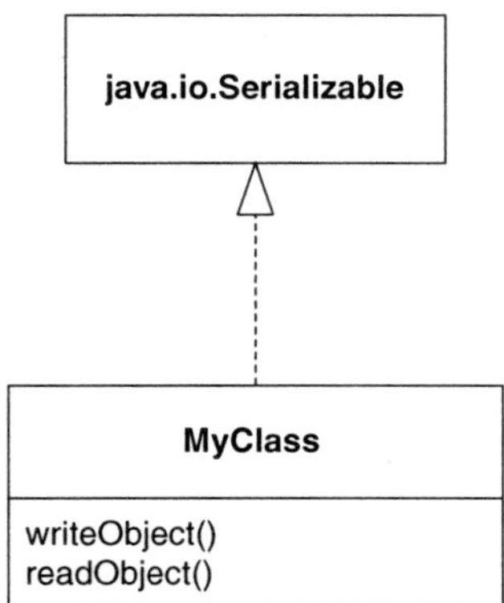

Figure A.3 The Java serialization API.

Thus, when you serialize an object, you also serialize all nontransient subobjects as well. This means you also serialize all nontransient sub-subobjects (the objects referenced from the subobjects). This is repeated recursively for every object until the entire reference graph of objects is serialized. This recursion is handled automatically by Java serialization (see Figure A.4). You simply need to make sure that each of your member objects implements the `java.lang.Serializable` interface. When serializing `MyClass`, object serialization will recurse through the dependencies shown, packaging the entire graph of objects as a stream. In Figure A.4, everything will be serialized except for transient long b, since it is marked as transient.

What Should You Make Transient?

How do you know which member variables should be marked transient and which should not? Here are some good reasons to mark an object as transient:

- The object is large. Large objects may not be suitable for serialization because operations you do with the serialized blob may be very intensive. Examples here include saving the blob to disk or transporting the blob across the network.
- The object represents a local resource or other data that cannot be meaningfully reconstructed on the target machine. Some examples of such resources are thread objects, database connections, and sockets.
- The object represents sensitive information that you do not want to pass in a serialized stream.

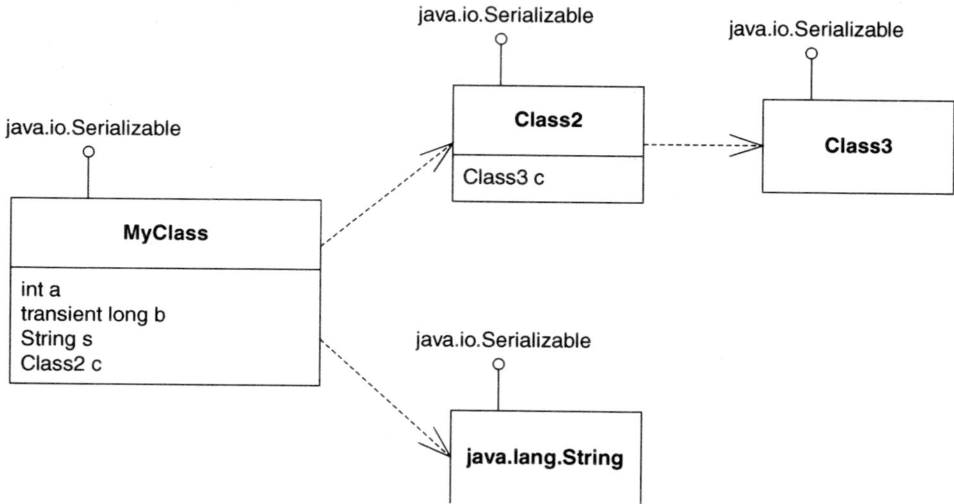

Figure A.4 Object serialization recursion.

Note that object serialization is not free—it is a heavyweight operation for large graphs of objects. Make sure you take this into account when designing your distributed object application.

Object Serialization and RMI

Java RMI relies on object serialization for passing parameters via remote method invocations. Figure A.5 shows what the `MyObject` object graph could look like. Notice that every field and subfield is a valid type for Java serialization.

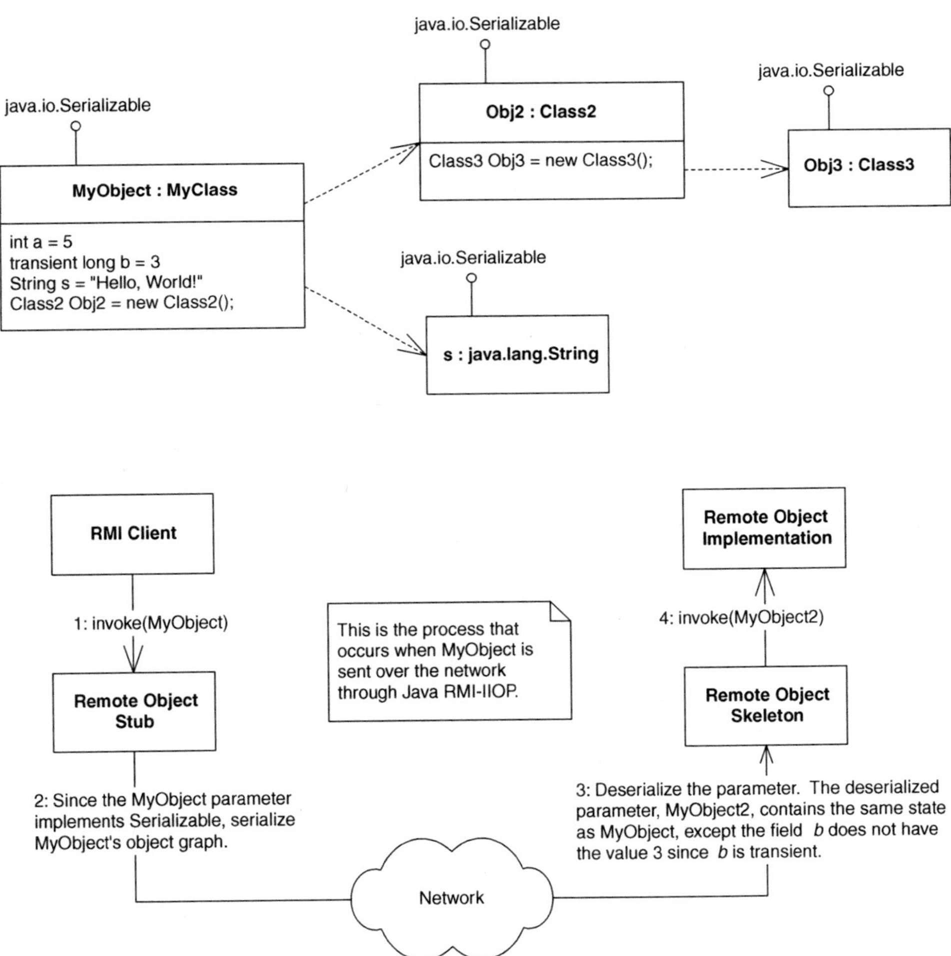

Figure A.5 Java RMI and object serialization.

Figure A.5 shows how RMI handles pass-by-value, where an entire graph of objects is serialized into a bit-blob, sent across the network, and then deserialized on the target machine.

Pass-by-Reference Semantics

Passing parameters by value can lead to inefficiencies. What if your referenced graph of objects is very large? What if you have lots of state to send across the network? The ensuing network lag from performing the invocation may be unacceptable.

There is another way to pass arguments. RMI *simulates* pass-by-reference semantics, which means the arguments are not copied over. Rather, a remote reference to client's parameters is copied over to the server.

If you want to pass a parameter by reference, the parameter must itself be a remote object. When the client calls the server, the RMI runtime sends a network reference to that remote object to the server. The server creates a stub object from that reference and can perform a callback on that stub, which connects the server to the remote object living on the client machine. Figure A.6 shows the process that occurs when `MyRemoteObject`, an instance of `MyRemoteClass`, is sent over the network through Java RMI.

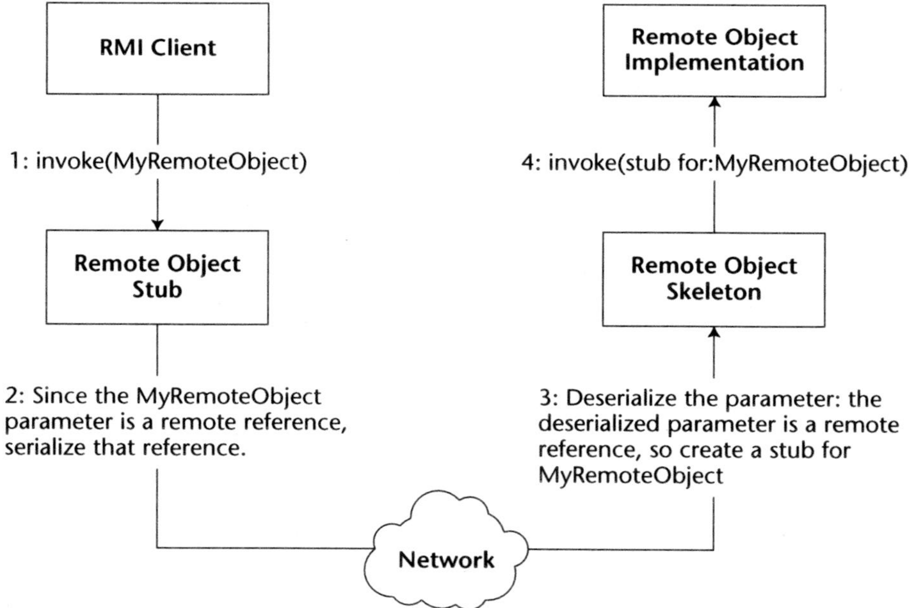

Figure A.6 Pass-by-reference with Java RMI.

The best way to understand this paradigm is by analogy. In the Java programming language, when you pass an object as a parameter, the object reference is copied. In RMI, when you pass an object as a parameter, the network reference is copied. Both of these strategies achieve pass-by-reference because they are cloning the thing that points to the object, rather than the object itself.

Because Java RMI references are also serializable, they are passable over the network as a bit-blob. This is why earlier we said that *all* parameters in Java RMI are passed by value. Thus, Java RMI only *simulates* pass-by-reference by passing a serializable reference, rather than serializing the original object. By making your parameters remote objects, you can effectively avoid the network lag in passing large objects. As usual, there is no such thing as a free lunch: In return for this reduced transfer cost, you will have to pay a price when accessing your object, because all accesses are remote invocations now.

In summary, we have the following rules for passing objects using Java RMI:

- All Java basic primitives are passed by value when calling methods remotely. This means copies are made of the parameters. Any changes to the data on the remote host are not reflected in the original data.
- If you want to pass an object over the network by value, it must implement `java.lang.Serializable`. Anything referenced from within that object must follow the rules for Java serialization. Again, any changes to the data on the remote host are not reflected in the original data.
- If you want to pass an object over the network by reference, it must be a remote object, and it must implement `java.rmi.Remote`. A stub for the remote object is serialized and passed to the remote host. The remote host can then use that stub to invoke callbacks on your remote object. There is only one copy of the object at any time, which means that all hosts are calling the same object.

CORBA Interoperability with RMI-IIOP

RMI-IIOP enables EJB applications to communicate with existing CORBA applications, as well as to integrate with existing investments written in non-Java languages, such as C++ and COBOL.

The *Common Object Request Broker Architecture* (CORBA) is a unifying standard for writing distributed object systems. The standard is completely neutral with respect to platform, language, and vendor. Many of the concepts in EJB came out of CORBA, which incorporates a host of technologies and is much broader in scope than J2EE.

As one of the key parts of the CORBA specification, the OMG has defined the *Internet Inter-ORB Protocol* (IIOP, pronounced "eye-op"). IIOP is the standard Internet protocol for CORBA and the transport layer underneath RMI-IIOP.

With RMI-IIOP, we can perform the following:

- **Combine client-side Java RMI with server-side CORBA.** We can write an object implementation to the CORBA API and write client code to the Java RMI API to call that CORBA object. This is shown in Figure A.7.
- **Combine client-side CORBA with server-side Java RMI.** We can write a remote object implementation with the RMI API and have a client written to the CORBA API to call that object. This is shown in Figure A.8.

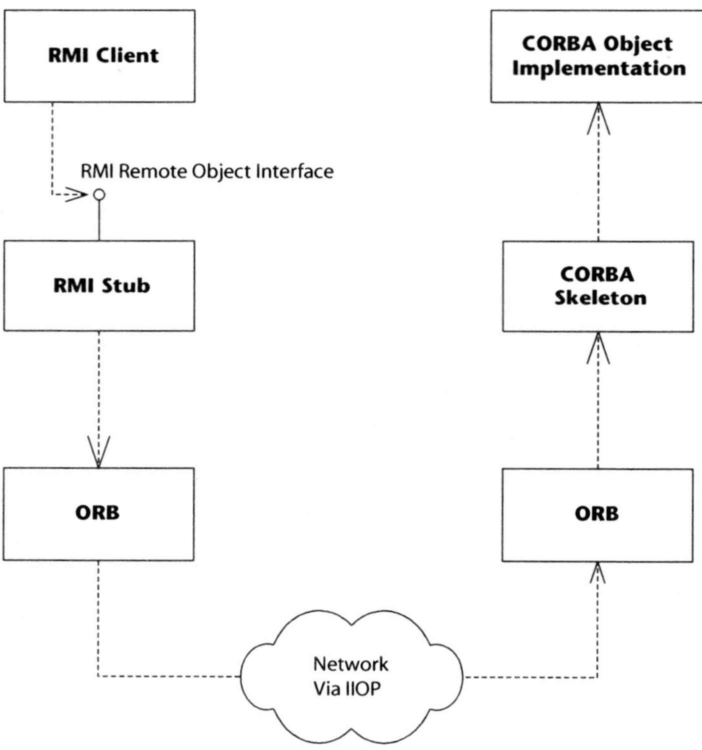

Figure A.7 An RMI client calling a CORBA object implementation.

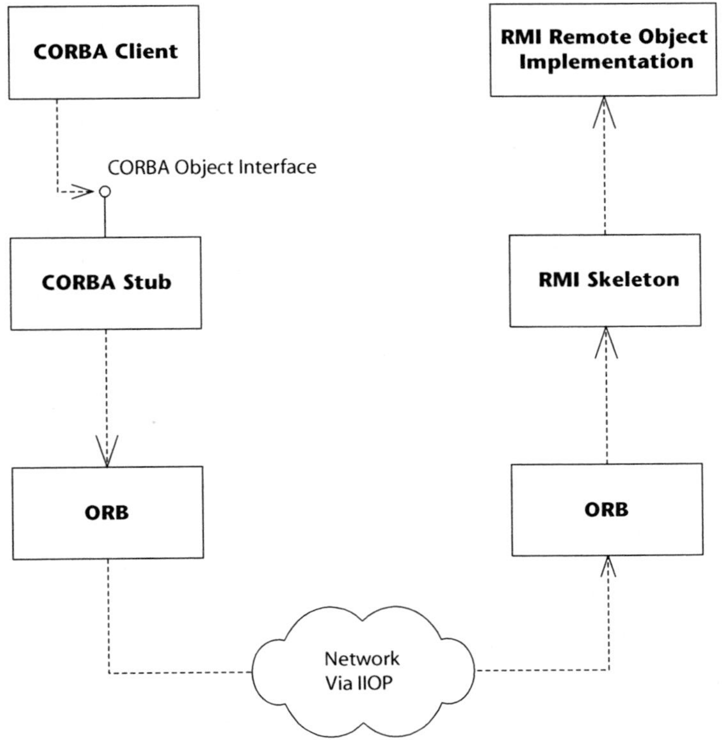

Figure A.8 A CORBA client calling an RMI remote object implementation.

The Big Picture: CORBA and EJB Together

CORBA and EJB have an interesting relationship. They compete with one another in some respects (due to CORBA Components), and at the same time, they complement each other. This is because CORBA is often the enabling technology that resides beneath the EJB level. Many EJB server vendors layer their EJB products on top of an existing CORBA infrastructure, and RMI-IIOP allows just this to happen.

CORBA-EJB interoperability has been a solid technology for years now, and it provides several benefits. The biggest benefit is that CORBA clients written in any language can call your enterprise beans.

Another benefit of CORBA-EJB interoperability is at the transaction and security level. Clients can mix calls to both CORBA objects and enterprise beans under the hood of the same transaction. Similarly, you should be able to construct a distributed transaction that spans heterogeneous EJB servers. And finally, you should be able to propagate security contexts from one EJB server to another, allowing for single sign-on between different EJB server vendors.

After this whirlwind tour of remote invocations, let's move on. For us to complete our RMI sample application, we need some way to publish the server and have the client locate that server. This process, called *bootstrapping*, is achieved via the JNDI. Let's put our RMI example on hold while we learn about JNDI. We'll return later to complete the example.

The Java Naming and Directory Interface

The Java Naming and Directory Interface (JNDI) is a Java API that provides a standard interface for locating users, machines, networks, objects, and services by name. For example, you can use JNDI to locate a printer on your corporate intranet. You can also use it to locate a Java object or a database. JNDI is used in EJB, RMI-IIOP, JDBC, and more. It is the standard Java way of looking up things by name over the network and is also used to manage an enterprise bean's environment.

Why Use JNDI?

In many cases, EJBs inside the container need not use JNDI directly because there are both declarative and programmatic means to refer to external resources by name.

Throughout this book, we have already seen examples of beans that use annotations that require the container to inject named environment resources. The container looks up these environment references in a dedicated JNDI environment naming context t `java:comp/env`.

Bean code can also access this context using the simple `javax.ejb.EJBContext.lookup(name)` method. In this case, the name argument is relative to the bean's `java:comp/env` context.

While these mechanisms rely on JNDI but are simpler and more convenient to use, they do not make the JNDI API redundant: Client code outside a container or more advanced applications that require access to multiple namespaces or that need to manipulate namespaces dynamically will still use the JNDI API.

Naming and Directory Services

To understand JNDI, you must first understand the concept of naming and directory services.

A *name* is like a reference in that it denotes an entity, for example an object or a person. The name is not the same as the referenced thing and has no meaning by itself ("What's in a name?"). Names are often preferred over other kinds of references because they are easier to use and remember than unwieldy references like phone numbers, SSNs, IP addresses, or remote object references.

A *naming service* is analogous to a telephone operator. When you want to call someone over the phone and you don't know that person's phone number, you can call your telephone company's information service operator to *look up* the person you want to talk with. You supply the telephone operator with the name of the person. The operator then looks up the phone number of the person you want to speak with and returns it to you. (The operator can even dial the number for you, connecting you to that person, but that is beyond what a pure naming service will do for you.)

A naming service is an entity that performs the following tasks:

- **It associates names with objects.** We call this *binding* names to objects. This is similar to a telephone company's associating a person's name with a specific residence's telephone number.
- **It provides a facility to find an object based on a name.** We call this looking up an object, or *resolving* a name. This is similar to a telephone operator finding a person's telephone number based on that person's name.

Naming services are everywhere in computing. When you want to locate a machine on the network, the *Domain Name System (DNS)* is used to translate a machine name to an IP address. If you look up www.wiley.com on the Internet, the name www.wiley.com is translated into the object (which happens to be a String) `208.215.179.146` by the DNS.

Another example of naming occurs in file systems. When you access a file on your hard disk, you supply a name for the file such as `c:\autoexec.bat` or `/etc/fstab`. How is this name translated into an actual file of data? A file system naming service can be consulted to provide this functionality.

In general, a naming service can be used to find any kind of object by name, such as a file handle on your hard drive or a printer located across the network. But one type of object is of particular importance: a *directory object* (or *directory entry*). A directory object differs from a generic object because you can store *attributes* with directory objects. These attributes can be used for a wide variety of purposes.

For example, you can use a directory object to represent a user in your company. You can store information about that user, such as the user's password, as attributes in the directory object. If you have an application that requires authentication, you can store a user's login name and password in directory object attributes. When a client connects to your application, the client supplies a login name and password, which you can compare with the login name and password that are stored as a directory object's attributes. You can store other attributes besides a login name and password, including a user's e-mail address, phone number, and postal address.

A *directory service* is a naming service that has been extended and enhanced to provide directory object operations for manipulating attributes. A directory is a system of directory objects that are all connected. Some examples of directory products are Novell eDirectory Netscape Directory Server, Microsoft Active Directory, or OpenLDAP. Your company probably uses a directory to store internal company information (locations of computers, current printer status, personnel data, and so on).

What does a directory look like internally? The directory's contents—the set of connected directory objects—usually forms a hierarchical treelike structure. Why would you want a treelike structure? A tree's form suggests the way a real-world company is organized. For example, the *root* (or top node) of your directory tree can represent your entire company. One branch off the root could represent people in the company, while another branch could represent network services. Each branch could have subtrees that decrease in granularity more and more, until you are at individual user objects, printer objects, machine objects, and the like. This is illustrated in Figure A.9.

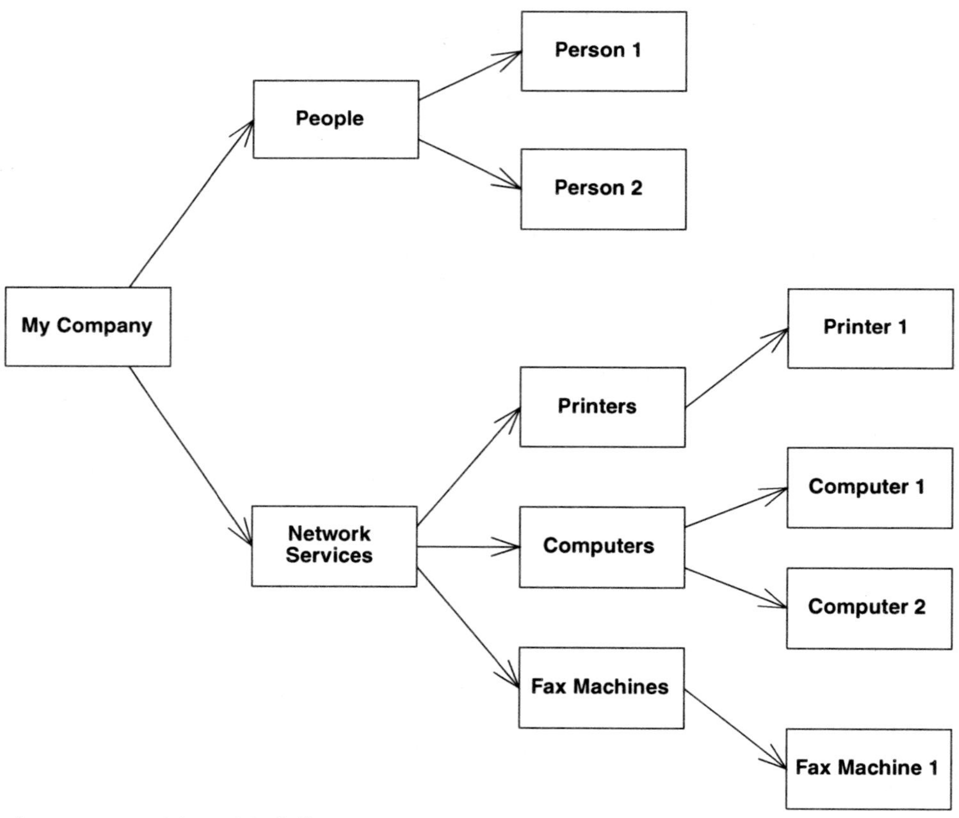

Figure A.9 A hierarchical directory structure.

All in all, directories are not very different from databases. A database can store arbitrary data, just as a directory can. Databases provide query operations to look up items in a database, just as directories do. You can think of a directory as a scaled-down, simplified database. In fact, most directories are implemented by a database behind the scenes.

Problems with Naming and Directories

There are many popular naming and directory products out today. Directory vendors differentiate their product lines by offering different types of services. Unfortunately, this leads to different naming and directory standards. And each directory standard has a different protocol for accessing the directory. For example, directories based on the *Lightweight Directory Access Protocol* (LDAP) are accessed differently than those based on the *Network Information System* (NIS) or Novell's *Network Directory System* (NDS).

This means that if you want to switch directory vendors, you need to rewrite all your client code that accesses the directory. It also means you need to download a new library, learn a new API, and test new code each time you use a different directory.

Initially, LDAP was meant to resolve this problem by becoming *the* ubiquitous protocol for directories. LDAP is straightforward and has been adopted quickly by the industry—IBM's Lotus Notes and Microsoft's Active Directory both are LDAP-based. However, not all directory products are LDAP-based.

Enter JNDI

JNDI is a system for Java-based clients to interact with naming and directory systems. JNDI is a *bridge* over naming and directory services, a beast that provides one common interface to disparate directories. Users who need to access an LDAP directory use the same API as users who want to access an NIS directory or a Novell directory. All directory operations are done through the JNDI interface, providing a common framework.

Benefits of JNDI

The following surveys the advantages that JNDI has to offer:

- You need to learn only a single API to access all sorts of directory service information, such as security credentials, phone numbers, electronic and postal mail addresses, application preferences, network addresses, machine configurations, and more.
- JNDI insulates the application from protocol and implementation details.

- You can use JNDI to read and write whole Java objects from directories.
- You can link different types of directories, such as an LDAP directory with an NDS directory, and have the combination appear to be one large, federated directory. The federated directory appears to the client to be one contiguous directory.

In J2EE, you can use JNDI for many purposes. These include:

- Using JNDI to acquire a reference to the *Java Transaction API* (JTA) *User-Transaction* interface
- Using JNDI to connect to resource factories, such as JDBC drivers or Java Message Service (JMS) drivers
- Using JNDI for clients and for beans to look up other beans

The JNDI Architecture

JNDI is made up of two halves: *the client API* and the *Service Provider Interface* (SPI). The client API allows your Java code to perform directory operations. This API is uniform for all types of directories. You will spend the most time using the client API.

The JNDI SPI is a framework for JNDI implementors: an interface that implementations of naming and directory services can be plugged into. The SPI is the converse of the API: While the API allows clients to code to a single, unified interface, the SPI allows naming and directory service vendors to fit their particular proprietary protocols into the system, as shown in Figure A.10. This allows client code to leverage proprietary naming and directory services in Java while maintaining a high level of code portability.

The JNDI architecture is somewhat like the Java Database Connectivity (JDBC) package:

- In JDBC, one uniform client API performs database operations. In JNDI, naming and directory service clients invoke a unified API for performing naming and directory operations.
- In JDBC, relational database vendors provide JDBC drivers to access their particular databases. In JNDI, directory vendors provide *service providers* to access their specific directories. These providers are aware of specific directory protocols, and they plug in to the JNDI SPI.

For example, the J2SE includes an LDAP service provider for free. The LDAP service provider knows how to map a JNDI client API operation into an LDAP operation. It then executes the LDAP operation on an LDAP directory, using the specific LDAP protocol.

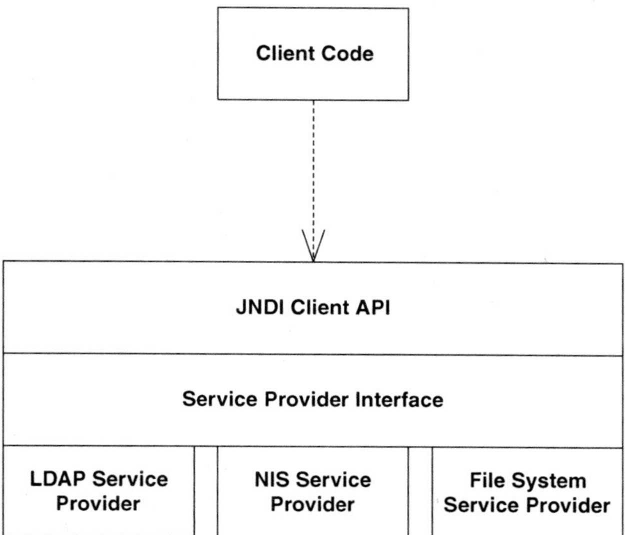

Figure A.10 The JNDI architecture.

A number of JNDI service providers are bundled with the core J2SE, including LDAP, RMI-IIOP, CORBA Naming Service and DNS, other providers available separately include NIS, Novell NDS, SLP, File System, and many more. The JNDI homepage (`http://java.sun.com/products/jndi`) has a list of service providers.

Java EE servers *bundle* a JNDI implementation with their product. Typically, this is a custom implementation provided by the Java EE server vendor. JNDI then just becomes another service provided by the server, along with RMI-IIOP, JMS, and so on. Many servers ship JNDI implementations that are fault tolerant, providing a high level of availability. These JNDI implementations are intended to integrate with the other Java EE services, such as RMI-IIOP, JDBC, EJB, and JMS.

JNDI Concepts

We begin our JNDI exploration with naming concepts. There are several kinds of names in JNDI:

- An *atomic name* is a simple, basic, indivisible name. For example, in the string `/etc/fstab`, `etc` and `fstab` are atomic names.
- A *compound name* is zero or more atomic names put together using a specific syntax. In the previous example, the entire string `/etc/fstab` is a compound name formed by combining two atomic names with a slash.

A *binding* is an association of a name with an object. For example, the file name autoexec.bat in the Windows file system has a binding to the file data on your hard disk. Your c:\windows folder is a name that is bound to a folder on your hard drive. Note that a compound name such as /usr/people/ed/.cshrc consists of multiple bindings, one to usr, one to people, one to ed, and one to .cshrc.

A *context* is a set of zero or more bindings. Each binding has a distinct atomic name. So for example, in the UNIX file system, let's consider a folder named /etc that contains files named mtab and exports. In JNDI, the /etc folder is a context containing bindings with atomic names mtab and exports. Each of the mtab and exports atomic names is bound to a file on the hard disk.

To expand this further, consider a folder named /usr with subfolders /usr/people, /usr/bin, and /usr/local. Here, the /usr folder is a context that contains the people, bin, and local atomic names. Each of these atomic names is bound to a subfolder. In JNDI terms, these subfolders are called *subcontexts*. Each subcontext is a full-fledged context in its own right, and it can contain more name-object bindings, such as other files or other folders. Figure A.11 depicts the concepts we have learned so far.

Naming Systems, Namespaces, and Composite Names

A *naming system* is a connected set of contexts that use the same name syntax. For example, a branch of an LDAP tree could be considered a naming system, as could a folder tree in a file system. Unfortunately, naming systems each have a different syntax for accessing contexts. For example, in an LDAP tree, a compound name is identified by a string such as cn=Benjamin Franklin, ou=People, o=Former-Presidents.org, c=us, whereas a file system compound name might look like c:\java\lib\tools.jar.

A *namespace* is the set of names contained within a naming system. Your hard drive's entire collection of file names and directories or folders is your hard drive file system's namespace. The set of all names in an LDAP directory's tree is an LDAP server's namespace. Naming systems and namespaces are shown in Figure A.12. This branch of a hard disk is an example of a naming system because it's a connected set of contexts. Within this naming system, the namespace is every name shown.

A *composite name* is a name that spans multiple naming systems. For example, on the Web, the URL http://java.sun.com/products/ejb/index.html is composed of the following namespaces:

- *http* comes from the *URL scheme-id* namespace. You can use other scheme-ids, such as ftp and telnet. This namespace defines the protocol you use to communicate.

- *java.sun.com* uses the DNS to translate machine names into IP addresses.
- *products, ejb,* and *index.html* are from the file system namespace on the Web server machine.

By linking multiple naming systems as in the preceding URL, we can arrive at a unified *composite namespace* (also called a *federated namespace*) containing all the bindings of each naming system.

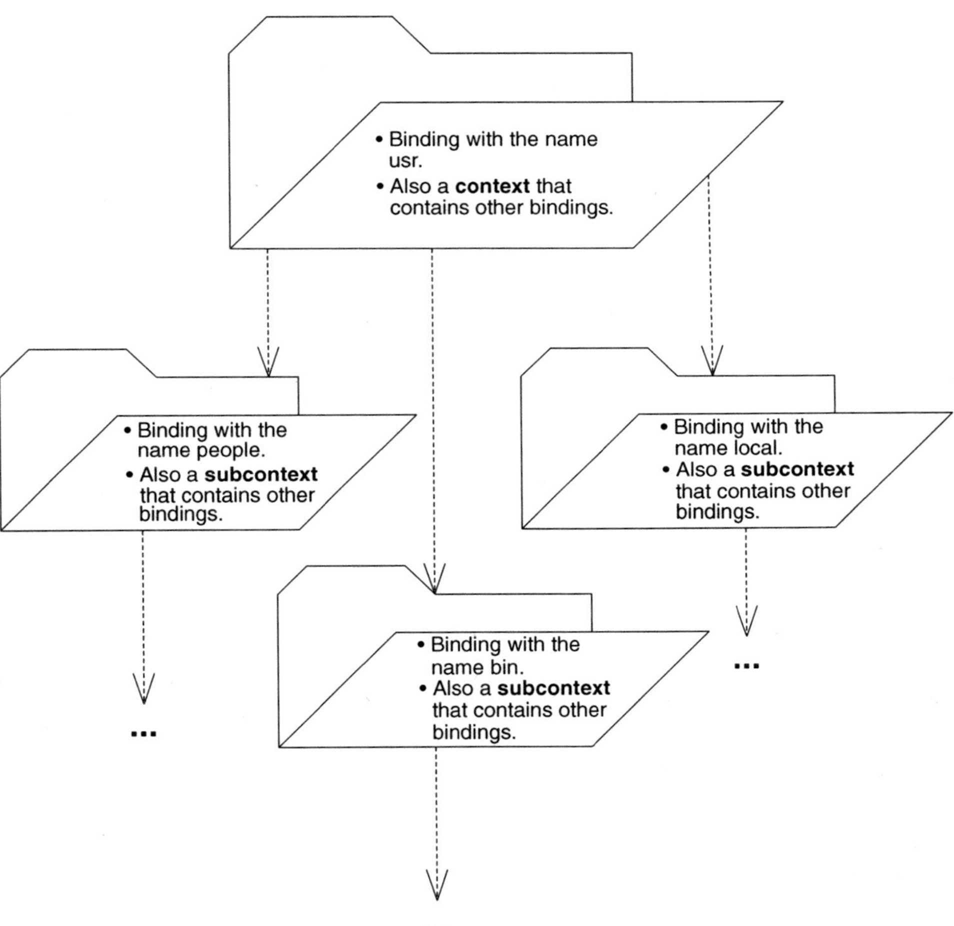

Figure A.11 JNDI naming concepts.

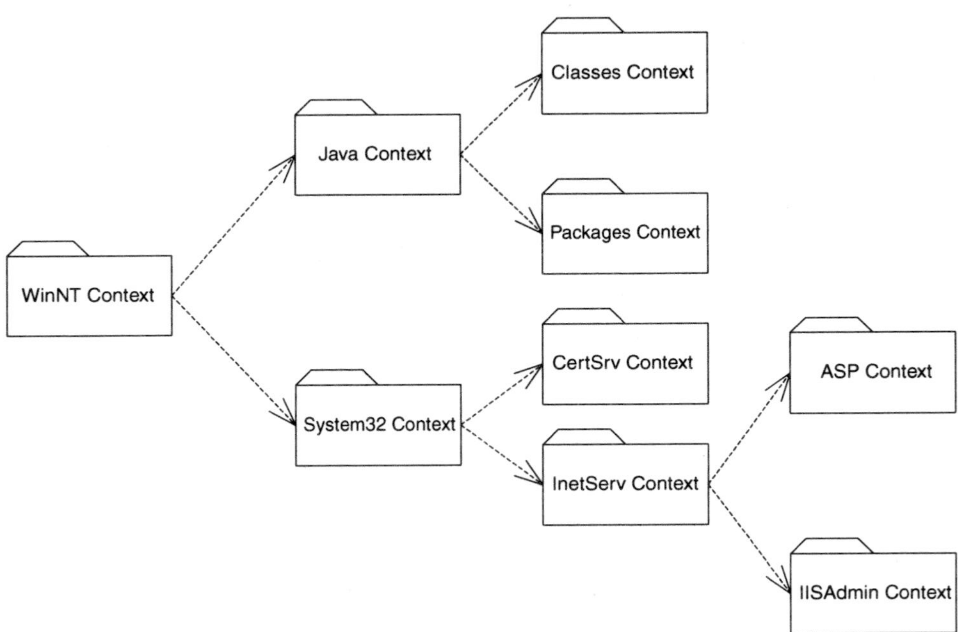

Figure A.12 Naming systems and namespaces.

Initial Context Factories

If you are to traverse a composite namespace, how do you know which naming system to look into first? For example, which namespace do you first look in when traversing the string `http://www.TheServerSide.com/events/index.jsp`?

The starting point of exploring a namespace is called an *initial context*. An initial context simply is the first context you happen to use. Frequently, the initial context will be the root node of a naming system, but this is not necessarily so. An initial context is simply a starting point for performing all naming and directory operations.

To acquire an initial context in JNDI, you use an *initial context factory*. An initial context factory is responsible for churning out initial contexts and is implemented by your JNDI driver. For example, there is an LDAP initial context factory, as well as a file system initial context factory. These initial context factories know the specific semantics of a particular directory structure. They know how to acquire an arbitrary context that you can use as an initial starting context for traversing a directory structure.

When you acquire an initial context, you must supply the necessary information for JNDI to acquire that initial context. For example, if you're trying to access a JNDI implementation that runs within a J2EE server, you might supply:

- The IP address of the J2EE server
- The port number that the J2EE server accepts requests on
- The starting location within the JNDI tree
- Any user name and password combination necessary to use the J2EE server

You could use this same paradigm to access an LDAP server—just substitute *LDAP server* for *J2EE server* in the preceding list.

Initial contexts and composite namespaces are illustrated in Figure A.13.

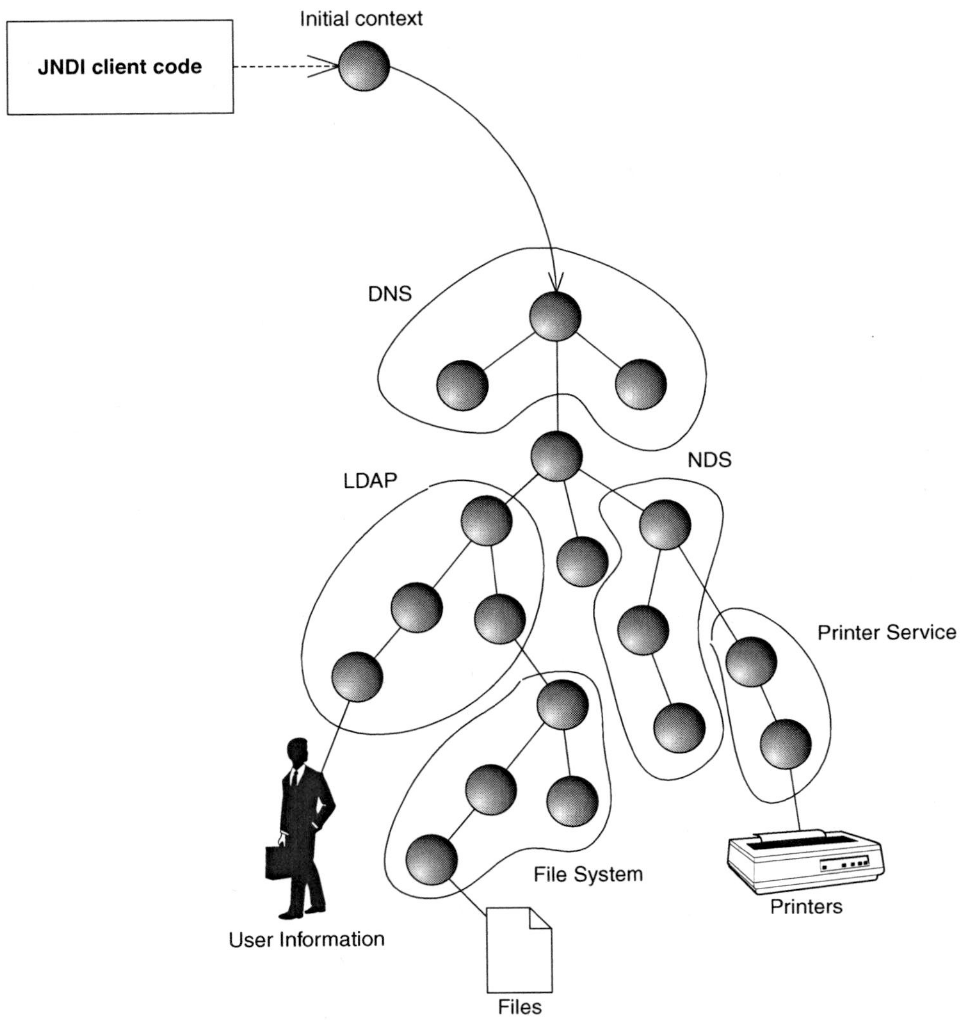

Figure A.13 A federated namespace with an initial context.

The naming contexts and subcontexts in Figure A.13 form a directed graph that you can navigate. In the figure as in most practical scenarios, these naming graphs are acyclic, but this is not required. An example of a cycle in a naming graph is a symbolic link in a subdirectory of the UNIX file system that links to a directory closer to the root. JNDI naming graphs are often referred to as JNDI trees. Note that in fact there is no restriction in JNDI that ensures that the graph is a tree. Naming graphs also need not have a single root node, and subcontexts can be bound in more than one context, so a single subcontext may be known under more than one name.

Programming with JNDI

Now that you've seen the concepts behind JNDI, let's put our theory into concrete use. Source A.3 shows a simple JNDI example.

```
package examples.jndi;

public class InitCtx {

    public static void main(String args[]) throws Exception {
      // Form an Initial Context
        javax.naming.Context ctx =
            new javax.naming.InitialContext(System.getProperties());
        System.err.println("Success!");
    }
}
```

Source A.3 InitCtx.java.

The code simply acquires an initial context and then the program completes. The specific JNDI driver that we use is based on the system properties passed in at the command line. For example, to connect to your file system, you would use the Sun Microsystems *file system* JNDI service provider, which is a driver that connects you to your own hard disk to browse the file system. You would then run the program as follows:

```
java
  -Djava.naming.factory.initial=
      com.sun.jndi.fscontext.RefFSContextFactory
  -Djava.naming.provider.url=file:c:\ examples.jndi.InitCtx
```

Note that the JNDI Driver (SPI) for the file system in not bundled with the J2SE, so you will have to download it separately and place it in your Java `classpath` in order to execute the previous command.

The `java.naming.factory.initial` parameter identifies the class of the JNDI driver. Then we identify the starting point on the file system that we want to begin navigating; specifically, the `c:\` folder. This starting point is structured in the form of a Uniform Resource Locator (URL). In JNDI, it is called the *provider URL* because it is a URL that the service provider accepts for bootstrapping.

We can reuse this same code to connect to an LDAP server as follows:

```
java
  -Djava.naming.factory.initial=com.sun.jndi.ldap.LdapCtxFactory
  -Djava.naming.provider.url="ldap://ldap.funet.fi:389/c=fi"
  examples.jndi.InitCtx
```

As you can see, this data-driven mechanism of performing JNDI has its advantages. It enables you to avoid recompiling your Java code, which is important if you ship your products only as `.class` files.

OTHER JNDI OPERATIONS

After acquiring the initial context, you could begin to execute JNDI operations, such as reading or writing data to and from the JNDI tree by using the other API calls available in JNDI. Here is a brief list of available operations that you can call on the context:

- `list()` **retrieves a list of bindings available in the current context. This typically includes names of objects bound in the JNDI graph, as well as subcontexts. In a file system, this might be a list of file names and folder names. If you're connecting to a proprietary J2EE server's JNDI implementation, you might see a list of bound objects as well as subcontexts to which you can navigate.**
- `lookup()` **resolves a name binding in the context, meaning that the operation returns the object bound to a given name in the context. The operation can also be used to move from one context to another context, such as going from** `c:\` **to** `c:\windows`**. The return type of** `lookup()` **is JNDI driver specific. For example, if you're looking up RMI-IIOP objects, you would receive a** `java.rmi.Remote` **object; if you're looking up a file in a file system, you would receive a** `java.io.File`**.**
- `rename()` **gives a context a new name, such as renaming** `c:\temp` **to** `c:\tmp`**.**
- `createSubcontext()` **creates a subcontext from the current context, such as creating** `c:\foo\bar` **from the folder** `c:\foo`**.**
- `destroySubcontext()` **destroys a subcontext from the current context, such as destroying** `c:\foo\bar` **from the folder** `c:\foo`**.**
- `bind()` **creates a new name binding in the current context. As with** `lookup()`**, JNDI drivers accept different parameters to** `bind()`**.**
- `rebind()` **is the same operation as bind, except that it forces a bind even if there is already something in the JNDI tree with the same name.**

Integrating RMI-IIOP and JNDI

Now that you've seen both RMI-IIOP and JNDI, let's see how to combine them and complete the RMI-IIOP example. There are essentially two uses of JNDI with RMI-IIOP:

- An RMI-IIOP server first binds a reference to one or more of its object in a JNDI context using the JNDI API.
- A client then uses JNDI to look up an RMI-IIOP server.

This process is shown in Figure A.14.

Your JNDI implementation is typically bundled with the Java EE server runtime. Therefore, when you start up your Java EE server, the JNDI service runs in-process to the Java EE server and starts up as well. Java EE servers also ship with a JNDI driver that can connect to that JNDI implementation, which clients call.

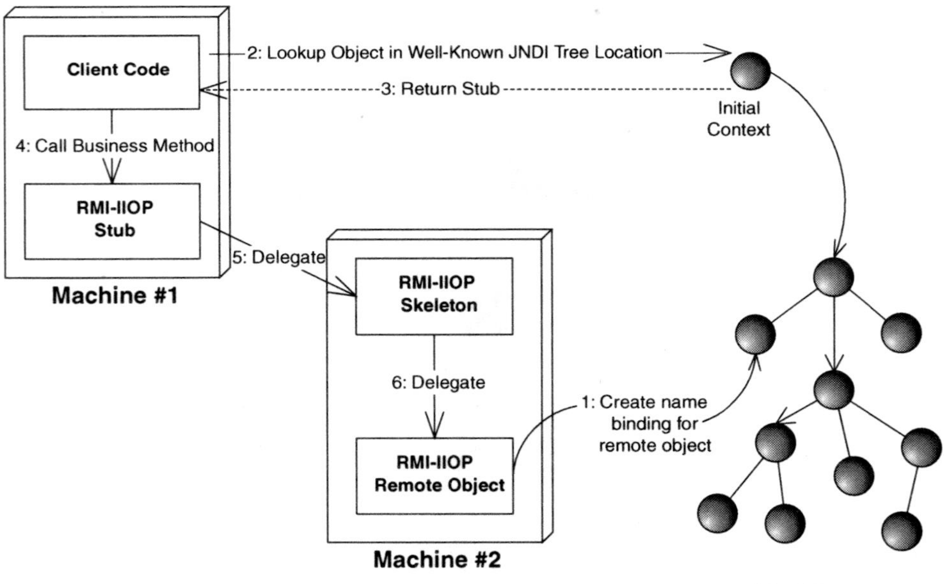

Figure A.14 Bootstrapping with JNDI.

Binding an RMI-IIOP Server to a JNDI Name

The source code for binding the RMI-IIOP server to a JNDI name is in Source A.4.

```
package examples.jndi;
import javax.naming.*;

/**
 * A helper class which starts our RMI-IIOP server
 */
public class Startup {

    /**
     * Our main() method starts things up
     */
    public static void main(String args[]) throws Exception {

        /*
         * Start up our PKGenerator remote object.  It will
         * automatically export itself.
         */
        PrimaryKeyGeneratorImpl generator =
            new PrimaryKeyGeneratorImpl();

        /*
         * Bind our PKGenerator remote object to the JNDI tree
         */
        Context ctx = new InitialContext(System.getProperties());
        ctx.rebind("PKGenerator", generator);
        System.out.println("PKGenerator bound to JNDI tree.");

        // wait for clients
        synchronized (generator) {
          generator.wait();
        }
    }
}
```

Source A.4 Startup.java.

The *Startup* class instantiates a remote object, acquires an initial context, binds the remote object to a name in the context, and then waits for a client to call. It assumes that your JavaEE server's JNDI implementation is already up and running. Note that you must supply your Java EE server's JNDI driver initialization parameters via the command line, as we showed earlier in this chapter when we ran our JNDI initial context example. Check your server's documentation or see the book's accompanying source code for this.

Looking Up an RMI-IIOP Server with JNDI

Our client code that looks up the RMI-IIOP object via JNDI is shown in Source A.5.

```
package examples.jndi;

import javax.naming.*;
import javax.rmi.*;

public class Client {

    public static void main (String[] args) throws Exception {

        // Lookup the remote object via JNDI
        Context ctx = new InitialContext(System.getProperties());
        Object remoteObject = ctx.lookup("PKGenerator");

        // Cast the remote object, RMI-IIOP style
        PrimaryKeyGenerator generator = (PrimaryKeyGenerator)
            PortableRemoteObject.narrow(
                remoteObject, PrimaryKeyGenerator.class);

        // Generate a PK by calling the RMI-IIOP stub
        System.err.println(generator.generate());
    }
}
```

Source A.5 Client.java.

The client code is self-explanatory, with one exception. After looking up the remote object, we perform the operation `javax.rmi.PortableRemoteObject.narrow()`. This is a static method on an RMI-IIOP class called `PortableRemoteObject`. This method casts the generic object that we looked up via JNDI to our RMI-IIOP interface type. This `narrow()` operation is required whenever you look up an RMI-IIOP object via JNDI. Why do we need it, and why don't we just cast it using a regular Java cast? The short answer is that the networking layer needs a chance to sneak in and create the necessary stub objects. Obviously, the code for these stubs must be available at this time. In most cases, that requires that the *rmic* command has been run previously to generate them.

As with the server, to run the client, you must supply your Java EE server's JNDI driver initialization parameters via the command line, as we showed earlier in this chapter when we ran our JNDI initial context example. Check your server's documentation or see the book's accompanying source code for this.

Summary

In this appendix, we've discussed how Java RMI-IIOP and JNDI are fundamental underlying technologies in an EJB deployment. We looked at the RMI-IIOP architecture, comparing it to traditional RPCs. We examined stubs and skeletons, parameter passing, and object serialization and pointed out the benefits of CORBA interoperability in EJB. We concluded our RMI-IIOP discussion by introducing a sample primary key generator RMI-IIOP server.

Next, we delved into JNDI. We looked at the basics of naming and directory concepts, and saw how to acquire an initial context. We then investigated how to bind and look up an RMI-IIOP object using JNDI.

APPENDIX B

Annotations

The use of metadata annotations is one of the most important new features in the EJB 3.0 specification. Annotations were added to the Java language in JSR-175 and have been generally available since the release of the Java 5 platform.

Annotations provide the syntax to write the required metadata for EJBs inside your source files. They can be used as an alternative to the standard XML deployment descriptor files. Annotations can also be combined with descriptor files. We have used annotations extensively throughout the book because they are mostly easier to read and closer to the actual code that developers write. You should not, however, think of annotations as the superior approach: there are cases when deployment descriptors are better suited.

This appendix gives a short, general introduction to programming with Java metadata annotations and explains when annotations should be used and when you should use descriptor files. We also provide a complete reference to the annotations used in EJB 3.

Introduction to Annotations

An annotation is a piece of text (a note) with which you can adorn your code. Annotations let you express information *about* code *in* the code.

Annotations are compiled and type-checked. If the appropriate retention policy is chosen, they can be accessed at runtime using Java reflection, but they cannot perform computations. While they are more expressive than a comment, annotations are still only descriptive.

Let's start with a quick example before we explain things in more detail. Imagine that we want to enforce some special development process rules within our company's build environment. We could do that based on letting developers categorize their classes to describe a class's test coverage, review stage, and suitability for outside publication. With annotations, we can attach that information to a class like this:

```
@CodeCategory(visibility = Visibility.PUBLIC,
              isUnitTested = true,
              isReviewed = true)
static class ClassTwo {
    // ...
}
```

Source B.1 A first annotation.

We could then write and use custom compile-time tools to check that no code goes into a final production build that was not previously reviewed and unit tested. We could even write code within our own classes that checks code categories at runtime, and we could output different logging information based on the code categorization.

If you haven't used annotations before, you will note the occurrence of the @-symbol outside a comment block. The @-sign is always a marker for annotations when used this way. Here, it marks the name `CodeCategory` as an annotation type name.

Where does this type come from? It was defined and compiled just like a Java interface or class. Here's the declaration of the annotation type `CodeCategory`:

```
package examples.annotations;

import java.lang.annotation.*;

enum Visibility {
    INTERNAL, PUBLIC
}

@Retention(RetentionPolicy.RUNTIME)
@Target(ElementType.TYPE)
public @interface CodeCategory {
    Visibility visibility() default Visibility.INTERNAL;
    boolean isUnitTested() default false;
    boolean isReviewed() default false;
}
```

Source B.2 Annotation type CodeCategory.

There are a few things that we can observe here:

- `CodeCategory` is marked with an `@`-sign before the keyword interface: this syntax declares that `CodeCategory` is an annotation type rather than a normal interface type.
- The annotation type has three members, each with a default value.
- The annotation type declaration is itself annotated with two annotations: `@RETENTION` and `@TARGET`. These annotations come from the java.lang.annotation package and are called meta-annotation types. Meta-annotations restrict the use of the types that they annotate:
  - The `@RETENTION` annotation determines if the target annotation should be visible only on the source code (*SOURCE*), compiled into the class file (*CLASS*), or even made available at runtime by the JVM (*RUNTIME*). The default retention policy for annotation types that are not explicitly marked is *CLASS*.
  - The `@TARGET` annotation specifies which code elements can be annotated with the new `CodeCategory` annotation type. The available options are types (including classes, interfaces, and enums), packages, methods, fields, or even annotation types. Without the `@TARGET` meta-annotation, an annotation type can be used on any kind of target.

    The `@TARGET` annotation is sometimes also used to mark types that can occur *only* in annotation type declarations, such as member types. To prevent the independent use of an annotation type, you may sometimes see the empty target annotation `@TARGET({})`.
- To access annotations at runtime, the Java reflection API has been extended. We can use the new `getAnnotation()` method on classes:

```
public static void printConvention(Object obj) {
    System.out.println(obj.getClass().
        getAnnotation(CodeCategory.class));
}
```

  Remember that we can access the `CodeCategory` this way only if the annotation type was marked with `@Retention(RetentionPolicy.RUNTIME)`.

Annotations for EJB

For EJBs, annotations are an alternative to the sometimes tedious and error-prone task of specifying the required metadata in XML descriptor files. You have already seen many examples of EJB annotations throughout this book.

As a quick reminder, here's the simple annotation that we used to describe a bean class as a stateful session bean with a remote interface and a life-cycle callback listener class:

```
@Stateful
@Remote(Count.class)
@Interceptors(CountCallbacks.class)
public class CountBean implements Count {

    public int count() {
        ...
    }
    ...
}
```

Source B.3 Annotated CountBean.java.

To outline the main differences, here's the equivalent XML descriptor file:

```
<?xml version="1.0" encoding="UTF-8" ?>
 <ejb-jar
   xmlns="http://java.sun.com/xml/ns/j2ee"
   xmlns:xsi="http://www.w3.org/2001/XMLSchema-
instance"xsi:schemaLocation="http://java.sun.com/xml/ns/j2ee
    http://java.sun.com/xml/ns/j2ee/ejb-jar_3_0.xsd"
    version="3.0">
 <enterprise-beans>
 <session>
  <ejb-name>examples.session.stateful_dd.Count</ejb-name>
  <remote>examples.session.stateful_dd.Count</remote>
  <ejb-class>examples.session.stateful_dd.CountBean</ejb-class>
  <session-type>Stateful</session-type>
  <transaction-type>Container</transaction-type>
    <lifecycle-callbacks>
     <callback-listener>
examples.session.stateful_dd.CountCallbacks
     </callback-listener>
  </session>
 </enterprise-beans>
</ejb-jar>
```

Source B.4 Ejb-jar file for CountBean.java.

As you can see, the three Java annotations in the source B.3 replace 16 lines of XML in source B.4. The main difference between the two files is that the annotations are directly expressed in the source file and attached to the code. They describe the EJB from within whereas the XML is external to the code and describes it from without. Both approaches have their place in EJB development. We will come back to this in a minute.

The remainder of this section briefly puts annotations in the context of other approaches for providing metadata and explains the advantages and disadvantages of this approach.

Background

Adding meta-information to Java program code has been done since Java exists. The earliest examples were the Javadoc tags (`@author`, `@return`, and so on) in comments that are used to generated API documentation in HTML format. The idea is to provide metadata in special source comments and let customized compilers or separate tools extract and handle the information. This approach was also used in many research implementations of early Java language extensions.

XDoclet

The most prominent example of this technique is the popular XDoclet tool that can, for example, be used to generate EJB deployment descriptor files in XML from EJB-specific source code comments provided by developers. Here's the session bean example in XDoclet syntax:

```
/**
 * @ejb.bean
 *    type="Stateful"
 *    name="Count"
 *    view-type="remote"
 */
public class Count ... {
}
```

Source B.5 XDoclet annotations in CountBean.java.

The main point to remember about the Javadoc/XDoclet approach is that the metadata is placed in comments. This means that it is *not* processed by the Java compiler. The metadata is not compiled to a regular class file and is available only at compile time. It is not accessible for runtime reflection unless mapped to custom-generated Java code that somehow represents the same information in standard Java.

Since the metadata syntax and semantics are not checked by the Java compiler, there must be specialized tools written for the custom metalanguage. This approach is very flexible and also easy to use and extend, but it means that the metadata itself is typically unstructured and untyped; that is, it will be error-prone to write.

NOTE There is no reason why a custom metalanguage could not rely on structured and typed artifacts or even on external Java classes. It just means someone must define and implement the proper language syntax and semantics in a compiler.

Annotations in Java

The metadata facility in Java 5 defines an annotation language that is part of the language itself. This has the following advantages when compared with the XDoclet approach:

- **Ease of use.** Annotations are checked and compiled by the Java language compiler, so no external tool is needed.
- **Portability.** Because the metadata facility is standardized, annotations are as portable as the rest of the code.
- **Type checking.** Annotations are instances of *annotation types*, which are compiled in their own class files.
- **Runtime reflection.** Annotations on a class can be kept in the class file and retained for runtime access.

Pros and Cons

With all these nifty features, annotations look like they might be used just about everywhere. However, the Java annotation facility in its current form also has its shortcomings:

- Unlike interfaces classes and exceptions, annotation types cannot form an inheritance hierarchy.
- Annotation member types are restricted to primitive types, String, Class, enum types, annotation types, and arrays of the preceding types.
- To annotate *existing* code, you must have access to the source code.
- Many developers have expressed their dislike of a syntax that leads to source code cluttered with @-signs. Of course, this is a matter of taste.

Having mentioned the more general criticism, we should also be clear about the pros and cons of annotations for EJBs. Here are the pros:

- Keeping the code and the metadata that describes it in sync is much easier with annotations directly on the source code.
- Compile-time checking on typed source code annotations helps you catch errors earlier than the XML compiler because it cannot detect semantic mismatches with the Java code. This must be checked by additional verifiers at or before deployment time.

For EJB, the one main argument against using annotations exclusively has already been mentioned: to work with the metadata for beans that you didn't write yourself, you would still need access to the source code. Adding metadata to beans that come in an Ejb-jar file without code is not going to work well unless you are allowed to disassemble the code, which is usually not much fun.

Fortunately, the EJB specification defines how annotations and XML descriptors can be *combined*: To give you full authority even over beans without source code, the specification requires that containers give descriptor files precedence over source code annotations. Thus, you can always overrule and redefine the metadata that comes embedded in a .jar file. In a process that requires different individuals to incrementally modify metadata, you should still consider using external XML descriptor files rather than annotations embedded in the source code.

EJB Annotation Reference

This section provides a complete reference of all annotation types used in the EJB 3 specification. In many cases, the absence of an annotation implies a reasonable default, so you only need to annotate if you want to deviate. The retention policy for EJB annotations is generally `RUNTIME`, so we don't list it separately for each annotation type.

Bean Type Annotations

This section lists annotations by the bean types to which they apply.

Session Bean Annotations

NAME	USE	TARGET	MEMBERS	DEFAULT	MEMBER DESCRIPTION
`@Stateless`	Marks a bean class as a stateless session bean.	TYPE	*String name()*	""	Defaults to the unqualified name of the bean class.
			String mappedName()	""	A product-specific name that the session bean should be mapped to.
			String description()	""	
`@Stateful`	Marks a bean class as a stateful session bean.	TYPE	*String name()*	""	Defaults to the unqualified name of the bean class.
			String mappedName()	""	A product-specific name that the session bean should be mapped to.
			String description()	""	
`@Init`	Specifies that a method on the bean class corresponds to a `create<METHOD>` method for an adapted EJB 2.1 EJBHome and/or EJBLocalHome client view.	METHOD	*String value()*	{}	Specifies the name of the corresponding `create<METHOD>` method of the adapted home. It must be specified when the *Init* annotation is used in association with an adapted home interface of a stateful session bean that has more than one create method. The *Init* method is only required for stateful session beans that provide a `RemoteHome` or `LocalHome` interface. The name of the adapted create method of the `Home` or `LocalHome` interface must be specified if there is any ambiguity.

(continued)

NAME	USE	TARGET	MEMBERS	DEFAULT	MEMBER DESCRIPTION
`@Remove`	Denotes a remove method of a stateful session bean. Completion of this method causes the container to remove the stateful session bean, first invoking the bean's PreDestroy method, if any.	METHOD	*boolean retainIf Exception()*	*false*	Allows the removal to be prevented if the method terminates abnormally.
`@Local`, `@Remote`	When applied to the bean class, this annotation lists the remote or local business interfaces of the bean in the *value* member. When applied to a business interface, the interface itself is marked as local or remote.	TYPE	*Class[] value()*	{}	An array of business interfaces and specified only when the annotation is applied to the bean class. It is only required if the bean class implements more than one interface (excluding *java.io.Serializable*, *java.io.Externalizable*, and any of the interfaces in the *javax.ejb* package).

Message-Driven Bean Annotations

NAME	USE	TARGET	MEMBERS	DEFAULT	MEMBER DESCRIPTION
`@MessageDriven`	Marks a bean class as a message-driven bean.	TYPE	*String name()*	""	Defaults to the unqualified name of the bean class.
			Class messageListenerInterface()	*Object.class*	Specifies the message listener interface of the bean. It must be specified if the bean class does not implement its message listener interface or implements more than one interface other than *java.io.Serializable*, *java.io.Externalizable*, or any of the interfaces defined by the *javax.ejb* package.
			ActivationConfigProperty[] activationConfig()	{}	
			String mappedName()	""	A product-specific name that the session bean should be mapped to.
			String description()	""	

Common Annotations for Session and Message-Driven Beans

This section lists annotation types that are common to both session beans and message-driven Beans. The table below organizes these annotations according to their use.

NAME	USE	TARGET	MEMBERS	DEFAULT	DESCRIPTION
Transactions					
`@TransactionManagement`	Specifies the transaction management demarcation type of a session bean or message-driven bean. If this annotation is not present, the bean has container-managed transaction demarcation.	TYPE	*TransactionManagementType value()*	*TransactionManagementType.CONTAINER*	The demarcation type can be either *CONTAINER* or *BEAN* See Chapter 10 on transactions for details.
`@TransactionAttribute`	Specifies that a business method is invoked within a transaction context by the container. This annotation can only be specified if container-managed transaction demarcation is used. It can be specified on the bean class and/or on methods of the class that are methods of the business interface. * On the bean class, it applies to all business interface methods of the class. * On a method, it applies it to that method only. * If applied at both the class *and* the method level, the method value overrides if the two disagree. If not present, and the bean uses container-managed transaction demarcation, the semantics of the REQUIRED transaction attribute are assumed.	METHOD, TYPE	*TransactionAttributeType value()*	*TransactionAttributeType.REQUIRED*	The transaction attribute type can be one of `MANDATORY`, `REQUIRED`, `REQUIRES_NEW`, `SUPPORTS`, `NOT_SUPPORTED`, `NEVER`. See Chapter 10 on transactions for details.

(continued)

NAME	USE	TARGET	MEMBERS	DEFAULT	DESCRIPTION
Interceptors and Life-Cycle callbacks					
`@Interceptors`	Designates one or more interceptor classes associated with a bean. Can be applied to the bean class or to a business method of the bean.	TYPE	*Class[] value()*		Lists all interceptor classes that are to be associated with the bean.
`@Around Invoke`	Designates an interceptor method	METHOD			See Chapter 8 for details on interceptors.
`@Exclude Default Interceptors`	When applied to a bean class, this annotation excludes the invocation of default interceptors for all business methods of the bean. When applied to a business method, it excludes the invocation of default interceptors for that method.	TYPE, METHOD			See Chapter 8 for details on interceptors.
`@Exclude Class Interceptors`	Excludes the invocation of class-level interceptors (but not default interceptors) for the given method.	METHOD			See Chapter 8 for details on interceptors.
`@Post Construct`	Designates a life-cycle callback method.	METHOD			
`@PreDestroy`	Designates a life-cycle callback method.	METHOD			

(continued)

(continued)

NAME	USE	TARGET	MEMBERS	DEFAULT	DESCRIPTION
`@Post Activate`	Designates a life-cycle callback method. Not applicable to message-driven beans.	METHOD			
`@Pre Passivate`	Designates a life-cycle callback method. Not applicable to message-driven beans.	METHOD			
Scheduling					
`@Timeout`	Designates a timeout method	METHOD			See Chapter 12 on scheduling for details on timeouts.
Exceptions					
`@Application Exception`	Applied to an exception to denote that it is an application exception and should not be wrapped but reported to the client directly. May be applied to both checked and unchecked exceptions.	TYPE			
Security					
`@Declare Roles`	Declares the security roles that are used the bean.	TYPE	*String[] value()*		See Chapter 11 on security for details.

(continued)

NAME	USE	TARGET	MEMBERS	DEFAULT	DESCRIPTION
`@Roles Allowed`	Specifies the security roles that are allowed to invoke the methods of the bean. Can be specified on the bean class and/or on methods of the class that are methods of the business interface: * On the bean class, it applies to all applicable interface methods of the class. * On a method, it applies it to that method only. * If the annotation is applied at both the class and the method level, the method value wins (if the two disagree). If the *@PermitAll* annotation is applied to the bean class, and *@RolesAllowed* is specified on an individual method, the value of the *RolesAllowed* annotation overrides for the given method.	TYPE, METHOD	*String[] value()*		A list of security role names.

(continued)

(continued)

NAME	USE	TARGET	MEMBERS	DEFAULT	DESCRIPTION
`@PermitAll`	Specifies that the specified method(s) are unchecked and may be called by all security roles. This annotation can be specified on the bean class and/or on the business methods of the class. On the bean class, it applies to all applicable business methods of the class. On a method it applies to that method only, overriding any class-level setting for the particular method.	TYPE, METHOD			
`@DenyAll`	Opposite of *@PermitAll.* Specifies that a particular method may not be invoked at all.	METHOD			
`@RunAs`	Sets the bean's *run-as* property. This annotation is applied to the bean class.	TYPE	*String value()*		The name of a security role.

(continued)

NAME	USE	TARGET	MEMBERS	DEFAULT	DESCRIPTION
References and Injection					
`@EJB`	Denotes a reference to an EJB business interface.	TYPE, METHOD, FIELD	*String name()*	""	Refers to the name by which the resource is to be looked up in the environment.
			Class beanInterface()	*Object.class*	The referenced interface type.
			String beanName()	""	The value of the *name* member of the reference bean's *@Stateful* or *@Stateless* annotation (or ejb-name element, if the deployment descriptor was used). The *beanName* allows disambiguation if there are multiple beans in the Ejb-jar that implement the same *beanInterface*.
			String mappedName()	""	A product-specific name that the bean reference should be mapped to. Applications that use mapped names may not be portable.
`@EJBs`	Declares references to EJB business interfaces.	TYPE	*EJB[] value()*		

(continued)

(continued)

NAME	USE	TARGET	MEMBERS	DEFAULT	DESCRIPTION
`@Resource`	Specifies a dependency on a resource in the bean's environment.	TYPE, METHOD, FIELD	*String name()*	*""*	The name by which the resource is known in the environment
			Class type()	*Object.class*	the resource manager connection factory type.
			AuthenticationType authenticationType()	*AuthenticationType .CONTAINER*	Specifies whether the container or bean is to perform authentication.
			boolean shareable()	*true*	Refers to the sharability of resource manager connections.
			String mappedName()	*""*	A product-specific name that the resource should be mapped to.
			String description()	*""*	
`@Resources`	Acts as a container for multiple resource declarations because repeated annotations are not allowed.	TYPE	*Resource[] value*		

Entity Annotations

As we pointed out earlier in this book, entities are not EJBs. We still list their annotations here.

(continued)

NAME	USE	TARGET	MEMBERS	DEFAULT	DESCRIPTION
`@Entity`	Marks a class as an entity class	TYPE	*String name()*	""	Defaults to the unqualified name of entity class. It is used to refer to the entity in queries.
Life-Cycle Callbacks					
`@Entity Listeners`	Specifies the callback listener classes to be used for an entity	TYPE	Class[] value()		
`@Exclude Superclass Listeners`	Specifies that the invocation of superclass listeners is to be excluded for the entity class (and its subclasses)	TYPE			
`@Exclude Default Listeners`	Specifies that the invocation of default listeners is to be excluded for the entity class (and its subclasses)	TYPE			
`@Pre Persist`	Specifies a callback listener method and may be applied to methods on the entity class or methods of an `EntityListener` class	METHOD			
`@Post Persist`	Specifies a callback listener method and may be applied to methods on the entity class or methods of an `EntityListener` class	METHOD			

(continued)

NAME	USE	TARGET	MEMBERS	DEFAULT	DESCRIPTION
`@Pre Remove`	Specifies a callback listener method and may be applied to methods on the entity class or methods of an `EntityListener` class	METHOD			
`@Post Remove`	Specifies a callback listener method and may be applied to methods on the entity class or methods of an `EntityListener` class	METHOD			
`@Pre Update`	Specifies a callback listener method and may be applied to methods on the entity class or methods of an `EntityListener` class	METHOD			
`@Post Update`	Specifies a callback listener method and may be applied to methods on the entity class or methods of an `EntityListener` class	METHOD			
`@PostLoad`	Specifies a callback listener method and may be applied to methods on the entity class or methods of an `EntityListener` class	METHOD			

(continued)

(continued)

NAME	USE	TARGET	MEMBERS	DEFAULT	DESCRIPTION
Queries and Query Result Mapping					
`@Flush Mode`	Designates the points at which entities are to be flushed to the database	METHOD FIELD	*FlushMode Type value()*	*FlushMode Type.AUTO*	If set to `AUTO`, flushes can occur at commit and before query execution when a transaction is active. If set to `COMMIT`, flushing will occur only at transaction commit.
`@Named Query`	Specifies a named EJB QL query	TYPE	*String name()*		The name assigned to the query and is used when creating a query object using *EntityManager* operations.
			String query()		Contains the EJB QL query string.
			QueryHint[] hints()	{}	A set of *QueryHints:* `@Target({})` `@Retention(RUNTIME)` `public @interface QueryHint {` `String name();` `String value();` `}`
`@Named Queries`	Specifies a set of `@Named` Query	TYPE	*NamedQuery[] value ()*		

(continued)

NAME	USE	TARGET	MEMBERS	DEFAULT	DESCRIPTION
@Named Native Query	Specifies a native SQL named query	TYPE	*String name()*		The name assigned to the query and is used when creating a query object using *EntityManager* operations.
			String query()		Contains the SQL query string.
			QueryHint[] hints()	{}	As above
			Class resultClass()	*void.class*	Refers to the class of the result.
			String() resultSet Mapping()	""	The name of a *SQLResultSetMapping*, as defined in metadata.
@Named Native Queries	Specifies a set of @Named NativeQueries	TYPE	*NamedNativeQuery[] value ()*		

(continued)

(continued)

NAME	USE	TARGET	MEMBERS	DEFAULT	DESCRIPTION
`@SqlResultSetMapping`	Specifies the mapping of the result of a native SQL query to entities and/or basic types	TYPE, METHOD	*String name()*		The name assigned to the mapping and is used to refer to it in the methods of the Query API.

			EntityResult[] entities()
			ColumnResult[] columns()
				{}
				{}
					Entities and columns are used to specify the mapping to entities and to basic values, respectively.
					`@Target({})`
					`@Retention(RUNTIME)`
					`public @interface EntityResult{`
					`Class entityClass();`
					`FieldResult[] fields() default {};`
					`String discriminatorColumn() default "";`
					`}`
					`@Target({})`
					`@Retention(RUNTIME)`
					`public @interface FieldResult {`
					`String name();`
					`String column();`
					`}`
					`@Target({})`
					`@Retention(RUNTIME)`
					`public @interface ColumnResult {`
					`String name();`
					`}`

(continued)

NAME	USE	TARGET	MEMBERS	DEFAULT	DESCRIPTION
References to the EntityManager and the EntityManagerFactory					
`@PersistenceContext`	Expresses a dependency on a container-managed EntityManager persistence context	TYPE, METHOD, FIELD	*String name()*	""	
			String unitName()	""	
			PersistenceContextType type	*TRANSACTION*	The name by which the EntityManager is known in the environment. It is not needed when dependency injection is used. The name of the persistence unit. It must be specified if there is more than one persistence unit within the referencing scope. Specifies whether a transaction-scoped or extended persistence context is to be used. The setting for the latter is `EXTENDED`.
`@PersistenceContexts`	Expresses a dependency on multiple container-managed EntityManager persistence contexts	TYPE	*PersistenceContext[] value()*		

(continued)

(continued)

NAME	USE	TARGET	MEMBERS	DEFAULT	DESCRIPTION
`@PersistenceUnit`	Expresses a dependency on an `EntityManagerFactory`	TYPE, METHOD, FIELD	*String name()*	""	The name of the EntityManagerFactory in the environment. It is not needed when dependency injection is used.
			String unitName()	""	The name of the persistence unit as defined in the `persistence.xml` file. It must be specified if there is more than one persistence unit in the referencing scope.

(continued)

NAME	USE	TARGET	MEMBERS	DEFAULT	DESCRIPTION
Object/Relational Mapping					
`@Table`	Specifies the primary table for the entity. Additional tables may be specified using SecondaryTable or SecondaryTables annotation. If no Table annotation is specified for an entity class, the default values apply.	*TYPE*	*String name()*	""	The table name, defaults to the entity name, if unset.
			String catalog()	""	The table's catalog name and defaults to the default catalog.
			String schema()	""	The name of the table's schema and defaults to the user's default schema.
			UniqueConstraint[] uniqueConstraints()	{}	Unique constraints that are to be placed on the table, only used if table generation is in effect. These constraints apply in addition to any constraints specified by the Column and JoinColumn annotations and constraints entailed by primary key mappings.

(continued)

(continued)

NAME	USE	TARGET	MEMBERS	DEFAULT	DESCRIPTION
`@SecondaryTable`	Specifies a secondary table for the annotated entity class, indicating that the data for the entity class is stored across multiple tables. If no `SecondaryTable` annotation is specified, all persistent fields or properties of the entity are mapped to the primary table.	*TYPE*	*String name()*	""	The table name.
			String catalog()		The table's catalog name and defaults to the default catalog.
			String schema()	{}	The name of the table's schema and defaults to the user's default schema.
			PrimaryKey JoinColumn[] pkJoinColumns()	{}	The columns that are used to join with the primary table. If not specified, the join columns reference the primary key columns of the primary table, and have the same names and types as the referenced primary key columns of the primary table.
			Unique Constraint[] unique Constraints()		Unique constraints that are to be placed on the table, typically only used if table generation is in effect. They apply in addition to any constraints specified by the `Column` and `Join- Column` annotations and constraints entailed by primary key mappings.

(continued)

NAME	USE	TARGET	MEMBERS	DEFAULT	DESCRIPTION
`@SecondaryTables`	Specifies multiple secondary tables for an entity.	TYPE	*Secondary Table[] value()*		
`@UniqueConstraints`	Specifies that a unique constraint is to be included in the generated DDL for a primary or secondary table.	{}	*String[] columnNames()*		An array of column names that make up the constraint.
`@Column`	Specifies a mapped column for a persistent property or field.	METHOD, FIELD	*String name()* *boolean unique()*	*""* *false*	The name of the column. Whether the property is a unique key. This is a shortcut for the *UniqueConstraint* annotation at the table level and useful when the unique key constraint is only a single field. Applies in addition to any constraint entailed by primary key mapping and to constraints specified at the table level.

(continued)

(continued)

NAME	USE	TARGET	MEMBERS	DEFAULT	DESCRIPTION
`@Column`			*boolean nullable()*	*true*	Whether the database column is nullable.
			boolean insertable()	*true*	Whether the column is included in SQL `INSERT` statements generated by the persistence provider.
			boolean updatable()	*true*	Whether the column is included in SQL `UPDATE` statements generated by the persistence provider.
			String column Definition()	*""*	The SQL fragment that is used when generating the DDL for the column.
			String table()	*""*	The name of the table that contains the column. If absent the column is assumed to be in the primary table.
			int length()	*255*	The column length. (Applies only if a string-valued column is used.)
			int precision()	*0*	The precision for a decimal (exact numeric) column. (Applies only if a decimal column is used.)
			int scale()	*0*	The scale for a decimal (exact numeric) column. (Applies only if a decimal column is used.)

(continued)

NAME	USE	TARGET	MEMBERS	DEFAULT	DESCRIPTION
`@JoinColumn`	Specifies a mapped column for joining an entity association. If no `@JoinColumn` annotation is specified, a single join column is assumed and the default values apply.	TYPE, METHOD, FIELD	*String name()*	*""*	The name of the foreign key column. If the join is for a `OneToOne` or `ManyToOne` mapping, the foreign key column is in the table of the source entity. If the join is for a `ManyToMany`, the foreign key is in a join table.
			String referenced ColumnName()	*""*	The name of the column referenced by this foreign key column. When used with relationship mappings, the referenced column is in the table of the target entity. When used inside a `JoinTable` annotation, the referenced key column is in the entity table of the owning entity, or inverse entity if the join is part of the inverse join definition.
			boolean unique()	*false*	Whether the property is a unique key. (cf. above)
			boolean nullable()	*true*	Whether the database column is nullable.
			boolean insertable()	*true*	Whether the column is included in SQL `INSERT` statements generated by the persistence provider.

(continued)

(continued)

NAME	USE	TARGET	MEMBERS	DEFAULT	DESCRIPTION
`@JoinColumn`			*boolean updatable()*	*true*	Whether the column is included in SQL `UPDATE` statements generated by the persistence provider.
			String columnDefinition()	""	The SQL fragment that is used when generating the DDL for the column.
			String table()	""	The name of the table that contains the column. If absent, the column is assumed to be in the primary table.
`@JoinColumns`	Supports composite foreign keys. Groups `JoinColumn` annotations for the same relationship or table association. When the `JoinColumns` annotation is used, both the name and the `referencedColumnName` elements must be specified in each such `JoinColumn` annotation.	METHOD, FIELD	*JoinColumn[] value()*		

(continued)

NAME	USE	TARGET	MEMBERS	DEFAULT	DESCRIPTION
`@Id`	Specifies the primary key property or field of an entity. The Id annotation may be applied in an entity or mapped superclass. By default, the mapped column for the primary key of the entity is assumed to be the primary key of the primary table. If no Column annotation is specified, the primary key column name is assumed to be the name of the primary key property or field.	METHOD, FIELD			
`@GeneratedValue`	Specifies generation strategies for primary keys. May be applied to a primary key property or field of an entity or mapped superclass in conjunction with the `Id` annotation.	METHOD, FIELD	*Generation Type strategy()*	*AUTO*	The strategy to generate the annotated entity primary key.
			String generator()	""	The name of the primary key generator to use. Default ID generator supplied by persistence provider.

(continued)

(continued)

NAME	USE	TARGET	MEMBERS	DEFAULT	DESCRIPTION
`@AttributeOverride`	Overrides the mapping of a property or field. May be applied to an entity that extends a mapped superclass or to an embedded field or property to override a mapping defined by the mapped superclass or embeddable class. If not specified, the column is mapped as in the original mapping.	TYPE, METHOD, FIELD	*String name()* *Column column()*		The name of the mapped property or field. The column that is being mapped to the persistent attribute. The mapping type will remain the same as is defined in the embeddable class or mapped superclass.
`@AttributeOverrides`	Overrides the mappings of multiple properties or fields.	TYPE, METHOD, FIELD	*AttributeOverride[] value()*		
`@EmbeddedId`	Denotes a composite primary key that is an embeddable class. May be applied to a persistent field or property of an entity class or mapped superclass. There must be only one EmbeddedId annotation and no Id annotation when the EmbeddedId annotation is used.	METHOD, FIELD			

(continued)

NAME	USE	TARGET	MEMBERS	DEFAULT	DESCRIPTION
`@IdClass`	Specifies a composite The names of the fields or properties in the primary key class and the primary key fields or properties of the entity must correspond and their types must be the same.primary key class that is mapped to multiple fields or properties of the entity. Applied to an entity class or a mapped superclass.	TYPE	*Class value()*		
`@Transient`	Specifies that a property or field of an entity class is not persistent.	METHOD, FIELD			

(continued)

(continued)

NAME	USE	TARGET	MEMBERS	DEFAULT	DESCRIPTION
@Version	Specifies a field or property of an entity class that serves as its optimistic lock value. The type of that field or property should be one of: int, Integer; short, Short; long, Long; Timestamp. Only a single Version property or field should be used per class. The Version property should be mapped to the primary table for the entity class. Fields or properties that are specified with the Version annotation should not be updated by the application.	METHOD, FIELD			
@Basic	Implicit mapping default for basic types. Can be applied to a persistent property or instance variable of any of the following types: Java primitive types, wrappers of the primitive types, java.lang.String, java.math.BigInteger, java.math.BigDecimal, java.util.Date, java.util.Calendar, java.sql.Date, java.sql.Time, java.sql.Timestamp, byte[], Byte[], char[], Character[], enums, and any other type that implements Serializable.	METHOD, FIELD	*FetchType fetch()*	*EAGER*	Whether the value of the field or property should be lazily loaded or must be eagerly fetched. The EAGER strategy is a requirement, the LAZY strategy is a hint to the persistence provider runtime.
			boolean optional()	*true*	A hint as to whether the value of the field or property may be null. It is disregarded for primitive types, which are considered nonoptional.

(continued)

NAME	USE	TARGET	MEMBERS	DEFAULT	DESCRIPTION
`@Lob`	Specifies that a persistent property or field should be persisted as a large object to a database-supported large object type. May be used in conjunction with the `Basic` annotation. A `Lob` may be either a binary or character type. The `Lob` type is inferred from the type of the persistent field or property, and except for string and character-based types defaults to `Blob`.	METHOD, FIELD			
`@Temporal`	Specifies that a persistent property or field should be persisted as a temporal type. May be used in conjunction with the `Basic` annotation. The temporal type must be specified for persistent fields or properties of type `java.util.Date` and `java.util.Calendar`. If the temporal type is not specified or the `Temporal` annotation is not used, the temporal type is assumed to be `TIMESTAMP`.	METHOD, FIELD	*TemporalType value()*	*TIMESTAMP*	The type used in mapping a temporal type. Possible values are *DATE, TIME, TIMESTAMP.*

(continued)

(continued)

NAME	USE	TARGET	MEMBERS	DEFAULT	DESCRIPTION
`@Enumerated`	Specifies that a persistent property or field should be persisted as an enumerated type. May be used in conjunction with the `Basic` annotation. If the enumerated type is not specified or the Enumerated annotation is not used, the enumerated type is assumed to be `ORDINAL`.	METHOD, FIELD	*EnumType value()*	*ORDINAL*	The type used in mapping an enum type. Possible values are: *ORDINAL, STRING.*
`@ManyToOne`	Defines a single-valued association to another entity class that has many-to-one multiplicity. It is not normally necessary to specify the target entity explicitly, since it can usually be inferred from the type of the object being referenced.	METHOD, FIELD	*Class targetEntity()*	*void.class*	The entity class that is the target of the association.
			CascadeType[] cascade()	{}	The operations that must be cascaded to the target of the association. Possible values are: *ALL, PERSIST, MERGE, REMOVE, REFRESH.* `ALL` is equivalent to the conjunction of `PERSIST`, `MERGE`, `REMOVE`, and `REFRESH`.
			FetchType fetch()	*EAGER*	Whether the value of the field or property should be lazily loaded or must be eagerly fetched. The `EAGER` strategy is a requirement, the `LAZY` strategy is a hint to the persistence provider runtime.
			boolean optional()	*true*	Whether the association is optional. If *false* then a non-null relationship must always exist.

(continued)

NAME	USE	TARGET	MEMBERS	DEFAULT	DESCRIPTION
`@OneToOne`	Defines a single-valued association to another entity that has one-to-one multiplicity. It is not normally necessary to specify the associated target entity explicitly, since it can usually be inferred from the type of the object being referenced.	METHOD, FIELD	*Class targetEntity()*	*void.class*	The entity class that is the target of the association.
			CascadeType[] cascade()	{}	The operations that must be cascaded to the target of the association. Possible values are: *ALL, PERSIST, MERGE, REMOVE, REFRESH.* `ALL` is equivalent to the conjunction of `PERSIST`, `MERGE`, `REMOVE`, and `REFRESH`.
			FetchType fetch()	*EAGER*	Whether the value of the field or property should be lazily loaded or must be eagerly fetched. The `EAGER` strategy is a requirement, the `LAZY` strategy is a hint to the persistence provider runtime.
			boolean optional()	*true*	Whether the association is optional. If *false* then a non-null relationship must always exist.
			String mappedBy()		The field that owns the relationship. Only specified on the inverse (nonowning) side of the association.

(continued)

(continued)

NAME	USE	TARGET	MEMBERS	DEFAULT	DESCRIPTION
`@OneToMany`	Defines a many-valued association with one-to-many multiplicity.	METHOD, FIELD	*Class targetEntity()*	*void.class*	The entity class that is the target of the association. (The parameterized type of the `Collection` when defined using generics.)
			CascadeType[] cascade()	{}	The operations that must be cascaded to the target of the association. Possible values are: *ALL, PERSIST, MERGE, REMOVE, REFRESH.* `ALL` is equivalent to the conjunction of `PERSIST`, `MERGE`, `REMOVE`, and `REFRESH`.
			FetchType fetch()	*LAZY*	Whether the value of the field or property should be lazily loaded or must be eagerly fetched. The `EAGER` strategy is a requirement, the `LAZY` strategy is a hint to the persistence provider runtime.
			String mappedBy()	*""*	The field that owns the relationship. Required unless the relationship is unidirectional.

(continued)

NAME	USE	TARGET	MEMBERS	DEFAULT	DESCRIPTION
`@JoinTable`	Used in the mapping of associations and specified on the owning side of a many-to-many association, or in a unidirectional one-to-many association. If the `JoinTable` annotation is missing, the default values of the annotation elements apply.	METHOD, FIELD	*String name()*	""	The name of the join table.
			String catalog()	""	The catalog of the table.
			String schema()	""	The schema of the table.
			JoinColumn[] joinColumns()	{}	The foreign key columns of the join table which reference the primary table of the entity owning the association (i.e., the owning side of the association).
			JoinColumn[] inverseJoinColumns()	{}	The foreign key columns of the join table which reference the primary table of the entity that does not own the association (i.e., The inverse side of the association).
			UniqueConstraint[] uniqueConstraints	{}	Unique constraints that are to be placed on the table. These are only used if table generation is in effect.

(continued)

(continued)

NAME	USE	TARGET	MEMBERS	DEFAULT	DESCRIPTION
`@ManyToMany`	Defines a many-valued association with many-to-many multiplicity. If the `Collection` is defined using generics to specify the element type, the associated target entity class does not need to be specified; otherwise it must be specified. Every many-to-many association has two sides, the owning side and the nonowning, or inverse, side. The join table is specified on the owning side. If the association is bidirectional, either side may be designated as the owning side.	METHOD, FIELD	*Class targetEntity()*	*void.class*	The entity class that is the target of the association. (The parameterized type of the Collection when defined using generics.)
			CascadeType[] cascade()	{}	The operations that must be cascaded to the target of the association. Possible values are: ***ALL, PERSIST, MERGE, REMOVE, REFRESH.*** ALL is equivalent to the conjunction of `PERSIST`, `MERGE`, `REMOVE`, and `REFRESH`.
			FetchType fetch()	*LAZY*	Whether the value of the field or property should be lazily loaded or must be eagerly fetched. The `EAGER` strategy is a requirement, the `LAZY` strategy is a hint to the persistence provider runtime.
			String mappedBy()	*""*	The field that owns the relationship. Required unless the relationship is unidirectional.

(continued)

NAME	USE	TARGET	MEMBERS	DEFAULT	DESCRIPTION
`@MapKey`	Specifies the map key for associations of type `java.util.Map`.	METHOD, FIELD	*String name()*	""	Designates the name of the persistent field or property of the associated entity that is used as the map key. If *name* is not specified, the primary key of the associated entity is used as the map key. If the primary key is a composite primary key and is mapped as `IdClass`, an instance of the primary key class is used as the key. If a persistent field or property other than the primary key is used as a map key, then it is expected to have a uniqueness constraint associated with it.

(continued)

(continued)

NAME	USE	TARGET	MEMBERS	DEFAULT	DESCRIPTION

`@OrderBy`	Specifies the ordering of the elements of a collection-valued association at the point when the association is retrieved.	METHOD, FIELD	*String value()*	""	The syntax of value is:
					`orderby ::= orderby_item [,orderby_item]*`
					`orderby_item::= property_or_field_name [ASC | DESC]`
					If `ASC` or `DESC` is not specified, `ASC` (ascending order) is assumed.
					If the ordering element is not specified, ordering by the primary key of the associated entity is assumed. The property or field name must correspond to that of a persistent property or field of the associated class. The properties or fields used in the ordering must correspond to columns for which comparison operators are supported.

(continued)

NAME	USE	TARGET	MEMBERS	DEFAULT	DESCRIPTION
`@Inheritance`	Defines the inheritance strategy for an entity class hierarchy. Specified on the entity class that is the root of hierarchy. An inheritance strategy specified by an entity class remains in effect for the entities that are its subclasses unless another entity class further down in the class hierarchy specifies a different inheritance strategy. If no inheritance type is specified, the `SINGLE_TABLE` mapping strategy is used.	TYPE	*InheritanceType strategy()*	*SINGLE_TABLE*	The inheritance strategy to use for the entity inheritance hierarchy. Possible values are: *SINGLE_TABLE, JOINED, TABLE_PER_CLASS*

(continued)

(continued)

NAME	USE	TARGET	MEMBERS	DEFAULT	DESCRIPTION
@DiscriminatorColumn	Defines the discriminator column for the SINGLE_TABLE and JOINED inheritance mapping strategies. The strategy and the discriminator column are only specified in the root of an entity class hierarchy or subhierarchy in which a different inheritance strategy is applied. The DiscriminatorColumn annotation can be specified on an entity class (including on an abstract entity class). . If the annotation is missing, and a discriminator column is required, the name of the discriminator column defaults to "DTYPE" and the discriminator type to STRING.	TYPE	*String name()*	*""*	The name of column to be used for the discriminator, defaults to "DTYPE".
			DiscriminatorType	*STRING*	The type of object/column to use as a class discriminator.
			String columnDefinition()	*""*	The SQL fragment that is used when generating the DDL for the discriminator column.
			int length()	*31*	The column length for string-based discriminator types. Ignored for other discriminator types.

(continued)

NAME	USE	TARGET	MEMBERS	DEFAULT	DESCRIPTION
`@DiscriminatorValue`	Specifies the value of the discriminator column for entities of the given type. The `DiscriminatorValue` annotation can only be specified on a concrete entity class. If the `DiscriminatorValue` annotation is not specified and a discriminator column is used, a provider-specific function will be used to generate a value representing the entity type. The inheritance strategy and the discriminator column are only specified in the root of an entity class hierarchy or subhierarchy in which a different inheritance strategy is applied. The discriminator value, if not defaulted, should be specified for each entity class in the hierarchy.	TYPE	*String value()*		The value that indicates that the row is an entity of the annotated entity type.

(continued)

(continued)

NAME	USE	TARGET	MEMBERS	DEFAULT	DESCRIPTION
`@PrimaryKeyJoinColumn`	Specifies a primary key column that is used as a foreign key to join to another table. The `PrimaryKeyJoinColumn` annotation is used to join the primary table of an entity subclass in the `JOINED` mapping strategy to the primary table of its superclass; it is used with a `SecondaryTable` annotation to join a secondary table to a primary table; and it may be used in a `OneToOne` mapping in which the primary key of the referencing entity is used as a foreign key to the referenced entity. If no `PrimaryKeyJoinColumn` annotation is specified for a subclass in the `JOINED` mapping strategy, the foreign key columns are assumed to have the same names as the primary key columns of the primary table of the superclass.	TYPE, METHOD, FIELD	*String name()*	""	The name of the primary key column of the current table.
			String referenced ColumnName()	""	The name of the primary key column of the table being joined to.
			String column Definition()	""	The SQL fragment that is used when generating the DDL for the column. This should not be specified for a `OneToOne` primary key association.
`@PrimaryKeyJoinColumns`	Groups `PrimaryKeyJoinColumn` annotations.	TYPE	*PrimaryKeyJoin Column[] value()*		

(continued)

NAME	USE	TARGET	MEMBERS	DEFAULT	DESCRIPTION
@Embeddable	Specifies a class whose instances are stored as an intrinsic part of an owning entity and share the identity of the entity. Each of the persistent properties or fields of the embedded object is mapped to the database table for the entity. Only Basic, Column, Lob, Temporal, and Enumerated mapping annotations may portably be used to map the persistent fields or properties of classes annotated as Embeddable.	TYPE			
@Embedded	Specifies a persistent field or property of an entity whose value is an instance of an embeddable class. The AttributeOverride and/ or AttributeOverrides annotations may be used to override the column mappings declared within the embeddable class, which are mapped to the entity table.	METHOD, FIELD			

(continued)

(continued)

NAME	USE	TARGET	MEMBERS	DEFAULT	DESCRIPTION
`@MappedSuperclass`	Designates a class whose mapping information is applied to the entities that inherit from it. A mapped superclass has no separate table defined for it. A class designated with this annotation can be mapped in the same way as an entity except that the mappings will apply only to its subclasses, since no table exists for the mapped superclass itself. When applied to the subclasses the inherited mappings will apply in the context of the subclass tables. Mapping information may be overridden in such subclasses by using the AttributeOverride annotation.	TYPE			

(continued)

NAME	USE	TARGET	MEMBERS	DEFAULT	DESCRIPTION
`@Sequence Generator`	Defines a primary key generator that may be referenced by name when a generator element is specified for the `GeneratedValue` annotation. A sequence generator may be specified on the entity class or on the primary key field or property. The scope of the generator name is global to the persistence unit (across all generator types).	TYPE, METHOD, FIELD	*String name()*	*""*	The generator name
			String sequence Name()		The name of the database sequence object from which to obtain primary key values.
			int initialValue()	*0*	The value from which the sequence object is to start generating.
			int allocationSize()	*50*	The amount to increment by when allocating sequence numbers from the sequence.

(continued)

(continued)

NAME	USE	TARGET	MEMBERS	DEFAULT	DESCRIPTION
`@TableGenerator`	Defines a primary key generator that may be referenced by name when a generator element is specified for the `GeneratedValue` annotation. A table generator may be specified on the entity class or on the primary key field or property. The scope of the generator name is global to the persistence unit (across all generator types).	TYPE, METHOD, FIELD	*String name()*	*""*	A unique generator name that can be referenced by one or more classes to be the generator for ID values.
			String table()	*""*	Name of table that stores the generated ID values.
			String catalog()		The catalog of the table.
			String schema()	*""*	The schema of the table.
			String pkColumnName()	*""*	Name of the primary key column in the table.
			String valueColumnName()	*""*	Name of the column that stores the last value generated.
			String pkColumnValue()	*""*	The primary key value in the generator table that distinguishes this set of generated values from others that may be stored in the table.
			int initialValue()	*0*	The initial value to be used when allocating ID numbers from the generator.
			int allocationSize()	*50*	The amount to increment by when allocating ID numbers from the generator.
			UniqueConstraint[] uniqueConstraints()	{}	Unique constraints that are to be placed on the table. These are only used if table generation is in effect. These constraints apply in addition to primary key constraints.

Summary

In this appendix, we've given you a short introduction to Java annotations as an alternative to writing XML descriptor files. We have also provided a complete list of all annotations defined in the EJB 3.0 specification as a reference.

Index

F

O

X

CPSIA information can be obtained at www.ICGtesting.com
Printed in the USA
BVOW02n1601260914

368013BV00021B/26/P